The SETTLEMENT *of* AMERICA

Volume 1

The SETTLEMENT *of* AMERICA

Encyclopedia of Westward Expansion from
Jamestown to the Closing of the Frontier

Volume 1

JAMES A. CRUTCHFIELD
CANDY MOULTON
TERRY A. DEL BENE

EDITORS

SHARPE REFERENCE

an imprint of M.E. Sharpe, Inc.

SHARPE REFERENCE

Sharpe Reference is an imprint of M.E. Sharpe, Inc.

M.E. Sharpe, Inc.
80 Business Park Drive
Armonk, NY 10504

© 2011 by M.E. Sharpe, Inc.

Cover photo: MPI/Stringer/Getty Images.

Library of Congress Cataloging-in-Publication Data

The settlement of America : encyclopedia of westward expansion from Jamestown to the closing of the frontier / edited by James A. Crutchfield, Candy Moulton, and Terry A. Del Bene.
    p. cm.
 Includes bibliographical references and index.
 ISBN 978-0-7656-1984-6 (alk. paper)
 1. United States—Territorial expansion—Encyclopedias. 2. West (U.S.)—Discovery and exploration—Encyclopedias. 3. West (U.S.)—History—Encyclopedias. 4. Frontier and pioneer life—United States—Encyclopedias. I. Crutchfield, James Andrew, 1938–
II. Moulton, Candy Vyvey, 1955– III. Del Bene, Terry Alan.

E179.5.S48 2012
978′.02—dc22   2010049478

Printed and bound in the United States

EB (c) 10 9 8 7 6 5 4 3 2 1

Publisher: Myron E. Sharpe
Vice President and Director of New Product Development: Donna Sanzone
Vice President and Production Director: Carmen Chetti
Executive Development Editor: Jeff Hacker
Project Manager: Henrietta Toth
Program Coordinator: Cathleen Prisco
Editorial Assistant: Lauren LoPinto
Text Design and Cover Design: Jesse Sanchez
Typesetter: Nancy Connick

Contents

Topic Finder

Contributors

History is not only the realm of historians. It is also the domain of historical writers—men and women who have devoted their lives to the study and documentation of the story of civilization from its beginnings to the present day. With few exceptions, all of the entries in this work were contributed by professional writers, some of whom have academic degrees in history, but all of whom have devoted most of their entire professional lives to the study and written presentation of the epic of American history.

They are members of an organization called Western Writers of America (WWA), an organization for which I have had the pleasure of serving as executive director for a number of years before retiring to concentrate on my own writing career. Candy Moulton, one of the co-editors of this project, is the new executive direc-

tor. Organized in 1953 by a small cadre of pulp fiction authors, WWA has grown over the years to become one the nation's largest and best-known professional writers' organizations and the leading voice for all genres of literature about the American West. Its primary purpose is the preservation and propagation of Western history and literature from the time of North America's first permanent European settlement at Jamestown, Virginia, in 1607, all the way through the closing of the western frontier at Wounded Knee, South Dakota, in 1890, and even to the West of today. Along the way, a vast number of eminent writers have contributed their talents to the story of America's rapidly expanding empire. Truly, the nonfiction writers represented here are the crème de la crème of today's documenters of the historical West in all of its manifestations.

Editors

James A. Crutchfield
Independent Scholar

Candy Moulton
Independent Scholar

Terry A. Del Bene
Independent Scholar

Contributors

Will Bagley
Western Writers of America

Gene Bryan
Independent Scholar

Sarah Badger Doyle
Independent Scholar

Ted Franklin Belue
Murray State University

Lenore Carroll
Western Writers of America

Jim Ersfield
University of New Mexico

Kent Blansett
University of Minnesota, Morris

Robert J. Conley
Western Carolina University

Jack E. Fletcher
Independent Scholar

Johnny D. Boggs
Western Writers of America

Sharon Cunningham
Western Writers of America

Patricia K.A. Fletcher
Independent Scholar

Kingsley Bray
Independent Scholar

David Dary
University of Oklahoma

Meg Frisbee
New Mexico State University

A. Dudley Gardner
Western Wyoming Community College

Jerome A. Greene
National Park Service

William Groneman III
Western Writers of America

Sarah Grossman
University of New Mexico

Melody Groves
Western Writers of America

Tamsen Hert
University of Wyoming Libraries

Paul A. Hutton
University of New Mexico

Jerry Keenan
Independent Scholar

Carol Krismann
University of Colorado, Boulder

Stoney Livinston
Independent Scholar

John Lubetkin
Independent Scholar

Dan Manning
Western Writers of America

Bill Markley
Western Writers of America

Leon C. Metz
Western Writers of America

Gregory F. Michno
Independent Scholar

Rod Miller
Independent Scholar

Mike Moore
Western Writers of America

Elaine M. Nelson
University of Minnesota, Morris

Bill O'Neal
Panola College

Eli Paul
Independent Scholar

James E. Potter
Nebraska State Historical Society

Lucia Robson
Western Writers of America

Quackgrass Sally
National Pony Express Association

Larry D. Sweazy
Western Writers of America

Rod Timanus
Western Writers of America

Herman J. Viola
Smithsonian Institution

Dale L. Walker
University of Texas, El Paso

Linda Wommack
Western Writers of America

Introduction

To properly understand what American westward expansion was, it is first necessary to appreciate what it was not. It was not a temporary movement of vast numbers of people thronging from one region to another, as was the case with the hoards of Huns who, in the fourth and fifth centuries, invaded and overran the plains and forests of Europe. Nor was it a highly structured migration completed within a finite time frame, such as the 1835–1840 overland trek of the Boers in South Africa. Finally, and perhaps most importantly, westward expansion in America was not confined to that great push from the western side of the Mississippi River that began in 1804, with Lewis and Clark's epic journey to the Pacific Ocean and back again, and continued through the Indian wars, the Rocky Mountain and Southwestern fur trade, the cattle frontier, the gold rush era, and the great age of railroad expansion.

So just what was the phenomenon known as the nation's westward expansion, sometimes called "manifest destiny"? Indeed, its movement rather resembled the tiny fingers of ocean water creeping upon the beach at high tide, some reaching much farther inland than others, only to recede and then advance again. Participants thought of the advance simply as a relocation from one place to another, a move demanded by desire or a hope for better living conditions. Its timing encompassed the period from the first permanent English settlement in North America in the early seventeenth century through the highly charged Indian massacre by the U.S. Army at Wounded Knee, South Dakota, in 1890.

That same year, the U.S. Census Bureau reported as follows: "Up to and including 1880, the country had a frontier of settlement, but at present the unsettled area has been so broken into by isolated bodies of settlement that there can hardly be said to be a frontier line." The realization of that auspicious event has been hailed by historians ever since to signify and define the closing of the American frontier and the end of the nation's westward expansion. The movement lasted nearly 300 years and spanned the North American continent from the Atlantic Ocean to the shores of the Pacific.

The Beginnings of Westward Expansion

An argument can be made that America's first flirtation with westward expansion occurred only one week after the English landfall at Jamestown, Virginia, on May 14, 1607. Beginning on May 21, Captain John Smith, one of the colonization company's leaders, and twenty-one companions made their way northwest up the James River for some 50 or 60 miles (80 or 96 km). When they arrived at the fall line—a natural boundary running north and south some 50 or 60 miles inland from the Atlantic Ocean, beyond which ships could not travel because of the rapids and falls in the streams—they retraced their tracks to Jamestown. For the next several decades, Jamestown residents and thousands of other colonists, representing several nationalities and living in settlements stretching from Georgia to New England, confined themselves to the narrow strip of land called the tidewater lying between the ocean and the fall line.

From the tidewater region, settlement gradually moved westward to encompass the Piedmont, the section squeezed between the tidewater and the eastern foothills of the Appalachians. By the mid-1700s, North America's two most dominant European groups, the British and the French, had positioned themselves for war. Although the British population outnumbered the French by about 1 million to 50,000, French influence among the Indian tribes of the upper Ohio River valley and along the rivers that flowed westward from the Appalachian Mountains was substantial. For years, control of the Ohio River region was of little importance, since few settlers had encroached upon the vast wilderness with intentions of permanently occupying it.

In 1747 and 1749, however, two British colonial land speculation concerns, the Ohio Company and the Loyal Company, made clear to Frenchmen and Indians alike that the British would introduce hundreds of settlers into the region.

The French and Indian War in North America—pitting elements of the French army and its Indian allies against the British army and American colonists—began in 1754 and dragged on until 1763, when a peace treaty signed at Paris ended the hostilities. France was expelled from much of North America, and the vacuum left by its departure from the Ohio River valley and adjoining territories provided a natural opportunity for American frontier families to move into the vacated lands. Hoping to curtail this colonial expansion, Great Britain's King George III issued his Proclamation of 1763 forbidding white encroachment beyond an imaginary line running along the crest of the Appalachian Mountains. The proclamation notwithstanding, tens of thousands of emigrants—primarily Scots-Irish, German, and English—poured across the mountains to new homes in the West.

One of the primary avenues westward was the Ohio River. From the close of the French and Indian War until the early 1800s, tens of thousands of emigrants, aboard canoes, pirogues, flatboats, keelboats, and just about any other vehicle that would float, descended this great stream to new lands in Kentucky and the Old Northwest Territory. Canals, especially the Erie Canal, although their time of greatest use was limited to a score of years, moved water-borne emigrants, as well as freight, from east to west in enormous numbers. The evolution of long-distance roads, however, provided easier access to the West for many travelers. To mention only a few, the Pennsylvania Road, which years later became part of the famed Lincoln Highway, provided a generation of emigrants with a simplified way to travel across southern Pennsylvania. The Wilderness Road through Cumberland Gap was used by North Carolinians and Virginians seeking new lands in Kentucky and Tennessee. The Cumberland—or National Road—which eventually stretched from Cumberland, Maryland, to St. Louis, Missouri, was responsible for the transportation of thousands of emigrants through the Appalachian Mountains, southwestern Pennsylvania, Ohio, Indiana, and Illinois to the Mississippi River. In New York, the Genesee Road connected Albany with Buffalo, far to the west near the shore of Lake Ontario.

By 1779, although most advancing frontier families had restricted their movement to the western edges of the Appalachian Mountain chain, two significant events heralded the future: the settlement of present-day central Kentucky (Boonesborough) and Middle Tennessee (Nashville), both colonies removed from their neighbors in the east by nearly 200 miles (320 km). Travelers' journals and diaries from this time are commonplace, and practically all of them describe the tremendous movement of migrants across the eastern United States. The old pioneer himself, Daniel Boone, reported through the pen of his protégé John Filson that, in 1773, he "sold my farm on the Yadkin {in North Carolina}, and what goods we could not carry with us; and on the twenty-fifth day of September, 1773, bade a farewell to our friends, and proceeded on our journey to Kentucke, in company with five families more, and forty men that joined us in Powel's Valley, which is one hundred and fifty miles from the now settled parts of Kentucke." F.A. Michaux, a noted French naturalist, toured the United States during the late eighteenth and early nineteenth centuries. In 1802, while traveling through the vast wilderness lying between Knoxville and Nashville, he wrote that the road through

> this part of the Indian territory cuts through the mountains . . . [and] it is as broad and commodious as those in the environs of Philadelphia, in consequence of the amazing number of emigrants that travel through it to go and settle in the western country. . . . About forty miles from Nasheville we met an emigrant family in a carriage, followed by their negroes on foot, that had performed their journey without any accident. Little boards painted black and nailed upon the trees every three miles, indicate to travelers the distance they have to go.

In western Pennsylvania, where the population had swelled in the years after the close of the French and Indian War, Joseph Doddridge left a vivid account of the constant movement of people westward during this period:

> The settlements on . . . [the western] side of the mountains commenced along the Monongahela, and between that river and the Laurel Ridge, in the year 1772. In the succeeding year they reached the Ohio River. . . . Land was the object which invited the greater number of these people to cross the mountain, for as the saying then was, "it was to be had here for the taking up." . . . Some of the early settlers took the precaution

to come over the mountains in the spring, leaving their families behind to raise a crop of corn, and then return and bring them out in the fall.

Just as the termination of the French and Indian War provided the opportunity and ambition for a major emigration west, so did the news of the U.S. victory in the War of 1812. With most British influence coming to an end in the Old Northwest, streams of settlers floated down the Ohio River and overland in search of their new tomorrows. "We have now fairly turned our backs on the old world and find ourselves in the very stream of emigration," declared English reformer Morris Birkbeck in a journal entry from 1817 during his stopover in western Pennsylvania on the way to his final destination in Illinois; "we are seldom out of sight, as we travel on this grand track towards the Ohio, of family groups, behind and before us, some with a view to a particular spot; close to a brother perhaps, or a friend, who has gone before, and reported well of the country."

Westward to the Pacific Ocean

Although much more expansion would occur east of the Mississippi during the early part of the nineteenth century, by then Americans had set their sights beyond the great river. The return of Lewis and Clark from their momentous journey to the Pacific Ocean in 1804–1806 set the stage for a ninety-year-long progression of Americans plodding their way west and gradually conquering and adding to the United States new territories stretching from Canada to the Mexican border.

The first to go forward were mountain men in search of beaver pelts to satisfy the growing demand for beaver fur, used in the rapidly expanding American and European hat industry. The mountain man era spanned from the first decade of the nineteenth century to the 1840s, when the beaver became virtually extinct in the streams of the Rocky Mountains and beyond. The journals and diaries of mountain men leave readers in awe at the vast number of miles these rugged individuals traveled in a year's time: one moment, perhaps in St. Louis—three months later in the heart of the Rocky Mountains—by fall in New Mexico. Mountain men provided much of the geographical data for many of the later maps of the trans-Mississippi West.

The U.S. army's first major conflict with Indians living west of the Mississippi occurred in 1823, when Colonel Henry Leavenworth and soldiers of the 6th U.S. Infantry battled side by side with fur traders against Arikara Indians along the upper Missouri River. For nearly the next seven decades, until the debacle called Wounded Knee, American troops subdued the Indians and escorted them to reservations, surveyed thoroughfares and railroad lines, built frontier forts, and did just about any other task required to move the country ever westward.

Important western byways gradually emerged, beginning with the Santa Fe Trail from Missouri to New Mexico in 1821, which opened U.S. commerce with the Republic of Mexico. When the Oregon Trail was pioneered across the Great Plains during the early, contentious days of the "the Oregon Question" with Great Britain, literally hundreds of wagon trains, conveying tens of thousands of families, groaned through the prairie grass and over mountain passes to the Pacific Ocean. Other trails quickly sprang up, to California, Utah, and other exotic destinations.

The discovery of gold in California in 1848 brought thousands of prospectors, miners, camp followers, and merchants to the West Coast, all in hopes of finding their fortunes. Other gold, as well as silver, strikes in Montana, South Dakota, Colorado, and Nevada prompted more Americans to pull up stakes in the East and migrate toward the setting sun.

After the Civil War, with the proliferation of millions of Texas Longhorn cattle that had been left to their own devices due to the shortage of ranchers gone off to war, a new industry sprang up on the Great Plains. The cattle business consisted of far more than simply rounding up cows and sending them up a trail to Montana. It involved an entire assemblage of crafts and trades to support the industry, and many prospective employees came from the East to try their hand at something new.

The final chapter in the nation's centuries-long movement west was the advent of the transcontinental railroad. Following receipt of land surveys provided by U.S. Army topographical engineers, monied men back east financed a plethora of lines running from the Mississippi River to the Pacific coast. By then, the bison, once numbering in the millions, were practically extinct, and the once-proud Plains Indians who depended on the bison for their livelihoods were little better off. Perhaps it is no accident that the "closing" of the American West coincided with the U.S. Army massacre of scores of innocent Sioux men, women, and children that day in late December 1890 at Wounded Knee, South Dakota.

The Closing of the Frontier

Indeed by 1890, the American frontier had been conquered. The great migration west had started with a dream by early American colonists to locate and possess land, supposedly better land, beyond the horizon and ended nearly 300 years later with the birth of a new giant on the world scene. Within two decades of the closing of the West, President Theodore Roosevelt, who himself had worked as a cowboy in Dakota Territory during his youth, announced to the world with the dispatch of the Navy's "Great White Fleet" that the United States was now a sea-to-sea, world-class power of international proportions and one to be dealt with respectfully.

That America's westward expansion was a defining moment in the nation's long history is hardly open to dispute. Along with such important events as the Revolutionary War and independence, the creation of the Constitution and Bill of Rights, the Civil War, World War I, the Great Depression, and World War II, it helped formulate who present-day Americans are, where they have been, and how they got where they are today. Equally certain is that a respectful understanding of this unique movement in world history will better prepare future generations for where they are going.

James A. Crutchfield

Maps

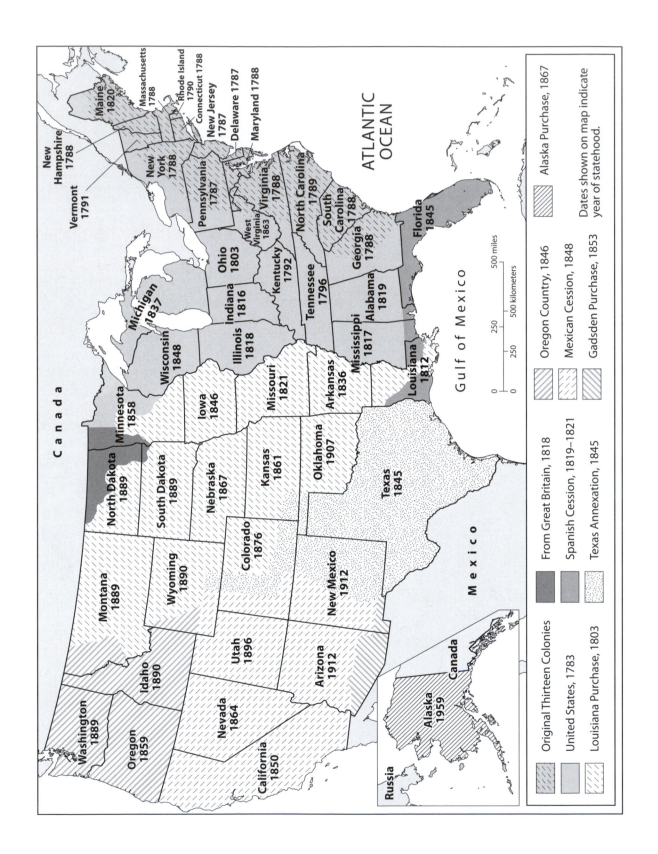

U.S. Territorial Expansion

Original Thirteen Colonies

United States, 1783

Louisiana Purchase, 1803

From Great Britain, 1818

Spanish Cession, 1819–1821

Texas Annexation, 1845

Oregon Country, 1846

Mexican Cession, 1848

Gadsden Purchase, 1853

Alaska Purchase, 1867

Dates shown on map indicate year of statehood.

ATLANTIC OCEAN

Gulf of Mexico

Canada

Mexico

Russia

500 miles

500 kilometers

New Hampshire 1788

Vermont 1791

Maine 1820

Massachusetts 1788

Rhode Island 1790

Connecticut 1788

New York 1788

New Jersey 1787

Delaware 1787

Maryland 1788

Pennsylvania 1787

West Virginia 1863

Virginia 1788

North Carolina 1789

South Carolina 1788

Georgia 1788

Florida 1845

Ohio 1803

Kentucky 1792

Tennessee 1796

Alabama 1819

Mississippi 1817

Louisiana 1812

Michigan 1837

Wisconsin 1848

Indiana 1816

Illinois 1818

Minnesota 1858

Iowa 1846

Missouri 1821

Arkansas 1836

North Dakota 1889

South Dakota 1889

Nebraska 1867

Kansas 1861

Oklahoma 1907

Texas 1845

Montana 1889

Wyoming 1890

Colorado 1876

New Mexico 1912

Washington 1889

Oregon 1859

Idaho 1890

Nevada 1864

Utah 1896

Arizona 1912

California 1850

Alaska 1959

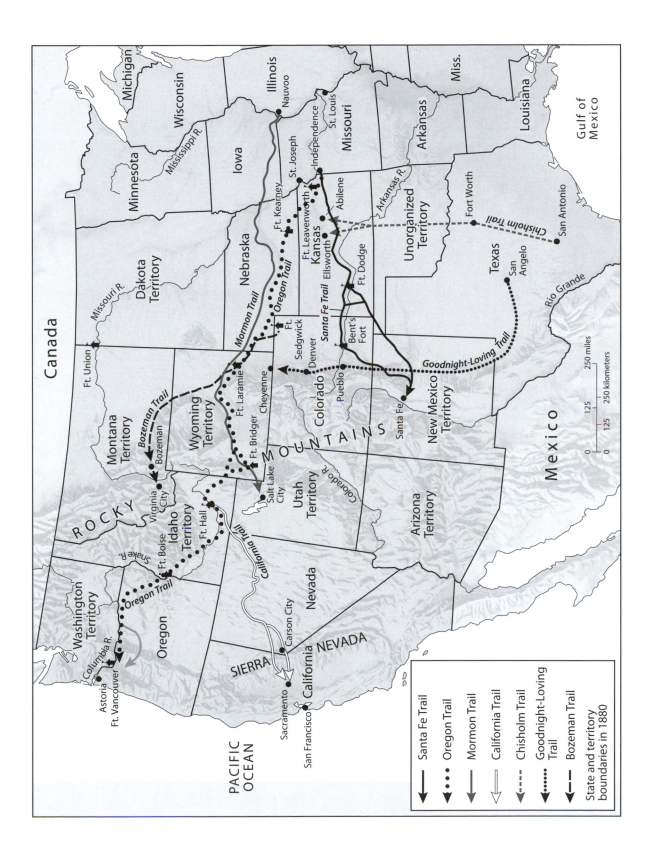

Western Overland Trails, 1820s–1860s

Essays

The Trans-Appalachian Frontier

Until 1804, when Captains Meriwether Lewis and William Clark began their journey up the Missouri River on President Thomas Jefferson's quest for the Pacific Ocean, America's first "West" consisted of the vast region lying east of the Mississippi River, west of the Appalachian Mountains, and south of the Great Lakes. Three centuries before, the Spanish—notably De Soto—had floated down the Mississippi, and, a century later, French voyageurs, missionaries, and explorers canoed the river's tributaries from the Great Lakes to the Gulf of Mexico, naming the land through which the mighty stream coursed Louisiana, to honor their sovereign, Louis XIV. For the English, after the establishment of Jamestown (1607) and Plymouth (1620), the New Eden beyond the Tidewater and Piedmont beckoned, igniting explorations across the Appalachians that led to Indian dispossession, four distinct "French and Indian Wars," numerous intertribal wars, and America's Revolution.

By 1650 English explorers realized that the headwaters of the New, Staunton, Clinch, James, Potomac, Holston, Yadkin, and Catawba rivers were linked by passable gaps and gorges through the mountains. Tales of a wide river meandering past a "high mountaine" and on to "a great sea" brimming with ships manned by men wearing red caps provoked English fear of French intrusion. Such talk fired the entrepreneurial dreams of Sir William Berkeley, governor of Virginia, and his aide, Captain Abraham Wood.

On August 27, Wood's party of seven and a Nottaway guide left Fort Henry at the Falls of the Appomattox River (present-day Petersburg, Virginia), headed southwest, and proceeded 125 miles (200 km) to the Pee Dee River. In a second attempt, Wood reached the New River. Wood later wrote a pamphlet about his trips and sponsored John Lederer, a German whose trek over the "Apalateans" allowed him a spectacular view of the Shenandoah Valley. Hoping to establish trade with the Cherokee, Wood funded James Needham to head southward to the headwaters of the Tennessee River, then to the village of Chota. For his killing of a Tuscarora tribesman, Needham was burned alive, but some visiting Shawnees rescued Needham's companion, Gabriel Arthur, taking him through Kentucky and across the Ohio River into Shawnee land; Arthur thus became one of the first Englishmen to see the new West. That same year, Wood sent Robert Fallam and Thomas Batts to the Ohio's upper tributaries "in order to reach the South Seas." They never reached the sea, but gained intelligence concerning France's hold on the Mississippi.

On June 17, 1673, Father Jacques Marquette and fur trader Louis Jolliet reached the mouth of the Wisconsin River and entered the Mississippi, floating downstream to the Illinois. Six years later, Robert de la Salle was exploring Louisiana with his Italian compatriot, Henri de Tonti. A decade later, brothers Pierre d'Iberville and Jean-Baptiste de Bienville (commandant of Biloxi) established colonies along the southern Mississippi basin and fended off small warships (corvettes) of England's sovereign, King William. William was determined the West would not fall into the hands of France or Spain, and the New World's first imperial war of expansion, King William's War (1689–1697), was named for him.

Yet it was the French who remained best informed about this first far West and knew of practical routes through the imposing barriers, knowledge that Governor Alexander Spotswood of Virginia was seeking. In 1714, after America's second expansionist clash (Queen Anne's War, 1702–1713), Spotswood led a party to the Blue Ridge Mountains of Virginia, naming his band "Knights of the Golden Horse-Shoe" in order to encourage gentlemen to venture and make discoveries and settlements. Despite this fanciful name, Spotswood was a practical man, wary of growing French presence.

Spotswood encouraged the creation of land companies, thus ushering in a new era of western expansion and imperial, colonial, and native clashes. Many land companies were short-lived. A few, such as the Mississippi Company, were corrupt, but others—the Loyal Land Company, the Transylvania Company, and Ohio Company—played pivotal roles in Anglo-European conquest.

Company rivalries were intense. The Loyal Land Company secured 800,000 acres (324,000 ha) and dispatched a surveying mission led by Dr. Thomas Walker, whose sojourn of 1750 earned him the distinction of being one of the first Englishman to enter Kentucky from the southeast, via Pine and Cumberland Gaps. Walker braved laurel-choked ravines and dense canebrakes. By meandering westward along the Cumberland River instead of taking the Great Warrior's Path, he missed reaching the bluegrass region; yet his expedition, if measured in expansionist terms, was singular. He renamed Cave Gap for the Duke of Cumberland, also giving the name to the Cumberland River and Cumberland Mountain. In a score of years, his route along the Rockcastle became a leg of the Wilderness Road. More critically, Walker's journal aided in the drawing of the three most influential maps in eighteenth-century expansion.

Within three years, Virginia's best two surveyors and cartographers, Joshua Fry and Peter Jefferson (father of the third president), used Walker's report to create the Fry-Jefferson Map of Virginia. Based on actual surveys instead of the vague reports of Indians and hunters, the Fry-Jefferson map had a threefold significance, depicting for the first time (1) western Virginia and Maryland's parallel Allegheny ridges, marking roads and rivers, mountains and settlements; (2) the Great Wagon Road (or Cumberland Road) of 455 miles (730 km) from the Yadkin River through Virginia to Philadelphia; and (3) the Trading Path to the Catawba and Cherokee towns and Moravian missions in North Carolina.

Colonial surveyor Lewis Evans utilized Dr. Walker's journal in creating Benjamin Franklin's 1755 "Map of the Middle British Colonies in America." During the same year, Major General Edward Braddock used Evans's map in his ill-fated expedition to the Forks of the Ohio during the last French and Indian War. Intended to spur trans-Appalachian migration, which it did as readily as the Fry-Jefferson Map, Evans's map added political insights as well as cartographic innovations and knowledge. In 1776 Governor Thomas Penal updated Evans's map and republished it in Thomas Jeffery's *American Atlas* and in *The Holster Atlas*, the standard guide among British soldiers during the Revolution.

The year Walker made his trek, Christopher Gist was on his three-pronged mission for the Ohio Company: to traverse the company's 200,000-acre (81,000-ha) tract to spy on the French, and to note Indian hostility toward the English. Gist traveled from Maryland through central Ohio to the Falls of the Ohio River, through Kentucky and southwestern Virginia, and back to North Carolina. His cabin was located only 20 miles (30 km) from the home of young Daniel Boone, who hunted with Nathaniel Gist, Christopher's son. (Few historians have noted this early Boone-Gist connection and its portentous impact upon trans-Appalachian settlement, considering Boone's future role as America's most famous pathfinder.) In 1751 Gist represented the Ohio Company's interests at Pennsylvania's Treaty of Logstown to gain Indian concessions for settlement between the Alleghenies and the Ohio, giving entrepreneurs George Croghan, Conrad Weiser, and William Trent trading rights and granting them permission to build two forts.

By the time of the last French and Indian War (1755–1763), with the West as the great prize for the imperial powers, a scattering of Franco- and Anglophiles were living in the Ohio River/Middle Mississippi basin. By the 1730s, French voyageurs and coureurs de bois (fur traders) had already established outposts along both banks of the Ohio River. By the 1740s, English traders were living at Lower Shawnee Town, wary of their precarious existence among the French and the Ohio Algonquians with their perennially shifting intertribal and imperial alliances. But high profits, unrestrained personal freedom, and adventure were too heady a brew for some to pass up. John Findlay was such a man.

Findlay eked out an existence as a trader or a tinker, roving with a packhorse or two along the cutting edge of America's Anglo frontier, living and dying in virtual anonymity. In 1755 Findlay was serving as a wagon driver for Major General Edward Braddock when he met a twenty-one-year-old North Carolinian, Daniel Boone, already a seasoned "long hunter." Findlay's tales of the West fired Boone's imagination.

The role of long hunters in American expansion cannot be denied. They were a unique fraternity of border men from Virginia, Pennsylvania, and North Carolina (including today's Kentucky and Tennessee, then part of Virginia and North Carolina, respectively) who hunted and trapped the vast eastern wilderness, often absent from their families for long periods of time, hence the name "long" hunters. Deerskins were valuable in the East and Europe, as were beaver and otter, sassafras and ginseng roots, smoked bear "bacon," and tallow. A hunter might earn more than $1,000 a year, though many died on the trail destitute. It was not unusual for them to break treaties and laws to trespass and poach on Indian land, adopting Indian skills and dress and supplanting Indians as the middlemen in the skin trade. Their glowing accounts of the West found eager ears back east. Elisha Wallen, Benjamin Cutbirth, Henry Knox, the Skaggs and Bledsoe brothers, Uriah Stone, Kasper Mansker, and, of course, Daniel Boone were long hunters, arguably the first Americans to push past the Blue Ridge. Long hunters signaled a new era of encroachment in the Ohio Valley. Indians saw the threat these bold intruders posed, yet had no consensus how to deal with them: violence was one response; accommodation another.

Already, company men of the Philadelphia firm of Baynton, Wharton, and Morgan were hunting from Kentucky's Green River and upper Illinois country to French Lick (Nashville). George Morgan's firm did a brisk business among the French and Indians, establishing trading posts in Kaskaskia, Cahokia, and Vincennes, competing with French and Spanish interests. The end of the French and Indian War brought the Proclamation of 1763, the vain attempt of Britain's King George III to halt western expansion and ameliorate "the Indian problem." On February 10, France signed the Treaty of Paris, ceding to England the land east of the Mississippi, south of the Ohio (excepting New Orleans), and west of the Blue Ridge Mountains.

On paper, England now possessed the West. Pioneers traveled the roads built by the British and their armies during the war. The Great Road went from the Holston to Long Island in the Tennessee country. General John Forbes's road across Pennsylvania followed the Trading Path to the Ohio's Forks, passing through Bedford, Raystown, Ligonier, and then Pittsburgh. Increased settler encroachment sparked fresh violence, halting westward migrations as quickly as they began.

In 1763 Pontiac's Rebellion and pan-tribal alliance so terrorized English settlers that immigration was stalled until the "conspiracy" was stamped out. The Crown in 1768 negotiated substantial treaties: the Fort Stanwix Treaty, in which the Iroquois, for £10,000 (nearly $50,000 in current currency) ceded to the English the tribe's much-disputed Ohio country claims; and the Treaty of Hard Labor, in which the Cherokees ceded to the English their Indian claims to much of the same territory. A third, the Treaty of Augusta, signed August 3, 1773, pitted the interests of the Creeks against the Cherokees. In the end, the British gained 2,100,000 acres (850,000 ha) of Georgia.

The treaties renewed migration but led to more dubiously chartered land settlement companies, encroachment by squatters, and land-grabbing schemes involving prominent easterners like George Washington, Patrick Henry, Benjamin Franklin, and New York Indian agent Sir William Johnson. Surveyors, traders—illegal and legal—and speculators flooded the region.

Pioneer, long hunter, and surveyor Daniel Boone (1734–1820) remains a legendary symbol of the trans-Appalachian West. Though Boone myths abound, his importance as a pivotal figure in western expansion can hardly be exaggerated. In 1765 Boone skirted eastern Kentucky. In 1769, Boone's party, led by John Findlay, reached the fabled bluegrass. Twice Indians captured them and one man was killed. In 1771 he returned home—broke. In 1773 he tried again. After the killing of his son James and the growing conflicts that in 1774 ignited Lord Dunmore's War, Boone settled east of the Blue Ridge.

Dunmore's War suspended migrations until the conflicts ended. More accurately, as the conflicts ebbed and flowed, the migrations increased and diminished correspondingly. Dunmore's War interrupted the Fincastle County, Virginia, surveying crews in central Kentucky, led by Captain Thomas Bullitt. The Virginians surveyed some 200,000 acres (81,000 ha) to be parceled off as military warrants to French and Indian War veterans before fleeing to the settlements, fearing attack—not, however, before James Harrod established Harrod's Town, America's first far western fort. That October, following the Battle of Point Pleasant, Chief Cornstalk signed the Treaty of Camp Charlotte, ceding Shawnee ancestral Kentucky claims to Virginia, the Shawnee vowing to live north of the Ohio, the new border between Indian and white lands.

As the West opened for settlement, Boone became its pathfinder. He had found an ally—lawyer and judge Richard Henderson of Salisbury, North Carolina, a founder of the Transylvania Company. Henderson schemed to buy from the Cherokees a large part of Kentucky, establish a colony, and sell grants and collect rents, making himself and his eight shareholders rich. In March 1775 at Sycamore Shoals (Elizabethtown, Tennessee), the Cherokees sold Henderson their Kentucky hunting rights for wares and cash equaling £10,000. Boone and thirty woodsmen blazed the Wilderness Road from the Holston River through Cumberland Gap to the Kentucky River, then to the site of Boonesborough, perhaps the most celebrated fort in the history of westward expansion. Henderson's Kentucky scheme failed, but the Wilderness Road became a major avenue westward.

Boonesborough, Harrod's Town, and St. Asaph's (alternately, Logan's Station) were major way stations in this western saga. Near Cumberland Gap in western Virginia, Joseph Martin's Station (1775) gave succor to wayfarers going west and directions about how to negotiate the bewildering mazes of buffalo paths that facilitated travel and trade. The Warrior's Path (Athiamiowee) began in the Carolinas, skirted Georgia and eastern Tennessee, and then crossed into Kentucky. One fork led to the Ohio River across from the Scioto; a second fork arced to the Upper Blue Licks and then to the Ohio. Athiamiowee received heavy traffic from warring Cherokees, Shawnees, and Catawbas.

Buffalo broadened, defined, and deepened these thoroughfares and expanded their range, transforming them into established "highways" leading to lakes and rivers, through dense stands of cane and around obstacles to springs, meadows, and salt licks. The Great Buffalo Path (Alanant-o-wamiowee) cut through north-central Kentucky from Big Bone Lick to Maysville, 225 miles (360 km) to the east. (Limestone Street in Lexington follows part of this old trace.) Boone's Wilderness Road eventually carried more than 300,000 people into Kentucky.

Similar trails from Indiana and Illinois joined at the Ohio near Lawrence, Indiana. Trails like the Cisca and Charlotte Pike opened trans-Appalachia from the southeastern colonies. The Natchez Trace and the Chickasaw Trail bisected the same region from the southwest. Not only did these pathways become the first roads into America's first West, but many of the same paths became wagon trails, had railroad tracks laid upon them, and evolved into highways and secondary roads.

Kentucky's statehood came in 1792. In 1796, the year of Tennessee's statehood, Kentucky governor Isaac Shelby widened Boone's old Wilderness Road, making it accessible to horse-drawn wagons of 1-ton burden; sections of the original Wilderness Road overlap U.S. Highway 25-E near Middlesboro.

Following the conquest of Kentucky and equally critical to America's push westward was the exploration and annexation of the region north of the Ohio River, called the Old Northwest, or Northwest Territory. Prior to the French and Indian War, this fertile veldt largely was inhabited by French settlers. By war's end, the Philadelphia firm of Baynton, Wharton, and Morgan was doing brisk business in Illinois and contiguous regions, marketing a wide variety of trade wares and weapons to the French, British troops and traders, and Indians. Government officials and well-heeled speculators like William Murray and John Murray (Lord Dunmore) began bartering with the Indians for land. Dunmore so raised the Indian's ire that he sparked a bloody regional war and soon fled to Virginia. In his wake, several land companies, notably the Illinois Company and Wabash Company, later to merge into the Illinois-Wabash Company, also purchased large tracts from Algonquians (like the Peoria and Kaskaskia). The British did not honor the transactions, and ultimately such transactions were banned by the Royal Proclamation of 1763.

In the 1770s, frontiersman Daniel Boone blazed the Wilderness Road through the Cumberland Gap in the Appalachian Mountains, opening the way west for thousands of pioneers. Painter George Caleb Bingham cast Boone's efforts in heroic light in 1851. *(MPI/Stringer/ Getty Images)*

After the American Revolution, the area quickly was subdued, but not without some of the most violent Indian wars in America's history. Thomas Jefferson was instrumental in this phase of expansion, in 1784 proposing that territories west of the Appalachians relinquish all territorial claims in favor of carving the region into states and gaining individual statehood. On July 13, 1787, the U.S. Congress unanimously passed the Northwest Ordinance, designating as the Northwest Territory the region east of the Mississippi, north and west of the Ohio River, and south of the Great Lakes. Two years later, Congress reaffirmed but amended the ordinance, expanding its territorial bounds. Ultimately this territory covered more than 260,000 square miles (670,000 sq km).

Not surprisingly, Indians stubbornly resisted this new wave of intrusion. Though the Northwest Ordinance guaranteed that Indian "land and property shall never be taken without their consent; and, in their property, rights, and liberty, they shall never be invaded or disturbed," such lofty words meant little. Indians often were viewed in one of two ways: either as savage obstacles to settlement or as primitive allies of the Crown and indigenous American enemies. White vigilante groups, a glut of traders awash in alcohol and guns, and swarms of squatters soon invaded the region. By 1786, with the establishment of Fort Harmar at the mouth of the Muskingum and Fort Finney at the mouth of the Great Miami, the Shawnee, Delaware, Miami, Wea, and other tribes began to flee into the Spanish territory of Missouri. The Ohio Company bought 1.5 million acres (600,000 ha) north of what is now Marietta, Ohio; an extra 300,000 acres (120,000 ha) were given to Revolutionary War veterans.

By 1790, 20,000 white settlers lived in the Ohio Valley. That same year General Josiah Harmar built Fort Washington near present-day Cincinnati. Understandably, many Indian leaders living north of the Ohio (like Little Turtle of the Miami tribe and Blue Jacket of the already relocated Shawnee tribe) refused to sign post–Revolutionary War treaties and took up the tomahawk against Americans in a new spate of bloodletting. Three pivotal battles ensued. The first (1790), with an army led by Harmar to the Indian towns along the Wabash, resulted in the disastrous ambush of Harmar's troops and his resignation. Harmar's successor as commander of the army, Arthur St. Clair, in November 1791 led his men to the Maumee River into America's most devastating Indian defeat: St. Clair's ineptitude resulted in the death of 632 soldiers and more than 200 camp followers. In 1794 at the Battle of Fallen Timbers, General "Mad" Anthony Wayne secured much of the Old Northwest, his memorable one-hour battle marking the last major Indian war of the eighteenth century.

As in the American land expansionist paradigms north of the Ohio—the Ordinance of 1787 and the creation of the Northwest Territory as a prelude to statehood—so too were the lands south of the Ohio added to Congress's oversight with the creation of the Southwest Territory on May 26, 1790. Before that and before the official deeming of this rich swath as a "territory," the area along the Appalachian ridge—literally, the eastern cutting edge of the first Far West—remained a unique cauldron of expansionist schemes and of conflicting alliances, such tensions often manifested both as anti-British and anti-Indian. Little wonder, with access to the Holston, Watauga, and Cumberland rivers, an array of buffalo traces, and the Cumberland Gap, that Virginia's border with eastern Tennessee and western North Carolina was a bustling nexus of long hunter camps; legal and illegal purveyors of deerskin, fur, and liquor; and home of leading figures like William Bean, William Blount, and John Sevier. Several pivotal Revolutionary War conflicts occurred here, most notably the Battle of King's Mountain.

The Regulator movement, the rebellion of 2,000 colonial North Carolinians over tariffs and the role of local authority, led to the Battle of Alamance on May 16, 1771, near today's Burlington. Governor William Tryon's troops ended the rebellion but helped precipitate America's Revolution and pushed the rebels further westward, into the Watauga Valley. But the powerful Cherokee nation held ancestral claim to the land and the Treaty of 1763 forbade colonists to travel west of the Appalachians. This meant the settlers were trespassers in a dangerous region. By 1772 the colonials had leased land from the Cherokees and drawn up the Articles of the Watauga Association, their government based loosely on that of Virginia. Inevitably, Cherokee-white conflicts began, resulting in the mutually duplicitous Treaty of Sycamore Shoals (1775), in which Richard Henderson's Transylvania Company acquired all the land lying in the great bend of the Cumberland River in present-day Tennessee, as well as a huge amount of real estate in Kentucky—all of it totaling some 20 million acres (8 million ha). A year later came war as South Carolina, North Carolina, Georgia, and Virginia sent militia against the Cherokee. By 1777 the region was reorganized as the Washington district and incorporated into North Carolina.

The coming Revolutionary War and related Chickamauga Wars altered the region's face, the land filling in with stockades and blockhouses, like Fort Nashborough (1779), Kilgore's Station (1779), Ziegler's (1790), Mansker's Station (1779), and a host of others scattered throughout modern Middle Tennessee. In 1779 James Robertson left the Watauga basin for the banks of the Cumberland, where he established Fort Nashborough (Nashville) in December. Four months later John Donelson's party explored the Holston, Clinch, and Cumberland rivers, pushing into Middle Tennessee, living in tents and hastily constructed camps. The rendezvous of Robertson's and Donelson's parties marks the beginnings of Nashville. In September 1780 came the British defeat at King's Mountain (in which Wataugans played a major role). By 1784 Wataugans were part of the short-lived state of Franklin, and in 1790 the Territory of the United States, South of the River Ohio—commonly called the Southwest Territory—was organized. President George Washington appointed William Blount as its first and only territorial governor.

By 1795 the population of the Southwest Territory numbered 77,262—far more than enough to qualify for statehood. Blount, after concluding the Treaty of Holston, moved the territorial capital to Knoxville and by the year of statehood (1796) served as U.S. senator from Tennessee. Blount played a major role in the establishment of Tennessee, as did John Sevier, the sole governor of the state of Franklin, three-term governor of Tennessee, and one-term U.S. representative. Sevier did much to end Tennessee's Cherokee Wars, served with distinction at the Battle of King's Mountain, and was a brilliant frontier leader within the Southwest Territory.

The relentless push across the Blue Ridge and beyond resulted in the last stand of Indians east of the Mississippi. The final uprising north of the Ohio, led by the great Shawnee warrior Tecumseh, ended in 1813 at the Battle of the Thames in southern Canada, the far northern theater of the War of 1812. Tecumseh, like Pontiac and Little Turtle, succeeded in putting together a large, well-organized pan-Indian alliance, his efforts aided by the spiritual vision of his brother, the prophet Tenskwatawa. When Tecumseh was killed, Indian hopes to regain the eastern lands died with him. For the Indians, at least, America's first Far West was no more.

Ted Franklin Belue

Further Reading

Alvord, Clarence Walworth, and Lee Bidgood. *The First Explorations of the Trans-Allegheny Region by the Virginians, 1650–1674*. Baltimore: Clearfield, 1996.

Draper, Lyman C. *The Life of Daniel Boone*. Edited by Ted Franklin Belue. Mechanicsburg, PA: Stackpole Books, 1998.

Henderson, Archibald. *The Conquest of the Old Southwest*. New York: Century, 1920.

Robinson, W. Stitt. *The Southern Colonial Frontier, 1607–1763*. Albuquerque: University of New Mexico Press, 1979.

Rohrbough, Malcolm J. *The Trans-Appalachian Frontier: People, Societies, and Institutions, 1775–1850*. New York: Oxford University Press, 1978.

Sosin, Jack M. *The Revolutionary Frontier: 1763–1783*. New York: Holt, Rinehart and Winston, 1967.

Indians

The history of the Americas, including the United States, has too often been taught as the westward movement of hardy pioneers into a vast, empty wilderness that they methodically tamed, eventually bringing civilization in their wake. This approach to history leaves out much that is basic to the true story. First of all is the definition of wilderness. A wilderness is an uninhabited area. The area that became the United States was not uninhabited, was not a wilderness. It was inhabited by approximately 500 tribes of people who would become known as American Indians.

Many of these tribes were as different from one another as night and day. They spoke tongues that belonged to different language families. Some of these languages, according to linguists, are as different from one another as are English and Swahili. In spite of this basic fact, many people still speak of "the dialects of the Indian language." Each of these tribes had its own civilization. Historian Francis Jennings has pointed out that the words "civilization" and "savagery," when they are used as absolutes, have no meaning other than that one is the opposite of the other. So no one was "bringing civilization" to the "wilderness." The newcomers were invading other people's land and bringing their own civilization to replace that which was already there. When the Europeans arrived, North America already had a panoply of egalitarian, rank, and hierarchical societies with complex cultural traditions, religions, economic systems, and political structures. Native American social structures ranged from empires of vast power and scope to small bands whose members were so isolated they believed themselves to be the only people on the planet.

Even that part of the story is often glossed over, leaving the reader with an unbalanced version of the truth. We are told about American Indian assimilation, meaning that the Indians learned a new culture from the whites. What actually happened is more properly termed acculturation. Two very different cultures came into contact with each other and each borrowed new ideas from the other. It was not a one-way street. White frontiersmen imitated the Indians in their dress. Colonists learned from Indians about farming methods and about the uses of local plants for foods and medicines. Among the Indian contributions were such common

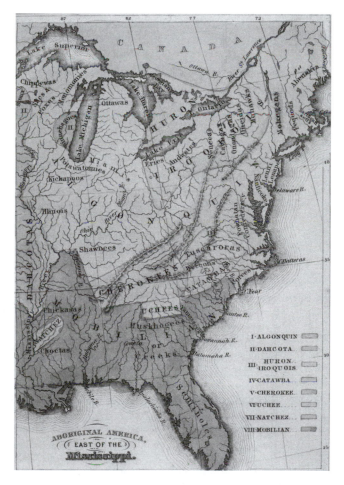

An early nineteenth-century map delineates Native American territories east of the Mississippi River prior to European contact. About 500 tribes, totaling 2 million people, occupied North America at the time of Columbus's arrival. *(Getty Images/Handout)*

commodities as aspirin, potatoes, tomatoes, and corn. Settlers also learned a new method of combat, which was eventually called guerrilla warfare. A visit to the modern Southwest quickly shows the influence of American Indians on the local architecture.

In order to bolster the idea of the savages in the wilderness and to justify the taking of Indian lands, European colonists early began talking and writing about the nomadic Indians, adding quickly that nomadic people could not own land because they simply wandered over it. This was the propaganda of conquest, not an honest mistake. When these fabrications were first made, the colonists had not yet met any nomadic Indians. The people whom the colonists met on the East Coast were settled farmers and fishermen, people who had much in common with the colonists.

However, the diseases brought by the colonists decimated the indigenous populations. The newcomers simply declared themselves to be the new chosen people and New England to be the new Promised Land, and like Gideon in the Old Testament, they claimed the right to smite the surviving local inhabitants and take over the land. Miles Standish even called his sword "Gideon." Indians were viewed as part of nature, and the Bible commanded the faithful to conquer nature and bend it to their own purposes. This attitude caused numerous wars between colonists and Indians, with the end of each war resulting in the whites' further acquisition of Indian land.

Many of the Indian nations quickly caught on to this scheme and, when the American Revolution broke out, some tribes—among them Cherokee, Mohawk, and Shawnee—allied themselves with the British, because British policy called for the containment of their colonies to the eastern seaboard. That meant keeping the colonists from encroaching further onto Indian land. But the war was lost by both the British and by their Indian allies, and the end of the Revolution and the establishment of the United States meant the beginning of westward expansion in a big way. The Native American allies of the United States would hardly fare better in the coming decades of expansion.

By 1802 President Thomas Jefferson had articulated his Indian removal plan, a way of getting all Indians out of the East and onto lands west of the Mississippi River. In 1803 he signed a compact with the state of Georgia agreeing to move all Indians beyond the borders claimed by Georgia. It was left for President Andrew Jackson, though, to finish the job. In 1830 Jackson managed to push through Congress his infamous Indian removal bill. Indian tribes were moved west forcibly, some into Kansas and some into

what would later be known as Oklahoma. Most moved without much protest, but the Seminoles in Florida held out and fought a major war with the United States, while the Cherokees chose instead to fight legal battles with the federal government. In the end, they lost as well and were moved west in 1838 over what became known as the Trail of Tears. (Many of these tribes had some holdouts who managed to stay behind and would later be recognized by the U.S. government.)

With the eastern Indian tribes mostly out of the way, white Americans began looking westward. The idea of the Promised Land and the chosen people was replaced by the notion of "manifest destiny," which declared that the government of the United States and its citizens had a divine right to inhabit and develop the continent from coast to coast. Momentous events soon followed. The first wagon train carrying white pioneers across the Great Plains made the journey in 1841. The discovery of gold in California brought a rush of hopeful prospectors beginning in 1849. California, which had been invaded by the Spanish beginning in the 1600s and had survived several previous discoveries of gold, became a lawless, brutal land where peaceful Indians were slaughtered like wild animals. One of the most touching illustrations of this brutality was the discovery in 1911 of Ishi, a California Indian (Yahi) who was the last survivor of his tribe, a man who spoke a language that no one else in the world could speak or understand.

The central plains of North America, known for a time as the Great American Desert, were originally considered permanent Indian country, unfit for habitation by any people other than Indians. They were just a place to pass through going from the East to the West. That idea was abandoned, though, in the late 1850s when gold and silver were discovered in Colorado and miners flooded into the lands of the Cheyennes and Arapahos.

According to Oliver LaFarge, the year 1796 "is a convenient date for the beginning of the era of the horseback culture of the High Plains." The Sioux and the Cheyennes were both mounted by then. The Blackfoot, Crow, Comanche, and other tribes followed quickly and became seminomadic buffalo hunters. White men who began settling in the Great American Desert encountered these horsemen of the plains. The 1850s saw what LaFarge called minor wars and then treaties, and the treaties always included land cessions from the Indians. It was also a time of settling Indians on reservations, particularly in California.

The Civil War delayed U.S. government action against Indians in the West, for the government

A family of Plains Indians transports their possessions on a travois, a triangular frame of long wooden poles with buffalo rawhide stretched between them. Some Plains Indian tribes were nomadic, others semisedentary. All were eventually displaced. *(MPI/Stringer/Getty Images)*

concentrated its military efforts on the Confederate Army in the South. Many Indians were involved in the Civil War, however. According to Herman J. Viola, at least 3,000 Indians fought for the North, the most prominent being Seneca General Ely S. Parker, who penned Lee's surrender at Appomattox Courthouse. The so-called Five Civilized Tribes in what is today eastern Oklahoma divided internally, some joining the rebellion and others either joining the Union cause or fighting to remain neutral. The most prominent Confederate Indian was General Stand Watie, a Cherokee who was the last Confederate general to surrender.

When tribal annuity payments were delayed in Minnesota by the war, the Santee Sioux asked their agent for more food. He told them to eat grass. Insulted and angered, four young Santee killed a white family in a dispute over a few eggs, setting off the "Minnesota uprising." The Sioux killed 500 white Minnesotans, but the uprising was put down in four weeks. In the aftermath, 307 Santee prisoners were sentenced to hang, but President Abraham Lincoln intervened, so only thirty-eight were executed.

Following the Civil War, ranchers in Texas drove their cattle onto the Great Plains, or what they called open range, while railroads crossed the plains and towns sprang up here and there. Indian lands were diminished by treaties. Senator John C. Calhoun pronounced that the country's "great mission is to occupy this vast domain." However, the federal government recognized that title to land remained in the hands of the original inhabitants, and that is why the treaties became so important. In order for the United States to own the land, it was necessary to obtain documents showing legal transfer of the title to the lands.

Treaties could be gotten by bribes, by threats, or by establishing peace at the end of a war, and warfare became a favored means to force the Indian nations into submission on the plains. In 1861 Arapahos, under the leadership of Chief Little Raven, gave up to the federal government all their land in Nebraska, Kansas, and Wyoming, retaining only a small portion in Colorado for a reservation. Often wars were started on very little pretext. For example, in 1854 a Sioux Indian slaughtered a lame cow that appeared to have been abandoned.

Its Mormon owner complained to the U.S. Army, and Lieutenant John L. Grattan, in violation of the Fort Laramie treaty of 1851, took thirty soldiers out to arrest the "thief." The soldiers and Lieutenant Grattan were killed, and the army sent out a punitive expedition commanded by General William Selby Harney.

Following the Santee Sioux uprising in 1862, government attempts to punish Santee hiding among other tribes spread the war to the northern and central plains. Some of the most horrific massacres of the century occurred as the military attacked villages, making women and children share the horrors of the battlefield in their own homes. Massacres at Bear River (Utah) in 1863 and Sand Creek (Colorado) in 1864 devastated the tribes and inspired the survivors to additional resistance.

After the Civil War one of the main tactics of the U.S. government was to encourage the slaughter of buffalo. The lessons of General William Tecumseh Sherman's wartime marches through Georgia and South Carolina were applied to the West. The Plains Indians depended on the buffalo not just for food, but also for many other necessities. They used every part of a buffalo. The hides became robes and tepee covers. Bones and horns were made into tools and weapons. The skulls were used as ceremonial objects. Even the dung had a use as fuel. If the Indians had neither food source nor the other products they developed from the buffalo herds, they could be subdued. As a result, the army looked the other way when buffalo hunters went onto Indian land to kill buffalo.

In the Southwest, the Navajos had been starved into submission during the Civil War by troops under Kit Carson, who had destroyed their crops, leaving them destitute and sending thousands to a concentration camp at Bosque Redondo, far removed from their homeland. Quanah Parker, the last Comanche holdout, surrendered in 1875 in Texas after General Ranald Mackenzie pulled a surprise raid on his camp, destroying the lodges, the crops, the food supplies, and 1,400 horses. The Nez Percés were forced onto reservations following their epic flight in 1877. Geronimo, the last Apache resister, finally surrendered in 1886.

The Sioux and Cheyennes provided the Indians' great victory over the U.S. Army in 1876 when they soundly defeated Lieutenant Colonel George Armstrong Custer's 7th Cavalry at the Little Bighorn River in Montana Territory. But in 1890 at Wounded Knee, South Dakota, the 7th Cavalry slaughtered perhaps 300 Sioux men, women, and children.

Historian Frederick Jackson Turner claimed that the year 1890 marked the end of the frontier. By then almost all Indians were confined to reservations, though remnants of the removed eastern tribes were hiding out in various locations in the East and the so-called Five Civilized Tribes—the Cherokee, Choctaw, Chickasaw, Creek, and Seminole—were still living in independent republics in what is today the eastern part of Oklahoma. That would not last much longer. Oklahoma statehood came in just seventeen years.

What followed for most of the tribes was the reservation period, a time marked by graft and corruption, when Indians were confined to the reservations and furnished with spoiled meat, bug-infested flour, and other inferior supplies; a time when Indian children were taken far away from their homes to boarding schools where they were often horribly mistreated and forced to abandon their language and culture.

Even the reservations did not stop the taking of Indian land. In 1887 Congress passed the General Allotment Act, also known as the Dawes Act, under which the tribes' communal lands were divided, with 160 acres (65 ha) going to heads of households and smaller amounts to individuals. The remaining land, called surplus, was opened up to white settlers. As one example, the Iowa tribe in Oklahoma retained 8,500 acres (3,500 ha) after allotment, while 200,000 acres (85,000 ha) were declared surplus. In addition, railroad rights of way took more land, and President Theodore Roosevelt took millions of acres of Indian land for national parks and national forests.

It was the Indian Citizenship Act of 1924 that first granted tribal members the right to vote. Even so, the government was slow to recognize the importance of its new citizens. Under President Franklin D. Roosevelt's New Deal, in 1933, the federal government reversed its long-standing Indian policy. John Collier was named Commissioner of Indian Affairs. Allotment was ended. The Indian Reorganization Act of 1934 provided ways for tribes to increase their land holdings and form tribal governments that would be recognized by the federal government.

When World War II started, Indians from all over the country joined the military services. Many of them met Indians from other tribes, often tribes they had never heard of before, and they discovered that they had much in common, often problems. At the war's end, these Indians joined together and formed national Indian organizations to fight these common problems. But the 1950s brought a shift in federal Indian policy. A new relocation program took Indians from their home communities and placed them in major cities like Chicago and Los Angeles. A new termination program called for an end to the special relationship between the tribes and the federal government. Nineteen tribes were affected by this policy before it was halted.

The 1950s also brought another reversal. The Indian population had been diminishing ever since the arrival of Christopher Columbus, and it was widely known as the vanishing race. In the 1950s, the Indian population began to increase, soon becoming the fastest-growing segment of the population of the United States.

The 1960s brought yet another reversal with the Indian Self-Determination Act, which led to other positive actions for the tribes since then. Today many Indian tribes have become major employers operating casinos. They use gambling profits for education and road construction. Some tribes have funded their own clinics and new schools. Others have begun to develop major tourism industries and museums where they can highlight their own cultures.

Robert J. Conley

Further Reading

Andrist, Ralph K. *The Long Death: The Last Days of the Plains Indians*. Norman: University of Oklahoma Press, 2001.

Billard, Jules B., ed. *The World of the American Indian*. Washington, DC: National Geographic Society, 1974.

Brown, Dee. *Bury My Heart at Wounded Knee*. 30th Anniversary Edition. New York: Macmillan, 2001.

Jennings, Francis. *The Invasion of America*. Chapel Hill: University of North Carolina Press, 1975.

Kroeber, Theodora. *Ishi in Two Worlds: A Biography of the Last Wild Indian in North America*. Berkeley: University of California Press, 1962.

La Farge, Oliver. *A Pictorial History of the American Indian*. New York: Crown, 1956.

Viola, Herman J. *After Columbus*. Washington, DC: Smithsonian Books, 1990.

Waldman, Carl. *Atlas of the North American Indian*. New York: Facts on File, 1985.

Wissler, Clark. *Indians of the United States*. Garden City, NY: Doubleday, 1966.

The Fur Trade

Early Trading in Furs

The trade in animal furs and hides (primarily beaver, but as time passed, to a lesser degree martin, fisher, mink, raccoons, deer, bear, and bison) between North American Indians and early entrepreneurs from several European countries set the stage for an industry that was to later play one of the most important roles in the westward expansion of the United States. Practically every European power that sent exploration (and exploitation) parties to the New World during the sixteenth, seventeenth, and eighteenth centuries had as a primary goal the cultivation of the rich trade among the natives in high-quality furs. The business began when the first explorers set foot on the shores of the North Atlantic. Furs were already an important item of commerce in Europe, and it was only natural that seafarers from Scandinavian—and later, from France, England, the Netherlands, and Spain—took a hard look at the New World for the presence of animal skins that could add profit to adventure. From that long-ago day around 1000 C.E. when Indians along the northeast coast of America presumably offered to trade to the Vikings packs of dried peltries, the contest for ascendancy in the American fur business had begun.

The first formalized fur-trading organization in North America was the Hudson's Bay Company (HBC), chartered in 1670 as an exclusive grant to Prince Rupert, Duke of Bavaria, from his cousin, King Charles II of England. Rupert's vision was to acquire immense wealth by exercising his sole right to trade with the numerous Indian tribes living in the huge territory drained by the Hudson Bay in eastern Canada. For many years, HBC held unchallenged control over its trading territory, eventually expanding it across Canada all the way to the Pacific Ocean. The company's first serious challenger was another Canadian-based establishment, the North West Company (NWC),

founded in 1783 when several smaller fur businesses known collectively as "pedlars" combined their resources. The two giants, HBC and NWC, merged operations in 1821, by which time the new entity, still called the HBC, controlled more than 3 million square miles (7.8 million sq km) of fur-rich Canadian territory, serviced by 173 posts. In time, HBC extended its influence across the border into U.S. territory under the guidance of luminaries such as Sir George Simpson, John McLoughlin, and Peter Skene Odgen.

In colonial America, trapping and trading in furs was big business as well. Before the revolution, when frontiersmen from east of the Appalachian Mountains traveled west in search of new lands for themselves and their families, it was often the "long hunters," so called because of the lengthy periods of time they would be gone from home, who led the vanguard. Much of Tennessee and Kentucky were first explored and settled by long hunters and their families between the 1760s and 1780s.

United States Fur Trade Regulation and the Beginnings of Private Enterprise

By the time the United States began to reflect its national identity, much of the exploitation of animal furs in the eastern part of the continent was rapidly coming to an end, primarily because the major fur-bearing mammals—such as beaver—had been extirpated from the region. In 1796 the U.S. Congress attempted to control the fur industry west of the Appalachian Mountains by passing legislation that called for the permanent establishment of "factories," or government-owned trading posts, to be used in the Indian trade. The government strictly regulated trafficking in furs, and the organization of the factory system left no place for private citizens to engage in any aspect of the business. Under the plan, quality trade goods were warehoused at various factories and used to barter with neighboring Indians who were persuaded to bring their furs to these posts for exchange.

While the federal government attempted to regulate the fur trade in the East through the implementation and administration of the factory system, French, English, and Spanish agents still held control over the fur business in the trans-Mississippi West. That so much of this foreign commerce was taking place on land that President Thomas Jefferson thought should rightfully belong to the United States deeply troubled him. For years, he had dreamed of an American empire that stretched all the way to the Pacific Ocean. However, every time he attempted to organize a mission to explore the vast wilderness expanses of the far West, he saw his plans thwarted.

In 1803, when President Jefferson got the chance to purchase Louisiana from war-torn France for $15 million, he jumped at the opportunity. Even before the papers were signed transferring 828,000 square miles (2.1 million sq km) of Louisiana to U.S. ownership, Jefferson had convinced Congress to appropriate a sum of money to finance an expedition to the Pacific. For the leader of this mission, the president chose his former personal secretary and close family friend Meriwether Lewis. Lewis selected his one-time army associate and comrade William Clark as his co-commander.

Lewis and Clark found an abundance of beaver beginning in the vicinity of today's Platte County, Missouri, all the way to the Pacific. The journals kept by the two captains, as well as those by Patrick Gass, John Ordway, and Joseph Whitehouse, contain scores of entries describing the beaver in his natural habitat and marveling at his seemingly endless numbers. When published accounts of the Lewis and Clark Expedition became available to the public, the beaver's future along the Missouri River, in the Rocky Mountains, and in other parts of the American West was sealed.

In late summer of 1806, when Lewis and Clark were on the final leg of their return trip from the Pacific Ocean, they were met by trappers Forrest Hancock and Joseph Dickson. Rumors had already begun to circulate back East about the large number of beaver and other fur-bearing animals that expedition members had found on their westward journey. The two trappers were traveling to the Rocky Mountains to capitalize on the abundance of beaver there. Hancock and Dickson were unfamiliar with the territory and prevailed upon John Colter, one of the expedition's best men, to guide them. Colter consulted with his commanders who agreed to release him from expedition service. Colter's return to the mountains that summer marked the beginning of America's leap into the western fur trade.

Hancock and Dickson had just vanished into the wilderness of the Rocky Mountains, and Lewis and Clark had only recently returned to St. Louis to a heroes' welcome, when a Louisiana-born, St. Louis–based Spaniard named Manuel Lisa decided to try his hand at the new western fur trade. In 1807 Lisa took a small detail of traders/trappers up the Missouri River as far as the confluence of the Bighorn and Yellowstone rivers, where his men built Fort Lisa, or Manuel's Fort as it is sometimes called.

Lisa returned to St. Louis and in 1809 organized the St. Louis Missouri Fur Company, more commonly known as the Missouri Fur Company. For the next couple of years, he sent his outfit's expeditions up its namesake stream, and his coffers alternated between full and empty as the company vigorously pursued its business. To facilitate this trade, Missouri Fur built one post in the Three Forks area in present-day Montana and another one across the Continental Divide on the Snake River. By 1811, when all three of the company's fur posts were abandoned because of the futility of trying to deal with the hostile Blackfoot tribe, Lisa shifted his center of operations downstream and established new headquarters at Council Bluffs.

Over the years, the Missouri Fur Company experienced several reorganizations, until finally, in 1819, Lisa became president. He was the only one of the original founders to remain active within the company. His crowning success was short-lived, however, for in August 1820 the entrepreneur died. His associate, Joshua Pilcher, took over the day-to-day operations. One of Pilcher's first acts was to reopen the upriver trade, and in the fall of 1821, upon the site of the old Fort Lisa, he built a new structure, which he called Fort Benton. Under Pilcher's management, the company soared to financial success, and the following year, more than $20,000 worth of furs was shipped downriver to St. Louis. With 300 men in the field, Missouri Fur was finally on its way to the success that had so often eluded its founder.

The Blackfoot menace resurfaced in the spring of 1823. Pilcher sent two traders, Robert Jones and Michael Immel, along with twenty-eight companions, into the Three Forks region of the upper Missouri River, again hoping to establish peaceful contact with members of the tribe. Affairs turned sour and the Indians killed Jones, Immel, and five others, taking about $16,000 worth of furs, traps, horses, and other equipment in the process. The final blow had been delivered to the Missouri Fur Company and the firm's decade-long domination of the Missouri River fur trade ended.

While the St. Louis–based outfit had wielded its influence over the Great Plains and eastern front of the Rocky Mountains, another company had established itself at the mouth of the Columbia River and made inroads into the wilderness from the west. In the spring of 1811, at about the same time Manuel Lisa was focusing his Missouri Fur Company's operations along the middle Missouri River, sixteen men made their way through the damp undergrowth of thick evergreen forest overlooking the Columbia River and began work on a stockaded fur post they called Astoria. Named for John Jacob Astor, the founder of the American Fur Company and its subsidiary, the Pacific Fur Company, the fort was intended to provide a home base for Astor's traders and trappers from which they competed with the powerful North West Company, owned and operated by Canadians.

Astor's scheme to develop his far-reaching fur empire was to send two separate parties, one by land and the other by sea, to the mouth of the Columbia. There, the center for Astor's Pacific operations was built. The overland party left Montreal in July of 1810, under the leadership of Wilson Price Hunt and Donald McKenzie. The ocean-bound group, aboard the ship *Tonquin*, set sail from New York two months earlier. The ship's party arrived at the Columbia first, and its crew immediately began work on Astoria.

Astor's dreams of dominating the western fur business were no more successful than Manuel Lisa's. By mid-1812, the United States and Great Britain were once again at war. In October of the following year, operatives of the North West Company, Astor's archrival along the Columbia, marched on Astoria and occupied the post. All of the furs, furnishings, and supplies were commandeered in exchange for a cash settlement worth only about one-third of the fort's actual value. In December the British formally occupied Astoria and changed its name to Fort George. Now, after only two-and-a-half years in the business, Astor's influence on the western trade was placed on hold, and he was relegated to his earlier interests around the Great Lakes. It would be almost a decade before his dominance was again felt in the trans–Mississippi River West.

It was not only the upper Missouri River basin and the Pacific Northwest that held the interest of the American fur-trading and trapping community. Manuel Lisa developed an early interest in trading with citizens of Santa Fe, but after several unsuccessful attempts, he returned to his Missouri River endeavors. By the second decade of the nineteenth century, however, other St. Louis–based fur traders were frequenting New Mexico and the southern Rocky Mountains region. Ezekiel Williams and several other Americans trapped the upper Arkansas River valley beginning in 1811. In the fall of 1815, Auguste P. Chouteau and Jules de Mun obtained licenses permitting them to trade and trap among the Arapaho Indians, who lived near the headwaters of the Arkansas River. Two years later, Spanish officials arrested both men, hauled them off to Santa Fe, confiscated their furs and trade goods worth $30,000, and imprisoned them for forty-eight days.

Dawn of the Mountain Man Era

In 1821 Mexico won its independence from Spain. Anxious to improve the republic's commercial relations with the United States, Mexican officials opened their lands to American trappers. During that year and the next, Jacob Fowler, Hugh Glenn, and eighteen other trappers/traders journeyed to the headwaters of the Arkansas, where they explored and trapped the region for several weeks.

In addition to Mexico attaining independence in 1821, the year was momentous for the western American fur trade on other fronts. In March, the giant British-controlled HBC and its Canadian competitor, the NWC, merged operations. The resulting establishment—and one that remains in business today—became one of the most powerful fur-trading establishments in North America, particularly after John McLoughlin took over the company's management in 1824. HBC flourished throughout the vast Northwest, dominating a region twice the size of Texas.

Five days after the merger of HBC and NWC, the U.S. Congress passed a bill that abolished the government-controlled factory system, thereby opening the doors to the lucrative American fur trade with the Indians to any and all comers. The legislation was engineered by Missouri senator Thomas Hart Benton at the urging of American Fur Company officials, including John Jacob Astor and his field lieutenant, Ramsey Crooks, who by now had a vision of reentering the Missouri River trade.

In 1822 another outfit was organized that had a tremendous effect on the western trade. Although the fur industry had by then become a business that accommodated both traders and trappers who worked for the same company, this new organization was about to change that relationship. The days of traders swapping trinkets with Indians for their furs—the procedure that had been followed in the East and around the Great Lakes for scores of years—were about gone. The era of the highly individualistic trapper, the fabled "mountain man" who lived off the land and trapped his own pelts, was about to begin.

On February 13, 1822, the *Missouri Gazette & Public Advertiser* carried a notice that marked the beginning of this fascinating period in American history:

> The Subscriber wishes to engage ONE HUNDRED MEN, to ascend the river Missouri to its source, there to be employed for one, two, or three years—For particulars, enquire of Major Andrew Henry, near the Lead Mines, in the County of Washington, (who will ascend with, and command the party) or to the subscriber at St. Louis.
>
> William Ashley

Several days later, the *St. Louis Enquirer* carried Ashley's announcement and, for the next few weeks, the notice also appeared in other Missouri newspapers. The far-ranging Rocky Mountain Fur Company, although not called by that name until sometime later, had its beginnings from the date of that advertisement. Before it, too, passed out of existence years later, the company had on its payroll—in addition to General Ashley and Major Henry—many legends of the fur trade, including Jedediah Smith, Jim Bridger, David E. Jackson, William and Milton Sublette, Etienne Provost, Robert Campbell, Thomas Fitzpatrick, Jim Beckwourth, Edward Rose, Mike Fink, Moses Harris, and Hugh Glass.

As successful as the Ashley-Henry firm eventually became, it, too, had its share of trouble during the early days. Although Henry established a strong presence at the confluence of the Yellowstone and Missouri rivers during the fall of 1822, the company lost $10,000 worth of trade goods that year when one of its boats was destroyed by the rapid currents of the fickle Missouri.

Then, an additional setback was experienced the following year when Ashley started upriver to re-supply Henry's trappers who had wintered on the Yellowstone. When the general reached the Arikara villages, located atop the steep west bank of the Missouri River in present-day South Dakota, the Indians attacked his two boatloads of men and supplies and forced them back downriver. After Ashley's traders fought an indecisive battle—reinforced by elements of the 6th U.S. Infantry Regiment under the command of Colonel Henry Leavenworth, along with employees from Joshua Pilcher's Missouri Fur Company—the season was late and Ashley again suffered a large financial loss to his company.

After the Arikara campaign of 1823, Ashley dispatched two trapping parties, one under the leadership of Andrew Henry and the other commanded by Jedediah Smith. During the winter of 1823–1824, the two groups trapped in the region beyond the Rockies and found an abundance of beaver there. When they delivered their furs back to the Missouri settlements during the summer of 1824, the trappers informed Ashley of this fact plus the news that they had discovered a way through the mountains that could be negotiated with wagons. The idea that wheeled vehicles could be used for transporting goods and supplies to the mountains, plus the revelation that the Missouri Fur Company was redoubling its efforts to dominate the Missouri River trade, convinced Ashley that his future lay deep in the Rocky Mountains.

Considering all of the recent developments, Ashley contemplated a method whereby he could resupply his men in the new area of operations by a more direct route. His solution to the dilemma, known ever since as the rendezvous system, revolutionized the entire western fur trade. The premise was very simple. Instead of maintaining distant fur posts at various sites in the mountains, Ashley employees purchased supplies, traps, weapons, liquor, and trade goods in St. Louis and the Missouri settlements and then hauled them overland to a preselected rendezvous site somewhere in the Rocky Mountains. There, during the warm days of summer, the trappers descended from the mountains, spent a week or two with the Ashley resuppliers, swapped their furs for the supplies and trade goods they needed, and were gone in time for the fall hunt.

The benefits of the rendezvous were mutual. Operating this type of resupply system allowed Ashley to obtain the best quality beaver pelts at the point of origin, rather than forcing him to compete with other fur merchants, all of whom were simultaneously trying to convince the Indians to bring them their best furs. The rendezvous allowed the trappers to acquire badly needed supplies and equipment in their home territory, thus saving them hundreds of miles of travel to and from the Missouri settlements. From a social standpoint, the rendezvous provided the opportunity for trappers to leave their lonely vigil in the remote mountains and to relax, drink, gamble, and socialize with the Indian women who frequented the gatherings.

Ashley's first rendezvous took place during the summer of 1825, and, although the general soon left the fur business altogether, the system continued to work for company owner and fur trapper alike. A total of fifteen annual rendezvous were held between 1825 and 1840, the only exception being 1831 when there was no gathering because the supply train did not reach the rendezvous site on time. The majority of the fifteen took place in the western part of today's Wyoming, although two of them occurred in eastern Idaho and four were held in northern Utah.

William Ashley's participation in the rendezvous scheme lasted only two years. After the 1826 gathering, he sold his fledgling fur company to Smith and two other former employees, David Jackson and William Sublette (Andrew Henry had already retired and Ashley had taken Jedediah Smith on as a partner for a brief time). The new firm, now called Smith, Jackson & Sublette, was purchased by the three men for perhaps as much as $30,000; the records of the transaction have been lost. The sum was payable to Ashley in beaver furs valued at $3 per pound.

Although he was now out of the day-to-day management of the fur company he had founded, General Ashley nevertheless agreed to furnish Smith, Jackson & Sublette with the merchandise and supplies it required and promised that he would refrain from doing business with competitors. As soon as he returned to St. Louis, however, Ashley attempted to enter into a business relationship with another fur outfit, his old competitor, Bernard Pratt & Company. Ashley's offer was to allow Pratt one-half interest in a new enterprise to be called William Ashley & Company, thereby allowing Ashley to circumvent his earlier commitment to Smith and his partners not to furnish supplies to other companies. Apparently, Ashley's plan was to place more trapping parties in the field, thus going into direct competition not only with his old company, but also with himself as supplier to that company. The partnership never materialized since Pratt instead sold out to Astor's American Fur Company, becoming its Western Department.

For the next four years, the three new partners in Ashley's old company went far afield in the Rocky Mountain wilderness, trapping furiously to maintain their competitive edge over the growing number of other outfits that put their own men into the mountains. Jed Smith made two trips to California during this time. On the last journey, after Umpqua Indians massacred many of his party in southern Oregon, Smith ended up at Fort Vancouver.

After four years of declining profits, Smith, Jackson & Sublette decided to leave the mountains for more lucrative livelihoods. At the 1830 rendezvous, they made arrangements for five associates—Thomas Fitzpatrick, Jim Bridger, Milton Sublette, Henry Fraeb, and Jean Baptiste Gervais—to buy them out. The new consortium called their enterprise the Rocky Mountain Fur Company (RMF). Unfortunately, although the five partners were master trappers and veteran mountain men, none had the business background to orchestrate a long-term, successful commercial endeavor as complex as the fur business.

Nevertheless, for the next four years RMF, still supported in the field by the rendezvous system, became the most famous name in the business and, during its brief span, carried scores of well-known trappers on its payroll. Competition from others, particularly the American Fur Company and two newcomers to the field—Benjamin Louis Eulalie de Bonneville and Nathaniel Wyeth—was ruthless. The five partners watched helplessly as profits declined and as the beaver became increasingly elusive.

Both the Bonneville and Wyeth outfits came to the mountains in 1832. Bonneville was a French-born American army officer on leave of absence from the military, ostensibly for the purpose of exploring and documenting the Rocky Mountains. When his leave began in August 1831, his official mission notwith-

Trade in animal pelts—especially beaver—was a vital industry in the early history of North America, luring trappers and traders west into the frontier. Artist Alfred Jacob Miller portrayed this Rocky Mountain trapper at the 1837 rendezvous. *(The Granger Collection, New York)*

standing, Bonneville immersed himself in the fur trade. Over the next two years, Bonneville and his companions, one of whom was the renowned Joseph R. Walker, went head-to-head with the other companies. By the mid-1830s, Bonneville was back on regular duty with the army, his foray into the mountains in search of furs complete.

Nathaniel Wyeth, a Boston ice merchant who wanted to try his hand at the western fur trade, lacked the skills to make his efforts successful. During his tenure in the mountains, he and his followers worked with the HBC, attempted to be the primary supplier for the RMF's annual rendezvous of 1834, and tried to do business with Bonneville's organization, all with little success. After building Fort Hall at the junction of the Snake and Portneuf rivers, the dejected Wyeth eventually returned to Boston, where he continued his career in the ice business.

The Southwest trade was also alive and well during the early 1830s. Charles Bent and his partner, Cerán St. Vrain, organized Bent, St. Vrain & Company, and along with Bent's brother, William, built Bent's Fort along the mountain branch of the Santa Fe Trail in present-day southeastern Colorado. For the next several years, Bent's Fort became the primary depository for furs trapped in the southern Rockies and the far Southwest.

In the meantime, the RMF had changed hands once more. At the 1834 rendezvous, RMF passed from its owners to a new outfit called Fitzpatrick, Sublette & Bridger. Before the ink on the contract had dried, the firm was defunct, and Fitzpatrick and Bridger hired on with the American Fur Company.

The Demise of the Mountain Man Era

The end of an era was rapidly approaching. Changing styles in men's fashion had witnessed the introduction of silk hats in Europe, and the new look rapidly cut into the demand for beaver fur. By the mid-1830s, practically every stream and creek in the American West had been culled, and the innocent rodent was almost extinct. Although the annual rendezvous continued to be held until 1840, profits from the fur trade dwindled dramatically with each passing year. Individual trappers still roamed the mountains in search of pockets of beaver populations that might have escaped the onslaught of the past two decades. But by and large, the scarcity of the animal, the decreased demand for its fur, and the mounting numbers of emigrants intent on crossing the Great Plains and Rocky Mountains into Oregon, all spelled doom to the once-lucrative fur business. The torch had passed, and the only vestige of the once-brilliant flame of this important period of national history was the gleam in the eyes of old fur trappers as they rekindled stories from the past.

During the brief, so-called "mountain man" era, few places in the trans-Mississippi West were untrodden by white men's feet. Literature is abundant with narratives of the lengthy journeys of these wilderness travelers. In studying this vastly important period of westward expansion, a researcher might come across a particular mountain man in Taos, New Mexico, on the first day of May and read about his adventures in Montana in late July, only to find him in St. Louis in the fall. These adventurers collectively traveled tens of thousands of miles across the Great Plains and Rocky Mountains, passing their newfound knowledge of the geography, natural history, and ethnology of the vast region to generations of future travelers, historians, and scientists.

James A. Crutchfield

Further Reading

Berry, Don. *A Majority of Scoundrels.* New York: Harper & Brothers, 1961.

Chittenden, Hiram Martin. *The American Fur Trade of the Far West.* New York: Francis P. Harper, 1902.

DeVoto, Bernard. *Across the Wide Missouri.* New York: American Legacy Press, 1981.

———. *The Year of Decision: 1846.* New York: Book of the Month Club, 1984.

Hanson, James A. *When Skins Were Money.* Chadron, NE: Museum of the Fur Trade, 2005.

Lavender, David. *The Fist in the Wilderness.* Garden City, NY: Doubleday, 1964.

Robertson, R.G. *Competitive Struggle: America's Western Fur Trading Posts, 1764–1865.* Boise ID: Tamarack Books, 1999.

Utley, Robert M. *A Life Wild and Perilous.* New York: Henry Holt, 1997.

Weber, David J. *The Taos Trappers.* Norman: University of Oklahoma Press, 1971.

Overland Trails

Overland trails were the routes of migration, commerce, and communication of nineteenth-century westward expansion. Over time these western overland trails evolved into a complex network or system of roads that became the primary means for expansion of the American West.

A trip along the overland trails was a great gamble and the adventure of a lifetime for many who took the bold step. Depending upon the destination, such journeys required a great investment of time (as much as six months of travel) and effort, plus considerable financial investment to put together an outfit including a wagon, team (or teams) of oxen, mules, or horses, and food and other supplies. The crossing involved great risk associated with difficult terrain, harsh weather, illness, accident, disease, and in some cases renegades who stole livestock or, very rarely, attacked wagon trains. Most overland travelers made the journey on foot, slogging through the inhospitable and almost unimaginable environments of the Great Plains, the Rocky Mountains, and the Great Western Desert at a snail's pace of a few miles a day. The thousands of unmarked graves that pepper the landscape that the trails crossed are testimony to the difficulty of the trek.

Trails to California, Oregon, and Utah

From the beginning of settlement on the eastern coast, Americans began looking westward. The mid-nineteenth-century overland trails continued the process of westward movement of population that began in colonial times. When eastern settlement reached the Missouri River by 1840, migration across the plains to the Pacific Coast was the inevitable next stage. The overland trails prior to 1840—fur trade and missionary trails on the central route, and the Santa Fe Trail, a commercial trail, on the southern route—were international trails, since parts of Oregon country were under British control, and the region from Texas to California were part of Mexico. It was the development of the overland emigrant trails during the next three decades that shaped the American West.

During the emigrant trails era people tended to move to places on the same general latitude as they left from, partly because the routes that developed across the West were primarily determined by topography. The Rocky Mountains presented a formidable north-south barrier, so two major routes evolved: the central corridor that went up the Platte River and over South Pass, and the complex of southern trails that went across the Southwest to southern California. Travelers from the East and Midwest took the central route; those from the South found their way to the southern trails.

From 1841 to 1869, an estimated 500,000 people traveled on the overland trails seeking land, gold, economic opportunities, or religious freedom and in the process settled the West. Although there were northern, central, and southern emigration routes, the central route through the South Pass of the Rockies (now known as the Oregon, California, and Mormon Trails) had the most traffic and is the best known today.

Each decade of the emigrant trails era had distinct characteristics. In the early 1840s, the trails to Oregon, California, and Utah were in their beginning stages, and the wagon trains needed guides to lead them over the undeveloped routes. By 1844, as emigration increased, expansionists called for the annexation of Oregon and Mexican territories. More routes developed, and emigration became a steady flow. Migration swelled in the 1850s, due to the California gold rush and increased settlement of the Northwest and Utah. New trails, alternates, and cutoffs were opened, and older trails were shortened or improved. By the mid-1850s, stagecoaches and freight trains regularly used the overland trails. The 1860s was a decade of further refinement, development, and increasing complexity in the network of emigrant travel, freight, and stage roads, telegraph lines, and railroad construction. The Civil War in the East combined with the passage of the Homestead Act and Conscription Act swelled the ranks of emigrants.

Overland Trail Improvement and the Coming of the Railroad

The increasing number of residents in the West demanded improved transportation and communication links with the eastern states, and the federal government responded. In 1853 Congress authorized western railroad surveys, which began the following year. In 1856 the Pacific Wagon Road Office was created for the construction and improvement of wagon roads, and an overland mail service was authorized. While federal involvement was important, the great advances of the 1860s—the Pony Express, the Overland Mail, the transcontinental telegraph, and the Union Pacific Railroad—were all private enterprises. At the same time, settlers, freighters, and gold rushers continued to travel the overland trails.

Most trail historians agree that westward mass migration by wagon on the overland trails began in 1841 with the first emigrant party, the Bidwell-Bartelson party, which traveled from Independence, Missouri, to California. En route, some of the party broke off and went on to Oregon country instead, thus opening an emigration route to the Pacific Northwest. Most historians also agree that the emigrant trails era all but ended with the completion of the transcontinental railroad in 1869. The overland trails were important avenues of migration across the unsettled areas on the Northern Plains and parts of the Southwest in the 1860s. While the era of mass migration was over after the completion of the transcontinental railroad, settlers continued traveling overland in wagons into the twentieth century due to financial necessity or lack of railroad access to the more remote areas in the West.

Shortcuts, Cut-offs, and Hazards on the Trail

The development of the overland trails was shaped by destinations. The names of the first major trails refer to their destinations: Santa Fe Trail, Oregon Trail, and California Trail. The Mormon Trail is also a destination trail, although it is named for the religious group that pioneered it to settle in the Salt Lake Valley. As the overland trails evolved over time, some trails were named for pioneering parties (the Cherokee Trail), other trail names were purely descriptive (the Overland Trail—named after the Overland Mail route), and still others referred to the river drainage they followed (the South Platte Trail, Smoky Hill Trail, Gila Trail). Most of the major cutoffs or alternates, however, were named for the people who opened them (Applegate Trail, Barlow Road, Sublette Cutoff, Hudspeth Cutoff, Beale Road, Goodale Cutoff, Bozeman Trail, Bridger Trail). The names of others, such as the Greenhorn Cutoff, describing a supposed shortcut that actually added length to the journey, are descriptive.

Certain parameters determined the routes of trails. One of the most important was terrain. Because emigrant and freight wagons had a narrow wheelbase relative to their height, they were extremely top-heavy. That meant they could not go on the side of a hill, but rather went up directly and over hills if there was no way to reroute and avoid such ascents and descents. Instead of traveling in heavily vegetated ravines, they generally stayed on ridge tops, which were sometimes so narrow the wagons had to travel in single file. Grade or slope was another important factor. If the trail route was very steep, strenuous measures had to be taken to pull up, let down, or brake the wagons. Finally, the routes were determined by the needs of people and livestock. People, and particularly animals, needed water every few miles, so they traveled between water sources the best way the terrain allowed. Also, each evening overlanders needed fuel to cook meals and feed for the stock.

Western terrain presented difficult obstacles and hazards that notably characterized the overland trails. Major rivers were often dangerous or impossible to ford. Ferries and occasional bridges were soon established. The final challenge to the earliest Oregon Trail travelers was floating down the treacherous Columbia River on the last leg of their journey, prompting emigrants to open the Barlow Road around the slopes of Mount Hood to the Willamette Valley in 1846. Desert crossings and the Sierra Nevada marked the last great challenges on the California Trail. The various routes to the summit were rocky and steep, making crossing the mountains the most difficult part of the entire California Trail.

Not only were the overland trails physically arduous, but also they crossed through areas occupied by Indian tribes. In the first decade of the emigrant trails era, relations between Indians and emigrants were generally cooperative and friendly. In the 1850s the tremendous environmental and social impacts of massive traffic over the trails caused Indian-white

At peak usage in the 1850s, the Oregon Trail carried up to 10,000 pioneers a year from western Missouri to the Pacific Northwest. A painting by William Henry Jackson depicts a wagon train on the trail at Devil's Gate in Wyoming. *(The Granger Collection, New York)*

relations to deteriorate, inflicting serious conflict. Harsh treaties and punitive military campaigns led to increasing Indian attacks on overland travelers in the 1860s. Yet throughout the era, the romanticized danger of Indian attacks was not as great as popularly believed, and harm or death caused by Indians was a minor occurrence compared to disease and accidents.

Trails vs. Roads, Emigrants vs. Immigrants

Emigrants called the routes they traveled roads—just like the farm and country roads where they came from. While today the term "road" means a thoroughfare that has been constructed, to nineteenth-century travelers anything a wagon could get over was a road, while a trail was a footpath or horse path that wagons could not go on. Surveyors in the 1850s and 1860s often noted an "Old Emigrant Road" on their survey plats, as opposed to a little-used "trail" for walkers or horses.

Fundamental to the concept of the emigrant trails is an understanding of the word "emigrant." Emigrants are people who leave their home region to settle in another place or country, as opposed to immigrants, who come into an area from another country to settle. In the emigrant trails era, emigrants saw themselves as leaving their eastern homeland and traveling overland to another home in the West. The basic concept is leaving one place for another within the same country. The gold rushers and those who followed them, the freighters and merchants, did not generally think of themselves as emigrants going to settle in a new place. To encompass the great variety of overland travelers in the mid-nineteenth century, modern writers often use terms such as "migrants" and "overlanders."

Trails of the Gold Rush

The well-known emigrant trails on the central route—the Oregon Trail, the California Trail, the

Mormon Trail, the Applegate Trail, the Barlow Road—were all opened in the pre–gold rush period when the majority of overlanders were families traveling to new homes in the Willamette Valley, northern California, or the Salt Lake Valley. After 1849, the first great year of the California gold rush, the trails changed rapidly and dramatically. The most important change was the proliferation of new routes. A myriad of new trails and cutoffs developed on the California Trail, and regional roads increased in California. More regional roads also developed in the Northwest to serve Oregon Trail travelers moving to new destinations.

The central Platte River–South Pass route had three general components: feeder routes, the main corridor (made up of alternates and cutoffs along the main route), and destination routes. At the eastern end, feeder routes on the north and south sides of the Platte River went from the jumping-off places like Nebraska City, Nebraska, and St. Joseph, Missouri, on the Missouri River and came together at Fort Kearny, in present-day central Nebraska. Trails went west from Fort Kearny on both the north and south sides of the Platte, now known as the Great Platte River Road, and through South Pass (now in central Wyoming) in a corridor made up of alternates and cutoffs. Farther west, destination routes departed from the main route and went to final destinations in Oregon, California, and Utah. In the Colorado gold rush, a new destination route left the main route west of Fort Kearny and went to Colorado along the South Platte River. In the 1860s, during the Montana gold rush, the Bozeman and Bridger trails left the Platte route farther west for destinations in Montana. Also in the 1860s, a northern overland route from Minnesota to Montana brought gold rushers from the East, and the Mullan Road was traveled from the West.

Southern Trails

The origins of the southern emigrant trails were different from the central trails like the Oregon and California trails. Rather than feeder routes to a main corridor, southern trails left from varying departure points and continued parallel to each other for some or all of the distance. Most of the southern trails to California were opened for emigrant traffic by the federal government, first during the war with Mexico in 1846 and later by the surveys attempting to find more direct overland routes to the Pacific coast. In spite of their military origins, the routes opened by General Stephen Watts Kearny's Army of the West and Lieutenant Colonel Philip St. George Cooke and the Mormon Battalion became authentic emigrant trails when they were heavily used by gold seekers in the early gold-rush years. Similarly, emigrant routes from Fort Smith, Arkansas, to Santa Fe and to El Paso were opened for emigrants by a military expedition under Captain Randolph Marcy in 1849.

Heavy emigrant traffic on the southern route began with the California gold rush. By the late 1840s several jumping-off places in eastern and southern Texas had been established that were used by gold seekers traveling to California. Texas was not the only departure point during the gold rush. The Santa Fe Trail changed from a commercial route to one also used by California-bound gold seekers. Other gold-rush trails developed as well, including the Fort Smith to Santa Fe trail that went along the Canadian River and the Fort Smith to El Paso trail across northern Texas. Most of the gold rushers on the southern route eventually joined the Gila Trail and continued to the Yuma crossing of the Colorado River and then across the desert to Warner's Ranch in southern California. It is estimated that at least 20,000 gold rushers traveled to California on the various southern trails in 1849.

Changes in the overland trails greatly accelerated in the 1860s. Before the Civil War, the first stagecoach lines linked cities on the Missouri River to Salt Lake City and San Francisco on the central route, and St. Louis to San Francisco on a southern route. After the war, the western trails and roads became a diverse, overlapping, and interconnected network of emigrant, mining, freighting, mail, and stage roads. The completion of the transcontinental railroad in 1869 ended the era of mass migration solely by wagon travel and marked the transition to regional roads connecting all parts of the developing West.

In the twentieth century, the story of westward expansion—the process of people moving westward across the continent and eventually filling it up—emerged as America's fundamental story. Trails made the process of settling the West possible. They were the iconic paths of westward expansion, the means of creating a continental nation. While individuals were the agents of expansion, the overland trails enabled them to accomplish it. Yet often overlooked in this dramatic story is the ultimate consequence of settling the West: the total disruption, conquest, and ultimate dispossession of the Indians who first inhabited the western landscape traversed by the overland trails.

Susan Badger Doyle

Further Reading

Buck, Don. "Those Who, What, When, Where Questions About Emigrants and Emigrant Trails." *News from the Plains*, Oregon-California Trails Association Newsletter (July 1994).

National Geographic Society. *Trails West*. Washington, DC: National Geographic Society, 1979.

Unruh, John D., Jr. *The Plains Across: The Overland Emigrants and the Trans-Mississippi West, 1840–60*. Urbana: University of Illinois Press, 1982.

West, Elliott. "American Pathways." In *Journeys to the Land of Gold: Emigrant Diaries from the Bozeman Trail, 1863–1866*, vol. 2, ed. Susan Badger Doyle. Helena: Montana Historical Society Press, 2000.

Western Writers of America. *Pioneer Trails West*, ed. Don Worcester. Caldwell, ID: Caxton Printers, 1985.

The Military Establishment

Importance of the Military Establishment in Westward Expansion

A bugle blast followed by charging cavalry troopers, sabers and pistols drawn, who chase away Indian warriors ready to finish off a small group of emigrants—this is what many people visualize when they think of the American military on the frontier. However, there is much more to the story than the simple fable portrayed by Hollywood. Although mountain men may have led the way, it was the soldiers of the military who provided the seeds for—and served as fundamental instruments of—westward expansion by the fledgling American democracy. They offered more than security to those who followed. The military brought people from cultures almost all over the world to the West. These individuals brought science, culture, technology, art, music, literature, engineering, and religion with them. They brought what was good and bad about society. They served as instruments in the collapse of American Indian tribal societies as well as proponents for the protection for those same tribes. The military payroll and military contracts promoted industry and agriculture in the West. Many of the soldiers chose to stay when their enlistments were up.

Early Military Affairs From the Revolution to the War of 1812

Misunderstandings and heavy-handedness on the part of Great Britain resulted in the American colonies declaring independence in 1776. The U.S. Congress raised an army to fight the British, who enlisted Indians to fight the Americans. British loyalists and their Indian allies conducted brutal frontier warfare, enraging many Americans and convincing them that independence was the correct choice.

Virginian George Rogers Clark led a military offensive in the Northwest Territory, capturing settlements under British control. By holding this territory, Clark procured what would become many of the Midwestern states. Several years after the 1783 Treaty of Paris, the federal government reduced the military due to a lack of funds and the people's mistrust of a standing army. Many settlers heading west were army veterans of the Revolution whom the government paid for their services with land grants.

In 1791 President George Washington led the army to put down the Whiskey Rebellion, an insurrection in western Pennsylvania over the payment of a federal tax on whiskey. The army's presence confirmed the federal government's authority to tax and its strong central role in keeping peace in the states.

At the Battle of Fallen Timbers, in 1794, in present-day Ohio, the U.S. army under the command of General "Mad" Anthony Wayne defeated a large, well-organized coalition of Indian tribes. The next year General Wayne negotiated the Treaty of Greenville with the defeated tribes, paving the way for further settlement of the Northwest Territory.

In 1803 the United States purchased Louisiana Territory from France. The transaction doubled the size of the United States. France transferred the territory to the United States in St. Louis on March 9, 1804. Captain Amos Stoddard, commanding an army artillery company, stood as the representative of the U.S. government. Captains Meriwether Lewis and William Clark, younger brother of George Rogers Clark, also attended. They led the Corps of Discovery, a military unit commissioned by President Thomas Jefferson to explore the new territory and to explain to the inhabitants that they were now part of the United States and that the nation desired peace and trade with all the peoples under its dominion. The Corps of Discovery left American territory and proceeded to the Pacific Ocean, attempting to find the fabled Northwest Passage that the United States could use as an easy route for trade with China. The Corps of Discovery was a success, but the route it found was not. The explorers kept detailed journals on people, topography, animals, and natural sciences. Upon their return in 1806, their exploration and findings led to further establishment of the U.S. claims to the entire Missouri and Mississippi river basins and the Oregon country.

The United States sent out other expeditions. One led by Lieutenant Zebulon Pike surveyed and collected scientific information in the southwest portion of the Louisiana Purchase in 1806–1807. When his party entered New Mexico, the Spanish captured them, but later released them.

In 1811 the Shawnee leader Tecumseh united tribes in the Old Northwest Territory and southern tribes east of the Mississippi to resist further advancement of American settlers. The Indian force attacked advancing U.S. troops and Indiana militia led by Governor William Henry Harrison. The army defeated the Indian force at the battle of Tippecanoe on November 7, 1811. This battle reduced Tecumseh's influence with the tribes in the Northwest.

Renewed friction between Great Britain and the United States broke out into the War of 1812, with much of the fighting taking place on the frontier. The battle of New Orleans was one of the most famous battles in the West. The Americans withstood the British attack and won the battle in January 1815. The United States retained New Orleans as an important port for the shipment of raw materials out of the Mississippi-Missouri river basin and the importation of finished goods.

From the End of the War of 1812 to the Civil War

In 1820 Major Stephen Long led a survey and scientific expedition up the Platte River to the Rocky Mountains of Colorado and then back by way of the Arkansas and Red rivers. Long's official map labeled the Great Plains "The Great American Desert." This false concept of the plains as a desert was portrayed on maps for fifty years, discouraging national expansion as thousands of emigrants bypassed the rich croplands of the plains on their way to farms in Washington, Idaho, and California.

America's mercurial policy toward the Indians during the early 1800s was to buy their land or forcefully evict them through battle, and then move them further west. The army and local militia led by Andrew Jackson fought a series of wars with the Creek and Seminole tribes in the south, and in 1832 American forces fought the Fox and Sauk tribes in the north in engagements known as the Black Hawk War. These wars paved the way for further settlement of the frontier.

In 1824 the federal government established the Office of Indian Affairs (OIA) as part of the War Department. In 1849 the OIA was transferred to the Interior Department, creating friction for the rest of the nineteenth century between the OIA and the military on how to administer the Indian tribes.

Between 1830 and 1840, the government supported the concept of a permanent Indian frontier, coinciding with the Great American Desert, beyond which all Indian tribes would be moved. In 1830 Congress passed, and President Andrew Jackson signed into law, the Indian Removal Act, which forced thousands of Indians, including Cherokees, Chickasaws, Creeks, and Choctaws, to move to the permanent Indian frontier. One of the federal government's most infamous removals used the military to force the Cherokee and other tribes to move west to modern-day Oklahoma. Thousands died as they traveled the Trail of Tears or were held in prison camps while awaiting the journey.

The army built Forts Gibson on the Arkansas River, Townson on the Red River, and Leavenworth on the Missouri River to keep the tribes from warring against American citizens and against each other. These forts served as staging points for military expeditions and regulated trade into Indian country. When Congress passed a law in 1832 prohibiting liquor among Indians, the military tried to enforce this law by inspecting wagons, pack animals, and trade vessels.

The army also had duties not involving fighting and controlling Indian tribes. These included exploration, surveying, mapping, scientific data collection, and building and maintaining transportation systems. The Army Corps of Engineers and the Corps of Topographical Engineers were responsible for many of these activities. The federal government merged the Corps of Topographic Engineers with the Corps of Engineers in 1863.

The army's first major building project was the National Road. Congress authorized the building of the road and the army began construction at Cumberland, Maryland, in 1811. Funding for the National Road was sporadic, ending when the army completed it in 1839 at Vandalia, Illinois. The army built the road using a new process, called macadamizing, which created a hard, stable surface. Thousands of pioneers used the National Road journeying west.

Lieutenant John Charles Frémont with the Corps of Topographic Engineers led a series of surveying and scientific expeditions to the West Coast from 1842 to 1845. Congress ordered 10,000 copies of Frémont's expedition reports published, including topographic maps, scenic illustrations, scientific observations, and a narrative of the expedition's travels. These publications established Frémont as a national celebrity, popularly called the Pathfinder. They also provided valuable information for people intent on moving into the West.

The Corps of Engineers and Corps of Topographic Engineers mapped the Great Lakes, the Missouri and Mississippi rivers, and their tributaries. They surveyed the nation's boundaries with Canada and Mexico. They cleared snags from rivers and surveyed and built roads for commerce and military movement. The corps built forts and coastal fortifications and built and repaired telegraph lines.

Between 1840 and 1860, the government spent a great deal of money on the military's western topographic and scientific expeditions. From 1853 to 1855, the Topographical Engineers surveyed the West for transcontinental railroad routes. The government published the reports in twelve volumes containing maps, illustrations, and information on topography, geology, plants, animals, and Indian tribes.

As the railroads were being built, the army protected them from Indian attacks. Former soldiers and officers worked for the railroads, bringing efficiency to the building and the running of the roads. The railroads were a help to the military, allowing it to move troops quickly and expensively to those places where they were needed. This eventually led to a reduction in the number of western forts.

When possible, the army shipped supplies and men by river and steamboats. Infantry marched and cavalry rode horses. Horse-drawn and ox-drawn wagons hauled supplies. General George Crook used pack mules in his campaigns. The army even used camels for transport and to haul supplies in the Southwest. The Camel Corps was in existence from 1855 until the Civil War. The camels did a good job, but they frightened horses and mules so the army eventually abandoned them.

In 1836 Americans living in Texas declared and won their independence from Mexico. In 1846 Texas joined the United States, setting off a war with Mexico. General Stephen Watts Kearny led his Army of the West over the Santa Fe Trail and occupied New Mexico without firing a shot. Americans and Hispanics in California revolted against Mexico and established the Bear Flag Republic, paving the way for its occupation by U.S. troops and naval ships.

American forces invaded Mexico and captured Mexico City in 1848. Many of the country's Civil War military leaders received valuable battlefield experience while serving in the Mexican-American War. At the signing of the Treaty of Guadalupe Hidalgo, in 1848, the United States territory again expanded by more than 1 million square miles (2.5 million sq km).

The army now had a vast new area to protect, not so much from Russian, British, Canadian, or Mexican invaders as from internecine violence perpetrated by the inhabitants of the area upon one another and upon newcomers flooding into the West. Hollywood lore shows abundant examples of the military's role in protecting wagon trains of settlers from Indian tribes defending their hunting grounds. Little is portrayed of the military's role in general policing of the West and its involvement in a broad range of economic, ethnic, and cultural disputes throughout the region. Disagreements between cattlemen and sheep herders, miners and ranchers, competing ranching interests, Mormons and non-Mormons, competing Indian tribes, Chinese and Irish miners, management and labor— such disputes often found the military squarely in the middle trying to maintain the peace. The army further served to protect the national borders and fulfill treaty obligations to combat raiding by inhabitants of the United States, be they filibusters or Indians, into neighboring countries. Soldiers hunted down thieves and murderers and often protected the court system until civil authorities were firmly established.

The army's fight against the Indian tribes was different from fighting a conventional war. It was more of a guerrilla war in which the army adopted many of the Indians' own tactics to use against them. Each tribe was different. The army had to know which tribes were friendly and which were enemies. The distinction between friend and foe changed not only in time, but also according to location. The Comanche could be at peace with Americans at one location, but at war with Texans, whom they considered different from Americans, at a different location. In 1849, in order to protect travelers on the trails, the government built new forts or bought strategic fur-trading posts and stationed soldiers at them—it built Fort Kearny in Nebraska and purchased Fort Laramie, Fort Hall, and Fort Vancouver along the Oregon Trail. The same process occurred along the other major trails and up the Missouri River, where old fur posts such as Fort Pierre and Fort Union were purchased and new forts—Sully, Randall, Rice, and Buford—were built.

As the army built forts, local economies developed around them. Farms and ranches supplied crops, cattle, and horses. The freighting business, destined to be used at military posts, was handled by private contractors, supporting the rudimentary transportation infrastructure in the West. Businesses sold luxury items and provided entertainment to the troops. The forts protected not only travelers, but also settlers. As the government moved tribes to reservations, the army not only kept the tribes on the reservations, but kept illegal settlers, thieves, and whiskey peddlers off.

The Church of Jesus Christ of Latter-day Saints, or Mormons, established their Zion in Utah in 1847, then part of Mexico, and were reluctant to recognize the federal authority over their own theocracy. The government sent the army to establish a U.S. presence in 1857–1858. After a brief conflict in which Mormon militia were responsible for the largest massacre of a wagon train in the history of westward expansion (Mountain Meadows), the Mormons eventually accepted the federal government's authority. A fort was established in Utah and an alternative trail route was identified around this potentially dangerous sect. Utah was reduced in size.

The Civil War Years

In 1861, with the outbreak of the Civil War, many army officers and soldiers on the frontier resigned to join the Confederacy. The Union and Confederate forces fought battles in the West. They fought many in Missouri, Arkansas, and the Southwest. The Union was able to hold on to California, Colorado, and the goldfields in Montana and eventually secured New Mexico Territory as well as Confederate Arizona Territory. The federal government gave Confederate prisoners the option to leave prison and serve on the frontier. Roughly 6,000 men switched from gray to blue uniforms and were called Galvanized Yankees (blue on the outside and gray on the inside). Western states and territories such as California, Nebraska, Nevada, Colorado, and Washington organized volunteer units to take the place of the regular army called east to fight in the war. One such unit, the First Nebraska Volunteers, originally an infantry unit, was later mounted and guarded the Oregon Trail in Nebraska Territory.

The Santee Sioux revolted and killed hundreds of Minnesotans in 1862. Minnesota called in volunteer units to fight and defeat the Sioux, many of whom fled to Dakota Territory and joined Sioux tribes living there. The pursuit of the Santee led to expansion of the war and involved large numbers of tribesmen who had nothing to do with the events in Minnesota. Fighting ranged over the northern and central plains, an area larger than that encompassed by the Civil War in the East. The emigrant trails became a central theater of conflict in this greater war. In 1863 the military massacred an encampment of mostly Bannocks in present-day Utah at Bear River.

Raids by hostile tribes of Arapahos and Southern Cheyennes in Colorado were an extension of the conflict sparked in Minnesota. In November 1864, John Chivington led a Colorado volunteer unit in an attack at Sand Creek on a peaceful Cheyenne village under the leadership of Black Kettle. Seeing the troops approach the village, Black Kettle raised an American flag to show that his people were peaceful. It did not matter; Chivington ordered an attack that killed many women and children as well as men. The troops mutilated bodies and took scalps to Denver for display. Peaceful tribes were horrified and began open warfare against the white invaders. A large segment of the American population was outraged, but the damage was done and the military spent years trying to reestablish peace.

After Sand Creek the Indians altered their strategies and tactics; instead of raiding targets of opportunity with small parties, they started choking off strong points with large forces. Indians stockpiled supplies for their villages and formed parties of as many as 1,000 warriors. Such vast forces easily brushed aside the small contingents of under twenty soldiers protecting the many telegraph and stage stations along the trail system. More than 200 miles (300 km) of stations along the Overland Trail were burned in the Bloody Summer of 1865. The town of Julesburg, Colorado, was sacked and burned twice that summer despite having a large fort nearby. It was only the influx of huge numbers of troops from the East after the surrender of the Confederacy that stemmed the tide of Indian victories.

The Post-Civil War Years

In 1865 the army began surveying the Bozeman Trail through Sioux territory without the tribe's permission, building a series of forts to protect travelers to the Montana goldfields. The Sioux resisted this trespass and fought against the army in Red Cloud's War, which ended with the 1868 Fort Laramie Treaty. The government abandoned the trail and forts and created the Great Sioux Reservation, which included the Black Hills, for the Sioux.

Following the Civil War, many Union officers of volunteer units returned to the regular army and influenced its policy during the last part of the nineteenth century. Ulysses S. Grant, who had been overall commander of the Union troops, became president of the United States, thereby vastly influencing Indian policy. Generals such as Philip H. Sheridan and William Tecumseh Sherman carried out those policies.

In 1868 General Sheridan sent Lieutenant Colonel George Armstrong Custer out at the head of the 7th Cavalry to attack the Cheyenne. He found them at

Washita, and attacking the village in the winter, he caught the Indians unaware. Black Kettle and other warriors, as well as women and children, were killed. The army now set upon a course of attacking villages in the winter to destroy the Indians' means of survival so they would have to surrender and go to reservations.

Presidents selected territorial governors because of their military careers. For example, President Rutherford B. Hayes appointed Lew Wallace, a Civil War officer and hero, as governor of the Territory of New Mexico. While contending with lawlessness, the Lincoln County War, and marauding Apaches, Wallace finished his great novel, *Ben Hur*.

The Oregon country had seen bloody warfare. Militia and regular troops battled Indian tribes during the Cayuse War (1847–1850) and the Rouge River Wars (1850s). These wars opened up Oregon and Washington for further settlement. In 1872–1873, a small group of Modocs fought the army on a bizarre battlefield through lava beds in northern California. They surrendered after a six-month standoff.

In 1874, after years of Comanche, Kiowa, and Cheyenne raids into Texas, General Sheridan initiated the Red River War; after a series of battles, the Indians surrendered and returned to their reservations.

In 1876 the government declared any Sioux not residing at their agencies hostile. Tensions had been

An 1875 photograph by Mathew Brady brings together five U.S. Army generals prominent during the Indian Wars *(left to right)*: Philip H. Sheridan, James W. Forsyth, Wesley Merritt, Thomas Devin, and George Armstrong Custer. *(Mathew Brady/Stringer/Getty Images)*

building ever since Custer had led an expedition through the Black Hills of the Great Sioux Reservation and reported placer gold in the streams. This report set off a gold rush, angering the Sioux. The military tried to stop the onrush, but was unsuccessful. The government decided it would be easier to buy the Black Hills from the Sioux. Many Sioux remained away from the agencies in the region of the Bighorn Mountains. The government sent out three columns of troops to trap the Sioux in a pincer movement and bring them to their reservation. On June 17, General George Crook's troops fought the Sioux at the Battle of the Rosebud. On June 25, Custer's 7th Cavalry found the Sioux and Cheyenne village on the Little Bighorn River. Custer divided his force and attacked. He and more than 200 men in his immediate command were killed. The other elements of his force just barely survived and were rescued when the rest of the joint columns from the north arrived at the scene of the battle. After the Battle of the Little Bighorn, the army was relentless in chasing down the hostile tribes until they were killed, surrendered, or escaped into Canada with Sitting Bull.

The Nez Percé had been friends with Americans since the Lewis and Clark Expedition, but after constant pressure from settlers and the loss of their homeland, some of the warriors killed a few settlers in 1877, and the Nez Percé War was on. The Nez Percé, led by Chief Joseph, tried to escape to Canada, but the army headed them off before most of them could escape. In all these battles, many of the soldiers were sympathetic to the Indians, but they had a job to do and they did it.

The Apaches had undertaken guerrilla warfare against the Mexicans for years and then against the Americans until 1886, when the Apache leader, Geronimo, surrendered to General Nelson Miles. Miles coordinated 5,000 troops and Apache scouts using a new method of signaling called a heliograph, essentially a solar telegraph that flashed messages long-distance by using mirrors and sunlight.

In 1890 the Sioux adopted a new religion sweeping through the Indian tribes. This new religion included a "Ghost Dance." Settlers and Indian agents became nervous that this new religion would turn violent. They asked for federal troops for protection and got it. After the attempted arrest and killing of Sitting Bull, a group under the leadership of Big Foot left the Standing Rock Reservation. The army, including the 7th Cavalry, intercepted and detained them at Wounded Knee. When the soldiers began to disarm the warriors, shots were fired and many people were killed. This frozen massacre site is recognized as the last of the army's participation in the Indian wars.

The army was made up of all sorts of men—farm boys, backwoodsmen, ne'er-do-wells, the well-educated, the illiterate, men from cities and towns as well as those who just got off the boat from England, France, Ireland, Germany, and every other European country. American Indians served with the military since the Revolution. On the frontier, they served as scouts and as auxiliary troops and eventually as regular troops.

During the Civil War, the Union allowed black soldiers to serve in the army; by the end of the war, 185,000 black soldiers had served. After the war, several exclusively black units (the 9th and 10th Cavalry Regiments and the 24th and 25th Infantry Regiments) were assigned to the West. These units served with distinction during the last half of the nineteenth century. The Indians called the African-Americans buffalo soldiers because their black curly hair resembled the hair of buffalo.

In the twentieth and twenty-first centuries, American Indians joined the military during both world wars and the wars in Korea, Vietnam, the Persian Gulf, Afghanistan, and Iraq. Throughout the life of the nation, the American military has been the nation's great experiment showing that all people, no matter what their background, can work together to defend the United States.

Bill Markley

Further Reading

Ambrose, Stephen E. *Nothing Like It in the World: The Men Who Built the Transcontinental Railroad, 1863–1869.* New York: Simon & Schuster, 2000.

Beers, Henry P. "A History of the U.S. Topographical Engineers, 1813–1863." *Military Engineer* 34 (June 1942).

Billington, Ray Allen. *Westward Expansion: A History of the American Frontier.* New York: Macmillan, 1949.

Downey, Fairfax. *Indian-Fighting Army.* New York: Bantam Books, 1963.

Goetzmann, William H. *Army Exploration in the American West, 1803–1863.* Lincoln: University of Nebraska Press, 1979.

Hutton, Paul Andrew. *Phil Sheridan and His Army.* Norman: University of Oklahoma Press, 1999.

Rickey, Don, Jr. *Forty Miles a Day on Beans and Hay.* Norman: University of Oklahoma Press, 1963.

Utley, Robert M. *Frontiersmen in Blue: The United States Army and the Indian, 1848–1865.* Lincoln: University of Nebraska Press, 1981.

Gold Rushes

A series of international gold rushes, from California in 1848 to Alaska at the end of the century, began the great mining frontiers that transformed the West. In contrast to the steady waves of agricultural migrations drawn to land and settlement, gold rushes were peaks of contagious excitement that attracted tens of thousands of adventurers all at once into rugged areas generally not suitable for agriculture. The rushes were fueled by a liberal policy of the U.S. government that allowed miners to take resources from publicly held lands, even ceding the ownership of the mining claims. While gold rushes were essential to developing the West, they were also short-lived, exploitive, and environmentally destructive. Each gold rush was a temporary boom followed by dispersal of the miners into other occupations or their departure to another mining boom. Gold rushes had important long-term effects on the West. White settlements suddenly sprang up in remote areas. New overland routes proliferated. The influx of masses of people in some areas provoked conflicts with Indians. The landscape was transformed. New territories and states were rapidly created. Businesses, services, and agriculture boomed in the mining camps, towns, and cities. As each rush ended and mining shifted from individual and egalitarian endeavor to industrial business and wage labor, large-scale mining industries significantly shaped the developing West.

Characteristics and Required Skills of a Gold Rusher

The most noticeable characteristic of gold-rush populations is the predominance of men—mostly young and single or without their families. Their goal was adventure and instant wealth rather than a commitment to a new life. The move was seen as temporary, and once the adventurers had obtained sufficient gold or money, they intended to return home. If they stayed, they often turned to other occupations and ei-

ther went home to bring their families back or sent for them.

Life in the goldfields was a constant adjustment to new circumstances and changing conditions. Mining camps were a mixture of Americans, foreigners, and ethnic minorities. They were transient communities thrown together under difficult circumstances. Most miners organized into mining companies, groups of six to eight who lived and worked together for mutual support and efficiency. Miners usually cooked for themselves, but also most camps had public eating-places. Shelters were crude and temporary, ranging from wagons or tents to frames with canvas sides and roof, although some were built of logs.

Most gold seekers did not find wealth, but the occasional rich strikes of the lucky few kept the rest motivated for a time. Once started, a gold rush kept going more on hope and rumor than reality. As the number of miners increased, the claims got smaller, opportunities diminished, and mining became more competitive. At the same time, the prices for food and other necessities were astronomical. Many miners were able to earn enough to make a living, but the net earnings of some miners fell so low that they were forced to remain in the gold camps because they did not have enough money for transportation back home.

Most gold rushes had relatively brief periods of activity, based on placer mining, or gathering gold that had been washed out of its original deposit into streambeds or gravels. The gold from placers was simpler to mine than veins or lodes, which required complex machinery and techniques to separate the gold from the rock in which it was encased. Thus, placer mining was ideally suited to the limited skills, equipment, and capital of the majority of gold seekers. The simplest means of placer mining was panning. The miner washed the sand and gravel out of the pan into a stream, leaving the heavier gold particles. The basic tools used for panning were the gold pan, pick, and shovel. Because the basic activity in the placer mines was digging with a pick and shovel, the mines were called "diggings."

Placer mining was extremely hard work under harsh conditions. Washing pans was slow and tedious, and machines were soon developed in the California gold rush. The first machines were rockers, or cradles, which were introduced in 1848. A rocker was a faster way of washing the dirt. The long tom, or tom, was introduced in late 1849. It was an improvement over the rocker, but took at least two men to keep the gravel and water flowing. A year later the sluice, a series of long wooden boxes, was developed. Machines allowed men to pool their labor and more efficiently mine the placers. These machines were used in every later rush in the West.

Since gold mining was such hard work, often with little return, many gold seekers realized that the way to make money was not to be a miner but to sell something or provide a service to other miners. The phenomenon of finding more profit in commerce and services than mining has been called "mining the miners." In every gold rush, a predictable "second rush" followed closely behind the first miners, bringing goods and services to the mining camps. While few miners became wealthy, entrepreneurs often did—and many amassed huge fortunes. The few women in the mining camps and towns played an important role. Many of them took advantage of the entrepreneurial opportunities for their domestic skills and made enormous profits.

The shift from mining by individuals and small groups to industrial mining using hydraulics and hard-rock mining marked the end of a gold rush. The inevitable introduction of vein or lode mining required considerable training, expensive and complex machinery, heavy capital investment, and wage labor, ending the opportunities for individuals to effectively work the placer mines.

The California Gold Rush

The California gold rush, 1848–1852, was the greatest of all the western gold rushes—in the number and variety of people involved, quantity of gold recovered, capital invested, and consequences. It also set the pattern for all the rushes that followed. Gold had been discovered in California several times since Sir Francis Drake's first-recorded gold finds in the sixteenth century. The California rush of 1848 began in January with James Marshall's discovery of gold on land owned by John A. Sutter. In a remarkable historical coincidence, his discovery was just nine days before the Treaty of Guadalupe Hidalgo was signed, by which the United States acquired California and large parts of the Southwest from Mexico. In the next few months, news of the gold discovery reached ports in the Pacific Ocean, Oregon, Mexico, and South America. Five thousand gold seekers from these areas went to California by the end of the year.

Meanwhile, reports of the discovery trickled to the rest of the world, but it was President James K. Polk's announcement of an "abundance of gold" in California in his State of the Union message in December that set off the great gold rush. The announcement headed off a worldwide depression, which was just starting at the termination of the Mexican-American War, saving European shipping industries and galvanizing great migrations to the goldfields. While most were Americans, gold seekers came from around the world. The first ships from overseas and the eastern American ports reached San Francisco in April 1849. Hundreds more arrived by the end of the year, bringing 41,000 passengers to San Francisco in 1849.

Although thousands of Americans left on ships in winter and early spring, most forty-niners traveled overland on two major routes during spring and summer. In the first year of the rush, 30,000 gold seekers left jumping-off places along the Missouri River and traveled over the central route—up the Platte River and through South Pass. The California Trail was 2,000 miles (3,200 km) long, took four and a half to five months to cross, and ended at the northern mines. Another 20,000 gold seekers traveled on southern routes—either the Santa Fe Trail or routes from Arkansas and Texas—crossing New Mexico and Arizona to destinations in southern California. After 1849 traffic dropped off sharply on the southern routes, but continued strong on the Platte route. In 1850 some 45,000 emigrants traveled the California Trail and traffic peaked in 1852 with more than 50,000.

Those men and women who pursued their fortunes in the California gold rush demonstrated a radical change from those who participated in the overland agricultural migration. They were economic opportunists rather than settlers—usually entire families—seeking land, new homes, or religious freedom in the West. An overwhelming proportion of the gold rushers were men—probably at least 80 percent and at times 95 percent. White, middle-class Americans dominated the gold rush as they had in agricultural migration; but in contrast to the more homogeneous rural and small-town agricultural settlers, a greater proportion of gold seekers were from urban eastern areas, represented all professions and occupations, and comprised a broader range of age, class, and ethnicity. The majority was born in the United States, but a large minority was from northern Europe and Canada.

During the peak gold rush period, 1848–1852, mining camps, towns, and cities in California grew rapidly. San Francisco, first known as Yerba Buena, was the most important port and city. The largest inland towns were Sacramento and Stockton, which served as distribution centers. Towns developed from temporary mining camps when they became commercial centers for a district or when an unusually rich strike drew large numbers of miners to the location. Over time, nearly half the mining population lived and worked in the mining district towns. Due to the tremendous increase in population and the desire of northerners to create a free (nonslave) state, California was admitted to the Union in September 1850.

The Colorado and Montana Gold Rushes

The next significant mineral rush was the Colorado gold rush, 1859–1862. Cherokee miners on the way to the California goldfields made the original gold discovery on Cherry Creek, near modern Denver. Thousands of men poured into the Colorado Rockies from other areas of the West and the eastern states. The number of gold seekers who rushed to Colorado in 1859 was second only to California in 1849. An estimated 50,000 men participated in the rush, and as many as half remained to work in the mines. The impact of the mass influx of gold seekers was typical of the initial year of a gold rush. In 1860, 97 percent of Colorado's 34,000 residents were male; 94 percent were fifteen to forty-four years old. After the peak years of the gold rush, Colorado became a center of settlement and urban development, adding a significant new concentration of American western population to those in California, the Pacific Northwest, and the Great Basin. As a direct result of the gold rush, Colorado Territory was created in 1861.

The Montana gold rush, 1863–1866, was the last of the three great western mining frontiers. The rush began with the discovery of gold at Bannack in 1862, followed by gold discoveries in Alder Gulch in 1863 and Last Chance Gulch in 1864. Gold seekers poured into Montana over the main overland trail, the Bozeman and Bridger trails, a northern overland route from Minnesota, and on steamboats coming up the Missouri River to Fort Benton. As in the California and Colorado gold rushes, the overall migration was predominantly male, at least 80 percent men and 20 percent women and children. Development in Montana followed the typical pattern. The gold rush resulted in the founding of towns and cities, agricultural production in the valleys, road and bridge building, and commercial businesses. The population rapidly increased to the number required for territorial status, and after several large gold nuggets were displayed in Washington, DC, Montana Territory was created in May 1864.

Other Significant Gold and Silver Rushes

There were also a number of minor gold rushes that did not draw immense numbers of participants and were more regional in scope, but nevertheless made important contributions to the development of the West. In 1859 the Comstock Lode in Nevada drew 17,000 gold rushers to an extraordinarily rich strike of silver and gold. A high percentage of the miners came from the declining placer mines in California, where by then industrialized mining offered less opportunity to the individual. While gold seekers soon came from eastern parts of the West, Californians predominated from the beginning and continued to do so after the rush ended and large company mines were opened. Supplies and equipment came primarily from California as well.

Of the thousands who rushed to the Comstock in 1859, only a few dozen made fortunes. Again, it was the speculators, developers, and entrepreneurs who became wealthy—some immensely so. The center of the rush, Virginia City, Nevada, grew to a population of 20,000, the second-largest city in the West at the time. President Abraham Lincoln was so impressed with the amount of Comstock silver contributed to the federal government that he encouraged Nevada to become a state. The process was so rapid that the state constitution had to be telegraphed to Washington. Nevada became the thirty-sixth state in October 1864.

Western miners next flocked to gold discoveries in Idaho on the Clearwater River in 1860 and on the Salmon River and in the Boise Basin in 1861. The increase in population enabled Idaho to become a territory in 1863. The Idaho gold rush produced large amounts of gold through 1865. In eastern Oregon significant discoveries were made in the Blue Mountain region, resulting in a gold rush in 1861–1864. Mining camps and towns sprang up around the region, and miners came in mainly from California, Oregon, and Washington. After the placers declined, the Oregon mines were noted for the large proportion of Chinese who mined in the area. In 1867 gold mining in the South Pass area spawned South Pass City and Atlantic City as the Sweetwater gold rush began. This mining activity is significant for its role in the establishment of Wyoming Territory. More important, it attracted women to the territory, which granted them suffrage after early South Pass City resident Esther Hobart Morris urged male residents of the community to support equal rights.

In 1874 Lieutenant Colonel George A. Custer led a military expedition to South Dakota to explore the Black Hills, which were held sacred by the Sioux and comprised part of their reservation. The region had been declared inviolable by the U.S. government and was off-limits to white intrusion. Custer's expedition discovered gold, setting off an immediate gold rush. The army was unable to stop the rush of eager miners onto the reservation. The federal government first attempted to purchase the Black Hills from the Sioux, but after negotiations failed the army launched military operations known as the Great Sioux War of 1876–1877 and subdued the militant factions. Meanwhile, the gold rush continued unabated in placer diggings around the region. In April 1876, the richest gold vein in western history was discovered near present-day Lead; it produced 10 percent of the world's gold supply over the next 125 years.

Two small rushes occurred in 1877. At Leadville, Colorado, rich silver-lead deposits were found at a nearly abandoned gold camp high in the mountains, and at Tombstone, Arizona, silver was discovered in an area controlled by Apaches. In 1883 gold was discovered in the Coeur d'Alene region of mountainous northern Idaho. A large crowd came into the region, but soon silver-lead ores proved more important than gold.

The final gold rush of the nineteenth century was the Klondike gold rush. Gold was discovered in August 1896 near Dawson, in the Yukon region of Canada. The Klondike gold rush began when news of the discovery reached Seattle on the steamship *Portland* in July 1897. Within six months 100,000 gold seekers had left for the Yukon, but only 30,000 completed the trip. The journey was long, cold, and extremely difficult. Klondikers (also called stampeders) had to walk most of the way, transporting hundreds of pounds of supplies on pack animals or sleds. There were only two routes: the Chilkoot Trail and the White Pass Trail. The Chilkoot Trail was steep and hazardous. The White Pass Trail, even worse, was called the "dead horse trail" for all the horses that died on it. On both trails illness and starvation were rampant.

As a result of the thousands of miners who were successful in completing the hazardous journey, Dawson temporarily became the largest city north of San

Jubilant sluice miners display a large gold nugget during the Klondike Gold Rush in 1897—the last of the great gold rushes of the nineteenth century. Some 30,000 fortune seekers made their way to the Yukon Territory; only the early few got rich. *(Hulton Archive/Stringer/Getty Images)*

Francisco, and other Canadian cities also had dramatic growth due to the gold rush. Unfortunately, few of those who struggled over the trails found gold. By the time they arrived, all the claims had been taken by the early few, who became immensely wealthy, and the newcomers had to work for wages to earn enough to return home. When gold was discovered at Nome, Alaska, in 1899, those still in Dawson rushed to the new goldfields, where most again failed to strike it rich.

The most important consequence of the western gold rushes was to accelerate westward expansion. Gold rushes caused unprecedented massive movements of people and commerce in an increasingly interconnected West. Indian tribes were pushed out of their lands by burgeoning mining settlements, causing further conflict with neighboring tribes as well as with the new white inhabitants of the region. The California gold rush created a virtually instant state on the West Coast. The subsequent desire to link California with the rest of the nation led directly to the start of the Pony Express and subsequent completion of the transcontinental telegraph and railroad. The development of Colorado and Montana in the aftermath of gold rushes accomplished the process of "filling in" the West.

Susan Badger Doyle

Further Reading

Fisher, Vardis, and Opal Laurel Holmes. *Gold Rushes and Mining Camps of the Early American West*. Caldwell, ID: Caxton Printers, 1979.

Holliday, J.S. *Rush for Riches: Gold Fever and the Making of California*. Berkeley: University of California Press, 1999.

———. *The World Rushed In: The California Gold Rush Experience*. Norman: University of Oklahoma, 2002.

Marks, Paula Mitchell. *Precious Dust: The American Gold Rush Era 1848–1900*. New York: William Morrow, 1994.

Paul, Rodman Wilson. *Mining Frontiers of the Far West, 1848–1880*. Albuquerque: University of New Mexico Press, 2001.

Wallace, Robert. *The Miners*. Alexandria, VA: Time-Life Books, 1976.

Wheeler, Keith. *The Alaskans*. Alexandria, VA: Time-Life Books, 1986.

Railroads

For many years after America's beginnings, the only means of transportation were walking; using horses, mules, or oxen for either riding or pulling a variety of wheeled vehicles; and operating manually powered watercraft on the country's lakes, rivers, and artificial canal network that connected some of the streams. It was the advent of the steamboat in the early part of the nineteenth century, however, that made water travel more economical and much faster.

Early Railroads

Shortly following the popularization of the steamboat, several enterprising entrepreneurs began developing a crude form of railroad. Among the early uses of the new technology was the hauling of rock and coal from quarries and mines. Passengers were also transported back and forth across short stretches of the countryside by hitching a horse to pull a modified stagecoach along a pair of iron rails laid parallel to each other. For all practical purposes, however, American railroads had their beginnings in the early 1830s, when small steam engines were first used to pull passenger cars similar to the older, horse-drawn models. The appearance of Peter Cooper's steam locomotive, the *Tom Thumb*, denotes America's first real infatuation with trains and the railroad.

On August 28, 1830, Cooper drove the *Tom Thumb* over 13 miles (21 km) of track belonging to the newly chartered Baltimore & Ohio Railroad at a speed of 4 miles (6.5 km) per hour. In front of the engine was a passenger car carrying twenty-four unbelieving riders. A few days after this initial experiment, Cooper, again driving the *Tom Thumb*, raced a horse-drawn carriage along tracks laid between Ellicott Mills, Maryland, and Baltimore. Although the horse and carriage quickly took the lead, Cooper eventually overtook them, only to lose the race when a belt on the *Tom Thumb*'s engine became disengaged.

Progress in this exciting new mode of travel was rapid. Within a few months other railroad companies, most prominently the Charleston & Hamburg (C&H) line in South Carolina, were experimenting with steam-driven trains. The C&H engine, named *The Best Friend*, developed a speed of 21 miles (34 km) per hour while pulling four cars full of passengers. With no load, the tiny engine accelerated up to 30 miles (48 km) per hour. But this was a trial run for *The Best Friend*, and many people believed that traveling this fast was not really practical. In fact, these unheard-of speeds frightened many spectators. One concerned critic, who happened to be a physician, proclaimed that such rapid movement would most likely give travelers some kind of brain disease and that the government, in order to protect innocent onlookers from a similar mental disorder while simply watching the flashing speed of the train, should be required to erect high fences on both sides of the railroad tracks to obstruct the view. Other observers were more futuristic in their predictions. Some foresaw the day when the steam-driven railroad would be the fastest and most economical mode of travel in the United States and, for that matter, in the entire world.

As trains became more and more common east of the Mississippi River, advanced technological developments also made them faster. With the higher speeds came more accidents and, consequently, more deaths among both passengers and crew. Philip Hone, a former mayor of New York City, wrote in his diary in late 1847 that incidents reported in his morning newspaper about railroad and steamboat accidents wherein dozens of people were killed or mutilated were as regular as drinking his breakfast tea.

Technological Advancements and the Push Across the Mississippi River

By the 1850s, trains consisting of many cars and pulled by powerful steam-driven locomotives were traveling among the major cities of the industrialized Northeast. To a lesser degree, the South was also being served by rail. Citizens had discovered that they could travel much faster, cheaper, and more conveniently by rail than by either roadway or canal. Also, the cost to ship agricultural produce and commercial freight—which when hauled overland via horse carriage or sent along America's inland waterways amounted to many dollars per ton—was reduced to mere pennies per ton by rail. America had literally found itself on the fast track.

In 1853 Congress passed legislation directing Secretary of War Jefferson Davis to oversee the completion of a comprehensive transcontinental railroad survey to determine the best route linking the Mississippi River region with the Pacific Ocean. Members of the U.S. Army Corps of Topographical Engineers surveyed four separate potential thoroughfares: from St. Paul, Minnesota, to the mouth of the Columbia River in Oregon; from St. Louis, Missouri, to California; from Fort Smith, Arkansas, to California; and from Fort Washita in present-day Oklahoma to California. The surveys had little effect on the eventual placement of the transcontinental railroad, but they did provide the nation's scientists with a wealth of knowledge about the botany, zoology, ethnology, and geology of the regions reconnoitered.

By 1854 the railroads in the East had pushed westward to the Mississippi River and, within two years, had crossed it, focusing national attention on the vast trans-Mississippi region. Almost a decade of overland travel across the Oregon and California trails, during which time tens of thousands of optimistic emigrant families had made the 2,000-mile (3,200-km) trek to the shores of the Pacific Ocean, had more than proved that the wave of the future for many Americans lay toward the setting sun. One of the most pressing issues now facing the westward-looking U.S. government was the implementation of a way to efficiently transport additional numbers of settlers into the far-off lands of Oregon and California, where they could start new lives, organize local governments, and work toward bringing those distant territories into the Union. Methods whereby developers could rapidly and economically tap into the seemingly unlimited natural resources of the immense region must also be provided, as well as the means for transporting the raw materials back to the marketplaces in the East.

During the 1856 presidential campaigns, both the Democratic and the newly formed Republican parties—and consequently, many Northern and Southern statesmen—advocated the construction of a transcontinental railroad. As the years passed, however, growing sectional differences caused more and more Southerners in Congress to change their minds about the massive project, since they believed that any railroad that eventually linked the Atlantic and Pacific oceans would benefit Northerners far more than themselves and their constituents. The secession from the Union of the Southern states in 1860–1861, along with the consequent resignation of all Southern members of Congress, removed the primary obstacle to the railroad's construction, and support for the long-awaited railroad project grew rapidly.

The divisiveness of the social and political issues—states' rights and slavery among them—that had plagued the United States for the past decade came into full focus in April 1861, when Confederate forces stormed and occupied Fort Sumter in South Carolina, triggering the Civil War. By that time, California, Oregon, and Kansas were already members of the Union as free states, meaning that slavery was legally outlawed within their borders. Texas was originally a slave state, but had seceded from the Union before the fall of Fort Sumter. Residents of practically all the rest of the vast, but sparsely populated territory lying beyond the western borders of the states (or seceded states) of Minnesota, Iowa, Missouri, Arkansas, and Louisiana had been given a choice by Congress that, when the time came, they could decide by popular vote whether to enter the Union as a slave or a free state. In the thinking of most Northern politicians, it was absolutely mandatory to link the cities of the eastern United States with the far western region beyond the Mississippi and to cultivate a climate of "free state" advocacy in its citizens. Supported by the intense lobbying activities of Theodore D. Judah, an experienced railroad builder and engineer, Congress authorized the construction of the transcontinental railroad.

On July 1, 1862, President Abraham Lincoln signed into law the Pacific Railway Act. The legislation called for officials of the recently established Central Pacific Railroad Company and those of a soon-to-be-organized entity, the Union Pacific Railroad Company, "to lay out, locate, construct, furnish, maintain and enjoy a continuous railroad and telegraph." The new Union Pacific line was to begin at Omaha, Nebraska Territory, and to generally follow the 40th parallel toward the western boundary of Nevada Territory. The Central Pacific's western terminus was placed at Sacramento, and workmen were to build its line eastward to the place where the two rail lines finally met.

The seemingly never-ending delays over the railroad's location and proposed construction—delays that dated back almost a decade to the time when the first cross-continent surveys were authorized by Congress—were extremely frustrating to Northern politicians who wanted to see the massive project completed. Unfortunately for them, seven years would pass between President Lincoln's signing of the enabling legislation that finally permitted the project to begin and the day when locomotives belonging to the two opposite-moving construction gangs finally met in the far-off Utah desert.

Engineering and Financial Considerations

One of the first problems to be dealt with was the gauge—the distance between the two rails—that the new roadbed would measure. Back in the East, there was no conformity in this regard among different railroads. Most tracks for Southern railroads were 5 feet (1.5 m) wide, while in sections around the Great Lakes and in portions of New Jersey and Pennsylvania, the distance between rails was 4 feet, 10 inches (1.5 m or 147 cm). Many New England companies used rails that measured only 4 feet, 8.5 inches (1.4 m) between them, while Missouri railroads used a 5 foot, 6-inch (1.7-m) design. In all, more than a dozen different gauges existed in the United States. Before the proposed transcontinental line could be started, the most reasonable gauge must be defined for it.

President Lincoln was authorized to dictate the gauge for the new line. After conferring with railroad officials from all over the country, as well as his own cabinet members, he settled on the standard used by the state of California: 5 feet. Lincoln's decision was hotly debated in Congress, since representatives from various states obviously wanted the new road to conform to the measurements of the railroads already in existence back home. It was not until March 1863, eight months after the Pacific Railway Act was signed by the president, that Congress took the matter of gauge size out of Lincoln's hands and proclaimed that 4 feet, 8.5 inches—the gauge size used in New England—would be the official standard for the transcontinental railroad.

An issue even more complex, confusing, and serious than the selection of the railroad's gauge was the manner in which the huge project would be financed. The Pacific Railway Act of 1862 contained several provisions that would offer assistance in getting the job done. First, the two railroad companies were granted, free of charge, a 200-foot (60-m) right-of-way on each side of the track, as well as the authority to use, again free of charge, "earth, stone, timber, and other materials for the construction thereof" from the public lands through which the track passed. Second, the companies were extended loans in the form of government bonds that amounted to between $16,000 and $48,000 per mile of track laid, with the stipulation that the loans be repaid over a thirty-year period at 6 percent annual interest; and, finally, millions of acres of government-owned land on either side of the rail line were forfeited outright to the companies for reselling and fund-raising.

This more than generous assistance rendered by the U.S. government failed to secure financial stability for the railroad companies. In the meantime, Theodore Judah had interested four prominent California businessmen—Mark Hopkins, Charles Crocker, Leland Stanford, and Collis P. Huntington—to invest heavily in the Central Pacific Railroad Company, thereby eventually putting the business on a sound fiscal footing. Likewise, Thomas C. Durant, later assisted by brothers Oakes and Oliver Ames, helped rescue the Union Pacific from financial ruin. In 1864 Congress passed another even more liberal act that, among other things, doubled the acreage given to the transcontinental railroad builders, thereby positioning the companies for even larger chances of success.

Success At Last

When Congress passed the Pacific Railway Act of 1862, a requirement of the legislation was that the transcontinental railroad be completed in time for the nation's centennial celebration in July 1876. To most of the people involved in the planning, design, and actual building of the proposed railroad, fourteen years seemed like a long time, and despite the serious and complex logistical problems involved, no one doubted that the target date could be met.

In early 1863 ground was broken for the Central Pacific line in Sacramento, California. Theodore Judah, the man who had done so much to sell the U.S. Congress on the feasibility of a transcontinental railroad, became the chief engineer for the eastward-moving Central Pacific line. Although Judah was anxious to get started in earnest, only 21 miles (34 km) of rails had been laid by the end of the year. In the meantime, Judah died, and the duties of actual construction of the railroad fell to Charles Crocker. Crocker had been lured to California during the early days of the gold rush, but soon discovered that more money could be made by selling supplies and equipment to the other miners than by being a prospector. Within a short period of time, he had become a millionaire in San Francisco.

In the East, construction was just as slow getting under way as it was in California. Despite a great deal of preliminary planning, the first rail in the Union

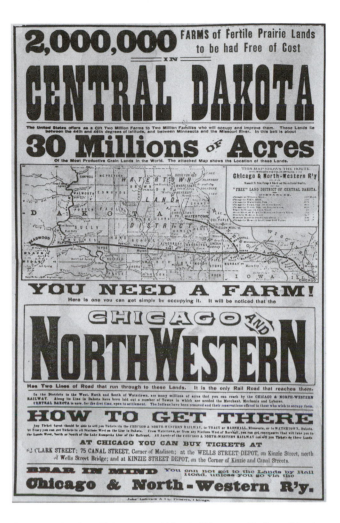

A poster for the Chicago and North-Western Railroad in the 1870s promotes free homestead land in Dakota Territory. By 1880 the U.S. rail network totaled 93,000 miles, having nearly doubled in each of the previous two decades. *(The Granger Collection, New York)*

Pacific line was not laid until July 10, 1865, three years after the passage of the Pacific Railway Act. In the beginning months, workers averaged putting down only 1 mile (1.6 km) of track per week.

The following year, General Grenville Dodge, a highly regarded Civil War veteran, was named chief engineer for the Union Pacific. Fresh out of college when he first became interested in railroad building, Dodge had eventually moved to Iowa, where he worked in rail construction until the Civil War began. During the war, Dodge attained the rank of major general of volunteers and not only witnessed considerable combat, but oversaw the construction of many railroad bridges and the repair of damaged railroads as well. By late December, nearly 300 miles (480 km) of rails stretched westward across the Great Plains. Advancing with the Union Pacific tracks were quickly thrown-up communities known as end-of-track or hell-on-wheels

towns. They were characterized by the temporary nature of their structures—often "buildings" made of canvas with dirt floors. Some of these hastily established towns, such as Julesburg, Cheyenne, Laramie City, and Green River, endured; others disappeared when the tracklayers moved on. A newspaper called *The Frontier Index* traveled with the tracks, too, with publication taking place in a railroad car.

The problems faced by Crocker and Dodge were many, but none were more serious than the shortage of labor and the timely procurement of building materials. During the early 1860s, unemployment was practically nonexistent in California for two reasons: the state was still only sparsely populated, and most unskilled laborers, who were the most adaptable for railroad work, were already employed in the gold diggings. So Crocker hired thousands of immigrant Chinese laborers, who earned about $25 a month for their twelve-hour, six-days a week job. The Chinese made excellent workers. Most of them came from the Pearl River delta area, located in Kwangtung Province in the southern part of China. In order to pay their fares to America, countless Chinese indentured themselves to their creditors and, in many cases, had to work for years to get out of debt.

Meanwhile, back in the East, Dodge had a larger and more accessible labor pool from which to select. Most of the Union Pacific's workers were either Irish immigrants or unemployed Civil War veterans, anxious for any job they could get after mustering out of the army and finding themselves suddenly out of work.

If the labor problem was less serious for the Union Pacific than it was for the Central Pacific, the problem of acquiring building supplies and construction equipment was much the same for both railroads. Although wood for the shaping of cross ties was abundant in the Sierra Nevada, practically all gear that the Central Pacific work crews needed had to be shipped by boat around the tip of South America and up the Pacific Coast to San Francisco. The iron rails, spikes, explosives, tools, locomotives, and every other item that could not be fashioned from wood took literally months to arrive in California.

Union Pacific workers had similar difficulties obtaining their equipment and supplies. The Union Pacific's eastern terminus was Omaha, which sat far out on the Great Plains and was separated by 140 miles (225 km) of prairie from the nearest railhead at Des Moines. Therefore, all building material had to be hauled overland to Omaha. Cross ties, ordered from Michigan and Pennsylvania, cost an exorbitant $2.50 each. And since most of the Union Pacific's route stretched across the treeless, barren Great Plains, not only railroad ties, but all the other materials and supplies as well were necessarily furnished from back East.

As far as terrain was concerned, the Union Pacific had the easier—albeit considerably longer—route, since it traversed relatively flat, treeless, and uncluttered territory. On the other hand, the Central Pacific workers were faced with the task of building the road over—and sometimes through—the high mountains of the Sierra Nevada and also building bridges and trestles over rapidly flowing rivers. By the end of 1867, Central Pacific work crews had laid only 136 miles (220 km) of track, while their eastern competitors had completed 540 miles (870 km).

Summer's heat and drought, winter's cold and dampness, hordes of bloodsucking mosquitoes, twelve-hour days of backbreaking toil, and poor food all combined to create a life of hardship, misery, and austerity for the laborers on the transcontinental railroad. As the work trains crossed the Great Plains, railroad workers were eyed suspiciously by the Indians along the way. To the Native Americans, the appearance of the "iron horse" was just one more indication that their way of life was rapidly disappearing.

In the end, the thousands of American, Chinese, and Irish workers prevailed, and as the spring of 1869 approached, rumors were already flying in both railroad camps that the meeting of the two lines was imminent. In April the building superintendent of the Central Pacific crew sent a message to his opposite number several miles away at the Union Pacific camp, wagering that his Chinese laborers could lay 10 miles (16 km) of track in a single day, an unheard-of proposition. On April 28, 4,000 Central Pacific workers laid 25,800 cross ties and 3,520 rails, driving 55,000 spikes and 14,080 bolts in the process and completing their task by 7:00 P.M. At times of heaviest activity, the men were putting into place an astounding 144 feet (44 m) of track per minute.

On May 10, 1869, the Union Pacific's Engine Number 119 and the Central Pacific's locomotive Jupiter approached each other at a place called Promontory Point, located near the northern shore of the Great Salt Lake in Utah Territory. Hundreds of people gathered for the historic occasion. The last remaining crosstie made from California laurel wood was placed, followed by the laying of the two final lengths of rail. The last spike, molded from solid gold mined in California, was driven into the tie by Leland Stanford, Central Pacific's president, and Thomas C. Durant, the vice-president of Union Pacific. A telegraph message was relayed across the country proclaiming, "Done."

The spanning of the United States by the first transcontinental railroad was one of history's most memorable engineering and construction feats. Even today, the sheer size and complexity of the project is mind-boggling. Nearly 25,000 workmen labored for five years to complete the road. It is estimated that 300,000 tons of rails, nearly 7 million bolts, more than 23 million spikes, more than 6 million crossties, and 1,700,000 anchor plates were used during the construction of the Union Pacific's eastern portion of the line (1,086 miles {1,748 km}). It is only logical to assume that the 688 miles (1,107 km) of the Central Pacific's tracks utilized parts and supplies equal to at least another 65 percent of those totals.

The continent had at last been bridged, the Atlantic and Pacific oceans had been connected, and—to make the occasion even more notable—the target date for the railroad's completion had been beaten by seven years.

There would be other railroads pushing across the West, bringing the opportunity associated with a steady form of transportation. In virtually all cases, the railroads brought development. Towns on the line generally prospered; towns that failed to get rail transportation often withered. Although the Northern Pacific, for example, crossing the northern territories, spawned wars with the northern Plains Indians, it had significant land grants associated with its development, and it gave rise to cities such as Bismarck, North Dakota. It also provided a way for early tourists to reach natural wonders such as Yellowstone and Glacier national parks.

James A. Crutchfield

Further Reading

Bowles, Samuel. *Across the Continent: A Summer's Journey to the Rocky Mountains, the Mormons, and the Pacific States, with Speaker Colfax*. Springfield, MA: Samuel Bowles & Company, 1865.

Dunbar, Seymour. *A History of Travel in America*. New York: Tudor, 1937.

Goetzmann, William H. *Army Exploration in the American West, 1803–1863*. Lincoln: University of Nebraska Press, 1979.

Kagan, Hilde Heun, ed. *The American Heritage Pictorial Atlas of United States History*. New York: American Heritage, 1966.

Keir, Malcolm. *The March of Commerce*. New Haven: Yale University Press, 1927.

Ketterson, Francis, Jr. *Golden Spike National Historic Site*. Washington, DC: National Park Service, n.d.

Nock, O.S. *Railroads Then and Now*. New York: Crown, 1975.

Wheeler, Keith. *The Railroaders*. New York: Time-Life Books, 1973.

Williams, Henry T., ed. *The Pacific Tourist*. New York: Henry T. Williams, 1877.

York, Thomas. *America's Great Railroads*. London: Bison Books, 1987.

Arts and Letters

Between the late eighteenth and late nineteenth centuries, as the United States expanded ever westward, Americans came to believe that the nation had a preordained mission to spread democracy and freedom all the way to the Pacific Ocean, a doctrine that became known as manifest destiny. During this period of extensive exploration, emigration, and settlement, many artists, painters, writers, and photographers depicted the West in words and illustrations. They conveyed images of the region's landscapes, Indians, and natural history and graphically related the opportunities offered by the West. Their efforts allowed Americans to gain a better understanding of the West, and this knowledge inspired settlers to first cross the Appalachian Mountains, then the Mississippi River, and finally the Great Plains and Rocky Mountains in their quest to reach the Pacific Ocean.

Nonfiction Writers

Many early Spanish and French explorers left accounts of the region west of the Mississippi River, but these were not readily accessible to most Americans interested in migrating there. It was not until after President Thomas Jefferson purchased Louisiana Territory in 1803, doubling the size of the nation with one scratch of the pen, that westward movement gained momentum. Jefferson sent Captains Meriwether Lewis and William Clark to explore Louisiana with instructions to bring back information on everything they saw relative to the Indians, wildlife, climate, and terrain of the newly acquired expanse. Their vivid account, published in two volumes in 1814 and titled *History of the Expedition under the Command of Captains Lewis and Clark, to the Sources of the Missouri, thence Across the Rocky Mountains and down the River Columbia to the Pacific Ocean*, contributed much to the early knowledge about the West, as did the journals of three of their companions, Patrick Gass's (1807); John Ordway's (lost for over a century before

it was rediscovered and published in 1916); and Joseph Whitehouse's (a complete version of whose narrative was not published until 1997). Before Lewis and Clark returned to St. Louis, Zebulon Pike was ordered to explore the southern portion of the region extending westward to the Rocky Mountains; upon his return, he also published a comprehensive narrative depicting his journey. Other explorers followed, including Stephen H. Long.

Many of the most important nonfiction works to come out of the West during this period were written by members of the U.S. Army Corps of Topographical Engineers and published as congressional documents by the federal government. From about 1838, when the corps was organized and placed under the command of Colonel John James Abert, until its demise during the Civil War, its members were key responders to the call of manifest destiny. Without them, their documentation skills, and their detailed maps, knowledge of much of the vast expanse between the Mississippi River and the Rocky Mountains would have been delayed for years.

Among the most noted of the engineers who provided written accounts of their explorations and findings were Colonel Abert's son, Lieutenant James W. Abert, who produced two books, *A Report of an Expedition on the Upper Arkansas and through the Country of the Comanche Indians* (1846) and *A Report and Map of the Examination of New Mexico* (1848). Lieutenant Colonel William H. Emory wrote *Notes of a Military Reconnoissance {sic} from Fort Leavenworth, in Missouri, to San Diego, in California*, which was released in 1848. Emory also contributed a monumental, three-volume study of the Mexican-American boundary survey of 1856–1859. Lieutenant John Charles Frémont, with the assistance of his wife, Jessie Benton Frémont, documented the findings of his survey of the Rocky Mountains in *Report of the Exploring Expedition to the Rocky Mountains in the Year 1842, and to Oregon and North California in the*

Years 1843–'44, released in 1845. The list of books produced by the Corps of Topographical Engineers is far too lengthy to list in this brief overview. Suffice it to say that even today the literature of the corps stands among the finest and most accurate bodies of documents ever issued about the American West.

Washington Irving, although best known for *The Legend of Sleepy Hollow* and *Rip Van Winkle*, both set in the East, produced several historical works that shed much light on the mysterious West. Following a tour on the western frontier in the early 1830s with a military party that traversed much of what is now eastern Oklahoma, he recounted his journey and his experiences with Indians and soldiers in *A Tour of the Prairies* (1835). In 1836 Irving also published the enormously successful, two-volume *Astoria, or Anecdotes of an Enterprise Beyond the Rocky Mountains*, which documented the history of John Jacob Astor's northwestern fur-trading empire headquartered at the mouth of the Columbia River.

Francis Parkman traveled the Oregon Trail as far west as Fort Laramie and described his experiences in a series of articles later published as a book, *The Oregon Trail: Sketches of Prairie and Rocky-Mountain Life*, in 1849. His work became something of a guide for California gold seekers and emigrants who enjoyed his colorful descriptive writing. Parkman is remembered as a master of narrative history and as one of America's first great historians.

In addition to assisting with her husband's reports of his explorations of the West, Jessie Benton Frémont, daughter of Missouri Senator Thomas Hart Benton and wife of John Charles Frémont, produced *Far Western Sketches* (1890) and three other books based upon her experiences.

Robert Louis Stevenson traveled to California in the middle 1870s and recounted his experiences in *Across the Plains*. Stevenson, of course, is better known as the author of *Treasure Island, Kidnapped,* and *The Strange Case of Dr. Jekyll and Mr. Hyde.*

Fiction Writers

The first fiction writer to produce "Westerns" was Friedrich Gerstäcker, a German, who wrote 150 very popular travel accounts and adventure novels, nearly all set in the American West. His *Rambling and Hunting Trips through the United States and North America* (1844) was followed by numerous novels set in the West. Gerstäcker was one of several German, Austrian, and Swiss authors who chose to write about the *American* West, often making it seem more glamorous and romantic than it was.

In 1853 Bret Harte, a native of Albany, New York, went to California, where he wrote for a literary journal. In 1868 he became editor of *The Overland Monthly*. Harte's story "The Luck of Roaring Camp" focused on life in a western mining camp and brought him national attention.

Mark Twain is sometimes called "the father of American literature." Following the Civil War, he traveled to Nevada Territory, where he got a job with a newspaper. He wrote *Roughing It* and provided material for *The Celebrated Jumping Frog of Calaveras County*. His later novels, *The Adventures of Tom Sawyer* and *Adventures of Huckleberry Finn*, are set along the Mississippi River.

Ned Buntline was a writer and publisher best known for his dime novels. He traveled widely in the West, meeting such figures as William F. (Buffalo Bill) Cody and "Wild Bill" Hickok. Buntline wrote a variety of stories about them, but also claimed that many of his stories about the West were based on his own adventures. Buntline's articles, filled with adventure, were, for the most part, historically inaccurate.

O. Henry traveled to Texas in 1882 and began his writing career. To provide money for living, he got a job as a bank clerk, but supposedly embezzled money and served three years in prison, from where he continued creating and selling his stories to magazines. Once out of jail, he went to New York, where he continued writing. His stories were widely published in national magazines.

Helen Hunt Jackson, widow of a United States army captain, traveled to Colorado in the fall of 1874. She married William Sharpless Jackson, a wealthy banker and railroad executive, in 1875 and turned to writing. Her nonfiction book, *A Century of Dishonor* (1881), condemned the government's Indian policy. She continued the theme in a novel, *Ramona* (1884).

Joaquin Miller, a native of Indiana, migrated to California during the gold rush and worked at various jobs, including newspaper writing. He wrote a number of popular works, including *Life Among the Modocs, An Elk Hunt,* and *The Battle of Castle Crags*, all based on his own experiences in the West. He also became a prominent poet.

Owen Wister, a Pennsylvania native, spent several summers in the West writing fiction set on the frontier. He wrote several books and stories but is best known for his novel *The Virginian* (1902), the story of a cowboy set in a highly mythologized version of the Johnson County War in Wyoming.

Zane Grey, a novelist, began writing about the West in 1908 when he produced *The Last of the Plains-*

men, a biography of C.J. "Buffalo" Jones. A New York publisher then encouraged Grey to write western novels, which included the best seller *Riders of the Purple Sage* (1912). Grey wrote seventy-eight books, seventeen of them published after his death; many remain in print, some recently released in new editions with original material once edited out but now restored to the text.

Artists

Many of the earliest and most significant American artists in the West traveled with government expeditions. Samuel Seymour joined Major Stephen H. Long's expedition as a landscape painter. The 1819–1820 expedition explored the Rocky Mountains and Platte River region, and then traveled down the Arkansas and Canadian rivers to modern Arkansas. Seymour made the earliest known sketches of the Royal Gorge and Pikes Peak in present-day Colorado. He later accompanied Long's 1823 expedition to the headwaters of the St. Peter's River in Minnesota. He is credited with beginning an era of western painting that lasted into the early twentieth century. Titian Ramsay Peale, son of the noted Philadelphia artist Charles Willson Peale, also traveled with Long's 1819 expedition to the Rocky Mountains, producing more than 100 drawings depicting western wildlife.

George Catlin, a painter and writer, specialized in portraits of Indians in the West. Between 1830 and 1836, he made five trips west, visiting about fifty tribes. Later, Catlin exhibited his paintings in the East and in Europe. In 1841 a monumental work titled *Manners, Customs, and Condition of the North American Indians* was published in two volumes containing about 300 engravings. Three years later, he published twenty-five plates in his *North American Indian Portfolio*. In 1848 his book *Eight Years' Travels and Residence in Europe* was published.

Seth Eastman was a West Point graduate who excelled in military painting and depictions of the Sioux Indians of the upper Midwest. He produced hundreds of sketches and paintings of Sioux everyday life, while his wife, Mary Eastman, captured for posterity many of the tribe's oral traditions, customs, and legends. To current scholars, Seth Eastman's collection of paintings of selected American forts is a gold mine of information about their exterior appearance and design elements at the height of their utility to the army.

Rudolph Friedrich Kurz, a native of Switzerland, sketched Indians and scenes at Fort Union on the Upper Missouri River during the early 1850s, two decades after Catlin, and executed hundreds of pencil

George Catlin, one of the foremost artists and ethnographers of the American Indian in the nineteenth century, produced an extensive firsthand record—in images and written accounts—of native life. Catlin posed for a portrait by William Fisk in 1849. *(The Granger Collection, New York)*

and ink drawings of tribal members along the river, years before the Montana gold fields were opened and the fur traders had deserted Fort Union.

Alfred Jacob Miller, a native of Baltimore, was hired by Sir William Drummond Stewart to graphically document his 1837 Rocky Mountains tour. The series of sketches became the basis for a gallery of paintings that are today one of the most valuable depictions of American Indian life. Miller is credited with being the only artist to capture firsthand renditions of a Rocky Mountain rendezvous when he attended the 1837 gathering of mountain men in the Green River valley of Wyoming.

Karl Bodmer, a Swiss painter, traveled along the upper Missouri River during the years 1832–1834 with his sponsor, Prince Maximilian of Wied, who had hired him to provide illustrations of the scientific journey. Bodmer produced some of the most important paintings ever made of life along the river before the encroachment of "civilization" all but annihilated many of the native tribes and much of their original lifestyles. Bodmer's works illustrated the prince's monumental narrative of the journey, titled *Travels in the Interior of North America during the Years 1832–1834*, the first English version of which appeared in 1843.

Thomas Moran, an artist of the Hudson River School, painted western landscape scenes during his tenure with the expeditions led by Ferdinand Hayden (Yellowstone) and John Wesley Powell (Grand Canyon) during the early 1870s. His images of the Yellowstone area inspired Congress to set aside more than 2 million acres (800,000 ha) of the region and designate it as the nation's first national park in 1872.

German artist Albert Bierstadt spent little time in the West, but during the mid-to-late 1800s, he produced beautiful, large landscape paintings suffused with golden light that caught the fancy of Americans and became very popular.

Two later painters, Frederic Remington and Charles M. Russell, worked mostly after the age of westward expansion, but both produced art depicting many scenes that actually occurred during that period of America's history. Remington, a classically trained artist from New York, achieved fame for his lifelike illustrations executed for *Harper's Weekly* magazine both before and during the Spanish-American War, in which he served as a war correspondent. His long career as an artist of the West yielded more than 2,700 paintings as well as numerous bronzes.

Russell, a self-educated Montana artist and kinsman to the noted Bent brothers of Bent's Fort fame, created more than 2,000 paintings of Indians, cowboys, and western landscapes in addition to many bronze sculptures. His heroic-sized mural titled *Lewis and Clark Meeting the Flathead Indians*, painted in 1912, hangs in the Montana state capitol at Helena.

Photographers

Photographers began working in the West soon after the daguerreotype process was discovered in 1839. The procedure produced detailed images on silver-coated, copper plates. The new photographic process, initially used to produce portraits of individuals, was used in Texas during the early 1840s and rapidly spread to California during and after the gold rush. In 1853–1854, Solomon Nunes Carvalho, a native of South Carolina, joined Frémont's fifth expedition west through Kansas and Colorado to Utah, searching for a railroad route. Carvalho, a skilled artist and photographer, made daguerreotypes on the journey. Most, however, have been lost. Carvalho was one of several artists who took up photography.

Another photographic process used wet plate collodion glass negatives from which paper prints could be produced. Carleton E. Watkins, a San Francisco photographer, became well known for his large landscapes of Yosemite, which were exhibited in the East in 1861. His views were among the first photographs made of Yosemite Valley. He made 30 mammoth views and 100 stereograph views that were among the first pictures of Yosemite seen in the East. Partly on the strength of Watkins's views, President Abraham Lincoln signed the 1864 bill that declared the valley inviolable.

Following the Civil War, photographers using the wet plate process took photographs on government survey expeditions and for railroads, documenting their construction across the nation. Andrew J. Russell photographed the construction of the Union Pacific, beginning in 1867, and the Central Pacific, along with photographer Alfred A. Hart. In 1867–1868, Alexander Gardner, prominent for his battlefield photos taken during the Civil War, photographed the proposed route of the Kansas Pacific Railroad west from Kansas City, Missouri. Meantime, William A. Bell photographed a proposed southern railroad route along the 32nd parallel.

Many other photographers recorded pioneer scenes, including Solomon Butcher in Nebraska; James P. Ball, a black photographer, who with his son operated in Helena, Montana; and Charles Roscoe Savage, who opened a studio in Salt Lake City and produced countless photographs of individuals and scenes of the area.

One of the better-known photographers, and an artist as well, was William Henry Jackson. He learned to draw as a boy and afterward, in 1858, became attracted to photography, landing a job in Troy, New York, retouching photographs. When the Civil War began, he enlisted but saw little military action, spending much time drawing sketches of camp life. Returning to photography when his enlistment was up, he soon went west and became a bullwhacker in Nebraska for an outfit bound for Montana. He resumed sketching and traveled to Salt Lake City and California. Soon realizing that he wanted to document the settling of the frontier, he opened a photographic studio in Omaha, Nebraska, in 1869. He photographed Indians and the building of the transcontinental railroad and was then hired to join an expedition exploring the Yellowstone River in Wyoming Territory. Later he photographed Mesa Verde and Yosemite before concluding his government work and opening a studio in Denver, Colorado. When he was eighty-one years old, he turned to painting and produced about 100 works dealing with historic themes such as the fur trade, the

California gold rush, and the Oregon Trail. He died at the age of ninety-nine.

Journalists

Close on the heels of the advance guard of America's westward expansion came the journalists and newspaper writers who documented the day-by-day lives of those who had gone before. From John P. Clum, who at the age of twenty-six organized the *Arizona Citizen* and, in 1880, began publishing the *Tombstone Epitaph*, to wealthy and controversial William Randolph Hearst Sr., who wrested control of the mighty *San Francisco Examiner* in 1887 at age twenty-four, literally hundreds of journalists scoured the wide spaces of America's newly explored frontier, not only for the benefit of the ever-growing local population, but for the enlightenment of readers back east as well.

Even before these latecomers, other journalists were active when Texas declared its independence from Mexico; when the great wagon trains rolled across the Great Plains on their way to New Mexico, Oregon, and California; when mountain men came out of the Rockies to resupply for the next season's hunt; and when gold and silver were discovered in California, Colorado, Montana, and dozens of other places.

Journalists recorded the pulse of the frontier; without the stories they filed, much knowledge of local affairs would be lost to researchers forever. The reports sent by journalists traveling with military expeditions enticed many people to move into the West, particularly during times of expansion when precious minerals were located in the Black Hills, California, and other locales.

Performing Artists

Although not as popular as the scores of writers, artists, photographers, and journalists who left behind their indelible marks on America's westward movement, performing artists were present and working on the frontier as well. As emigration moved westward, many theater companies left the eastern seaboard and established themselves first in the Mississippi and Ohio River valleys, then in the trans-Mississippi West.

Important actors and impresarios of the early period were such luminaries as Edwin Booth (brother to Abraham Lincoln's assassin, John Wilkes Booth), Edwin Forrest, Louisa Lane Drew (matriarch of the famed Barrymore acting family), Noah Ludlow, and Sol Smith. Performances rendered at theaters across the country encompassed a wide diversity, from plays based on Shakespeare's *Julius Caesar* and *Hamlet* to lighthearted minstrel shows performed by black-faced, white actors.

The drawings, paintings, books, newspaper and journal articles, reports, photographs, and theatrical performances produced during the period of westward expansion not only provided a record for future generations, but in their time rendered important insights about the West for easterners. Their importance was paramount in contributing to the desires of hundreds of thousands of Americans to pick up stakes and head toward the setting sun.

David Dary

Further Reading

Ewers, John C. *Artists of the Old West*. Garden City, NY: Doubleday, 1973.

Goetzmann, William H. *Army Exploration in the American West, 1803–1863*. Lincoln: University of Nebraska Press, 1979.

Karolevitz, Robert F. *Newspapering in the Old West*. Seattle: Superior Publishing, 1965.

Rossi, Paul A., and David C. Hunt. *The Art of the Old West*. New York: Alfred A. Knopf, 1971.

"Touring West: 19th Century Performing Artists on the Overland Trails." New York: New York Public Library, 2001.

Wheeler, Keith. *The Chroniclers*. Alexandria, VA: Time-Life Books, 1976.

A–Z Entries

Abert, James William (1820–1897)

As a twenty-four-year-old lieutenant in the United States Army Corps of Topographical Engineers, James William Abert was chosen by John Charles Frémont to command the surveying team that explored and mapped the Canadian River, providing the United States government in 1845 with the first comprehensive map of north Texas. Of equal interest to historians is the written and illustrated report Abert appended to his map. His writing is precise and engaging, showcasing a sharp eye for natural history as well as a talent for amateur ethnography. His portraits of members of the Kiowa and Comanche tribes are carefully drawn, and the illustrations accompanying his descriptions of the flora of the southwest are clear and beautiful.

Due to the success of this initial command, the war with Mexico in 1846 brought additional opportunities for Abert. With his colleague Lieutenant William G. Peck, he was commissioned to survey the settlements along the Rio Grande as part of the war-related effort to map the territory of New Mexico. For the official report of this second survey, Abert turned his minutely observed line drawings of the landscape, wildlife, and people of the territory into lithographs. In his personal journal and his official reports, Abert comes across as both engaging and modest. He was very well liked by the men under his command, at least one of whom explicitly contrasted his respect for Abert with his irritation at the high-handed and arrogant manner of Frémont.

Born in Mount Holly, New Jersey, on November 18, 1820, James William Abert was the son of Colonel John J. Abert, commander of the Corps of Topographical Engineers. After attending Princeton University, Abert graduated in 1842 from the United States Military Academy, ranked fifty-fifth in a class of fifty-six men. Despite his unremarkable record at West Point, he consistently ranked at or near the top of his class in drawing. Abert's artistic skill helped him stand out in the Corps of Topographical Engineers and, along with his undeniable political connections, it was probably a factor in Frémont's initial decision to entrust Abert with command of the Canadian River survey.

After the Mexican-American War, Abert never returned to the southwest. From 1848 to 1850, he taught drawing at West Point. During the Civil War, he served in the Union Army in the Shenandoah Valley in 1861 and 1862. He was promoted to major in the U.S. Army Corps of Engineers in 1862, but a catastrophic fall from his horse forced his retirement from active duty in 1864. Abert enjoyed a long and varied civilian career. After running a mercantile business for a few years, he worked as the Examiner of Patents in Washington, DC, between 1869 and 1871. He was a professor of English at Missouri State University and the president of the Kentucky Examining Board of Teachers of Public Schools. He died at his home in Kentucky on August 10, 1897.

Sarah Grossman

See also: Army of the West; Corps of Topographical Engineers; Frémont, John C.

Further Reading

Abert, James William. *Expedition to the Southwest: An 1845 reconnaissance of Colorado, New Mexico, Texas, and Oklahoma.* Introduction and notes by H. Bailey Carroll; Introduction to the Bison Books edition by John Miller Morris. Lincoln: University of Nebraska Press, 1999.

———. *Western America in 1846–1847; the original travel diary of Lieutenant J.W. Abert, who mapped New Mexico for the United States Army. With illus. in color from his sketchbook.* Edited by John Galvin. San Francisco: J. Howell, 1966.

Goetzmann, William H. *Army Exploration in the American West, 1803–1863.* New Haven: Yale University Press, 1959.

Adams, John Quincy (1767–1848)

Sixth president of the United States, John Quincy Adams was also a senator, representative, secretary of state, minister to the Netherlands, Russia, Prussia, Portugal, and Great Britain, poet, professor, swimming enthusiast, scholar, author, philosopher, lawyer, treaty negotiator, founder of the National Republican Party, abolitionist leader, son of a U.S. president, and sylvaculturalist, among many other pursuits.

Adams was born on July 11, 1767, in Braintree, Massachusetts. As a child, he witnessed the Battle of Bunker Hill (also called Breed's Hill) from a nearby height above the family farm. John Quincy's patriot father, John Adams, who became the second president of the United States, instilled in his son a great love of national service. Young Adams accompanied his father to the courts of Europe to drum up assistance for the American Revolution. At fourteen John Quincy, who was a master of languages even at a young age, served as translator for the U.S. envoy to Russia. He returned to Paris to rejoin his father and viewed the signing of the Treaty of Paris of 1783, which ended the American Revolution.

Adams graduated from Harvard University and began a career in law. Being connected to the pantheon of founding fathers was a great benefit for John Quincy, who at the age of twenty-six was appointed Minister to the Netherlands by President George Washington. A series of foreign postings followed. In 1797 President John Adams took the advice of his friend George Washington and appointed John Quincy to be Minister to Prussia. From these positions the younger Adams was a witness to the continental wars set off by the French Revolution and the subsequent Napoleonic period.

In 1803 Adams was elected senator from Massachusetts as a Federalist and became one of the few New Englanders to support President Thomas Jefferson's purchase of Louisiana Territory. In 1805 Adams took on extra duties as professor of rhetoric and oratory at Harvard. Three years later President James Madison appointed Adams Minister to Russia, where he was living during Napoleon's disastrous 1812 invasion. In 1814 Adams was the chief negotiator for the Treaty of Ghent, ending the War of 1812. He served as Minister to Great Britain between 1815 and 1817, where he laid the groundwork for the Rush-Bagot Convention of 1817, a treaty to demilitarize the U.S.-Canadian border. He further crafted an agreement to fix the U.S. boundaries at the Rocky Mountains. In 1817 Presi-

dent James Monroe appointed Adams as his secretary of state (1817–1825), a post that involved Adams in the acquisition of Florida, the drafting of the Monroe Doctrine—which prohibited further European colonies in the Americas—and negotiating the Adams-Onís Treaty, which wrung concessions out of Spain regarding the western boundary of the Louisiana Purchase.

In the controversial election of 1824, Adams won the presidency, declaring no party affiliation. Voting for the four candidates who ran that year resulted in no majority in either popular or electoral votes. The issue was sent to the House of Representatives for a decision. The candidate with the lowest total of electoral votes, Henry Clay, threw his support to Adams which assured John Quincy the election. The supporters of the election's loser, Andrew Jackson, howled "corruption" when Adams appointed Clay as his secretary of state. Jackson vowed to run again in 1828.

The presidency of John Quincy Adams was a troubled one. The divisive election, combined with internal squabbling over protective tariffs, made it difficult for Adams to promote his legislative agenda. He attempted to encourage infrastructure development including roads, harbors, canals, a national observatory, a national university, naval expansion, and a national bank. His signing of the Tariff of 1828 (or the Tariff of Abominations) created sufficient discord so as to make it almost impossible to move further legislation forward. The Adams administration suffered from the president's practice of not removing supporters of his political rivals from appointed positions. Adams chose only to remove individuals for incompetence rather than political allegiances. Accordingly many Jacksonians were in positions to aid Jackson's election campaign. Clay and Adams worked to put together a new political party, the National Republican Party, an effort that did not take hold.

In the election of 1828 Andrew Jackson defeated Adams in a landslide victory. Adams did not attend the inauguration of the seventh president. However, not content to retire from public life, he was elected to the House of Representatives in 1831 and served there until his death in 1848. While in the House he became one of the most prestigious abolitionists in the nation. In 1841 he argued the case before the Supreme Court of those former slaves who took their freedom back by seizing their slave ship, the *Amistad*. John Quincy turned down several prestigious appointments in his lifetime, including the presidency of Harvard and a seat on the U.S. Supreme Court. He did not support President James K. Polk's declaration of war against Mexico in 1846, which eventually led to the acquisition of a large portion of land in the American West. He viewed the war as a blatant attempt to expand the number of slave-holding states. He suffered a stroke in 1846 but recovered sufficiently to return to Congress, where he died on February 21, 1848, in the Capitol Building, while preparing a speech.

Adams's role in the story of westward expansion stems from the negotiation of the Adams-Onís Treaty of 1819 (or the Transcontinental Treaty), which added Florida but ceded claims to most of Rocky Mountain West and Oregon. Additionally, he helped to promote much of the infrastructure in the Midwest, which became a springboard for westward emigration. His long-term fight against slavery affected how that institution was restricted in the Western territories. Adams did not survive to participate in the monumental struggle over bleeding Kansas and the subsequent Civil War, but was an omnipresent spirit in the halls of Congress.

Terry A. Del Bene

See also: Adams-Onís Treaty (1819); Jackson, Andrew; Louisiana Purchase (1803); Missouri Compromise (1820).

Further Reading

Miller, William Lee. *Arguing About Slavery.* New York: Alfred A. Knopf, 1996.

Nagel, Paul C. *John Quincy Adams: A Public Life, A Private Life.* Cambridge, MA: Harvard University Press, 1997.

Adams-Onís Treaty (1819)

This friendship treaty between the United States and Spain set a firm boundary between the Louisiana Purchase and Spanish lands. Negotiated between John Quincy Adams, U.S. secretary of state, and Luis de Onís, Lord of Rayaces, representing the king of Spain, the treaty also is referred to as the Transcontinental Treaty or the Florida Treaty. The formal name of the agreement is *Treaty of Amity, Settlement and Limits Between the United States of America, and His Catholic Majesty.* Adams's role in obtaining concessions from the Spanish government was made easier due to Andrew Jackson's aggressive pursuit of Seminoles, brigands, and escaped slaves into Spanish lands during the First Seminole War (1817–1818). During that campaign, Jackson attacked Spanish strongholds, demonstrating the weak hold Madrid maintained in Florida. Florida was a plum ripe for picking. The Spanish government recognized that it was going to lose Florida one way

or the other and chose to salvage concessions out of the United States.

The document covered a wide range of grievances between Spain and the United States, including losses to privateers. The treaty ceded Spanish claims to Florida and Oregon north of the 42nd parallel. The United States ceded all claims to Texas west of the Sabine River. The United States agreed to recognize Spanish land grants pre-dating the treaty and a commission was set up to adjudicate claims with former Spanish subjects up to a total cost of $5 million. Freedom of religion was guaranteed to former Spanish subjects and both powers agreed to the return of deserters from ships' companies.

For a brief span, Spain controlled all or parts of Texas, California, New Mexico, Arizona, Colorado, Nevada, Utah, and Wyoming, which were considered safe from American expansion. The settling of the western boundary for the Louisiana Purchase made the settlement of Oregon Territory somewhat less complex.

The Adams-Onís Treaty was signed by the emissaries on February 22, 1819. The king of Spain ratified it on October 24, 1820. The U.S. Senate advised ratification on February 19, 1821. President James Monroe completed the ratification process by signing the treaty on February 22, 1821.

Terry A. Del Bene

See also: Adams, John Quincy; Louisiana Purchase (1803).

Further Reading

Brooks, Philip C. *Diplomacy and the Borderlands: The Adams-Onís Treaty of 1819.* Berkeley: University of California Press, 1939.

Adobe Walls, Battles of

Two noted battles of the Indian Wars took place a decade apart in the vicinity of Adobe Walls, the crumbling remains of an abandoned trading post erected by William Bent in the Texas Panhandle.

The First Battle of Adobe Walls, on November 26, 1864, was one of the largest engagements ever fought in the West between whites and Indians. Famed frontiersman Kit Carson had joined the U.S. Army when the Civil War began, commanding large numbers of New Mexico volunteers against Confederate invaders and hostile Indians. Late in 1864 Colonel Carson was ordered to attack the winter camps of Comanches and Kiowas who conducted ferocious raids into New Mexico.

In November Carson led 400 men into the Texas Panhandle. The force included the 1st Cavalry of New Mexico Volunteers—a regiment organized by Carson—supported by two mountain howitzers and seventy-five Ute and Apache scouts. Several enemy encampments were situated along the Canadian River near Adobe Walls, and as Carson's column neared their targets, 3,000 Kiowas, Comanches, Apaches, and Arapahos launched an attack.

The battle began just after breakfast on Friday, November 26, when the Indians attacked and surrounded the soldiers, pressing their assault with heavy rifle fire and brilliant horsemanship. The fight raged all day, but by early afternoon the Indian warriors had suffered close to 200 casualties, while only 2 soldiers had been killed and 10 wounded.

When the Indians at last withdrew, Carson ordered a retreat down the river, intending to destroy a nearby village. The Indians attacked again, firing the tall grass at Carson's rear. Carson retaliated by setting a blaze in his front, then moving to high ground on his right flank. The furious Indian charge was checked largely by the efficient operation of the mountain howitzers under the direction of Lieutenant George Pitts. Carson's men dismantled a Kiowa-Apache village, killing Chief Iron Shirt in the process.

By the time darkness fell, Carson had twenty-five wounded men on his hands and almost no ammunition. He marched his men in the direction of his supply train, locating the twenty-seven wagons and single ambulance within three hours. By the morning of Saturday, November 27, Carson's men were ready to fight again, but the Indians warily stayed out of howitzer range all day. On Sunday Carson prudently headed back toward New Mexico, despite the protests of many aggressive or foolhardy soldiers. Only George A. Custer in 1876 had ever faced as large a number of hostile warriors.

A decade after the First Battle of Adobe Walls, another notable incident exploded in the area. By 1874 the Indian way of life on the Great Plains was threatened as vast herds of buffalo disappeared under the onslaught of hordes of hide hunters. There was a desperate response to the messianic promises of Comanche medicine man Isa-tai, who pledged magical protection from hunters' bullets. Warrior societies excitedly planned a war of extermination against the hide hunters in Comanche lands, beginning with a camp near Adobe Walls.

The tiny cluster of sod buildings included two general stores, a saloon, and a blacksmith shop, all recently built to serve buffalo hunters in the Panhandle.

There were 28 men and 1 woman—wife of one of the merchants—sleeping in and around the buildings when more than 600 Comanche, Kiowa, Arapaho, and Cheyenne warriors attacked at dawn on November 27, 1874. Three hunters were killed outside the buildings, but most of the men found refuge inside the structures. The professional hunters, forted up behind thick walls and armed with powerful Sharps buffalo rifles, broke the charge with deadly fire. The courageous young war leader, Quanah Parker, was shot in the shoulder and his horse was killed. The hunters repulsed a second charge, although the warriors carried off their dead and wounded under fire.

Unwilling to charge the fortified riflemen again, the warriors conducted a desultory siege. One of the merchants accidentally shot himself and died in front of his horrified wife. But sharpshooter Billy Dixon triggered a famous shot, knocking a warrior off his horse on a ridge seven-eighths of a mile from the camp. Dixon later praised "the valor" of Bat Masterson who, at age twenty, was the youngest member of the defenders.

The great war party soon broke off the siege and scattered, although there were numerous attacks on isolated hunting camps across the Panhandle. The Second Battle of Adobe Walls triggered the Red River War of 1874–1875. This massive military convergence in the Panhandle featured army columns hounding Comanche and Kiowa bands onto their reservations in the southeastern corner of Indian Territory. Parker and 400 diehard followers were the last to leave the plains and move onto the Fort Sill Reservation in June 1875.

Bill O'Neal

See also: Carson, Kit; Hide Hunters; Parker, Quanah.

Further Reading

Estergreen, M. Morgan. *Kit Carson, a Portrait in Courage.* Norman: University of Oklahoma Press, 1962.

Haley, James L. *The Buffalo War.* Norman: University of Oklahoma Press, 1985.

Sides, Hampton. *Blood and Thunder: The Epic Story of Kit Carson and the Conquest of the American West.* New York: Anchor Books, 2006.

Alamance, Battle of

On May 16, 1771, in a brief confrontation that some historians call the first battle of the American Revolution, North Carolina Regulators met head to head with the well-heeled troops of Royal Governor William Tryon at Alamance Creek, near the town of Hillsborough, North Carolina. Although the Regulators outnumbered Tryon's troops by about two to one (2,000 frontiersmen to 1,000 royal soldiers), they were decisively defeated within two hours, resulting in great numbers of the disenfranchised pioneers casting their lots to migrate even further west, across the Appalachian Mountains, to the Watauga colony in present-day Tennessee. One Baptist church, which prior to 1771 numbered just over 600 members, was reduced to a mere 14 following the battle.

The Regulators had their beginnings as far back as 1755, when a group of settlers living along the Yadkin River in North Carolina organized themselves against a rising trend of outlawry in the region. Daniel Boone and others allied themselves with the movement as its members attempted to bring law and order to what at the time was America's westernmost frontier.

Following several years of sporadic activity, the Regulation movement was reborn in the mid-1760s with a new agenda: to extract from the royal government the appointment of unprejudiced juries, to demand a public accounting of collected taxes, and to redress other numerous wrongs. Affairs got out of hand in September 1770, when about 150 Regulators marched into a session of the Superior Court being held in Hillsborough, making their demands known to everyone present. Several attorneys and bystanders were horsewhipped and publicly ridiculed. The Regulators demanded that all business of the sitting court be retried according to the Regulators' guidelines, but the presiding judge, Richard Henderson, instead deserted the court and returned to his home, leaving everyone in a state of confusion. On a rampage of destruction, the Regulators torched Henderson's home, barn, and stables, without the foresight to know that in a few brief years, it would be Henderson who would help open vast expanses of western land to settlement through the auspices of his land speculation enterprise, the Transylvania Company.

The Regulator movement died with the Battle of Alamance, but the earlier westward migrations of scores of North Carolina families was greatly augmented by the frontier fighters for justice. After the battle, out of grace with the royal government and with little hope for a comfortable life in their homeland, little else remained but for them to pack up and move west as well.

James A. Crutchfield

See also: Boone, Daniel; Cumberland Gap; Long Hunters; Watauga Settlements.

Further Reading

Crutchfield, James A. *Tennesseans at War: Volunteers and Patriots in Defense of Liberty.* Nashville: Rutledge Hill Press, 1987.

Henderson, Archibald. *The Conquest of the Old Southwest.* New York: Century Company, 1920.

Alamo, The

The Alamo in San Antonio, Texas, had its origins as the mission San Antonio de Valero, established by Spanish missionaries in 1718. Soon after building started at one site, the mission was moved to its present location in 1724. Friars began construction on a mission church in 1744, but the building collapsed. A new church, today's Alamo, was started in 1756, but it was never completed and remained roofless for years. San Antonio de Valero struggled along with a constantly dwindling number of Indian converts and occupants until 1793, when the mission ceased to exist and its property was secularized.

The mission became known as the Alamo in the early 1800s. A Spanish cavalry unit arrived in San Antonio in 1803 to reinforce a unit already stationed there. The new unit was called the Second Flying Company of San Carlos De Alamo de Parras. The soldiers and their families settled in an area just south of the mission, forming a separate community from the town of San Antonio de Bexar across the San Antonio River to the west. Over time the cavalry unit's name was shortened to the Alamo Company and its area became known as the Barrio de Alamo. Eventually the name became permanently attached to the most imposing structure in the barrio, the San Antonio de Valero mission.

The siege and battle of the Alamo (February 23–March 6, 1836) is the event for which the Alamo is best remembered. Mexico won its independence from Spain in 1821 and opened the borders of Texas to settlement in the following years. Tensions arose between the newly arrived American settlers and the government of Antonio López de Santa Anna during the early 1830s. These tensions erupted into open rebellion against Mexico in October 1835 when a small Mexican army unit from San Antonio de Bexar traveled to the town of Gonzales to retrieve a cannon that had been loaned to the town's citizens. Eighteen men from Gonzales met the Mexican troops and refused to surrender the gun. They stalled in negotiations while Texan reinforcements arrived and swelled their number to 150 men. Thus fortified, they sent the Mexican force reeling back to San Antonio after a short fight, thereby starting the Texas Revolution.

A slowly organizing Texan volunteer army besieged a Mexican force under General Martin Perfecto de Cós at San Antonio two months later. The Texans, led by Benjamin Milam, assaulted the town from December 5 to December 10, driving the Mexican troops across the river and into the Alamo. When Cós finally surrendered, he and his men were released under parole.

Command of San Antonio now fell to Lieutenant Colonel James Clinton Neill, who, with a force of about eighty men, had the responsibility of defending both the town and the Alamo. Recognizing the danger inherent in his position, Neill sent requests to the nascent Texas government for men, supplies, and money. In late January 1836, James Bowie arrived with a company of volunteers, answering Neill's call for aid, and Lieutenant Colonel William Barret Travis soon followed with a small company of Texan cavalry. Another small group of newly arrived volunteers from the United States under Davy Crockett joined the garrison in February.

A problem in the command of the San Antonio garrison occurred when Neill was called away from the post and he appointed Travis—the highest-ranking regular army officer present—to take command pending his return. Volunteer troops objected since they traditionally were allowed to elect their own officers. When Travis agreed to an election, the volunteers chose Bowie, who exceeded his authority for a time, attempting to exert control over the whole garrison as well as the town. The two leaders finally resolved their conflict and agreed to jointly command the garrison.

While the Texans bickered, Santa Anna marched north with an army to retake San Antonio and all of Texas. His cavalry vanguard arrived outside San Antonio on February 22 with the Texans unaware of its presence. When the Mexican cavalry hesitated at a river crossing, waiting for the main body of the army to arrive, they lost the advantage and potential to surprise the Texans. Thus, when Santa Anna took possession of the town on the following afternoon, the forewarned Texans retreated to the walls of the Alamo. Santa Anna's troops raised a red flag signaling no quarter from the bell tower of the San Fernando church in the center of town, and the Texans responded by firing a cannon. Upon hearing that the Mexicans had called for a meeting before the shot was fired, Travis and Bowie sent emissaries out to see if negotiations were possible, but were rebuffed by Santa Anna's aides. The Mexican general made it clear that the only option was surrender.

While the Mexican army occupied San Antonio, conducted a loose encirclement of the Alamo, and harassed the Texans with sporadic cannonade, the Texans settled in for a prolonged siege and waited for reinforcements. Bowie, ill and incapacitated after the first day, handed over full command of the garrison to Travis. The young lieutenant colonel, determined to hold the Alamo until reinforcements arrived, dispatched a series of couriers to the Texan government and colonies with appeals for assistance. In one letter of February 24, addressed to the people of Texas and all Americans in the world, Travis described the precariousness of his situation and the steadily increasing number of Mexican troops arrayed against him. He declared that he would never surrender or retreat and that if help did not arrive he would "sustain myself as long as possible and die like a soldier."

Santa Anna launched a small probing attack against the Alamo's south wall at 10:00 A.M. the following day. Texan rifle and artillery fire repelled the attack, and several of the men within the Alamo sallied out to burn huts that had given cover to their enemy. Travis reported exultantly in another letter that many of the Mexicans were wounded, but the Texan force in the Alamo had not "lost a man." The siege dragged on as some of Travis's entreaties for aid began to pay off. A group of about thirty-four men from the town of Gonzales, led by couriers John W. Smith and Albert Martin, reached the Alamo on March 1; however, Santa Anna's force also increased. The battalions of Aldama, Toluca, and his combat engineers, the Zapadores, arrived in San Antonio on March 3, giving Santa Anna the troops he needed to storm the fort.

Travis received further encouragement on the same day when courier James Butler Bonham arrived with a letter from Travis's close friend Robert M. Williamson, commander of the Texan Ranging Corps, who encouraged Travis and his men to sustain themselves until help arrived. Williamson indicated that 60 men had left Gonzales for the Alamo and another 300, under command of Colonel James Walker Fannin, were on the way from Goliad, with a similar number marching toward the Alamo from local towns. When reinforcements arrived from Gonzales in the predawn hours of March 4, the Texan numbers swelled to about 250 men.

This additional support for the defenders may have been the catalyst that convinced Santa Anna to storm the Alamo before more reinforcements arrived. Santa Anna launched his attack at dawn on Sunday, March 6. Stalled for a time along the north wall in the face of Texan artillery and small arms fire, he seemed on the verge of being repelled when he committed his reserves. Mexican soldiers poured over the north wall by sheer force of numbers while the diversionary column gained a foothold on the southwest corner of the compound.

With enemy troops entering the Alamo from the north and south, Travis's men were forced to abandon their positions. At least three groups of Texans fought on but were cut down outside the Alamo's walls. Others took cover in the former mission's buildings, where they were overcome in room-by-room combat.

Travis died at his post at the north wall. Bowie died in his sickbed. The exact place and manner of Crockett's death remain unknown. The battle ended sometime around 6:00 A.M. Santa Anna entered the Alamo and in keeping with his policy of no quarter ordered the execution of several Texan survivors, later burning the bodies. Mexican troops reoccupied the Alamo after the battle. The Texans would turn the tide in favor of their revolution six weeks later when they defeated Santa Anna at the Battle of San Jacinto. Following that loss, the Mexican occupiers destroyed and burned most of the Alamo's walls and buildings before retreating to Mexico.

The Alamo's surviving buildings, the church and long barracks, were later used as a quartermaster depot for the U.S. Army, a Confederate Army post during the Civil War, and a civilian-owned warehouse. The U.S. Army added the famous bell-shaped top to the church's facade in 1850, making the Alamo one of the most identifiable buildings in America today.

The city of San Antonio grew up and around the former mission San Antonio de Valero. The efforts of the Daughters of the Republic of Texas, led by Clara Driscoll and Adina de Zavala, in the early twentieth century saved what was left of the Alamo. Today it is preserved by the Daughters of the Republic of Texas as a historical site and shrine to the defenders of the Alamo.

William Groneman III

See also: Bowie, James; Crockett, Davy; Fannin, James Walker; Goliad, Battle of; San Jacinto, Battle of; Santa Anna, Antonio López de; Texas Revolution and Independence; Travis, William Barret.

Further Reading

Groneman, William, III. "The Alamo." In *The Way West*, ed. James A. Crutchfield. New York: Forge Books, 2005.

———. *Eyewitness to the Alamo*. Rev. ed. Plano: Republic of Texas Press, 2001.

Lindley, Thomas Ricks. *Alamo Traces*. Lanham, MD: Republic of Texas Press, 2003.

Nelson, George. *The Alamo: An Illustrated History*. Uvalde, TX: Aldine Books, 1998.

Alaska Purchase (1867)

What began as "Seward's Folly," "Seward's Icebox," and President Andrew Johnson's "Polar Bear Garden," ultimately became a wise investment in Pacific Rim real estate. In 1867, for a mere $7.2 million, U.S. secretary of state William Seward (1801–1872) purchased from Russia 600,000 square miles (1.6 million sq km) of Alaskan wilderness filled with fur-bearing animals, timber, gold fields, and valuable minerals.

Russia had claimed Alaska as early as 1741 after explorer Vitus Bering's expedition landed near Yakutat. The Russian-American Company was established to take advantage of the wealth of sea otter pelts, and in 1790 the town of Kodiak was founded. The Russian-American company eventually spread settlements as far south as northern California. However, the company's interests in Alaska waned as the sea otter pelt industry slumped and, after acquiring regions within their own northern and eastern borders, its focus shifted as its finances stretched thin. In the meantime, the Russian government feared that Great Britain would attempt to occupy Alaska and that the Americans, who had recently discovered gold in California, would soon march up the coast and take control of Alaska.

In the United States, Manifest Destiny was in full swing. The idea of westward expansion was popular, especially with Secretary of State Seward, a presidential hopeful, who believed that Great Britain would evacuate Canada, thus leaving Canadian natives requesting American territorial status. Logically, Alaska would be included in the process. He endorsed the idea of American expansion, believing that eventually the United States would include all of North America.

Combined with the desire to continue positive relationships with Russia and realizing the bargain price of $7.2 million, Seward continued his push for the purchase of Alaska. Opposition, however, came from politicians and the media alike. No one really knew what the region represented. Some believed that the United States was purchasing a wasteland from a country that never really owned it. Russia stood to gain considerable money for a region it had acquired for nothing.

PREPARING FOR THE HEATED TERM.

King Andy and his man Billy lay in a great stock of Russian ice in order to cool down the Congressional majority.

An 1867 political cartoon on the purchase of Alaska, titled "Preparing for the Heated Term," depicts Secretary of State William H. Seward *(left)* and President Andrew Johnson *(right)*, hauling a large chunk of Alaskan ice to cool congressional tempers. *(The Granger Collection, New York)*

Talks of purchasing Alaska had started as early as 1860, but the American Civil War split the country and it would not be until 1866 that negotiations resumed. Ultimately the treaty hammered out between Seward and the Russian minister never mentioned the name "Alaska," but referred to the territory as "Russian lands on the North American continent." Signed on March 30, 1867, the treaty won easy approval from the U.S. Senate, but the House of Representatives, busy with plans to impeach President Johnson, was in no hurry to provide funding. Months later, the House finally approved the $7.2 million price tag, but the United States had already taken possession of the new territory in October 1867, when the American flag was raised at Sitka.

Sitka served as the territorial capital for the next thirty years, but raising the American flag over the small village did little to trigger a stampede. Only a handful of people ventured north; travel was difficult and expensive. Fish, timber, and mining industries had yet to develop. Most Americans knew very little about the new acquisition and even Congress ignored it. For the first seventeen years, few real government facilities existed outside those provided by the army since Alaska was a military district with no civilian laws. In 1877 the army withdrew its troops, relinquishing Alaska's rudimentary government to the Treasury Department, which in turn yielded it to the U.S. Navy. During those early years, most of the native people were unaware of the sale and transfer of power, continuing to govern themselves through long-standing customs and traditions.

In 1896 the great Klondike gold strike convinced even the harshest critics that Alaska was a valuable addition to American territory. Alaska attained its statehood in 1959, and today, its capital, Juneau, oversees a land full of wildlife, mines, seafood production, oil, and natural gas. Seward, one of Alaska's most picturesque cities, was named for William Seward.

Melody Groves

See also: MacKenzie, Donald; Manifest Destiny; Territorial System.

Further Reading

Jensen, Ronald J. *The Alaska Purchase and Russian-American Relations.* Seattle: University of Washington Press, 1975.

Taylor, John M. *William Henry Seward: Lincoln's Right Hand.* Dulles, VA: Potomac Books, 1996.

Allison Commission

In the summer of 1875, President Ulysses S. Grant approved the appointment of a commission "to treat with the Sioux Indians for the relinquishment of the Black Hills" of Dakota Territory, part of the Great Sioux Reservation created by the 1868 Fort Laramie Treaty. After Lieutenant Colonel George Armstrong Custer's 1874 expedition confirmed rumors of gold in the Black Hills, hundreds of miners flooded into the region in violation of the treaty. When the U.S. Army's half-hearted efforts failed to keep miners out of the Hills, the government decided that the solution lay in purchasing the region from the Sioux.

The Allison Commission, named for its chairman, U.S. senator William B. Allison of Iowa, included former congressman Abram Comingo, Brigadier General Alfred H. Terry, Reverend Samuel D. Hinman, G.P. Beavais, W.H. Ashby, and A.G. Lawrence. Scholars have characterized the commission as lacking both experience in dealing with Indians and receiving only vague instructions governing its negotiations.

The council was held near the Red Cloud and Spotted Tail agencies in northwestern Nebraska because the Indians refused to meet at the Missouri River. Gathered with the Oglalas and Brulés were Yanktonai, Two Kettle, Blackfeet, and Sans Arc delegations from the Standing Rock and Cheyenne River agencies in Dakota Territory, some Cheyennes and Arapahos, and a few nonagency—meaning those who were not confined to reservations—Sioux. The principle nonagency bands under Sitting Bull and Crazy Horse did not attend.

The commissioners reached Red Cloud Agency on September 4, 1875, but wrangling between Red Cloud and Spotted Tail over the specific meeting place delayed the council. The commission finally fixed a site near the banks of the White River, about 6 miles (10 km) northeast of Red Cloud Agency and its nearby military post, Camp Robinson (near today's Chadron, Nebraska).

The first formal session finally opened September 20. Estimates of Indian numbers vary, but certainly several thousand were present during the council. The commissioners were divided over what proposal to offer, and negotiations were complicated by poor interpretation on the part of the translators and differences of opinion among the Indians. Some were adamantly opposed to selling the Black Hills, while others were more receptive. Because Article 12 of the 1868 treaty prevented a direct cession of reservation land without the agreement of three-fourths of all adult male Indians, the commission first offered to lease mining rights for $400,000 per year. If the Sioux would sell the Black Hills, the government would pay them $6 million.

At the session on September 27, the leading chiefs stated that before they would give up the Black Hills, the government must agree to support the Sioux for "seven generations" or as long as any should live. At one point $70 million was mentioned as the purchase price, perhaps an interpreter's error. Nevertheless Indian demands exceeded what the commissioners were authorized to offer, and negotiations ended on September 29 without an agreement.

After Custer's defeat at the Little Bighorn in 1876, Congress authorized another commission, which forced the Sioux to cede the Black Hills by threatening to cut off their government rations and annuities.

James E. Potter

See also: Black Hills Expeditions; Crazy Horse; Fort Laramie, Treaty of (1868); Red Cloud; Sioux; Sitting Bull; Spotted Tail.

Further Reading

Olson, James C. *Red Cloud and the Sioux Problem*. Lincoln: University of Nebraska Press, 1965.

"Report of the Commission Appointed to Treat with the Sioux Indians for the Relinquishment of the Black Hills." *Report of the Secretary of the Interior* (Washington, DC: GPO, 1875), 1: 686–702.

American Fur Company

John Jacob Astor incorporated the American Fur Company (AFC) on April 6, 1808, when he was granted a charter by the state of New York. The company had two divisions: the Eastern Department, at Michilimackinac in present-day Michigan, and the Western Department, in St. Louis. By 1827 the company monopolized the Missouri River Indian trade, and by 1831 its employees covered the largest and best areas.

The average pay for the trappers and traders who worked in the field for AFC was about $130 per year. A list of them reads like a Who's Who in the Rocky Mountain fur trade, including such luminaries as Thomas Farnham, George Davenport, Joshua Pilcher, William Vanderburgh, Andrew Drips, Kenneth McKenzie, William Laidlaw, Ramsey Crooks, Pierre Chouteau Jr., Alexander Culbertson, James Kipp, Peter and Thomas Sarpy, Charles Larpenteur, Alexander Harvey, Warren Ferris, and Lucien Fontenelle.

Astor's wealth was a great asset to the company. Not wanting to answer too many questions about his business, Astor revealed to the U.S. government that AFC had a capital of over $1 million in 1831 and had harvested over 500,000 animal hides in the years 1829, 1830, and 1831. Reportedly, in 1831 alone, AFC gathered furs worth an estimated $30,000.

Some of the trading posts under AFC's control were a post at Blacksnake Hills; a post among the Oto tribe; Fort Tecumseh, a small house 70 miles (115 km) above the Arikara villages; the Mandan post; Fort Union; Fort Cass; and a post near the mouth of Maria's River, called Fort Piegan. Fort William, later called Fort Laramie, was purchased by AFC in 1834.

Trade goods for AFC were collected in New York every spring and sent up the Missouri River to the different posts. The furs received in exchange for these goods were counted, weighed, repacked, and shipped to New Orleans. There they were transported to New York City, unpacked, bound into bales, and shipped to markets in Europe and China.

A long-standing feud between the Rocky Mountain Fur Company (RMF) and AFC finally ended when the two companies divided the trapping territory between them, each promising not to interfere in the other's section.

The AFC was the first monopoly in the western part of today's United States. It had a lot of power, backing, and influential managers and employees. The company was so large that for a while it maintained its own route between Fort Laramie and Fort Pierre, along which employees could send their goods by steamboat to St. Louis.

The company reorganized in 1848, giving about half of the stock to the five most important administrators: Alexander Culbertson, James Kipp, William Laidlaw, Andrew Drips, and Fredrick Labone.

Mike Moore

See also: Astor, John Jacob; Astoria; Chouteau Family; Crooks, Ramsay; Fontenelle, Lucien; Fort Laramie; Fort Union (North Dakota); McKenzie, Kenneth; Pilcher, Joshua; Rocky Mountain Fur Company; Stuart, Robert.

Further Reading

Chittenden, Hiram. *Fur Trade of the Far West.* Lincoln: University of Nebraska Press, 1986.

Ferris, Warren. *Life in the Rocky Mountains.* Denver: Old West Publishing, 1983.

Quaife, Milo, ed. *Forty Years a Fur Trader on the Upper Missouri: The Personal Narrative of Charles Larpenteur.* Lincoln: University of Nebraska Press, 1989.

American Horse (1840–1908)

Born as Wasechun-tashunka to Sitting Bear in the Black Hills of South Dakota in 1840, American Horse was an Oglala Sioux chieftain during the Sioux Wars of the 1860s and 1870s. He grew to become an influential, levelheaded leader.

American Horse stood out among other Sioux during the Bozeman Trail War in December 1866, in which 81 troops from Fort Phil Kearny were ambushed and killed in the Battle of the Hundred Slain, or the Fetterman fight. Red Cloud and American Horse led 1,000 Sioux, Cheyenne, and Arapaho tribesmen in that ambush. The conflict led to the 1868 Treaty of Fort Laramie in which the United States, realizing that the Sioux could inflict devastating injury to the army, agreed to abandon Forts Phil Kearny, C.F. Smith, and Reno in exchange for peace.

In a move that ultimately opened thousands of acres of land to settlement, American Horse was one of the signers of a later treaty between the Sioux and the United States government in 1887. The Yankton Treaty, although opposed by many Sioux, was approved and ultimately divided Sioux lands by half, ceding what later became North and South Dakota in 1889. In 1891 American Horse traveled to Washington, DC, where he and his delegation managed to gain government support for improved rations and humane treatment of the Sioux.

Along with other Sioux leaders, American Horse joined Buffalo Bill's Wild West Show and toured the United States. The show consisted of "historical" scenes interspersed with sharp shooting, riding tricks, and extravagant rodeo events. Buffalo Bill's show glorified historical events, but grew wildly popular as entertainment, even in Europe. As the Indians became less of a "real life" threat on the frontier, popularity of their acts grew exponentially. The Sioux staged historic battle reenactments such as Custer's Last Stand and even signed autographs. Buffalo Bill made sure the Indians of his troop were well treated and respected.

American Horse died at Pine Ridge, South Dakota, in December 1908.

Melody Groves

See also: Arapaho; Bozeman Trail; Carrington Family; Cheyenne; Crazy Horse; Fort Laramie, Treaty of (1868); Fort Phil Kearny (Wyoming); Ghost Dance; Red Cloud; Red Cloud's War; Sioux; Sitting Bull.

Further Reading

Demallie, Raymond J. *Sioux Indian Religion: Tradition and Innovation.* Norman: University of Oklahoma Press, 1989.

Hyde, George E. *Red Cloud's Folk: A History of the Oglala Sioux Indians.* Norman: University of Oklahoma Press, 1987.

Kasson, Joy S. *Buffalo Bill's Wild West: Celebrity, Memory, and Popular History.* New York: Hill & Wang, 2001.

Apache

The Apaches were an Athapascan-speaking people whose ancient history is not well understood. Scholars agree about neither the origins of the Apaches nor the reason for their migration to the American Southwest. Athapascan peoples inhabited large expanses of the North American subarctic and sent offshoots south, encompassing vast areas of the West.

The Apaches and their linguistic cousins, the Navajo, took hundreds if not thousands of years to arrive in the southwestern United States from their former homes in Alaska and Canada. The final split between the eastern and western Apaches probably took place between 1300 and 1400 C.E. This late date helps explain the large number of shared cultural characteristics among the various Apache subgroups. Apache homelands encompassed most of Arizona, western New Mexico, and a portion of northern Mexico.

The derivation of the term "Apache" is not known. Some say it is from the Yuman word *e-patch*, which roughly means "man." Others say it comes from the Zuni word *apachu*, meaning "enemy." The Apaches called themselves *tinneh*, *dine*, *tinde*, or *inde*, which translates to "man" or "people."

The Apaches, as we know them today, consist of several subgroups, not all of them uniformly agreed upon by authorities. Jicarillas, Lipans, and Kiowa-Apaches form the eastern division. Mescaleros, Western Apaches, and Chiricahuas constitute the western division. These groups are further subdivided and known by various names. For example, the names Mimbrenos, Copper Mines, Warm Springs, Mogollons, and Gilas were all used to identify the easternmost of the Chiricahua subgroup.

Apaches, as documented in history, maintained a nomadic, mainly hunting and gathering economy, inhabiting huge tracts of land, well into the historic period. This lifestyle was supplemented by some horticultural practices. Women planted corn, beans, and squash in verdant valleys in the spring and the Apaches returned on their seasonal round to harvest whatever crops had survived with this minimal care. This economy was also supplemented by trading and raiding with adjacent cultures. Apaches are renowned in literature and arts as a warrior culture, coming into conflict with neighboring tribes, the Spanish, the Mexicans, the Confederate Army, the U.S. Army, and American settlers and miners.

The Apaches followed no supreme leader. A man led only so long as his followers agreed to comply with his orders. The Chiricahua subgroup produced many famous leaders who commanded supreme respect, none

Geronimo *(right)*, the great warrior of the Chiricahua Apaches, poses with members of his tribe in 1886, the year he finally surrendered. Geronimo, known for his guerrilla raids against encroaching Mexican and U.S. forces, was the last Apache leader to submit. *(MPI/Stringer/Getty Images)*

the least of which was Cochise. But even the followers of Cochise were free to leave his band if they chose to do so. Other important Apache leaders were Geronimo, Mangas Coloradas, and Victorio.

Apaches were cunning and fierce in battle and knew no equal as guerrilla fighters. Rarely did they choose to stand toe-to-toe and fight it out with the U.S. Army and its superior firepower. The Apaches chose the time and place for skirmishes, waiting patiently for the advantages of time, position, and numbers to be favorable to them. When the situation did not favor the Apaches, they merely faded into the landscape and waited for another day. Their tactical inventiveness earned them a fearsome reputation. They were among the last of the American tribes to be pacified, an event that stretched U.S. resources to the breaking point and required the help of numerous Apaches as allies.

In October 1872, Cochise agreed to accept a reservation in southeastern Arizona, encompassing an area about 60 miles (100 km) on a side and including the Dragoon and Chiricahua Mountains. After his death in 1874, the United States removed the Chokonen Chiricahuas from the reservation and imprisoned them in Florida.

Today the Apache tribes are scattered. The San Carlos and White River reservations in Arizona, two of the largest, are home to most of the Western Apaches. The Mescalero reservation in New Mexico is home to many of the Eastern Apaches, and the Mescaleros consider themselves Chiricahua descendants. The Chihennes live on a small reservation in Oklahoma where they were joined by some of the few surviving Chokonens of the Chiricahuas. To this day, the Chiricahuas have no reservation in their homeland in southern Arizona. Once taken prisoner and removed, they were never allowed to return. Such was the bitter hatred and fear of them felt by the citizens and government of the United States.

Stoney Livingston

See also: Cochise (Cheis); Geronimo; Lozen; Victorio.

Further Reading

Lockwood, Frank C. *The Apache Indians*. Lincoln: University of Nebraska Press, 1987.

Roberts, David. *Once They Moved Like the Wind*. New York: Touchstone, 1993.

Sweeny, Edwin R. *Cochise: Chiricahua Apache Chief*. Norman: University of Oklahoma Press, 1991.

Terrell, John Upton. *Apache Chronicle*. New York: World, 1972.

Arapaho

There are three distinct groups of Arapahos: the Northern, who live on the Wind River Reservation in central Wyoming; the Southern, who are situated on the Canadian River in Oklahoma; and the Gros Ventres, who live near the Milk River in northern Montana. In all cases they share lands with other tribal groups.

The expedition of Pierre La Verendrye made early contact with the Arapahos in about 1742–1743 near present-day Pierre, South Dakota. Like other Plains Indians, the Arapahos relied on hunting and gathering for their sustenance, following game herds, such as the bison. Thanks to a close association with the Cheyenne Indians, the Southern Arapahos were assigned to a shared reservation with the Southern Cheyennes when reservation lands were allocated under the Dawes Act in 1887. They also received treaty annuities in connection with the Southern Cheyennes. As a result the Arapahos intermarried with the Cheyennes and experienced language, cultural, and religious assimilation because of their close ties. Even so, the tribes were governed separately.

By the nineteenth century, the trading relationship between the U.S. government, encroaching white settlers, and the Arapahos had deteriorated into active conflict that led to further loss of tribal lands. One of the most notorious events affecting the tribe occurred in November 1864, when some Arapahos were encamped at Sand Creek with Black Kettle's Cheyennes. Their village came under attack by Colonel John M. Chivington, commanding Colorado volunteers. About 160 Arapahos and Cheyennes, including women, children, and elders, were killed. These tribal members had earlier been assured they would be safe if they remained in camp at Sand Creek.

Arapaho resistance to westward expansion grew after what became known as the Sand Creek Massacre. Arapaho warriors were instrumental in the attempts to close down the Overland Mail Route and its vital telegraph stations during the bloody summer of 1865. More than 200 miles (325 km) of stage stations were burned out in a series of highly effective large-scale raids.

There are presently some 6,000 Northern Arapahos and 11,000 Southern Arapahos. They have worked to preserve their language, although only the elders remain truly fluent. A project of the Disney Corporation introduced a version of the children's film *Bambi* in Arapaho in an effort to preserve the language. Arapaho elder Alonzo Moss translated the original script into Arapaho, and he and other Northern Arapaho tribal members performed the voices.

Terry A. Del Bene and Candy Moulton

See also: Black Kettle; Cheyenne; Chivington, John M.; Sand Creek Massacre.

Further Reading

Trenholm, Virginia Cole. *The Arapahoes, Our People.* Norman: University of Oklahoma Press, 1970.

Arikara

The Indian tribe originally known as the Arickaree, or popularly the Rees, was also called Sahnish. It was descended from the Caddoans, from whom its language is derived. A seminomadic people, the Arikaras inhabited an area of the Missouri River valley that stretched from Nebraska, including Kansas, to the Dakotas. Archeologists have confirmed the presence of Arikaras in the area now known as Omaha, Nebraska. Their migration west has been considered "aimless" by some historians, but the Arikara people claim that the migration originated from a directive by Neesaau ti naacitakUx, the Chief Above, through a communication with the sacred being Mother Corn.

The Arikaras lived in half-circle earth lodges (similar to those of the Hidatsas and Mandans) from 40 to 75 feet (12–23 m) in diameter, partially underground to maintain consistent temperatures throughout the seasons. The roofs were constructed of willow branches, dry grass, and a layer of sod. The Arikaras also used the tepee as a dwelling, but rarely and only in areas where the construction of earth lodges was not practicable.

The Arikaras were primarily farmers and adept traders, but also hunted bison to supplement their diet when crops were not substantial enough to sustain the tribe. The hunters created elaborate fence systems in order to drive the bison into small pens where they were killed. Another hunting technique involved setting fires in order to panic the bison sufficiently to allow the hunters to drive them off cliffs. Crops included corn ("maize"), beans, squash, tobacco, pumpkins, and watermelons.

The crops grown by the Arikaras provided valuable commodities for trading with other Indian tribes. The Teton Sioux, neighbors of the Arikaras, depended on them as a major supplier of their food. In exchange, the warrior Sioux provided many items, such as so-phisticated weaponry, that the Arikaras were less able to produce for themselves.

Arikara men wore buffalo robes, leggings, and moccasins. Women most often wore full-length, fringed dresses of antelope skins. Arikara religion was based on medicine and magic, called the Shunuwanuh. Ceremonies were performed from midsummer to fall. The Sun Dance was performed for agricultural purposes, and the Child Dance allowed outsiders into the tribe. The legend known as the Address to Mother Corn involves the soul, the Sishu, which was believed to be responsible for everything people do in their lives. Animals were also believed to possess Sishu, but nonliving objects did not.

Meriwether Lewis, William Clark, and the Corps of Discovery encountered the Arikara near the Grand River in 1804. Three villages numbered about 3,000 members at the time. Lewis and Clark spent five days with the Arikaras, who were friendly to the explorers. The tribe agreed to send a representative to meet President Thomas Jefferson and also to seek peace with the neighboring Mandans and Hidatsas at the behest of Lewis and Clark.

In 1823 after attacking General William H. Ashley's trapping expedition on the Missouri River, the Arikaras were involved in what is now called the Arikara War. The U.S. Army responded to the attack with 230 soldiers, 750 allied Sioux warriors, and 50 trappers, all under the command of Colonel Henry Leavenworth. The conflict was the first documented "war" between the army and a Native American tribe west of the Mississippi River.

It is believed that the first outbreak of smallpox that nearly decimated the Arikaras occurred in the 1780s. The most severe outbreak came in 1856, in the Star Village at Beaver Creek, and took half of the population. In 1862 the Arikaras joined the Mandans and Hidatsas at Like-a-Fishhook Village, where they become known as the Three Affiliated Tribes. Today, the Arikaras reside on the Fort Berthold Reservation in North Dakota.

Larry D. Sweazy

See also: Arikara War; Ashley, William Henry; Clark, William; Hidatsa; Leavenworth, Henry; Lewis, Meriwether; Mandan.

Further Reading

Campbell, Lyle. *American Indian Languages: The Historical Linguistics of Native America.* New York: Oxford University Press, 1997.
Parks, Douglas R. *Myths and Traditions of the Arikara Indians.* Lincoln: University of Nebraska Press, 1996.

Arikara War

The Arikara War is often referred to as America's first Plains Indian war, as it was the first major armed conflict between the U.S. Army and a recognized Native American nation living west of the Mississippi River.

The Arikaras, also known as the Rees, were a nomadic, agricultural society, occupying lands along the Missouri River from Nebraska to the Dakotas. Adept traders and usually friendly to explorers, such as Lewis and Clark, the Arikaras were not known as a warring tribe at the beginning of the nineteenth century—but that soon changed. With more white settlers encroaching on their land in the early 1820s, the Arikaras were drawn into conflicts with the settlers and the neighboring Teton Sioux.

The Arikara War began in present-day South Dakota in the spring of 1823, when General William H. Ashley and his fur-trading party were ascending the Missouri River on their way to the confluence of the Missouri and the Yellowstone rivers. The Arikaras' attack lasted a reported fifteen minutes and left a dozen of Ashley's men dead. The survivors retreated downriver and reported the attack to government officials. Six weeks later, the United States responded to the attack with 230 soldiers, 750 allied Teton Sioux warriors, and 50 trappers, all under the command of U.S. Army Colonel Henry Leavenworth.

Leavenworth, a former lawyer from New Haven, Connecticut, had been brevetted the rank of colonel after the Battle of Niagara during the War of 1812. He had served as an Indian agent and had overseen the construction of Fort St. Anthony today's Minnesota in 1820. His retaliation against the Arikaras occurred on August 9, 1823. Fifty tribesmen were killed in a fierce battle. Six days later, Leavenworth charged his men with the task of destroying the village along the Missouri River, and it was burned to the ground. An American post was eventually built on the spot as a message to the Crows and Blackfoot that the United States would not tolerate "unfriendly" Indians.

The defeat of the Arikaras was swift, but Leavenworth became the center of great debate because he did not entirely annihilate the tribe. His lenient approach to the conflict with the Arikaras generated controversy within government circles and subjected him to criticism in the newspapers. Most Americans of the time favored the subjugation of all Native American tribes and nations. At the time the United States was competing directly with Great Britain for control of the Missouri River. Both nations wanted total access to areas north of the river and west to the Pacific coast. After the Arikara War, fur trading and exploration expanded, leading to other conflicts.

The Arikaras left the area, eventually settling with the Skidi tribe on the Loup River. They returned to the Missouri River two years later and continued to migrate northward, as far as the Heart River by the 1850s. Continued conflicts and outbreaks of smallpox reduced the Arikaras to a much smaller population than they had been prior to the Arikara War. They joined the Hidatsas and Mandans, whose numbers were also reduced by war and epidemics.

In 1862 the tribes moved to Fort Berthold in what is now North Dakota. In 1880 the Fort Berthold Reservation was created, and the Arikaras have lived there ever since. With the Hidatsas and Mandans, they are now known as the Three Affiliated Tribes.

Colonel Henry Leavenworth survived the debate over his treatment of the Arikaras and went on to build several military outposts in the West, including present-day Fort Leavenworth in Kansas. He received the full rank of brigadier general in 1833.

Larry D. Sweazy

See also: Arikara; Ashley, William Henry; Clark, William; Hidatsa; Leavenworth, Henry; Lewis, Meriwether; Mandan.

Further Reading

Barnhill, John H. "Nester: The Arikara War." *Montana: The Magazine of Western History* 52 (Autumn 2002).

Nester, William R. *The Arikara War: The First Plains Indian War, 1823*. Missoula, MT: Mountain Press, 2001.

Armijo, Manuel (c. 1792–1853)

Manuel Armijo was New Mexico's governor when General Stephen Watts Kearny's Army of the West occupied Santa Fe in August 1846, during the Mexican-American War. He was born about 1792 of poor parentage in present-day New Mexico, when the region was still under Spanish control. Little is known about his early life, but after he joined the military, his star rose rapidly and he advanced through the ranks. New Mexico won its independence from Spain in 1821, and Armijo was appointed governor in 1827, serving for two years.

Following more years in the army, Armijo reclaimed the governorship in 1837, when he squashed a rebellion in northern New Mexico and executed the provisional governor. Except for a brief period during 1844–1845, he held the office until being ousted by the U.S. occupation in 1846. During his tenure, he was remembered for awarding a large number of land grants to both Mexicans and Americans, sometimes making himself a silent, behind-the-scenes partner. He was also primarily responsible for the persecution of several Americans involved in the Texan–Santa Fe Expedition of 1841, sending most of them to Mexico City where they were held as prisoners until their eventual release.

When news arrived in Santa Fe of the imminent arrival of Kearny's American army, Armijo proclaimed loudly that he would defend the territory until the end and called upon his fellow citizens to arm themselves for battle. However, unknown to only but a few insiders, he had actually already agreed to sell out to the Americans in a secret meeting held in Santa Fe on August 12, 1846, nearly a week before Kearny's army rode into the capital and declared it and the surrounding region to be under the protection of the United States.

After allowing the American army to occupy Santa Fe without a fight, Armijo fled to Mexico in disgrace, where he was tried, but acquitted, of treason. Returning to New Mexico after the war, he operated a ranch until his death, but never again was involved in politics. He died a rejected and disappointed man on December 9, 1853, and, out of respect for the one-time official and foe, the New Mexico Territorial Assembly adjourned its session for his funeral.

James A. Crutchfield

See also: Army of the West; Kearny, Stephen Watts; Maxwell Land Grant Company; Texan Santa Fe Expedition.

Further Reading

Crutchfield, James A. *Tragedy at Taos: The Revolt of 1847.* Plano: Republic of Texas Press, 1995.

Weber, David J. *The Mexican Frontier, 1821–1846: The American Southwest Under Mexico.* Albuquerque: University of New Mexico Press, 1982.

Army of the West

On May 13, 1846, after being advised two days earlier by President James K. Polk that the Mexican army had violated American territory along the Rio Grande, the U.S. Congress declared war on Mexico, earmarking $10 million and 50,000 army troops for the effort. Less than one month later a command known as the "Army of the West" was organized and dispatched to New Mexico and California.

Within days of the declaration of war, Colonel Stephen Watts Kearny, in charge of the First United States Dragoons stationed at Fort Leavenworth, Missouri, was ordered to command the new army that would consist of elements of his dragoon regiment and volunteer forces. Recruits were drawn from the Mormon companies that were already traveling somewhere on the Great Plains on their way to the Great Salt Lake (the famed Mormon Battalion). Additionally, ten companies of Missouri volunteers—eight of infantry and two of artillery—were organized and placed at Kearny's disposal.

In late June, Kearny rode out of Fort Leavenworth, accompanied by a mixed command of 1,658 men, consisting of 300 troopers of his own First Dragoons, 856 riflemen of the First Regiment of Missouri Mounted Volunteers, 250 artillerymen from St. Louis, 145 infantrymen from Missouri, and 107 Laclede Rangers from St. Louis. Traveling with the soldiers were 3,658 mules, 14,904 cattle, 459 extra horses, 1,556 wagons, 12 six-pounder cannons, and 4 twelve-pounder howitzers. The army's first destination, after picking up the Santa Fe Trail, was Bent's Fort, located 537 miles (865 km) to the west along the Arkansas River in present-day southeastern Colorado.

The journey to Bent's Fort, although extremely hot and dry, progressed largely without incident. In late July, as lead elements of the army approached the trading post, mountain man Thomas "Broken Hand" Fitzpatrick delivered to Kearny a letter from New Mexico's governor, Manuel Armijo, stating that the American invasion of Mexican territory would be opposed vigorously. On August 2, when Kearny and the army broke camp at Bent's Fort, crossed the Arkansas River, and headed southwestward toward Raton Pass, they knew they were violating Mexican territory, and the battle-trained colonel ordered his men to be doubly alert.

Raton Pass, separating present-day Colorado and New Mexico, was crossed uneventfully and on August 14, the Army of the West approached the small New Mexican village of Vegas (now Las Vegas, New Mexico), located about 60 miles (100 km) from Santa Fe. Reports were soon received that 600 Mexican soldiers were encamped in a pass a few miles away, fully prepared to defend it. Kearny, now promoted to brigadier general, addressed the villagers and guaranteed them that the American army had no hostile intentions toward the public and that American rule would be far more tolerable than that under which they had lived.

The defending Mexican army never appeared in the pass, thus allowing Kearny and his troops to make their way to San Miguel, where again rumors were flying, this time of a 1,000-man Mexican army ready to attack the Americans in nearby Apache Pass. The American soldiers—unaware that Kearny, through the diplomacy of Santa Fe trader James Wiley Magoffin and Captain Philip St. George Cooke, had secretly negotiated with Governor Armijo several days earlier to give up his defensive plans—were baffled when they approached the pass on August 18 and found no enemy army there. Armijo deserted his position and fled to Mexico, leaving the perplexed Army of the West to ride unopposed into Santa Fe.

Following the peaceful occupation of Santa Fe, General Kearny prepared for the second half of his mission—the winning of California. Before leaving the New Mexican capital, however, he directed that fortifications to be named Fort Marcy, in honor of Secretary of War William L. Marcy, be built upon a neighboring eminence. Just prior to departing for California, Kearny appointed several Americans and Mexicans with American sympathies to posts of authority, including Charles Bent as governor.

On September 25, Kearny and 300 of his First Dragoons left Santa Fe for the Pacific coast. The Mormon Battalion, under the command of Captain Cooke, soon followed them. The First Missouri Volunteers, commanded by Colonel Alexander W. Doniphan, remained in Santa Fe until the Second Missouri Volunteers, led by Colonel Sterling Price, relieved them. Doniphan then marched to Chihuahua, Mexico, where his regiment became part of General Jonathan E. Wool's army. Half of the artillery accompanied Doniphan to Chihuahua and the remainder stayed in Santa Fe.

Marching westward along the Gila River in current southern New Mexico and Arizona, Kearny's army crossed the Colorado River into California on November 25. For the next several days the column crossed the unforgiving desert of southern California, pestered by extreme heat, lack of water, dying mules and horses, and marauding wolves. On December 6, at a small village called San Pasqual, the remnants of the Army of the West held off Mexican troops, but not before losing thirty-one men dead and disabled, among them General Kearny with serious wounds. Mexican-American hostilities ceased in California on January 8, 1847, when the army resisted an enemy attack along the San Gabriel River, near Los Angeles.

The life of the Army of the West was brief. From its establishment in early June 1846 until its demise following the American victory at Los Angeles in January 1847, its members had traveled hundreds of miles—from Fort Leavenworth, Missouri, all the way to southern California—against grueling, sometimes almost impossible, odds. The organization's impact on the American conquest of the Southwest cannot be overstated.

James A. Crutchfield

See also: Armijo, Manuel; California, Conquest of; Doniphan, Alexander William; Fitzpatrick, Thomas "Broken Hand"; Kearny, Stephen Watts; Magoffin, James Wiley; Mormon Battalion; Santa Fe Trail.

Further Reading

Clark, Dwight L. *Stephen Watts Kearny: Soldier of the West.* Norman: University of Oklahoma Press, 1961.

Crutchfield, James A. *The Santa Fe Trail.* Plano: Republic of Texas Press, 1996.

———. *Tragedy at Taos: The Revolt of 1847.* Plano: Republic of Texas Press, 1995.

Walker, Dale L. *Bear Flag Rising: The Conquest of California, 1846.* New York: Forge Books, 1999.

Ashley, William Henry (c. 1778–1838)

William H. Ashley, one of the most important figures in the American fur trade and the man credited with the creation and implementation of the "rendezvous" system among fur trappers and traders, was born in Chesterfield County, Virginia, around 1778. He settled in Ste. Genevieve, Missouri, in 1802, becoming a mine operator. Later serving as a lieutenant colonel during the War of 1812, he moved to St. Louis in 1819, and became lieutenant governor of the soon-to-be new state of Missouri in 1820. The following year, he was appointed to the post of brigadier general of the Missouri militia.

Ashley soon formed a partnership with Major Andrew Henry and, in February 1822, he advertised for 100 "enterprising young men" to accompany Henry in an ascent of the Missouri River to its source. The resulting organization was the genesis of the Rocky Mountain Fur Company (RMF), although the firm was not called by that name until some years later. The 1822 expedition was less than a total success, but the men built a small stockade at the mouth of the Yellowstone, while Ashley returned to St. Louis to re-supply for the following year. The journey upriver in 1823 became a disaster when Arikara Indians refused to allow Ashley's party to pass their villages. The U.S. Army intervened, but the affair was resolved indecisively and Ashley lost a great deal of money and time.

Failing in his bid for the Missouri governorship in 1824, Ashley once again headed for the mountains. In July 1825, at Henry's Fork of the Green River, he hosted the first annual rendezvous, an event that placed fur-rich mountain men who had trapped the mountains during spring and winter in contact with outfitters from St. Louis bearing badly needed supplies and equipment. With this initial gathering of the trappers held for the purpose of disposing of their furs and re-supplying for the upcoming trapping season, Ashley began a tradition that was to last for sixteen years.

Ashley personally directed the rendezvous of 1826, at which time he and Major Henry sold their fledgling fur company to Jedediah Smith, David Jackson, and William Sublette. Back home in St. Louis, Ashley continued to serve as the provider of rendezvous supplies to his old company. In 1831, upon the death of an incumbent Missouri congressman, he was elected to the U.S. House of Representatives and was reelected in 1832 and 1834. In 1836 he failed once again to win the elusive governorship of Missouri.

William Ashley played an important role in the history of America's westward expansion. One of his biographers, Harvey L. Carter, wrote: "Few individuals can be said to have exercised a greater influence on the course of the fur trade of the Far West. . . . The innovations that he introduced can be said to have revolutionized the business." Ashley died of pneumonia on March 26, 1838, and left an estate valued at $50,000.

James A. Crutchfield

See also: Arikara War; Henry, Andrew; Rendezvous; Rocky Mountain Fur Company.

Further Reading

Clokey, Richard E. *William H. Ashley: Enterprise and Politics in the Trans-Mississippi West.* Norman: University of Oklahoma Press, 1980.

Astor, John Jacob (1763–1848)

A butcher's son born in Waldorf, Germany, near Heidelberg, on July 17, 1763, John Jacob Astor immigrated

German-born John Jacob Astor amassed America's first great fortune by creating a fur-trading empire from the Great Lakes to the Pacific Northwest. In 1808 he organized the American Fur Company, which dominated the industry for many years. *(The Granger Collection, New York)*

with his family to England when he was seventeen, and to America in 1784. He joined a brother in New York and there demonstrated his entrepreneurial talents, selling musical instruments for a time, and then discovering the profits to be made in furs. He tramped the New York countryside buying beaver, fox, marten, mink, and other pelts from farmers and independent trappers and from the Iroquois and other tribes of the region. From his profits he launched an import-export business and within a decade had agents trading furs in China for silks, tea, and spices. By the end of the century he was buying pelts from as far west as Mackinaw, Michigan, and the Great Lakes region, had begun trading with fur companies in Montreal, was shipping his furs on his own vessels to buyers around the world, and had amassed a personal wealth of $250,000—an enormous fortune for the time.

In 1808 Astor established the American Fur Company, which in its fifty-six-year history became the most powerful of all North American fur enterprises, dominating the Great Lakes region and much of the Mississippi Valley and, at its peak, controlling three-quarters of the American fur trade. In 1810 he organized the Pacific Fur Company for a massive incursion into the American Northwest. He built a chain of forts westward from St. Louis to the Pacific with a headquarters entrepôt, Astoria, near the Columbia River estuary. There he challenged the Hudsons's Bay Company's dominance of the fur trade west of the Rocky Mountains.

Although the fort and subsequent town of Astoria were built, Astor's operations on the Pacific Rim were unsuccessful. He lost his base of operations at the mouth of the Columbia River during the War of 1812 and turned his attention to the fur-rich Rocky Mountains and Great Plains and to successfully lobbying for the elimination of government-operated fur-trading posts, thereby opening the field to private companies such as those he owned.

Astor resumed active trade with China in 1815 and maintained a fleet of vessels to trade European and American goods for those of China. For a brief time he even experimented with smuggling Turkish opium into China, but since the trade earned only small profits he abandoned it.

Astor was married to Sarah Todd of New York in 1790 and the couple had five children. He retired from import-export enterprises in 1834 and until his death at age eighty-four on March 29, 1848, concentrated on such business interests as real estate investment, hotels, insurance, banking, and railroads. He became the wealthiest American of his era, leaving an estate valued at $20–$30 million, a portion of which he bequeathed to the Astor Library and many philanthropies.

Dale L. Walker

See also: American Fur Company; Astoria.

Further Reading

Irving, Washington. *Astoria*. Philadelphia: Carey, Lea, & Blanchard, 1836; various reprint editions.

Porter, Kenneth W. *John Jacob Astor, Business Man*. Cambridge, MA: Harvard University Press, 1931.

Terrell, John Upton. *Furs by Astor: The Full Story of the Founding of a Great American Fortune*. New York: William Morrow, 1963.

Astoria

Intended as the chief Northwest fur-trading depot of John Jacob Astor's Pacific Fur Company, Fort Astoria was constructed in 1811 on the southern shore of the Columbia River estuary near Fort Clatsop, the encampment in which the Lewis and Clark expedition spent the winter of 1805–1806. Although it failed to achieve Astor's dream of overtaking the dominance by England's mighty Hudson's Bay Company (HBC) in the fur industry west of the Rocky Mountains, Fort Astoria remained historically significant. As fort and town, it became the first permanent American settlement on the Pacific coast, served as the hub of exploration of the Oregon country, and was important in American disputes with England over claims to the region.

As the far western anchor of Astor's fur empire, Fort Astoria was an ambitious enterprise but one ill timed and therefore short-lived. Construction began in the early spring of 1811 by a company of laborers brought around Cape Horn on the trade vessel *Tonquin* commanded by Captain Jonathan Thorne. By May a crude log stockade ringed with cannon emplacements protected a trading post, blacksmith shop, dwellings, and sheds. The fort's principal trade lay in the inland furs, particularly the much-prized beaver, and sea otter pelts, brought forward by the Clatsop and Chinook people whose ancestral lands surrounded the fort.

Three months after the *Tonquin* disembarked, the party that constructed Fort Astoria along with Captain Thorne and his reduced ship's complement departed the Columbia for the short voyage north to Russian America (Alaska) before returning to New York. Near Nootka Sound, off Vancouver Island, Thorne and his twenty-seven crewmen were massacred by coastal natives with whom they had hoped to engage in a trade for furs.

In February 1812, the fort's population increased markedly when a party of Pacific Fur men led by Astor lieutenant Wilson Price Hunt reached the mouth of the Columbia after a harrowing sixteen-month overland journey from St. Louis. These men and the original builders of Fort Astoria included company partners, clerks, craftsmen, artisans, trappers, seamen, and laborers—a polyglot crew of Scotsmen, Americans, French Canadians, Sandwich Islanders, and Indians.

Hunt's tenure as chief factor at Fort Astoria proved to be brief. The War of 1812 between the United States and Great Britain spilled over into the faraway Oregon country, then controlled chiefly by the Hudson's Bay Company and its rival, the Canadian-based North West Company. In 1813, under Astor's order, Hunt negotiated the sale of Fort Astoria to the North West Company, which renamed the post Fort George. After HBC absorbed the North West Company in 1821, its men occupied Fort George as the main post in the Oregon Country until 1825, when headquarters were removed to Fort Vancouver in present-day Washington State.

Fort George reverted to the name Astoria after the Anglo-American boundary treaty of 1846, and became part of the Territory of Oregon, organized on August 14, 1848, by an act of Congress.

Dale L. Walker

See also: Astor, John Jacob; Hudson's Bay Company; Hunt, Wilson Price; North West Company; Stuart, Robert.

Further Reading
Irving, Washington. *Astoria*. Philadelphia: Carey, Lea, & Blanchard, 1836; various reprint editions.

Terrell, John Upton. *Furs by Astor: The Full Story of the Founding of a Great American Fortune*. New York: William Morrow, 1963.

Walker, Dale L. *Pacific Destiny: The Three-Century Journey to the Oregon Country*. New York: Forge Books, 2000.

Atkinson, Henry (1782–1841)

A native of Person County, North Carolina, Henry Atkinson, whose role in the American army's conquest of the trans-Mississippi West is unparalleled, joined the U.S. Army as a captain of the 3rd Infantry Regiment in 1808. In his first venture west, he served at several military outposts. Rising through the ranks rapidly, Atkinson was stationed in New York, where he saw action as a colonel in the War of 1812, fought against Britain, and commanded the 6th Infantry Regiment ("The Regulars") in 1815.

In 1819 Atkinson was chosen to lead an expedition to the Yellowstone country by Secretary of War John C. Calhoun. With the American fur trade nearly dormant during the War of 1812, the trip was intended to put British fur traders on notice that the Americans were back in business. Success was not immediate. The trip was poorly planned and lacked proper support, allowing Atkinson and his men to journey no further than Council Bluffs, Iowa.

In the following year, Stephen H. Long began a government-supported venture from Council Bluffs. Not only was his presence a warning to the British fur traders, but also the original Atkinson expedition mission was expanded and he was charged with finding the sources of the Platte, Arkansas, and Red rivers.

In 1820 Atkinson was sent to St. Louis and took command of the Western Department of the Army, which eventually grew to oversee all military activity west of the Mississippi River.

Ambitious and successful in military organization, he jumped at the chance to mount a second expedition to the Yellowstone region in 1825. Thoroughly planned and supported this time, the expedition was a success. Of note on this trip was his meeting with William Henry Ashley near the mouth of the Yellowstone River. Ashley's men, known as Ashley's Hundred, had previously been involved with the Arikara Indians along the Missouri River in a skirmish that triggered the Arikara War.

After establishing his post at Jefferson Barracks, south of St. Louis, Atkinson sent Colonel Henry Leavenworth to establish a presence on the frontier in Kansas, at the site that is now Fort Leavenworth. Ironically, Leavenworth had created a storm of controversy when he had quelled the Arikaras in the Arikara War, but did not follow up on his victory. Atkinson faced similar criticism for his actions in the Black Hawk War, named after the noted Sauk Indian chief.

Promoted to brevet brigadier general, in 1832 Atkinson was in command of military operations in the Black Hawk War. When confronted by Atkinson's superior numbers, Black Hawk attempted to surrender, but a battle ensued in which many women and children were killed as they fled across the Mississippi River. Five federal soldiers were killed, and nineteen others were wounded. Atkinson's strategy in the Battle of Bad Axe, or the Bad Axe Massacre, effectively ended the war. The Black Hawk War was the last major Indian conflict east of the Mississippi River. Ultimately Atkinson was nearly ostracized for his overall handling of the Black Hawk War and for the casualties taken. His reputation was tainted, while his subordinates, future president Zachary Taylor and Henry Dodge, prospered.

In 1840 General Atkinson participated in his last major campaign when he oversaw the removal of the Winnebago Indians from Wisconsin. The Winnebago were resettled in Iowa, where Fort Atkinson was established.

Henry Atkinson died at Jefferson Barracks on June 14, 1842.

Larry D. Sweazy

See also: Arikara War; Ashley, William Henry; Black Hawk War (1832); Calhoun, John C.; Dodge, Henry; Leavenworth, Henry; Long, Stephen H.; Taylor, Zachary.

Further Reading
Nichols, Roger L. *General Henry Atkinson: A Western Military Career*. Norman: University of Oklahoma Press, 1965.

Trask, Kerry A. *Black Hawk: The Battle for the Heart of America*. New York: Henry Holt, 2006.

Attacullaculla
(c. 1712–1778)

Attacullaculla (sometime spelled "Attakullakulla"), a Cherokee leader, was born about 1712. He first appears in history as one of the seven Cherokee who sailed to England in 1730 with Sir Alexander Cuming, an adventurer who had explored the Southern Appalachian Mountains and befriended the Cherokee. Attacullaculla then was known as Ookanaka (probably Uka Unega meaning White Owl), and he was called "Owen Nakan" by the English. Cuming had gone to the Cherokee town of Tellico and claimed to have named Moytoy (Ama-edohi) emperor of the Cherokee and obtained the Cherokees' declaration of loyalty to King George II. (The "emperor" was almost certainly, at least in the Cherokees' minds, nothing more than a trade commissioner.) Seven Cherokees, including Ookanaka, accompanied Cuming to England. The Cherokees returned home about four months later after attending an audience with the king. They had their portraits painted in new English outfits by either Hogarth or Markham and signed Articles of Agreement having to do with trade and other issues. Ookanaka learned to speak some English.

Six years later, Ookanaka was influential enough to cause the Cherokees to reject French overtures and maintain trade relationships with the English. In 1740 he was captured and carried north by the Ottawas, where he became friends with Pontiac and some of the French. He seems to have become influential with the Ottawas, even as a captive. Ookanaka returned to Cherokee country in 1748 and he found the South Carolina traders cheating the Cherokees. His years with the Ottawas had turned him toward the French, and he helped to instigate a war against South Carolina.

Ookanaka then acquired a new name. He was called Ada-gal'kala, meaning "Leaning Wood." The English wrote it as "Attacullaculla" and called him the "Little Carpenter." The nickname was a play on the meaning of his Cherokee name and carried the additional meaning that he could craft a bargain, since he was already known as a skilled diplomat.

When the Cherokees entered into a treaty with South Carolina, Governor James Glen of that colony wanted the "Little Carpenter" delivered up to him for having started the war. The Carpenter adroitly explained his way out of this trouble. When he discovered that the French could not provide the trade goods the Cherokees wanted, the Carpenter shifted his allegiance again to the British. When discussing trade relations with the governor of South Carolina, the Carpenter represented himself as the spokesman for the Cherokees.

The Carpenter exercised considerable influence over the Cherokees for several years and convinced the British to appoint his friend John Stuart superintendent of the British southern colonial district. In 1762 the Carpenter began referring to himself as the president of the Cherokee Nation. In 1775 he and other Cherokee elders signed an agreement with the Transylvania Company to sell present-day Kentucky and Middle Tennessee. The sale was opposed by Dragging Canoe, a particularly anti-American leader, and his followers. The outbreak of the American Revolution interfered with their attempts to thwart the sale. At the end of the war, the United States held the Cherokees to the bargain, pushing aside the Transylvania Company while acquiring Kentucky for the new nation. The Carpenter continued to serve in the capacity of principal chief for the Cherokees until his death in 1778 around the age of sixty-six.

Robert J. Conley

See also: Boone, Daniel; Boonesborough, Kentucky; Cherokee; Cherokee Wars; Land Speculation Companies; Watauga Settlements.

Further Reading

Conley, Robert J. *A Cherokee Encyclopedia.* Albuquerque: University of New Mexico Press, 2007.
———. *The Cherokee Nation: A History.* Albuquerque: University of New Mexico Press, 2005.
Woodward, Grace Steele. *The Cherokees.* Norman: University of Oklahoma Press, 1963.

Audubon, John James
(1785–1851)

American ornithologist, naturalist, and wildlife artist, John James Audubon was born out of wedlock, of French parentage, in Santo Domingo (Haiti) on April 26, 1785. His father, Jean Audubon, had a successful career as a merchant ship captain and slave dealer; his mother, Jeanne Rabin, a Creole house servant, died a few months after his birth. He spent his youth in Nantes, in northwestern France, and was raised by Jean Audubon's wife, who encouraged John James's early interest in nature and art. Much of his formal education was obtained at the naval academy of Rochefort-sur-Mer.

In 1803, when he was eighteen, Audubon's American life began when his father, determined to keep his son from conscription in Napoleon's army, sent him to family-owned lands called Mill Grove near Philadelphia. There Audubon's passion for hunting, bird-watching, and sketching came to fruition. At Mill Grove he also performed his first ornithological experiments when he banded several small birds, *Sayornis phoebe*, and determined they were migratory, returning to their nesting and breeding areas in the spring of each year.

In April 1808, Audubon married English-born Lucy Bakewell, daughter of a prominent family whose property adjoined Mill Grove. Soon after their marriage, the Audubons moved to Kentucky, where, between 1808 and 1820, John James engaged in a mining effort and other business experiments, including operation of a dry-goods store. In his spare hours he continued his bird studies, documenting, describing, and making watercolor paintings of the birds he observed in his travels from the Great Lakes to Louisiana, the eastern seaboard to the Mississippi. He also worked as a portrait painter, art teacher, and taxidermist, while Lucy tutored, taught school, and cared for their two sons.

In 1826, after difficulties finding an American publisher for his portfolio of bird paintings, Audubon sailed to England and there and in Scotland was able to finance publication of his seminal work, Birds of America. The portfolio of 435 lifelike and life-sized paintings and drawings was printed in 26 by 37 inch (66 x 94 cm) color engravings and sold by subscription in groups of five sheets, later to be bound in leather. The first edition of about 175 sets took twelve years (1827–1838) to make its way to print. This "Havell Edition" was named for the eminent London engraver Robert Havell Jr., who produced the aquatint engraving of all but the first ten plates of the portfolio. Audubon's text for his Birds of America, titled Ornithological Biography, appeared in five volumes between 1831 and 1839 in collaboration with the Scottish naturalist William MacGillivray.

In 1831 Audubon returned to the United States. With exhibits of his bird prints in the Library of Congress and the Athenaeum, Boston's renowned museum and library, his fame was ensured. He traveled extensively, studying mammals as well as birds, making new paintings, and seeking subscribers for his books.

In 1843 Audubon fulfilled his dream of traveling to the wilds of the trans-Mississippi region when he completed an expedition to the headwaters of the Missouri River. At Fort Union he was treated like royalty and enjoyed studying the many species of bird and mammal life that were new to him because of his eastern upbringing. Although he hunted bison, he was quick to criticize the wanton killing of the magnificent beast, predicting that it, like the great auk before it, would quickly disappear from the face of the earth.

Upon Audubon's return from the West to his New York home, his health declined but he still had the energy to produce one more monumental work—*The Viviparous Quadrupeds of North America*—issued in a portfolio of 150 drawings from 1845 to 1848. He suffered a stroke during production of the work, which was completed by his son, John Woodhouse Audubon. John James Audubon died on January 27, 1851, at his home on the Hudson in northern Manhattan, New York, and is buried at Trinity Cemetery in New York City.

The Audubon Society, incorporated in 1905, with chapters in most of the fifty states, is dedicated not only to bird studies, sanctuaries, protection of habitats, and conservation work, but also to many other environmental causes.

Dale L. Walker

See also: Fort Union (North Dakota); Grinnell, George Bird.

Further Reading

Audubon, Maria. *Audubon and His Journals.* Langhorne, PA: Chelsea House, 1983.

Ford, Alice. *John James Audubon.* Norman: University of Oklahoma Press, 1964.

Herrick, Francis Hobart. *Audubon the Naturalist: A History of His Life and Times.* New York: Appleton, 1917.

McDermott, John Francis, ed. *Up the Missouri With Audubon: The Journal of Edward Harris.* Norman: University of Oklahoma Press, 1951.

Streshinsky, Shirley. *Audubon: Life and Art in the American Wilderness.* New York: Villard Books, 1993.

Austin, Moses (1761–1821)

Moses Austin, whose grandiose ideas to settle Spanish-held Texas with 300 American families were cut short by his premature death, was born in Durham, Connecticut, on October 4, 1761. In 1783, he moved to Philadelphia, Pennsylvania, to join his brother Stephen in the mercantile business. The brothers also opened lead-mining operations in Virginia under the name of Moses Austin and Company, and imported both British miners and smelter operators to run this first-of-its-kind business in the United States. After several successful years the brothers fell on hard financial times, losing all their holdings and capital by 1797.

With a wife and young family to support, Austin traveled to Louisiana Territory, then under Spanish control, to investigate rumors of rich lead deposits located in present-day Missouri. Finding the rumors to be true, he relocated to Missouri in 1798, acquired land and mining rights from local authorities, and founded the town of Potosi as the center of his business operations. He brought with him American workers and their families to operate the mines and ore smelters and to colonize the new village. When the Louisiana Territory was purchased by the United States in 1803, he became a prominent and prosperous citizen in Missouri, serving as an appointed justice on the Court of Common Pleas and as a founding member of the Bank of St. Louis.

Once again, however, Austin suffered severe financial setbacks, brought about by stiff competition in the lead-mining industry, the War of 1812, and the failure of the Bank of St. Louis in 1819. He divested himself of most of his holdings in order to pay his creditors and, while attempting to return to the mercantile business, he formulated a plan to regain his fortune and social status.

Armed with the bold idea of relocating American families to settle the Spanish-held Texas frontier, with himself as the leader of their colony, Austin set out on horseback in 1820 to present his proposal to the Spanish governor. Following a journey of 800 miles (1,300 km) and several months, he arrived in San Antonio de Bexar only to be ordered to immediately return home before being able to present his plan to officials. However, a fateful intervention by an old friend in San Antonio, the Baron de Bastrop, gained an audience for Austin with the governor anyway and, once the governor listened to the idea, he approved it and forwarded it to Mexico City for endorsement. Within weeks word came back that the request had been granted, allowing Austin, with the official commissions in hand and now in partnership with Bastrop in the new venture, to return to Missouri in January 1821 to make arrangements for the new colony's launch. He took ill on the return journey, however, and barely survived the trip home. Austin died on June 10, 1821, leaving his son Stephen with the responsibility of carrying out his audacious settlement plans.

Rod Timanus

See also: Austin, Stephen F.; Empresario System; Texas Revolution and Independence.

Further Reading

Fehrenbach, T.R. *Lone Star: A History of Texas and the Texans.* New York: Macmillan, 1991.

Gracy, David B. *Moses Austin: His Life.* San Antonio: Trinity University Press, 1987.

Austin, Stephen F. (1793–1836)

The future "Father of Texas" was born in Wythe County, Virginia, on November 3, 1793. Stephen F. Austin was the oldest child of ambitious frontiersman Moses Austin, who moved his family in 1798 to Missouri, which was then a Spanish possession. Moses opened lead mines and operated a general store.

Stephen Austin was sent east to a school in Connecticut, then to Transylvania University in Lexington, Kentucky. After returning to Missouri—by then a territory of the United States—in 1810, the young man worked closely with his father. Stephen became a member of the Missouri territorial legislature and served as adjutant of a militia battalion. The family business was wrecked by the panic of 1819, and Stephen moved to Arkansas. Engaging in land speculation, he accepted an appointment as a circuit judge. Before the end of 1820 Stephen relocated to New Orleans, where he studied law.

By this time Moses Austin was pursuing a contract with the Spanish government of Mexico to become a Texas colonizer, or *empresario*. Despite Mexican efforts to settle its northern province, Texas remained a wilderness. With American settlers relentlessly moving westward, Mexican officials reluctantly decided to open Texas to these capable frontiersmen. American pioneers were unsurpassed at civilizing wilderness regions, and it was the responsibility of the *empresarios* to select orderly settlers, who became Mexican citizens. Moses Austin returned to Arkansas with a contract to settle 300 families—and with an illness that would prove fatal. On his deathbed Moses asked Stephen to fulfill the Texas contract. Although initially unenthusiastic about the wilderness venture, Stephen dutifully obeyed his father's last wishes. With a strong education for the day, as well as a background of service in frontier government, the conscientious Stephen proved better as a colonizer than the restless Moses.

Stephen began recruiting settlers, and in 1822 his first colonists arrived by ship on the Texas coast. At this early stage a revolution displaced the Spanish, and Austin had to renegotiate his agreement with the new Mexican government. He became fluent in Spanish and acquainted with numerous Mexican officials, and ultimately he was able to offer prospective colonists large land grants—often as many as 4,605 acres (1,864 ha). American settlers flocked to Austin's colony, and

Austin negotiated new agreements for hundreds of additional families. Within a few years Austin's colony teemed with farms and new settlements.

The capital of his colony was San Felipe de Austin, a log cabin village on the Brazos River. As *empresario*, Austin exercised almost complete civil, judicial, and military control over his colony, which became the largest and most successful in Texas. Although his contracts awarded him vast tracts of land, he had no time to develop his personal property.

By the 1830s, Mexican officials, concerned with the rapidly growing Anglo presence in Texas, made clumsy efforts to control the colonists. Austin reluctantly agreed to present a petition of protest to the Mexican government in April 1833, but he was arrested by the orders of dictator Antonio López de Santa Anna. Incarcerated for more than two years, Austin found his health undermined and his loyalty toward Mexico changing to the cause of Texas independence.

When war broke out in 1835, Austin was elected general of the Texas volunteers, although soon he was sent to seek loans and other support in the United States. General Sam Houston led Texas to a spectacular victory at San Jacinto, and then was swept into the presidency of the Republic of Texas over Austin. Houston appointed Austin secretary of state, but soon thereafter, the overworked Austin contracted pneumonia and died on December 27, 1836.

Bill O'Neal

See also: Austin, Moses; Empresario System; Houston, Sam; Santa Anna, Antonio López de; Texas Revolution and Independence.

Further Reading

Barker, Eugene C. *The Life of Stephen F. Austin.* Nashville: Cokesbury Press, 1925.

Cantrell, Gregg. *Stephen F. Austin: Empresario of Texas.* New Haven: Yale University Press, 1999.

B

Baker, James (1818–1898)

Mountain man James Baker was born on December 19, 1818, at Belleview, Illinois. Jim, as most people knew him, was 6 feet tall (183 cm), of Scottish descent with reddish-blond hair, a good shot, and humble. Some accounts say he was covered from head to toes in scars from bear fights, riding accidents, and Indian battles. In 1838 he ran away from home and joined the American Fur Company, working for the outfit for about eighteen months. Returning home at the expiration of his contract in 1840, he did not like the quietness of life in Illinois, so he went west again the following year. He joined a wagon train led by Tom Fitzpatrick and traveled with it until it reached the Green River country in Wyoming.

Baker then joined Jim Bridger and his men to trap in the mountains and, shortly afterward, participated in the most famous conflict of his life—the battle of Little Snake River. Bridger asked for volunteers to warn his other companions that hostile Indians were nearby. After two days of hard riding, Baker and two others arrived at the other camp, located at the confluence of the Little Snake River and Battle Creek near today's Colorado-Wyoming border. The Indians soon attacked and demanded the trappers' horses. Baker later reported that the twenty-three trappers were pitted against about 500 Cheyennes and Arapahos who made forty charges, sometimes coming within fifteen paces of the group. The trappers constructed a crude fort from cottonwood logs, threw up a breastwork of dead horses, dug pits to protect themselves, and hid behind stumps. Several were wounded in the fight and four were killed. All four were buried in a common grave there. The battle turned only when the Indian leader had his horse shot out from under him. After dark, the trappers left on a six-day hike to Bridger's camp.

Following the fight, Baker continued trapping and gravitated to the lands of the Shoshone, in time being adopted into their tribe. He won the chief's daughter, Marina, as a reward for his bravery in helping to recover her when she was captured by a band of Blackfoot who attacked their camp. His second wife was also a Shoshone named Meeteese (Little Traveler), whom he called Mary.

Baker built a cabin next to Clear Creek that later became known as Baker's Crossing, near Denver. He later constructed a toll bridge and store at the same place. Baker could speak several Indian dialects. In 1865 he served as a guide and interpreter for D.C. Oakes, the agent for the Utes, and later interpreted for Captain Randolph Marcy on his march to Fort Union, New Mexico.

Baker was chief scout at Fort Laramie during the 1850s. His portrait in stained glass can be seen in the dome at the Colorado state capital. When Denver became too busy and crowded for him, he returned to the Snake River region where he built a large, two-story log cabin that can still be seen at the Little Snake River Museum. Remembered as one of the last mountain men, Baker died on May 15, 1898, near Braggs, Wyoming.

Mike Moore

See also: American Fur Company; Bridger, Jim; Fitzpatrick, Thomas "Broken Hand"; Fort Laramie; Shoshone.

Further Reading

Baker, Leighton. *Jim Baker, the Redheaded Shoshoni.* Tavares, CO: Golden Lifestyles Books, 1993.

Barbed Wire

The introduction of barbed wire in the nineteenth century dramatically altered the western landscape and its people. This technological innovation was the first method that utilized wire to secure and restrain cattle and other property on the American Great Plains. Before the invention of barbed wire, ranchers relied on various raw materials such as mud, brush, stones, and trees to create barriers for their livestock. Yet these materials were not abundant in the Great Plains region. Landowners therefore needed an economical type of fencing to enclose cattle and protect crops throughout these western lands.

No one individual is credited as the inventor of barbed wire, but Joseph F. Glidden of Dekalb, Illinois, is often recognized as the "father of barbed wire." In 1874 Glidden was the first to receive a patent for his innovation, in which he placed barbs at intervals along a smooth strand of wire and twisted another strand of wire around it to hold the barbs in place. The sharp points of the wired fence, known as "the devil's rope," could cause injury to animals and humans who encountered the barrier. However, after one run-in with the fence, another was unlikely.

Barbed wire was both beneficial and controversial upon its introduction to Great Plains farmers and ranchers. On the one hand, it was cheap, easy to install, and durable against the most extreme weather conditions experienced in the region. It also allowed ranchers to practice various breeding methods with their livestock separated in closed-off spaces. On the other hand, barbed wire prevented cattle from escaping severe weather conditions experienced throughout the Great Plains. In the event of a blizzard, cattle instinctively head away from the storm. But when ranchers installed barbed wire, herds drifting before storms piled up against the sharp fences and froze to death in great numbers. Tensions also arose between open range cattlemen and cowboys and the landowners who created new boundaries with barbed wire. This fencing prevented ranchers' and cowboys' access to public watering holes, pastures, and passages. The struggle over the use of barbed wire on public lands led to the violent protests of the "fence-cutter wars." The state of Texas even passed a law that made fence-cutting a felony crime. The end of the fence-cutting wars also marked the end of open-range cattle grazing.

The introduction of barbed wire ushered in a new era of modern ranching in the vast lands of the American West. The Great Plains region is still "wired," and barbed wire's legacy remains fixed in the western landscape.

Elaine M. Nelson

See also: Cattle Frontier; Glidden, Joseph; Open Range.

Further Reading

McCallum, Henry D., and Frances T. McCallum. *The Wire That Fenced the West*. Norman: University of Oklahoma Press, 1965.

Bartlett, John Russell (1805–1886)

John Russell Bartlett was appointed commissioner of the U.S. Boundary Survey in the wake of the Mexican-American War, despite his lack of experience as either a surveyor or a topographer. A bibliographer and scholar who lived most of his life in Rhode Island, Bartlett was to assist in the survey of the U.S.-Mexican border. His term as commissioner was beset by financial troubles and political discord. In spite of this difficult tenure, his *Personal Narrative of Explorations and Incidents in Texas, New Mexico, California, Sonora, and Chihuahua* remains one of the most comprehensive and engaging travel narratives of the southwestern United States and northern Mexico from the mid-nineteenth century.

Born on October 23, 1805, in Providence, Rhode Island, Bartlett developed political connections stemming from his position as the manager and proprietor of a bookstore in downtown New York that specialized in literary and scientific publications. When John Charles Frémont resigned his position as boundary commissioner in 1850, Bartlett's friends pushed his name forward as the replacement. He was the fourth man appointed to the job within a two-year period: the first appointee died before he could travel to the border; the second was removed from office after a brief tenure; and Frémont resigned before he could begin work.

The boundary commission, formed by the Treaty of Guadalupe Hidalgo in 1848, was a bi-national organization whose decisions were considered binding components of the treaty negotiations. As commissioner, Bartlett was criticized for overspending his congressional appropriation, but he achieved notable early success by establishing a good relationship with his Mexican counterpart, Pedro García Conde. Ironically, Bartlett's and García Conde's rapport was at the root of Bartlett's undoing as commissioner. According to the treaty, the border was to follow the course of the Rio Grande from the Gulf of Mexico upstream to the southern boundary of New Mexico and then head westward toward the Gila River. The maps that both

García Conde and Bartlett carried, however, incorrectly marked the southern border of New Mexico as a point some 30 miles (50 km) north of where it was actually located. In the interest of maintaining cordial relations with García Conde, Bartlett agreed to use this more northern boundary as the starting point for the survey. Bartlett's compromise over this territory was bitterly opposed by the official surveyor, A.B. Gray. Bartlett himself did not understand what the fuss was about; he thought the disputed desert territory was worthless for either settlement or mining. However, Gray understood the value of the territory as a potential route for a southern transcontinental railway and considered Bartlett's compromise to be the politically antagonistic decision of a Yankee trying to undermine the economic expansion of the South.

Ultimately, the dispute over the location of the Bartlett-Conde line, in conjunction with political dissatisfaction with the boundary commission's profligacy, led to Bartlett's removal as boundary commissioner in 1853—an ironic outcome, as the contested territory was included in the Gadsden Purchase the following year. Bartlett returned to Providence, where he remained until his death on May 28, 1886. In addition to his work with the boundary commission, he was also the author of several books, including a guide to regional colloquialisms, *The Dictionary of Americanisms* (1848); *The Progress of Ethnology* (1847); and his *Personal Narrative* (1854).

Sarah Grossman

See also: Emory, William H.; Gadsden Purchase (1853); Guadalupe Hidalgo, Treaty of (1848); Mexican Boundary Survey.

Further Reading

Bartlett, John Russell. *Personal Narrative of Explorations and Incidents in Texas, New Mexico, California, Sonora, and Chihuahua, connected with the United States and Mexican Boundary Commission During the Years 1850, '51, '52, and '53.* New York: D. Appleton, 1854.

Hine, Robert V. *Bartlett's West: Drawing the Mexican Boundary.* New Haven: Yale University Press, 1968.

Rebert, Paula. *La Gran Línea: Mapping the United States–Mexico Boundary, 1849–1857.* Austin: University of Texas Press, 2001.

Beale Wagon Road

In 1857 Edward Fitzgerald Beale accepted a commission to survey a wagon road along the 35th parallel from Fort Defiance, New Mexico, to the Colorado River, where it would connect to the Mojave Road to Los Angeles. The proposed road was intended to be a practical military and emigrant road across the Southwest. Beale began the road survey at Zuni Pueblo in August 1857 and reached the Colorado River in October. The expedition used twenty-five camels as pack animals. In January 1858 he went eastward on the road with a military escort to determine the feasibility of traveling during wintertime. That year he was authorized to extend the road eastward to Fort Smith, Arkansas. In 1859 Beale and a construction crew of 100 men worked on the road, relocating some sections and developing springs to provide the travelers with a water source. In the summer of 1860, Beale traveled over the entire road to inspect it. In his official report he suggested that $100,000—in addition to the $210,000 that had already been spent—was needed to build bridges and dams. The funding was never authorized due to the Civil War.

Emigrant use of the Beale Wagon Road began in 1858 with four separate wagon trains. The first train was the Rose-Baley train. The Rose party reached the Colorado River first and prepared to cross, while the Baley party was still 10 miles (16 km) behind in the mountains. Mojave Indians, armed only with bows and arrows, attacked the train at the river. The emigrants held them off with their firearms, and when the Mojave leader was killed, the other Indians retreated. Eight emigrants were killed and several were wounded in the battle. The emigrants turned around, rejoined the rest of the train at the mountain camp, and started back to Albuquerque, a distance of 500 miles (800 km). Near Sitgreaves Pass they met the Cave wagon train, which shared food and animals with them and also turned back. The large combined train was constantly harassed by Hualapai Indians. Just as their provisions and spirits were perilously low, they met the large Smith wagon train. Revived somewhat, they all continued toward Albuquerque. A fourth train turned around when it heard of the Indian difficulties. The army sent provisions and an escort to bring the emigrants to Albuquerque, where they remained for the winter.

Many of the 1858 emigrants accompanied Beale's road-building expedition in 1859 and safely reached Los Angeles. During the summer a peace treaty was concluded with the Mojave Indians and Fort Mojave was established at the Colorado River crossing to protect travelers. In the following years thousands of emigrants and gold miners used the Beale Road. The road was also traversed by large livestock drives. From 1858 to 1877 more than 600,000 Texas Longhorn cattle were driven over the route to California, and more than 1 million merino sheep were herded eastward to New Mexico from 1871 to 1882. Although the completion of the Atlantic and Pacific Railroad in 1883 brought an end to the Beale Wagon Road, its importance as a major transportation route continued as U.S. Route 66 and modern Interstate 40 were built in the same general corridor.

Susan Badger Doyle

See also: Corps of Topographical Engineers.

Further Reading

Baley, Charles W. *Disaster at the Colorado: Beale's Wagon Road and the First Emigrant Party*. Logan: Utah State University Press, 2002.

Bowman, Eldon G., and Jack Smith. *Beale's Road Through Arizona*. Flagstaff, AZ: Flagstaff Corral of Westerners International, 1979.

Briggs, Carl, and Clyde Francis Trudell. *Quarterdeck & Saddlehorn: The Story of Edward F. Beale, 1822–1893*. Glendale, CA: Arthur H. Clark, 1983.

Dodge, Bertha S. *The Road West: Saga of the 35th Parallel*. Albuquerque: University of New Mexico Press, 1980.

Goetzmann, William H. *Army Exploration in the American West, 1803–1863*. Lincoln: University of Nebraska Press, 1979.

Bear Flag Revolt

The brief uprising of settlers in California's Sacramento Valley in the summer of 1846, known as the Bear Flag Revolt, served as a prelude to the American takeover of California in the Mexican-American War of 1846–1848. Months before news reached California that the administration of President James K. Polk had declared war against Mexico (on May 13, 1846), seedlings of rebellion were planted in the sunny farmlands north of San Francisco. There, in 1841, the Swiss-born adventurer John A. Sutter built a fort near the junction of the American and Sacramento rivers on a parcel of the 50,000 acres (20,230 ha) of land granted to him by Mexican authorities. With the passage of years, Sutter's Fort became a refuge for the growing influx of American pioneers reaching California. Inevitably, as rumors reached the Pacific of strained relations between the United States and Mexico, the fort became the locus of anti-Mexican sentiment. In December 1845, Captain John C. Frémont, the celebrated "Pathfinder" of the U.S. Army Topographical Corps of Engineers, led an expedition

of sixty-two armed men into Sutter's Fort en route to Monterey. In the old capital, Frémont met with the American consul to California, Thomas O. Larkin, then with Mexican officials, explaining that he and his men were exploring the eastern flanks of the Sierra Nevada and mapping an overland route to Oregon Territory. He was permitted to winter in California providing he bivouacked his men inland and not among settled coastal areas.

The timing of Frémont's arrival in California, five months before the opening of the war with Mexico, as well as his somewhat nebulous mission, struck many as peculiar. He was the son-in-law of Senator Thomas Hart Benton of Missouri, the most influential expansionist in Congress, and was viewed by some as Benton's confidential agent sent to California to report on the Mexican armed forces and defenses. Whatever his mission, the Pathfinder overstayed his welcome in the Monterey vicinity and General José Castro, commander of Mexican forces in northern California, ordered him to leave the province.

At Klamath Lake in southern Oregon, on May 9, 1846, Frémont's party was intercepted by U.S. Marine Corps lieutenant Archibald Gillespie, an agent and courier for President Polk who carried confidential dispatches from Washington. These papers and oral messages, believed to contain news of imminent war with Mexico, resulted in Frémont's return to Sutter's Fort, where he arrived on the eve of the first overt act of the Bear Flag Revolt.

On June 10, a contingent of Sacramento Valley settlers led by trapper Ezekiel Merritt ambushed a Mexican officer and his nine men who were leading a horse herd to General Castro at Santa Clara. Merritt and his raiders left the Mexicans with one horse each and brought the remaining animals back to Sutter's Fort. Apparently with Frémont's sanction, Merritt and about twenty other Americans then seized the small Mexican garrison in Sonoma, 30 miles (50 km) north of San Francisco, on June 14, raising over the *presidio* a crude flag depicting a silhouette of a grizzly bear, a red star, and the words "California Republic" on a white field. The rebels captured the local military commander, Colonel Mariano G. Vallejo, and his family and escorted them to Sutter's Fort, where Frémont ordered them jailed. (Ironically, Vallejo was a supporter of United States annexation of California.)

The Bear Flaggers had a small skirmish with a Mexican force on June 24 at Olompali, a rancho north of San Francisco, which resulted in the death of one of General Castro's cavalrymen and the wounding of several others, while the Americans escaped unscathed.

A day later, Frémont, in command of ninety men, arrived in Sonoma, where he took command of the rebels and "captured" the nearby settlement of San Rafael. At an Independence Day banquet in Sonoma, Frémont announced the creation of the California Battalion of Volunteers, but events to the south two days earlier would put an end to such plans.

On July 2, 1846, Commodore John D. Sloat of the U.S. Navy sailed into Monterey Bay on his flagship *Savannah* and on July 7 occupied Monterey, raising the American flag over California. Two days later, with news of the American occupation of California being carried to Sonoma by Lieutenant Joseph W. Revere, grandson of that other news-bearer, Paul Revere, the Bear Flag was lowered from its mast in the public plaza and the Bear Flag Republic came to an end twenty-five days after its creation.

Dale L. Walker

See also: Benton, Thomas Hart; California, Conquest of; Frémont, John C.; Manifest Destiny; O'Sullivan, John L.; Sutter, John A.

Further Reading

Bancroft, Hubert H. *History of California*. San Francisco: History Company, 1886. Reprint, Santa Barbara: Wallace Hebberd, 1969.

De Voto, Bernard. *The Year of Decision, 1846*. Boston: Little Brown, 1943.

Walker, Dale L. *Bear Flag Rising: The Conquest of California, 1846*. New York: Forge Books, 1999.

Beaver

The North American beaver, *Castor canadensis*, and its European counterpart, *Castor fiber*, are the second largest rodents on earth (the capybara, *Hydrochoerus hydrochaeris*, of Central and South America, is the largest). They share the fate of near-extirpation from over harvesting by trappers for their fur.

Semi-aquatic and mostly nocturnal, beavers are a riparian mammal, making food of the roots and tubers of water lilies and other aquatic plants, and of thistles, clover, apples, tree-bark, and similar flora near their river habitat, from which they never travel far. Known for felling small trees for their food supply and for the dams they build to protect their lodges, the beaver pulls the peeled logs and branches underwater in the lodge and reservoir building process; the above-water portion of the lodge, the family home, is sealed with mud.

Beavers mate for life; litters consist of one to six young that quickly learn to swim using their broad, flat tails as rudders and propelled by their webbed back feet, their ears sealed and eyes protected by membrane when underwater. In adulthood they are usually 2 feet (61 cm) long with 10 inches (25 cm) of tail and can weigh up to 60 pounds (23 kg). Their life span ranges from fifteen to twenty years.

The beaver's commercial value to Europeans lay in the animal's soft and waterproof under-fur, which became a precious commodity among Europe's wealthy and fashionable set for its use in felt hat-making—stovepipes, tricorns, ladies' riding helmets—and in coat and cape linings, muffs, and adorning coats. Other valued products from the beaver were its tail, considered a delicacy and eaten skinned and fried by the mountain men who trapped the animal; and the rodent's anal glandular secretion, *castoreum*, used as a tincture in perfumes, and as a medical nostrum believed effective in curing headaches and fevers.

The French, during their occupancy in Canada in the sixteenth and seventeenth centuries, were the first to discover the value and desirability of the beaver's fur and to trap and export the pelts. Through their monolithic Hudson's Bay Company, the British brought the fur trade—with the beaver the prize fur-bearer—to its zenith between 1760 and 1816. Numerous American fur enterprises active from the Rocky Mountains southward to Mexico, northward to Canada and westward to the Pacific, added to the beaver slaughter, which in peak years amounted to 100,000 dressed furs (worth up to $6 a pound in St. Louis) annually.

By 1850 the American fur trade had collapsed. Among the factors were changes in European fashion (including the use of silk over beaver felt in hat-making), changes in the economic climate and pursuits of Americans in the Western states and territories, and the decline of the trapper trade: mountain men were beginning to guide pioneer wagon trains westward. By then the beaver population had drastically dwindled. The animal became an endangered species by the early 1900s, not only from over-trapping, but also because of changes in the animal's wetlands habitat from draining of streams and ponds for farming. It remains endangered in some areas, as does *Castor fiber* in Europe.

Dale L. Walker

See also: American Fur Company; Hudson's Bay Company; Missouri Fur Company; North West Company; Rocky Mountain Fur Company; Smith, Jackson & Sublette.

Further Reading

Leonard, Lee R., III. *The World of the Beaver.* New York: J.B. Lippincott, 1964.

Maser, Chris. *Mammals of the Pacific Northwest: From the Coast to the High Cascades.* Corvallis: Oregon State University Press, 1998.

Muller-Schwarze, D., and Lixing Sun. *The Beaver: Natural History of a Wetland Engineer.* Ithaca, NY: Cornell University Press, 2003.

Becknell, William
(c. 1787–1856)

William Becknell, sometimes called the "father" of the Santa Fe Trail, was born in Amherst County, Virginia, in 1787 or 1788. By the time the War of 1812 commenced, Becknell had already immigrated to Missouri, where he served for two years as a U.S. Mounted Ranger under the command of Daniel Morgan Boone.

In June 1821, Becknell advertised in the *Missouri Intelligencer* for men to accompany him on a trading mission "to the westward for the purpose of trading Horses & Mules, and catching Wild Animals of every description." The expedition left Arrow Rock, Missouri, on September 1, 1821, and the outward journey carried the small party along what is known today as the primary route of the Santa Fe Trail. Upon reaching the border of New Mexico, Becknell learned from Spanish soldiers that Mexico had only recently won its independence from Spain and that American traders were welcome in the country. The expedition reached Santa Fe on November 16, 1821.

Encouraged by the reception of American traders in the New Mexican capital, Becknell arrived back in Franklin, Missouri, on January 30, 1822. He immediately began making plans for an even larger trading mission to commence later in the spring. Accordingly, on May 22, 1822, he again departed Arrow Rock with twenty-one men and three wagons. This trip represented the first time that wagons were used on the Santa Fe Trail, and their utilization necessitated that Becknell find an alternative path for the last one-third of his trip in order to avoid the treacherous height and poor condition of the trail over Raton Pass. He pioneered what is now called the "Cimarron Cutoff," connecting the neighborhood of present-day Dodge City, Kansas, with Fort Union, New Mexico, and a course that was flatter, albeit hotter and dryer, than the original mountain road.

Becknell made a handsome profit on the goods carried on his second trip to Santa Fe. He quickly tired of the Santa Fe trade, however, and went west again in the summer of 1824, this time as a fur trapper instead of a merchant. Eastern goods had flooded the Santa Fe markets since the trail had been opened three years earlier, and Becknell thought that a trapping trip into the Colorado and Wyoming Rockies would pay better returns than another trading mission to New Mexico.

The progress of his trapping party was hindered by an extremely harsh winter and, in early 1825, he and his men returned to New Mexico, arriving there in April. Proceeding home to Missouri shortly afterward, Becknell dropped his second career as rapidly as he had his first. Later in the year, he was recruited to assist in the official United States survey of the Santa Fe Trail, and, following that mission, he served in the Missouri House of Representatives and as a captain in the Missouri militia during the Black Hawk War of 1832. During the Texas struggle for independence from Mexico in 1836, he commanded a company of mounted soldiers, called the "Red River Blues." He eventually settled near Clarksville, Texas, and lived a prosperous life until his death on April 25, 1856.

James A. Crutchfield

See also: Black Hawk War (1832); Santa Fe Trail; Texas Revolution and Independence.

Further Reading

Beachum, Larry M. *William Becknell—Father of the Santa Fe Trade.* El Paso: Texas Western Press, 1982.

Beckwourth, James P.
(1798–1866)

Storyteller, fabricator, raconteur, prevaricator, liar—of all the labels applied to those who stretch the truth, mountain man and adventurer James P. Beckwourth personified them all.

Born in Fredericksburg, Virginia, on April 26, 1798, Beckwourth was the third of thirteen children. His father, of Irish and English descent, served as an officer in the Revolutionary War. His mother was African-American. When Jim was seven or eight, the family migrated to St. Louis, a move that introduced him to the life of exploration.

In 1824 Beckwourth accompanied General

The legendary African-American mountain man, fur trader, and scout James P. Beckwourth is credited with discovering the Beckwourth Pass through the Sierra Nevada mountains and founding a trading post in 1842 that became the city of Pueblo, Colorado. *(MPI/Stringer/Getty Images)*

William Ashley's third annual fur-trapping and trading expedition up the Missouri River, searching for beaver. What followed was a life of adventure that transformed him into a "mighty warrior, hunter and all-around hard nut," wrote author Bernard DeVoto in the preface to T.D. Bonner's *Life and Adventures of James P. Beckwourth*.

During his travels Beckwourth was one of the first trappers to cross South Pass. He trapped in the Great Salt Lake and Cache valleys of present-day Utah and explored along the Bear, Weber, and Green rivers. He took part in the first rendezvous, held in 1825, and in 1828 he was captured by Crow Indians, who eventually adopted him into the tribe. He married a Crow woman, Pine Leaf, and was looked upon as a war chief by the tribe.

Beckwourth's adventures carried him from the Yellowstone region to El Rio Bravo, from Salt Lake to Santa Fe, and from Missouri to Florida. At one point or another, he was a business associate with the Sublettes, the Bents, and Louis Vasquez. When the

fur trade waned, Beckwourth went to California and started a trading post and inn, catering to emigrants. After leaving California, he returned to Missouri, then ventured to Denver and opened a store.

Beckwourth's place in history was assured when T.D. Bonner chanced upon him in California in 1854 and two years later wrote *The Life and Adventures of James P. Beckwourth*. Many others were taken with this man, noting both his good and bad qualities. J. Frank Dobie, in his *Life and Literature of the Southwest*, called Beckwourth "the champion of all Western liars." Bernard DeVoto opined that Beckwourth's profession as a mountain man ordained him to be a liar. Francis Parkman thought him treacherous, but at the same time praised him for his daring courage.

In late 1864 Beckwourth was asked to scout for Colorado and New Mexico volunteers commanded by Colonel John Chivington, who was looking for "hostile" Cheyenne and Arapaho camps on Sand Creek. The brutal weather took its toll on Beckwourth, and he relinquished his scouting duties, therefore not participating in the tragedy that became known as the Sand Creek Massacre.

In 1866 the aging mountain man was sent on a peace mission to his old friends the Crows, and a great feast was prepared in his honor. Soon after his arrival, he fell ill and died. Beckwourth's unremarkable passage from the stage of history does not diminish the important role this African-American played in the exploration and settlement of the West.

Gene Bryan

See also: Ashley, William Henry; Bent Brothers; Chivington, John M.; Crow; Sand Creek Massacre; Sublette Brothers; Vasquez, Louis.

Further Reading

Bonner, T.D. *The Life and Adventures of James P. Beckwourth: Mountaineer, Scout, Pioneer and Chief of the Crow Nation of Indians.* Lincoln: University of Nebraska Press, 1972.

Dobie, J. Frank *Guide to Life and Literature of the Southwest.* Dallas: Southern Methodist University Press, 1952.

Parkman, Francis. *The Oregon Trail.* Boston: Little, Brown, 1927.

Bent, St. Vrain & Company

An 1830 partnership of expediency between a fur trapper and a Santa Fe trader led to the formation of a company that dominated trade in the Southwest for nearly two decades. Charles Bent of Missouri, the veteran of numerous back-and-forth trips on the Santa Fe Trail, formed a cooperative arrangement with Cerán St. Vrain, an American of French extraction then residing in New Mexico, to sell the goods freighted from the United States. St. Vrain, already successful in the fur business and a Santa Fe trader himself, continued to accumulate furs for the enterprise, which Bent hauled eastward.

Charles Bent's brother, William, an experienced mountain man and trapper, joined the firm after establishing trading posts along the Arkansas River, including Fort William in 1831, near what is now Pueblo, Colorado. During 1833–1834, the company built another structure, also called Fort William, but popularly called Bent's Fort, near the mouth of the Purgatoire River. The firm then built Fort St. Vrain on the South Platte River in 1837 and a second Bent's Fort on the Canadian River in 1842. Each of these outposts successfully served, in turn, the Indian trade, traffic along the Santa Fe Trail and other trade routes, fur trappers, the military, and gold-rush emigrants.

The company grew into other enterprises, including control of vast expanses of land from both Mexican land grants and under license from the United States. Sheep raising, horse-trading, and dealing in mules were among the ventures. Whether by design or happenstance, political and romantic alliances aided the success of Bent, St. Vrain & Company. Cerán St. Vrain, in 1831, became a Mexican citizen; William Bent married into the Cheyenne tribe through his union with Owl Woman, a chief's daughter; Charles Bent married a member of the Jaramillo family, powerful in both Taos and Santa Fe; and the U.S. Army was always welcome at company outposts. As political upheaval and warfare swept through the area periodically, the company effectively juggled these alliances, maintaining, for the most part, business as usual during Indian wars, territorial disputes, and, finally, the 1846 Mexican-American War.

However, the entanglements eventually played a role in the ruination of Bent, St. Vrain & Company. An 1843 U.S. Army expedition bivouacked at Bent's Fort contracted with the firm for supplies but left without paying. Later, troops en route to the Mexican War consumed vast quantities of company stores. Upon U.S. seizure of New Mexico, Charles Bent was appointed territorial governor. Owing to his alliances with the Jaramillos and the unpopularity of his business practices, he was murdered by rival factions in the Taos Revolt of 1847.

Thus ended, for all practical purposes, Bent, St. Vrain & Company. While briefly reorganized as St. Vrain & Bent, St. Vrain, as senior partner, sold his interest within a matter of months and his business dealings with William Bent soon faded.

Rod Miller

See also: Bent Brothers; Bent's Fort; Mexican-American War; Santa Fe Trail; St. Vrain, Cerán; Taos Revolt.

Further Reading

Hafen, LeRoy R. *The Mountain Men and the Fur Trade of the Far West.* Lincoln: University of Nebraska Press, 1983.

Lavender, David. *Bent's Fort.* Lincoln: University of Nebraska Press, 1972.

LeCompte, Janet. *Pueblo, Hardscrabble, Greenhorn: Society on the High Plains, 1832–1856.* Norman: University of Oklahoma Press, 1981.

Bent Brothers

Bent, Charles (1799–1847)

Charles Bent, the eldest of four Bent brothers who made their names in the western fur trade—the others were William, George, and Robert—was born in Charleston, Virginia (now West Virginia) on November 11, 1799. When Charles was six years old, he moved to St. Louis with his parents, Silas and Martha. There, in the town that was the gateway to the West, he grew to manhood amid the sights and sounds of the trapper and trader communities.

As a young adult, Bent joined the Missouri Fur Company and spent considerable time on the upper Missouri River, although his exact position with the company is unknown. Later, in 1825, he became a partner in the reorganized Missouri Fur Company. The firm's lack of success, however, prompted Bent to look in other directions for his future, and he soon became involved with the newly opened Santa Fe trade. When his first organized trip to New Mexico rewarded him handsomely, Bent became convinced that the wave of the future pointed to the Southwest, and he totally immersed himself in a profitable commerce with the remote New Mexican villages.

In 1830 Bent and Cerán St. Vrain, a well-to-do Missouri trader among the Indians of the southern plains, established Bent, St. Vrain & Company, which soon became the foundation of a trading empire covering hundreds of thousands of square miles of present-day Wyoming, Utah, Colorado, New Mexico, Arizona, Texas, Oklahoma, Kansas, and Nebraska. The company built an adobe fort—first known as Fort William, after Charles's brother, and later as Bent's Fort—on the north bank of the Arkansas River, near what is today La Junta, Colorado.

Charles Bent became so completely absorbed with the southwestern trade that he established a permanent home in Taos, a small Mexican-Indian town north of Santa Fe. He married an affluent Mexican widow, María Ignacia Jaramillo, and, although he retained his American citizenship, became deeply involved in the town's civic affairs, soon establishing himself as one of its most prominent, well-respected residents. In late 1846, when General Stephen Watts Kearny and the Army of the West arrived in Santa Fe and claimed New Mexico for the United States, he appointed Charles Bent to the office of civilian governor for the territory.

Bent was well qualified for the position since he was so well known and respected in the region. For a short time after his appointment, it appeared that affairs would remain peaceful. However, after Kearny and most of the army left for California to pursue the Mexican War, the civilian population of northern New Mexico became decidedly unstable. Growing suspicious of the Americans and the new regime that followed the military takeover of the area, both the Indians and the Mexicans cast their allegiances to the previous Mexican government rather than supporting the new American authorities.

By the fall of 1846, revolt was in the air in New Mexico. Charles Bent had only recently returned to his home in Taos from his governor's duties in Santa Fe when he was confronted during the early morning hours of January 19, 1847, by a band of hostile Mexicans and Indians from the nearby Taos Pueblo. He was attacked, wounded several times, and subsequently scalped while still alive. Mrs. Bent and her sister, Josefa (Mrs. Kit) Carson, along with the Bent children, escaped the horrific scene by crawling through a hole hacked out with a spoon in one of the building's adobe walls. Later, captured by the angry mob of attackers outside in the courtyard, the women and children witnessed Governor Bent's agony as he died before their eyes. American authorities were quick to respond to the murder of Bent. In early February, a U.S. Army force commanded by Colonel Sterling Price marched on Taos Pueblo, destroyed the church there in which several of the rebels had hidden, and forced the Indian leaders to sue for peace.

The Bent brothers and Cerán St. Vrain were among the most successful traders on the southwestern frontier. For years their company dominated commerce along the mountain route of the Santa Fe Trail, and Bent's Fort became a mecca for fur trappers, soldiers, freighters, and southern Plains Indians of several different tribes. Charles Bent, as senior partner of the organization, contributed immeasurably to the westward expansion of the United States.

Bent, George (1814–1847)

George Bent was born in St. Louis, Missouri, on April 13, 1814, the third of the four fur-trader sons born to Silas and Martha Bent. Around 1832, he joined his brothers, William and Charles, in the fur trade business on the southern plains. He assisted in the construction of Bent's Fort on the Arkansas River and eventually became a partner with his brothers and Cerán St. Vrain in Bent, St. Vrain & Company. Bent worked for several years with his brothers in handling and expanding their business, while dividing his time between the fort and a home in Taos. After the murder of his brother, Charles, in Taos in January 1847, George was appointed foreman of the grand jury that heard testimony about the events that took his brother's life. He died suddenly of a fever at Bent's Fort on October 23, 1847, less than a year after the death of Charles.

Bent, Robert (1816–1841)

Robert Bent, the youngest of the four Bent brothers, was born in St. Louis, Missouri, on February 23, 1816. At the age of sixteen, he accompanied his brother George to Bent's Fort and there he went to work for his two other brothers, Charles and William. Whether or not Robert was ever made a partner in Bent, St. Vrain & Company is uncertain, but he assisted in the administration of the fort, sharing with George the responsibilities of its management when Charles and William were away. On October 20, 1841, while he accompanied a wagon train along the Santa Fe Trail, Comanche Indians killed and scalped him.

Bent, William (1809–1869)

William Bent, the second Bent brother, was born in St. Louis, Missouri, on May 23, 1809, several years after his family had moved there from Virginia. William was deeply influenced by his older brother Charles, who, by 1822, had already established himself as a successful fur trapper and trader among the Indians on the upper Missouri River. By 1824, William was trapping along the upper reaches of the Arkansas River.

After Charles Bent and Cerán St. Vrain established Bent, St. Vrain & Company in 1830, William was invited to join them as a partner. Bent's Fort, completed in 1833 on the Arkansas River, was originally called Fort William, after the younger Bent, since he was the supervisor of its construction. In time, William became the major driving force in the day-to-day management of the fort's activities, and it was he who primarily guided the company through its successful trading operations among the many Indian tribes of the southern plains.

In 1837 Bent married a Cheyenne named Owl Woman. His influence among the Indians through his marriage contributed tremendously to the pursuit of peace between the various Plains tribes and the rapidly encroaching whites. When Bent's Fort was destroyed in August 1849—either by fire or by William's own hand, depending upon which source one believes—William built a new fort a few miles east of the old one, but, by 1856, weary of a lifetime of trading, he left the business altogether.

After the death of Owl Woman, Bent married twice more, both times to Indian women. When the Colorado militia marched on the Cheyennes at Sand Creek in November 1864, two of William's sons, George and Charles, fought with the Cheyennes, while another, Robert, was forced to ride with the volunteers. William himself was so ingrained with the Indian lifestyle and so loyal to his Cheyenne kinsmen that he was guarded by troops to keep him from forewarning the Indians of the impending attack.

Like his older brother Charles, William Bent was a legend among the fur trapping and trading brotherhood of the southern Great Plains. His success as a trader at Bent's Fort has earned him a name not to be forgotten in the annals of the western American fur trade. He died on May 19, 1869, at his ranch in Colorado.

James A. Crutchfield

See also: Army of the West; Bent, St. Vrain & Company; Bent's Fort; Sand Creek Massacre; Santa Fe Trail; Taos Revolt.

Further Reading

Crutchfield, James A. *Tragedy at Taos: The Revolt of 1847.* Plano: Republic of Texas Press, 1995.

Lavender, David. *Bent's Fort.* New York: Doubleday, 1954. Reprint, Lincoln: University of Nebraska Press, 1972.

Benton, Thomas Hart (1782–1858)

One of America's foremost promoters of westward expansion during the first half of the nineteenth century was U.S. senator Thomas Hart Benton of Missouri. Benton, who became the first man to serve thirty years in the Senate, was a product of the Tennessee frontier, where he lived as a young man. Born in Orange County, North Carolina, on March 14, 1782, he was the son of Jesse Benton, a wealthy plantation owner. Around 1801, some ten years after his father's death, Thomas, along with his mother, seven brothers and sisters, and the family slaves, moved to Williamson County, Tennessee, to claim part of his late father's western estate.

The family took up residence west of the small town of Franklin, the county seat, on several thousand acres located near the Natchez Trace, close to the Indian boundary line. Young Benton practiced law in Franklin and was later elected to the Tennessee legislature.

As a U.S. senator from Missouri (1821–1851), Thomas Hart Benton was a leading advocate of western expansion, free land for settlers, and the doctrine of manifest destiny. *(Stock Montage/Hulton Archive/Getty Images)*

In time he developed a close friendship with Andrew Jackson and was one of the general's regimental commanders of Tennessee forces recruited in 1812 to assist in the war effort against Great Britain.

A falling-out with the older and more influential Jackson in 1813 sent young Benton packing to Missouri, where he edited a St. Louis newspaper before returning to politics and being elected the first U.S. senator from the newly admitted state. It was during his senatorial years that Benton wielded immense influence in the shaping of the American West. He was a leading spokesman for Manifest Destiny and was one of a growing number of powerful statesmen who believed that it was a natural conclusion for white Americans to conquer and develop the West. It was also Benton who, with the assistance of Ramsay Crooks and John Jacob Astor's American Fur Company, destroyed the government factory system of trade with the Indians, thus leaving the vast Rocky Mountain region wide open for domination by private trappers and traders.

In time Benton mended his differences with Andrew Jackson, and throughout much of his Senate tenure he provided strong support for "Old Hickory" when he became the nation's seventh president. When another Tennessean, James K. Polk, became president several years later, Benton was equally supportive of him and his western land acquisition policies.

Thomas Hart Benton was the father-in-law of John C. Frémont, who in his own time became famous for his explorations of the vast region lying between the Rocky Mountains and California. No doubt Benton's own keen interest in the West was whetted even more by the illustrious and adventuresome career of his daughter Jessie's husband. Indeed Frémont's successes would not have been possible without Benton's tremendous influence among Washington politicians.

In 1850 Benton was defeated for his long-held senate seat, but three years later, he returned to Washington as a congressman. When he died on April 10, 1858, the American West was on the threshold of a new chapter in its long and varied history. The old days of fur trapping and major exploration had passed, but the time of the cattle barons, the cowboys, the prospectors, the sodbusters, and the settlers was just beginning. Benton played a major role in America's westward expansion and was, no doubt, a leading factor in the successful domination of the United States over enormous new regions.

James A. Crutchfield

See also: Factory System; Frémont, John C.; Manifest Destiny.

Further Reading

Chambers, William N. *Old Bullion Benton: Senator from the New West.* Boston: Atlantic Monthly Press, 1956.

Smith, Elbert B. *Magnificent Missourian: The Life of Thomas Hart Benton.* Philadelphia: J.B. Lippincott, 1958.

Bent's Fort

Located on the north bank of the Arkansas River, 8 miles (13 km) east of La Junta, Colorado, Bent's Fort was built in 1833 by Charles and William Bent (1799–1847 and 1809–1869) and trapper-trader Cerán St. Vrain (1802–1870), all from St. Louis. The Bents were experienced fur traders who often camped on the Arkansas, close to the stream the French called the Purgatoire. The area, well known to the Sioux, Cheyenne, Arapaho, Kiowa, Ute, Pawnee, and Comanche tribes, formed the greatest untouched pastureland and buffalo domain the brothers had ever seen. They recognized the potential there for an emporium for trade among the tribes, especially for buffalo robes and beaver hides. The location could also serve as a way station for trade wagons headed south into New Mexico on the Santa Fe Trail.

With St. Vrain as the brothers' partner and with Mexican laborers hired in Taos, New Mexico, Bent's Fort (originally named Fort William) rose quickly, constructed of adobe bricks of mud and straw, strengthened with wool fibers, and with cottonwood logs for roof supports and palisades. Its configuration was a rough rectangle, 180 by 130 feet (54 x 40 m) with walls measuring 14 to 18 feet (4.25–5.5 m) and over 2 feet (0.6 m) thick with guard towers at the main, north side, entrance, and on the eastern rampart, which had a swivel cannon on its parapet. Outside the rear wall was a large horse and mule corral; a graveled central compound held a wagon park and fur presses. Around the compound perimeter were lodging spaces, council rooms, offices, and cottonwood-beamed shops with overhanging roofs, hard clay floors, and whitewashed walls. Eventually these were occupied by coopers, joiners, wheelwrights, blacksmiths, carpenters, and other tradesmen. Sixty to 100 employees worked at the fort in peak season.

For fifteen years the fort operated successfully as Indian traders came to the "Big Lodge" to barter their buffalo robes, beaver hides, and horses for arms, galena, powder, saddlery, blankets, axes, sugar, tobacco, beans, flour, beads, hoop iron for arrowheads, brass wire and tacks for decorating, and alcohol. Mountain men came as well, some with their Indian wives and children, to sell their furs and buy supplies.

The fort's prosperity declined drastically during and after the Mexican-American War of 1846–1848. Charles Bent was murdered at his home in Taos in 1847 by a mob of Mexicans and Pueblo Indians, and the following year William Bent and Cerán St. Vrain dissolved their partnership. By then the fur trade had declined to near extinction; the southern buffalo herds had been thinned and driven from their grazing lands, and in the spring of 1849, California-bound gold rushers came through bringing cholera with them, killing half of the Southern Cheyennes and spelling the virtual end of Indian trade at the fort.

On August 21, 1849, after failing in negotiations to sell the fort to the army, William Bent loaded twenty wagons with goods from the fort and headed downstream with his family and employees. After making camp, he rode back alone and torched the fort, destroying its wooden structures.

Bent's Fort was reconstructed in 1976 and is administered by the National Park Service.

Dale L. Walker

See also: Bent Brothers; Bent, St. Vrain & Company; Santa Fe Trail; St. Vrain, Cerán; Taos Revolt.

Further Reading

Clark, Dwight L. *Stephen Watts Kearney: Soldier of the West.* Norman: University of Oklahoma Press, 1961.
Lavender, David. *Bent's Fort.* New York: Doubleday, 1954.
Magoffin, Susan Shelby. *Down the Santa Fe Trail and Into Mexico: The Diary of Susan Shelby Magoffin, 1846–1847.* New Haven: Yale University Press, 1926. Reprint, Lincoln: University of Nebraska Press, 1982.

Bidwell, John
(1819–1900)

Sometimes called the "Prince of Pioneers" for his selflessness and courage, John Bidwell of Chautauqua County, New York, in 1841 led the first party of emigrants to travel overland from Missouri to the Pacific coast.

Born on August 5, 1819, he ventured west at age twenty with seventy-five dollars in cash after unsuccessful attempts at farming in New York and Ohio. Pursuing teaching in Platte County, Missouri, he was influenced by lectures and newspaper articles on the opportunities and glories of California. He formed the Western Emigration Society at the end of 1840 and within a month had signed 500 members from Missouri, Arkansas, Kansas, and Kentucky, eager to journey westward. All who came forward agreed to furnish their own "outfits," consisting of wagons, draft animals, weapons, food, and supplies, and to rendezvous at Sapling Grove, a few miles west of Independence, Missouri, prepared for the journey across the Rocky Mountains to California.

On the departure date of May 9, 1841, only sixty-nine people, including five women and several children, plus a dozen wagons and a hundred or more horses, mules, and oxen, formed Bidwell's overland party. He said later, only slightly tongue in cheek, that all the party really knew about their imminent journey was that California lay west. Luckily Bidwell heard of a group of missionaries being led to the Oregon country by the veteran mountain man Tom Fitzpatrick, who, after Bidwell's entreaties, agreed to guide the New Yorker and his people as far as Fort Hall in southern Idaho.

At Soda Springs, on the northernmost bend of the Green River in Idaho, Bidwell's party split, half traveling on to Oregon with Fitzpatrick, Bidwell's group of thirty-two drifting south to the Humboldt River, then making the grueling passage across the Sierra Nevada range into California. They reached the Sacramento River on November 4, six months and 2,000 miles (3,200 km) from Missouri.

Soon after reaching the Sacramento Valley, Bidwell went to work at Sutter's Fort as John A. Sutter's business manager, a position he fulfilled faithfully and honestly, winning the love and admiration of his employer. In 1848, on the eve of the great gold rush, Bidwell tried placer mining (in which gold is easily extracted from surface deposits) on the Feather River, took out a sizable fortune in gold, and purchased the 22,000-acre (8,900-ha) Rancho Chico north of Sacramento.

He served in the Mexican-American War, rising to the rank of major and, later, brigadier general of the California militia; served in the California state senate and in the U.S. Congress; and was an unsuccessful Republican candidate for governor of California in 1890 and Prohibition Party candidate for president of the United States in 1892. Bidwell left a record of his travels to California in his book *Echoes of the Past*, published in 1900. He died in Chico, Butte County, California, on April 4, 1900.

Dale L. Walker

See also: Burnett, Peter Hardeman; Oregon Trail; Sutter's Fort.

Further Reading

Bidwell, John. *Echoes of the Past.* Chicago: R.R. Donnelley & Sons, 1928. Reprint, New York: Arno Press, 1973.

———. *John Bidwell and California: The Life and Writings of a Pioneer, 1841–1900.* Ed. Michael J. Gillis and Michael F. Magliari. Spokane, WA: Arthur H. Clark, 2003.

Hurtado, Albert L. *John Sutter: A Life on the North American Frontier.* Norman: University of Oklahoma Press, 2006.

Billings, Frederick (1823–1890)

Frederick Billings, born September 27, 1823, in Vermont, was a lawyer and businessman who played the major role in the development of the Northern Pacific Railroad and its policies. Billings, Montana, is named in his honor. After graduating from the University of Vermont at age twenty, he practiced law. Caught by "Yellow Fever," he joined the gold rush to California in early 1849. There he became one of the region's leading and wealthiest attorneys. During the Civil War, Billings played an active role in keeping California in the Union, but in 1864, he permanently returned to Vermont. A friend of Northern Pacific president J. Gregory Smith, Billings purchased a one-twelfth interest in the Northern Pacific Railroad in 1869 and joined its board of directors the following March.

A major goal of the Northern Pacific was to attract northern European immigrants through the sale of federally owned lands, and in 1870 the Northern Pacific's board selected Billings to chair its Land Committee. Billings was soon quarreling with Smith and his backers and was given little support to survey and get title to land paralleling completed track, an estimated 2.9 million acres in Minnesota. Working closely with Jay Cooke, Billings also undertook a $1 million-plus effort to attract immigrants, but was stymied by European politics when the 1870 Franco-Prussian War resulted in Scandinavian countries temporarily prohibiting emigration to the United States.

Following the Northern Pacific's 1873 bankruptcy, Billings played a key role in keeping the railroad operating. The survival of the Northern Pacific Railroad was in doubt, for it had financial obligations to more than 11,000 often warring bond holders, as well as outside creditors and political forces wanting its dissolution. Financial matters were not resolved until mid-1875, leaving the railroad existent but without a penny of credit. Given his unquestioned ability, Billings was chosen to be chairman of the Northern Pacific's executive committee.

With operational economies and increasing land sales, construction was renewed in 1876. Primary efforts were on the west coast to reach western Cascade Mountains coal deposits 40 miles (65 km) from Tacoma, and other spurs were initiated in Minnesota and Dakota. In 1878 Billings put together a $2.5 million bond package for tracks to be laid between Bismarck, North Dakota, and the Yellowstone River at Glendive Creek, construction beginning the next spring.

Billings assumed the Northern Pacific Railroad's presidency upon Charles P. Wright's resignation for health reasons in May 1879. Highly respected, Billings was soon closeted with Anthony Drexel and J.P. Morgan to finance the railroad's completion, which resulted in a $40 million first mortgage bond issue dated January 1, 1881.

Because of Billings's reputation and Wall Street support, the western part of the Northern Pacific's route was suddenly seen as a competitive threat by the president of the Oregon Railway & Navigation Company, Henry Villard. In a series of complex legal and financial moves, including the famous "blind pool" with which he purchased Northern Pacific stock, Villard seized control of the Northern Pacific Railroad in June 1881, soon forcing Billings to resign. After a brief period, and to everyone's surprise, Billings and Villard entered into an effective working relationship. Villard appointed Billings chairman of the Northern Pacific's executive committee that September and asked him to make one of the major speeches at the dedication ceremonies two years later. With Villard's 1884 resignation, Billings had the opportunity to become president again but declined for health reasons and devoted the last years of his life to philanthropy, travel, and family affairs. He died on September 30, 1890.

M. John Lubetkin

See also: Cooke, Jay; Northern Pacific Railroad; Pacific Railway Act (1862); Pacific Railway Act (1864); Villard, Henry.

Further Reading

Hedges, James B. *Henry Villard and the Railways of the Northwest.* New York: Russell & Russell, 1930.

Mickelson, Sig. *The Northern Pacific Railroad and the Selling of the West.* Sioux Falls, SD: Center for Western Studies, 1993.

Winks, Robin W. *Frederick Billings: A Life.* Berkeley: University of California Press, 1991.

Bison, American

The American bison *(Bison bison)*, sometimes erroneously called the buffalo, was the most important animal to the Plains Indians, providing for much of their needs. Ancestors of the bison originally crossed the Bering Sea land bridge linking Asia with North America thousands of years ago and humans have hunted them ever since their own arrival in North America.

The modern bison is currently North America's largest land mammal. It is a powerful animal—muscular in front, with a massive head with horns and a hump on its back between the shoulder blades to help support the head. A bull weighs approximately 2,000 pounds (750 kg) and a cow approximately 1,100 pounds (410 kg). Bison graze on grasses and forbs, forming herds with usually a dominant bull as leader. As a bull ages he is pushed out of the herd by younger, stronger bulls, living solitary for the rest of his life.

Estimates of the number of bison in North America before the arrival of Europeans range from 30 to 70 million animals. Whatever the actual count, a vast number of bison migrated on the Great Plains in a north-south seasonal pattern. Bison ranged as far north as the Arctic Circle and as far south as Mexico.

Before the arrival of horses and firearms, Indians hunted bison on foot using a variety of methods. One way was to lure or chase bison over steep cliffs, called buffalo jumps, killing or severely crippling them in the fall. Another was to "impound" them within a cul-de-sac, giving hunters time to rain missiles upon the milling animals, killing and wounding as many as possible.

With the arrival of the horse, Indians were able to race close enough to bison to shoot them with bows and arrows or to spear them with lances. Firearms were a technological advancement making it easier for Plains Indians to kill bison.

The bison was very closely associated with Plains Indian religious beliefs and culture. Natives used the animals as all-purpose sources for food, shelter, clothing, weapons, tools, utensils, religious items, toys, and games. They even used bison dung, called buffalo chips, as fuel.

As the frontier expanded westward, hunting pressure increased on the bison. By 1832 they had become extinct east of the Mississippi River. As bison hides or robes became popular on the East Coast for use as lap blankets, traders bartered manufactured goods with Indian tribes for the robes and then shipped the robes back east. The increased demand for robes led tribes to hunt bison for more than their needs. Bison tongue was a nineteenth-century delicacy.

Settlers heading west killed bison for food. Most of these hunts did not seriously decrease the size of the herds until after the Civil War, with the construction of the railroads across the plains. Contract hunters then killed thousands of bison to feed railroad laborers. Later, professional hunters slaughtered tens of thousands of bison only for their hides and tongues, leaving the

Native peoples relied on bison as a source of food, skins for clothing and shelter, bones for tools, and dung for fuel. A lithograph by George Catlin recreates a buffalo hunt by Plains Indians in the 1830s. *(The Granger Collection, New York)*

stripped carcasses to rot on the prairie. The government encouraged the bison slaughter, thereby depriving free-roaming Indian tribes their source of food and forcing them to become dependent on the government and to move onto reservations. This relocation allowed home-steaders to overspread and settle on the plains where both Indians and bison had earlier roamed. Later, work-ers scoured the plains picking up millions of pounds of bison bones to grind for fertilizer.

By the end of the nineteenth century, fewer than 1,500 bison remained. The government took measures to protect them, and private individuals such as James "Scotty" Philip, Samuel Walking Coyote, and Charles Goodnight strove to round them up onto private pre-serves and protect them from total annihilation.

According to the National Bison Association, there are currently 350,000 bison in North America. Many are in private herds and are raised for commercial purposes.

Bill Markley

See also: Cody, William Frederick (Buffalo Bill); Good-night, Charles; Hide Hunters.

Further Reading

Dary, David A. *The Buffalo Book: The Full Saga of the American Animal.* Chicago: Swallow Press, 1974.

Hasselstrom, Linda, and David Fitzgerald. *Bison, Monarch of the Plains.* Portland, OR: Graphic Arts Center, 1998.

Lott, Dale F. *American Bison.* Berkeley: University of California Press. 2002.

McHugh, Tom. *The Time of the Buffalo.* New York: Alfred A. Knopf, 1972.

Black Hawk (1767–1838)

Born in 1767 in the Sauk tribal village of Saukenuk, on a bluff overlooking the Rock River at present-day Rock Island, Illinois, Black Hawk (tribal name Ma-ca-tai-me-she-kia-kiak) rose among his people to be-come a war chief and the central figure in the 1832 war to regain the lost homelands of the Sauk nation.

As a young man, Black Hawk hunted and trapped along the Rock River and its confluence with the Mis-sissippi and participated in war parties against such Sauk enemies as the Osages, Santee Sioux, and Chip-pewas. He recalled in his autobiography that at age fifteen he killed and scalped an enemy warrior and that by the time he was eighteen he began to lead attacks against the foes of his people.

The Sauks were allied with the Meskwaki (Fox) people and in the War of 1812 both tribes fought for the British in battles on the borders of Lake Erie, in Ohio, Illinois, Wisconsin, and Iowa. In May 1813, Black Hawk took part in the siege of Fort Meigs (commanded by General William Henry Harrison) on the Maumee River at Perrysburg, Ohio. On July 21, 1814, the war chief led 500 Sauk fighters in one of the far western actions of the war, the battle at Campbell's Island in the Mississippi River adjacent to the city of East Moline where, arrayed against a U.S. Army keelboat contingent of 120 men, the Sauks were victorious. On September 6, Black Hawk and his fighters were part of a British force of thirty men that defeated American troops under Major Zachary Taylor at Credit Island in the Mississippi River off Davenport, Iowa.

He returned to Saukenuk after the war and there learned he had been replaced as war chief by Keokuk, a rival who had sided with the Americans in the late war. "Keokuk, who has a smooth tongue, and is a great speaker," Black Hawk said in his *Autobiography*, "was busy in persuading my band that I was wrong—and thereby making many of them dissatisfied with me." The chiefs were to remain at odds in the conflict of 1832 in which Black Hawk led Sauks and occasional allies in a five-month campaign against Illinois and Michigan Territory militia and the U.S. Army. The conflict grew out of an 1804 treaty in which the Sauk and Fox tribes agreed to vacate tribal lands in Illinois and move to the west side of the Mississippi.

After the Black Hawk War ended in August 1832, the Sauk leader and his band were incarcerated at Jef-ferson Barracks in St. Louis for eight months, then, in April 1833, were transported by steamboat and rail to Washington, DC, on the order of President Andrew Jackson. Black Hawk and his comrades met the presi-dent and his secretary of war, Lewis Cass, former gov-ernor of Michigan Territory, and toured several eastern states, always to throngs of curious onlookers.

After Black Hawk returned to his people, he lived peacefully in a Sauk village on the Des Moines River in southeast Iowa. He dictated his autobiography to Antoine LeClaire, a government interpreter living at Fort Armstrong, Rock Island, Illinois. The book was published in 1833. The great chief died after a brief illness on October 3, 1838.

Dale L. Walker

See also: Black Hawk War (1832); Harrison, William Henry; Sauk; Taylor, Zachary.

Further Reading

Hodge, Frederick W. *Handbook of American Indians North of Mexico.* Washington, DC: Smithsonian Institution, Bureau of American Ethnology, 1910.

Jackson, Donald, ed. *Black Hawk: An Autobiography.* Champaign: University of Illinois Press, 1964.

Josephy, Alvin M., Jr. *The Patriot Chiefs: A Chronicle of American Indian Resistance.* New York: Viking, 1961.

Trask, Kerry A. *Black Hawk: The Battle for the Heart of America.* New York: Henry Holt, 2005.

Black Hawk War (1832)

An 1804 treaty signed by the governor of Indiana Territory, William Henry Harrison (the future ninth president of the United States), and two representatives of the Sauk people lay at the root of the Black Hawk War. By the treaty the Sauks and their neighbors, the Meskwaki, or Fox, tribe agreed to vacate their lands east of the Mississippi River to allow for white settlement, in exchange for a stipend of $2,500. However, the real Sauk leaders, the war chief Black Hawk among them, announced that the treaty was invalid: the men who had met with Governor Harrison had no authority to sell tribal lands and in any event such a transaction required the acquiescence of the entire Sauk tribal council.

The Sauks shared lands along the upper Mississippi with the Fox people, occupying small villages from the Des Moines River in Iowa north into Wisconsin and the larger settlement of Saukenuk at the mouth of the Rock River in northern Illinois. In the War of 1812 both tribes sided with British forces. The Indian combatants, led by Black Hawk, expected that with the British victorious their lost homelands would be restored. Instead, the Americans gained control of the northwest frontier and in 1816 reaffirmed the 1804 treaty. The original document stipulated that the tribes could continue to occupy the territory in question until the federal government requested them to move west across the Mississippi. In 1828 that request arrived and the tribes were given a year's notice to vacate the treaty district.

Some of the Sauk chiefs, notably Keokuk, a member of the tribal council, opposed disputing the treaty believing it futile to confront American military forces. Black Hawk, however, was not disposed to surrender tribal lands without resistance. With his "British Band" (so called because of the war chief's War of 1812 service) he began a series of forays across the Mississippi, hoping to gain allies. For many months he and his band, ranging from 100 to 500 fighting men and many noncombatants, returned to Iowa. Black Hawk believed he would be aided by his Fox neighbors in regaining their mutual homelands, but the Fox were only intermittently willing to risk peace against overwhelming odds and fear of reprisals by the federal government.

Inevitably, blood was spilled in the incursions by the displaced Indians in their crossings of the Mississippi. The first armed conflict of the war, the so-called Battle of Stillman's Run, took place on May 14, 1832, a few miles north of Rockford in

The Bad Axe Massacre of August 1–2, 1832, was the final engagement of the Black Hawk War. At the mouth of the Bad Axe River in southwest Wisconsin, the army gunboat *Warrior* and soldiers on the bluffs above killed most of 400 Sauk and Fox warriors. *(The Granger Collection, New York)*

far north-central Illinois. There a force of 275 state militiamen commanded by the thirty-nine-year-old Massachusetts-born Major Isaiah Stillman clashed with about fifty of Black Hawk's Sauk followers. The ragtag militia force fled in a panic, twelve of them killed in the rout. (Twenty-three-year-old Abraham Lincoln, a captain of the Illinois militia, is said to have helped bury the dead.)

On May 24, 1832, again not far from Rockford, a group of Fox warriors fell on a small party led by the Indian agent Felix St. Vrain, killing him and three of his companions.

A major engagement with over 600 militiamen from Illinois and Michigan Territory and about 100 Sauk warriors, called the Battle of Wisconsin Heights, was fought near present-day Sauk City, Wisconsin, on July 21, 1832. Militia casualties were trivial but the Sauks and their allies lost over fifty men killed. Smaller engagements, little more than skirmishes, were fought on the northern Illinois boundary, spilling over into Wisconsin, at places called Indian Creek, Kellogg's Grove, Plum River, Horseshoe Bend, and Blue Mounds.

The war ended on August 1–2, 1832, near the mouth of the Bad Axe River of Wisconsin when Black Hawk and his mixed force of warriors tried to cross the Mississippi and were caught in fierce fire from an army gunboat on the escape route of the river and musketry from U.S. Army regulars and militiamen from the bluffs above. Sioux fighters working for the Americans killed all but about 70 of the more than 400 Sauk and Fox fighters in the river and killed and scalped many of those who swam to the east bank of the river, including a number of women and children. The army and militia suffered about two dozen casualties.

Black Hawk did not witness the August 2 massacre; he surrendered that day to army authorities at Fort Crawford, Prairie du Chien, Wisconsin.

Three future presidents saw action in the Black Hawk campaign: Captain Abraham Lincoln of the Illinois militia, U.S. Army colonel Zachary Taylor of Virginia, and Lieutenant Jefferson Davis of Kentucky, who became president of the Confederate States of America in 1861.

Dale L. Walker

See also: Black Hawk; Davis, Jefferson; Harrison, William Henry; Sauk; Taylor, Zachary.

Further Reading

Efflandt, Lloyd H. *Lincoln and the Black Hawk War.* Rock Island, IL: Rock Island Arsenal Historical Society, 1992.

Jung, Patrick J. *The Black Hawk War of 1832.* Norman: University of Oklahoma Press, 2007.

Nichols, Roger L. *General Henry Atkinson: A Western Military Career.* Norman: University of Oklahoma Press, 1965.

Trask, Kerry A. *Black Hawk: The Battle for the Heart of America.* New York: Henry Holt, 2006.

Black Hills Expeditions

The Black Hills, a group of mountains rising 4,000 feet (1,220 m) above the surrounding plains of South Dakota and Wyoming, were the scene of the last major gold rush in the continental United States.

The Black Hills, with an area of 6,000 square miles (15,540 sq km), are oval in shape, roughly 125 miles (200 km) long from north to south and 65 miles (105 km) wide from east to west. The dome of the Black Hills began to rise 48 million years ago while erosion exposed its granitic core. Gold and other minerals located in veins in the hard rock eroded out over countless years and water deposited them in streambeds. Pine forests covering the Black Hills gave them a dark color in the distance, so the Lakota named them *Paha Sapa*, Black Hills. The Lakota and Cheyenne considered Paha Sapa sacred and only spent short amounts of time there cutting lodge poles and hunting. They did not live there.

The first European explorers to enter the Black Hills were the brothers François and Joseph de la Vérendrye in August 1742. They came from Three Rivers, Canada, searching for a route to the Pacific Ocean. Lewis and Clark, leaders of the Corps of Discovery, carried maps showing the location of the Black Hills as they headed up the Missouri River in 1804. Even at that time, there were reports of gold there. In 1811 Wilson Price Hunt and his men on their way to Oregon may have passed through the Black Hills; in 1823 Jedediah Smith led a party of fur trappers through. As the years went by, there were occasional reports of trappers, hunters, and miners entering the Black Hills, but the Lakota and Cheyenne took a dim view of whites entering the region, often killing intruders.

David Dale led a geological survey in the region of the Black Hills in 1852; Dr. John Evans, a member of the expedition, created the first map of a portion of the Black Hills. During Colonel William S. Harney's 1855 Sioux Expedition to punish the Lakota for the 1854 Grattan Massacre near Fort Laramie, the punitive expedition briefly entered the region. Lieutenant Gouvernor K. Warren, a topographic engineer with the

Cavalry and covered wagons muster for the Black Hills Expedition led by Lieutenant Colonel George Armstrong Custer in 1874. During the mission, 1,000 men explored the Black Hills of Dakota Territory and scouted potential locations for a fort. *(Kean Collection/Getty Images)*

expedition, scouted for fort locations and took detailed notes that draftsmen later added to the general map of the trans-Mississippi West. In 1857 Warren and a young geologist, Ferdinand V. Hayden, along with a seventeen-man military escort made the first comprehensive scientific and topographic expedition to the Black Hills. Leaving Fort Laramie they headed northeast. At Inyan Kara Mountain to the west of the Black Hills, they met a band of Lakota who warned them not to enter the area. Warren and Hayden complied with this demand and did not enter, but they did circle the foothills. Warren recorded their route and kept detailed field notes, and Hayden observed the geology, finding traces of gold in some of the creeks. The government did not publish their report until 1875.

In 1859 Captain William F. Raynold's scientific expedition, which included Hayden and was guided by mountain man Jim Bridger, traveled past the northern Black Hills on its way to explore the tributaries of the Yellowstone. Raynold's team panned the streams coming out of the region, finding traces of gold.

During the Powder River War in 1865, three columns of troops skirted the Black Hills, but did not enter them. In August 1866, Hayden explored the area with a small military escort, finding small quantities of gold. The report of gold excited prospectors and speculators who wanted to begin their own search for paying quantities of gold in the Black Hills, but the Lakotas opposed any entry. The Lakotas concluded a peace treaty with the U.S. government at Fort Laramie in

1868, establishing the Great Sioux Reservation, which included the Black Hills. Lieutenant General William T. Sherman, commander of the Military Department of Missouri, restricted civilian gold exploration expeditions from approaching the Black Hills.

In 1873 the Dakota Territory Legislative Assembly asked Congress for a scientific expedition to the Black Hills and asked that the area be opened for settlement. In 1874 General Phil Sheridan directed Lieutenant Colonel George Armstrong Custer to explore the Black Hills and determine a site for a future military post to guard travelers headed to the Montana mining districts. On July 2 Custer set out in a southwesterly direction from Fort Abraham Lincoln on the Missouri River with 1,000 cavalry and infantry troops supported by 110 wagons hauling equipment and supplies, 3 Gatling guns, a rifled cannon, and a 16-piece band. The expedition arrived at the northern Black Hills and entered them on July 24. The expedition geologist, Newton Horace Winchell, stated that he saw no gold, but miners brought along on the expedition and many of the soldiers said that they did. Custer's Scout Charlie Reynolds rode to Fort Laramie with a report mentioning that the expedition had found gold. Although he downplayed the occurrence of gold, newspapers and promoters sensationalized the report; the *New York Daily Tribune*, for example, printed the headline "New Gold Country."

Mining parties and associations formed to travel to the Black Hills even though the military continued to stop and evict them. The most famous of these associations was the Gordon Party, named after John Gordon, its guide. On December 23, 1874, the Gordon prospectors reached French Creek and built Gordon Stockade near present-day Custer, South Dakota. They began to find placer gold in French Creek. On April 5, 1875, the army located the Gordon prospectors and escorted them from the Hills, but they told anyone who would listen that there was lots of gold in the Black Hills.

Wanting to know just how much gold might be found there in order to determine if it was worthwhile to buy the region from the Lakotas, the government organized a scientific expedition in 1875. Geologists Walter P. Jenney and Henry Newton led the expedition. They had fifteen assistants, an escort of 400 soldiers led by Lieutenant Colonel Richard L. Dodge, and a guide named California Joe Milner. The infamous Calamity Jane disguised herself as a man and joined the expedition. Jenney and several assistants investigated the mineral resources while Newton, Dr. Valentine T. McGillycuddy, topographer, and H.P. Tuttle, astronomer, worked on the topographical survey. Congress published their preliminary report and map late that year.

Simultaneous with the Black Hills Expedition of Newton and Jenney, prospectors continued to encroach, and the government made an attempt to buy the Black Hills from the tribes. The initial negotiations failed. After an intensive military campaign, which included the battles of the Rosebud and Little Bighorn, the tribes accepted a new treaty on October 27, 1876, relinquishing the area and paving the way for the settlement of the Black Hills. Even so, to this day, the Lakota have not accepted payment for Paha Sapa.

Bill Markley

See also: Bridger, Jim; Cheyenne; Custer, George Armstrong; Custer Expedition; Fort Laramie; Fort Laramie, Treaty of (1868); Grattan Massacre; Harney, William S.; Hayden, Ferdinand; Hunt, Wilson Price; Lakota; Lewis and Clark Expedition; Red Cloud's War; Sheridan, Philip H.; Sherman, William Tecumseh; Sioux; Smith, Jedediah.

Further Reading

Grafe, Ernest, and Paul Horsted. *Exploring With Custer: The 1874 Black Hills Expedition.* Custer, SD: Golden Valley Press, 2002.

Gries, John Paul. *Roadside Geology of South Dakota.* Missoula, MT: Mountain Press, 1996.

Parker, Watson. *Gold in the Black Hills.* Pierre: South Dakota State Historical Society Press, 2003.

Schubert, Frank N. *Vanguard of Expansion: Army Engineers in the Trans-Mississippi West, 1819–1879.* Washington, DC: Government Printing Office, 1980.

Black Kettle (c. 1803–1868)

Black Kettle was a Cheyenne chief whose endless attempts to make peace with the U.S. government proved futile, eventually resulting in a massacre in which nearly half of his people were killed at Sand Creek in present-day Colorado in 1864.

Little is known about Black Kettle's early life, but he participated in a few skirmishes, and then grew into a chief and peacemaker by 1854. At that time he was chosen to be a member of the Council of Forty-Four, a group of chiefs who were entrusted to lead their people with wisdom. Whether he desired to establish true peace with whites, thus guaranteeing his people land and life, or merely sought his own personal gain is up for speculation.

In 1858 Black Kettle and several southern Cheyenne chiefs told a government agent that they wished to make a new treaty following their losses in a battle on Solomon's Fork in 1857. It was not until 1860 that he accepted gifts and signed the treaty. However, the other chiefs and most of his tribe wanted no part of the treaty, and many of his own followers turned against him.

Undeterred, Black Kettle continued negotiating treaties and peace deals with government agents. In 1864 warriors of Black Kettle's and associated bands made devastating raids along the Little Blue and Platte rivers, killing more than fifty people and taking seven hostages. Still desiring peace, Black Kettle told the white authorities that he would negotiate a trade for the seven captives in return for amnesty. Major Edward Wynkoop at Fort Lyon, Colorado, tried to make a separate peace treaty in direct violation of his orders. On the Smoky Hill River in Kansas, he and 125 soldiers tried to get the captives back, but the Indians refused to cooperate.

On November 29, 1864, Colonel John Chivington led the Colorado volunteers against a combined Cheyenne-Arapaho encampment near Sand Creek in Colorado. At least 120 Indians died, mostly women and children, and eighty-one soldiers were killed. Black Kettle, who survived the attack, was chastised by his tribe for trying to make peace. Although his status as council chief was threatened, he continued to urge peace, but the majority of council chiefs voted for war. When the Cheyenne, Arapaho, and Lakota villages moved north to fight, Black Kettle and eighty families moved south.

In 1865 Black Kettle and three other chiefs signed a treaty on the Little Arkansas River giving away their homeland between the Arkansas and Platte rivers. This enraged the other tribes. Then, in 1866, Black Kettle, Little Robe, and a few other chiefs told the authorities they had changed their minds. Wynkoop and other officials promised $14,000 worth of gifts if the chiefs would sign another treaty, the Medicine Lodge Treaty, which they did.

Black Kettle's attempts to lead his people to peace were greatly ignored. Indians throughout the West were revolting. Then, in late November 1868, Lieutenant Colonel George M. Custer and his 7th U.S. Cavalry attacked Black Kettle's camp on the Washita River in present-day western Oklahoma without warning. Black Kettle and his wife were killed, along with scores of other Indians.

Melody Groves

See also: Chivington, John M.; Sand Creek Massacre; Washita Engagement.

Further Reading

Brill, Charles J. *Custer, Black Kettle, and the Fight on the Washita.* Norman: University of Oklahoma Press, 2002.

Greene, Jerome A., Douglas D. Scott, and Christine Whitacre. *Finding Sand Creek: History, Archaeology, and the 1864 Massacre Site.* Norman: University of Oklahoma Press, 2006.

Hardorff, Richard G. *Washita Memories: Eyewitness Views of Custer's Attack on Black Kettle's Village.* Norman: University of Oklahoma Press, 2006.

Hatch, Thom. *Black Kettle: The Cheyenne Chief Who Sought Peace, but Found War.* Hoboken, NJ: John Wiley, 2004.

Blackfoot

The Blackfoot are a powerful confederation of Algonquian-speaking tribes including the Northern Blackfoot (Siksika, meaning "person having black feet"), Bloods (Kainai or Ká-íaa, meaning "many chiefs"), and Piegans (Pikani, Pekuni, or Pi-kániwa, likely meaning "spotted robes"; spelled Peigan in Canada). Today the Blackfoot call themselves Niitsi-tapi, "the real people." The three tribes spoke the same language, but governed themselves independently.

They were not friendly to Americans or to Indian neighbors. Indeed, the Blackfoot were the most warlike of all the Northern Plains tribes during the early period of westward expansion. They fought their Indian neighbors—Crows, Sioux, Cheyennes, Assiniboines, Snakes, Kutenais, and Flatheads—as well as encroaching white, particularly American, trappers. The Black-

foot raided along the route known as the Old North Trail, which crossed the Northern Plains. Their ferocity came, in part, from the fact that early on they obtained firearms from French-Canadian traders, which gave them a decided advantage against their foes.

The Blackfoot territory extended from the Yellowstone River to the North Saskatchewan River in Canada and from the Rocky Mountains to the Cypress Hills. The Blackfoot proper occupied the most northern territory and currently occupy land along the Bow River east of Calgary, Canada. The Bloods are located south of them, on the Oldman, Belly, and St. Mary rivers west of Lethbridge, Canada, with the Northern Peigan tribe farther west on the Oldman River. In Montana, the southern branch of the Piegan tribe, the Blackfoot Nation, occupies the upper Missouri River drainage.

This confederation of tribes relied on hunting and gathering, in the early period forming elaborate drive lines that forced buffalo over the edge of a cliff, allowing tribal members to slay them for the meat, hides, and other products they provided. These buffalo jumps became important killing areas, the most predominant being Head-Smashed-In near today's Fort McLeod, Canada, which has been declared a world heritage site. Other smaller buffalo jumps can be identified all across traditional Blackfoot territory.

A party of Piegan fought with Meriwether Lewis on the Marias River when the U.S. Corps of Discovery returned from its two-year exploration of a northern route to the Pacific Northwest. Lewis killed one of the tribesmen, and his companion Reuben Field killed another, earning longtime enmity from the Blackfoot confederacy, which was thereafter extremely hostile to American fur trappers and traders.

Until 1830 the Blackfoot traded exclusively with the British Hudson's Bay Company, but that year Scotsman Kenneth McKenzie, a partner in the American Fur Company, and Jacob Berger, a Hudson's Bay man, convinced the Blackfoot to trade with the American Fur Company. Later American Fur built several trading posts to serve the Blackfoot trade in a profitable, albeit rocky relationship. The most effective of the posts were Fort Union, in western North Dakota, and Fort Benton, in Montana. Both were adjacent to the Missouri River, which provided good transportation for material goods.

The Blackfoot were of no significant consequence during the period of the Plains Indian wars, in large measure because their numbers had already been seriously diminished by diseases such as smallpox, which had been introduced among them by white travelers.

Today the 1.5 million-acre (607,500 ha) Blackfoot Reservation, in north central Montana with its headquarters in Browning, is home to approximately 15,550 members. In Canada, reserves are provided for the Blackfoot, Peigan, and Blood tribal factions.

Candy Moulton

See also: American Fur Company; Hudson's Bay Company; Lewis and Clark Expedition; McKenzie, Kenneth.

Further Reading

Barbour, Barton H. *Fort Union and the Upper Missouri Fur Trade.* Norman: University of Oklahoma Press, 2001.

Ewers, John C. *Indian Life on the Upper Missouri.* Norman: University of Oklahoma Press, 1988.

———. *Plains Indian History and Culture: Essays on Continuity and Change.* Norman: University of Oklahoma Press, 1997.

Grafe, Steven L., ed. *Lanterns on the Prairie: The Blackfeet Photographs of Walter McClintock.* Norman: University of Oklahoma Press, 2009.

McClintock, Walter. *The Old North Trail: Life, Legends and Religion of the Blackfeet Indians.* Lincoln: University of Nebraska Press, 1992.

Blue Water Creek, Battle of

In 1855 an attack by a large force of U.S. soldiers on a small Plains Indian village proved a pivotal episode in the first war between the American government and the Lakota people. The Battle of Blue Water Creek, like many of the engagements between the two foes, was less a set-piece, conventional battle than a surprise army raid on a mixed community of Indian men, women, and children. That this particular group consisted of the suspected perpetrators of the 1854 Grattan Massacre lent legitimacy to the government's punitive actions.

The Sioux Expedition, also called the Harney Expedition after Colonel William S. Harney, its volatile commander, set forth in midsummer 1855 from Fort Kearny, Nebraska Territory, along the Platte River route for Fort Laramie. Harney commanded an infantry and mounted force of 600 regulars, the largest and best equipped yet seen on the central Great Plains. Another contingent traveled up the Missouri River via a flotilla of steamboats to garrison Fort Pierre, located in the heart of Sioux country. In general, Harney's orders were to restore the vital transportation and communication networks between East and West and, in particular, to punish those responsible for the annihilation of Lieutenant Grattan's command. On September 2, Harney arrived at Ash Hollow, an overland trail landmark on the North Platte River in present-day western Nebraska. Learning that a Brûlé Lakota village was camped 8 miles (12 km) northwest, Harney had his chance to carry out those orders.

On the morning of September 3, Harney split his command, sending his mounted force, led by Lieutenant Colonel Philip St. George Cooke of the 2nd Dragoons, to circle around and block a northern escape. Harney used his remaining foot soldiers to attack from the south. Cooke's cavalrymen performed their task flawlessly and kept out of sight; thus the Lakotas knew nothing of either force's presence until the villagers saw Harney's approaching men.

Little Thunder, the Brûlé leader of the village, rode out to fathom the army's intentions and to buy his now panicked and fleeing people some time. The ensuing parley accomplished nothing, and Little Thunder returned to his people, barely ahead of the first volley of rifle fire. Harney's men advanced as they fired, using recently issued long-range rifles employing the newly developed minié ball technology. The soldiers' deadly fire pushed the Indians north where Cooke's command waited. After Cookes's position was generally known, the battle devolved into a full-blown rout, the path of retreat stretching for miles. Soldiers on horseback chased the escaping Indians, many on foot, for hours, rarely distinguishing between warriors and noncombatants. When the tally was taken later, some eighty-six Lakotas had been killed and about seventy taken captive at a cost of the death of five soldiers.

Harney took little time to report a great victory to his superiors. The safety of overland travel had been restored and the resumption of westward expansion ensured. The command continued overland to Fort Laramie, then to Fort Pierre, where a peace conference officially brought this first Sioux war to a close in the spring of 1856. Warfare in the Platte Valley, along the Overland Mail Route, near the Powder River, and along the Bozeman Trail, though, followed in the 1860s. Harney's reputation as an Indian fighter at Blue Water Creek lasted through his lifetime; his tactics became a model for later students such as John Chivington and George Custer.

R. Eli Paul

See also: Bozeman Trail; Chivington, John M.; Cooke, Philip St. George; Custer, George Armstrong; Grattan Massacre; Harney, William S.; Lakota; Sioux.

Further Reading

Adams, George Rollie. *General William S. Harney: Prince of Dragoons*. Lincoln: University of Nebraska Press, 2001.

Mattes, Merrill J. *The Great Platte River Road: The Covered Wagon Mainline Via Fort Kearny to Fort Laramie*. Lincoln: Nebraska State Historical Society, 1969.

Paul, R. Eli. *Blue Water Creek and the First Sioux War, 1854–1856*. Norman: University of Oklahoma Press, 2004.

Bodmer, Karl (1809–1893)

As he tramped through the forests of his native Switzerland, young Karl Bodmer little dreamed that, as an adult, he would become one of the foremost artists of the American West. Born on February 6, 1809, in Riesbach, he studied painting under the tutelage of his uncle, the painter Johann Jakob Meier. When he was nineteen years old, the aspiring artist moved to Koblenz, Germany, where he hoped to be appreciated more than he was in his homeland.

It was while Bodmer was in Koblenz that he came to the attention of the naturalist Prince Alexander Philip Maximilian of Wied-Neuwied. The prince was planning a trip to America and was looking for an artist to take along to graphically portray all that he saw on his journey. In May 1832, the pair, along with the hunter and taxidermist of the expedition, David Dreidoppel, boarded an American ship near Rotterdam and began their voyage to the United States.

The party arrived in Boston in July and, after considerable delay due to a cholera epidemic that was spreading rampant along the eastern seaboard, finally began the westward journey. By the spring of 1833, the Prince's entourage was in St. Louis; from there, on April 10, it headed up the Missouri River aboard the American Fur Company's steamboat, *Yellowstone*. Bodmer had just missed by a few months meeting another great painter of the West, George Catlin, who had descended the Missouri aboard the same boat the previous year.

Seventy-five days after leaving St. Louis, Maximilian, Bodmer, and Dreidoppel arrived at Fort Union. From there, they took a keelboat to Fort McKenzie. All the time, Bodmer painted with an intensity that drove him to depict scores of landscapes, Indians, and the only known white eyewitness rendering of a battle among Indians—the skirmish between the Blackfoot tribe camped outside Fort McKenzie and a party of Crees and Assiniboins.

Bodmer's paintings of several prominent Blackfoot leaders at Fort McKenzie were among his greatest works of art. The Blackfoot had only recently established a fragile peace with the white trapper and trader community, and Bodmer's portraits of many of the tribe's members were among the first ever to be completed.

Downriver, after leaving Fort McKenzie, Bodmer and his party wintered with the Mandans around Fort Clark. He saw and painted many of the same Indians that Catlin had painted a year earlier. It is quite interesting to compare the two men's portraits of the same individual, each displaying a unique style of painting.

Following his tour of the American West, Bodmer returned to Europe, never to visit the United States again. He produced all of the magnificent illustrations for Prince Maximilian's voluminous treatise on the journey, entitled *Travels in the Interior of North America*. Although in later years he gained some degree of fame as a landscape artist, it is for his careful rendering of the American Indian and the wilderness in which he lived that Bodmer is best remembered. The artist died in Barbizon, France, on October 30, 1893.

James A. Crutchfield

See also: Blackfoot; Catlin, George; Mandan; Maximilian, Prince Alexander Philip.

Further Reading

Hunt, David C., Marsha V. Gallagher, and William J. Orr. *Karl Bodmer's America*. Lincoln: University of Nebraska Press, 1984.

Maximilian, Prince Alexander Philip. *Travels in the Interior of North America*. New York: Taschen, 2001.

Bonneville, Benjamin Louis (1796–1878)

Had Washington Irving not memorialized Benjamin L. Bonneville in his popular book of the period, *The Rocky Mountains; or, Scenes, Incidents, and Adventures in the Far West; Digested from the Journal of Capt. B.L.E. Bonneville*, the exciting life of the French-born military figure might have been lost to modern-day readers. Born near Paris, on April 14, 1796, young Benjamin and his family were close friends of the American Revolutionary firebrand and author of *Common Sense*, Thomas Paine. In 1803 Bonneville's mother brought him and his two brothers to the United States, where they lived on Paine's farm in New Rochelle, New York.

On his seventeenth birthday, Bonneville entered the U.S. Military Academy, from which he graduated two-and-a-half years later with the rank of brevet second lieutenant of artillery. For the next several years he fulfilled a number of assignments in various locations, including New England, Mississippi, Arkansas, and Texas.

On May 1, 1832, Bonneville, along with the noted mountain man Joe Walker and a large assemblage of men, horses, mules, and supplies, left Fort Osage, Missouri, for a trip to the Rocky Mountains. Bonneville arranged for a twenty-six-month leave of absence from the army and during that time he intended to explore the mountains, study the Indian tribes living in the vast region, observe the terrain and geography of the area, and attempt to gain a foothold in the highly competitive fur trade. Bonneville and Walker worked together most of the time, although they and their respective exploring parties occasionally separated for time's sake. It was Bonneville who sent Walker on the California mission that resulted in Walker's discovery of Yosemite Valley. Although William Sublette had penetrated the eastern front of the Rocky Mountains two years earlier with heavy supply wagons on his way to the 1830 rendezvous, it remained for Bonneville to drive the first loaded wagons completely across the crest of the Rockies through South Pass, thus proving once and for all that the mountains were not impassible to vehicular traffic.

Returning to the army after his leave had expired (actually, he had exceeded his leave of absence by fourteen months and upon his arrival at Washington, DC, he learned that he had been dropped from the roles, later to be restored), Bonneville participated in the Second Seminole and the Mexican-American wars. He was assigned command of the Military Department of New Mexico in 1855 and, during his stay in the Southwest, he saw combat service against the Apache Indians. He also served in a noncombatant role in the Civil War, eventually being brevetted to brigadier-general at the conflict's close.

Settling on a farm near Fort Smith, Arkansas, in 1871, the elderly Bonneville married a twenty-two-year-old woman and lived there for the rest of his life. At the time of his death, on June 12, 1878, he was the oldest retired army officer (age eighty-two) in the United States.

James A. Crutchfield

See also: Mexican-American War; Walker, Joseph R.

Further Reading

Irving, Washington. *Adventures of Captain Bonneville*. Washington, DC: National Geographic Society, 2003.

Boone, Daniel (1734–1820)

Daniel Boone was the quintessential frontiersman, and his explorations of the trans-Appalachian Mountain wilderness firmly established him as one of America's earliest proponents of westward expansion.

Boone was born into a Quaker family near Reading, Pennsylvania, on November 2, 1734. Although circumstances denied him a formal education, he learned enough wilderness skills as a youth to prepare him for the role he was to play in history. About 1750 the Boone family migrated to the Yadkin River valley of North Carolina. Early in the French and Indian War and barely in his twenties, Boone served as a wagon driver and blacksmith on General Edward Braddock's disastrous 1755 march upon the French-held Fort Duquesne at the Forks of the Ohio River.

Following his short stint in the war, Boone turned his attention to the fabled land of Kentucky, then the westernmost expanse of the Virginia colony, making three trips between 1767 and 1773. In 1775 as agent for land speculator Richard Henderson, he laid out the road that eventually came to be known as the Wilderness Road connecting present-day upper East Tennessee with the site of Boonesborough in central Kentucky. In the years following, thousands of easterners followed the road westward to the promised lands of Kentucky and Tennessee.

In 1778 Boone, now firmly established at Boonesborough, escorted a salt-gathering party into the nearby wilderness, where he was captured by a party of Shawnee, taken across the Ohio River to their villages, and eventually adopted into the tribe as Chief Blackfish's son. With a surreptitious plan in mind, Boone accompanied several Shawnees to Detroit, where he convinced the unsuspecting British lieutenant governor, Henry Hamilton, that Boone would persuade his Kentucky countrymen to surrender Boonesborough and cast their lot with the British. Upon his return to Ohio, Boone escaped from the Shawnees and made his way back to his home fort, where he apprised his associates of an impending attack by the British and their Shawnee allies. In the meantime, one of the other Kentuckians captured during the salt-gathering

Boonesborough, Kentucky

mission had already escaped, returned to Kentucky, and convinced most of Boone's followers that their leader had sold out to the British and intended to surrender Boonesborough.

When Boone personally supervised the strengthening of the fort and prepared its inhabitants for the upcoming battle, his friends realized that his agreement with the British was merely an elaborate ruse to give him time to get back home and prepare for the region's defense. After an unsuccessful, nine-day siege of Fort Boonesborough, the Shawnee and British called off the attack and returned to Ohio. Boone was court-martialed for his so-called conspiracy with the enemy, but was acquitted and promoted to major of the militia.

In 1799 Boone and his family moved across the Mississippi River to present-day Missouri, then part of the vast Spanish-held Louisiana Territory. His faithful wife of fifty-seven years, Rebecca, died in 1813, and the following year he was awarded an 850-acre (340 ha) land grant, a gift from a grateful U.S. Congress for his services to the country. He sold the land to pay off debts. Boone died in St. Charles, Missouri, on September 26, 1820. His remains, along with those of Rebecca, were reinterred in Frankfort, Kentucky, in 1845.

Daniel Boone and his brother, Squire, represented the first generation of an illustrious family whose name has become synonymous with the American frontier. Two of Daniel's sons, Nathan and Daniel Morgan Boone, as well as one of his grandsons, Albert Gallatin Boone, played a number of roles associated with westward expansion. Nathan fought in the Black Hawk War and was a member of the U.S. Dragoons. Both Nathan and his brother, Daniel Morgan, helped organize the Missouri militia, and Albert was a fur trapper who worked with General William H. Ashley along the upper Missouri River.

James A. Crutchfield

See also: Boonesborough, Kentucky; Cumberland Gap; Long Hunters; Shawnee.

Further Reading

Bakeless, John. *Daniel Boone: Master of the Wilderness.* Philadelphia: J.B. Lippincott, 1939.

Brown, Meredith Mason. *Frontiersman: Daniel Boone and the Making of America.* Baton Rouge: Louisiana State University Press, 2008.

Draper, Lyman C. *The Life of Daniel Boone.* Edited by Ted Franklin Belue. Mechanicsburg, PA: Stackpole Books, 1998.

Faragher, John Mack. *Daniel Boone: The Life and Legend of an American Pioneer.* New York: Holt Paperbacks, 1993.

Boonesborough, founded by Daniel Boone and Judge Richard Henderson in April 1775 as part of the Transylvania Company venture, was located on the Kentucky River in central Kentucky and was one of the most important fortified settlements on the early southern frontier. Boone's efforts to settle and protect his namesake fort from Indian attack added to his reputation as a frontiersman and brought him national attention.

Henderson's Transylvania Company was one of many land speculation organizations formed during the eighteenth century. The enterprising judge purchased the rights to 20 million acres (8 million ha) of wilderness land in present-day Kentucky and Tennessee from the Cherokees during the Treaty of Sycamore Shoals, held in mid-March, 1775, at a site along the Watauga River in upper East Tennessee. His intention was to establish a colony to be called Transylvania, and he hired Boone to blaze a road from the treaty grounds to his newly acquired land and lead emigrants to settle it. Following an old Indian hunting trail, the Warriors' Path, Boone guided his companions through Cumberland Gap in the southern Appalachian Mountains to the site of Boonesborough. The thoroughfare through the mountains became known as the Wilderness Road.

The settlement had several distinct characteristics. Nearby salt springs provided a valuable industry for the newly arrived pioneers. Boone ordered that the community be well fortified, which made it a harbor for all settlers in the area. Boonesborough was the capital of the would-be colony of Transylvania and hosted the first legislative assembly west of the mountains. The General Assembly of Virginia made Boonesborough the first town officially established in Kentucky. Twenty-six cabins and four blockhouses comprised the settlement in 1775.

Prone to attack, Boonesborough endured several Indian assaults. The inhabitants expected hostilities, and Boone drove them to finish the fortifications in March 1777. The most serious attack occurred during a two-week siege in September 1778. Shawnees had captured Boone in February, but he had escaped to warn the settlement of the impending Indian raid. The defenders of Boonesborough faced a force of about 450 natives, including Wyandots, Mingos, Cherokees, and Shawnees, as well as a few French Canadians. Although the fort's defenders were outnumbered, under Boone's leadership they successfully repelled the attackers.

During its heyday, Boonesborough continued to be the hub of activity in the remote area, but Judge Henderson's claim to the Transylvania colony was weak and the territory remained part of Virginia until Kentucky became a state in 1792. By the beginning of the nineteenth century, Boonesborough was in decline. Efforts to reclaim the community began in the 1930s to honor the two-hundredth anniversary of Boone's birth in 1734. Fort Boonesborough State Park opened in 1963.

Meg Frisbee

See also: Boone, Daniel; Cumberland Gap; Land Speculation Companies.

Further Reading

Caruso, John Anthony. *Appalachian Frontier: America's First Surge Westward.* Revised Edition. Knoxville: University of Tennessee Press, 2003.

Faragher, John Mack. *Daniel Boone: The Life and Legend of an American Pioneer.* New York: Henry Holt, 1992.

Henderson, Archibald. *The Conquest of the Old Southwest.* New York: Century Company, 1920.

Boudinot, Elias (1802–1839)

Elias Boudinot was born in Georgia in 1802, the son of David Watie (Uweti), a Cherokee Indian, and Susannah Reese. His name at birth was Buck Watie. In 1818, he, along with his cousin John Ridge, enrolled in the Cornwall mission school in Connecticut. Elias Boudinot, president of the American Bible Society, took a special interest in Buck and became his benefactor, causing Buck to change his own name to Elias Boudinot. In 1824–1825, both Ridge and Boudinot outraged the citizens of Cornwall by marrying white girls. The two young Cherokees and their wives were forced to flee from Cornwall for their lives.

Back home in the Cherokee Nation, Boudinot found affairs in turmoil because of the insistence of the state of Georgia that the Cherokees be removed. He organized a lecture tour to Pennsylvania and New York in an attempt to sway public opinion in favor of the Cherokee case. He managed to raise enough money to establish a Cherokee Nation newspaper. On February 21, 1828, the first edition of the *Cherokee Phoenix* was published in both English and Cherokee, Sequoyah having but recently presented the Cherokees with his syllabary for writing the Cherokee language. Elias Boudinot was the editor. The paper served much the same purpose as had Boudinot's lectures.

Boudinot, John Ridge, and John's father, Major Ridge, were staunch supporters of the Cherokees' right to remain in their homeland, carrying their case all the way to the U.S. Supreme Court and winning a favorable decision. But when President Andrew Jackson refused to enforce the Court's ruling, they realized they were playing a losing game and became supporters of removal. From that point on, they and Principal Chief John Ross became bitter enemies. In the meantime, Boudinot had somehow managed to find the time to become the first American Indian novelist with the publication of *Poor Sarah, or, the Indian Woman*, in 1833.

On December 29, 1835, Boudinot, the Ridges, and others gathered in Georgia with U.S. commissioners and signed the notorious Removal Treaty, or the Treaty of New Echota, which called for the total removal of all Cherokees from their ancient homeland to territory west of the Mississippi River. The treaty was illegal and fraudulent because none of the signers were official Cherokee Nation government representatives. However, that fact did not bother the federal government, and the treaty was ratified in the U.S. Senate.

Boudinot, the Ridges, and others of the so-called Treaty Party made the move west to what is now Oklahoma. After the general removal of the Cherokee Nation, which was finally completed in 1839, Boudinot, Major Ridge, and John Ridge were all assassinated on June 22, 1839, by followers of Chief John Ross. Boudinot was enticed away from the home he was working on by men pretending to need some medicine. As he walked down a lane with them, other men came out of the trees on each side of the lane and stabbed and hacked him to death.

Robert J. Conley

See also: Cherokee; Indian Removal Act (1830); Jackson's Indian Policy; New Echota, Treaty of (1835); Trail of Tears.

Further Reading

Conley, Robert J. *A Cherokee Encyclopedia.* Albuquerque: University of New Mexico Press, 2007.

———. *The Cherokee Nation: A History.* Albuquerque: University of New Mexico Press, 2005.

Dale, Edward Everett, and Gaston Litton. *Cherokee Cavaliers: Forty Years of Cherokee History as Told in the Correspondence of the Ridge-Watie-Boudinot Family.* Norman: University of Oklahoma Press, 1940.

Gabriel, Ralph H. *Elias Boudinot, Cherokee and His America.* Norman: University of Oklahoma Press, 1941.

Boundary Commissions

Two important boundary commissions delineated the borders of the United States with Mexico and Canada during the period of westward migration.

The first commission, authorized in 1849 and begun in 1850, involved development of the boundary between the United States and Mexico. President James K. Polk in early 1849 appointed John B. Weller, an Ohio congressman, to establish the survey that corresponded with the work of General Pedro Garcia Conde, representative of Mexico. This boundary commission had been authorized under terms of the Treaty of Guadalupe Hidalgo in 1848.

Under Weller's direction, the initial point of the survey was determined, but then the commission adjourned. John C. Frémont was soon appointed to replace Weller, but resigned the position. In June 1850, John Russell Bartlett of Massachusetts took over the American part of the survey.

Bartlett's force included a military escort and a significant team of engineers, surveyors, and assistants supervised by Lieutenant A.W. Whipple of the Corps of Topographical Engineers. The principal surveyor was John Bull. The work, which started in early September 1850, included identification and notes about the northern part of Sonora and Chihuahua, in Mexico, and the potential for a railroad route across the region.

The surveyors marched from San Antonio to El Paso del Norte, arriving in early November. This survey did not establish the boundary line, however, because the Gadsden Purchase, in 1853, led Mexico to cede additional lands to the United States. As a result, the work continued until 1856 under the direction of four different commissions. The final boundary was delineated that year under the direction of Major W.H. Emory for the United States and Jose Salazar Ylarregui and J. Mariano Monterde, scientific commissioners on behalf of the Republic of Mexico.

The second important boundary commission involved location and marking of the northern boundary between the United States and Canada, in the region between Lake of the Woods, in present-day Wisconsin, and the Continental Divide in today's Glacier National Park, Montana. It defined the northern borders of Minnesota, North Dakota, and Montana and was jointly conducted by British and American boundary commission teams.

The U.S. Commission was organized by the secretary of war under the direction of Captain Francis Ulric Farquhar and Major William Johnson Twining. The boundary survey team worked from 1872 through the summer of 1874. As part of their duties, boundary commissioners marked the border at points three miles apart. Where the boundary passed through timber, surveyors cut a swath and also erected monuments of earth or stone. Farther west, on the open plains, they used earth and stone markers, which were eventually replaced with iron monuments.

In 1874, the final year of the commission work, the survey parties organized at Fort Buford, beside the Missouri River in western Dakota Territory. Altercations with northern Plains Indians the previous year along the Yellowstone River predicated the need for military escorts for the survey parties, including members of the 7th Cavalry commanded by Major Marcus Reno, a West Point graduate who would two years later fight at the Battle of the Little Bighorn.

This survey party not only mapped and marked the boundary with Canada, but also provided other information that would be used in subsequent years by military officials as they forced native people onto reservations.

Candy Moulton

See also: Corps of Topographical Engineers; Frémont, John C.; Gadsden Purchase (1853); Guadalupe Hidalgo, Treaty of (1848); Mexican-American War.

Further Reading

Campbell, Archibald, and William Johnson Twining. "Reports upon the survey of the boundary between the territory of the United States and the possessions of Great Britain from the Lake of the Woods to the summit of the Rocky Mountain: Authorized by an act of Congress approved March 19, 1872." United States Northern Boundary Commission. United States Department of State. Washington, DC: Government Printing Office, 1878.

Goetzmann, William H. *Army Exploration of the American West 1803–1863.* Lincoln: University of Nebraska Press, 1979.

Rees, Tony. *Arc of the Medicine Line.* Lincoln: University of Nebraska Press, 2007.

Bowie, James (c. 1796–1836)

Although not the inventor of the famous "Bowie" knife, it is James Bowie whose name has forever been associated with the deadly weapon. His exact birth date (1795 or 1796) and birthplace (Sumner County, Tennessee; Burke County, Georgia; Logan County, Kentucky have all been suggested) are unknown, but

Frontiersman and adventurer James Bowie burnished his already larger-than-life image by dying with the other defenders of the Alamo on March 6, 1836. His brother Rezin invented the deadly Bowie knife, but Jim made it famous in one bloody fight in 1827. *(MPI/Stringer/Getty Images)*

he settled in the bayou country of Louisiana as a teenager. As an adult he was personable and a natural-born leader, but he was driven all his life to rise above his humble beginnings and pursued the acquisition of wealth and prestige through whatever avenues he could, legal or illegal.

By 1819 Bowie, along with his brothers Rezin and John, were partners with the pirate Jean Lafitte in the illegal importation of slaves into Louisiana. Although the slave trade was profitable and virtually risk-free, Bowie soon yearned for an even faster way to accumulate the wealth he desired. His stint as a slave runner lasted only a year before he found a more lucrative endeavor—dealing in the purchase and sale of fraudulent Spanish land grants and claims. Over the next several years, he amassed land, cash, and social status through that enterprise.

A single event on a sandbar in the Mississippi River just west of Natchez in 1827, however, forever etched the legend of James Bowie in history. Bowie

was present as members of two opposing factions witnessed a pistol duel between two enemies. The duel was inconclusive, with both men missing their marks, but old animosities and rivalries caused the witnesses to attack each other. In the melee, Bowie was clubbed over the head, shot twice at close range, and stabbed repeatedly. Despite his wounds, he managed to draw a large knife that his brother Rezin had designed and severely crippled one attacker and killed a second one before the bloody brawl ended. Miraculously, Bowie survived his wounds.

Later, when authorities investigated his questionable land dealings, even Bowie's new reputation as a ferocious knife fighter could not halt the wheels of justice. He resettled in the Mexican province of Texas in 1830, seeking to continue his quest for wealth and status, unfettered by American law. He became a Mexican citizen, and in 1831 married Ursula Veramendi, the daughter of the mayor of San Antonio de Bexar. When Ursula died of cholera in 1833, Bowie never recovered from his grief and began drinking heavily and neglecting his health.

At the onset of the Texas Revolution in 1835, Bowie joined the revolutionary forces and took part in the siege of San Antonio, again distinguishing himself in battle. He became co-commander of the American garrison at the Alamo in 1836, being ordered there by General Sam Houston. Bowie's health failed shortly after the Mexican Army arrived to retake San Antonio and he relinquished his command to William Barret Travis. He took to his sickbed, remaining ill for the entire siege, and, when Mexican soldiers overran the Alamo on March 6, 1836, he was killed along with all the other defenders.

Rod Timanus

See also: Alamo, The; Texas Revolution and Independence; Travis, William Barret.

Further Reading
Davis, Clifford C. *Three Roads to the Alamo.* New York: HarperCollins, 1998.
Hopewell, Clifford. *James Bowie Texas Fighting Man.* Waco, TX: Eakin Press, 1994.

Bozeman, John (1835–1867)

John Marion Bozeman was born in Pickens County, Georgia, in 1835. In 1860 he left his wife, Lucinda, and three young daughters to join the Colorado gold rush. Discouraged by the diminishing returns in the Colorado mines, he left for the new goldfields in what soon became Montana Territory. Shortly after arriving at Grasshopper Creek, he had more bad luck and lost interest in mining. By the spring of 1863 Bozeman was looking for new opportunities.

At Bannack, in present-day Montana, Bozeman enlisted veteran trail guide John Jacobs to aid him in opening a shortcut to the Montana goldfields from the main emigrant road along the North Platte River, one that would lie east of the Bighorn Mountains and follow the Yellowstone River. When Bozeman and Jacobs attempted to lead a wagon train over this new route in the summer of 1863, the train was confronted by angry Cheyenne and Sioux warriors 140 miles (225 km) out on the trail. Jacobs and the train turned back, but Bozeman and a small group of men went through Wyoming's Bighorn Basin to Montana on horseback. Bozeman remained in Montana that winter and served with the Vigilantes of Montana who organized in December 1863 to combat lawlessness in the mining camps.

In 1864 Bozeman successfully led a wagon train to Montana over his new Bozeman Trail. This was his only trip over the entire Bozeman Trail with a wagon train. He accompanied the train to Virginia City and then turned around and went back to the site of the town of Bozeman. On August 9 he participated in the town meeting at which the new town was named for him. He settled in Bozeman and farmed, recorded land claims, recruited new businesses, and was elected probate judge.

In the summer of 1866 Bozeman set up a ferry at the Yellowstone ford, just east of what is now Springdale, Montana. By September he closed the ferry, reportedly because of Indian problems, and returned to Bozeman, where he continued his other business interests. In April 1867, Bozeman and Tom Cover started for Fort C.F. Smith to secure a flour contract for the new mill in Bozeman. On April 18, a few miles east of modern-day Livingston, Montana, on the pack trail on the south side of the Yellowstone River, Bozeman was killed and Cover was wounded in an encounter with five Piegan Indians. Bozeman's body was buried at the site and was later removed to the cemetery in Bozeman.

But for his untimely death, Bozeman likely would have continued as a local, marginally successful businessman in Bozeman. Undoubtedly, his death at the hands of Indians near the trail named for him contributed to his legendary fame.

Susan Badger Doyle

See also: Bozeman Trail; Vigilantism.

Further Reading

Burlingame, Merrill G. *John M. Bozeman: Montana Trailmaker.* Bozeman: Museum of the Rockies, Montana State University, 1983.

Doyle, Susan Badger, ed. *Journeys to the Land of Gold: Emigrant Diaries from the Bozeman Trail, 1863–1866.* 2 vols. Helena: Montana Historical Society Press, 2000. Abridged edition, *Bound for Montana: Diaries from the Bozeman Trail.* Helena: Montana Historical Society Press, 2004.

Bozeman Trail

The Bozeman Trail was a shortcut from the main Platte overland road to the Montana goldfields. Its 450-mile (725-km) route left the North Platte River at two different places between present-day Douglas and Casper, Wyoming, went northwest through the Powder River Basin along the eastern base of the Bighorn Mountains—a region occupied and contested by Sioux, Cheyenne, Arapaho, and Crow tribes—crossed the Bighorn River in Montana, went west up the Yellowstone River valley, crossed the Gallatin Range at Bozeman Pass, and descended to Bozeman in the Gallatin Valley. In the spring of 1863, John Bozeman and John Jacobs scouted this route east from Montana to the main overland road on the North Platte River. They organized a wagon train at Deer Creek Station and led the train over the new route 140 miles (225 km) to where they were stopped by a large war party of Cheyennes and Lakotas and were turned back to the main overland road.

The first successful wagon trains traveled over the Bozeman Trail to Montana in 1864. Four large trains of 1,500 emigrants and 450 wagons left the North Platte River at Richard's Bridge. One of the trains had a serious fight with Indians, and four men were killed. In early 1865 the federal government closed the Bozeman Trail to emigrant traffic, and in the summer General Patrick E. Connor led a punitive campaign against the Northern Plains tribes in the Powder River Basin. Conner, guided by Jim Bridger, opened a new route from the North Platte River and established Fort Reno at the Powder River crossing. At the same time Connor was campaigning, James A. Sawyers led a federally funded wagon road expedition from the Niobrara River to Virginia City mostly following the Bozeman Trail.

In the summer of 1866, 2,000 people and 1,200 wagons in numerous trains traveled the trail. A large proportion of these were freighters. The early travelers encountered difficult river crossings but no problems with Indians. The establishment of Fort Phil Kearny in July and Fort C.F. Smith in August prompted Red Cloud and his allies to resist activity along the Bozeman Trail. An attack on July 17, followed by seven days of raids along the trail from the North Platte to the Bighorn River, signaled the start of Red Cloud's War. At least two dozen emigrants, freighters, traders, and soldiers were killed in the raids.

In the spring of 1867, the army opened an alternate route between Phil Kearny and C.F. Smith, but by then the trail was solely a military road to the forts. One small emigrant train traveled the Bozeman Trail in 1867. Red Cloud's warriors frequently raided military supply and mail trains along the trail and military herds and work camps near the forts. Four major fights occurred near Forts Phil Kearny and C.F. Smith from December 1866 through November 1867, including the disastrous Fetterman Massacre. When the Union Pacific Railroad was completed past Cheyenne in the spring of 1868, the high costs of protecting the Bozeman Trail were no longer necessary. The army abandoned the forts on the trail that summer, a precondition to Red Cloud's negotiating a treaty in November. Red Cloud's alliance signed the Fort Laramie Treaty of 1868, creating the Great Sioux Reservation. The Bozeman Trail was used in military campaigns in 1876–1877 and as a telegraph, stage line, and settlement route in the 1880s.

Susan Badger Doyle

See also: Bozeman, John; Carrington Family; Fort Laramie, Treaty of (1868); Red Cloud; Red Cloud's War; Sioux.

Further Reading

Doyle, Susan Badger. "The Bozeman Trail, 1863–1868: The Evolution of Routes to Montana." *Overland Journal* 20, no. 1 (Spring 2002): 2–17.

———, ed. *Journeys to the Land of Gold: Emigrant Diaries from the Bozeman Trail, 1863–1866.* 2 vols. Helena: Montana Historical Society Press, 2000. Abridged edition, *Bound for Montana: Diaries from the Bozeman Trail.* Helena: Montana Historical Society Press, 2004.

Hebard, Grace Raymond, and E.A. Brininstool. *The Bozeman Trail.* 2 vols. Cleveland: Arthur H. Clark, 1922. Reprint, Lincoln: University of Nebraska Press, 1990.

Johnson, Dorothy M. *The Bloody Bozeman: The Perilous Trail to Montana's Gold.* New York: McGraw-Hill, 1971. Reprint, Missoula, MT: Mountain Press, 1983.

Bridger, Jim (1804–1881)

Of all the fur trappers and traders who made up the brotherhood of the mountain men, probably none lived a more interesting life than Jim Bridger. He was born in Richmond, Virginia, on March 17, 1804, just two months before Lewis and Clark left St. Louis on their momentous "voyage of discovery." The two captains could not have known, of course, that in their native state of Virginia, a child had entered the world who would capitalize on their geographical findings to such an extent that he would be recognized in his own lifetime as one of the outstanding authorities on the Rocky Mountains and the ever-expanding West.

Bridger received little formal education; as a teenager he was apprenticed to a blacksmith in St. Louis. In 1822, when General William Ashley advertised for men to accompany Major Andrew Henry to the headwaters of the Missouri River, the youth eagerly applied for a job. On one of his first trips afield, the greenhorn Bridger, along with an older companion, John Fitzgerald, left a fellow trapper, Hugh Glass, for dead after he had been mauled by a grizzly bear. Bridger, influenced by the older Fitzgerald, finally consented to desert Glass—who seemingly was drawing his last breath—or be left to face the hostile wilderness alone. Glass did not die but instead survived his ordeal and made his way back to civilization with a vow to kill the two men who had left him to the elements. Glass eventually confronted Bridger, but forgave him, chalking up the youth's error in judgment to his inexperience in the wilderness.

In the fall of 1824, while trapping in the vicinity of the current junction of the borders of Idaho, Wyoming, and Utah, Bridger and a few companions explored the Bear River downstream to its confluence with the Great Salt Lake. He thus supposedly became the first white man to visit that heretofore-unknown body of water. Upon tasting the lake's salty waters, Bridger is purported to have declared that the group had apparently chanced upon the shores of the Pacific Ocean.

In 1826 William Ashley sold his fur outfit to Jedediah Smith, David Jackson, and William Sublette. Bridger remained as an employee of the new company, and on August 4, 1830, became one of the principals who bought out Smith and his partners and formed the reorganized Rocky Mountain Fur Company.

Bridger was born in the year that is usually recognized as the one that opened the western fur trade. In 1843, after the beaver were all gone and the prairie ally misled the Donner Party about the suitability of Hastings' Cutoff. Bridger hoped the Cutoff would reinvigorate trade at Fort Bridger, but his fabrications helped turn the Donner Party into one of the most infamous wagon companies in westward expansion, as they became trapped in the Sierras, subsisting on human flesh.

Bridger lived to be an old man for the times. He died on his farm in Missouri on July 17, 1881. One of his biographers has suggested how sad it is for today's students of the Rocky Mountain fur trade that no one took the time to interview this true hero of the American West in his autumn years and to record all of the marvelous stories that he could have told. Instead he lived his late life in solitude, never being visited and, no doubt, casting longing eyes ever westward toward the beloved Rocky Mountains of his youth.

James A. Crutchfield

See also: Fort Bridger; Glass, Hugh; Rocky Mountain Fur Company.

Further Reading

Utley, Robert M. *A Life Wild and Perilous: Mountain Men and the Paths to the Pacific.* New York: Henry Holt, 1997.

Vestal, Stanley. *Jim Bridger: Mountain Man.* Lincoln: University of Nebraska Press, 1970.

Fur trader, mountain man, and guide Jim Bridger is believed to have been the first white man to see the Great Salt Lake (1825). He established Fort Bridger (1843), an important trading post and supply station on the Oregon Trail in what is now Wyoming. *(The Granger Collection, New York)*

and plains were choked with emigrants, he established Fort Bridger in western Wyoming, a post that served as a resting and trading stop for weary westward travelers along the Oregon Trail. Bridger's retirement from the active fur trade in 1843 signified the end of the mountain man era of American history.

Bridger made his mark on western expansion, becoming a walking atlas of the Rocky Mountain West and showing the way to others. He regularly was sought out to provide detailed information about the paths through the mountains. He was the first white man to encounter Bridger Pass, which later became a focal component of the Overland Trail. He pioneered a route to Montana, the Bridger Trail. He tried to get the Mormon pioneers to change their destination from the Valley of the Great Salt Lake to the Hopi Mesas. When it was clear they were intent on their original destination he provided valuable information about the trail ahead. Not all the information Bridger provided was accurate, however. In 1846 he intention-

Bridger Trail

In January 1864, John M. Jacobs was in Denver, working with others to organize a wagon train he planned to guide over the route he and John Bozeman attempted but failed to open the previous summer. The party's principal organizer was Reverend L.B. Stateler, but when the *Denver Rocky Mountain News* published a letter highly critical of Jacobs, the plans fell through. Without Jacobs, Stateler and a train of 300 people traveled from Denver to Fort Laramie, where Jim Bridger met them and agreed to guide them and others over a route west of the Bighorn Mountains. Bridger was familiar with the region from many years of trapping, trading, and guiding exploring expeditions.

Bridger led the first train, departing the main overland trail near Red Buttes, 12 miles (19 km) southwest of present Casper, Wyoming. The trail went northwest, forded the Bighorn River and Greybull River, crossed a divide, and descended Clarks Fork to Rock Creek in Montana. The Bridger Trail converged with the Bozeman Trail where it crossed Rock Creek. From there both trails were the same. The route, pioneered by Bridger, went west to the Yellowstone River crossing. At the Shields River a few miles west of the crossing, the Bridger Trail diverged, and most Bridger Trail travelers descended to the vicinity of Bozeman in the Gallatin Valley from Bridger Pass, 10 miles (16 km) north of Bozeman Pass.

Ten wagon trains of about 2,500 people in nearly 700 wagons traveled the Bridger Trail in 1864. Bridger's train departed May 20, closely followed by a small train of experienced traders known as the Independents. John Jacobs, who followed Bridger's track, led the third train. During the trip, Jacobs angered and alienated the members of the train as much as he had the year before. Trader and Indian agent Major John Owen led the final train of the season in September and October. Owen's train was guided by Bridger, who had traveled eastward on the trail from Virginia City back to Fort Laramie.

The Bridger Trail was opened as an alternative to the Bozeman Trail in 1864. It was considered safer from Indian interference than the Bozeman Trail, but because it went through the arid Bighorn Basin, it could not sustain the same amount of wagon traffic as the better-watered route through the Powder River Basin. That, combined with the federal government closing the Bozeman Trail to emigrants the following year, ended travel on the Bridger Trail as a main route to Montana after its only year of use.

Susan Badger Doyle

See also: Bozeman, John; Bozeman Trail; Bridger, Jim.

Further Reading

Carley, Maurine, comp. "Bridger Trail Trek." *Annals of Wyoming* 39, no. 1 (April 1967): 109–28.

Detzler, Jack J., ed. *Diary of Howard Stillwell Stanfield, 1864–65.* Bloomington: Indiana University Press, 1969.

Lowe, James A. *The Bridger Trail: A Viable Alternative Route to the Gold Fields of Montana Territory in 1864.* Spokane, WA: Arthur H. Clark, 1999.

———. "The Bridger Trail: An Alternative Route to the Gold Fields of Montana Territory in 1864." *Annals of Wyoming* 70, no. 2 (Spring 1998): 12–23.

Buffalo Soldiers

When American Indians of the West saw black troops for the first time, they thought their curly hair resembled the woolly mane of the bison. These Indians coined the term "buffalo soldiers" as a gesture of respect to the steady, courageous blacks in blue. The troops accepted their moniker proudly, with the 10th Cavalry incorporating a buffalo into their regimental crest.

By the end of the Civil War, almost 200,000 African-American soldiers were serving with the United States Colored Troops, various state militias, and the navy. The Colored Troops had performed with great valor against Confederate forces. With the great conflict over, the army greatly reduced its strength, but maintained six regiments of Colored Troops—the 9th and 10th Cavalry and the 38th, 39th, 40th, and 41st Infantry. In 1869 further downsizing reduced the infantry to twenty-five regiments, and the four African-American units were consolidated into the 24th and 25th regiments.

Although all enlisted men in these regiments were African Americans, officers were white men. Racial beliefs of the post–Civil War era dictated a negative view of service with former slaves, and numerous officers, including George Armstrong Custer and Eugene Carr, declined commissions with black regiments. The first black graduate of West Point, Second Lieutenant Henry O. Flipper, Class of 1877, was assigned to the 10th Cavalry. Unfortunately, Lieutenant Flipper encountered severe prejudice from other officers, and in 1882 he was court-martialed on trumped-up charges.

Despite widespread bias, many officers found a professional home in the black regiments. Colonel Benjamin Grierson, leader of "Grierson's Raid" during the Civil War, commanded the 10th Cavalry from 1866 to 1890, while Colonel Edward Hatch led the 9th from 1866 to 1890. Colonel George Andrews commanded the 25th Infantry for twenty-one years, and Colonel Joseph Potter was in charge of the 24th for thirteen years. There was similar longevity among many company officers.

Buffalo soldiers often served long enlistments. A high desertion rate was experienced among white enlisted men, many of them immigrants who had joined the army as a first job through which they could learn English. For black men, however, the nineteenth-century army offered a career. With an opportunity to demonstrate the potential of their race, buffalo soldiers developed *esprit de corps* and unit pride. Morale was high, and in the field buffalo soldiers demonstrated stamina, discipline, and courage. Desertion rates were low and re-enlistment rates high among the buffalo soldiers. Black regiments also had fewer courts-martial for drunkenness. But military service was not easy for buffalo soldiers, who suffered discrimination and hostility from the very settlers and townspeople they protected.

Black regiments were stationed in the West, remaining at isolated posts without relief throughout the Indian Wars. Fort Davis in far West Texas, for example, was garrisoned by the 9th Cavalry from 1867 to 1875; by the 10th Cavalry from 1875 to 1885; by the 25th Infantry from 1870 to 1880; and by the 24th from 1869 to 1872 and in 1880.

From their frontier outposts buffalo soldiers campaigned ceaselessly and became involved in vicious combat. The two cavalry regiments saw extensive action in New Mexico, Arizona, and Texas against the Apache, with the 9th earning a reputation for always arriving in the nick of time to save settlers or fellow soldiers. The 24th and 25th fought elements of the Northern Plains nations, including Sioux and Cheyenne. For their valor, thirteen buffalo soldiers were awarded the Medal of Honor, along with seven of their officers.

Following the end of the Indian Wars, the buffalo soldiers maintained their hard-earned reputation when they fought in the Spanish-American War and campaigned in the Philippines. In 1916 they served under General John "Black Jack" Pershing—nicknamed because he had once commanded the 10th Cavalry—in his expedition against Pancho Villa. Men of the four regiments continued to be known as buffalo soldiers until the 1950s, when the army was totally integrated.

Bill O'Neal

See also: Apache; Cheyenne; Sioux.

Further Reading
Carroll, John M., ed. *The Black Military Experience in the American West.* New York: Liveright, 1971.
Glasrud, Bruce, and Michael N. Searles. *Buffalo Soldiers in the West: A Black Soldiers Anthology.* College Station: Texas A&M University Press, 2007.
Leckie, William F. *The Buffalo Soldiers: A Narrative of Negro Cavalry in the West.* Norman: University of Oklahoma Press, 1984.
Nalty, Bernard C. *Strength for the Fight: A History of Black Americans in the Military.* New York: Free Press, 1986.

Burnet, David G. (1788–1870)

Born in 1788 in New Jersey, David Gouverneur Burnet was the fourteenth child of Dr. William Burnet, who had served in the Continental Congress and as a surgeon general in the Continental Army. Several of David's older brothers achieved prominence, but although David—orphaned in childhood—strove to attain his own measure of greatness, he suffered many disappointments throughout his long life.

After receiving a sound education and preparing for a legal career, Burnet sought adventure as a young man. He turned up in Texas in 1826 seeking an *empresario* grant. Burnet and Lorenzo de Zavala received a colonization contract to settle 300 families, but failure to enlist colonists in the United States led to the sale of the contract to a land company.

Back in New Jersey in 1830, Burnet married Hannah Este, with whom he had four children, but only William lived to adulthood. Burnet brought his bride to Texas in 1831, building a small home on the San Jacinto River and installing a steam sawmill. The mill lost money for four years and Burnet sold it in 1835. By then, the struggle for Texas independence had erupted. An articulate attorney, Burnet was selected as a delegate to the Convention of 1835, but he was not a strong advocate for independence and was not returned to the Convention of 1836. In March the delegates wrote and signed a declaration of independence, as well as a constitution for the Republic of Texas. Delegate Sam Houston was appointed to command an army of Texas volunteers, while an interim government—a president, vice-president, and five cabinet members—was elected to serve until regular elections could be held. With a feeling that the interim president should not be a delegate, the Convention elected David G. Burnet, whose vice-president was Lorenzo de Zavala.

With Texan forces annihilated at the Alamo and at Goliad, and Mexican forces marching eastward, General Houston conducted a strategic retreat. Collecting more volunteers as he withdrew, he drilled and organized his men on the march; but frightened citizens fled alongside the army, creating an unsavory withdrawal called "The Runaway Scrape." Burnet led the criticism of Houston's strategy and sent orders to return and fight. After Houston's brilliant triumph at San Jacinto in April 1836, the interim president displayed petty jealousy. Clearly exerting scant control over Texas, Burnet directed that elections scheduled for December 1836 be moved up to September, and Sam Houston was overwhelmingly elected president. Burnet's interim presidency lasted from March 17 to October 22, 1836.

In 1838 Burnet was elected vice-president alongside President Mirabeau B. Lamar. Three years later Burnet was defeated for the presidency by Sam

Houston, following a vitriolic campaign. Subsequent efforts to attain appointive positions failed. Burnet's wife died in 1858 and his only son, William, was killed in battle during the Civil War. During Reconstruction, in 1866, the Texas Legislature appointed Burnet and O.M. Roberts to the U.S. Senate, but the Senate refused to seat them. Alone and with no money, Burnet died in Galveston in 1870.

Bill O'Neal

See also: Alamo, The; Empresario System; Goliad, Battle of; Houston, Sam; Lamar, Mirabeau B.; Santa Anna, Antonio López de; Texas Revolution and Independence.

Further Reading

Fields, Dorothy Louise. "David Gouverneur Burnet." *Southwestern Historical Quarterly*, 49 (October 1945).

Henson, Margaret Swett. "Burnet, David Gouverneur." *The New Handbook of Texas.* Vol. 1. Austin: Texas State Historical Association, 1996.

Burnett, Peter Hardeman (1807–1895)

Peter H. Burnett, the man who in 1849 led the new state of California from the chaotic days of the gold rush into mainstream America, was born in Nashville, Tennessee, on November 15, 1807, the son of early settlers in the Middle Tennessee region. At age ten, Burnet and his family (the second "t" was added to the name later) moved to Missouri. Peter later returned to Tennessee, trying his hand at various jobs and studying law before once again migrating to Missouri in 1832.

He was admitted to the Missouri bar, but also operated a mercantile establishment until the Panic of 1837 forced him out of business. An appointment as district attorney in northwestern Missouri finally provided Burnett with a steady income, but he was so far in debt from his earlier mercantile losses that he became dissatisfied with the job. Burnett turned his eyes toward Oregon, where many of his neighbors were beginning to emigrate. A recently introduced bill in Congress, if passed, would grant families 1,600 free acres (650 ha) of fertile Oregon land for simply settling there. He organized a wagon train and, in May 1843, began the long trip to the Columbia River along with almost 1,000 other people, thousands of cattle, and nearly 120 wagons. On June 1, several miles from the departure point (near Independence, Missouri), Burnett

was elected captain of the wagon train, a position that placed him in charge of the welfare and progress of the entire operation.

The Oregon legislature, in 1845, elected the transplanted Tennessean to the post of judge of the territorial Supreme Court. He resigned the office after a year-and-a-half and took up the full-time practice of law. When gold was discovered in California in 1848, Burnett struck out for the Sacramento valley, arriving on October 29. He began prospecting for gold, and after only a few weeks of mining he had saved enough cash to enable him to resume his law practice. His first client was John Sutter Jr., who hired him to manage the financial affairs of his father, the very man upon whose property gold had been discovered in the first place.

The California in which Burnett settled in 1848 was a hotbed of political activity, most of it focused on the statehood issue. Congress was being urged to allow California into the Union, but since an equal number of slave and free states already existed, officials were hesitant to admit the region for fear of tipping the scales of power one way or the other. Elections were called for in November 1849, even before statehood had been achieved, and Burnett announced his candidacy for governor. He won over his closest competitor by a vote of 6,716 to 3,188. Taking office in December, he served only thirteen months before resigning in January 1851, for personal reasons which he never explained in his letter of resignation. After he left the governor's office, Burnett again practiced law, served on the California Supreme Court, and guided the Pacific Bank of San Francisco as its president. In 1880 he penned his autobiography, entitled *Recollections and Opinions of an Old Pioneer.* He died in 1895, an eighty-eight-year-old veteran of life on several American frontiers.

James A. Crutchfield

See also: California, Conquest of; Oregon Trail.

Further Reading

Burnett, Peter. *Recollections and Opinions of an Old Pioneer.* Santa Barbara, CA: Narrative Press, 2004.

Burr, Aaron (1756–1836)

Aaron Burr's significance to America's westward expansion centers around his plot, along with co-conspirator General James Wilkinson, to separate the western portion of the infant United States from the rest of the nation and to organize the region into a new country with a strong allegiance to Spain.

Born in Newark, New Jersey, on February 6, 1756, Burr was the son of the president of the College of New Jersey (now Princeton University). He graduated from the college at the age of sixteen and afterward studied law, then joined the Continental Army as war with Great Britain became imminent. He quickly rose in rank from private to lieutenant colonel before being forced to resign in 1779 due to ill health. During his time in the army, he served brilliantly with Colonel Benedict Arnold and Major General Richard Montgomery at Quebec in December of 1775, was aide-de-camp to generals George Washington and Rufus Putnam, and commanded the fort at West Point.

After the revolution, Burr resumed the study of law and was admitted to the New York bar in 1782. A series of rapid successes in the political arena culminated with his election as third vice-president of the United States during President Thomas Jefferson's first administration from 1801 to 1805. In July 1804, while in office, and purportedly in response to critical remarks made by Alexander Hamilton, the de facto leader of the opposition Federalist Party, Burr killed Hamilton in a duel held in New Jersey on the west bank of the Hudson River.

The once-popular Burr now found himself out of grace with the American people. He was burned in effigy in towns across the country and friends who once had been closest to him now distanced themselves. One confidant, however, James Wilkinson, the commanding general of the army and newly appointed governor of Louisiana, continued to court the former vice-president's favor and, over a period of time, the two men spawned their idea for an independent country to be carved out of the westernmost states. In July 1806, Wilkinson dispatched Lieutenant Zebulon Pike to explore the distant regions of present-day Colorado and New Mexico, with orders to learn all he could about the Spanish presence there. Realizing the repercussions that could occur if the real purpose of the mission were ever revealed, Pike's journey was designated one of discovery, much as that of the recently departed Lewis and Clark Expedition.

Within months after Pike left St. Louis, Wilkinson had a change of heart about his and Burr's grandiose conquest of the Southwest, primarily prompted by the fact that Burr was now a wanted man following exposure of his imperialistic scheme and its publication in all of the nation's newspapers. Perfectly willing to turn state's evidence against his one-time partner, Wilkinson redeemed himself with President Thomas Jefferson while Burr tried to escape authorities. In January 1807, he was arrested along the Natchez Trace in Mississippi Territory and eventually taken to Richmond, Virginia, for trial, where Wilkinson testified against him. Miraculously, he was acquitted of the treason charges and released, a tired and broken man. Following a brief residency in Europe, he returned to the United States, resumed his New York law practice, and died on Staten Island on September 14, 1836.

James A. Crutchfield

See also: Jefferson, Thomas; Pike, Zebulon M.; Pike Expedition; Wilkinson, James.

Further Reading

Isenberg, Nancy. *Fallen Founder: The Life of Aaron Burr.* New York: Penguin, 2007.

Wandell, Samuel H., and Meade Minnigerode. *Aaron Burr.* New York: G.P. Putnam's Sons, 1925.

Butterfield Stage

Before 1859 no single road connected the east and west coasts of the United States. California's forty-niners, who had rushed to the goldfields, now demanded quicker communication across the country. In response, the U.S. Post Office sent out a plea for help. John Butterfield, former mayor of Utica, New York, and friend of President James Buchanan, responded. He proposed a road connecting St. Louis, Missouri, with San Francisco, California.

Within twelve months, Butterfield selected a 2,800-mile (4,500-km) southern route; purchased 1,200 horses, 600 mules, and 800 sets of harnesses; and hired 1,000 men as surveyors, conductors, drivers, veterinarians, wranglers, and blacksmiths. He ordered 250 wagons, surveyed thousands of miles of roadway, graded fording sites, opened new roads or improved old ones, procured several thousand tons of hay and fodder, built 200 way stations 20 miles (32 km) apart, dug 100 wells, and created the run schedule. He accomplished all this at a cost of $600,000.

Concord and Celerity stagecoaches, built in Concord, New Hampshire, were painted either red or green with bright yellow running gear. Inscribed with the letters *O.M.C.* (Overland Mail Company), the Concords weighed 3,000 pounds (900 kg) each with a load capacity of two tons. Celerity coaches (also referred to as mud wagons) were used in more rugged areas and across the desert, since their wheels were narrower than the Concords'. Both coach bodies were set on leather straps, which caused many passengers to get motion sickness.

The coaches held nine people, riding three abreast. The six passengers squeezed into the back and middle rows faced forward, while the three in the front row faced the rear. The facing passengers had to ride with their knees dovetailed, baggage on their laps (when it did not fit up top) and mail pouches beneath their feet. The coaches traveled day and night, stopping ten minutes at way stations and forty minutes for meals. The stage averaged 120 miles (190 km) in twenty-four hours. It took eight days just to cross Texas.

Initially the fare ran $100 in gold for those traveling east from San Francisco, but $200 for those heading west. After a few months of grumbling and confusion, the compromise price of $150 in gold was established, regardless of direction.

During its two and a half years of service, the Butterfield Stage always arrived at its final destination within the twenty-five-day contract time. The service proved so reliable that the British government sent official correspondence to British Columbia via the Butterfield Stage Line.

By early 1861, war with the Apache in Arizona and New Mexico heated up and the spread of the telegraph was rendering the stage obsolete for mail delivery in certain areas. The Civil War rang the final death knell on the Butterfield Stage. To prevent the possibility of the Overland Mail Company's property falling into Confederate hands, the U.S. Postmaster General ordered the company to discontinue service and move all the coaches, livestock, and equipment north to the Central Overland Trail. Once that happened, the Confederates seized all the Butterfield stations in Texas.

John Butterfield, now in failing health, stepped down as president of his company and died in 1869. The Butterfield Stage Line had stitched together a growing nation. In fact, John Butterfield created the first reliable line of communication by establishing the longest mail route in the world at that time.

Melody Groves

See also: Overland Mail; Overland Telegraph Company; Overland Trail; Pony Express.

Further Reading

Hackler, George. *The Butterfield Stage in New Mexico.* Las Cruces, NM: Barbed Wire Press, 2005.

Ormsby, Waterman L. *The Butterfield Overland Mail.* San Marino, CA: Huntington Library and Art Gallery, 1942.

Tompkins, G.C. *A Compendium of the Overland Mail Company on the South Route 1858–1861 and the Period Surrounding It.* El Paso, TX: Talna, 1985.

C

Calhoun, John C. (1782–1850)

Frederick Jackson Turner, whose highly important "frontier theory" explained the significance of the moving western frontier to the overall picture of American history, once wrote that a proper biography of John C. Calhoun would constitute the political history of the United States from the War of 1812 to the Compromise of 1850. Indeed, Calhoun's presence on the national scene helped create the legacy of much of this nearly forty-year period when the country evolved from a group of provincial states to a large consortium of entities reaching all the way to the Pacific Ocean.

Calhoun was born in the Abbeville District of South Carolina on March 18, 1782, at a time when many of his fellow Carolinians were migrating to new homes on the westward slopes of the Appalachian Mountains. His family was of modest means, but he managed to attend Yale College, later receiving his law degree from Litchfield Law School in Connecticut. In 1811 he was elected to the U.S. House of Representatives, where, along with Kentucky's Henry Clay and Tennessee's Felix Grundy, he led a small group of southern and frontier congressmen known as the War Hawks, who were intent on seeing the United States go to war with Great Britain.

Calhoun served in the administrations of four presidents: as James Monroe's secretary of war for eight years (1817–1825), as John Quincy Adams's vice-president for four years (1825–1829), as Andrew Jackson's vice-president for three years (1829–1832), and as John Tyler's secretary of state for one year (1844–1845). As secretary of war, Calhoun was responsible for Indian affairs and the administration of the army and its role as defender of the frontier. Under his management, the army expanded the number of forts and roads constructed and sent survey parties up the Missouri and Mississippi rivers. The highly publicized Yellowstone Expedition of 1819–1820, under the command of Stephen Long, was completed under his direction.

Calhoun prematurely left the Jackson administration over political differences with the president, but soon returned to Washington, DC, as a senator whose primary interest was promoting states' rights over the desires of federal government. As a southerner, he advocated slavery, and he spent the rest of his senatorial career and his brief time as Tyler's secretary of state attempting to guarantee new states entering the Union the right to enter as slave states, a position that practically every northern statesman held in contempt. He was an early supporter of Texas annexation, and as secretary of state, he orchestrated a questionable treaty with the republic's leaders to allow Texas to evolve from a republic to full statehood. When James K. Polk replaced Tyler in 1845, he chose James Buchanan to succeed Calhoun at the State Department, largely due to Calhoun's apparent disinterest in providing a solution to the Oregon question with Great Britain. Calhoun soon adopted a new crusade: his opposition to the nation's declaration of war with Mexico.

Calhoun's last battles were his opposition to the 1846 Wilmot Proviso, which outlawed slavery from being introduced into any state that in the future might be carved from territory ceded to the United States at the termination of the Mexican-American War, and the Compromise of 1850, a garbled package of legislation that started out to reinforce the Wilmot Proviso but, when passed, included an assortment of laws primarily aimed at equalizing the number of future "slave" versus "free" states to be admitted to the Union. Calhoun, too sickly to make his arguments known during the legislation's floor debate, had an associate read his remarks. The Compromise of 1850 was enacted during five separate meetings of Congress. The last four sections were approved after Calhoun died on May 31, 1850.

James A. Crutchfield

See also: Clay, Henry; Compromise of 1850; Missouri Compromise (1820); Texas Annexation.

Further Reading

Bartlett, Irving H. *John C. Calhoun: A Biography.* New York: W.W. Norton, 1994.

Peterson, Merrill D. *The Great Triumvirate: Webster, Clay, and Calhoun.* New York: Oxford University Press, 1988.

California, Conquest of

In 1846, Alta (Upper) California was a distant and long-neglected territory of Mexico whose populace owed little allegiance to a faraway central authority and the governors it sent out, principally to collect taxes and oversee the province's trade with the outside world. Many Californians favored annexation by the United States or England. For its part, and as an extension of the perceived "Manifest Destiny" of the country's expansion to the Pacific Ocean, the United States coveted the province, especially for its strategic San Francisco Bay. For several years Americans had been trickling into northern California to hunt, trap, and farm in the rich Sacramento Valley where the Swiss impresario John A. Sutter had constructed a fort on a parcel of the 50,000 acres (20,000 ha) granted him in 1841 by Mexican authorities. In addition to its role as a way station for newcomers to California, Sutter's domain served as the staging area for the conquest of California, beginning in December 1845, when U.S. Army topographer John C. Frémont led an exploring party there.

Frémont's role in the Bear Flag Revolt, the opening event of the conquest, is open to question, but on June 14, 1846, whether encouraged or incited by him, a band of American settlers in the Sacramento Valley invaded the mission settlement of Sonoma. There, the insurgents raised their homemade Bear Flag and declared California to be free and independent of Mexican rule. The brief uprising ended in the first week of July when Commodore John D. Sloat, commander of the U.S. Pacific Fleet, sailed into Monterey Bay and raised the American flag over the customs house.

At the end of July, Commodore Robert F. Stockton, a veteran of the War of 1812 and engagements against Barbary pirates in the Mediterranean, succeeded to Sloat's command. In Monterey he greeted Frémont, who had arrived in the town two weeks earlier with his scout and guide Kit Carson and 160 volunteers. Frémont and his battalion were dispatched on a warship to San Diego and took possession of the town on July 29. Stockton led the takeover of Los Angeles, capital of Alta California, on August 13. (In October, the Los Angeles garrison of fifty Americans was overwhelmed by a mob of angry Californios—native Californians of Spanish or Mexican ancestry—and was forced to abandon the town.)

Meantime, the final pivotal figure of the conquest, Brigadier General Stephen Watts Kearney, a tough and resourceful soldier of service dating from 1812, was approaching California after an epic march from Fort Leavenworth, Kansas. He commanded an army of 300 dragoons (medium cavalry) and over 1,000 infantrymen. His orders were to annex Santa Fe, capital of New Mexico province, and march on to capture and claim Alta California for the United States.

Kearny and the army reached Santa Fe on August 18 and the New Mexico capital capitulated to the Americans without resistance, after which the general departed Santa Fe on September 25, 1846, with 300 dragoons, wagons, cannons, and supplies, heading west for California.

On October 6, 200 miles (320 km) south of Santa Fe, Kearny's column intercepted some horsemen led by Kit Carson, bound for Washington, DC, with dispatches from Commodore Stockton announcing that California was now an American possession. This was the first Kearny had heard the news and while it stunned him he determined to march on. He ordered 200 dragoons back to Santa Fe, sent Stockton's dispatches on to Washington with another courier, and prevailed upon Carson to guide the much-reduced force to California.

After a grueling desert crossing, Kearny and his remaining men reached San Pasqual, an Indian village east of San Diego, and on December 6, 1846, fought a battle in the morning mist against a detachment of Californio lancers. The Americans suffered casualties of twenty killed and eighteen wounded (including Kearny) to minor losses among the Mexican troops. A relief party dispatched by Stockton escorted Kearny and his exhausted men into San Diego.

Upon Kearny's recovery and with the objective of recapturing Los Angeles, a joint army-navy force of 600 men commanded by Kearny and Stockton engaged Mexican militiamen on the San Gabriel River on January 8, 1847, and at the village of La Mesa the following day. These battles on the approaches to Los Angeles, and the reoccupation of the town on January 10, ended hostilities. Frémont, now designated lieutenant colonel, reached Los Angeles with his mounted riflemen after the battles and negotiated the capitulation treaty on January 13. The paper was signed by Frémont and General Andrés Pico, commander of Mexican forces in southern California, at an adobe ranch house in Cahuenga Canyon in present-day North Hollywood.

Dale L. Walker

See also: Bear Flag Revolt; Frémont, John C.; Kearny, Stephen Watts; Manifest Destiny.

Further Reading

Clark, Dwight L. *Stephen Watts Kearny: Soldier of the West.* Norman: University of Oklahoma Press, 1961.

Hubert H. Bancroft. *History of California.* San Francisco: The History Company, 1886. Reprint, Santa Barbara: Wallace Hebberd, 1969.

Walker, Dale L. *Bear Flag Rising: The Conquest of California, 1846.* New York: Forge Books, 1999.

Winders, Richard B. *Mr. Polk's Army: The American Military Experience in the Mexican War.* College Station: Texas A&M University Press, 1997.

California Trail

The northern overland wagon road to California evolved dynamically between 1841 and 1869 into a complicated network of established roads and risky cutoffs created from existing Indian trails, fur trade routes, and the Oregon Trail. At the same time, the southern routes to the Pacific coast carried tens of thousands of travelers from Missouri, Arkansas, and Texas across today's American Southwest.

The northern trail had multiple beginnings and endings that compare best to the strands of a frayed rope. From the Missouri River, trails left Independence, St. Joseph, Fort Leavenworth, Council Bluffs, and smaller settlements; over time these jumping-off points shifted northward. Geography wove the strands together between Fort Laramie and South Pass, but at the Continental Divide, the rope unraveled again. Alternate routes went to Fort Hall, Fort Bridger, and Salt Lake as guides and government explorers constantly worked out better approaches to the trail's greatest challenges: the Great Basin and the Sierra Nevada. Over three decades, emigrants crossed this final barrier via Walker, Sonora, Carson, Donner, Henness, Beckwith, Fandango, and Noble's passes.

Major cutoffs left the trail west of South Pass (Greenwood/Sublette, Kinney, Slate Creek), at Soda Springs (Hudspeth), Fort Bridger (Hastings, Hensley's

Salt Lake, the Simpson–Pony Express route), the Black Rock Desert (Lassen, Noble, Honey Lake), and Reno (Beckwith). A major alternate, the Cherokee Trail, connected Arkansas with the trail at Fort Bridger, while in 1859 the Lander Cutoff at South Pass became the first government wagon road in the trail system.

The Bidwell-Bartleson party initiated wagon travel to California in 1841 when thirty-three hardy pioneers blazed a road around the north end of the Great Salt Lake to reach the Humboldt River near today's Elko, Nevada, but no one ever used it again. Following a trace he had explored in 1833 and 1834, Joseph R. Walker led the first train on what became the main California Trail up Raft River to the Humboldt in 1843. A year later Caleb Greenwood and Paiute leader Truckee helped the Stephens-Murphy-Townsend party take the first wagons across the Sierra over what became Donner Pass, the route that the transcontinental railroad and Interstate 80 later followed. Wagons finally made it from Independence to Sutter's Fort at Sacramento in one season in 1845. Emigration boomed in 1846, but the year is best remembered for the disaster that befell the Donner Party when blizzards trapped the train in the Sierra.

The war with Mexico dramatically slowed Western emigration in 1847 and 1848, but the conflict made California part of the United States. The discovery of gold there in 1848 inspired the largest voluntary migration in history, and some 75,000 Americans crossed the plains to California in 1849 and 1850. Cholera decimated the gold seekers; the "rush" swept away nearly every blade of grass, and it also established the pattern followed in later mineral rushes to the Comstock, Pike's Peak, and Montana. During the 1850s the trail became an established national wagon road and overland stage and mail route. Overland freighting to supply military posts and the new settlements at Salt Lake, Denver, and Carson Valley became a big business with both enormous profits and devastating risks. During its last decade, the California Trail saw the Pony Express come and go, with the telegraph and an explosion in western migration following the Civil War.

Native peoples provided essential resources and aid to the wagon trains that pioneered the trail. During its first years, conflict with Indians was minimal; historian John Unruh estimated that between 1840 and 1860, Indians killed 362 emigrants, while emigrants killed 426 Indians. Violence escalated as the principal Indian nations along the trail—the Pawnees, Lakotas, Cheyennes, Arapahos, Absarokas, Shoshones, Utes, and Northern Paiutes—recognized the relentless nature of overland emigration and its devastating impact on their essential resources of grass, game, wood, and water. The withdrawal of the few federal troops stationed along the road in 1861 encouraged young warriors, often against the counsel of the more experienced men, to begin organizing systematic attacks on overland freighting, stage coaches, and a few wagon trains.

Hard figures are illusive, but before the completion of the transcontinental railroad in 1869, more than 250,000 people crossed the California Trail. The number of pioneers starting out was higher, but disease, drowning, gunshot accidents, and stampedes killed as many as 5 percent of those who traveled across the plains.

Throughout its existence, the California Trail was the driving agent of change in the American West and ultimately transformed the region.

Will Bagley

See also: Bidwell, John; Cherokee Trail; Donner Party; Fort Bridger; Fort Hall; Fort Laramie; Forty-Niners; Lander Cutoff; Oregon Trail; Overland Trail; South Pass; Walker, Joseph R.

Further Reading

Buck, Don. "Those Who, What, When, Where Questions About Emigrants and Emigrant Trails." *News from the Plains*, Oregon-California Trails Association Newsletter (July 1994).

National Geographic Society. *Trails West*. Washington, DC: National Geographic Society, 1979.

Unruh, John D., Jr. *The Plains Across: The Overland Emigrants and the Trans-Mississippi West, 1840–60*. Urbana: University of Illinois Press, 1982.

Western Writers of America. *Pioneer Trails West*. Ed. Don Worcester. Caldwell, ID: Caxton Printers, 1985.

Campbell, Robert (1804–1879)

Born in 1804 in Aughlane, Tyrone County, Ireland, Robert Campbell migrated to St. Louis in 1824. There, he became ill with a severe hemorrhage of his lungs, and his physicians suggested he undertake a trip to the mountains to improve his health. He signed on with General William H. Ashley's 1825 trading and trapping expedition, and the trip, despite its inherent hardships and dangers, completely restored his health. For the next two decades and more, Campbell distinguished himself along with the likes of Jedediah Smith, Jim Bridger, Joe Meek, and most assuredly William Sublette as one of the hardy breed that became known as "mountain men."

Like the rest of the mountain men, Campbell's adventures in the Rocky Mountains, particularly his encounters with the Indians and the wild beasts that inhabited the region, made him a legend. Among his many adventures, he was a participant (and survivor) of the Battle of Pierre's Hole in July 1832, just prior to that year's rendezvous. Campbell, Milton, Sublette, and Antoine Godin were among the trappers who encountered the Gros Ventre Indians that day on the west side of the Teton Mountains. The fight continued throughout the afternoon, and the Gros Ventres withdrew sometime during the night.

Following the 1832 rendezvous, Campbell and William Sublette formed a partnership with the express purpose of taking on Kenneth McKenzie and the Hudson's Bay Company (HBC) on the upper Missouri River. They established a number of forts and trading posts as part of that plan.

While racing HBC's Nathaniel Wyeth to the Green River rendezvous in 1834, Campbell and Sublette stopped long enough at the confluence of the Laramie and North Platte rivers to establish a trading post to cache supplies for later trading. They named the post Fort William (they had built and abandoned a Fort William near Fort Union earlier). Later, after they sold the fort, the name was changed to "Fort John on the Laramie," which was later shortened to Fort Laramie. This was the first permanent American settlement in Wyoming.

Campbell withdrew from the field the next year and became a successful banker and merchant in St. Louis and a sometime consultant to the federal government on Indian affairs. He was a commissioner with Father Pierre De Smet to seek a treaty with the Indians in the 1851 conference at Fort Laramie and was appointed by President Ulysses S. Grant to a similar post in 1869.

A bronchial ailment claimed Campbell's life on October 16, 1879, in Saratoga Springs, New York.

Gene Bryan

See also: Bridger, Jim; De Smet, Pierre-Jean; Fort Laramie; Hudson's Bay Company; McKenzie, Kenneth; Meek, Joseph L.; Pierre's Hole, Battle of; Rendezvous; Smith, Jedediah; Sublette Brothers; Wyeth, Nathaniel Jarvis.

Further Reading

Chittenden, Hiram C. *The American Fur Trade of the Far West*. Lincoln: University of Nebraska Press, 1986.

Hafen, Leroy, and Frances Young. *Fort Laramie and the Pageant of the West*. Lincoln: University of Nebraska Press, 1984.

Roberts, Phil. *Readings in Wyoming History*. Laramie, NE: Skyline West Press, 1996.

Carlisle Indian Industrial School

Founded in 1879 by Richard Henry Pratt (1840–1924), the Carlisle Indian Industrial School in Carlisle, Pennsylvania, was considered a "noble experiment" for its efforts to assimilate American Indian children into the culture of the United States.

Pratt's experience with Indians began with his service as an officer with the Buffalo Soldiers in the 10th U.S. Cavalry Regiment, where he commanded the Indians who served as scouts for the unit. In 1875 Pratt was sent to Fort Marion, Florida, an Indian prisoner-of-war camp, where his duty was to "civilize" the captives. He required them to discard their traditional clothing and food and to cut their braids, and he taught them English.

The captives, primarily Apaches, were released from Fort Marion in 1878, but assimilation techniques had been successful enough to allow Pratt to convince Secretary of the Interior Carl Schurz, Secretary of War George W. McCrary, and a number of benefactors to use a deserted military base in central Pennsylvania as the site of a school to teach and assimilate Indian children.

Students were recruited from Dakota Territory. Pratt's first stop was at Spotted Tail's Rosebud reservation. Spotted Tail was not initially receptive to Pratt's offer to educate the children of the tribe, citing his mistrust of whites, because of broken treaties and trespassing into the Black Hills, as his reasons. Pratt was persistent, ultimately convincing Spotted Tail that future treaties would be more difficult for the whites to break if the English language and customs were fully understood by the Indians.

Pratt's next stop was the Pine Ridge reservation, where he met with Red Cloud and other members of his tribe and told them of Spotted Tail's agreement to send children to the school. Between these two reservations, a total of eighty-two children were recruited, including Red Cloud's grandson. Other members of Pratt's team recruited children from the Kiowa and Cheyenne tribes.

In the meantime, the school had hired a full complement of teachers and instructors. Not surprisingly, school life was modeled on military training. Soon after arrival, the boys' long hair was cut. Uniforms were issued to boys, and girls wore Victorian-style dresses. The children were assigned to "companies" and marched to and from the dining hall and classes.

Classes were divided between academics and trades. Reading, writing, and arithmetic were taught in the mornings, with carpentry, gardening, and blacksmithing for the boys, and domestic duties, like cooking and sewing, for the girls, in the afternoons. Discipline was of utmost importance and enforced with military rigidity. Marching drills were practiced daily, and the children were assigned rank, with the teachers and instructors

The Carlisle (Pennsylvania) Indian Industrial School was one of dozens of boarding schools established by the federal government in the nineteenth century—most of them on reservations—to educate and assimilate young Native Americans. (Library of Congress)

acting as officers. A military justice system was created with students doling out the consequences for offenses. The most severe offenses sent the children to confinement at the guardhouse. The guardhouse, built during the Revolutionary War, still stands.

Every student was required to take music lessons. A band was formed that played at football games, school ceremonies, and at every presidential inaugural parade during the existence of the school. Organized sports, including football, were also introduced to the students.

To further the assimilation process, Pratt created the outing system. During the summer months when there was no school in session, Pratt hired out the Indian children to non-Indian families instead of returning them to their tribal life. The outing system provided cheap labor to local farmers, and some children remained on the farms and attended public schools. Pratt considered this proof of the school's ability to assimilate Indian children into white society.

The health of the students was an immediate issue at Carlisle Indian Industrial School. Tuberculosis and smallpox outbreaks took the lives of several students. Separation from their families and tribe caused illnesses. It was common practice to send ill children back to their families, but some died at the school and are buried in a cemetery on the premises.

Richard Henry Pratt retired as the school's superintendent in 1904. At the end of the school's existence in 1918, over 10,000 representing more than thirty-nine tribes had passed through its halls. The graduation rate was 8 percent. Today, the Carlisle Indian Industrial School is remembered mostly for its star football player, Jim Thorpe, and for its football team, the Carlisle Indians. The team was coached by Glenn Scobey "Pop" Warner, one of the founders of the football program for children, the "Pop Warner Little Scholars." The football team retains the best winning percentage (.647) of any defunct college.

Larry D. Sweazy

See also: Buffalo Soldiers; Indian Policy; Red Cloud; Spotted Tail.

Further Reading

Pratt, Richard Henry. *Battlefield and Classroom: Four Decades with the American Indian, 1867–1904.* Norman: University of Oklahoma Press, 2004.

Witmer, Linda F. *The Indian Industrial School, Carlisle, Pennsylvania, 1879–1918.* Carlisle, PA: Cumberland County Historical Society, 1993.

Carrington Family

Three individuals—one man and two women—were among those present at the Fetterman Massacre near present-day Sheridan, Wyoming, in December 1866. The man, Colonel Henry B. Carrington, was the commander of the U.S. army post Fort Phil Kearny, situated in the midst of hostile Sioux and Northern Cheyenne territory. His wife, Margaret, was with him at the post, and following the massacre accompanied him back East to other commands. The other woman, Frances (Fannie) Grummond, was the wife of an officer at the fort, and following his death in the massacre returned to her hometown of Franklin, Tennessee. Years later, when she learned of the death of Margaret Carrington, she began a correspondence with her old acquaintance that culminated in her marriage to the widowed Carrington.

Henry Beebe Carrington (1824–1912)

Henry B. Carrington was born on March 2, 1824, in Connecticut and reared by his mother and grandmother. He aspired to attend the U.S. Military Academy but failed to pass the physical, and instead studied law at Yale. He moved west to Ohio, married Margaret Sullivant, and later became adjutant general of the state, during which period he oversaw reorganization of the militia. In 1861 he became colonel of the 18th U.S. Infantry Regiment, and the following year was promoted to brigadier general of volunteers, spending his years of Civil War service recruiting and training soldiers rather than on the front lines. He mustered out of the volunteers in August 1865 and later rejoined the regular army, again as a colonel.

On March 10, 1866, Carrington became commanding officer of the army's Mountain District, formed to protect the Bozeman Trail, and was subsequently sent to establish three forts—Reno, Phil Kearny, and C.F. Smith—to provide protection for travelers headed to the gold fields in Montana. Eventually, he established his headquarters at Fort Phil Kearny, located along the Bozeman Trail in north-central Wyoming. He was present at negotiations with Indians at Fort Laramie in the spring of 1866. He expected a peaceful assignment garrisoning Forts Reno, Phil Kearny, and C.F. Smith, but Red Cloud and other Sioux leaders did not want white men in their hunting area, which had been delineated for them under terms in the 1851 Horse Creek Treaty. At an 1866 meeting in Fort Laramie the majority of Indians agreed to leave the soldiers alone, but Red Cloud walked out, vowing to defend the territory.

The wagon train Carrington commanded, which included an army band and civilian workers needed to cut wood and build the fort, left Fort Laramie in May 1866. They carried with them tools and a sawmill for preparing building materials, but not enough seasoned troops or sufficient arms and ammunition to defend the forts they would construct. Carrington soon learned the depths to which the Indians opposed the construction of the forts he was destined to build. As soon as they stopped at the site of Fort Phil Kearny, his command saw Indians who harassed soldiers continually when they were on woodcutting details. The occupants of the fort effectively became prisoners, forced to stay inside because of Indian forays.

Captain William J. Fetterman, a cavalry officer seasoned in Civil War battles, arrived in November and declared that with eighty men he could wipe out the Sioux nation. He and other battle-experienced officers thought Colonel Carrington a coward because he would not take offensive action against the marauding Indians.

Officers attempted to ambush the Sioux on December 6, but failed. Nevertheless, the restless officers wanted to pursue the tribesmen. On December 21, 1866, Fetterman, against Carrington's orders, followed a party of Lakota and Cheyenne over Lodge Trail Ridge, where tribesmen including Red Cloud and Crazy Horse were waiting in ambush. Before relief could be organized, Fetterman and his entire command were annihilated.

In January, Carrington was ordered to close the fort and withdraw to Fort Caspar, located on the North Platte River to the south. The troops left Fort Kearny in the middle of a blizzard. Carrington was labeled a coward in the press and President Ulysses S. Grant called for a court martial, but a special commission that investigated the events exonerated him.

Carrington spent the balance of his career trying to give his side of the story. He taught at a military school in Indiana, served on military boards, and was a prolific writer. His first wife, Margaret Carrington, wrote *Absaraka, Home of the Crows*, probably with his collaboration. This memoir served to restore his reputation. His second wife, Frances Grummond, wrote another memoir of the events at Fort Phil Kearny. Carrington died in Boston on October 26, 1912.

Margaret Carrington (1831–1870)

Margaret Sullivant, born in 1831 of a prominent Kentucky family, was one of a small, literate group of army wives who recorded life in the frontier garrisons after the Civil War. She was the first wife of Colonel Henry Carrington, commanding officer of Fort Phil Kearny at the time of the Fetterman fight. She married Henry in 1851 and bore six children, two of whom survived to adulthood.

In March 1866, when Colonel Carrington received orders to move into Dakota Territory and garrison three forts along the Bozeman Trail, Margaret accompanied him. Lieutenant General William Sherman encouraged officers' wives to keep diaries so that the adventure could be recorded. Using her contemporary writings, Margaret wrote *Absaraka, Home of the Crows*, published in 1868. It is probable that Henry added details of the building of the fort and the fight involving Fetterman; he is the main character in the book and it rationalizes his role in the Fetterman debacle.

Margaret began her record with her concerns for hospitality to Sherman at Fort Laramie and continued on the trail over the plains along the Platte River to the foothills of the Big Horn Mountains where the fort was built. She thought the clear air was good for her sons' health. She describes the beautiful landscape, from which the wives and children were gradually cut off by danger from Indian raids. The group became virtual prisoners inside the fort, but continued their domestic life and celebrated army rituals and social events. Margaret welcomed mountain man Jim Bridger into her home, where she read Shakespeare to him. He cautioned her and others at the fort about the Indians.

After the Fetterman massacre, Margaret mourned the victims and the survivors and took into her home Fanny Grummond, the pregnant bride of one of the officers killed in the massacre. When they were ordered to desert the fort, their wagon train moved out into a blizzard. Margaret called upon her reserves of fortitude as she described the ordeal of the frozen ride to Fort Caspar, with her children wrapped in furs, lying next to a blazing stove in the army ambulance.

Afterward, Henry tried to salvage his army career and Margaret wrote her memoir, dedicated to General Sherman. She died a few years later, in 1870, of tuberculosis, leaving behind her vivid account of life in a frontier garrison.

Frances Courtney Carrington (1845–1911)

Frances Courtney, the second wife of Colonel Henry Carrington, was born in 1845 in Franklin, Tennessee. During the Civil War and the intense fighting in her hometown in November 1864, her family was in sympathy with the Union cause and young Fannie caught the eye of Union officer George W. Grummond. They married in August 1865 and moved to several army posts until Grummond joined the 2nd U.S. Cavalry. The Grummonds arrived at Fort Phil Kearny in present-day Wyoming in the fall of 1866.

Fannie, though inexperienced with frontier life, was a considerate, spirited woman and joined the social life at the fort, thrilled to observe the formal garrison flag-raising, the first between the Platte River and Montana Territory. Like other frontier army wives, she showed that it was possible for women to live in areas of the largely unsettled West, thus encouraging westward expansion.

The Sioux, under Red Cloud, had taunted the soldiers since they arrived at the site in July 1866. The warriors harassed woodcutters on detail, stole horses and cattle, and killed soldiers and civilian workers. Civil War veteran officers stationed at the fort were eager to engage the Indians and grew contemptuous of their commander, Colonel Henry Carrington, who saw the building of the fort as his task, not fighting Indians.

On December 21, 1866, Lieutenant Grummond joined Captain William J. Fetterman in pursuit of a sizable group of Sioux and Cheyenne warriors, who set a trap and ambushed the soldiers killing all eighty-one men before relief could arrive.

Margaret Carrington, the colonel's wife, took the pregnant and now widowed Fannie Grummond into her home as the garrison mourned and later left Fort Phil Kearny for Fort Caspar. After Fanny's son was born, she applied for an army pension but learned that Grummond had been previously married and had two children, whose mother had also applied for pensions. Even though the first union was not officially ended until twenty days after Grummond married Fanny, both marriages were ruled valid.

When Margaret Carrington died in 1870, Fannie wrote to Henry Carrington. They exchanged letters and were married in 1871. She finished her memoir, *My Army Life, A Soldier's Wife at Ft. Phil Kearney*, which resembles Margaret Carrington's *Absaraka, Home of the Crows*. Both books discuss the same events and feature Henry as the main character. The last third of Fannie's book reported the events of a 1908 reunion of individuals who had been at Fort Kearny during the Fetterman fight in which Grummond was killed. Fannie died in 1911 in Boston of tuberculosis. She is remembered for her writings, which inspired many to continue the work of settling the West.

Lenore Carroll

See also: Bozeman Trail; Cheyenne; Crazy Horse; Fort Phil Kearny (Wyoming); Red Cloud; Red Cloud's War; Sioux.

Further Reading

Carrington, Frances C. *My Army Life and the Fort Phil Kearney Massacre*. Lincoln: University of Nebraska Press, 2004.

Carrington, Margaret. *Absaraka, Home of the Crows*. Lincoln: University of Nebraska Press, 1983.

Monnett, John H. *Where a Hundred Soldiers Were Killed: The Struggle for the Powder River Country in 1866 and the Making of the Fetterman Myth*. Albuquerque: University of New Mexico Press, 2008.

Smith, Shannon D. *Give Me Eighty Men: Women and the Myth of the Fetterman Fight*. Lincoln: University of Nebraska Press, 2008.

Carson, Kit (1809–1868)

The Western counterpart of another frontier hero, Daniel Boone, Kit Carson was born on Christmas Eve, 1809, near Richmond, Kentucky, within a few miles of the fort and settlement that Boone founded in 1775. Kit's father, Lindsey Carson, a Revolutionary War veteran, moved with his family to Howard County, Missouri, in 1812 and, in 1823, Christopher (he was called Kit from childhood) became apprenticed to a saddle-maker in the settlement of Franklin.

In the summer of 1826, the sixteen-year-old Carson joined a trade caravan heading out on the Santa Fe Trail to Kansas, Colorado, and the adobe towns of the province of New Mexico. From Santa Fe he made his way to Taos, center of the fur trade in the Southwest, and there learned the crafts and survival methods of the mountain men. He worked as a dollar-a-day teamster on trade wagons and rode with his merchant-employers through Yaqui and Apache Indian country into Chihuahua, Mexico, where his facility in the Spanish language enabled him to serve as an interpreter.

In 1828 he joined the first of many California expeditions, traveling with a brigade of forty men led by veteran trapper Ewing Young, and returned to Taos in 1831. During the next decade he trapped throughout the Rocky Mountains, on the Platte, Sweetwater, Yellowstone, Snake, Bear, and Green rivers with such renowned mountain men as Thomas "Broken Hand" Fitzpatrick, Jim Bridger, and Joe Meek. For a time he worked as a trapper for the Hudson's Bay Company, partnered with Bridger on the Yellowstone and with fur trader Lucien Fontenelle on the Yellowstone, Gallatin, and Madison rivers of Montana.

Carson's reputation as an Indian fighter grew in forays against the Sioux and Blackfoot, implacable enemies of the white trapper-intruders, and against the Comanches in their tribal lands along the Arkansas River in Colorado. In 1838 Carson joined a trading expedition into Navajo country and worked for a time as a hunter out of Bent's Fort on the Arkansas River. In Missouri in 1842 he met John C. Frémont of the U.S. Army Corps of Topographical Engineers, then preparing the first of his four western explorations, and was hired as a guide at $100 a month. Carson's biographers like to point out that it was he who found the paths through the Rockies to Oregon and California for Frémont, the "Pathfinder." To Frémont's credit, when he wrote his memoirs in 1887, Carson was given credit not only for his work as guide and hunter but for his vast knowledge of Indian lore, his loyalty, courage, "frank speech and address," and his "prompt, self-sacrificing, and true" character.

In 1842 Carson led Frémont's mapping expedition through the South Pass of the Rockies and into the

THE YOUTH'S COMPANION HISTORIC MILESTONES

KIT CARSON · · HUNTER AND TRAPPER · · IMPLACABLE FOE OF HOSTILE INDIANS BUT FRIEND AND PROTECTOR OF THOSE THAT WERE PEACEFUL · · TRAIL MAKER · PATHFINDER · GUIDE · · INCOMPARABLE SCOUT AND LOYAL AND EFFICIENT SOLDIER · · THE LAST OF THE OLD FRONTIERS-MEN AND ONE OF THE GREATEST

Frontier scout, Indian fighter, trapper, guide, and soldier, Kit Carson became a legend in his own lifetime, his exploits dramatized in dime novels, magazines, songs, and poems. Carson could read none of them; he was illiterate. *(Library of Congress)*

Wind River Range. In the spring of 1843 he rejoined Frémont in exploring the Great Salt Lake and Great Basin, the party making a dangerous winter crossing of the Sierra Nevada, following the Oregon Trail to Fort Vancouver.

Between the end of the first expedition and the start of the second, Carson returned to Taos and, in February 1843, married Josefa Jaramillo, the fifteen-year-old sister-in-law of his friend Charles Bent of Bent's Fort. Kit had been twice married in Indian ceremonies—to an Arapaho girl in 1835 who died shortly after the birth of their daughter, and later to a Cheyenne woman—but Josefa was to be his life's partner, and their twenty-five-year marriage produced seven children. He built a cabin for her on the Little Cimarron River near Taos and started a small farming operation before he rejoined Frémont at Bent's Fort in the summer of 1845. By the time this expedition reached Sutter's Fort that November, the United States was poised for a war with Mexico.

Carson rode with Frémont in June 1846 in the capture of the Mexican garrison at Sonoma during the short-lived Bear Flag rebellion and in the subsequent march south to Monterey. He also served as General Stephen Watts Kearny's guide from New Mexico to California, fighting in the two battles en route to San Diego, at San Pasqual in December 1846 and the engagement on the San Gabriel River the following January that ended the conquest of California chapter of the Mexican-American War.

After the war, Carson engaged in farming operations in Rayado, New Mexico, while still serving as occasional guide and scout and joining trapping expeditions around the Southwest. During this calm period of his life Carson dictated his life story to a friend and the manuscript was used as the basis for an 1858 biography. He served as government agent to the Indians in northern New Mexico until the outbreak of the Civil War, and then resigned to become a colonel in the 1st New Mexico Volunteer Infantry. As an army officer he served at the Battle of Valverde in southern New Mexico in February 1862 in a long scorched-earth campaign against the Navajos (1863–1864), and in a military expedition in November 1864 against an estimated 5,000 Kiowas, Comanches, and Arapahos on the Canadian River. The significant battle of the campaign took place at an old trading post in the Texas Panhandle called Adobe Walls and resulted in Indian casualties of about 60 compared to 6 men killed and 25 wounded in Carson's force of 400 soldiers and Indian scouts.

After visits to Washington, New York, and Boston, Carson returned to New Mexico in April 1868, suffering from chest and neck pain and a chronic bronchial condition. He lived to see the birth of his and Josefa's seventh child, but his beloved wife died ten days later. He survived Josefa by exactly one month, dying of a cerebral hemorrhage on May 23, 1868, at Fort Lyon, Colorado, where he had gone for treatment of his lung problems. In January 1869, Carson and Josefa were reburied, side-by-side, in Taos.

Dale L. Walker

See also: California, Conquest of; Frémont, John C.; Long Walk; Navajo; Young, Ewing.

Further Reading

Carter, Harvey L. *"Dear Old Kit": The Historical Christopher Carson.* Norman: University of Oklahoma Press, 1968.

Dunlay, Thomas W. *Kit Carson and the Indians.* Lincoln: University of Nebraska Press, 2000.

Roberts, David. *A Newer World: Kit Carson, John C. Frémont and the Claiming of the American West.* New York: Simon & Schuster, 2000.

Sides, Hampton. *Blood and Thunder: The Epic Story of Kit Carson and the Conquest of the American West.* New York: Doubleday, 2006.

Cashman, Nellie
(c. 1850–1925)

Ellen (Nellie) Cashman was born in Queenstown, County Cork, Ireland, somewhere between 1850 and 1854. She stood just over five feet tall, with delicate features and luminous, dark eyes. She immigrated to the United States with her sister Fanny in the late 1860s. In 1869 the sisters headed west on the transcontinental railroad, and when Nellie's sister found a husband in San Francisco, Nellie moved on.

In 1872 she opened a short-order restaurant in Virginia City, Nevada. She moved to Tombstone, Arizona, months before the shoot-out in front of the OK Corral. From there, she joined the rush to the newly discovered gold fields in Upper British Columbia, where she staked a successful claim and ran a boardinghouse for other miners.

In her search for gold and silver Cashman struck pay dirt several times, but she spent most of her money helping those in need, from a Catholic hospital to individual prospectors down on their luck. She also canvassed friends, including "Black Jack," the doyen of Tombstone's populous flock of soiled doves. John Clum, the editor of the *Tombstone Epitaph,* wrote: "If she asked for a contribution—we contributed." When her sister Fanny died, Nellie took on the care of Fanny's five children. Cashman became known throughout the West as the Miners' Angel, the Saint of the Sourdoughs, and the Angel of the Camps. Several of those she helped went on to become influential men who grubstaked her in turn for her mining ventures.

For fifty years Cashman made her home in the boomtowns and mining camps of the West, from Mexico to Alaska. She even went to Africa in search of diamonds, but she preferred the wilderness north of the Arctic Circle. Stories of her exploits abound. In the middle of winter she hired six men to help her take 1,500 pounds (680 kg) of provisions to prospectors suffering from scurvy in northern Canada. A party of soldiers sent out to rescue her found her camped on the ice, cooking her evening meal by the heat of a wood fire and humming a lively tune. Later Cashman was involved in a ship's mutiny in Mexico. She joined the stampede across the treacherous Chilkoot Pass in Alaska. She even helped build boats to ride the Yukon River rapids to Dawson City, where she opened a restaurant, general store, and hotel. At almost seventy years of age, she drove a dog team, alone, 750 miles (1,200 km) across Alaska. She never married.

Nellie Cashman died in 1925, possibly of pneumonia, in a hospital her seemingly boundless energy had helped to build.

Lucia Robson

Further Reading

Clum, John P. *Nellie Cashman: The Angel of the Camp* (reprinted from the *Arizona Historical Review,* 1931).

Ledbetter, Suzann. *Nellie Cashman: Prospector and Trail Blazer.* El Paso: Texas Western Press, 1993.

Reiter, Joan Swallow. *The Women.* New York: Time-Life Books, 1978.

Catlin, George
(1796–1872)

George Catlin was a man born to a mission. Early in life, he had always been interested in Indians. Indeed, his mother, as a young girl, had been held captive by one of the Pennsylvania tribes, and perhaps the vivid stories she told when he was a small boy instilled in him his life-long curiosity about his wilderness neighbors.

Catlin was born on July 26, 1796, in Wilkes-Barre, Pennsylvania, when that part of the state was still close to the western frontier. Always restless, young Catlin had difficulty deciding what to do with his future. In 1818, he began the practice of law, but soon decided that his real interest was painting. He moved to Philadelphia in 1823 and opened a portrait studio, pursuing a form of art in which he was extremely talented. When he once observed a delegation of American Indians visiting government officials in the East, he realized what he wanted to do with his life, vowing then to visit and paint as many tribes in their own homelands as the remainder of his life would permit.

In 1830 Catlin visited St. Louis and accompanied William Clark to Prairie du Chien and Fort Crawford. Later, he toured Fort Leavenworth and painted among the Kansa villages located on the Kansas River. A year later, he was a guest among the Pawnee, Omaha, and Oto tribes, but it was in 1832, when he traveled far up the Missouri River aboard the American Fur Company's new steamboat, *Yellowstone,* that he saw his first really "pristine" Indians.

Now Catlin was in his own element. He painted Crows, Blackfoot, Sioux, and Mandans, all tribes that had experienced little exposure to the westward wanderings of Americans. In 86 days on this journey, Catlin painted 135 pictures ranging from portraits of chiefs to landscapes and natural scenes. Luckily, during the trip he documented the Mandan tribe, which a short time afterward was decimated by a smallpox epidemic. In 1834, he visited the Kiowa and the Comanche tribes and, the following year, he traveled to the upper Mississippi River homelands of the Ojibway, Sauk, Fox, and Eastern Sioux peoples.

After several seasons of painting west of the Mississippi, Catlin returned east and exhibited his work to the public. His art was only modestly received in the United States and abroad and, in time, he disposed of most of his paintings, which, fortunately for future generations, were purchased by the Smithsonian Institution. Catlin's value to fur trade history and the westward movement lies in the fact that he captured on canvas the looks and lifestyles of many tribes during the heyday of the trade period, just prior to the introduction of the white man's ways and customs. He died in Jersey City, New Jersey, on December 23, 1872.

James A. Crutchfield

See also: Bodmer, Karl; Disease; Mandan; Miller, Alfred Jacob.

Further Reading

Dippie, Brian W., Therese Thau Heyman, Christopher Mulvey, and Joan Carpenter Troccoli. *George Catlin and His Indian Gallery.* Washington, DC: Smithsonian American Art Museum, 2002.

McCracken, Harold. *George Catlin and the Old Frontier.* New York: Bonanza Books, 1959.

Cattle Brands

Ever since humans first conceived the notion of private property, they have placed some kind of identifying mark on their possessions. The Egyptians were branding cattle, for instance, as far back as 2,000 B.C.E., and, during the darkest days of U.S. history, when slavery was prevalent, brand markings were frequently used on men, women, and children.

The practice of branding cattle was already widespread in Europe in the fifteenth century when Columbus "discovered" America; years later, when Spanish conquistadors landed in Mexico, they brought brand-marked cattle with them. It was only a matter of time before the cattle moved northward with the adventurous Spanish, who often maintained large herds with them as they explored far and wide across New Spain. Later, Mexican *vaqueros* inherited the idea and, from them, Texas cowboys adopted the procedure, which proved particularly valuable for claiming the thousands of free-roaming feral cattle grazing the Texas landscape following the Civil War.

In the early days, the only permanent way to mark a cow was to burn the brand into the hide, usually on the left hip, which fortunately did not harm the animal. Cattle were also sometimes identified by earmarks, a unique design that was cut into one or both ears. Even today in the West, brands are important identification marks for livestock, including cattle, sheep, and horses; in some cases tattoos, freeze brands, metal tags in the animal's ear, earmarks, and even implanted microchips are used instead of and sometimes along with hot iron brands.

The number of brands developed and utilized over the years was as numerous as the owners who needed a way to identify their cattle, and the design of the marks was as varied as the vivid imaginations of the men who created them. One important rule was always followed when devising brands: the design of the mark should be difficult, if not impossible, to alter. Many are the tales of stolen cattle that had their marks "rebranded" with a similar, yet slightly different brand.

This type of brand altering—often accomplished with a single hot iron known as a running iron—was common among rustlers and led to some of the great range wars in the West.

Branding was done during the spring and fall roundups. Cowboys would ride far and wide gathering the newborn calves and branding them following the code of the West, where the calf was given the same brand as the cow it nursed. The procedure was clearly explained by America's cowboy-president, Theodore Roosevelt:

> A fire is built, the irons heated, and a dozen men dismount to, as it is called, "wrestle" the calves. The best two ropers go in on their horses to catch the latter; one man keeps tally, a couple put on the brands, and the others seize, throw, and hold the little unfortunates. A first-class roper invariably catches the calf by both hind feet, and then, having taken a twist with his lariat around the horn of the saddle, drags the bawling little creature, extended at full length, up to the fire, where it is held before it can make a struggle. . . . If there are seventy or eighty calves in a corral, the scene is one of the greatest confusion. The ropers, spurring and checking the fierce little horses, drag the calves up so quickly that a dozen men can hardly hold them; the men with the irons, blackened with soot, run to and fro; the calf-wrestlers, grimy with blood, dust and seat, work like beavers; while . . . the tallyman shouts out the number and sex of each calf. The dust rises in clouds, and the shouts, cheers, curses, and laughter of the men unite with the lowing of the cows and the frantic bleating of the calves to make a perfect babel.

As the number of brands increased in any particular state or territory, the job of maintaining them became quite laborious, and in some jurisdictions an elected official was responsible for recording and keeping up with the marks and their ownership. Brand marks often were published in a brand book, which was simply a directory of brands distributed by the local cattlemen's association. Stock producers also routinely published their brands in newspapers, giving notice to residents and landowners.

James A. Crutchfield

See also: Cattle Frontier; Open Range.

Further Reading

Arnold, Oren, and John P. Hale. *Hot Irons: Heraldry of the Range.* New York: Cooper Square, 1972.

Pelzer, Louis. *The Cattlemen's Frontier.* Glendale CA: Arthur H. Clark, 1936.

Roosevelt, Theodore. *Ranch Life and the Hunting Trail.* New York: Winchester Press, 1969.

Cattle Frontier

Cattle are not native to North America. The first cattle, along with the first horses, arrived in the Western Hemisphere in 1494 on Christopher Columbus's second voyage to the New World. The cattle frontier truly began in Mexico, where *vaqueros* worked cattle on large ranches, called *haciendas*, primarily in Chihuahua, Coahuila, Nuevo León, and Durango. The cattle range eventually spread northward, into today's New Mexico by 1598, to south and east Texas by the 1690s, and southern California a century later. Like the cattle, the *vaqueros*, and later American cowboys, adapted to the ranges.

Once Mexico declared its independence from Spain in 1821, white settlers in Texas slowly learned the methods of ranchers. One of those newcomers, Samuel Maverick, began farming and ranching in Matagorda County in the 1840s. Since the early days in New Spain, cattle had been branded as proof of ownership, but Maverick left many of his cattle, especially calves, unbranded. By the late 1850s, unbranded cattle were being called mavericks.

Up to the Civil War, cattle had been part of the rural culture in the eastern United States, but not on a large scale, and only Southerners had experience working cattle on horseback. After the war, that would change.

By 1865, with sirloin steaks selling in New York City for 25 to 35 cents a pound, Texas entrepreneurs realized the wealth to be had if they could get cattle to those markets. Plus, many maverick cattle roamed across the state, more or less free for the taking. Cattle were rounded up, branded, and empires were born.

The era of the long cattle drives thus began. Cattle had been herded to shipping points well before the Civil War, but never in such numbers as cowboys drove Texas Longhorns north to the railroads at Sedalia, Missouri, or Baxter Springs, Kansas. Within a few years, other trails, such as the Chisholm and the Western, brought Longhorns from southern Texas to Kansas cow towns such as Abilene, Ellsworth, Newton, Wichita, Caldwell, and Dodge City. These cattle markets moved westward with the railroads and to comply with quarantine lines established to prevent Texas fever, often fatal to northern cattle and spread by Longhorns immune to the tick-borne disease.

Cowboys were hired to work cattle on the ranches and drive herds to railheads or other pastures. An estimated one-third of those hired hands were African Americans, predominantly former slaves, and a somewhat larger proportion were of Mexican descent, especially in the

CATTLE MEN READ THIS!

Great Inducements to those who wish to

Ship Cattle on the U. P. Railroad !!

Having entered into special arrangements with the U. P. R. R. Company, by which I can ship Cattle East at greatly reduced rates, and having selected a point between Carter and Church Buttes Stations some ten miles East of the former place, near the junction of the Big and Little Muddies, and having Constructed Commodious Lots and Extensive Enclosures, and the Company having put in a Switch capable of holding 40 Cars, I will be Prepared to Commence Shipping on or before the 15th of the Present Month, and will be able to promptly ship any Number of cattle that may be Offered.

Persons driving Cattle from Montana and Idaho, and passing by Soda Springs and the Bear Lake Settlements, will cross over from Bear River to the head of Little Muddy and follow down that stream, over a good road, to within a mile and a half of the junction of the Little with the Big Muddy, where they will cross a bridge and find a rich pasture, extending many miles; good water & perfect security for their stock, within convenient distance of the stock yards.

The cattle yards are in an enclosure of some 400 acres, and stock scales and all conveniences for shipping will be furnished. If parties do not wish to ship themselves, I will purchase, at good prices, all shipping cattle that may be offered. As cattle are now bearing excellent prices East, it would be well for persons to bring their Cattle forward as soon as possible.

For further particulars, address

W. A. CARTER,
Fort Bridger, Wyo. Ter.

Fort Bridger, July 2, 1877.

W. G. Jay
Clerk, Operating
Ogden, Utah.

An ad for the Union Pacific Railroad at Fort Bridger, Wyoming Territory, seeks cattle for shipment east in 1877. The establishment of railheads on the western frontier prompted the great cattle drives of the 1860s to 1880s. *(The Granger Collection, New York)*

Southwest. Although eventually glorified by pulp novels and movies, the work of the cowboy was far from glamorous. On a trail drive, a cowboy would be likely to work eighteen hours a day, seven days a week, in all types of weather, for maybe a dollar a day and meals. Profanity became a staple of their language.

The cattle frontier spread out of Texas, especially after Indian tribes were subjugated, opening rangelands across the West. Texas cattlemen Charles Goodnight and Oliver Loving blazed a cattle trail into New Mexico and Colorado territories. Other routes brought cattle to Nebraska, Wyoming, Montana, and the Dakotas. John Chisum established a sprawling ranch along the Pecos River in New Mexico, running more than 100,000 head of cattle. John Slaughter, who had learned the cattle business from *vaqueros*, started a ranch in southern Arizona. Goodnight eventually operated ranches in southern Colorado and in the Texas Panhandle. The Swan Land and Cattle Company made Alex Swan one of the largest landowners in Wyoming. Rufus Thompson Buell arrived in California and carved a cattle and horse ranch, along with a dairy farm, out of the former Rancho San Carlos de Jonata land grant. In the Texas Panhandle, the XIT Ranch covered 3 million acres (1.2 million ha), while ranchers Conrad Kohrs and Granville Stuart controlled millions of acres in Montana.

Books such as James S. Brisbin's *Beef Bonanza* (1881), Major W. Shepherd's *Prairie Experiences in Handling Cattle and Sheep* (1884), and Walter Baron von Richthofen's *Cattle-Raising on the Plains of North America* (1885) glamorized the industry and encouraged foreigners to invest heavily in American ranches.

With the boom, however, came violence. Before the Taylor Grazing Act of 1934 regulated grazing on public lands, ranchers fought farmers, sheepherders, or other ranchers for water and/or grazing rights. Some ranchers lynched rustlers and horse thieves. In 1889 powerful Wyoming ranchers hanged Ellen Liddy "Cattle Kate" Watson and homesteader Jim Averill, charging them with rustling without the benefit of a trial. Range wars erupted in Pleasant Valley, Arizona, from 1886 to 1892, and in Johnson County, Wyoming, in 1892. Cow towns saw their share of bloodshed, too, although probably not as frequently or as violently as depicted in Western films and fiction.

Despite fluctuating markets, the beef bonanza lasted until the disastrous winter of 1886–1887 left thousands of cattle dead and many ranches bankrupt. Yet the cattle frontier brought significant improvements in agrarian practices, too. Windmills and barbed wire were introduced. Fenced pastures replaced vast open range. Seeing a need to improve beef, ranchers introduced breeds such as the Angus, Brahma, and Hereford. In the early 1900s at the King Ranch in Texas, Shorthorn cows were bred with Brahma bulls, resulting in the Santa Gertrudis, which the U.S. Department of Agriculture recognized as a purebred in 1940.

The cattle frontier has never faded in the West. Although always a gamble, ranching remains a vibrant industry throughout the United States, with current cattle and calf production valued at $35.7 billion.

Johnny D. Boggs

See also: Barbed Wire; Chisholm Trail; Goodnight, Charles; Goodnight-Loving Trail; Johnson County War; Open Range; Texas Trail; Western Trail.

Further Reading

Abbott, E.C. "Teddy Blue." In *We Pointed Them North: Recollections of a Cowpuncher*. Norman: University of Oklahoma Press, 1939.

Dary, David. *Cowboy Culture: A Saga of Five Centuries*. New York: Alfred A. Knopf, 1991.

McCoy, Joseph G. *Historic Sketches of the Cattle Trade of the West and Southwest*. Columbus, OH: Long's College Book Company, 1951.

Central Pacific Railroad

The Central Pacific Railroad was the western segment of America's first transcontinental railroad. It stretched eastward from Sacramento through Nevada and finally to Utah, meeting with the Union Pacific line at Promontory Summit in 1869. The feat of traversing the rugged Sierra Nevada was one of the greatest engineering and management accomplishments of the nineteenth century.

The Central Pacific was organized in California in 1861. Theodore Judah, a rail engineer who had surveyed a passage through California's Sierra Nevada mountain range, sought to forge a railroad that would use this route as part of a transcontinental line uniting the west coast of America with the rest of the nation, a dream that consumed him.

Judah initially looked for financial supporters in San Francisco, to no avail. He then solicited support in Sacramento, where he finally secured a partnership composed primarily of a handful of businessmen who would create the line. They were led by the "Big Four": Leland Stanford, Mark Hopkins, Collis Huntington, and Charles Crocker. The viability of the fledgling railroad was bolstered in July 1862 when President Abraham Lincoln signed the Pacific Railroad Act, authorizing a transcontinental railroad that would join the Central Pacific with the Union Pacific Railroad. Construction of the Central Pacific commenced in 1863.

Although the two railroads received handsome loans and land subsidies from the federal government, initial progress was slow. The Civil War was consuming labor, materials, investment monies, and the attention of the country. Conflicts between Judah and the Big Four, as well as challenges presented by the imposing Sierra Nevada, also limited progress of the rail line eastward. By the end of the Civil War in April 1865, roughly 50 miles (80 km) of track had been built by the Central Pacific.

Despite unusually severe winter weather in the next several years, the Central Pacific was able to forge its rail tracks ahead at an increasing pace. Charles Crocker, Samuel Montague, and James Strobridge, who had assumed the railroad's engineering and construction duties after the death of Judah in 1863, poured huge amounts of labor, much of it performed by Chinese immigrants, into the building effort. Meanwhile, Collis Huntington essentially cornered the market for iron rails, sending them to California on a fleet of merchant ships chartered by Central Pacific. Wagon roads were built parallel to the future railroad tracks, and work trains were assembled and run to supply the thousands of workers with the food, water, and materials they needed to continually grade the right-of-way and lay tracks. Timber for ties was harvested in the mountains being traversed, tons of snow were cleared by armies of shoveling workers, and engineering and technical innovations and solutions were invented along the way as the tracks reached around, through, and over the mountains of California and western Nevada.

Once the major mountains were cleared, the Central Pacific undertook an all-out race with the Union Pacific. Every mile completed meant more land and financial subsidies and incentives for the Central line rather than the Union Pacific. The company surveyed, graded, and established right-of-way well ahead of actual line construction in order to claim and hold additional miles. Between 1867 and 1869, the Central Pacific completed nearly 600 miles (965 km) of line, at one point laying down more than 10 miles (16 km) in a single day. The two railroads' locomotives touched noses on May 10, 1869. Ceremonial spikes were driven home, and America united its coasts with a single band of rails, completing the transcontinental railroad.

The Central Pacific hoped to reap a bonanza of financial rewards from this momentous undertaking. It completed a line from Sacramento to San Francisco and, by the acquisition of several California railroads and additional construction, built a solid infrastructure of rail lines throughout the state. Financial prosperity, while not immediate, eventually made the Big Four and other investors wealthy. In 1885 the Central Pacific was leased to the Southern Pacific Railroad, which operated the line under its auspices until 1959, when the two lines merged into a new entity called the Southern Pacific. Ultimately, in a move laden with historical irony, the Union Pacific acquired the Southern Pacific Railroad in 1996, making it the largest railroad company in the United States. Once bitter rivals, the Central Pacific and Union Pacific are now united organizationally, echoing the physical union that was marked by a golden spike at Promontory, Utah, in 1869.

James Ersfeld

See also: Chinese Immigration; End-of-Tracks Towns; Judah, Theodore D.; Judah Survey; Pacific Railway Act (1862); Railroad Land Grants.

Further Reading

Kraus, George. *High Road to Promontory: Building the Central Pacific across the High Sierra.* Palo Alto, CA: American West, 1969.

Charbonneau, Jean Baptiste (1804–1866)

Jean Baptiste Charbonneau was born at Fort Mandan on February 11, 1804. His father and mother, Toussaint Charbonneau and Sacagawea, had recently joined the Lewis and Clark Expedition as interpreters for the journey up the Missouri River exploring the Louisiana Territory. Expedition leader William Clark was especially protective and fond of the infant during the trip, nicknaming him "Pomp," after the Roman emperor Pompey. While his father Toussaint was one of the oldest members of the expedition at age forty-five, Jean Baptiste certainly was the youngest.

Following the expedition, Jean Baptiste's parents took him to St. Louis to live with William Clark, at Clark's request, to be educated. Under Clark's sponsorship, Jean Baptiste attended the St. Louis Academy, learning to speak English and French. He was also schooled in history, classical literature, science, and mathematics. In 1823 eighteen-year-old Jean Baptiste met Prince Paul Wilhelm of Wurttemberg, who had come to North America on a natural history expedition financed by his uncle, King Frederick of Germany. The prince invited Jean Baptiste to return to Germany with him, and for the next six years young Charbonneau traveled throughout Europe and Africa, learning to speak four more languages while residing in the royal German household.

Returning to America in 1829, Jean Baptiste also returned to the wilderness. He became a hunter and trapper in present-day Utah and Idaho, served as an army scout, and accompanied explorers such as Jim Bridger and Jim Beckwourth on many of their expeditions. In 1846 he was the guide for the Mormon Battalion on its journey from Santa Fe to San Diego during the Mexican-American War. He remained in California and served briefly as the mayor of the town of Mission San Luis Rey. During the California gold rush of 1849, Charbonneau worked claims along the American River near Sacramento without success. After nearly ten years of fruitless searching for gold, and despite his previous education, he was forced to clerk in a hotel in Auburn, California, in order to survive.

In 1866, while on his way to newly discovered gold fields in Montana to seek his fortune, Jean Baptiste Charbonneau died of bronchial pneumonia near a place called Inskip Station in Oregon. He was sixty-one years old.

Rod Timanus

See also: Charbonneau, Toussaint; Clark, William; Fort Mandan; Lewis, Meriwether; Lewis and Clark Expedition; Sacagawea.

Further Reading

Ritter, Michael L. *Jean Baptiste Charbonneau, Man of Two Worlds.* Charleston, SC: BookSurge, 2004.

Charbonneau, Toussaint (1759–1840)

Toussaint Charbonneau, the consort of Sacagawea of Lewis and Clark Expedition fame, was born in 1759 near Montreal, Canada. In his middle years, about 1796, he began to live among the Indians, primarily the Hidatsa and Mandan tribes, as a fur trapper and hunter in what is now North Dakota. By 1804 he had acquired, either through purchase or as winnings in a game of chance, two Shoshone women to serve as companions or slaves, Sacagawea and Otter Woman. When the Lewis and Clark Expedition arrived at the Mandan village where Charbonneau was living at the time, he hired on as an interpreter for the Corps of Discovery. With Sacagawea and their infant son, Jean Baptiste, he traveled to the Pacific Ocean and back with the expedition. Except for his occasional cooking skills, Charbonneau was not very highly regarded by the two leaders in their journals as a very productive member of the group, and Captain William Clark once reprimanded him for striking Sacagawea in a fit of anger.

When the expedition returned to the Mandan village in 1806, Charbonneau collected his pay and stayed behind while the rest of the group went back to St. Louis. In 1809 he and Sacagawea traveled to St. Louis to collect a land bounty owed him for his services on the expedition and to leave his young son in the care of William Clark so that the child might get a formal education. Charbonneau tried his hand at farming his land, but soon tired of the enterprise and returned to the West in 1811, where he took employment with the Missouri Fur Company. According to some sources, Sacagawea died in 1812, shortly after giving birth to Charbonneau's second child at Manuel Lisa's Fort, in today's South Dakota, where Charbonneau was working at the time. The next year, Charbonneau also sent his infant daughter, Lisette, to live with Clark.

Over the next several years Charbonneau was employed by the U.S. government as an interpreter for many expeditions to the upper Missouri River. He provided services for foreign dignitaries and government officials visiting the area of the Mandan village where he continued to live. Charbonneau died in 1840 at the age of eighty.

Rod Timanus

See also: Charbonneau, Jean Baptiste; Clark, William; Lewis, Meriwether; Lewis and Clark Expedition; Sacagawea.

Further Reading

Morris, Larry E. *The Fate of the Corps: What Became of the Lewis and Clark Explorers After the Expedition.* New Haven: Yale University Press, 2004.

Cherokee

As far back as anyone knows, there was no Cherokee Nation, but rather individual, autonomous Cherokee towns, bound together by common language, culture, and clans. The towns were scattered over all or parts of the present-day states of North Carolina, South Carolina, Tennessee, Kentucky, Georgia, Alabama, Virginia, and West Virginia. The language was

A silversmith, trader, and native warrior, Sequoyah invented an eighty-five-character script—or syllabary—for the Cherokee language, making reading and writing possible. The syllabary helped unify the Cherokee people and aided their efforts to resist removal. *(Library of Congress)*

Iroquoian, spoken by the Mohawk, Oneida, Onondaga, and Tuscarora tribes. "Cherokee" is not a Cherokee word. The people today known as the Cherokees originally called themselves either *Ani-yunwiya* (the Real People) or *Ani-Kituwagi* (Keetoowah People). Keetoowah is said to have been the original Cherokee town out of which all other towns grew.

The Cherokees have several clans. Most of what would be considered legal matters—matters for courts to decide today—were in the old Cherokee days matters for the clans to consider. Clan law was the basis of Cherokee society. It was the glue that held everything together. Cherokee clans were matrilineal, meaning that an individual's descent was traced strictly through the female line.

Affairs began to change for the Cherokees when English traders arrived and settled among them, beginning in 1673. In a short time there were mixed-blood Cherokee families, and the Englishmen became the heads of their families. Mixed-blood Cherokee children took their white fathers' surnames. The power and influence of Cherokee women were seriously undermined. The Cherokees, like other nations, became dependent on European trade goods and embroiled in European power struggles. At times, these power struggles caused divisions among the Cherokees.

One great change came about when the English, frustrated by trying to deal with individual Cherokee towns, urged the Cherokees to appoint an "emperor." The Cherokees complied, thinking of the new officeholder as a trade commissioner rather than a ruler. The role of the trade commissioner or emperor eventually evolved into the role of "President of the Nation" or principal chief.

During the American Revolution, a significant number of Cherokees joined the British in fighting against the American rebels. They did so because the British were trying to keep the colonists in the colonies and off of Indian land. When the Revolution concluded, these Cherokees, under the leadership of Dragging Canoe, also known as Chickamaugas, continued the fight, but the British ceased supplying them with arms. Then, with the death of Dragging Canoe, the movement slowly fell apart, and new treaties were signed.

The government of the Cherokee Nation continued to formalize, and when the U.S. government's removal policy went into effect in the 1820s, the Cherokee Nation opposed it in the courts. The Cherokees also outlined opposition by influencing public opinion. Nevertheless, the Nation was removed in 1838 to present-day northeast Oklahoma. Following Cherokee involvement in the Civil War and the area's organization into Indian Territory, the Cherokee Nation was all but dissolved in 1907 when Oklahoma became a state. In 1973 the Cherokee Nation was revitalized, with new elections and a new constitution. Today it is a thriving American Indian nation.

Robert J. Conley

See also: Cherokee Wars; Chickasaw; Choctaw; Creek; Indian Removal Act (1830); Jackson's Indian Policy; Trail of Tears.

Further Reading

Conley, Robert J. *The Cherokee Nation: A History.* Albuquerque: University of New Mexico Press, 2005.

Cherokee Trail

The Cherokee Trail from Fort Gibson (on the Texas Trail) to Fort Bridger became the major thoroughfare to the West from Arkansas, southwestern Missouri, East Texas, and the Cherokee Nation. Approximately 900 miles (1,450 km) in length, the trail today is the longest branch of the California National Historic Trail. An estimated 25,000 to 35,000 people (10 to 15 percent of the total western migration) and approximately 100,000 head of livestock traveled over this trail before 1861. The longest Texas cattle drives recorded were made by Arkansas cowboys to California and by Mormons to Utah.

In April 1849, a combined wagon train of California gold seekers from Washington County, Arkansas, and the Cherokee Nation, captained by Lewis Evans, left the Grand Saline crossing of the Grand (Neosho) River. Traveling northwest, blazing the first wagon road through present-day Oklahoma and south central Kansas, they struck the Santa Fe Trail near what is now Galva. The train proceeded west along the Arkansas River to Bent's Old Fort and on to Pueblo, Colorado. Traveling north along the front range of the Rocky Mountains to Elk Mountain, Wyoming, the train turned west to cross the North Platte River, north to today's Rawlins, Wyoming, west across the Red and Great Divide deserts to the Green River, and on to Fort Bridger to join the main California Trail.

In the spring of 1850, four separate Cherokee-white wagon trains (two from Arkansas, one from southwestern Missouri, and one from the Cherokee Nation) followed Evans's route to the South Platte crossing at present-day Denver. In 1858 members of this train and others returned to start the Pike's Peak gold rush. On entering the Laramie Plains, the trains turned west (just north of the border), constructing a wagon road over the fur-trader route to Fort Davy Crockett. Rafting the Green River at the current Buckboard crossing, the trains proceeded to Fort Bridger.

By 1851 Cherokees were driving cattle to California. In 1852 emigrations to Oregon and California continued, and in 1854 Texas cattle were driven to California and Mormons were migrating to Utah. The trail continued in use in 1859 as gold seekers went to Pike's Peak and in 1864 as gold seekers migrated from Colorado to Idaho and Montana. The Cherokee Trail, named in 1859 by both Lieutenant Randolph Marcy and surveyors of Kansas Territory, had by 1854 become the major north-south road. The route had toll ferries over several rivers: one on the Cache La Poudre, two on the North Platte (1849 and 1850 crossings), and two on the Green River (1849 and 1850 crossings). The traffic on the eastern Cherokee Trail gave rise to Fuller's post office and ranch in 1855 and the settlement of El Dorado, Kansas, in 1857.

Numerous jumping-off places, branches, and cutoffs evolved over the life of the trail. Early cutoffs included the Sweetwater from Rawlins north to the Sweetwater River; Lodgepole (Pole Creek) from the South Platte through the Black Hills to the Cherokee Trail at the Little Laramie River; and Bridger Pass from the North Platte to Bitter Creek, surveyed and built by the U.S. Army from 1856 to 1858 and used heavily by emigrants, cattle drovers, and the military from 1859 on. In May 1860, Denver's *Rocky Mountain News* published a guide titled "Route from Denver to Fort Bridger, via Cherokee Trail" over Bridger Pass. In 1862 the Overland Stage and Mail moved its route from the beset South Pass route to the well-used Cherokee Trail. Through the years this Bridger Pass route became known as the Overland Trail. The last documented overland emigrant wagon went over Bridger Pass in 1898.

The Smoky Hill Trail, the most direct route west to the Pikes Peak goldfields, has two of its three branches striking and coming west on the Cherokee Trail into Denver. Many Cherokee Trail remains can be seen today.

Patricia Fletcher and Jack Fletcher

See also: California Trail; Fort Bridger; Overland Trail.

Further Reading

Worcester, Don, ed. *Pioneer Trails West.* Caldwell, ID: Caxton Printers, 1985.

Cherokee Wars

Cherokees first met the English in 1673 at the Cherokee town of Chota on the Little Tennessee River. The English were quick to note that the main occupation of the Cherokees was war. There was no central Cherokee government; each Cherokee town was autonomous. At the time, the Cherokees were engaged in intermittent warfare with the Catawbas, Shawnees, Tuscaroras, and other Indian tribes.

Trade relations were established quickly with the English colonies, and in 1740 1,000 Cherokees joined Georgia colonists to fight the Spaniards at St. Augustine. About 1754 Cherokees joined Virginia to fight the French. Two years later, a group of Cherokees returning home through Virginia was attacked by local settlers, who killed twenty-four of the Indians. The Virginians possibly mistook the Cherokees for other Indians since the colonial governor was paying bounties on scalps of enemy Indians. The angry Cherokees then retaliated against the settlers, causing the British to retaliate in force.

In 1760 Colonel Archibald Montgomery invaded the Cherokee country with a battalion of Highlanders and four companies of Royal Scots, burning many of the towns and killing sixty Cherokees and taking forty prisoners. From there he marched into the Cherokee Overhill country (now East Tennessee), intending both to punish the Indians and relieve Fort Loudoun, a nearby British fortification that was under siege by the Cherokees. Montgomery was met by a large force of Cherokees who ambushed him in a deep valley. Admitting defeat, the colonel retreated to Charlestown, leaving Fort Loudoun to its inevitable fate: surrender on August 8, 1760.

In 1761 Colonel James Grant went into the Cherokee country seeking revenge. He destroyed fifteen towns and 1,500 acres (600 ha) of farmland, sending 5,000 Cherokees into the hills homeless and destitute. Eventually, Attacullaculla, the great Cherokee diplomat, negotiated a peace at Charlestown, South Carolina.

In 1775 Cherokees under the leadership of Attacullaculla and Oconostota met at Sycamore Shoals in what is now upper East Tennessee to negotiate the sale of most of contemporary Kentucky and much of Middle Tennessee to the Transylvania Company. The deal was struck, but Dragging Canoe and his followers strongly objected. When the American Revolution broke out shortly afterward, Dragging Canoe and his men, who came to be known as Chickamaugas, allied themselves with Great Britain and fought against the Americans.

In July 1776, the Cherokee chief, Old Abram, and his followers were defeated by settlers at Island Flats, near present-day Elizabethton, Tennessee. By 1779 conditions among the East Tennesseans were so unbearable that Virginia governor Patrick Henry ordered the destruction of every Cherokee village known to harbor offending Indians. Evan Shelby's surprise attack upon the towns inhabited by Dragging Canoe and his followers sent 500 warriors fleeing.

After the site of Nashville, 200 miles (320 km) to the west, was settled in 1779–1780, the Cherokee menace, aggravated by other warring tribes in the region, continued. For more than a decade, the settlers of the middle Cumberland River valley lived in fear of almost monthly reprisals by the local tribes. Finally, in 1794, Nashvillians, upon the order of General James Robertson, mounted a war party and decimated several Cherokee towns along the Tennessee River in today's Chattanooga area. A permanent peace was at last established with the warring tribes. The Cherokee Nation never again went to war against the United States.

The Cherokee Nation became embroiled in the U.S. Civil War, with Cherokees fighting on both sides. Stand Watie, in charge of Confederate Cherokee forces, was among the last of the Confederate leadership to surrender.

Robert J. Conley

See also: Attacullaculla; Cherokee; Nashville; Watauga Settlements.

Further Reading

Conley, Robert J. *The Cherokee Nation: A History*. Albuquerque: University of New Mexico Press, 2005.

Woodward, Grace Steele. *The Cherokees*. Norman: University of Oklahoma Press, 1963.

Cheyenne

A tribe of the Algonquian linguistic family, the Cheyennes were militantly opposed to white expansion in Indian lands and were involved in many of the violent white versus Indian conflicts of the West in the period between the Civil War (1861–1865) and the early 1880s.

While remembered as buffalo-hunting horsemen of the Great Plains, the Cheyennes and their close allies, the Arapahos, were farmers with stable villages in northern Minnesota from the mid- to the late eighteenth century. The introduction of the horse in western America by the Spanish changed the lives of the Cheyennes, transforming them in the space of less than a century from obscure farm folk to nomadic buffalo hunters, fierce horseback warriors, and one of the major tribes of the western Plains.

Both the Cheyenne and Arapaho people, after conflicts with the Sioux and Chippewa tribes of the Upper Mississippi, migrated across the Missouri River. With the building of Bent's Fort on the Arkansas River in 1833, a segment of the Cheyenne populace moved south to settle on the Arkansas, becoming known as the Southern Cheyenne, while the remainder of the tribe, the Northern Cheyenne, continued a nomadic life in the North Platte–Yellowstone River region. The division of the Cheyennes was made official by the Fort Laramie Treaty of 1851.

The 1860s and 1870s were a bloody period in which the tribe was tested time and again against the encroaching American settlers. While making peace with erstwhile foes such as the Sioux, Kiowas, and Comanches, the Cheyennes were relentless enemies of white trespassers on Indian lands and of the state and federal troops that protected the invaders.

While the Cheyennes fought against settlers in Texas, Colorado, Kansas, and Nebraska in these critical years, retaliatory atrocities by United States and state military forces overshadowed the Cheyenne raids. The most egregious of these atrocities was the Sand Creek Massacre near Fort Lyon, Colorado. On November 29, 1864, a force of several hundred Colorado militia volunteers attacked a sleeping Cheyenne-Arapaho village under Chief Black Kettle. The militiamen, commanded by Colonel John M. Chivington, killed and mutilated at least 150 people in the encampment, including women and children.

The Medicine Lodge Treaty of 1867 relocated the Southern Cheyenne, Arapaho, Comanche, and Kiowa tribes to reservations in Indian Territory, yet the bloodshed was far from over. On November 27, 1868, an attack by the U.S. 7th Cavalry under Lieutenant Colonel George A. Custer killed Black Kettle and sixty other Cheyennes at their winter camp on the Washita River in Indian Territory. Reports of Cheyenne casualties ranged from 30 to100, including noncombatants.

The Cheyennes took part in the Red River War of 1874–1875 with other tribes of the southern plains— Kiowa and Comanche—crossing the Red River into Texas and being soundly defeated by army regulars. The Cheyennes aided the Sioux at the Battle of Rosebud Creek in Montana on June 17, 1876, and at the culminating battle of the Little Bighorn River eight days later.

In 1878 the Northern Cheyenne made a final act of resistance when Little Wolf, Dull Knife, and 300 others of the tribe, mostly noncombatants, escaped the reservation in Indian Territory and made a dash north toward their Montana homelands. Many were captured and confined at Fort Robinson, Nebraska; in a desperate attempt to escape on the night of January 9, 1879, sixty-four of the prisoners were killed.

The modern Northern Cheyenne reservation is at Lame Deer, Montana, and the Southern Cheyenne share a reservation with the Southern Arapaho in Oklahoma.

Dale L. Walker

See also: Arapaho; Bent's Fort; Black Kettle; Chivington, John M.; Comanche; Custer, George Armstrong; Dull Knife; Fort Robinson; Kiowa; Medicine Lodge, Treaty of (1867); Red Cloud's War; Sand Creek Massacre; Sioux; Washita Engagement.

Further Reading

Berthrong, Donald J. *The Southern Cheyennes.* Norman: University of Oklahoma Press, 1963.
Fowler, Loretta. *The Arapaho* (Indians of North America series). New York: Chelsea House, 1989.
Grinnell, George Bird. *The Cheyenne Indians: Their History and Ways of Life.* 2 vols. New Haven: Yale University Press, 1923.
———. *The Fighting Cheyennes.* New York: Scribner's, 1915.
Sandoz, Mari. *Cheyenne Autumn.* New York: McGraw-Hill, 1953.

Cheyenne-Deadwood Trail

The discovery of gold in the Black Hills of Dakota Territory in the early 1870s created the need for good trails to transport goods, equipment, and people to Deadwood and other Black Hills mining camps. The first and one of the most important trails to the Black Hills region was the Cheyenne-Deadwood Trail.

There had always been rumors of gold in the streams of the region, but the Black Hills, or *Paha Sapa*, as the Lakota Indians named them, were part of the Great Sioux Reservation reserved for the Lakota and other tribes and off-limits to whites. In 1874 Lieutenant Colonel George A. Custer led a military and scientific expedition into the Black Hills searching for a good location for a future fort and potential gold deposit sites in the area. Some of the men found gold dust in French Creek in the southern mountains. Custer sent one of his scouts, "Lonesome Charlie" Reynolds,

Reports of a gold strike led to the founding of Deadwood, Dakota Territory, in 1876 and a trail that connected it with Cheyenne, Wyoming Territory. Deadwood became notorious as the site of the murder of Wild Bill Hickok. *(Fotosearch/Stringer/Getty Images)*

southwest to Fort Laramie, Wyoming, with news of the gold discovery. Lonesome Charlie quickly spread the word and prospectors began to enter the Black Hills illegally.

Many prospectors rode the Union Pacific Railroad to Cheyenne, Wyoming. From Cheyenne they traveled the established trail to Fort Laramie and beyond to Red Cloud Agency, located in current northwest Nebraska at the southern edge of the Black Hills. The military attempted to stem the mad rush to the mountains, but to no avail. From Red Cloud Agency and later following a more direct route by way of Raw Hide Buttes, the prospectors headed to the new boomtown of Custer on French Creek in the Black Hills.

In August 1875, gold was discovered on Whitewood Creek in the northern mountains and the town of Deadwood soon sprang into existence. Giving up its attempt to keep people out, the government tried to buy the Black Hills from the Lakotas.

The route from Cheyenne naturally extended beyond Custer to Deadwood along three branches—one to the east circled the mountains to the north, the central branch followed stream valleys and cut across ridges in the central region, and the western route circled the mountains to the north. Men constantly worked to improve the trail and find new shortcuts. On August 25, 1877, Captain W.A. Stanton, chief engineer with the army's Department of the Platte, finished his survey of the most direct route of the Cheyenne-Deadwood trail, measuring it as 266 miles (428 km) long from Cheyenne to the Deadwood Post Office. Along the trail

were road ranches where horses could be changed and travelers could buy a meal and a drink.

Travelers along the trail walked, went on horseback, or rode in wagons or stages. Two of the most famous Old West characters who traveled the Cheyenne to Deadwood trail were Wild Bill Hickok and Calamity Jane Cannary. The Cheyenne and Black Hills Stage, Mail, and Express Company began transporting people to the Black Hills in January 1876, with the first Concord stagecoach arriving in Deadwood on September 25; after that, regular stage service was established to that town. Teamsters, also called bullwhackers because of the long whips they swung and cracked in the air over their draft animals, brought goods to the mountains in freight wagons hooked together and pulled by massed teams of oxen or mules.

The trail often was treacherous. Rains turned the route into a quagmire of mud. Drifting snow brought traffic to a halt. People traveled the route under constant threat of attack from Native American tribes. The Lakotas, not happy with the incursions of whites into their territory, attacked parties traveling the trail, often resulting in murder and robbery. Lawless whites also preyed on travelers, especially targeting gold shipments from the mountains. Special wagons were constructed with plate iron to withstand robberies, and armed guards riding shotgun were hired to protect the shipments, but at times, these were no match for ingenious bandits. Robbers were able to stop and rob two famous armored stages, the Monitor and Old Ironsides.

In 1886 the construction of railroads to the Black Hills began. On February 19, 1887, the last stage left Cheyenne for Deadwood, bringing a colorful era to a close.

Bill Markley

See also: Black Hills Expeditions; Custer, George Armstrong; Custer Expedition; Fort Laramie; Fort Laramie, Treaty of (1868); Lakota; Sioux.

Further Reading

Brown, Jesse, and A.M. Willard. *The Black Hills Trails: A History of the Struggles of the Pioneers in the Winning of the Black Hills.* Rapid City, SD: Rapid City Journal, 1924.

Parker, Watson. *Gold in the Black Hills.* Pierre: South Dakota State Historical Society Press, 2003.

Spring, Agnes Wright. *The Cheyenne and Black Hills Stage and Express Routes.* Lincoln: University of Nebraska Press, 1948.

Tallent, Annie D. *The Black Hills, or Last Hunting Grounds of the Dakotahs.* Sioux Falls, SD: Brevet Press, 1974.

Chickasaw

The Chickasaw Indians, a Muskogean-speaking tribe, were natives of today's northern Mississippi. They claimed lands as far north as the western portions of the current states of Tennessee and Kentucky.

Before Memphis was founded in the early nineteenth century, the site was known as Chickasaw Landing. As one of the so-called Five Civilized Tribes that was affected early on in the nation's history by various Indian Removal acts, the tribe's population of approximately 4,000 citizens and 1,000 slaves experienced the full brunt of American expansion.

The Chickasaws and their southern neighbors, the Choctaws, were linguistically related and often intermarried. Most authorities believe that at some time in the distant past, the two tribes were one. Tribal traditions of both peoples relate that they migrated to present-day Mississippi from west of the Mississippi River and that the two tribes separated at a place called Nanih Waiya, literally, the hill of origins, located in Winston County, Mississippi. From there, so the ancient stories go, the two populations went separate ways to claim their neighboring homelands. The Chickasaws established their capital in the region surrounding modern-day Tupelo, Mississippi, in an area they called "Old Fields."

During America's colonial period, the Chickasaws demonstrated antagonism toward French administrators in the lower Mississippi River valley and, in early 1736, they decisively defeated a large French and Choctaw army led from New Orleans by Jean-Baptist le Moyne, Sieur de Bienville, the brother of French Louisiana's governor. The tribe maintained a strong loyalty to the British, however, but after the establishment of the United States, its warriors became staunch allies with the new nation, often fighting side-by-side with Americans against neighboring Indian tribes such as the Creek.

The Chickasaws readily responded to southern white lifestyles and by the beginning of the nineteenth century had abandoned their traditional clothing and housing customs, adopting the styles and mores of their white neighbors instead. Some became astute entrepreneurs and owned sizable pieces of property, farms, ferries, gristmills, and salt springs. They embraced slavery—an institution they maintained after their expulsion from Mississippi in 1836 until the Civil War, but even then, in defeat with their Confederate allies, they staunchly resisted the harsh and unpopular restrictions of Reconstruction.

The Chickasaw removal from Mississippi to Indian Territory in present-day Oklahoma, was precipitated by the conclusion of the Treaty of Pontotoc Creek four years earlier in 1832. Chief Levi Colbert at first settled his tribe as a distinct district within the Choctaw reservation, maintaining the relationship until 1856, when the Chickasaws relocated within Indian Territory and formed their own government. Following the Civil War and the demands of Reconstruction, assaults by timber and railroad interests resulted in the passage in 1906 of the Burke Act, which disbanded the tribe the following year.

Decades of protest during the first half of the twentieth century by the remnant population of the Chickasaw Nation to federal authorities regarding the confiscation of their status and property met with no success. Finally, in 1971, the tribe was permitted to elect its own governor, and in 1983, limited self-government was allowed, under the supervision of the U.S. Bureau of Indian Affairs.

James A. Crutchfield

See also: Cherokee; Choctaw; Creek; Creek Wars; Indian Removal Act (1830); Jackson's Indian Policy.

Further Reading

Foreman, Grant. *The Five Civilized Tribes: Cherokee, Chickasaw, Choctaw, Creek, Seminole.* Norman: University of Oklahoma Press, 1982.

Malone, James H. *The Chickasaw Nation.* Whitefish, MT: Kessinger Publishing, 2007.

Chief Joseph
(1840–1904)

In 1877 Nez Percé chief Joseph, following a 1,500-mile (2,400-km) flight with hundreds of his kinspeople, including women, children, and the elderly, surrendered his rifle to Lieutenant Colonel Nelson Miles and General Oliver O. Howard and made the definitive statement of his life: "From where the sun now stands I will fight no more forever." Born in the Wallowa Valley of modern-day northeastern Oregon in April 1840 to a Nez Percé headman and his wife, the child was given the name Hin-mah-too-yah-lat-kekt—"Thunder Traveling to Loftier Mountain Heights"—when he was still a boy.

Joseph's life spanned a period of great change for his tribe. Missionaries moved into Nez Percé country shortly before Joseph was born; as a child he and his family lived at the Spalding Mission in Idaho and learned English and Christian ways in the classroom of missionary Eliza Spalding. When Joseph's father realized such influences would permanently change Nez Percé culture and belief, he rejected mission life and teachings, and returned to traditional tribal custom at a time when increasing numbers of emigrants were traveling into the Pacific Northwest via the Oregon Trail. By 1855, when the first of several treaty councils took place allowing escalating encroachment onto Nez Percé lands by white settlers, the Christian missions were abandoned.

Hin-mah-too-yah-lat-kekt took over leadership of the Wallowa band of Nez Percé Indians while in his twenties, assuming the mantle of headman from his father, who had become known as Chief Joseph and would thereafter be called Old Joseph. The younger leader also took the name Chief Joseph, and was familiarly called Young Joseph by settlers and other men with whom he interacted. Although erroneously referred to in early biographies as a war chief, he actually was a peace chief for his band, and tried diplomacy to resolve issues over tribal territory, successfully remaining with his band in the Wallowa Valley until forced out in May 1877 under provisions of a treaty negotiated in 1863 that the Nez Percé called the Thief Treaty.

Just days before the Nez Percé were to report to the Indian Reservation at Lapwai, Idaho, hostilities broke out between some tribesmen and white settlers, leading to an attack on the tribe at White Bird Canyon on June 17, 1877. Reluctant to turn to violence, Chief Joseph nevertheless remained with the tribal bands as they fled from that first battle site across Idaho, Montana, Yellowstone National Park, and Wyoming. They engaged in other battles and skirmishes at Clearwater in Idaho (July 11–12), the Big Hole in western Montana (August 9), at Camas Meadow in Idaho (August 20), at Cow Island in Montana (September 23), and finally at the Bear's Paw in northern Montana, where they were under siege by frontier army troops commanded by Miles from September 30 to October 5, when Joseph finally surrendered along with 448 of his followers.

During the flight, Chief Joseph assumed the role of guardian of the Nez Percé people and caretaker for the tribe's tremendous horse herds. He almost single-handedly saved the herd from capture during the battle at the Big Hole, ensuring the people's ability to escape from the soldiers under the command of Colonel John Gibbon. His younger brother, Ollokot—called Frog—served as the war leader of the Wallow band of Nez Percés. Other Indian leaders during the 1877 war and flight were Nez Percés White Bird, Looking Glass, Toolhoolhoolzote, and Lean Elk (also called Poker Joe) and Husis Kute (or Naked Head), a Palouse who had joined with the Nez Percé in their attempt to remain off the reservation.

One group led by White Bird successfully reached sanctuary in Canada with Sitting Bull, a Hunkpapa Sioux who had gone there after the 1876 battle at the Little Big Horn. Some of the people with White Bird remained in Canada for the rest of their lives, but most eventually returned to the reservation in Idaho. Chief Joseph and his band were forced into exile in Indian Territory, where he began a new fight—to return to the Columbia Basin. He succeeded in 1886. Some of the exiles returned to the Idaho reservation, but Chief Joseph and his most loyal supporters were ordered to the Colville Reservation in Washington, where he died on September 21, 1904. His grave is in Nespelem, Washington.

Chief Joseph had several wives and children, including Heyoom-yo-yikt, his oldest wife also known as Bear Crossing, and Sound of Running Feet, his twelve-year-old daughter who escaped Bear's Paw to go to Canada with White Bird before eventually returning to Lapwai, Idaho.

Chief Joseph was the second Indian inducted into the North American Indian Hall of Fame in Andarako, Oklahoma. Several towns, schools, a dam, a canyon, a mountain, and annual events ranging from powwows to rodeos were named for him. His image became part of the official image of the Nez Percé tribe in Idaho and has been rendered on two different postage stamps and a U.S. Treasury Department $200 bond.

Candy Moulton

See also: Howard, Oliver O.; Nez Percé; Stevens Treaty (1855); Thief Treaty (1863).

Further Reading

Greene, Jerome. *Nez Perce Summer: The U.S. Army and the Nee-Mee-Poo Crisis*. Missoula: Montana Historical Society, 2000.

Josephy, Alvin, Jr. *The Nez Perce Indians and the Opening of the Northwest*. New York: Houghton Mifflin, 1997.

McWhorter, Lucullus V. *Hear Me, My Chiefs! Nez Perce Legend and History*. Caldwell, ID: Caxton Press, 2000.

Moulton, Candy. *Chief Joseph: Guardian of the People*. New York: Forge Books, 2006.

Chinese Immigration

The Chinese were an important component of settlement throughout much of the West. Workers traveled across the Pacific Ocean to the west coast, moving eastward as new territory opened.

During the mid-1800s, China's Guangdong province was in turmoil. Guangdong, along with its capital, Canton, had always been a hotbed of rebellion against the Manchu rulers, who 200 years earlier had invaded China from Manchuria, conquered the nation, and replaced the Ming dynasty. Periodic rebellions resulted in the deaths of millions of people. In 1847 British banks cut off funding to businesses in Guangdong for over a year, throwing 100,000 men out of work. Desperate husbands, fathers, and sons grasped at rumors of Gum Shan—Gold Mountain.

James Marshall discovered gold in California in 1848. A Chinese man living there wrote to a friend in Canton about the discovery. Soon everyone in Guangdong was talking about Gum Shan, where a person could pick gold nuggets off the ground. The Chinese portion of the California gold rush was on.

The plan was to find enough gold in Gum Shan so families back home in Guangdong could live comfortably. Once the Chinese prospectors achieved this goal, they intended to return home. Chinese miners were so efficient at mining in California that their Caucasian neighbors became jealous and began restricting the Chinese miners' rights and their ability to mine.

In 1862 the federal government authorized construction of the Central Pacific Railroad, starting from the West, and the Union Pacific railroad, beginning at the Missouri River. In 1865 the Central Pacific Railroad's owners took advantage of the Chinese labor force, men who worked faster and cheaper than their Caucasian counterparts did. Soon hundreds of Chinese were employed by the company. Without the expertise of the Chinese in explosives and working on cliffs, it would have taken longer and been more expensive to build the Central Pacific, especially through the rugged Sierra Nevada. On May 10, 1869, when the railways were joined from east and west to create the transcontinental railroad, most of the Chinese were out of a job.

Chinese prospectors and businessmen spread throughout the West along with other pioneers. Wherever there was a new mineral strike, the Chinese soon were in that mining district—California, Arizona, Nevada, Montana, Idaho, Washington, and Colorado. The predominantly Caucasian population developed prejudices against the Chinese based on their race, different language, work ethic, dress, and culture—all creating friction. To lessen hard feelings, Chinese worked old placer mines that Caucasians believed were useless. They went into businesses that offered little competition to Caucasians, such as restaurants, laundries, and stores. Most Chinese lived the American dream—they were independent business owners.

In 1874 Lieutenant Colonel George Custer's expedition through the Black Hills of Dakota Territory discovered gold, triggering a gold rush. In the fall of 1875, prospectors entered Deadwood Gulch and discovered gold along Whitewood Creek. Chinese prospectors joined the throng of miners in Deadwood. Some acquired placer mining claims while others established laundries. The laundry operators saved the wash water from the miners' clothes and sluiced it, recovering gold dust, literally mining the miners. The 1898 Black Hills Residence and Business Directory listed eleven restaurants in Deadwood, seven of which were Chinese owned. The Chinese also worked as house servants, cooks, barbers, physicians, lumberjacks, and gamblers. They owned real estate and businesses, including hotels and stores.

In 1882 Congress passed the Chinese Exclusion Act. This had a profound impact on America's Chinese population. The act cut off almost all new immigration, excluding women, to the United States from China. Prejudice against the Chinese at times erupted into mob violence and murder. Mobs looted and burned Chinese homes. Mobs beat and murdered Chinese immigrants in Denver, Colorado; Rock Springs,

Wyoming; and Montana mining camps. Tacoma and Seattle, Washington, forcibly expelled the Chinese. Conflict arose in Deadwood and Idaho mining camps, though less so compared to other western towns.

Despite being the victims of continuing prejudice, the Chinese built joss houses where they conducted Buddhist and other Chinese religious ceremonies. The joss house also served as a meetinghouse where the Chinese gathered for relaxation and fellowship. The Chinese loved their holidays and invited non-Chinese to participate, the most spectacular holiday being the Chinese New Year. This fifteen-day celebration usually took place in February with the start of the new moon. During the celebration, Chinese merchants closed their shops and took a vacation from work. The Chinese populace decorated their houses with banners, paintings, and lanterns. They shot off fireworks and firecrackers day and night, and they marched in parades accompanied by bands. They paid off debts, invited everyone to visit their homes, and gave the visitors gifts.

The Chinese had provisions in their contracts with the companies that had brought them to America. If they died here, the companies shipped their bones back to China. After the body had been in the ground for two years, workers dug up the bones, wrapped them in newspaper or cloth, placed them in zinc-lined boxes, and returned them to China.

Due to the Chinese Exclusion Act, there were few Chinese families in America in proportion to single Chinese men. The Chinese population slowly drifted either back to China or to large western towns by the end of the nineteenth century.

Bill Markley

See also: Central Pacific Railroad; Mining Industry.

Further Reading

Chang, Iris. *The Chinese in America*. New York: Penguin Books, 2004.

Zhu, Liping. *A Chinaman's Chance: The Chinese on the Rocky Mountain Mining Frontier*. Boulder: University Press of Colorado, 1997.

Zhu, Liping, and Rose Estep Fosha. *Ethnic Oasis: The Chinese in the Black Hills*. Pierre: South Dakota State Historical Society Press, 2004.

Chisholm Trail

The cattle trail that became synonymous with the Texas cowboy was named for a man who never drove cattle, and who blazed a trail that never entered Texas.

Jesse Chisholm (1805–1868), a Scots-Cherokee trader, in 1865 established a post on the North Canadian River just west of present-day Oklahoma City and began hauling goods to Wichita, Kansas, about 220 miles (355 km) away. He died shortly after Texas cattlemen began using part of his trail for their own profit.

The end of the Civil War brought a demand for beef in the east (eclipsing pork as the primary meat on dinner tables), and with the arrival of the Kansas Pacific Railway in Abilene, Kansas, entrepreneur Joseph G. McCoy began building cattle pens, loading chutes, a bank, and a fancy, three-story hotel (which cost $15,000) called the Drover's Cottage. McCoy then sent the word to Texas cattlemen; with luck, cattle might bring $3 a head in Texas, but prices could hit $40 a head in Kansas. The Texas and Pacific Railway did not reach Fort Worth, Texas, until 1876, but even then, driving cattle perhaps 1,000 miles (1,600 km) to Kansas proved significantly cheaper than shipping them by rail from Texas. In 1867, the first cattle drovers came north from Texas, discovering Chisholm's trail and following it into Kansas, then continuing on to Abilene. That year, 35,000 head of cattle were shipped from Kansas.

Ranchers and trail bosses—contractors like John Blocker, Jesse Driskill, Richard King, Seth Mabry, Abel "Shanghai" Pierce, and Ike Pryor—often sent several herds, usually numbering about 2,000 head, up the trail each year. Typically, cattle and crew (trail boss, cook, horse wrangler, and about ten cowboys) traveled between 8 and 12 miles (13–19 km) a day.

The trail became known as the Great Texas Cattle Trail, but also was called the Kansas Trail, Abilene Trail, McCoy's Trail, or merely the Trail. By the 1870s it was dubbed the Chisholm Trail and stretched from the railheads to the heart of cow country in South Texas.

Though never clearly defined except at river crossings, the trail followed the Old Shawnee Trail from the Rio Grande to the Brazos River in Waco, where it broke away from the Shawnee and moved northwest to Fort Worth, crossing the Red River into Indian Territory and fording the Washita, Canadian, and Cimarron rivers before entering Kansas.

Abilene's heyday ended in 1871, when 600,000 head of cattle were shipped, after local merchants grew weary of rowdy cowboys. Other towns—Newton (1871), Ellsworth (1871–1875), Wichita (1872–1876), and Caldwell (1880–1885)—quickly replaced Abilene. The arrival of homesteaders, barbed wire, and quarantine laws that prevented the transport of Texas longhorns for fear of "Texas fever," a tick-spread disease often fatal to northern cattle, eventually closed the trail. By the late 1870s, more cattlemen were following the Western Trail to Dodge City, Kansas, but the Chisholm Trail remained in use until 1885. During its brief existence, an estimated 5 million Texas longhorns followed the trail to Kansas.

Johnny D. Boggs

See also: Barbed Wire; Cattle Frontier; Western Trail.

Further Reading
Gard, Wayne. *The Chisholm Trail.* Norman: University of Oklahoma Press, 1954.

Worcester, Don. *The Chisholm Trail: High Road of the Cattle Kingdom.* Lincoln: University of Nebraska Press, 1980.

Chivington, John M. (1821–1894)

Rarely in the history of the United States has a character emerged with a conflicting reputation equal to that of John Milton Chivington. While revered as a Union hero of the Civil War for saving New Mexico and Colorado from the clutches of the Confederacy during the battle at Glorieta, New Mexico, Chivington was equally reviled as the bloodthirsty perpetrator of the Sand Creek Massacre.

Chivington was born on January 27, 1821, near Lebanon, Ohio. He was a huge man physically, standing at 6 feet, 5 inches (2 m) and weighing 260 pounds (120 kg). A Methodist preacher, he was often referred to as a raging bull both in the church pulpit and in battle; he soon earned the sobriquet "the fighting parson." He migrated from Ohio to Kansas and later to Colorado. In 1861 Chivington asked Territorial Governor William Gilpin of Colorado for a "fighting commission" with the Colorado Volunteers, raised to resist the threat of Texan Confederates streaming through New Mexico and seizing the precious metal mines of Colorado. Chivington was made a major with the 1st Colorado Volunteers and rode forward under Colonel John Slough to Fort Union, New Mexico, in March 1862. From there the Union forces from Colorado engaged a column of Confederate troops under the overall command of General Henry Hopkins Sibley.

The first day's battle at Apache Pass, near present-day Glorieta, New Mexico, resulted in the Confederates being repulsed from their advance toward Fort Union. Two days later, the Texans reengaged the Colorado volunteers several miles east, at Glorieta Pass, where a fierce fight ensued. The Confederates were slowly pushing the Union forces back when Chivington detached a detail around the southern flank of the Confederate force where Sibley's supply train was encamped at Pigeon Ranch. Chivington's troops destroyed the bulk of the Texans' supplies there, forcing Sibley's troops to disengage from the battle and retreat to Santa Fe. From there, facing the prospect of beleaguered or nonexistent supply lines stretching all the way from western Texas through hostile Apache territory, Sibley began a steady withdrawal from New Mexico. The victory at Glorieta, the "Gettysburg of the West," kept the Confederacy from seizing valuable western U.S. territory and resources. Chivington was considered a hero of this campaign.

Chivington remained in the Colorado Volunteers for a short period before resuming his spiritual career in Denver City. When Indian hostilities erupted in 1864, he was among the whites who rallied to avenge several brutal outbreaks of Indian violence. He again became an officer of volunteers raised to punish local Indians for various real and imagined atrocities. On November 29, 1864, his force of 250 troops descended on a shared Cheyenne and Arapaho encampment near Big Sand Creek in eastern Colorado and killed 150 Indian men, women, and children in a bloody massacre. Word of this action soon reached Denver, and Chivington was court-martialed in May 1865. He was censured for his actions, but did not serve any prison time. His reputation, however, was irreparably soiled. Chivington spent the next thirty years of his life in Colorado and the Midwest, dying of cancer on October 4, 1894.

Jim Ersfeld

See also: Black Kettle; Sand Creek Massacre.

Further Reading
Alberts, Don E. *The Battle of Glorieta: Union Victory in the West.* College Station: Texas A&M University Press, 1998.

Hoig, Stan. *The Sand Creek Massacre.* Norman: University of Oklahoma Press, 1974.

Whitford, William C. *The Colorado Volunteers in the Civil War.* Glorieta, NM: Rio Grande Press, 1971.

Whitlock, Flint. *Distant Bugles, Distant Drums: The Union Response to the Confederate Invasion of New Mexico.* Boulder: University Press of Colorado, 2006.

Choctaw

In the nineteenth century, the Choctaw Indians were considered one of the Five Civilized Tribes (with the

Cherokee, Chickasaw, Creek, and Seminole), so called because they were peaceable and had adopted many of the customs and cultural practices of their white colonist neighbors.

Both the Choctaw and Creek people are believed to have a common ancestry in the Mississippian culture, which existed from about 700 C.E. until the advent of European explorers in the southeastern United States. The first historical records of the Choctaws are the accounts of the expedition into central Alabama of the conquistador Hernando de Soto. In October of that year, De Soto led his Spaniards against a native force commanded by a young Choctaw chief named Tuscalusa. In a battle at the Choctaws' fortified village of Mabila (or Mauvila) in October 1540, De Soto's Spaniards suffered heavy losses of men and horses before retaliating, killing hundreds of Tuscalusa's people and burning their village to the ground.

An agricultural people of the Muskogean linguistic group, the Choctaws held some 23 million acres (9.3 million ha) in all, located largely in Mississippi, with small enclaves in Alabama, Louisiana, and Florida. These lands were ceded to the U.S. government by a series of treaties between 1786 and 1830. The final cession, of about 11 million acres (4.5 million ha) of the Choctaws' Mississippi lands, was given over to the federal government in exchange for some 15 million acres (6.1 million ha) in Indian Territory (Oklahoma). This transaction was made official in the Treaty of Dancing Rabbit Creek (in Noxubee County, mid-eastern Mississippi), signed on September 27, 1830, between tribal representatives and U.S. negotiators. The Rabbit Creek document had special historical significance as the first treaty enacted under the Indian Removal Act, signed into law by President Andrew Jackson in May 1830.

The Choctaws were also the first of the Five Civilized Tribes to walk the Trail of Tears, the long walk from the Deep South to Indian Territory. After the Choctaws, the Seminoles underwent removal in 1832, the Creeks in 1834, the Chickasaws in 1837, and finally the Cherokees in 1838.

At the time of the Treaty of Dancing Rabbit Creek, nearly 20,000 Choctaws occupied their ancestral lands; between 1831 and 1833 about 12,500 followed the Trail of Tears, of whom an estimated 2,500 died en route of disease, starvation, exposure, and acts of violence against them. The French political philosopher and historian Alexis de Tocqueville (1805–1859), touring the American South in 1831, watched the Choctaw exodus during a stopover in Memphis, Tennessee, and wrote in his classic book, *Democracy in America* (1835): "In the whole scene there was an air of ruin and destruction, something which betrayed a final and irrevocable adieu; one couldn't watch without feeling one's heart wrung."

Some 6,000 to 7,000 Choctaws remained in Mississippi to suffer under the intimidation and abuse of the white populace. Even so, those forming what came to be called the Mississippi Band of Choctaw Indians became the first Native Americans to be declared U.S. citizens. The Choctaws of Indian Territory were granted autonomy as the Choctaw Nation until 1906, when they too were granted U.S. citizenship.

The Choctaw Nation of Oklahoma is situated in 11,000 square miles (28,500 sq km) of land in southeastern Oklahoma with its tribal capital at Durant; the Mississippi Choctaw Indian Reservation is located in parts of nine counties throughout the state, with the largest concentration of tribal members in Neshoba County in east-central Mississippi.

Dale L. Walker

See also: Cherokee; Chickasaw; Creek; Indian Removal Act (1830); Jackson's Indian Policy; Trail of Tears.

Further Reading

De Rosier, Arthur H. *The Removal of the Choctaw Indians.* Knoxville: University of Tennessee Press, 1970.

Debo, Angie. *The Rise and Fall of the Choctaw Republic.* Norman: University of Oklahoma Press, 1961.

Foreman, Grant. *The Five Civilized Tribes: Cherokee, Chickasaw, Choctaw, Creek, Seminole.* Norman: University of Oklahoma Press, 1982.

Galloway, Patricia Kay. *Choctaw Genesis, 1500–1700.* Lincoln: University of Nebraska Press, 1998.

Kidwell, Clara Sue. *The Choctaws in Oklahoma: From Tribe to Nation, 1855–1970.* Norman: University of Oklahoma Press, 2007.

Chouteau Family

The Chouteau family was one of the most influential on the American frontier. Members of the family's network extended over several generations, expanded the fur trade throughout the Missouri River basin, opened new territory for settlement, and maintained the peace with influential tribes. They established fur-trading posts that became major cities and towns, including St. Louis; Kansas City; Salina, Oklahoma; and Fort Pierre, South Dakota. However, the family's American dream had a sad beginning in France's colonial outpost, New Orleans, with a husband abandoning his teenage wife and young son.

René Chouteau, out to make his fortune, sailed from France to Louisiana, finding a job as a New Orleans tavern keeper. In 1748 twenty-five-year-old René married fifteen-year-old Marie Thérèse Bourgeois, a New Orleans native who had lost her father when she was six years old. Marie Thérèse and René had a son, Auguste, born in 1750. Family tradition recounts that René was abusive, cutting Marie Thérèse's face and leaving a scar. Several years after the birth of Auguste, René deserted his family, sailing back to France. With her husband gone and her father dead, Marie Thérèse called herself the widow Chouteau.

A ship carrying French colonists led by Pierre de Laclède Liguest arrived at New Orleans in 1755. Pierre and Marie Thérèse met and fell in love. They wanted to live as husband and wife, but René Chouteau was still alive in France. The Catholic Church and the French government did not recognize divorce; Marie Thérèse and Pierre lived together as husband and wife anyway. They had four children—a son, Pierre, born in 1758, followed by three daughters. Since Marie Thérèse Chouteau and Pierre de Laclède were not legally married, they gave the children the last name of Chouteau.

In 1763 Laclède traveled up the Mississippi River, taking thirteen-year-old Auguste with him. After selecting a site for a trading post near the confluence of the Missouri and Mississippi rivers, he returned downriver to Fort Chartres for the winter. On February 14, 1764, Laclède placed Auguste in charge of a work crew and sent them to the trading post site to begin clearing the land and building the post. When Laclède arrived in early April, he liked what Auguste had accomplished and named the trading post St. Louis. It soon grew into one of the most important cities of the frontier. As Laclède and his workers completed the post and settlers were establishing farms and businesses, they learned that France had secretly traded Louisiana to Spain. The Spanish authorities treated Laclède and later the Chouteau brothers well, giving them trading rights with the tribes up the Missouri and Mississippi rivers.

Laclède worked to establish good relationships with the Indians, including the Osage tribe in what is now the state of Missouri. The Osages were one of the most powerful tribes in North America. They acquired firearms early on from Europeans and dominated neighboring tribes. It was good news for Laclède that the Osages considered the French their friends and desired French goods.

Laclède's trading post was an instant success with the Osages and other tribes. The Osages respected Laclède and the two Chouteau brothers, Auguste and Pierre. To cement that trust and develop a close friendship, the Osages invited the two boys to live with them; thus Auguste and Pierre spent long periods of time with the Osages, learning their ways and becoming their close friends.

Even though business with the tribes was booming and Laclède was a good businessman, he was headed into debt because he was always willing to extend credit. Traveling to New Orleans in 1778 to compile a shipment of goods, Laclède died on the return trip. Marie Thérèse died at home in St. Louis in 1814. Auguste and Pierre eventually paid off Laclède's debts. They became successful businessmen in St. Louis, branching out from the fur trade into mining and real estate.

When the United States purchased Louisiana Territory from France (Spain, in the meantime having retroceded the vast region back to France in 1800), Auguste and Pierre wholeheartedly embraced the new government. Opening their homes to Meriwether Lewis and William Clark when the Corps of Discovery visited St. Louis, the brothers supplied the explorers with provisions, workmen, and maps. As the expedition was heading up the Missouri River, Pierre Chouteau led a delegation of Osage leaders to Washington, DC, where they met with President Thomas Jefferson. A few days after the meeting, the government appointed Pierre agent of Indian affairs for the District of Upper Louisiana. The Chouteau brothers continued their friendship with both Lewis and Clark after the return of the Corps of Discovery.

Auguste and Pierre remained trading partners and friends with the Osages. They were instrumental in keeping the tribe on the U.S. side against the British during the War of 1812. The brothers provided leadership in St. Louis and Missouri government, but above all they were fur traders. Most of the sons of Auguste and Pierre as well as their sister's sons formed partnerships and continued with the fur trade. Auguste died in 1829 and Pierre died in 1849.

Chouteau, Auguste Pierre (1786–1838)

Auguste Pierre Chouteau, Pierre's oldest son, was born in 1786. Nicknamed A.P., he graduated fourth in his class from West Point in 1806. He resigned from the army in 1807 and returned to his love, the fur trade. The Osages liked A.P. very much. During the War of 1812, he was a leader in the territorial militia.

A.P. established a trading post in present-day

Salina, Oklahoma, and led several trading and fur-trapping expeditions further west. On one trip, he and his men went into Spanish territory. The Spanish military captured them and took them to a Santa Fe prison. The authorities released them after forty days, but retained their furs and trade goods.

A.P. was friends with Sam Houston and Washington Irving, and his good reputation was known to President Andrew Jackson. He died in 1838 at his home in Salina and was buried with full military honors.

Chouteau, Pierre, Jr. (1789–1865)

Pierre's second oldest son, Pierre Jr., nicknamed Cadet, was one of the great fur traders of the frontier. Pierre Jr., born in 1789, grew up in the fur trade. He became a partner in and later bought the American Fur Company, building trading posts and establishing a system of trade throughout the Missouri River basin. Along with Kenneth McKenzie, the innovative Pierre Jr. convinced the other American Fur Company partners to build a steamboat, the *Yellow Stone*, and take it upriver to their trading posts. In 1832 the boat traveled up the Missouri River as far as Fort Pierre, in present-day South Dakota. The following year, the vessel was able to make it up the Missouri River all the way to Fort Union in what is now western North Dakota. Pierre Jr. and McKenzie showed that steamboat travel was practical on the Missouri River. Steamboats greatly increased the profits of the American Fur Company and expanded commerce on the Missouri River.

Pierre Jr. allowed George Catlin to travel on his riverboats. Catlin sketched and painted members of the tribes he met in his travels up the river. Later Pierre Jr. traveled upriver to Fort Union on one of his steamboats accompanied by Prince Maximilian of Wied-Neuwied, who was studying the American Indians and natural sciences. The prince brought along his artist, Karl Bodmer, who sketched and painted members of various tribes they encountered. The artwork created by Catlin and Bodmer provided outstanding images of the peoples of the Great Plains.

Pierre Jr. invested in mining, railroads, and property. In later years, he lived in New York City. In 1865 he died a wealthy man. Fort Pierre and Pierre, the capital of South Dakota, are named in his honor.

Bill Markley

See also: American Fur Company; Bodmer, Karl; Catlin, George; Fort Union (North Dakota); Laclède Liguest, Pierre de; Maximilian, Prince Alexander Philip; McKenzie, Kenneth; Osage.

Further Reading

Barbour, Barton H. *Fort Union and the Upper Missouri Fur Trade.* Norman: University of Oklahoma Press, 2001.

Christian, Shirley. *Before Lewis and Clark: The Story of the Chouteaus, the French Dynasty That Ruled America's Frontier.* New York: Farrar, Straus and Giroux, 2004.

Foley, William E., and David C. Rice. *The First Chouteaus: River Barons of Early St. Louis.* Urbana: University of Illinois Press, 2000.

Hoig, Stan. *The Chouteaus: First Family of the Fur Trade.* Albuquerque: University of New Mexico Press, 2008.

Robertson, R.G. *Competitive Struggle: America's Western Fur Trading Posts, 1764–1865.* Boise, ID: Tamarack Books, 1999.

Chuck Wagons

The famous Texas Panhandle cattleman, Charles Goodnight, is generally credited with the invention of the chuck wagon. In the early days, when cowboying was a local affair and herders were out on the range for only a few days at a time, wranglers generally carried their food with them. Sometimes pack horses or mules might be utilized when additional supplies needed to be hauled. However, with the advent of the genuine cattle drive, when huge herds of Longhorns were driven hundreds of miles from home ranches in Texas northward to Kansas and, later, to the open ranges of Wyoming and Montana, a more complex and sophisticated method of feeding the men had to be developed.

The answer was the chuck wagon. In 1866 Goodnight purchased an old government wagon, drastically modified it, added axles of iron, and placed a large wooden box, or cabinet, on its rear. The lid on this "chuck" box was fitted with a swinging leg that allowed the lid to be used as a preparation table. The box was divided into conveniently sized compartments in which "Cookie," as the drive's chef was usually called, stored all sorts of rations and equipment, from salt and baking powder to beans and coffee to tin utensils and cooking ware.

The chuck wagon, driven by the cook, always traveled in advance of the cattle and the cowboys for two reasons: to avoid the dust created by the thousands of hooves and in order to set up camp and get the evening meal under way by the time the tired cowboys arrived. Skimpy as the food on a cattle drive might have been, eating was the highlight of each day for the weary cowboys after long hours in the saddle. Consequently, cooks were hired for their ability to turn out a good

The horse-drawn chuck wagon, a kind of mobile kitchen and pantry, was devised for use on long cattle drives. "Chuck" was slang for food; a "cookie" drove and ran the wagon. The food was simple, but the evening meal was the highlight of the day. *(The Granger Collection, New York)*

meal on what little supplies they could carry in the chuck wagon. Most were older men—often cowboys too old to withstand the rigors of the trail drive on the back of a horse.

Like so many inventions, the chuck wagon was developed to solve a very real problem, in this case, the transporting of quantities of food and supplies across many miles and over several weeks. Goodnight's redesign and perfection of a standard horse-drawn wagon into the utilitarian vehicle that it soon became contributed greatly to the success of the late 1800s cattle drive.

James A. Crutchfield

See also: Cattle Frontier; Goodnight, Charles; Open Range.

Further Reading
Dary, David. *Cowboy Culture: A Saga of Five Centuries.* New York: Alfred A. Knopf, 1991.

Cimarron Cutoff
See **Santa Fe Trail**

Clark, William (1770–1838)

Although indelibly linked with Meriwether Lewis and the transcontinental expedition of 1804–1806, William Clark also had a varied career as soldier, explorer, cartographer, Indian agent, and territorial governor. Over 6 feet (1.8 m) tall, robust and tireless, he became an ideal frontiersman and, when called upon, the perfect partner to Lewis in the Corps of Discovery, his contributions to the success of the expedition incalculable.

Clark was the sixth son in a Virginia plantation family of ten children, born on August 1, 1770, near the Rappahannock River. His brothers all served in the Revolutionary War; the most celebrated of them, George Rogers Clark, eighteen years William's senior, was commander of the Kentucky militia. It was from George that William learned the skills that made him an outstanding wilderness soldier.

At age nineteen, Clark began service in the Kentucky militia, fighting Indians in the Ohio Valley. He was commissioned in the regular army in 1792 and became a proficient mapmaker and fort builder as he earned promotion to the rank of captain. In August

1794, he fought in General Anthony Wayne's army at the Battle of Fallen Timbers in northwest Ohio against a confederation of tribes of the Northwest Territory. It was at Fallen Timbers that he met and befriended the young ensign and fellow Virginian, Meriwether Lewis.

Clark resigned from the army in 1796 to manage his family's plantation and remained so occupied until June, 1803, when he received a letter from Lewis asking that he join him in sharing the command of the expedition being organized to effect President Thomas Jefferson's plan for a transcontinental exploration of the continent. Clark accepted the invitation with alacrity and in October joined Lewis at a point on the Ohio River opposite Louisville, Kentucky (founded in 1778 by George Rogers Clark). The commanders reached St. Louis in December and spent six months organizing the Corps of Discovery, its members, boats, supplies, and instruments, and the guesswork maps of the terra incognita ahead of them.

The expedition of forty-two members set out on the Missouri River on May 14, 1804, and returned to St. Louis on September 23, 1806, after a total of over 8,000 miles (13,000 km) traveled and every objective met or surpassed. Among Clark's contributions to the mission were his planning and supervision of the Corps' winter camps and quarters, his mapmaking, his journals (written with an amusing abundance of misspellings) that served as a priceless adjunct to Lewis's meticulous but gap-filled notebooks, and his geniality, somewhat in contrast to Lewis's often melancholy moods.

Between 1807 and 1813, Clark served as Indian agent for Louisiana Territory and brigadier general of its militia, after which service he was appointed governor of the newly formed Missouri Territory. He married Julia Hancock of Fincastle, Virginia, in January 1808. (Their son was named Meriwether Lewis Clark.)

Upon Missouri's achieving statehood in 1820, William Clark became a candidate for the governorship but failed to win the election. In 1822 he was named Superintendent of Indian Affairs in St. Louis and held that post until a few months before his death on September 1, 1838.

Dale L. Walker

See also: Jefferson, Thomas; Lewis, Meriwether; Lewis and Clark Expedition; Louisiana Purchase (1803); Louisiana Territory.

Further Reading

Foley, William E. *Wilderness Journey: The Life of William Clark*. Columbia: University of Missouri Press, 2006.
Holmberg, James J., ed. *Dear Brother: Letters of William Clark to Jonathan Clark*. New Haven: Yale University Press, 2002.
Jones, Landon Y. *William Clark and the Shaping of the West*. New York: Hill & Wang, 2004.

Clay, Henry (1777–1852)

Known as a flamboyant, spellbinding orator and for over forty years a dominant American statesman-politician, Henry Clay is best remembered as the "Great Pacifier" who championed the 1820 Missouri Compromise, a series of laws that, among other measures, prohibited slavery in the western territories. The legislation eased tensions over the volatile issue of extending slavery to new states and territories.

Born on April 12, 1777, on his preacher-father's 460-acre (190-ha) farm near Richmond, Virginia, Henry was the seventh of his mother's sixteen children (nine by Henry's father, seven by her stepfather). As a youngster he spent his spare hours at the Richmond courthouse, where, at age ten, he heard speeches by future presidents James Madison and James Monroe and future Supreme Court chief justice John Marshall as they debated ratification by Virginia of the U.S. Constitution.

When Henry was fifteen, his family moved to Kentucky, but he stayed behind to work in a grocery store. His father arranged for him to serve as a clerk to George Wythe, a formidable legal mind and judge of the Chancery Court of Virginia. Clay was admitted to the Virginia bar before his twenty-first birthday and soon thereafter moved to Lexington, Kentucky, where he established a successful circuit-riding law practice, traveling to different towns and achieving some notoriety for defending criminal cases and for his fiery courtroom oratory. He became an immensely popular lawyer and state lawmaker known for his propensity for gambling and roistering with friends as well as for his legal and political skills.

In 1811, Clay—newly elected to the U.S. House of Representatives—was named Speaker of the House on the first day of his first session, a unique event in the history of the institution. He served in the House of Representatives from 1811 to 1825 and was thrice elected speaker. As the guiding spirit among the War Hawks of the House, he advocated war against the British for violation of maritime laws and became a central figure behind the subsequent War of 1812 and in the peace commission when the war ended.

In the national election of 1824, Clay was among the presidential candidates but lost the race to John

Quincy Adams of Massachusetts. Adams's appointment of Clay as secretary of state was called by critics a "corrupt bargain" given the enmity between Clay and Adams during the campaign. In all, Clay made five attempts to win the presidency: in 1824 he was defeated by Adams; in 1832 he was defeated by Andrew Jackson; in 1840 he lost the nomination as a Whig candidate to William Henry Harrison; in 1844 he was defeated by James Knox Polk; and in 1848 he lost the nomination as a Whig candidate to Zachary Taylor. A founding member of the anti-Jackson Whig Party, Clay was a proponent of the American Plan, a system to improve the national economy by exacting tariffs to protect American industry, establishing a national bank, and improving the country's transportation system.

In 1957 a special congressional committee, chaired by Senator John F. Kennedy of Massachusetts, named the five greatest U.S. senators, among whom were Henry Clay of Kentucky, Daniel Webster of New Hampshire, and John C. Calhoun of South Carolina, the colleagues known as "The Great Triumvirate" for their lasting impact on American history.

Henry Clay died in Washington, DC, on June 29, 1852, at the age of seventy-five.

Dale L. Walker

See also: Calhoun, John C.; Compromise of 1850; Elections, Presidential; Missouri Compromise (1820).

Further Reading

Baxter, Maurice G. *Henry Clay and the American System*. Lexington: University Press of Kentucky, 1995.

Peterson, Merrill D. *The Great Triumvirate: Webster, Clay, and Calhoun*. New York: Oxford University Press, 1988.

Remini, Robert V. *Henry Clay: Statesman for the Union*. New York: W.W. Norton, 1993.

Schurz, Carl. *Life of Henry Clay*. 2 vols. New York: Houghton Mifflin, 1888.

Clyman, James (1792–1881)

Probably James Clyman's most important contribution to the story of westward expansion is the set of recollections that he compiled. Published in book form in 1984 as *Journal of a Mountain Man*, the volume gives valuable insights into the early days of the upper Missouri River fur trade.

Clyman was born in Fauquier County, Virginia, on February 1, 1792, on land leased by his father from President George Washington. When he was fifteen, his family moved to Stark County, Ohio, but his dislike for farming sent him further west to Indiana, then to Illinois, where he learned to survey, a profession that would come in handy later.

Moving again, this time to St. Louis, he joined General William H. Ashley's fur-trapping expedition on its second trip up the Missouri River in 1823. Ashley quickly recognized that the intelligent young man would make a welcome addition to the rough-and-tumble assemblage he had gathered in St. Louis, and, since Clyman could both read and write, the general hired him as clerk on one of his keelboats.

Clyman was present during the disastrous attack upon Ashley's expedition by the Arikara Indians and left an important account of the affair. After a shaky peace was established with the Indians, he was assigned to accompany Jedediah Smith and others to the Continental Divide. On this mission, Smith was mauled by a grizzly bear and it was up to Clyman to patch him up. In his graphic account of the backwoods surgery, Clyman dryly pointed out that the harrowing experience "gave us a lisson on the charcter of the Grissly Baare which we did not forget."

During his later travels throughout the west, Clyman ventured with other notable companions, including Tom Fitzpatrick and William Sublette. He eventually settled down near Danville, Illinois, and operated a store, but when the Black Hawk uprising started, he volunteered to serve as quartermaster for Henry Dodge's Mounted Rangers. He later went to Oregon in 1844, then to California in 1845. Meeting members of the ill-fated Donner and Reed parties at Fort Laramie, he tried to persuade them not to follow the Hastings Cutoff route across the Sierra Nevada.

Clyman's journal is standard reading for anyone interested in the early West. It is written with no periods—indeed, with hardly any punctuation—and with phonetic spelling on some words. But what comes across are the thoughts of a clear thinker, combined with some of his own poetry and not a little bit of homespun philosophy, such as "the human mind can never be satisfied, never at rest."

James Clyman died in the Napa Valley of California on December 27, 1881.

Mike Moore

See also: Arikara War; Ashley, William Henry; Black Hawk War; Donner Party; Smith, Jedediah.

Further Reading

Clyman, James. *Journal of a Mountain Man*. Ed. Linda M. Hasselstrom. Missoula, MT: Mountain Press, 1984.

Cochise (Cheis) (c. 1810–1874)

His Apache name was Cheis or Chees. White men called him Chees, Kachise, Cachees, Cochil, and Cochise. There were other forms, spellings, and pronunciations but they all described one man—one of the fiercest guerrilla fighters who ever lived and the undisputed leader of the Chokonen Chiricahua Apaches in the 1860s and early 1870s.

His birth date is unknown, but is presumed to be about 1810. As an adult, Cochise was taller than average for an Apache, standing about 5 feet 10 inches (1.6 m) tall. He was well-proportioned and physically capable as a fighter. It was his physical capability, lack of fear, cunning, and aura that led to his leadership of the Chiricahuas.

Cochise lived most of his life in relative obscurity. Were it not for a single incident, he might have remained unknown and unimportant in the annals of American history to anyone other than members of his own tribe. In late January 1861, a boy named Felix Ward was kidnapped from a ranch south of Tucson. Cochise was called to a meeting in Apache Pass with Lieutenant George Bascom in early February. Anticipating no trouble, Cochise arrived with his wife, brother Coyuntura, two or three warriors (assumed to be his nephews), and two of his children, in the late afternoon of February 4. Inside the meeting tent, Bascom asked Cochise about the disappearance of Felix Ward. Cochise denied any knowledge of the incident and offered to help find the boy. Convinced that Cochise was lying, Bascom advised him that he was to be detained until the boy was returned. Cochise drew a knife, cut a hole in the tent, ran through the ring of soldiers surrounding the tent, and escaped in the darkness though wounded in the leg by a rifle ball. He was never taken by surprise again.

During the following two weeks, Cochise and his people captured four whites and killed several Mexicans. Cochise tried to use the whites as barter for his wife, children, brother, and nephews to no avail. Bascom remained steadfast that the hostages were to be released only upon the return of Felix Ward. Cochise's people tortured and killed their white captives, whose burned bodies were discovered on February 18, 1861. The following day, on orders from Bascom's superior officer, Coyuntura and the three warriors were hanged from oak trees, high enough above the ground so that wolves could not reach the bodies and they would remain undisturbed for all to see. Thus began the Cochise War, a war of depredation and incalculable deaths, lasting more than a decade.

Almost every raid on a ranch or settlement and almost every violent death of a white or Mexican in the region over the next decade was blamed on Cochise. There is no doubt he was guilty of many of them, but when other incidents occurred, there is little or no evidence that he was even in the United States. The U.S. Army sent more than one-fifth of its manpower to the Southwest to subdue Cochise and his band of Chokonens, numbering no more than 400 at most. Generals George Crook, Oliver Howard, and others were involved in the campaigns, but no one was able to force Cochise to surrender. He outwitted them at every turn.

Refusing several offers to settle on reservations in New Mexico and on the San Carlos in Arizona, Cochise insisted that he would fight forever before moving his people from their traditional homeland in southeastern Arizona. General Howard, anxious to see an end to the Apaches' reign of terror, agreed to give Cochise what he wanted: the Chiricahua and Dragoon Mountains in Arizona. Cochise was granted a reservation, 55 miles (88 km) on each side, encompassing much of southeastern Arizona, including Apache Pass, where his brother and nephews had been hanged in 1861. He accepted the reservation with the understanding that Tom Jeffords, the only white man known to have gained his friendship, be appointed agent for the reservation.

The Chiricahua Reservation became official in December 1872. Attacks on whites dwindled while Cochise lived. He guaranteed safe passage for the stage lines and kept his promise. Raids by Apaches into Mexico continued, though not led by Cochise. The leader explained that while he tried to talk his warriors out of such folly, they were free to do as they pleased in Mexico for the Chiricahuas had no treaty with that country.

In the spring of 1874, Cochise grew gravely ill. He is thought to have had stomach or colon cancer. On June 7, Tom Jeffords met Cochise for the last time. Cochise said he would die at midmorning the next day. Though agreeing that the chief would die very soon, Jeffords had to leave Cochise's camp that night because he had rations to distribute. Cochise died the following morning. He was buried in a secret place, known only to some members of his tribe and Tom Jeffords. His burial site has never been found.

Stoney Livingston

See also: Apache; Crook, George; Howard, Oliver O.

Further Reading

Carlson, Vada F. *Cochise: Chief of the Chiricahuas.* New York: Harvey House, 1973.

Sweeney, Edwin R. *Cochise: Chiricahua Apache Chief.* Norman: University of Oklahoma Press, 1995.

Cody, William Frederick (Buffalo Bill) (1846–1917)

If Daniel Boone epitomized America's first major thrust westward, then William F. Cody, known as Buffalo Bill, personified the ending of the frontier. With his re-creation of the last days of the "Wild West," he and his traveling band of entertainers thrilled a generation of people who had, themselves, barely missed living in the last days of the Old West.

William Frederick Cody got his nickname—Buffalo Bill—from his prowess at hunting buffalo to feed railroad workers. From 1883 to 1913 his Wild West Show fostered the romantic image of the cowboy and the myth of the American West. *(Hulton Archive/Stringer/Getty Images)*

Less than three months before the United States and Mexico went to war in May 1846, Cody was born near Le Claire, Iowa, on February 26. During his first twenty years of life, he pursued several jobs: express rider for Russell and Waddell (later expanded to Russell, Majors and Waddell), freighter, miner, fur trapper, Pony Express rider, and soldier with a band of Kansas guerrilla fighters during the Civil War.

After the war, Cody hunted buffalo (actually the American bison) on the Great Plains, supplying railroad crews with fresh meat. His hunting prowess earned him the name "Buffalo Bill" by admirers, and a series of successful scouting missions for the U.S. Army furthered his reputation as a man to be respected. During his years as a scout, he participated in multiple expeditions and skirmishes against various Indian tribes on the Great Plains. In 1872 Cody was awarded a Medal of Honor, which was later rescinded because he had served as a civilian rather than as a member of the military.

By then, he had met E.Z.C. Judson (who wrote under the pseudonym Ned Buntline), a journalist best remembered for his lionization of Cody and other westerners in a series of dime novels. Cody had also begun acting as a hunting guide to prominent visitors to the Great Plains, among them the Grand Duke Alexei Romanov, a member of the Russian royal family. With his reputation assured by the likes of Judson and Romanov, Cody traveled to Chicago in 1872 to appear in a Judson-written play titled *The Scouts of the Plains.* Although the play was short on literary and theatrical merit, many authorities point to it as the beginning of America's enduring interest in the West.

Returning to the plains, Cody resumed his job with the army and served as chief scout in General George Crook's 1876 Yellowstone Expedition. During these years, he also continued his acting career both in the East and in the West, traveling back and forth to pursue one or the other. He partnered in a ranching operation with brothers and famed army scouts Frank and Luther North, but soon lost interest, his heart having been captured by show business. In 1882 Cody launched his famous Wild West Show, which for the next quarter of a century toured much of the United States (including the 1892 Chicago World's Columbian Exposition) and Europe, featuring at one time or another such legends as Sitting Bull and Annie Oakley.

On January 10, 1917, as war waged in Europe, Cody died an impoverished man in Denver, Colorado. His life span covered the period from the Mexican-American War to World War I. In addition to the founding of Cody, Wyoming, the gateway to Yellowstone National Park, his legacy to a generation of Americans was the re-creation of the Wild West that he so loved and that his audiences had barely missed.

James A. Crutchfield

See also: Crook, George; North, Frank Joshua; North, Luther Hedden; Pawnee Scouts; Russell, Majors and Waddell; Sitting Bull.

Further Reading
Cody, William F. *The Life of Hon. William F. Cody: Known as Buffalo Bill, the Famous Hunter, Scout, and Guide.* Lincoln: University of Nebraska Press, 1978.

Russell, Don. *The Lives and Legends of Buffalo Bill.* Norman: University of Oklahoma Press, 1960.

Colter, John (c. 1775–1813)

Several generations of historians have rightfully called John Colter the "first" mountain man since it was he who left the returning Lewis and Clark Expedition in 1806 to set out with two westward-bound adventurers headed for the Rocky Mountains to try their hand in the fur business.

Colter was born in Virginia about 1775, but as a youth he followed his family to a new homestead near Maysville, Kentucky. There, in October 1803, he joined Lewis and Clark as one of the nine "young men from Kentucky," referred to in the official journals of the expedition. Young Colter was appointed hunter for the group and, following a few disciplinary problems in winter camp, he became a valuable addition to the entourage.

After receiving his commanders' permission to leave the expedition in mid-1806, Colter headed back up the Missouri River with his two newfound friends, but the partnership soon dissolved and by the following year he had joined Manuel Lisa's trapping party along the upper Missouri River. Lisa was quick to recognize the value of the young but experienced Colter, and he sent him on a mission to spread the word among the neighboring Indian tribes that the newly built Fort Raymond, situated at the confluence of the Yellowstone and Bighorn rivers, was open for business. It was while on this trek that Colter became the first white man to see the miraculous hot springs and geysers of the region around present-day Yellowstone National Park. For years afterward, until more whites confirmed Colter's seemingly unbelievable tales, the legendary region was known as "Colter's Hell."

Although he is well remembered as an explorer and trapper, Colter's claim to fame lies in his astounding escape from Blackfoot Indians in the fall of 1808. He and a friend, John Potts, were trapping in the vicinity of the Three Forks of the Missouri when they were suddenly confronted by a war party of Indians. The Blackfoot killed Potts outright and took Colter prisoner. His captors allowed him to run for his life, and after he was stripped naked and given a 400-yard (365-m) head start, the race was on. In an amazing demonstration of endurance, Colter managed to escape his foes, even killing one of them during the ordeal. Seven days later, the still naked, sun-parched Colter limped barely alive through the gates of Fort Raymond.

In 1810 Colter left the mountains and returned to civilization in Missouri, declaring that he should be cursed if he ever visited the wilderness again. He kept his promise, settled down, married, and began to raise a family. Just three years later, in 1813, the man who had survived the wilds of the Rocky Mountains and the wrath of the Blackfoot Indians died in the settlements following a siege of jaundice. He was not yet forty years old.

James A. Crutchfield

See also: Lewis and Clark Expedition; Lisa, Manuel.

Further Reading
Harris, Burton. *John Colter: His Years in the Rocky Mountains.* Casper, WY: Big Horn Book Co., 1952.

Mattes, Merrill J. *Colter's Hell & Jackson Hole.* NP: Yellowstone Library and Museum Association and the Grand Teton Natural History Association, 1962.

Oglesby, Richard Edward. *Manuel Lisa and the Opening of the Missouri Fur Trade.* Norman: University of Oklahoma Press, 1963.

Comanche

Closely related to the Shoshone people of the eastern Rockies of Montana and the largest tribe of the Shoshonean language group, the Comanches migrated early in the eighteenth century to the southern Great Plains. As nomadic buffalo hunters they were among the finest horsemen of the West and among the most fearsome, with great prowess in the use of lance and bow and arrow, and with a fervent love of battle. The Comanches' record of internecine warfare included fights, usually over stolen horses, with nearly every tribe on the plains: Apache, Osage, Tonkawa, Ute, Pawnee, Cheyenne, Arapaho, Lakota, Kansas, Crow, Choctaw, Wichita, Kickapoo, Creek, and others. The name "Comanche" derived from a Ute word roughly translating to "people who fight us"; the Comanches were called "lords of the Plains" by whites who grudgingly admired them.

Driven by the seasonal wanderings of the buffalo herds, Comanche bands roamed a huge territory known as Comanchería, from the Red River to the Rio Grande, from the Rocky Mountains on the west to the fringes of the vast Llano Estacado ("Staked Plains") of the west Texas tablelands. But while buffalo hunting occupied the tribe for its subsistence, from the early eighteenth century the Comanches established a reputation as marauders—bloodthirsty killers, kidnappers, and thieves. So great were Comanche depredations against settlers in Texas alone that the Texas Rangers were organized in 1835 primarily to counter their raids.

In 1853 at Fort Atkinson, Kansas (then Indian Territory), after years of suffering smallpox and cholera epidemics, many Comanche bands joined former enemies in a treaty with the U.S. government. The document pledged that "Peace, friendship, and amity shall hereafter exist between the United States and the Comanche and Kiowa, and Apache tribes of Indians. . . . that they will abstain from all hostilities whatsoever against each other, and cultivate mutual good-will and friendship."

Fourteen years later the federal government arranged a peace council at Medicine Lodge Creek, Kansas. The Comanches, Kiowas, Kiowa-Apaches, Cheyennes, and Arapahos were represented, and most signed a far-reaching treaty in which the tribes agreed to permit railroads to be built through their lands and to live peaceably on the 4,800 square miles (12,400 sq km) of a reservation set up for them in Indian Territory. In return, the government promised protection from mercenary hide hunters who were killing off the buffalo and to provide schools and churches for the reservation as well as annual annuities.

However, two of the strongest Comanche bands were absent from the parley, one of which had among its members one who would become the most dynamic and influential of all Comanche leaders, Quanah Parker. He was born about 1852 near modern-day Wichita Falls, Texas, in the Noconi band of the Comanche people, and named Quanah—"Fragrant" in the Comanche tongue. His father was Peta Nocona, son of a powerful medicine man; his mother was a white woman named Cynthia Ann Parker, taken captive in May 1836, when 300 Comanches attacked a white settlement on the Navasota River in east Texas.

In June 1874, seven years after the Medicine Lodge Creek treaty, 700 Comanches under Quanah Parker attacked a camp of white hide hunters in the heart of buffalo country, a place called Adobe Walls in the Texas Panhandle. The attack failed, and after a winter and spring of fighting, Quanah's band and the remaining "free" Comanches surrendered at Fort Concho, in west Texas, in June, 1875.

By end of the century, the Comanches had settled on the reservation in Southwest Oklahoma, farming, raising cattle, and leasing grazing land to area ranchers.

Dale L. Walker

See also: Adobe Walls, Battles of; Indian Captivity; Medicine Lodge Creek, Treaty of (1867); Parker, Cynthia Ann; Parker, Quanah.

Further Reading

Fehrenbach, T.R. *Comanches: The History of a People*. New York: Alfred A. Knopf, 1974.

Hamalainen, Pekka. *The Comanche Empire*. New Haven, CT: Yale University Press, 2008.

Noyes, Stanley. *Los Comanches: The Horse People*. Albuquerque: University of New Mexico Press, 1993.

Wallace, Ernest, and E. Adamson Hoebel. *The Comanches: Lords of the South Plains*. Norman: University of Oklahoma Press, 1952.

Compromise of 1850

At the end of the Mexican-American War, the United States added huge tracts of land to its possessions. These acquisitions from Mexico created a national crisis. The country was tearing itself apart trying to maintain a balance between slave states and free states, and the new territories forced the question of whether the new lands were going to allow slavery. Henry Clay, one of the nation's preeminent politicians, offered a resolution for the dilemma. Clay's recommendations were voted down after six months of heated debate, which witnessed some of the best oratories of legends such as Daniel Webster, John C. Calhoun, and Clay himself. Senator Stephen A. Douglas resurrected Clay's suggestions as a series of bills. In 1850 Congress passed five new acts, which together encompassed the Compromise of 1850. The bills that became these acts were carefully crafted to maintain the precarious balance between slave and free states. Texas entered the Union as a slave state and California as a free state. The huge land base claimed by Texas was reduced and incorporated into new territories. The selling of slaves in the nation's capital was eliminated in return for a stronger law for capturing and returning escaped slaves throughout the nation.

Congress passed a bill creating western and northern boundaries for the new state of Texas. This act required Texas to relinquish all of its former territorial claims outside of the established boundary. Texas further had to turn over all forts, arsenals, and public buildings to the United States. Texas received $10 million for its relinquishment of territory and public property. The act established a territorial government in New Mexico, an area claimed by Texas. A companion act established the state of California. A third act established the territory of Utah, an area encompassing portions of modern Wyoming, Nevada, and Utah.

The fourth bill passed created significant conflict over the course of the next few years. Congress amended the fugitive slave act to expand the capabilities of territories and states to capture and return escaped slaves. The expanded act made it illegal to assist or harbor fugitive slaves and provided for civil damages to the injured property owner. Free states found themselves in the uncomfortable position of spending large sums of money to hunt down fugitive slaves and return them to captivity. Since some states had forbidden slavery within their borders after the establishment of the Union, being forced to participate in the enslavement of others was a direct assault upon what were considered their states' rights. The final bill in the compromise eliminated the sale of slaves within the District of Columbia. The right to hold slaves within the District of Columbia was defended vociferously and was not altered by the bill.

The Compromise of 1850 was a small bandage placed upon a large gaping wound. The amendments to the fugitive slave act served to increase sectional tensions. Civil war followed in Kansas in 1857, and was joined in 1861 by the remainder of the nation.

Terry A. Del Bene

See also: Calhoun, John C.; Clay, Henry; Douglas, Stephen A.; Mexican-American War.

Further Reading

Potter, David M. *The Impending Crisis*. New York: Harper & Row, 1976.

Conestoga Wagon

The Conestoga wagon, named for a valley in Lancaster County, Pennsylvania, became an established type of heavy-duty transport during the mid-1700s and varieties of its basic design continued their popularity well into the era of the nation's westward expansion. The original Conestogas were in demand by eastern industries such as gristmills, distilleries, tanyards, mines, and ironworks for hauling raw materials and finished products. Traveling a rate of 12 to 14 miles (20–23 km) per day, goods were conveyed by as many as 3,000 Conestoga wagons between Philadelphia and Lancaster during America's colonial period. Three pairs of specially bred draft horses were used in a common six-up hitch configuration, with nigh and off horses at lead, swing, and wheel positions.

Pennsylvania Dutch craftsmen built individual Conestogas with the distinctive characteristics of radically slanted endgates and sway-bellied sideboards topped by eight to twelve bentwood bows to support sheets of waterproofed sailcloth or homespun. Generally produced in three sizes, the wagons carried from 2 to 5 tons (1.8–4.5 mt). Farmers normally utilized smaller versions that required fewer draft animals to pull lighter loads. Conestoga wagons were designed with curved floorboards to force the load inward with every bump while traveling. Beautifully proportioned, yet practical, Conestogas were considered the covered wagon of their era.

The Conestoga wagon box, an open storage compartment, was positioned upon its framework of bolsters, hounds, coupling poles, and axletrees. Dished wooden-spoke wheels with 4-inch-wide (10-cm) iron rims varied slightly in diameter from 4 feet (1.2 m) in front to 5 or 6 feet (1.5–1.8 m) at the rear. The wheels were held in place by a linchpin, giving the classic vehicle yet another distinctive feature. Following precision work by wainwright and wheelwright, a blacksmith normally finished "ironing" each wagon, often ornamentally, prior to the wagon getting a paint job of traditional red running gear and blue sideboards. Attachments to accommodate a freighter included a feedbox, toolbox, water bucket, jack, axe, and tar pot filled with a sticky wheel lubricant. Conestogas remained on the job for over a century with slight modifications to original design. Even so, the manufacture of overland vehicles en masse surpassed outdated methods of handcrafting wagons as the frontier was extended westward.

The Conestoga teamster, much like the post–Civil War cowboy, was romanticized. Clothed in buckskins

The Conestoga wagon, designed by the Pennsylvania Dutch in the mid-1700s for hauling freight, could carry loads of up to 5 tons, pulled by teams of specially bred horses. Eight or more wooden bows supported a canvas or homespun cover. *(The Granger Collection, New York)*

or homespun and protected from sun and rain by a wide-brimmed hat, the man in charge rode aboard a lightweight saddle cinched to the nigh wheeler or walked to the left of his wagon. He commanded the team with loud cracks from a 7-foot (2-m) blacksnake whip, being careful to avoid contact with living horse-flesh. The lazy board might be used for a makeshift seat, advantageous for working the handbrake on a downhill grade.

Directional commands to the draft animals were transferred through a jerk line that looped forward along the harness rings of the nigh swing horse, and then up to the nigh leader where it separated at its neck and connected to the bit. A steady pull and a loud "haw" meant go left. A few quick jerks and "gee" was the right turn signal. A jockey stick linked the left front horse to its mate, the off leader, forcing it to honor each turn, while the rest of the team merely followed the leaders. Each horse had heavy leather traces, called tugs, which were connected back to wooden singletrees, in turn attached to doubletrees. The wheel team's doubletree pivoted on the wagon tongue and was held in place by the handle of an iron wagon ham-

mer, used to insert or remove the linchpins, allowing wheels to be greased daily.

Conestogas were utilized as supply wagons for General George Washington's army at Valley Forge, transported cannons from Cornwall, Pennsylvania, to Continental soldiers, carried $600,000 in silver loaned by France to the fledgling American government, and hauled gunpowder during the War of 1812. For sixty years following the Revolutionary War, the chief use of Conestoga wagons was hauling freight and farm produce across the Appalachian Mountains.

In later years, the American overland transportation era, once so dominated by Conestoga wagons, underwent significant changes. These began with the advent of the Santa Fe Trail during the 1820s as a highway of commerce from Missouri to New Mexico and the blossoming popularity of the Oregon Trail starting in the early 1840s, whereupon tens of thousands of emigrants made their way across the Great Plains to new homes in the trans-Mississippi West. Later, as speedy and powerful steam locomotives arrived on the scene, the trusty four-wheeled freight wagon, unrestricted by iron rails, was placed into service assuming different characteristics and setting a course to meet demands required for future transportation.

Dan R. Manning

See also: Oregon Trail; Prairie Schooner; Santa Fe Trail.

Further Reading

Ammon, Richard. *Conestoga Wagons*. New York: Holiday House, 2000.

Omwake, John. *The Conestoga Six-Horse Bell Teams of Eastern Pennsylvania*. Cincinnati: Ebbert & Richardson, 1930.

Shumway, George, et al. *Conestoga Wagon, 1750–1850*. York, PA: George Shumway and Early American Industries Association, 1966.

Cooke, Jay (1821–1905)

Jay Cooke's impact on westward expansion was far reaching and predicated by his agreeing to finance the Northern Pacific Railroad, which pushed the frontier 400 miles (645 km) westward to the Missouri River (Bismarck, North Dakota) between 1870 and 1873. The construction contributed to the creation of Yellowstone National Park, brought about the decision to build the Canadian Pacific Railroad, set off a surge in emigration to western Minnesota and eastern Dakota, and ignited the Great Sioux War. Then on September 18, 1873, the collapse of Cooke's banking house directly triggered the Panic of 1873.

Cooke was born on August 10, 1821, in Sandusky, Ohio, where his father was one of the community's founders, a classic frontier entrepreneur. As a teenager Cooke worked in St. Louis, acquiring a lifetime interest in the Northwest. Offered a job in a Philadelphia banking house, Cooke was so brilliant that, on his twenty-first birthday, he received one-eighth interest *gratis*. In 1861, with a moderate stockpile of personal wealth, he started his own firm, soon taking the lead role in selling Pennsylvania war bonds. By mid-1865 he had sold over $1.6 billion in war bonds for the Union, approximately 27 percent of all the money raised to pay the war's cost, his scrupulous honesty making him a hero to the public and the military.

By war's end Cooke was the nation's leading banker, having made a fortune using inside information against anti-government speculators including J.P. Morgan. Cooke's life held many contradictions; while he was active in the abolitionist movement, at one point hiding one of John Brown's sons after Harper's Ferry, he refused to let African-American soldiers ride his trolley cars in Washington during the war. A man of deep and sincere religious conviction, Cooke nevertheless was second to none in bribing congressmen. His philanthropic activities were legendary, but also he designed his own 75,000-square-foot (7,000 sq m) marble home, then the country's largest and most opulent. He was a generous manager and operated his banking house on a meritocracy system, but unilaterally made all final decisions of importance.

Cooke anticipated becoming President Ulysses S. Grant's secretary of the Treasury in 1869, but was bypassed by the president in favor of another supporter. Cooke, who had been making Minnesota railroad and land investments, then jumped at the chance to finance the Northern Pacific Railroad. He raised just over $20 million for the railroad, but his major initiatives were thwarted by the onset of the Franco-Prussian War, Canadian and British interests who feared western Canada was going the way of Texas and California, congressional allies of the Central Pacific and Union Pacific railroads, and Northern Pacific mismanagement and corruption. By the late 1870s, he was being increasingly drawn into the railroad's daily affairs. As President J. Gregory Smith's management became increasingly illogical and complaints about his honesty and management system increased, Cooke found himself taking an active role in the railroad's affairs to the detriment of his banking house.

In 1872, convinced of Smith's dishonesty, Cooke forced his resignation, but then had no operational replacement for months. Meanwhile, Cooke's younger banking partners, angry at his inability to develop new business and at the time he was spending on Northern Pacific matters, became increasingly concerned about the company's future. Making matters worse, publicity concerning Indian attacks on the railroad's surveyors dried up bond sales. By mid-1873, both Cooke's banking house and the Northern Pacific were all but out of cash. His New York partners then rebelled, literally shutting the doors to his Wall Street office.

Cooke lived in retirement after 1873 and died on February 2, 1905, seemingly content after emerging from bankruptcy with a few million dollars.

M. John Lubetkin

See also: Billings, Frederick; Northern Pacific Railroad; Pacific Railway Act (1862); Pacific Railway Act (1864); Villard, Henry; Yellowstone Surveying Expeditions.

Further Reading

Josephson, Matthew. *The Robber Barons*. New York: Harcourt, Brace & World, 1962.

Lubetkin, M. John. *Jay Cooke's Gamble: The Northern Pacific Railroad, the Sioux and the Panic of 1873*. Norman: University of Oklahoma Press, 2006.

Cooke, Philip St. George (1809–1895)

Philip St. George Cooke was a career officer in the U.S. Army for five decades, playing leadership roles in the exploration of the West and serving with distinction in the Mexican-American War, the Civil War, and several Indian conflicts. He was a cavalry tactician, an army administrator, and a battlefield commander, attaining the rank of brevet major general at the end of the Civil War. Ironically, he is also remembered for being the father of a Confederate general and the father-in-law of the South's most famous cavalry commander, J.E.B. Stuart.

Born in Leesburg, Virginia, on June 13, 1809, Cooke graduated from West Point in 1827 and initially served in the 6th Infantry Regiment. He was assigned to various posts in the West, participating in the Black Hawk War. He joined the 1st Dragoons in 1833 and was promoted to first lieutenant. During the Mexican-American War, Cooke rode with Colonel Stephen Watts Kearny's Army of the West and accompanied Missouri trader James Magoffin to Santa Fe to help broker a bloodless takeover of the city in August 1846. He then commanded the Mormon Battalion during much of its westward trek to California in 1846–1847, shepherding the men, women, and children from Santa Fe to San Diego. By this time Cooke had attained the brevet rank of lieutenant colonel.

After the Mexican-American War, Cooke served with the 2nd U.S. Dragoons in campaigns against the Sioux and in peacekeeping posts in "Bleeding Kansas." He participated in the Utah Expedition of 1857–1858 and the little known Utah War. Cooke was then promoted to colonel and took command of the 2nd Dragoons. After observing the Crimean War for the U.S. Army, he returned to Utah, where he commanded the Department of Utah in 1860–1861.

Before the Civil War, Cooke had written a manual of cavalry tactics that was later published in 1862. The U.S. Army never made its contents official doctrine, since many cavalry officers disagreed with Cooke's approach to mounted warfare. When the war began, he was the commanding officer of the 2nd Dragoons, one of five cavalry regiments in the regular U.S. Army.

Initially posted in Washington, DC, Cooke became a brigadier general in November 1861. The following spring General George B. McClellan, commander of the Army of the Potomac, mounted his Peninsula Campaign against Richmond. McClellan chose Cooke to command a large cavalry force in this army, and Cooke subsequently participated in several of the campaign's most significant battles. He led cavalry attacks at both Yorktown and Gaines' Mill in Virginia, both of which resulted in high casualties and arguable results. He was removed from field command after the Peninsula Campaign and served out the rest of the war in various administrative posts. The debacle of the Peninsula Campaign and his family members' commitment to the Confederacy undoubtedly caused Union officials to keep Cooke away from the battlefield. He continued serving in the army in other administrative jobs, including commanding the Department of the Platte, until his retirement in 1873. He wrote his memoirs in his later years and died in Detroit on March 20, 1895.

Jim Ersfeld

See also: Armijo, Manuel; Army of the West; Black Hawk War (1832); Magoffin, James Wiley; Mexican-American War; Mormon Battalion; Utah War.

Further Reading
Cooke, Philip St. George. *The Conquest of New Mexico and California in 1846–1848*. Chicago: Rio Grande Press, 1964.
Young, Otis E. *The West of Philip St. George Cooke, 1809–1985*. Glendale, CA: Arthur H. Clark, 1955.

Cordoba, Treaty of (1821)

Mexico's eleven-year struggle for independence was resolved by the Treaty of Cordoba. The insurgency had begun shortly after Napoleon I deposed King Carlos IV of Spain and replaced him with one of Napoleon's brothers. The French hold on New Spain was short-lived, but the revolution continued even after a Spanish monarchy had been restored. Augustin de Iturbide, a colonel in the Royal Army, switched sides at a critical juncture and, together with insurgent forces, systematically captured the population centers of Mexico. Commander in Chief de Iturbide was adept at bringing the splintered rebel forces together and eventually invested Mexico City itself. The king of Spain replaced his viceroy, Juan Apodaca, with the captain-general of New Spain, Juan de O'Donoju.

Realizing that Spanish control of New Spain was at an end, the Spanish government agreed to negotiate with the rebels in the town of Cordoba. The treaty included three guarantees: that the new government would recognize and establish the Catholic Church, that the Mexicans would have independence, and that the new nation would establish equality between the classes. De Iturbide and de O'Donoju signed the treaty on August 24, 1821. De Iturbide included a clause in the treaty that allowed him to seize power. The treaty allowed for a Mexican emperor if no European prince arrived to govern the nation. De Iturbide thus became the first emperor of Mexico; his reign was a troubled and short one.

Despite the ratification of the treaty, the transition to an independent Mexico was not easy. Spanish troops remained in the country for another eight years. The Spanish congress denounced the treaty in 1822 and the Mexican congress rebuked the plan and the treaty in 1823. With the collapse of the treaty, a constitutional convention drafted the Constitution of Mexico, which was adopted on October 4, 1824. General Guadalupe Victoria became the first constitutional president of Mexico. Emperor Augustin I retired to Europe.

Terry A. Del Bene

See also: Becknell, William; Gregg, Josiah; Santa Fe Trail.

Further Reading

Grabman, Richard, David Bodwell, and Joaquin Ramon Herrera. *Gods, Gachupines and Gringos: A People's History of Mexico.* Mazatlán, Mexico: Editorial Mazatlán, 2008.

Corps of Topographical Engineers

One of the nation's most successful initiatives in its surge westward over the thousands of square miles of mountains and plains of the trans-Mississippi region was the Corps of Topographical Engineers. With a staff never exceeding more than thirty-six officers, the Corps, over its brief lifespan of twenty-five years, explored, surveyed, documented, and mapped the burgeoning United States. In the words of William H. Goetzmann, in *Army Exploration in the American West, 1803–1863*, the corps was a "central institution of Manifest Destiny" that "functioned as a department of public works for the West."

The corps traced its origins to a small, dedicated government unit called the Topographical Bureau, formed in 1813, but greatly reduced in size following the War of 1812. As more and more emigrants pushed into the Ohio River valley and the Old Northwest, the bureau's size was again increased to deal with internal projects—canals, roadways, and river channel improvement—in the East. In 1829 Colonel John James Abert was appointed head of the bureau, a position he held until 1838 when the Corps of Topographical Engineers replaced the Topographical Bureau. Abert then took over the helm of the corps, a position he held for twenty-three of the corps' twenty-five years of existence.

The engineers of the corps followed upon the footsteps of another dynamic group in America's drive to the Pacific Ocean: the mountain men. Between the mountain men and the topographical engineers, hardly a township of the trans-Mississippi region was left unvisited. While the rugged, highly independent mountain men were shrewd, self-educated entrepreneurs who followed their trade for a combination of adventure and profit, the engineers were highly structured, well-educated scientists (only eight of the seventy-two officers who served in the corps over its lifespan were not West Point graduates) whose interests revolved around the topography, geology, botany, zoology, and ethnology of the region they were exploring. The mountain man's prize was a beaver pelt; the engineer's, a well-executed map of virgin territory that would assist generations of future emigrants.

It is difficult to assign meaningful degrees of importance to the men of the corps and to the many missions that they accomplished. One leader and his legacies were as significant as the next, although some assignments were much more involved than others and required more time and energy.

John C. Frémont, who became the Republican Party's first presidential candidate, began his military career as a lieutenant in the corps. Over the next eight years he participated in or led five expeditions that carried him from St. Louis to Fort Vancouver, in present-day Washington, and from Devil's Lake in what is now North Dakota to Monterey, California, and the shores of the Pacific. Probably more than any other topographical engineer—in part because he was the son-in-law of the powerful Missouri senator Thomas Hart Benton and had Benton's support and political assistance—Frémont epitomized the profession and entered the history books as the most noted member of the corps.

Others made equal marks upon the exploration and mapping of the West. During the Mexican-American

War (1846–1848), men of the corps rode with units of the regular army throughout the Southwest. Colonel Abert's son, Lieutenant James W. Abert—along with Lieutenants William H. Emory, William G. Peck, and William H. Warner—accompanied Colonel Stephen Watts Kearny's Army of the West on its conquest of New Mexico and California. Captain George W. Hughes and Lieutenants Lorenzo Sitgreaves and William B. Franklin were part of General John Wool's invasion of Mexico and the long march to Saltillo.

Following the war with Mexico, topographical engineers participated in two Mexican-American boundary surveys (1849–1855) to determine the boundary lines between the two countries established by the Treaty of Hidalgo and, later, the Gadsden Treaty. Emory, now a brevet major, filled the role of chief astronomer on the first survey, under the direction of Commissioner John Russell Bartlett, and was assisted by Lieutenants Amiel Weeks Whipple and Edmund L.F. Hardcastle. Emory and Lieutenant Nathaniel Michler divided the command of the second project.

While Emory and his associates were busy on the Mexican border, other topographical engineers were working on projects that would be critical to the nation's continually growing interest in westward emigration. A number of wagon roads linking remote points on the frontier were surveyed and laid out across the central and southern Great Plains. Captain Howard Stansbury explored and mapped the valley of the Great Salt Lake in 1849. Other important projects in which the corps participated were the transcontinental railroad surveys (1853–1855), site selection for strategic army forts and installations, and studies for the improvement of navigation on several rivers. Much knowledge of the high plains of present-day Nebraska, Montana, the Dakotas, and Wyoming, was gained by Lieutenant Gouverneur K. Warren and Captain William F. Raynolds.

No other group contributed more to America's westward movement than the Corps of Topographical Engineers. Its members lived up to the name bestowed upon them by Frank N. Schubert in the title of his study of the corps, the "vanguard of expansion." Not only did men of the unit produce detailed and accurate maps of previously uncharted regions, but also they authored and illustrated voluminous studies of the natural and ethnological history of the areas—studies that still are used by scholars today.

By the outbreak of the Civil War in 1861, many of the open spaces on maps of the American West had been filled in, thanks to the Corps of Topographical Engineers. As the war raged in the East, several engineers left the ranks to return home and join the Confederacy, while others were granted reassignment to combat units in the Union Army. These men, on both sides of the conflict, served their armies with distinction. The corps' commander, Colonel Abert, grew infirm and retired. On March 3, 1863, the corps was merged into the army's regular Corps of Engineers, the construction unit of the army that survives today.

James A. Crutchfield

See also: Abert, James William; Army of the West; Beale Wagon Road; Emory, William H.; Frémont, John C.; Gadsden Purchase (1853); Mexican Boundary Survey; Railroad Surveys, Transcontinental; Stansbury Expedition.

Further Reading

Goetzmann, William H. *Army Exploration in the American West, 1803–1863.* Lincoln: University of Nebraska Press, 1979.

Schubert, Frank N. *Vanguard of Expansion: Army Engineers in the Trans-Mississippi West, 1819–1879.* Washington, DC: Government Printing Office, 1980.

Traas, Adrian George. *From the Golden Gate to Mexico City: The U.S. Army Topographical Engineers in the Mexican War, 1846–1848.* Washington, DC: Government Printing Office, 1992.

Cox, Ross (1793–1853)

Young Irish-born Ross Cox arrived at Fort Astoria, Oregon, in May 1812, aboard the ship *Beaver*. Born in Dublin, Ireland, in 1793, he eventually immigrated to New York City, where in 1811 he hired on as a clerk with John Jacob Astor's Pacific Fur Company at a salary of $100 per year. Soon after disembarking at Astoria, located near the mouth of the Columbia River, he was assigned to march inland with a work party of trappers to build and equip a new fort on the Spokane River. He became lost when he wandered off into the forest and his companions left him behind. For two weeks he experienced a harrowing ordeal in the wilderness—with no weapons, no horse, nor any supplies—before friendly Indians found him.

Following the completion of the new post, called Fort Spokane, Cox departed the next spring and returned to Astoria. There he learned that war had been declared between the United States and Great Britain. He also discovered that his company's headquarters on the Columbia River had been occupied by trappers employed by the North West Company, a large Canadian outfit, and that they had renamed it Fort

George. With little choice, Cox hired on as a clerk with the new owners.

For the next several years, Cox traveled extensively between Fort George and the interior fur posts belonging to the North West Company, dealing with several Indian tribes, including the Flathead, Pend d'Oreille, Spokane, and Walla Walla. In 1816, he was placed in charge of Fort Okanogan, which had been built in 1811 and was the first United States settlement in present-day Washington. In late 1816, although he was still a young man, Cox retired from the fur trade and visited Fort George one last time. He then made an overland journey to Montreal and from there sailed to Dublin, where he married, wrote for a local newspaper, and served as a clerk for the city police department. Much of his later life—until his death in Dublin in 1853—remains a mystery. Fortunately for future generations, however, he left behind a valuable book, *Adventures on the Columbia River*, which documented his experiences in the wilds of the Pacific Northwest.

James A. Crutchfield

See also: Astor, John Jacob; Astoria.

Further Reading

Cox, Ross. *Adventures on the Columbia River.* Santa Barbara, CA: Narrative Press, 2003.

Dryden, Cecil. *Up the Columbia for Furs.* Caldwell, ID: Caxton Printers, 1949.

Crazy Horse (1840–1877)

War leader of the Oglala Lakota (Sioux), Crazy Horse is best known for his involvement in the Battle of the Little Bighorn, June 25, 1876, in which Lieutenant Colonel George Armstrong Custer and his command were annihilated by the combined force of Lakota and Northern Cheyenne warriors.

Crazy Horse, like all Oglala war leaders, had earlier made a reputation in battles with frontier soldiers and enemy tribesmen. He was born in the fall of 1840 to Rattle Blanket Woman and Crazy Horse, a family name he would eventually take. He was first called Curly Hair. As a child he learned Lakota ways and became known for his generosity, especially to elderly members of the tribe. He was a contemporary of such important northern Plains leaders as Sitting Bull, Gall, American Horse, and Red Cloud.

The first armed confrontation between the frontier military and Sioux tribesmen took place in 1854 at the Grattan fight (Grattan Massacre) near Fort Laramie. The following year young Curly Hair was at the edge of the fighting when General William Harney attacked a Sioux camp in what became known as the Battle of Blue Water Creek. Shortly after this, the boy set off on a vision quest. He drew strength and direction for his life from this pivotal action. Four years later, as a young warrior, he rode with Cheyenne allies; still later he would fight against the Crows.

In 1857 Curly Hair engaged with fellow tribesmen in a battle with some Arapahos, during which he proved his daring and war prowess. Following this fight, he was given the name Crazy Horse by his father, who himself took the name Worm. Subsequently Crazy Horse married, had a daughter who died at a young age, and participated in intertribal battles and altercations with the frontier military, including the July 1865 battle at Platte Bridge and the 1866 Fetterman fight (Fetterman Massacre), all leading up to the battle at the Little Bighorn in 1876.

Crazy Horse became one of the most important war chiefs on the northern Plains, recognized both within his Oglala Lakota band and by other tribal leaders. He was charismatic yet reclusive, apparently never had his photograph taken (although some purported photos of him have surfaced), and was strongly loyal to the people in his camp. From his first observations of western encroachment into tribal territory in the 1850s, he firmly resisted the advance of white settlement and any cooperation with whites. The 1851 Horse Creek Treaty allowing for the building of roads and the establishment of army military posts, as well as subsequent treaty agreements, were never accepted by Crazy Horse and his immediate followers. With them he strongly resisted gold mining incursions into the Black Hills and fought to retain the Powder River Basin country of present Wyoming, which was traditional tribal territory.

Crazy Horse surrendered to military authorities in the spring of 1877, most likely because of the illness of his wife, Black Shawl, who had tuberculosis. He settled in a camp near Camp Robinson, in northwestern Nebraska, where he lived peacefully through the summer. In August, however, when military authorities asked Crazy Horse (then a sergeant in the Indian Police) to assist in bringing the Nez Percé Indians led by Chief Joseph under control, the chief's message was misinterpreted, leading some military leaders to believe that Crazy Horse intended to return to the warpath. He was subsequently taken to Camp Robinson, and when military officials attempted to place him in the guardhouse, he was fatally stabbed. He died in the late evening on September 5, 1877, with his father, Worm, his uncle Touch-the-Clouds, and Dr. Valentine T. McGillycuddy, an army surgeon who had treated his wound, by his side. His parents took the body and buried it at an undisclosed location in Lakota Territory.

Candy Moulton

See also: American Horse; Blue Water Creek, Battle of; Chief Joseph; Custer, George Armstrong; Fort Robinson; Gall; Grattan Massacre; Harney, William S.; Horse Creek Treaty (1851); Powder River Expedition (1865); Powder River Expedition (1876); Red Cloud; Red Cloud's War; Sitting Bull.

Further Reading

Bray, Kingsley M. *Crazy Horse: A Lakota Life.* Norman: University of Oklahoma Press, 2006.

Brininstool, E.A. *Crazy Horse: The Invincible Ogallalla Sioux Chief.* Los Angeles: Wetzel, 1949.

Buecker, Thomas R., and Eli Paul, eds. *The Crazy Horse Surrender Ledger.* Lincoln: University of Nebraska State Historical Society, 1994.

Clark, Robert A., ed. *The Killing of Chief Crazy Horse: Three Eyewitness Views by the Indian, Chief He Dog, the Indian-White, William Garnett, the White Doctor, Valentine McGillycuddy, with commentary by Carroll Friswold.* Lincoln: University of Nebraska, Bison Books, 1988.

Hardorff, Richard G. *The Death of Crazy Horse: A Tragic Episode in Lakota History.* Lincoln: University of Nebraska Press, 2001.

Marshall, Joseph, III. *The Journey of Crazy Horse.* New York: Viking, 2004.

Creek

Ethnological studies indicate that the Creek (Muscogee or Muskogee) people were descended from the Mississippian culture of the American Southeast, an agricultural, mound-building people of the era of about 800 to 1500 C.E. Originally, the Creeks were a scattered confederacy of agricultural tribes rather than a single unit, occupying villages in the rich river bottomlands of Tennessee, Alabama, and central and southern Georgia. The modern city of Macon, Georgia, is the location of Ocmulgee Old Fields, where ancient funeral mounds and temple ruins are located in the city's Ocmulgee National Monument. The monument, ancestral home of the Creeks and their forebears, preserves evidence of 12,000 years of habitation by the area's Native American people.

As with the Choctaws and other southeastern tribes, the Creeks' first encounter with Europeans occurred in 1540 when the rapacious Spanish conquistador Hernando de Soto explored the region. The Muscogee people came to be called "Creeks" by British traders who encountered the tribe living along the Ocmulgee River and its waterways in central Georgia. ("Okmulgee" is a Creek word said to mean "boiling or bubbling water.")

The Creeks were divided in their loyalties in the American Revolutionary War. The Upper Muscogees were allied with the British and fought with the Cherokees, Chickasaws, Shawnees, and others against the American patriots. These pro-British Creeks occupied riparian areas in Georgia and Alabama. The Lower Muscogees (the terms, geographical in nature, were of British origin), who were located largely in villages on the Chattahoochee River along the Georgia-Alabama border, remained neutral throughout the war.

With the end of the war in 1783, Creek homelands fell under the laws of the new United States. A consequence of this was the elevation of Georgia to statehood in 1788 and white settlers invading Creek territory. In this period rose one of the heroes of tribal history, the Creek statesman Alexander McGillivray (c. 1759–1793), who organized Indian opposition to the encroachment. The son of a Scots trader and a French-Indian mother, McGillivray signed a treaty in 1790 that ceded a large portion of Creek lands to the United States in exchange for federal recognition of Creek sovereignty in the remaining tribal territory.

An Upper Muscogee faction known as the Red Sticks (for their red-painted war clubs) sought to fight the incursion into their lands by white settlers and the attempts to "civilize" the tribe. The Red Sticks went to war against Americans in August 1813 by attacking Fort Mims, an army post near Mobile, Alabama. The war, which lasted a year, cost the Creeks at least 3,000 casualties and half of their homelands.

As one of the Five Civilized Tribes (with the Cherokees, Chickasaws, Choctaws, and Seminoles), so called for their adoption of many of the customs and social practices of white colonists, the Creeks were subject to President Andrew Jackson's Indian removal policy. In 1834 most of the tribe followed the Trail of Tears—the long road of exile to designated lands in Indian Territory (Oklahoma).

Today, the Creek (officially Muscogee) Nation is headquartered in Okmulgee, in east-central Oklahoma, with the tribe integrated into the larger population of the state. Other Muscogee tribal towns are Wetumka and Okemah, Oklahoma, and Atmore, Alabama. There are also small tribal enclaves in Georgia and Florida.

Dale L. Walker

See also: Cherokee; Chickasaw; Choctaw; Creek Wars; Indian Removal Act (1830); Jackson, Andrew; Jackson's Indian Policy; Trail of Tears.

Further Reading

Debo, Angie. *Road to Disappearance: A History of the Creek Indians.* Norman: University of Oklahoma Press, 1979.

Ethridge, Robbie. *Creek Country: The Creek Indians and Their World, 1796–1816.* Chapel Hill: University of North Carolina Press, 2003.

O'Brien, Sean Michael. *In Bitterness and in Tears: Andrew Jackson's Destruction of the Creeks and Seminoles.* Guilford, CT: Lyons Press, 2005.

Creek Wars

The Creek (Muscogee) people and many other tribes of the southeastern United States took part in the Yamasee War of 1715–1718, a conflict between native people and white colonists in what was later known as South Carolina. This little-known but consequential fight came close to ending white settlement in the battle area and nearly exterminated the nearby Yamasee tribe.

Of far more importance to tribal history than the Yamasee War, or the many internecine wars in which the Creeks were involved, was the Creek War of 1813–1814, also known as the Red Stick War. This bloody struggle began with clashes within the Muscogee, or Creek, nation over the paramount issues of acculturation—adapting to white policies, laws, and social systems—and the increasing incursions by white settlers into Indian lands.

The Upper Muscogees, who came to be called the Red Sticks for their red-painted war clubs, occupied riparian villages in Georgia and central Alabama. They had allied with the British in the American Revolution and were aggressively opposed to the idea of acculturation, which was espoused by U.S. Indian agent Benjamin Hawkins (1754–1816). He organized farms, mills, and trading posts and taught agricultural techniques, livestock-raising, and other "civilized" skills and ideas to the Creeks. But the Red Sticks, influenced by their prophets and the nativist, anti-American eloquence of the Shawnee leader Tecumseh, rejected the white

teachings and vowed to resist further white takeover of tribal lands. Inevitably, the Red Sticks clashed with the Lower Muscogee people (often called White Sticks), who resided along the Georgia-Alabama border and were allied with the American colonists. Worse, the Red Sticks went to war against the Americans.

On August 30, 1813, a Red Stick band attacked Fort Mims, an American outpost 40 miles (64 km) north of Mobile, Alabama. The Red Sticks captured the fort by surprise and massacred between 350 and 500 of its occupants, including women and children. Army and militia retaliation was swift and deadly. Tennessee militia, U.S. Army regulars, and Cherokee, Choctaw, and Lower Muscogee warriors commanded by General Andrew Jackson began a scorched earth campaign against the Red Sticks. In November, at the village of Talishatchee in Alabama, nearly 200 Red Stick warriors were killed. Militiaman David Crockett, who participated in the battle, later said, "We killed them like dogs."

Jackson's Creek campaign (considered part of the War of 1812) reached its climax on March 27, 1814, at the Horseshoe Bend of the Tallapoosa River in central Alabama. The battle resulted in nearly 900 Red Stick warriors killed against fifty American dead. On August 9, the Creeks signed the Treaty of Fort Jackson (near Montgomery, Alabama), ceding 23 million acres (9.3 million ha)—more than half their homelands in Alabama and Georgia—to the United States. The White Sticks, which had aided Jackson's campaign, were also forced to sign the treaty.

In 1834 the Creeks, one of the designated Five Civilized Tribes, were subject to President Jackson's Indian removal policy and followed the 1,000-mile (1,600-km) Trail of Tears to Indian Territory (Oklahoma). In 1836 a faction among the Creeks who remained in the area of the Chattahoochee River between Georgia and Alabama took part in an uprising protesting mistreatment by encroaching white settlers. The two-month Second Creek War ended with some 2,500 Creeks marched to Montgomery for subsequent removal to Oklahoma.

Dale L. Walker

See also: Creek; Jackson, Andrew; Tecumseh; Trail of Tears.

Further Reading

Debo, Angie. *Road to Disappearance: A History of the Creek Indians.* Norman: University of Oklahoma Press, 1979.

Groneman, William, III. *David Crockett.* New York: Forge Books, 2005.

Martin, Joel W. *Sacred Revolt: The Muskogees' Struggle for a New World.* Boston: Beacon Press, 1991.

Saunt, Claudio. *A New Order of Things: Property, Power, and the Transformation of the Creek Indians, 1733–1816.* New York: Cambridge University Press, 1999.

Crockett, Davy (1786–1836)

David Crockett, hero of the battle at the Alamo during the Texas fight for independence from Mexico, was born on August 17, 1786, in present-day Greene County, Tennessee, one of nine children of John and Rebecca Hawkins Crockett. Crockett left his home at a young age and spent much of his time on the road, working a variety of jobs such as cattle driver, freighter, and hatter, often paying off his father's debts. His formal education totaled six months.

Crockett married Mary (Polly) Finley in 1806. Their union produced three children: John Wesley (1807), William (1809), and Margaret (1812). After Polly's death in about 1815, Crockett married Elizabeth Patton, a widow with two children, and together they had three more children: Robert Patton (1816), Rebecca Elvira (1818), and Matilda (1821).

Crockett and his first wife lived on Bean's Creek in Franklin County, Tennessee, near the Alabama border when the Creek Indian War broke out in 1813. He volunteered for service with the U.S. Army, serving as a scout and hunter and taking part in the battles of Tallusahatchee, Talladega, and Enotochopco. After a furlough, he returned to service in 1814, pursuing the Creek through the swamps of southern Alabama and western Florida. Crockett left military service in 1815 with the rank of sergeant.

Upon returning home, Crockett farmed, an occupation he found "wan't the thing it was cracked up to be," hunted, and served as a lieutenant in Franklin County's 32nd Militia Regiment. He also suffered his first bouts of malaria, probably contracted during his journeys through western Florida.

By 1818 he had moved his family west to Shoal Creek, where he served the new community as a magistrate, justice of the peace, town commissioner, and lieutenant colonel of the 57th Regiment of Militia. Crockett entered politics in 1821 when he was elected to the Tennessee state legislature. During this time he and Elizabeth suffered a financial blow when a flood destroyed their newly established dam, grist and powder mills, and distillery.

Crockett soon moved his family yet again, this time to the Obion River country in western Tennessee, near the stream's confluence with the Mississippi River. He won another term in the legislature in 1823, representing five counties in western Tennessee, but lost a more ambitious bid for the U.S. Congress in 1825. He did not abandon politics, however, winning a seat in the U.S. House of Representatives in 1827 and again in 1829. He lost the next election of 1831, but returned to Congress for the last time in 1833. Throughout his political career Crockett fought for the right of his constituents—the poor squatters of western Tennessee—to own the land they settled and developed. His stand brought him into conflict with President Andrew Jackson and other Tennessee political leaders, including future president James K. Polk. Crockett's stubborn opposition to Jackson on every issue led to his drift from the Democratic Party to that of the Whigs.

Crockett's reputation as an eccentric backwoods member of Congress achieved national attention through production of the play *The Lion of the West* (1831), featuring a character loosely based on him, and the publication of *Life and Adventures of Colonel David Crockett of West Tennessee* (1833). Crockett, dissatisfied with his portrayal in the latter work, published his autobiography, *A Narrative of the Life of David Crockett of the State of Tennessee*, in 1834. His book proved very popular; historians agree that it remains a classic of American history and autobiography.

The author toured the Northeast in 1834, visiting Philadelphia, New York City, Boston, and other stops, sponsored by the Whigs. He promoted his book, enjoyed celebrity treatment, and delivered an anti-Jackson speech at stops along the way.

Crockett left for the Mexican territory of Texas in the autumn of 1835 after losing the election of that year. He intended to explore Texas well before relocating there permanently with his family. He arrived in Texas just after settlers of the territory had launched a revolt against the government of Mexico. Crockett offered his services, volunteering for the newly formed Texan army in January 1836 at Nacogdoches, Texas. One month later he arrived in San Antonio de Bexar, joining the Texan garrison there under the command of William Barret Travis and James Bowie.

The Mexican army, led by Generalissimo Antonio López de Santa Anna, arrived on February 23 and besieged the Texans in the former Spanish mission San Antonio de Valero, then known as the Alamo. The siege lasted thirteen days until Santa Anna's troops took the fort by storm. Crockett died in the Alamo on March 6, 1836.

William Groneman III

See also: Alamo, The; Bowie, James; Fannin, James Walker; Goliad, Battle of; Texas Revolution and Independence; Travis, James Barret.

Further Reading

Crockett, David. *A Narrative of the Life of David Crockett of the State of Tennessee*. 1834. Lincoln: University of Nebraska Press, 1987.

Groneman, William, III. *Death of a Legend: The Myth and Mystery Surrounding the Death of Davy Crockett*. Plano: Republic of Texas Press, 1999.

———. *David Crockett: Hero of the Common Man*. New York: Forge Books, 2005.

Crook, George (1829–1890)

George Crook battled American Indian warriors for four decades between the 1850s and the 1880s, and was recognized as an unorthodox, courageous, and resourceful commander, eventually becoming known among his respectful Indian foes as the "Grey Fox."

Crook was born on September 23, 1829, and raised on an Ohio farm. At the age of eighteen he was admitted to West Point, where Philip Sheridan, who would also become a noted army general, was his roommate. Graduating near the bottom of his class in 1852, Crook was commissioned a lieutenant of the 4th Cavalry, serving for eight years on the Pacific Coast. He helped build military posts, escorted explorers' parties, and campaigned against Indians in the Rogue River and the Yakima wars. The innovative young officer learned to fight frontier-style, emulating guerilla tactics of the Indians and subsisting off the land while in the field. He respected his opponents. With equal eccentricity he determined to drill his troops and instruct them in marksmanship.

When the Civil War began, Crook obtained the colonelcy of the 36th Ohio Volunteer Infantry, witnessing heavy combat and sustaining severe wounds. Under General Sheridan, he led a cavalry division and commanded a corps, rising to major general of volunteers.

Crook returned to the frontier in 1867 as a lieutenant colonel of the 23rd Infantry. From Boise, Idaho Territory, he took the field in pursuit of Paiute raiders. Free to develop his innovative methods of Indian fighting as commander of the Department of the Columbia, he pacified the area within a year.

Crook exacted loyalty, affection, and supreme effort from his men. He incessantly pumped his sub-ordinates for information, but never revealed his plans to them. He did not bother his officers with detailed instructions, expecting them to exercise initiative. Two keys to Crook's success against various hostile tribes were his use of pack trains, which he perfected to a science and which provided far greater mobility than wagon trains, and his liberal employment of Indian scouts.

In 1871 Crook was placed in charge of the Department of Arizona, where the ferocious and resourceful Apaches raided at will. Crook hounded the hostiles ceaselessly, and by 1873 most Apaches were on reservations. He was promoted to brigadier general to fill the vacancy of the recently slain E.R.S. Canby. Crook thus bypassed numerous officers, and his controversial promotion was bitterly resented by many men with greater seniority. Aware of his own talents and industriousness, Crook scorned his critics and was as outspokenly contemptuous of them as he had been of ineffective officers during the Civil War.

General George Crook earned a reputation as one of the U.S. Army's most effective Indian fighters, with successes in the Snake War (1864–1868), the Apache Wars of the 1870s and 1880s, and the Great Sioux War of 1876–1877. *(Kean Collection/Getty Images)*

After gold was discovered in the Black Hills in 1874–1875, General Crook was given command of the Department of the Platte, in anticipation of trouble with the Sioux and Cheyenne tribes. He commanded the Newton-Jenney Expedition in 1875, which conducted a survey of the Black Hills to determine the existence and extent of the gold deposits reported the previous year by an expedition led by Lieutenant Colonel George A. Custer. When hostilities erupted in June 1876, he led more than 1,200 men in the Battle of the Rosebud, one of the most significant clashes of the Indian Wars. Crook lost the battle and withdrew from active fighting while awaiting reinforcements, perhaps contributing indirectly to Custer's disastrous defeat a week later.

He remained in the field through the summer and fall of 1876, leading his men in a horrific expedition across the western Dakotas in September that became known as the Horsemeat March or Starvation March, when his command ran out of supplies and had to eat their horses for survival. While on this particular march, they also engaged Lakota Sioux at Slim Buttes in the first major battle after Little Bighorn.

An inveterate outdoorsman, Crook habitually ranged ahead of his column in the field on solitary hunting and scouting forays. During his years in the West he killed animals of virtually every known species and caught almost every type of fish. He eventually became a taxidermist and preserved his own trophies. Crook often made significant contributions to the mess tables of his men with his hunting and fishing. When his men saw smoke ahead, animals were brought forward to pack whatever meat he had provided. His personal probes also taught him a great deal about the plant life and terrain of the areas in which he was stationed, information that he utilized in planning his campaigns. He almost always refused an escort, not wanting to overwork his men. Crook shunned uniforms, preferring to wear canvas clothes and a straw hat. He liked to ride a mule, with a rifle or shotgun balanced across his pommel for quick use. He seldom—some sources say never—used liquor, tobacco, tea, coffee, or profanity. He was tall, lean, erect, and sported a forked beard.

In 1882 General Crook returned to Arizona, where restless Apaches were raiding off their reservations. He launched a relentless effort, including a landmark campaign into the Sierra Madre Mountains of Mexico in 1883. Two years later Geronimo led a relatively minor breakout, but when civilians, newspapers, and even General Sheridan criticized his methods, Crook resigned. Crook's rival, Nelson A. Miles, ultimately accepted Geronimo's surrender.

Incensed by the removal to Florida of his faithful Apache scouts, Crook waged a fruitless correspondence to see justice done. In 1888 he was promoted to major general and assigned to the Division of the Missouri. Crook and his wife, Mary, moved to headquarters in Chicago, where he died of a heart attack on March 21, 1890.

Bill O'Neal

See also: Apache; Black Hills Expeditions; Custer Expedition; Geronimo; Sheridan, Philip H.

Further Reading

Bourke, John Gregory. *On the Border with Crook*. Boulder, CO: Johnson Publishing, 1962.

———. *With General Crook in the Indians Wars*. Palo Alto, CA: Lewis Osborne, 1968.

Crook, George. *General George Crook: His Autobiography*. Norman: University of Oklahoma Press, 1946.

Thrapp, Dan L. *General Crook and the Sierra Madre Adventure*. Norman: University of Oklahoma Press, 1972.

Crooks, Ramsay (1787–1859)

Ramsay Crooks, the man largely responsible for the abolition of the U.S. government–operated fur trade with the Indians (the factory system), was born on January 7, 1787, near Glasgow, Scotland, the son of a shoemaker and his wife. Following the father's death, the family migrated to Montreal in 1803, young Crooks himself moving to St. Louis by early 1807. There, in the town that was already deeply involved in the western fur trade—although Lewis and Clark had only returned from the Pacific the previous year—he immersed himself in the Missouri River Indian trade. For three years, he operated a small fur company with Robert McClellan, before hiring on with John Jacob Astor's much larger Pacific Fur Company.

During 1810–1812, Crooks accompanied Wilson Price Hunt and his overland party from St. Louis to Astoria, located at the mouth of the Columbia River. One month after he arrived on the shores of the Pacific Ocean, Crooks prepared to return to St. Louis as one of Robert Stuart's party, arriving there in April 1813. It was on this trip that Crooks and the others discovered and traversed South Pass, a natural passageway through the Rocky Mountains, although their direction was from west to east.

For the next several years, Crooks worked primarily in the Great Lakes region and along the Ohio River, where he became a valuable lieutenant of John Jacob Astor and his rapidly growing fur empire. At one point in his career, he owned at least one-fifth of Astor's American Fur Company. In 1822, it was Crooks, with the help of Missouri senator Thomas Hart Benton, who lobbied Congress to abolish the government factory system so that privately owned fur interests could obtain a larger portion of the ever-growing and very lucrative western fur trade.

Upon Astor's exit from the fur business in 1834, Crooks bought out the Northern Department of American Fur and continued its operation in the Great Lakes region for eight years, before the company—weakened by the Panic of 1837—finally succumbed in 1842.

Until his death in New York City on June 6, 1859, Crooks remained a prominent fur merchant, with a reputation for honesty and integrity in his business affairs with both fellow fur men and Indians, as well as in his personal life. He had one daughter, born in 1817, by a Chippewa Indian woman and took full responsibility for her upbringing and education. His marriage to Emile Pratt, daughter of St. Louis fur entrepreneur, Bernard Pratt, in 1825, produced nine children, six of whom preceded him in death. Crook is buried in Greenwood Cemetery in Brooklyn, New York.

James A. Crutchfield

See also: American Fur Company; Astor, John Jacob; Benton, Thomas Hart; Factory System; Hunt, Wilson Price; Stuart, Robert.

Further Reading

Lavender, David. *The Fist in the Wilderness*. Garden City, NY: Doubleday, 1964.

Crow

Originally known as the Absarokees (pronounced ab-zor-keys), which in the Hidatsa language means "children of the large-beaked bird," the Crow Indians generations ago lived in the northeastern United States in the "Land of Many Lakes." Today the Crows refer to themselves as Apsáalooke or Bíiluuke, which translates as "our side." As they note, to be Bíiluuke implies common genetic ancestry and, most important, common language, spiritual beliefs, and social structure.

Linguistically the tribe is Siouan. Other tribes in that region, including the Cree, Ojibwa, and Chippewa, forced the Crow people to migrate west into the woodlands of present-day Wisconsin and eventually across the Mississippi River onto the Great Plains. While living in the woodlands, the Crows were adept farmers, but after migrating west into what is today North and South Dakota, they became primarily hunters and gathers, ultimately claiming a territory encompassing much of northeastern Wyoming and southern Montana.

In moving west, the Crows divided into two main bands: the River Crows, who lived along the Yellowstone, Milk, and Missouri rivers in today's Montana, and the Mountain Crows, who had territory in the high ranges of northern Wyoming and southern Montana. A third band, the Kicked in the Bellies, was closely related to the Mountain Crows. All three groups believed in First Maker; took part in Sun Dances, vision quests, and other tribal ceremonies; and had strong family units as well as a clan system, which diminished in prominence during the nineteenth century.

Their first contact with European explorers came in 1743 when the La Vérendrye brothers ventured through Crow territory on an exploratory trip. On his return from the Pacific coast in 1806, Captain William Clark met Crow tribal members along the Yellowstone River in southern Montana at the site he would name Pompey's Pillar. In the early 1800s, fur trappers and traders moved into Crow country, establishing forts and posts where they could trade with the native inhabitants. The Crows signed their first treaty with the United States in 1825, leading to friendly relations. The first erosion of their western territory came from internecine battles with enemy tribes, particularly the Sioux and Blackfoot, and in 1851 they entered into another treaty with the United States, negotiated at Fort Laramie, that established "boundaries" for the tribes.

By the time the Crows agreed to provisions of an 1868 treaty negotiated at Fort Laramie that again reduced their territory, they had already been pushed into a smaller region as a result of conflict with other tribes. The Crows sided with the U.S. military, providing scouts for frontier army troops, including some who rode with the 7th Cavalry during the lead-up to the Battle of Little Bighorn in 1876.

Among the important Crows were Red Bear, a warrior and River Crow chief from about 1807 to the 1860s; Rotten Tail, a River Crow leader during the 1840s and a medicine man and pipe carrier (war party commander); Plenty Coups, a Mountain Crow leader who was a visionary, diplomat, and last principal chief of the Crow tribe; Medicine Crow, who became chief about 1870 and led the tribe during the period of assimilation; Pretty Eagle, a reservation-era leader, recognized as a head chief in 1890; White-Man Runs Him, Curly, and Hairy Moccasin, scouts for Custer; Woman Chief, a Gros Ventre by birth who was taken captive and raised by the Crows, among whom she became an important war leader.

Today the Crow Nation has a population of about 10,000 and a reservation on a reduced portion of their historic territory located primarily in Montana, with some territory in the Northern Big Horn Mountains of Wyoming. They hold an annual gathering, Crow Fair, near Hardin, Montana, where they share traditional dances and music, crafts, and handiwork.

Candy Moulton

See also: Custer, George Armstrong; Fort Laramie, Treaty of (1868); Lewis and Clark Expedition.

Further Reading
Linderman, Frank B. *Pretty Shield: Medicine Woman of the Crows.* Lincoln: University of Nebraska Press, 1972.

Medicine Crow, Joseph. *From the Heart of the Crow Country: The Crow Indians' Own Stories.* Foreword by Herman J. Viola. Lincoln: University of Nebraska Press, 2000.

Cumberland Gap

During the last quarter of the eighteenth century and during the first decade of the nineteenth, Cumberland Gap—a passageway through the southern Appalachian Mountains that is also referred to as the Wilderness Road—became one of America's most important thoroughfares for westward migration into the Ohio River valley.

From the first permanent English settlement at Jamestown, Virginia, in 1607 until the mid-1700s, European settlers had contented themselves with occupying the narrow strip of land between the Atlantic Ocean and the eastern slopes of the Appalachians. The culmination of the French and Indian War, however, and the signing of the Treaty of Paris in 1763, transferred millions of acres of previously French-claimed land to England, and despite King George III's Proclamation of 1763 forbidding settlement on all lands lying west of the crest of the Appalachians, land-hungry colonials immediately cast their eyes toward the setting sun.

Thomas Walker (1715–1794), a Virginia-born physician and agent for the Loyal Company, a land speculation concern, was among the first to explore the southern part of the Appalachians lying along the present-day Tennessee-Kentucky-Virginia border. In April 1750, Walker and a few companions discovered what in later years became known as Cumberland Gap, an easy passageway through the lofty mountains. The gap was named in honor of King George II's second son, the Duke of Cumberland. Nearly twenty years later, Daniel Boone passed through the gap during his exploration of the region. Just prior to Richard Henderson's treaty with the Cherokee at Sycamore Shoals in March 1775, Boone, with thirty axmen to assist him, again set out westward and blazed a trail from the Long Island of the Holston River (present-day Kingsport, Tennessee) to the bluegrass country of Kentucky, where he founded Boonesborough. Initially called Boone's Trace, the path later became known as the Wilderness Road.

Between 1776 and 1810, an estimated 200,000 to 300,000 emigrants passed through Cumberland Gap on their way from the eastern settlements to the fertile lands of Kentucky and the Ohio River valley. By 1800, Kentucky (1792) and Tennessee (1796) had become states of the Union. In the meantime, the Wilderness Road, now improved to accommodate wagons and other wheeled vehicles, began witnessing eastern-bound traffic as well, primarily produce—corn whiskey, livestock, and turkeys—headed for eastern markets.

As eastern canals, improved roads, and railroads progressively populated the countryside during the early to middle 1800s, traffic declined along the Wilderness Road. Although considered a strategic position by both the Union and Confederate high commands during the Civil War (General Ulysses S. Grant called it the "Gibraltar of America"), Cumberland Gap and its surrounding lands saw little action during the conflict. In 1940 the Cumberland Gap National Historical Park was authorized by Congress, finally opening in 1955.

James A. Crutchfield

See also: Boone, Daniel; Boonesborough, Kentucky; Land Speculation Companies; Proclamation of 1763.

Further Reading
Kincaid, Robert L. *Wilderness Road.* Indianapolis: Bobbs-Merrill, 1947.

Steele, William O. *The Old Wilderness Road: An American Journey.* New York: Harcourt, Brace & World, 1968.

Custer, Elizabeth Bacon (1842–1933)

Elizabeth Bacon Custer was born in 1842 in Monroe, Michigan. She was the only surviving child of Daniel Bacon, a wealthy businessman. She attended schools in Monroe and Grand Rapids, where she was taught to embody the Victorian virtues of piety, submissiveness, religiosity, and domesticity.

Libbie, as she became known, knew George Armstrong Custer, or Autie, from childhood, but he did not propose until 1863. They were married in 1864 and Libbie escaped an ordinary life in Monroe for the excitement of life as an army bride in Washington, DC. Her beauty, charm, wit, and humor served to advance Autie's career in Washington just as his bravery and daring advanced it on the battlefield. Custer's cook and housekeeper, Eliza Brown, took care of their domestic needs while Libbie learned how to become an officer's wife.

Following the end of the Civil War, Custer was assigned to New Orleans, and then Texas, and Libbie accompanied him, often riding sidesaddle for hours. She accepted the hardships of an officer's wife as the price she paid to be with her "bo." She lived in a tent, washed in a basin, did her hair without a mirror, and dressed in the dark for an early departure as the regiment traveled across Louisiana and Texas.

After serving in Texas, Custer was assigned to the 7th Cavalry at Fort Riley, Kansas. Libbie led the young wives' social activities and reveled in riding across the plains with Autie. Custer fought Indians across Kansas, Oklahoma, and Texas. In 1867 he was court-martialed for, among other reasons, cruelty to deserters and being insensitive to his troops. Custer and Libbie lived at Fort Leavenworth during his punishment, but General Philip Sheridan wanted him in the field, so after nine months the Custers returned to Fort Riley and Custer resumed chasing Indians across Kansas. They later moved to North Dakota, where Libbie was living at Fort Abraham Lincoln at the time of Custer's death.

After Custer's defeat and death at the Battle of the Little Big Horn in 1876, Libbie developed a career as the hero's widow, writing the *Complete Life of General George Armstrong Custer*, defending her late husband's actions, vaunting his bravery, and cultivating the myth of "the general." She worked for the Society of Decorative Arts in New York City and eventually overcame her grief to write three books: *Boots and Saddles* (1885),

Tenting on the Plains (1887), and *Following the Guidon* (1890). While Libbie wrote primarily of lighthearted times on the plains, the books served to promote Custer's reputation and counteract criticism of his actions and personality. She drew vivid pictures of life as an army wife and the successful books led to a career on the lecture circuit.

She left notes for a book about their Civil War experiences, which she never finished. Out of deference to Mrs. Custer, many people withheld negative comments about Custer, waiting until her death, but she outlived most of the critics, dying in 1933 at the age of ninety.

Lenore Carroll

See also: Custer, George Armstrong; Washita Engagement.

Further Reading

Custer, Elizabeth Bacon. *Boots and Saddles, Or Life in Dakota with General Custer*; various reprint editions.

———. *Following the Guidon*; various reprint editions.

———. *Tenting on the Plains: With General Custer from the Potomac to the Western Frontier*; various reprint editions.

Leckie, Shirley A. *Elizabeth Bacon Custer and the Making of a Myth*. Norman: University of Oklahoma Press, 1998.

Merrington, Marguerite. *The Custer Story: The Life and Intimate Letters of General George A. Custer and His Wife Libbie*. Lincoln: University of Nebraska Press, 1987.

Custer, George Armstrong (1839–1876)

No frontier soldier is more famous, or more controversial, than the golden-haired cavalier George Armstrong Custer. Born in New Rumley, Ohio, on December 5, 1839, and raised in Monroe, Michigan, Custer won an appointment to West Point in 1857, graduating four years later as the goat of his class. A meteoric rise followed his appointment as a second lieutenant in the 2nd Cavalry. Excellent staff service with Civil War generals George B. McClellan and Alfred Pleasonton won Custer a brigadier's star in 1863 in an effort to energize the moribund Union cavalry. It proved a wise appointment as the young general impressed both friend and foe and especially a northern press corps eager for colorful heroes with reckless courage and flamboyant style. When General Philip H. Sheridan took command of the Army of the Potomac's cavalry in 1864, he found a kindred spirit in Custer, whom he soon promoted to major general

General George Armstrong Custer (*second from left*) poses with his brother Tom (*far right*) and a Sioux scout (*far left*) in 1876, shortly before the fateful Battle of the Little Bighorn. Custer and the entire 7th Cavalry, including his two brothers, were killed. *(Time & Life Pictures/Getty Images)*

in command of the 3rd Cavalry Division. Custer performed spectacularly in the Shenandoah and Appomattox campaigns. Sheridan purchased the table on which Lee's surrender terms had been signed and presented it to Custer's bride, Elizabeth.

With the war over, Custer returned to his regular army rank of captain, although he held the brevet rank of major general. In the army reorganization of 1866, he secured a commission as lieutenant colonel of the new 7th Cavalry. Since the regiment's colonels always remained on detached duty, Custer actually commanded the 7th and put the stamp of his romantic personality upon it. He promptly adopted the buckskin jacket and broad-brimmed hat of the plainsmen, while keeping his signature crimson scarf and shoulder-length hair.

Custer's first western campaign, the dismal 1867 Hancock expedition against the southern plains tribes, ended with his court-martial and suspension for a year. General Philip Sheridan, feeling Custer had been made

a scapegoat for Hancock's failures, brought him back in the fall of 1868 to lead his strike force against the Cheyennes. The 7th Cavalry scored a smashing victory over Black Kettle's Washita village in western Oklahoma on November 27, 1868. Although some branded Custer's attack as a slaughter of innocents, the 7th's commander emerged as the most famous Indian fighter on the western frontier.

Reconstruction duty in Kentucky was followed by assignment to the northern plains, where Custer's 7th guarded railroad survey parties and battled the Sioux in the Yellowstone country in 1873. In 1874 he led a 1,200-man expedition to explore South Dakota's Black Hills. His report of gold in the hills led to a white stampede into Sioux country that forced bands under Sitting Bull and Crazy Horse to war.

Custer was to command the expedition against the so-called hostiles, but instead became embroiled in the scandal involving the sale of post sutlerships by President Ulysses Grant's venal war secretary, William W. Belknap. Custer's congressional testimony against Belknap won him Grant's enmity and he was stripped of his command. Grant reluctantly gave in to pleas from Sheridan and General Alfred Terry to at least restore Custer to command of the 7th Cavalry for the army's upcoming campaign against the northern tribes.

Sheridan's plan called for three columns to move against Sitting Bull's people along the Yellowstone River and its tributaries—General George Crook to move north from Fort Fetterman in central Wyoming; Colonel John Gibbon to push east down the Yellowstone from Fort Ellis, Montana; and General Terry, with Custer's 7th, to move east from Fort Abraham Lincoln on the Missouri River. There was no real plan for the columns to act in concert, but it was hoped that one of them would drive the Sioux toward another column. The only worry was that the Indians might elude the troops and escape.

Terry and Custer joined Gibbon's column on the Yellowstone on June 21, 1876. A plan was devised whereby Custer was to follow a large Indian trail up Rosebud Creek while Terry and Gibbon moved up the Bighorn River. They would reunite on the Little Bighorn on June 26. It was assumed that Custer's 7th would strike the Sioux, driving the fleeing Indians into the column of either Terry or Crook. Terry gave Custer wide latitude to use his own discretion. Unknown to all was that Crook had been defeated by Crazy Horse on the Rosebud on June 21 and had retreated to refit and await reinforcements.

Custer pushed rapidly up the Rosebud and then

followed an Indian trail to the Little Bighorn River, his Crow and Arikara scouts soon discovering a large Indian camp along the river. Custer had hoped to rest his troopers for a day while giving Terry time to move south, but he was discovered by Sioux scouts and decided to attack immediately on June 25 before the villagers could scatter. With no idea of the size of the enemy force before him, but absolutely confident of himself and his regiment, Custer divided his command into four parts. Major Marcus Reno was ordered with three companies to cross the river and attack the village; Captain Frederick Benteen's three companies were sent to the left to block any escape route; Custer led five companies onto the bluffs above the river to strike the village from the right; and Captain Thomas McDougall was left with a company to guard the pack train.

Everything immediately went wrong. The villagers—at least 2,000 warriors and perhaps more—did not flee but put up a spirited resistance. Reno, promptly repulsed with heavy losses, retreated to the bluff above the river where he was joined by Benteen and McDougall. Benteen had received a written order to hurry with the pack train to reinforce Custer, but now relinquished command to the stampeded Reno and hunkered down with his men. Custer was left to his fate.

Custer and his five companies, some 212 men, were denied the river crossing and formed a skirmish line along the ridge to await Benteen. The Indians rolled up the lines, pushing them back into a circle atop a high hill where Custer, his two brothers and a nephew, and about fifty other men made a last stand. Every man with Custer perished.

Custer's Last Stand immediately overshadowed the rest of the officer's career and became one of the best-known battles in American history. The defeat enraged the American people, who quickly embraced Custer as a heroic martyr to the cause of national expansion, and led to the prompt crushing of the Sioux by Sheridan's troops and the opening of the Black Hills and much of Dakota, Wyoming, and Montana to white settlement. Sheridan, who knew Custer best, remembered him fondly, but others had a darker view, and in time they prevailed. By the late twentieth century Custer had become an absurd caricature of arrogance and incompetence that was blamed for all the wrongs committed against Native Americans by a guilt-ridden generation. In fact, he was a brave, if rash, young soldier who gave his life for his country to ensure its continental destiny. He died in obedience to the orders of a faithless government that did not deserve so fine a sacrifice. In

so doing he created a great historical controversy and a towering legend.

Paul Andrew Hutton

See also: Black Kettle; Crazy Horse; Crook, George; Custer, Elizabeth Bacon; Custer Expedition; Grant, Ulysses S.; Sheridan, Philip H.; Sitting Bull; Washita Engagement.

Further Reading

Custer, Elizabeth B. *Boots and Saddles*. Norman: University of Oklahoma Press, 1962.

Donovan, James. *A Terrible Glory: Custer and the Little Bighorn*. Boston: Little, Brown, 2008.

Elliott, Michael A. *Custerology*. Chicago: University of Chicago Press, 2008.

Hutton, Paul Andrew, ed. *The Custer Reader*. Norman: University of Oklahoma Press, 2004.

Utley, Robert M. *Cavalier in Buckskin*. Norman: University of Oklahoma Press, 2001.

Custer Expedition

The 1874 Custer Expedition into the Black Hills of Dakota Territory triggered a gold rush leading to the Lakotas' loss of their sacred Black Hills and to the development of the mineral, timber, and grazing industries for white settlers. The pine-forested Black Hills, or *Paha Sapa* in Lakota, were part of the Great Sioux Reservation and belonged to the tribe as specified in the 1868 Treaty of Fort Laramie. The Black Hills were thus off-limits to whites.

There had always been rumors of large deposits of gold in the Black Hills; early expeditions to the region had found a few gold flecks in some of the streams. These reports excited prospectors and speculators who wanted to begin their own search for gold in the region. However, the Lakotas opposed any entry. Lieutenant General William T. Sherman, commander of the Military Department of Missouri, did not allow any civilian gold-seeking expeditions to approach the Black Hills. His troops actively prevented prospectors from traveling to the area and evicted any who initially eluded the troops.

In 1873, however, the Dakota Territory Legislative Assembly asked Congress for a scientific expedition to explore the Black Hills and requested that the federal government open the area for settlement. In 1874 General Philip Sheridan directed Lieutenant Colonel George Armstrong Custer to explore the mountains and determine a site for a future military post to guard travelers headed to the Montana mining districts, to survey and map the area, and to record the topography and geology.

Custer based his expedition out of Fort Abraham Lincoln, Dakota Territory. The army had built the fort in 1872 on the west bank of the Missouri River across from the new settlement of Bismarck, located at the end of the line for the Northern Pacific Railroad. Custer, commanding the 7th Cavalry, took ten companies from that unit and also two infantry units to guard 110 supply wagons. He had with him a sixteen-piece mounted military band; Indian scouts, including his favorite Arikara scout, Bloody Knife; and white civilian scouts, including Lonesome Charlie Reynolds. Other notable members of the expedition were Major George A. Forsyth, who had been in command of scouts at the Battle of Beecher Island (September 17–19, 1868) in Colorado against Cheyenne Dog Soldiers and Oglala Lakota warriors; Colonel Fred Grant, son of President Ulysses Grant; and two of Custer's brothers, Captain Tom Custer and Boston Custer, who was the civilian forage master.

The War Department assigned Captain William Ludlow of the Corps of Engineers and six enlisted men to survey the topography and to create maps of the Black Hills area. Newton Winchell, Minnesota's state geologist and a professor at the University of Minnesota, rode with Custer to record rocks, minerals, and geologic formations. George Bird Grinnell, from Yale University, was along to collect fossils. Acting as his assistant was Luther North, who had formed the Pawnee Scouts. Aris Donaldson acted as botanist. The *St. Paul Pioneer* paid Donaldson to provide reports for that newspaper. In addition to Donaldson, Custer invited along four other newspaper reporters who provided the public with detailed reports on the expedition, and he hired William Illingsworth, a St. Paul, Minnesota, photographer, to record the images of the expedition. Illingsworth's photographs, which are valuable as a historic record of the expedition, also show how the Black Hills' vegetation has changed since 1874. Sarah "Sally" Campbell, an African-American, was Custer's cook; she became the first non-Indian woman to enter the Black Hills. Horatio N. Ross and William T. McKay, experienced miners, were also part of the expedition, but scholars have been unable to agree upon their official status. Some believe that they were hired as civilian teamsters, while others believe they were personally hired by Custer to search for evidence of gold.

Custer and his troops—an expedition of 1,000 men—set out in a southwesterly direction from Fort Abraham Lincoln on July 2, 1874. Crossing the treeless prairie, they entered the northern Black Hills on July 23. They slowly journeyed on a southerly route past flower-filled valleys, swift-flowing creeks, and large stands of pine trees. They climbed peaks and hunted wild animals.

Although the expedition failed to find significant gold deposits, Custer eventually sent Reynolds south to Fort Laramie, Wyoming, with a report that some gold had been located. Reynolds told anyone who would listen that paying quantities of gold had been found, prompting reporters to dispatch to their newspapers sensationalized accounts of the "discovery" of the precious metal.

The Custer Expedition turned north and left the Black Hills on August 15, passing Bear Butte, sacred to the Cheyenne, Lakota, and many other tribes. The travelers returned to Fort Abraham Lincoln on August 30. Ludlow, working with his surveyors and the scientists, published his scientific report and three maps in 1875.

As a result of the early reports by Reynolds and the dispatches published in newspapers, gold seekers illegally rushed to the Black Hills. The U.S. Army failed to keep them all out, especially after a second expedition led by Walter P. Jenney and Henry Newton in 1875 confirmed that there was gold in the region. Custer's Black Hills expedition led to a series of events that eventually caught the 7th Cavalry, Lonesome Charlie Reynolds, Bloody Knife, and the Custer brothers at the Battle of the Little Big Horn.

Bill Markley

See also: Black Hills Expeditions; Cheyenne; Custer, George Armstrong; Fort Laramie; Fort Laramie, Treaty of (1868); Grinnell, George Bird; Lakota; North, Luther Hedden; Sheridan, Philip H.; Sherman, William Tecumseh; Sioux.

Further Reading

Connell, Evan S. *Son of the Morning Star*. New York: Harper & Row, 1984.

Grafe, Ernest, and Paul Horsted. *Exploring With Custer: The 1874 Black Hills Expedition*. Custer, SD: Golden Valley Press, 2002.

Hutton, Paul Andrew. *Phil Sheridan and His Army*. Norman: University of Oklahoma, 1985.

Parker, Watson. *Gold in the Black Hills*. Pierre: South Dakota State Historical Society Press, 2003.

Davis, Jefferson (1808–1889)

Although best known for serving as the first and only president of the Confederate States of America from 1861 to 1865, Jefferson Davis's earlier role as U.S. secretary of war in President Franklin Pierce's administration (1853–1857) had important ramifications for the nation's westward expansion.

Born in Christian County, Kentucky, on June 3, 1808, Davis attended Jefferson College, near Natchez, Mississippi, and Transylvania College at Lexington in his home state. While a senior at Transylvania, he was appointed to the U.S. Military Academy at West Point, from which he graduated in June 1828, ranking twenty-third in a class of thirty-two. For the next few years Davis served in the army, but never attained a higher rank than first lieutenant in a dragoon regiment.

In 1835, following an uneventful military career, Davis resigned from the army and married Sarah Knox Taylor, daughter of the future Mexican-American War hero and president of the United States Zachary Taylor. Within three months, Sarah died from malaria and the grief-stricken Davis took up a career as a plantation owner in Mississippi. Ten years later, two life-changing events occurred: he married Varina Howell, a Natchez belle who would have tremendous influence on his later career, and he won election to the U.S. Congress as a Democrat. He took time off from his public life to serve in the Mexican-American War as colonel of the First Mississippi Rifles, seeing action at the Battle of Buena Vista, where he was wounded.

Davis returned home to Mississippi a hero and was appointed to the U.S. Senate, soon resigning to run unsuccessfully for governor. When Franklin Pierce became president of the United States in 1853, Davis consented to become his secretary of war, a position he filled with distinction throughout Pierce's entire administration. It was in this role that Davis had responsibility for inaugurating the four great transcontinental railroad surveys carried out by members of the U.S. Army Corps of Topographical Engineers. He used his considerable influence as a cabinet member to force the passage of the Kansas-Nebraska Act and drew upon his military experience to implement improvements for the army.

When Pierce left the White House in 1857, Davis returned to a seat in the Senate, where he served until Mississippi seceded from the Union in January 1861. A few weeks after the secession, upon reaching home, Davis was informed that he had been elected provisional president of the Confederate States of America. The following year, he was inaugurated as permanent president, taking office in the first Confederate capital at Montgomery, Alabama, and then, moving to Richmond, Virginia, when the capital moved.

When Richmond fell in April 1865, Davis and some of his cabinet attempted to flee, hoping to reestablish the government elsewhere. However, he was captured near Irwinville, Georgia, a few weeks later along with his wife and entourage. Tried for treason and sentenced to prison at Fort Monroe, Virginia, Davis was incarcerated for two years before finally being released by federal authorities. He returned to Mississippi, locating near Biloxi, and, over the next few years penned his memoirs, *The Rise and Fall of the Confederate Government*, published in 1881. Davis died on December 9, 1889.

James A. Crutchfield

See also: Corps of Topographical Engineers; Kansas-Nebraska Act (1854); Railroad Surveys, Transcontinental.

Further Reading

Goetzmann, William H. *Army Exploration in the American West, 1803–1863.* Lincoln: University of Nebraska Press, 1979.

Dawes, Henry L. (1816–1903)

Born in Cummington, Massachusetts, on October 30, 1816, Henry Laurens Dawes was a lawyer, teacher, and politician throughout the nineteenth century. In his political career, Dawes is most notable for his role as the chair of the Senate Committee on Indian Affairs, where he authored the General Allotment Act of 1887. Also known as the Dawes Act, this law significantly reshaped the western landscape and drastically altered Indian communities throughout the United States.

In 1839 Dawes graduated from Yale College. He was admitted to the Massachusetts state bar in 1842. During the years before he started his legal career, he taught in Greenfield, Massachusetts; then he practiced law in North Adams and Pittsfield. During his years as a teacher and a lawyer, he also served in an editorial capacity for both the *Greenfield Gazette* and the *Transcript* before beginning his long career in state and national politics. In 1848–1849 and 1852, Dawes served in the Massachusetts legislature and in 1850 was elected to the state senate, where he held one term in office. In 1853 he joined the Massachusetts Constitutional Convention.

Between 1857 and 1875, Dawes was a Republican member of the U.S. House of Representatives. During these years he was recognized for his writings on antislavery and Reconstruction legislation. He was also influential in his role as the chair of several House committees, including the Committee on Elections, the Committee on Appropriations, and the Ways and Means Committee. Dawes also established the beginning of daily weather reports, which led to the creation of the U.S. Weather Bureau.

From 1875 to 1893, Dawes served as a U.S. senator from Massachusetts. During this period, he drafted legislation that contributed significantly to the government's ongoing political efforts to assimilate Indian populations throughout the country. His political legacy is tied to his role as the writer and legislative sponsor of the General Allotment Act of 1887. Also known as the Dawes Severalty Act, it was an aggressive effort to detribalize Indian communities and assimilate them into mainstream American society. This policy divided tribal lands into small private plots that were dispersed to individual members and families in each tribe. The allotment of these lands was intended to provide Indians with the tools to become American citizens.

As a proponent of this legislation, Dawes has been described as having a genuine interest in the long-term survival of Native Americans. Along with many other government and nongovernment reformers during this era, he believed that the Indians' lifeways impeded their progress in American society, economy, and politics. However, this sincerity cannot outweigh the fact that the Dawes Act represents one of the most aggressive chapters in the history of the United States' relations with Indians during the nation's expansion into the West.

Dawes died at Pittsfield, Massachusetts, on February 5, 1903.

Elaine M. Nelson

See also: Dawes Severalty Act (1887); Indian Policy.

Further Reading

Prucha, Francis Paul. *The Great Father: The United States Government and the American Indians*. Lincoln: University of Nebraska Press, 1986.

Wunder, John R. *Retained by the People: A History of American Indians and the Bill of Rights*. New York: Oxford University Press, 1994.

Dawes Severalty Act (1887)

Also known as the General Allotment Act, the Dawes Severalty Act was proposed by Senator Henry L. Dawes of Massachusetts. The act established a commission that was in charge of distributing Indian lands in 160-acre (65-ha) parcels to the heads of families and 80-acre (32-ha) plots to individual males. The process of distributing allotments to individual members stretched back to the Indian Peace Commission of the 1860s. The process was not new to Indian policy, but the wholesale adoption and renegotiation of previously protected treaty lands was novel.

If individuals failed to select an allotment, the commission provided one to them. To prevent the automatic sale of allotments, the government held all allotments in trust for a period of twenty-five years. The government was then supposed to sell off all surplus Indian lands to nontribal members. This policy lasted until John Collier's administration and the Indian Reorganization Act of 1934.

The Dawes Act was one of the most devastating and destructive policies to tribal sovereignty in history. It carried out earlier policies of assimilation by forcing native peoples to assume a capitalist and proprietary relationship with property. Reformers like Henry Dawes believed that his legislation provided economic stability to reservation communities and promoted the process of assimilation.

Many of the reformers' ideas backfired and caused irrevocable damage to tribal governments and culture. The act liquidated tribal lands, while individual ownership further aided in the checker-boarding effect on many reservations. As nontribal members purchased lands, the territorial jurisdiction of many tribal governments was harmed. The authority and sovereign powers of the tribal government were thus further eroded.

Many allotments were lost to bank foreclosures, confiscation by the Internal Revenue Service, and fraudulent lease arrangements. As allotments entered the probate courts they often were subdivided into tiny parcels, insufficient to support the owners. Many of these allotments were compromised further by the relocation and termination policies of the 1950s. During relocation, families had to abandon their allotments to participate in the program, which moved thousands of Indians to urban centers. Around 100 million acres (40 million ha) of tribal lands were lost due to the allotment process of the Dawes Act.

Kent Blansett

See also: Dawes, Henry L.; Indian Policy.

Further Reading

Washburn, Wilcomb. *The Assault on Indian Tribalism: The General Allotment Law (Dawes Act) of 1887.* Philadelphia: J.B. Lippincott, 1975.

Wunder, John R. *Retained by the People: A History of American Indian and the Bill of Rights.* New York: Oxford University Press, 1994.

De Smet, Pierre-Jean (1801–1873)

Pierre-Jean (Peter John) De Smet was a Catholic priest who traveled west in 1840 to answer the Flathead tribe's request for a Christian missionary. He was probably the most important non-Protestant missionary to the western Indians during the period of his ministry.

De Smet was born January 30, 1801, in Dendermonde, East Flanders, Belgium. Migrating to America when he was twenty, he desired to become a Jesuit priest and spent the next ten years studying at St. Louis University and in Europe before going west to minister

to Native Americans. His first mission, among the Potawatomis during 1838–1839, failed because of the influence of whiskey recently introduced to the tribe. In the West, he served the Pend d'Oreilles, Koetenays, Cauldrons, Okinaganes, Kalispells, and Yankton Sioux. He founded the first Catholic mission in the Northwest, St. Mary's, built in 1841, for the purpose of converting the Flatheads. The tribe had sent a delegation of three prominent men east to seek knowledge of Christianity and request missionaries to return with them.

When he went west, De Smet joined a growing number of missionaries. The Catholics had an advantage when dealing with French-speaking fur company employees and their families, since most were of this faith. It was the fur companies who provided shelter, food, means of travel, protection, and all the comforts the missionaries had when traveling. The Catholic priests were different from Protestant missionaries in the West. Not only did they act and talk differently, the priests wore black robes, had a very formal ritual, and remained unmarried. There was always competition and friction among the various religious groups for the souls of individuals.

In April 1840, De Smet left Westport, Missouri, with members of the American Fur Company (AFC) bound for the annual rendezvous to be held on the Green River in present-day western Wyoming. On July 5, he held his first mass and addressed the people who attended in French and English, his translator relaying the words to the Flatheads and Shoshones in their own tongues. During the service, the Canadians sang in French and Latin, the natives in their own language. Leaving the rendezvous, De Smet arrived at St. Louis on December 31.

De Smet performed his ministry well; he baptized famed mountain man Jim Bridger's children and gave the last sacraments to Bridger's associate Lucien Fontenelle, who died in his arms. De Smet also baptized Fontenelle's four children and their mother in 1838; the oldest became his godson. At the 1840 rendezvous, he baptized several hundred of the Flathead tribe. At the 1851 Fort Laramie treaty council, he offered communion and baptized children and adults under a hide tepee.

Besides his missionary work, De Smet wrote *Origin, Progress and Prospects of the Catholic Mission to the Rocky Mountains* in 1843, *Letters and Sketches*, also in 1843, and *New Indian Sketches* in 1863, a story of the conversion of Louise Sighouin, of the Coeur d'Alenes, a daughter of the tribe's chief. He left the mountains in 1846 and died in St. Louis on May 23, 1873.

Mike Moore

See also: Bridger, Jim; Fontenelle, Lucien; Rendezvous.

Further Reading

De Smet, Pierre Jean. *New Indian Sketches* (1863). Seattle: Shorey Book Store, 1974.

——. *Origin, Progress and Prospects of the Catholic Mission to the Rocky Mountains* (1843). Reprint, Fairfield, WA: Ye Galleon Press, 1986.

Donnelly, Joseph. *Wilderness Kingdom: Indian Life in the Rocky Mountains, 1840–1847*. New York: Holt, Rinehart and Winston, 1967.

Laveille, E. *The Life of Father De Smet*. New York: P.J. Kennedy, 1915.

Denver and Rio Grande Railroad

The Denver and Rio Grande Railroad (D&RG) was a multigauge railroad in the heart of the West's rugged Rocky Mountains that provided accessible transportation for both passengers and freight during the developing years of Colorado as a territory and state. Built initially as a narrow-gauge railroad supporting mining activities in Colorado and New Mexico, it evolved into a successful passenger carrier as well, providing travelers with awe-inspiring views while transporting them to their destinations. It was the first major rail carrier in the West initially designed along a north-south axis, and it traversed mountainous terrain at one time believed to be impossible to cross. Over the course of its history, its management was involved in a series of bitter disputes and complicated relationships with other rail carriers in the region. Because of these unique characteristics, it was sometimes dubbed "Rebel of the Rockies."

Construction on the D&RG began in 1870. The rail line was the brainchild of a Union Civil War general, William Jackson Palmer. Its initial route ran from Denver to Colorado Springs, then a town of only ten people. Palmer wanted the line to extend all the way to El Paso and then into Mexico, transporting minerals, supplies, and people to and from the rich mining sites being developed in those areas. Many factors caused significant changes to this plan, resulting in a complex and lengthy rail line that ultimately reached as far west as Salt Lake City, Utah, and south to Santa Fe, New Mexico.

As the D&RG forged southward and westward in the 1870s, it became embroiled in a dispute with the Atchison, Topeka, and Santa Fe Railroad (AT&SF), which was also expanding into southern Colorado and northern New Mexico. A short "war" ensued, with armed emissaries from each line threatening the other. A legal conflict followed, resulting in the D&RG being forced to briefly lease its right-of-way and equipment to the AT&SF. Although the D&RG would finally establish service to Santa Fe, it now turned its attention to westerly routes, where progress would be impeded more by Rocky Mountain barriers than by competing railroads.

The D&RG rail line attacked its westward expansion head-on with a multipronged approach comprising the acquisition of small, local railroads, Herculean engineering feats that conquered incredibly rugged terrain, and flexible, sometimes redundant, use of narrow- and standard-gauge rail construction. The result was an extensive line of freight and passenger rail service through the core of the Rocky Mountains. By the start of the twentieth century, the D&RG had established itself as an important rail line in Colorado and Utah. With the acquisition of the Denver and Salt Lake Western Railroad in 1931 and access to the Moffat Tunnel in 1947 secured through merger, the now-designated D&RGW became the dominant rail carrier between Denver and Salt Lake City. Its preferred method of operation was to use fast, flexible trains that transported freight to desired destinations more quickly than its competitors. Continued expansion of service and migration to standard-gauge rail tracks kept the D&RGW viable in the twentieth century.

The railroad continued to defy both conventional traditions and industrial trends as rail service evolved in the 1900s, maintaining the last private passenger service (the *Rio Grande Zephyr*) from Salt Lake City to Denver, despite the rest of the industry's abdication to Amtrak. The D&RGW bought the Southern Pacific Railroad in 1988, adopting the Southern Pacific name for the new company. Finally, in 1996, the company was sold to the Union Pacific Railroad, ending the long history of a fiercely independent and unique railroad. The D&RG was a bold pioneer, establishing the "Scenic Line of the World" by creating routes, as its motto stated, "through the Rockies—not around them."

Jim Ersfeld

Further Reading

Athearn, Robert G. *Rebel of the Rockies: A History of the Denver and Rio Grande Western Railroad*. New Haven: Yale University Press, 1962.

Beebe, Lucius, and Charles Clegg. *Rio Grande: Mainline of the Rockies*. Berkeley, CA: Howell-North Books, 1962.

Disease

Illnesses of any kind posed serious problems for early Westerners. Conditions that today are considered relatively mild, such as a head cold or diarrhea, could then be life threatening. On the fringes of the frontier, an illness might not necessarily kill a person, but left many patients weak, unable to care for themselves, and susceptible to other, more serious medical problems.

Health problems suffered by many early travelers were, for the most part, those that cause little concern today since modern medical treatment and ruthless pursuit of the origin of diseases have eliminated a plethora of maladies once commonplace and quiet deadly. Cholera, smallpox, tuberculosis, measles, diphtheria, whooping cough, and malaria are relatively uncommon in the United States, but posed severe difficulty for people on the move through unfamiliar land, among strangers, and with no medical assistance available.

Cholera is an acute diarrhea illness caused by a bacterial infection of the intestine, leading to rapid loss of body fluids, dehydration, and shock. Without treatment, death can occur within hours. People get cholera not from casual contact, but rather from drinking contaminated water or eating food with *Vibrio cholerae* bacteria in it. Part of the difficulty in treating the disease in the early days was that many people believed it to be an airborne malady; hence, caregivers unaware of how the disease was transmitted would share drinking vessels with infected patients. The proof that cholera was water-borne was provided by John Snow in 1854, decades after America's first surge west of the Appalachians and at about the same time as the trans-Mississippi migration was taking place in earnest.

In the early West, cholera was often considered not so much a disease as a kind of malaise in the air or as a scourge that was punishment from God. People could be vaccinated against smallpox, but not against cholera. The disease spread rapidly; in 1833 it swept through St. Louis, killing over 500 people. In July of the same year, the steamer *Yellow Stone* had a cholera outbreak on board that killed all of the crew except the captain.

Smallpox was a terrible disease that probably took the most lives in the West. Some authorities estimate that as many as 15,000 Indians died of smallpox along the upper Missouri River in 1837–1838. Its spread was so rapid and universal that the U.S. government paid doctors fifty cents a person to vaccinate members of the

tribes closest to the Missouri River and eastern plains. Congress had passed legislation to extend vaccination to all Indians in a systematic way and appropriated $12,000 for the program. Although survivors of the disease obtained immunity, following generations had no such protection.

The devastating 1837 smallpox outbreak began when an Indian stole a blanket from a person dying of the disease aboard a steamboat. Wrapping himself in the blanket, he unknowingly carried off the disease to his tribe. Fur trader Charles Larpenteur reported that the infected man's tribe was reduced by more than one-half as a result of the illness. It was during this time that doctors began to vaccinate Native Americans; however, inoculation then was a much different process than it was in later times. The doctor would stick a needle into the scabs of a healthy smallpox

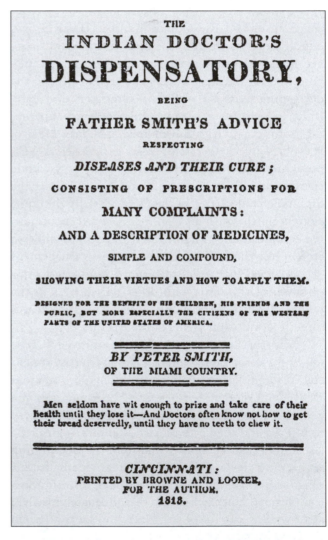

A medical pamphlet published for Native Americans in 1818 prescribed a variety of herbal treatments. Diseases contracted from whites, such as smallpox and measles, decimated the Indian population. *(MPI/Stringer/Getty Images)*

survivor and use the dirty needle to pierce the skin of a healthy person, hoping that the needle had picked up some of the dead virus, thereby giving the recipient of the inoculation a mild case of the disease, but serious enough for his body to begin manufacture of antibodies. In many instances it took several inoculations to achieve the desired results. The initial attempts to inoculate the Indians did not go well. Larpenteur wrote that the pox sample should have been taken from a very healthy person, but that the man from whom the virus was obtained was in extremely poor health and that the operation proved fatal to most of the people inoculated.

During the expansion of the West, influenza or simple colds upset people's normal routines and caused the deaths of many individuals. The most common remedies were calomel, mustard rubs, opium, camphor, bed rest, diluted brandy, and bloodletting. The many bands of Indians could treat the victims little better, having only sweats and natural medicine to fight disease.

Contaminated drinking water resulted in much sickness. Dysentery was acquired either by drinking alkali water or by a drastic change of diet. Many individuals suffered when fresh meat was all they had to eat.

Whether maladies were called fevers, chills, or agues, all of them had an impact on large numbers of people. Missionary Samuel Parker noted in 1838 that since 1829, fever and ague had killed hundreds of Indians below the falls of the Columbia River. Recurring bouts of ague, a form of chills and fever, were so predictable that events like travel had to be planned around them. Shaking ague sometimes manifested itself by an urge to yawn and stretch, fingernails turning blue, and complaints of cold sensations that worsened, leading to the chattering of teeth, waves of fever, and aching of the back and head. After profuse sweating, the illness eased. This illness many times did not kill the victims, but seriously weakened them, making them susceptible to other illnesses.

In the autumn of 1833, the populace of St. Louis was afflicted with a yellow fever epidemic that did not dissipate until December. Some references to "camp," yellow," or "mountain fever" might have actually been describing typhoid. With ten days or longer of incubation, typhoid, caused by a bacillus, brought on aches, red rashes, bronchitis, coughing, abdominal pain, fever for two or more weeks, diarrhea, and delirium. Near the end, the afflicted victim suffered from ulcers caused by bacteria along the intestinal lining, leading to perforation and internal hemorrhaging. Laudanum, a tincture

of opium, was commonly prescribed for typhoid, but it simply relieved the pain without providing a cure.

A variety of diseases, such as Rocky Mountain spotted fever and plague, were passed on by ticks and fleas. Brigham Young suffered from tick fever in 1847 during the Mormon emigration to the valley of the Great Salt Lake; because of his condition, he fell behind the lead elements of the pioneer companies.

Mike Moore

See also: Mandan.

Further Reading

Bethard, Wayne. *Lotions, Potions and Deadly Elixirs: Frontier Medicine in America.* New York: Roberts Rinehart, 2004.

Dary, David. *Frontier Medicine: From the Atlantic to the Pacific, 1492–1941.* New York: Alfred A. Knopf, 2008.

Robertson, R.G. *Rotting Face: Smallpox and the American Indian.* Caldwell, ID: Caxton Press, 2001.

Steele, Volney. *Blister, Bleed and Purge: A History of Medicine on the American Frontier.* Missoula, MT: Mountain Press, 2005.

Doak's Stand, Treaty of (1820)

By 1820 the U.S. government's Indian policy was shifting toward promoting the removal of Native American tribes settled in lands east of the Mississippi River. The treaty signed at Doak's Stand—formally named *A treaty of friendship, and accommodation, between the United States of America and the Choctaw nation of Indians, begun and concluded at the Treaty Ground, in said nation, near Doak's Stand, on the Natchez Road*—was a first step toward removal of the Choctaws from present-day Mississippi to Arkansas. Through this document the Choctaws ceded roughly 5 million acres (2 million ha) of prime cotton-growing territory in exchange for tracts of land of unknown, but assumed lesser value across the Mississippi—lands that, incidentally, were taken back by the U.S. government five years later.

Major General Andrew Jackson served as one of the primary negotiators. Realizing that his budget of $50,000 was insufficient to acquire the support of the Choctaws, Jackson invested money in a feast with abundant whiskey, hoping that the liquor might smooth the negotiations. Choctaws started arriving on October 2, 1820. Formal negotiations began on October 10, although the government representatives had been busy throughout the intervening period. Despite the food and liquor provided over several days, the Choctaws resisted Jackson's ploy and refused to exchange lands. This refusal forced Jackson to play his trump card, the implied threat of military action annihilating the Choctaws. Even with such heavy-handed tactics, the negotiations were lively and Jackson offered up roughly 13 million acres (5.3 million ha) in exchange for the Choctaw concessions in Mississippi. The treaty was signed by the U.S. representatives, Mingoes, headmen, and scores of warriors on October 18, 1820.

Article 4 of the treaty allowed Choctaws to stay on small parcels of land east of the Mississippi River "and remain without alteration until the period at which said nation shall become so civilized and enlightened as to be made citizens of the United States." For those who wished to move, there were trade goods and a promise of sufficient corn to make the move from the ceded lands. Article 7 provided that 54 square miles (140 sq km) of the Choctaws' ceded lands were to be sold, with proceeds going to support Choctaw schools. Other provisions paid Choctaw warriors for service in the First Seminole War, established federal control of the use of alcohol on Choctaw lands, and dealt with selling additional lands to allow annuities to remain in Choctaw hands.

As an instrument of removal, the Doak's Stand Treaty was flawed. Most Choctaws chose to remain in Mississippi, despite intense pressure to move west placed upon them by federal agents. Removal was accomplished through subsequent treaties such as the Dancing Rabbit Creek Treaty of 1830.

Terry A. Del Bene

See also: Choctaw; Indian Removal Act (1830); Jackson, Andrew; Jackson's Indian Policy.

Further Reading

Kappler, Charles J., ed. *Indian Treaties, 1778–1883*. Mattituck, NJ: Amereon House, 1972.

Dodge, Henry (1782–1867)

Henry Dodge was important to the nation's expansion across the Midwest as a longtime law enforcement officer, mining entrepreneur, military commander, governor of Wisconsin Territory, and U.S. senator from Wisconsin following statehood. He was born on October 12, 1782, at Post Vincennes, Indiana, and, in 1796 his family moved to the Ste. Genevieve district

of Louisiana (now Missouri), where the self-educated Dodge married and served as sheriff. During his sojourn in Missouri, he was involved with Aaron Burr in the former vice-president's southwestern settlement scheme, but withdrew his support when Burr was arrested and tried for treason. He also served as a major general in the Missouri militia and saw action in the War of 1812.

By 1827 Dodge supported a wife, who bore him nine children, and owned several slaves. The family moved to present-day Wisconsin, where Dodge reentered the lead mining business, an interest he had pursued in Missouri. Five years later, he distinguished himself in the Black Hawk War, participating in the action at Wisconsin Heights and in the Battle of Bad Axe. As part of his military responsibilities, he fulfilled a presidential appointment as major and commander of a newly organized mounted ranger battalion whose mission it was to patrol the Santa Fe Trail, provide protection on the Illinois-Wisconsin border, and keep peace in Indian Territory (now Oklahoma) among native tribes and recently arrived eastern tribes of Indians.

When the U.S. Dragoons Regiment was organized in 1833, partly to replace the unsuccessful mounted rangers battalion, Dodge was appointed the unit's first commander. The following year he and his command left Fort Gibson and explored present-day Oklahoma as far as the Pawnee villages, the first time the army had ever visited the tribe. The next year, the regiment departed Fort Leavenworth, traveled up the Platte River, then the South Platte, and headed south along the front range of the Rocky Mountains, exploring the Arkansas River and part of the Santa Fe Trail on the return trip. The first expedition, although plagued with sickness and logistical problems and slowed by the intense heat, was, nevertheless, considered successful, as was the second one, which covered about 1,600 miles (2,600 km) and provided a great deal of information about the little-explored region through which it passed.

Dodge held his colonelcy with the dragoons for three years before resigning to become governor of the newly created Territory of Wisconsin. He served as chief executive until 1841, then again from 1845 to 1848, when the territory was admitted to the Union as the thirteenth state on May 29, 1848, and he was elected as one of the state's first two U.S. senators. Retiring from politics in 1857, Dodge lived the rest of his life in Burlington, Iowa, where he died on June 19, 1867.

James A. Crutchfield

See also: Black Hawk; Black Hawk War (1832).

Further Reading

Prucha, Francis Paul. *The Sword of the Republic: The United States Army on the Frontier, 1783–1846.* New York: Macmillan, 1969.

Donation Land Claim Act (1850)

The acquisition of vast tracts of territory in the West created a problem for the young American Congress: how to dispose of the land. The Organic Act of 1843 for Oregon Territory included provisions for giving land to settlers but it was not an efficient system. In 1850 Congress voided the clauses in Oregon's Organic Act and established new procedures through the Donation Land Claim Act, also called the Donation Land Act.

This legislation, the handiwork of territorial delegates to Congress, provided for the establishment of a surveyor-general and a budget for his office and operations. The terms of geodetic and topographic surveys were established as well as a maximum cost per mile of survey.

The law first dealt with existing occupants of the territory by allowing white and half-breed (meaning mixed white/Indian) men to acquire for free one-half of a square mile (320 acres [130 ha]) of land. The grant recipients had to be over eighteen years old and either be a United States citizen or to have declared the intention to become a citizen prior to December 1, 1850. If the applicant had cultivated the land for four consecutive years and married within one year of December 1, 1850, the grant was expanded to a full square mile (640 acres [260 ha]). The act provided that half of the land be granted to the spouse and could be inherited and held by heirs to the property.

White emigrants to the territory between December 1, 1850, and December 1, 1853, were entitled to one-quarter of a square mile of land (160 acres [65 ha]) or one-half of a square mile (320 acres [130 ha]) if they married within one year of attaining the age of twenty-one. This largess applied only to citizens who were older than twenty.

None of the land grants included mineral rights. An individual could own only one land patent and the surveyor-general assured the accuracy of the grant by establishing the claim stakes and mapping the claim.

Grant recipients were required to cultivate the land for four consecutive years to receive their patents. Military posts and any lands deemed by the president as necessary for public uses were exempted, and no lands cultivated after the critical dates established in the act were eligible for a grant.

The act also set aside 72 square miles (116 sq km) of land for the use of the Territory of Oregon for purposes such as the building of a university. The act affirmed existing claims of land by communities and the Willamette Milling and Trading Companies. The act was in effect for roughly five years and was used for more than 7,000 grants.

Terry A. Del Bene

See also: Homestead Act (1862); Stevens Treaty (1855).

Further Reading

Davis, William C. *The American Frontier.* Norman: University of Oklahoma Press, 1992.

Lindgren, H. Elaine. *Land in Her Own Name.* Norman: University of Oklahoma Press. 1996.

Doniphan, Alexander William (1808–1887)

Before his achievements in the Mexican-American War of 1846–1848, Alexander Doniphan had practiced law in Lexington, Missouri, and Liberty, Missouri, served three terms in the state legislature as a Whig, and, in 1838, been appointed brigadier general of the Missouri militia. He was a native of Mason County, Kentucky, born on July 9, 1808, and a graduate of Augusta College, a small Methodist school in Bracken, Kentucky. He married Elizabeth Jane Thornton in 1837 and they had two sons.

Doniphan earned a measure of fame in 1838 when he refused to carry out an order by his superior officer in the Missouri militia. The issue was the culmination of efforts to expel members of the Church of Jesus Christ of Latter-day Saints (known as Mormons) and the church's founder, Joseph Smith, from the state. As a member of the state legislature, Doniphan had sponsored a bill in 1836 to create Caldwell County in northwestern Missouri expressly for Mormon settlement. The bill passed into law but rabid anti-Mormon sentiment grew as more of Smith's followers bought land and settled in the state. In November 1838, in the town of Far West, Caldwell County, Doniphan and his militiamen were ordered to arrest Joseph Smith and other church leaders, gather them in the public square, and execute them by gunfire. Major General Samuel D. Lucas, commander of the state militia, signed the order, but Doniphan adamantly refused to enforce it, calling it a license for cold-blooded murder and promising his superior serious repercussions if anyone was executed. Smith was subsequently jailed, the other prisoners escaped custody, and Doniphan was not reprimanded for disobeying the order.

With the declaration of war with Mexico in May 1846, the U.S. War Department ordered the organization of an Army of the West at Fort Leavenworth, Kansas, to take control of the provinces of New Mexico and Alta California. The force of close to 1,700 men, drawn principally from Missouri and under the overall command of General Stephen Watts Kearny, included eight companies of the First Regiment of Missouri Mounted Volunteers, led by Doniphan, now a colonel.

Following the occupation of Santa Fe in August 1846, Doniphan helped formulate the laws that would govern the new United States territory of New Mexico, and in December, some months after Kearny's departure for California, Doniphan rode south with 856 men and a huge supply train, bound for Chihuahua, Mexico.

Doniphan's march became legendary in the annals of the war. His ragtag battalions routed a Mexican force at Brazito near El Paso and captured Ciudad Chihuahua on February 28, 1847, after defeating a Mexican army of 4,000 a few miles north of the city, suffering only twelve casualties. He then marched his men 600 miles (1,000 km) southeast to Saltillo, capital of the state of Coahuila, in the aftermath of the capture of the city by Brigadier General John E. Wool, commander of American forces in the Chihuahua campaign.

Following the war, Doniphan returned to practice law in Missouri. In February 1861, as a slaveholder and strong Unionist he served as a delegate to the Washington Peace Conference at a time when seven southern states had seceded from the Union. He was offered a command in the Union Army but declined. He died in Richmond, Missouri, on August 8, 1887.

Dale L. Walker

See also: Army of the West; Kearny, Stephen Watts; Mexican-American War; Mormon Battalion; Mormon Church.

Further Reading

Dawson, Joseph G. *Doniphan's Epic March: The 1st Missouri Volunteers in the Mexican War.* Lawrence: University Press of Kansas, 1999.

Hughes, John T. *Doniphan's Expedition.* College Station: Texas A&M University Press, 1997.

Launius, Roger D. *Alexander William Doniphan: Portrait of a Missouri Moderate.* Columbia: University of Missouri Press, 1997.

Donner Party

In his *Emigrants' Guide to Oregon and California*, Lansford W. Hastings wrote: "The most direct route, for the California emigrants, would be to leave the Oregon route, about 200 miles east from Fort Hall; thence bearing west southwest, to the Salt Lake; and thence continuing down to the bay of San Francisco." This route became known as Hastings' Cutoff although it did not actually reduce the number of miles the emigrants had to travel to reach California. Plus, following this advice led to a tragedy of unbelievable proportions for families and individuals of the Donner Party.

In 1846 the families of James Reed and Jacob and George Donner left their homes in Springfield, Illinois, for California. They journeyed to Independence, Missouri, in April to join their wagons with others headed west. The group departed from Independence on May 12. While they were late getting started, there was no urgency in their travel along the trail. Sarah Keyes, Margaret Reed's mother, died at Alcove Spring near the Big Blue River. They spent five days burying Mrs. Keyes and crossing the Big Blue. Ruth Whitman, writing about Tamsen Donner, stated: "They planned the journey as a summer holiday, but it took months longer than they had anticipated." Reaching Fort Laramie in late June, the party decided to follow Hastings' Cutoff. Mountain man James Clyman, returning east along the route with Lansford Hastings, advised James Reed, an old friend, not to follow the new route, as "it could be fatal."

At Fort Bridger on July 28, the Donner Party found that even though Hastings had promised to meet them there and guide them to California, he had departed with another party. Edwin Bryant, who had traveled with them earlier on the journey, left a letter for them at Fort Bridger advising against the cut-off. The letter was never delivered and they continued on. There is speculation that the fort's owners, Jim Bridger and his partner, Louis Vasquez, withheld the letter to ensure the success of their post by not discouraging emigrants to use Hastings' Cutoff.

There was no wagon route through the Wasatch

Mountains and the emigrants had to blaze their own, further delaying their progress. Once in the valley of the Great Salt Lake, several additional days were lost crossing the Great Salt Desert. Rejoining the California Trail along the Humboldt River, the party suffered additional setbacks. James Reed was banished for killing teamster John Snyder during a violent argument, and the party was reduced by three more members through abandonment, disappearance, and an accidental shooting. By the time they reached the Sierra Nevada, it was late October and snow was falling. The party needed just one more day for the leading families to ascend the high peaks and reach Sacramento, only 150 miles (240 km) away, but the snowfall was so deep that they were stranded. The winter of 1846–1847 was among the worst in Sierra history.

Finding one cabin and building two more, part of the Donner Party settled near today's Donner Lake. The two Donner families, a few miles behind the others, set up camp at Alder Creek Valley. They did not build cabins, but instead erected tepee-like structures that let smoke exit through the top; canvas, quilts, and hides were draped over the wood to provide cover. Food was in short supply and the livestock that remained was left to roam. When a blizzard struck and buried the animals, the starving families could not locate their carcasses.

In December fifteen of the strongest individuals set out for civilization. Later known as the "Forlorn Hope," this group of ten men and five women encountered a violent storm on Christmas night. Caught in the middle of a blizzard with no shelter, four from the group perished. In order to survive, the remaining members consumed their dead colleagues, also murdering and cannibalizing two *vaqueros* (herdsmen) sent by Sutter who had brought them supplies before the party became trapped. In January the party finally reached a Miwok Indian village. It was not until mid-February, however, that the first of several rescue parties reached the Sierra camps, where cannibalism had been practiced as well. Raising rescue parties was difficult due to the number of men involved in the Bear Flag Rebellion and the war against Mexico. It was after the rescue parties arrived that the survivors in the Sierra camps practiced cannibalism. Many people had died waiting for relief, and others died on the way out. The last survivor was brought out in the spring. Of the eighty-nine emigrants who departed from Fort Bridger in July, only forty-five survived.

Recalling the trip, Virginia Reed Murphy wrote: "We were full of hope and did not dream of sorrow." The ordeal of the Donner Party was not in vain. The

Mormons, emigrating west the next year, used much of the Donner trail through the Wasatch to reach the Salt Lake valley. In 1849 Captain Howard Stansbury, exploring the Great Salt Lake valley, came across some of the wagons, supplies, and carcasses left the by the Donner Party near Pilot Peak. In his official report he commented on Hastings' Cutoff and described the incidents of 1846: "A portion of his [Hastings's] company, which had followed at some distance behind him, becoming belated in crossing the Sierra Nevada Mountains, a number of them perished, and the remainder were reduced to the revolting necessity of living upon the bodies of their dead comrades, until they were rescued by relief from Sutter's Fort."

Tamsen Emerson Hert

See also: California Trail; Fort Bridger; Manifest Destiny; Mexican-American War; Mormon Trail; Oregon Trail; Stansbury Expedition.

Further Reading

Johnson, Kristin, ed. *"Unfortunate Emigrants": Narratives of the Donner Party.* Logan: Utah State University Press, 1996.

King, Joseph A. *Winter of Entrapment: A New Look at the Donner Party.* Toronto: P.D. Meany, 1992.

McGlashan, C.F. *History of the Donner Party, A Tragedy of the Sierra.* Stanford, CA: Stanford University Press, 1947.

Mullen, Frank, Jr. *The Donner Party Chronicles: A Day-by-Day Account of a Doomed Wagon Trail, 1846–1847.* Reno: Nevada Humanities Committee, 1997.

Rarick, Ethan. *Desperate Passage: The Donner Party's Perilous Journey West.* Oxford and New York: Oxford University Press, 2008.

Stewart, George R. *Ordeal by Hunger: The Story of the Donner Party.* Lincoln: University of Nebraska Press, 1960.

Douglas, Stephen A. (1813–1861)

Although born in Brandon, Vermont, Stephen Arnold Douglas became known as the brilliant U.S. senator from Illinois who met an obscure congressman from his home state named Abraham Lincoln in a series of debates in the senate campaign of 1858.

Douglas, who came to be known as the "Little Giant" for his short stature and expansive mind, migrated to Illinois at age twenty and in the town of Jacksonville studied law and joined the bar. He was elected to the state legislature in 1836, became secretary of state in 1840, a judge of the Illinois Supreme Court in 1841, a member of the House of Representatives in 1843, and of the U.S. Senate in 1847.

In Congress, Douglas was a tireless expansionist. He favored the annexation of Cuba and all of the Oregon Territory over any British claims, and supported the Mexican-American War in the James K. Polk presidency. He also chaired the influential Senate committee that guided newly acquired territories to statehood. With Henry Clay he drafted the bills that made up the Compromise of 1850, a bill calling for "popular sovereignty"—the people of the area in question deciding *yea* or *nay*—on the question of extending slavery into the new territories gained in the war with Mexico. In addition, he introduced the Kansas-Nebraska bill to the Senate in 1854, which called for the citizens of the new territories to decide on the slavery question. This act of Congress gave impetus to the abolitionist cause and fostered a movement toward civil war that included the activities of the Border Ruffians (the proslavery Missourians who crossed into the new Kansas Territory); the Jayhawkers (the derisive name for abolitionists); and the violent insurrectionist acts of John Brown and others that gave rise to the designation "Bleeding Kansas."

Douglas was twice in contention for the presidency, in 1852 when Franklin Pierce won the Democratic Party's nomination, and in 1856, when Douglas threw his support to James Buchanan.

Illinois congressman Abraham Lincoln, who held opposite views to Douglas on the slavery issue in the lands of the vast Louisiana Purchase, challenged the incumbent for his Senate seat in 1858. The two met in a series of seven three-hour debates on the slavery issue between August 21 and October 15 that year. Democrat Douglas won re-election to his Senate seat but Republican Lincoln, a one-term congressman, won a national exposure for views against the spread of slavery.

The slavery issue dogged and divided the Democratic Party at its convention in Charleston, South Carolina, in April 1860, and with southern delegates walking out in Charleston and again in Baltimore. The northern wing of the party nominated Douglas as their presidential candidate. The southern wing responded by meeting in Richmond and nominating John C. Breckenridge of Kentucky, vice president in the James Buchanan administration, but Lincoln won the election by nearly a half-million votes. (Between election day in November 1860 and Lincoln's inauguration in March 1861, seven states seceded from the Union.)

Douglas selflessly offered his services to Lincoln to promote the Union cause and toured several border states for that purpose. In late spring of 1861, however, he fell ill with typhoid fever and died on June 3 in Chicago.

Dale L. Walker

See also: Clay, Henry; Elections, Presidential; Kansas-Nebraska Act (1854); Oregon Question

Further Reading

Capers, Gerald M. *Stephen A. Douglas: Defender of the Union.* Boston: Little, Brown, 1959.

Johannsen, Robert W. *The Frontier, the Union, and Stephen A. Douglas.* Urbana: University of Illinois Press, 1989.

———. *Stephen A. Douglas.* New York: Oxford University Press, 1973.

Milton, G.F. *The Eve of Conflict: Stephen A. Douglas and the Needless War.* Boston: Houghton Mifflin, 1934.

Drouillard, George (c. 1775–1810)

George Drouillard, one of the most valued and respected members of the Lewis and Clark Expedition, was likely born about 1775, probably in Canada, the son of a French-Canadian father and a Shawnee Indian mother. Little is known about his childhood, but in late 1803 he was recruited by Captain Meriwether Lewis at Fort Massac in Illinois Territory to act as interpreter, guide, and hunter for the Corps of Discovery's exploration of the newly acquired Louisiana Territory. Drouillard was fluent in French and English, possessed natural wilderness survival skills, and was proficient in Indian sign language. Evidence exists that he may have spelled his name Drouilliard, with a second "i," but he was always referred to in the journals kept by Lewis and Clark as Drewyer. In the two years it took for the expedition to reach the Pacific Ocean and return to St. Louis, he would prove his worth on numerous occasions.

Without Drouillard's skill in sign language, Lewis and Clark would never have been able to communicate with the various Indian tribes they encountered on their journey, and his efforts secured the good will and aid of the Oto, Mandan, Shoshone, Nez Percé, and Clatsop tribes, thus ensuring the success of the expedition. He was also an expert hunter who regularly provided fresh meat for the cooking pots, and he always remained calm and unruffled when a tense or dangerous situation arose. In one incident he stopped one of the expedition boats from capsizing on the Missouri River in a stiff gale by calmly taking the tiller from the inexperienced man handling it and steering into the wind, thus saving valuable instruments and supplies, as well as the occupants.

Upon the successful return of the expedition in 1806, Drouillard drew his pay, secured the free acres of land in the new territory that each member of the party was awarded, bought the acreage of two other members of the expedition to add to his own for a total of 960 acres (390 ha), and headed back west. By 1807 he was a member of Manuel Lisa's first trapping expedition up the Missouri and Yellowstone rivers to the mouth of the Big Horn River, where he helped build a trading post. He then proceeded to travel several hundred miles to inform surrounding Indian tribes that the new trading post was open for business. During the years 1808–1809, Drouillard continued his association with Lisa and the Missouri Fur Company, acting as representative in the field for two of Lisa's partners in the company, both of whom preferred to stay home in St. Louis rather than venture into the wilderness.

In May 1810, while trapping with Lisa and thirty others near the Jefferson and Madison rivers, Drouillard was attacked by Blackfoot Indians while separated from the main body of men, who were engaged in constructing a fort. He managed to kill two of his attackers before being killed himself. His comrades later found his horribly mutilated remains and buried him where he had fallen.

Rod Timanus

See also: Lewis and Clark Expedition; Lisa, Manuel; Missouri Fur Company.

Further Reading

Ambrose, Stephen E. *Undaunted Courage: Meriwether Lewis, Thomas Jefferson, and the Opening of the American West.* New York: Touchstone/Simon & Schuster, 1996.

Bakeless, John, ed. *The Journals of Lewis and Clark.* New York: Mentor/Dutton Signet, 1964.

Skarsten, M.O. *George Drouillard: Hunter and Interpreter for Lewis and Clark and Fur Trader, 1807–1810.* Spokane, WA: Arthur H. Clark, 2003.

Dull Knife (1810–1883)

Dull Knife was a Northern Cheyenne leader who tried to protect his people and preserve the Cheyenne way of life as the United States expanded into Cheyenne territory. Born in 1810, he grew up in the Powder River country in present-day Montana and Wyoming. His Cheyenne name was Morning Star, but the Lakotas and his white contemporaries knew him by his Lakota name, Dull Knife.

After Colonel John Chivington and his Colorado volunteers attacked Black Kettle's Southern Cheyenne camp on Sand Creek in 1864, Dull Knife and other Cheyenne leaders joined their southern relatives in attacking military targets as well as settlers and emigrants.

Dull Knife and the Northern Cheyenne fought in Red Cloud's War against the government when the military built forts along the Bozeman Trail. Dull Knife and Two Moons lead their Cheyenne warriors against Fort C.F. Smith. The Cheyennes caught thirty soldiers and civilians outside the fort on a hay-cutting detail. The soldiers and civilians were able to withstand the Cheyennes' attack with new repeating rifles in what would become known as the Hayfield Fight.

Under the terms of the 1868 Fort Laramie Treaty, the government abandoned the Bozeman Trail and three forts built along the route. Dull Knife, one of the chiefs representing the Cheyennes, signed the treaty.

Dull Knife did not participate in the Battle of the Little Bighorn in June 1876, having left Red Cloud Agency during that time as the government had stopped food rations. During the winter of 1877, Colonel Ranald Mackenzie's troops and Pawnee warriors found Dull Knife's camp in the Bighorn Mountains and attacked at daybreak. The Pawnees captured the horse herd, and Cheyenne men, women, and children were killed as they awoke and attempted to flee. The Cheyenne camp was destroyed by the soldiers, the Cheyenne horses shot. It took three days of walking through bitter weather for Dull Knife and his people to reach Crazy Horse's Oglala Lakota camp, where the Oglalas clothed, fed, and gave them shelter.

In the spring of 1877, Crazy Horse's Oglalas, along with Dull Knife and other Cheyenne chiefs and their people, surrendered at Camp Robinson, Nebraska. The Cheyennes thought they would be living with the Lakotas on the Great Sioux Reservation according to the terms of the Fort Laramie Treaty, but the government, concerned about the close alliance between the Northern Cheyennes and Lakotas, sent the Northern Cheyennes to Indian Territory (modern-day Oklahoma) to live with the Southern Cheyennes. There the Northern Cheyennes began to sicken and die.

On September 9, 1878, Dull Knife and another Cheyenne chief, Little Wolf, led 297 men, women, and children north to return to their homeland. They fought a running battle against the military as well as civilians who followed them and attempted to intercept them. After crossing the Platte River and entering the Sand Hills of Nebraska, Dull Knife and Little Wolf split up. Dull Knife headed toward Red Cloud Agency with 150 people, and Little Wolf continued on to the Cheyenne homeland in southern Montana.

On October 23, as an early blizzard hit, Dull Knife's people were intercepted by cavalry troops from Fort Robinson. The troops escorted the Cheyennes to the fort and gave them living space in one of the barracks. But soon the government decided that the Cheyennes had to return to Indian Territory.

On the night of January 9, 1879, Dull Knife and his followers broke out of the barracks. Over the course of two weeks, they kept up a running battle with the troops. In the end, the soldiers killed sixty-four men, women, and children, including one of Dull Knife's daughters, before recapturing most of the others. Dull Knife and a few other people eluded capture and made it to Pine Ridge Agency, but even there they were held as prisoners. Little Wolf and his people were captured in the spring.

The Northern Cheyennes were eventually given a reservation in Montana, and Dull Knife lived out the rest of his life there, dying in 1883.

Bill Markley

See also: Black Kettle; Bozeman Trail; Cheyenne; Crazy Horse; Fort Laramie; Fort Laramie, Treaty of (1868); Fort Robinson; Lakota; Mackenzie, Ranald Slidell; Red Cloud; Red Cloud's War; Sand Creek Massacre.

Further Reading

Adams, Alexander. *Sunlight and Storm: The Great American Plains.* New York: G.P. Putnam's, 1977.

Brown, Dee. *Bury My Heart at Wounded Knee: An Indian History of the American West.* New York: Henry Holt, 2001.

Debo, Angie. *A History of the Indians of the United States.* London: Folio Society, 2003.

Sandoz, Mari. *Cheyenne Autumn.* New York: Avon Books, 1964.

Dunbar-Hunter and Freeman-Custis Expeditions

Thomas Jefferson was elated over the United States purchase of Louisiana Territory from the French gov-

ernment in 1803. The president's innate curiosity about the history, geography, and natural resources of the vast region prompted him to send several exploration parties into the field to observe and document everything of interest that they found. The Lewis and Clark Expedition up the Missouri River, across the Rocky Mountains, and down the Columbia River to the Pacific Ocean is well known, as is, although to a lesser extent, the mission that sent Lieutenant Zebulon Pike to the Southwest in quest of the source of the Red River. However, two other exploring parties were sent out at about the same time and, although neither was successful in attaining its original goals, they nevertheless added a great deal of information to the growing knowledge of what lay beyond the Mississippi River.

In 1804 William Dunbar (1749–1810), a Louisiana transplant from Scotland, was charged with leading an expedition up the Arkansas River to its source and down the Red River to its junction with the Mississippi. His partner was George Hunter (1755–1823), a Revolutionary War veteran, also from Scotland by way of Philadelphia. Accompanying them were Hunter's son and twelve soldiers commanded by a sergeant, all aboard a 50-foot (15-m) long oar-powered flatboat equipped with a mast, sail, and cabin. Osage Indian hostility in the region that lay between the two rivers made the proposed journey impractical. Instead, the party traveled up the Red River to the Black, up the Black to the Quachita, then up that watercourse to the site of present-day Hot Springs, Arkansas. Beginning at Natchez, Mississippi, on October 16, 1804, the group returned on February 2, 1805.

The second expedition, led by Thomas Freeman (?–1821) and Peter Custis (c. 1780–1842) left Fort Adams, 60 miles (100 km) south of Natchez, on April 28, 1806, to explore and map the Red River. Freeman, a native of Ireland who had assisted in the surveying of Washington, DC, and Custis, a Virginia-born senior medical student at the University of Pennsylvania, were accompanied by U.S. Army captain Richard Sparks, Lieutenant Enoch Humphreys, nineteen soldiers, and an unnamed slave, aboard two 25-foot (7.5-m) long flatboats and a pirogue. By June 7, the expedition reached a huge log jam on the river that prohibited it from traveling further. Over the next few days, with the assistance of a local guide, the group made its way through a network of swamps, bayous, downed trees, and shallow water to the upstream side of the log jam. In late July, they were met by 300 Spanish troops near present-day New Boston, Texas, who insisted they go no further. Vastly outnumbered, Freeman gave the command to turn around and proceed down the river, reaching Fort Adams in early September.

Although both expeditions were technical failures, they provided a great deal of new information about areas that had previously been little explored.

James A. Crutchfield

See also: Jefferson, Thomas; Lewis and Clark Expedition; Pike Expedition.

Further Reading

White, David A., ed. *News of the Plains and Rockies, 1803–1865.* Spokane, WA: Arthur H. Clark, 1996.

Duniway, Abigail Scott (1834–1915)

Abigail Duniway, the mother of suffrage and equal rights for women in the Northwest, was a successful writer, newspaper publisher, milliner, journalist, and lecturer. She was a tireless promoter of women's rights for fifty years and was the first woman to cast a vote in Oregon.

Born Abigail Jane Scott in a small log cabin near Groveland, Illinois, in 1834, she was the third of twelve children, nine of whom survived childhood. Her education was sporadic at best for she was needed on the family farm. In 1852, during a time of economic depression and amid stories of grand opportunities in Oregon, her father decided to emigrate despite her mother's poor health. Her father gathered a group of thirty wagons and set out, appointing Abigail as journal keeper. At the time, she was seventeen. It was a journey of tragedy for her. Not only did her mother and youngest brother die of cholera, but also a young man whom she loved was swept away in the Snake River.

The family arrived in Oregon in October and settled on a farm near Lafayette while Abigail taught school. In 1853 she met and married Benjamin Duniway, who lived on an isolated ranch in Clackamas County. During the time she bore two of her four children and worked on the ranch, she also wrote her first novel. *Captain Gray's Company*, the first novel commercially published in Oregon, did not receive good reviews but it was the first of many based on her Overland Trail experiences. In 1855 the Duniways sold their ranch and bought a farm outside Lafayette. However, Abigail's husband guaranteed a loan for a friend who could not pay. Farm prices fell and the weather was disastrous, resulting in the loss of the farm. Benjamin became a teamster but was run over by a runaway wagon, disabling him for the rest of his life.

Now the sole source of income, Abigail opened a boarding school and taught there as well. In 1865 she sold the school and began a larger one in Albany, Oregon. She also opened a millinery shop, selling fine hats and clothing. On a buying trip, she met women in the suffrage movement, thus beginning her long commitment to equal rights for women. After attending the California Woman Suffrage Convention in December 1870, she moved the family to Portland, learned the newspaper business, and began her weekly newspaper, *The New Northwest*. The paper focused on all aspects of women's rights and the legal inequities facing women. Abigail also began her career as a lecturer, persuading Susan B. Anthony to extend her planned tour of the West into the Northwest. Abigail managed Anthony's tour, introduced her at events, and also spoke extemporaneously. Over the next twenty years, she crossed the country four times and spoke to large crowds of women. She also wrote seventeen novels, which were serialized in her newspaper. Her lectures pinpointed the suffrage issue as more complicated than just the vote; she also argued for women's financial autonomy, their rights to own property, the protection of their health, and the limitation of pregnancies.

In 1887—as a result of a rift with the national suffrage movement, which had begun to ally with temperance forces, and the death of her only daughter—Abigail ceased publication of her newspaper and moved her family to Idaho. Although she did not drink alcohol, she strongly believed that allying with temperance would stop votes supporting suffrage for women. In 1894 the family moved back to Portland and she revived the Oregon Suffrage Association. Another push for the vote ended in defeat, due mostly to Abigail's brother, publisher of the *Oregonian*, who editorialized against it. However, Abigail's attendance at the state legislature resulted in several measures that awarded married women greater personal and property rights.

In 1912, just before Abigail's seventy-eighth birthday, Oregon passed a women's suffrage amendment granting women the right to vote. She had been an advocate for women's suffrage for over fifty years, and the governor asked her to be the first woman to vote. Abigail died in 1915 at age eighty-one of a foot infection.

Carol Keenan and Carol Kinsmann

See also: Oregon Trail; Woman Suffrage.

Further Reading

Duniway, Abigail Scott. *Path Breaking: An Autobiographical History of the Equal Suffrage Movement in the Pacific Coast States.* New York: Schocken Books, 1914.

Moynihan, Ruth Barnes. *Rebel for Rights: Abigail Scott Duniway.* New Haven: Yale University Press, 1983.

Scott, Abigail Jane. *Journal of a Trip to Oregon.* Edited by David Duniway. Lincoln: University of Nebraska Press, 1997.

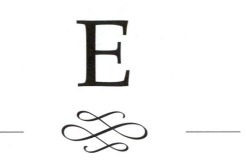

E

Eastman, Seth (1808–1875), and Mary Eastman (1818–1877)

Seth and Mary Eastman are known for their meticulous records of the everyday life, rituals, and legends of the Dakota Sioux of the 1840s. Seth was a military artist and painted Indian life at Fort Snelling in Minnesota Territory, as well as many other works, while Mary recorded Indian legends and customs for her books and magazine articles.

Seth Eastman was born in Brunswick, Maine, in 1808. Because he had a passion for military life as well as drawing during his youth, he received an appointment to West Point, graduating in 1829 with an average record, but first in his class in drawing. His first assignment was to Fort Crawford in Wisconsin, but the following spring he moved on to Fort Snelling on the upper Mississippi River. Peaceful Indian tribes, mostly Dakota Sioux, surrounded the fort. While there, Seth lived with Stands Like a Spirit, daughter of the Indian chief Cloud Man, and their daughter was born. Such relationships were common among the soldiers and Indians at the time.

However, shortly after the child was born, Seth was assigned to the Topographical Engineers and moved to Connecticut. In January 1833, he was ordered to West Point to teach topographical drawing. It was there that he met Mary Henderson, the Virginia-born daughter of the assistant surgeon of the U.S. Army. She was well educated, with a curious mind. They married in 1835. In 1837 Seth published his *Treatise on Topographical Drawing*, which became West Point's first textbook on the subject. By 1840 he was a captain and had become an established painter in oils with seventeen landscapes hung in National Academy of Design spring shows.

After a brief stint in Florida dealing with the Seminoles, Seth was ordered back to Fort Snelling. The entire family, including three children, was welcomed by the Indians, who liked and respected Seth and were curious about Mary. Her first impression of the Indians was one of fear and fascination. Mary was accepted and began recording tribal customs and legends. She has been called the first ethnologist because of the faithful, authentic, and detailed accounts in her book, *Dakotah or, Life and Legends of the Sioux Around Fort Snelling*. Checkered Cloud, an elderly Sioux medicine woman, who recounted tribal legends, befriended her. Seth illustrated the book, and many of Mary's interviews took place during his sittings. His output of drawings and paintings was prolific during this time and, like Mary, he was interested in authenticity and detail. Neither was a romantic, and they focused only on what they heard and saw to record a way of life.

In 1848 Seth was ordered to Texas and Comanche country although he had hopes of an assignment to illustrate Henry R. Schoolcraft's proposed and congressionally authorized history of the Indian tribes of the United States. Mary left for St. Louis, where she managed his artistic career and continued her own literary pursuits. *Dakotah* was published in 1849 to great acclaim, and in 1852 she wrote an answer to *Uncle Tom's Cabin* titled *Aunt Phillis's Cabin; or Southern Life as It Is*. The latter was a best seller although it received poor reviews. Other magazine articles and books followed with varying degrees of success. Meanwhile, Mary lobbied Henry H. Sibley, the congressional delegate for the Minnesota Territory, for a furlough in Washington for Seth so he could work on the Schoolcraft project. This was denied although he did obtain a leave in December 1849, and was finally assigned to the Commissioner of Indian Affairs so he could illustrate Schoolcraft's five-volume work.

In May 1855, Seth returned to Texas and in the following October he was promoted to major. He was in poor health by this time and, after several other assignments, he became the mustering and disbursing officer for Maine and New Hampshire in April 1861. In 1863 he retired with disability and was brevetted a brigadier general for his Civil War services. Returning to Washington in 1867, he was commissioned by Congress to paint nine canvases illustrating Indian life for the House Committee on Indian Affairs and seventeen views of military forts for the House Committee on Military Affairs.

Seth died in 1875 while painting his favorite view and the last fort in the series, West Point. Mary died following a stroke two years later. Seth's works are on view in the Corcoran Gallery of Art, the Capitol in Washington, DC, the Minneapolis Institute of Arts, and the Thomas Gilcrease Institute of American History and Art in Tulsa, Oklahoma.

Carol Krismann

See also: Corps of Topographical Engineers; Schoolcraft, Henry Rowe; Sioux.

Further Reading

Boehme, Sarah E., Christian F. Feest, and Patricia Condon Johnston. *Seth Eastman: A Portfolio of North American Indians.* Afton, MN: Afton Historical Society Press, 1995.

Eastman, Mary Henderson. *Dakotah or, Life and Legends of the Sioux Around Fort Snelling.* Includes Rena Neumann Coen. "Mary Henderson Eastman: A Biographical Essay." Afton, MN: Afton Historical Society Press, 1995.

McDermott, John Francis. *Seth Eastman: Pictorial History of the American Indian.* Norman: University of Oklahoma Press, 1961.

———. *Seth Eastman's Mississippi: A Lost Portfolio Recovered.* Urbana: University of Illinois Press, 1973.

McNeil, W.K. "Mary Henderson Eastman, Pioneer Collector of American Folklore." *Southern Folklore Quarterly* 39:3 (1975).

Elections, Presidential

The presidential elections of the mid-nineteenth century were among the most pivotal in American history. The nation was divided by many issues, the most pernicious of which was slavery. As the nation spread its influence and population into the vast tracts of the West, the issue of slavery loomed over the expansion like a smothering shadow. The most successful politicians of these decades were adept at maintaining the delicate balance of power between slave and free states. The dangerous balancing act resulted in a period of twenty-four years during which no president served two consecutive terms.

Election of 1844

Incumbent John Tyler was in a weak position as he sought reelection in 1844. He had been thrown out of the Whig Party for bolting the party, forcing him to run as a third-party candidate under the National Democratic Party. The Whig Party nominated Henry Clay for president with Theodore Frelinghuysen as vice-president. The Democratic Party—not the same party that Tyler had helped form—had a hotly contested nomination process that required a supermajority to win. Front-runner Martin Van Buren was bested on the ninth ballot by James K. Polk, a candidate whose name was first raised on the eighth ballot. Polk's running mate was George Mifflin Dallas, who accepted the nomination after Silas Wright refused it. Other candidates for president included James Birney, who ran under the Liberty Party on an anti-slavery platform. His running mate was Thomas Morris. The candidacy of the first president and prophet of the Church of Jesus Christ of Latter-day Saints, Joseph Smith, was terminated when Smith was murdered by a mob in Missouri.

The overarching issues of the election were the annexation of Texas and the expansion of American influence into Oregon Territory. Clay was against expansion and Polk was pro-expansion. Polk attempted to balance charges that the annexation of Texas was of benefit to the slave states by including in his expansionist platform the free territory of Oregon. Clay was compelled eventually to support the annexation of Texas provided it would not result in a war with Mexico. Tyler withdrew from the election in August.

The election was close. It was the last presidential election in which the states were allowed to have voting on different days. Personal attacks filled the newspapers. Clay was labeled a drunkard and Polk a coward. Front-runner Clay's early lead melted away. The Liberty Party acted as a spoiler for important electoral votes. Just fewer than 2,700,000 votes were cast of which the Liberty Party received 2.3 percent. The Democrats and James Polk garnered 49.5 percent of the popular vote and 170 electoral votes out of 275. The Whigs received 48.1 percent of the popular vote, but only 105 electoral votes of the 138 needed to win. Polk won the election by combining victories in numerous southern states with those in a coalition of pro-expansion northern states.

Through this election the American public had given the government its approval for continued westward expansion.

Election of 1848

With his health failing, President Polk kept his promise not to seek reelection. Polk had expanded the nation even more than Thomas Jefferson. The Treaty of Guadalupe Hidalgo—ending the Mexican-American War and signed in early 1848—left the nation with vast tracts of new lands in the Southwest. These almost immediately became pawns in the power struggle between pro- and anti-slavery forces.

The Whig Party latched onto the popularity of Mexican-American War hero General Zachary Taylor and nominated him for president, along with Millard Fillmore for vice-president. The Democrats countered with the nomination of the former secretary of war, Lewis Cass, and his running mate General Orlando Butler. Martin Van Buren and Charles Francis Adams ran a third-party ticket under the Free Soil Party.

The issue of whether the new territories could allow slavery dominated the election. Cass supported a system by which each territory would decide the matter on its own. On the other hand, Taylor, owned hundreds of slaves and the election soon devolved into almost continuous character assassination. Cass was labeled as corrupt and dishonest while Taylor was painted as brainless, crude, greedy, and vicious.

This was the first presidential election in which all the states voted on the same day, except for South Carolina, which had its state legislature choose the electors. A total of 2,879,184 votes were cast. The Free Soil Party garnered 10.1 percent of the popular vote, hurting the Democratic Party severely by siphoning off many of its votes. Cass was able to collect roughly 42.5 percent of the popular vote, resulting in 127 of the 290 electoral votes. Taylor did not receive a majority popular vote, reaching only 47.3 percent. However, he won 163 electoral votes, which amounted to seventeen over the required 146. Taylor managed to win a mixture of northern and southern states in his victory.

Taylor's election resulted in a continuation of the power struggle between pro- and anti-slavery forces with the West as the battleground. Taylor's death in office on July 9, 1850, put Millard Fillmore into office for the remainder of the term.

Election of 1852

The festering dispute over slavery seemed to divide the nation more deeply with each year. Incumbent Millard Fillmore was passed over by the Whig Party in 1852 in favor of another Mexican-American War hero, General Winfield "Old Fuss and Feathers" Scott. Fillmore had been unable to parlay the apparent success of the Compromise of 1850 into the solid support of his own party. The party split along sectional lines with Daniel Webster tying up the New England votes. It took fifty-three ballots for Scott to win the nomination, relying almost exclusively on votes from northern states. Scott's running mate was William Alexander Graham. The sectional crises pulled the Whig Party apart and 1852 was the final year that the party ran a nominee for the presidency.

The Democrats did not expect to have a chance of winning in 1852. The nomination was sought by such notables as Stephen Douglas, William Marcy, Lewis Cass, and James Buchanan. The Democrats picked an

THE BUFFALO HUNT.

A political cartoon from 1848 presents an optimistic view of the presidential prospects of Martin Van Buren, the candidate of the new Free Soil Party. He was soundly defeated by both Democrat Lewis Cass (*left*) and Whig Zachary Taylor (*right*), who won the election. *(Library of Congress)*

unlikely candidate, General Franklin Pierce of New Hampshire, after forty-nine ballots. Pierce's running mate was William R. King of North Carolina.

Once again there was a third-party candidate run by the Free Soil Party, in the person of John Hale, but the party's success as a spoiler in the 1848 election was not repeated.

The electorate had little to choose from in terms of differences between the party platforms. Voter turnout was exceptionally low. Many Whigs chose not to vote because of concerns about either the pro-slavery platform or Scott's anti-slavery proclivity. The Whigs managed to drive away voters from both branches of their party. Pierce succeeded in keeping his views on slavery ambiguous, making him more palatable to much of the electorate.

Of the roughly 3 million votes cast, the Free Soil Party garnered 4.9 percent of the popular vote. Pierce received roughly 50.8 percent of the popular vote and Scott received roughly 43.9 percent. The close popular vote margin for the top two candidates was not reflected in the Electoral College, where Pierce pulled off one of the most lopsided electoral victories in history, taking 254 of the 296 votes. He found himself tested as sectional differences, which took down the Whig Party, threatened to split the nation as well. Under Pierce the great sectional division came to a crisis that even the creative Kansas-Nebraska Act could not avert.

Election of 1856

With the fall of the Whig Party, its remnants gathered together new allies and formed new entities, the Republican Party and the Native American Party. The Republican Party soon rose to national prominence. Incumbent Franklin Pierce found himself, like so many of his predecessors, passed over for nomination to a second term. The Democrats selected James Buchanan, one of the better-qualified men to run for the presidency. Former president Millard Fillmore ran for the Native American (Know-Nothing) Party, a group focused on anti-foreigner (mainly anti-Catholic) issues. The Republicans selected John C. Frémont, dubbed "the Pathfinder" for his far-reaching explorations of the West, as their first candidate.

The issues during the campaign were broad, including the potential annexation of Cuba and the troubles in Kansas, but ultimately came back to the slavery debate. Democrats supported popular sovereignty and had a decidedly pro-slavery bent. The Republican platform condemned the twin abominations of slavery and polygamy in the new territories. The Know-Nothings ran against immigration and naturalization. For all the passion of the election campaigns, none of the candidates did much to promote his election. Few gave speeches. People were concerned that a Republican victory might lead to the secession from the union of many southern states.

Slightly more than 4 million votes were cast in the election. Millard Fillmore was a surprise, receiving roughly 21.6 percent of the popular vote but only eight electoral votes of the 296 available. The Republican Party, characterized as a radical group, received about 33.1 percent of the popular vote, all from northern states. This translated into 114 electoral votes of the

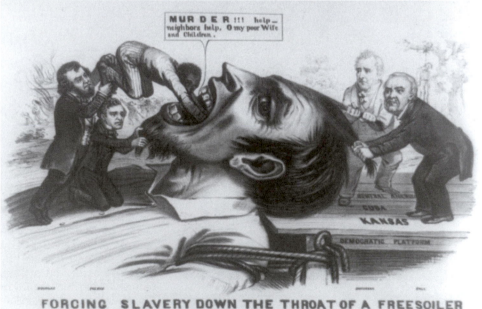

FORCING SLAVERY DOWN THE THROAT OF A FREESOILER

A cartoon in 1856 criticizes Democrats for seeking to extend slavery. A giant Free-Soiler is held down by James Buchanan and Lewis Cass (*right*), while Franklin Pierce and Stephen A. Douglas (*left*) force a black man, symbolizing slavery, down his throat. (*Library of Congress*)

149 necessary to win. James "Buck" Buchanan managed to attain a minority vote victory with his 45.3 percent popular vote and 174 electoral votes.

Buchanan served in troubled times. Kansas was bleeding, there was war in Utah, riots in New York City and Washington, DC, and a banking collapse. Under Buchanan, the failed policies of attempting to pander to both sectional factions led to increasing hostility, threatening civil war.

Election of 1860

The failed policies of President Buchanan served to increase national division. Buchanan did not run for reelection, but his vice-president, John C. Breckenridge, was happy to take his place on the ballot. The contentious election of 1860 served as the spark that ignited the national powder keg.

The Democratic Party convention in Charleston, South Carolina, was deeply divided over the party platform. Southern delegates demanded a platform that strongly supported slavery. Stephen A. Douglas led a northern faction, which still promoted popular sovereignty. Angry Southern delegates walked out of the convention. After fifty-four ballots, Douglas still did not have sufficient votes to win the nomination. The convention adjourned and met later in Baltimore, where Douglas was finally nominated. The convention nominated Benjamin Fitzpatrick for vice-president but he refused to run, and Herschel V. Johnson was nominated in his stead.

Southern Democrats met in Richmond and nominated John C. Breckenridge and Joseph Lane as their ticket. A coalition of former Whigs and Democrats came together to form the Constitutional Union Party, which met in Baltimore and nominated John Bell and Edward Everett as its ticket. The Republican convention had its moments of drama, but it took Abraham Lincoln only three ballots to garner the necessary votes. He overcame front-runner William H. Seward, who was thought by many to be too radical.

The players had been cast and the stage set for one of the most divisive elections in U.S. history. Most candidates had the good sense to venture sparingly into the public eye, allowing others to carry forth their messages. Douglas broke with convention and managed a nationwide speaking tour. Northern Democrats espoused preservation of the Union and recommended continuation of the principle of popular sovereignty. Southern Democrats promoted the expansion of slavery, while the Constitutional Union Party recommended preservation of the Union as it was, with slavery recognized in the Constitution. The Republican platform was critical of the expansion of slavery in the territories, but promised to leave the institution alone where it existed. Republicans also promoted a transcontinental railroad, homesteading legislation, and protective tariffs.

Almost 4,700,000 votes were cast in a high voter turnout of 81.2 percent of the electorate. Abraham Lincoln solidly won in the northern states, amassing 180 electoral votes—152 electoral votes were necessary to win. Lincoln managed this stunning achievement while gaining under 40 percent of the popular vote and winning only eighteen states. Breckenridge managed to win eleven states in the Deep South, tallying slightly over 18 percent of the popular vote and seventy-two electoral votes. John Bell was popular in the border states and won roughly 12.6 percent of the popular vote and thirty-nine electoral votes. The hapless Douglas won only Missouri and New Jersey, garnering twelve electoral votes and 29.5 percent of the popular vote.

Lincoln's election started a rush by southern states to secede from the Union. The ineffectual, lame-duck president, Buchanan, failed to act as southern states appropriated federal property. The difficult question whether the secessionists could be brought back into the Union without a civil war was left to the new president. The question was finally resolved after four years of war and the deaths of well over 600,000 Americans. The West was settled thereafter without the institution of slavery and by a national government with greater strength and power than it had before the war. The Republicans fulfilled their platform by promoting a transcontinental railroad and by providing for homesteading of the vast tracts of lands available in the West.

Terry A. Del Bene

See also: Compromise of 1850; Douglas, Stephen A.; Frémont, John C.; Homestead Act (1862); Kansas-Nebraska Act (1854); Missouri Compromise (1820); Pacific Railway Act (1862); Pacific Railway Act (1864); Polk, James K.; Scott, Winfield; Taylor, Zachary; Tyler, John.

Further Reading

Frank, Beryl. *The Pictorial History of the Democratic Party.* Secaucus, NJ: Castle Books, 1980.

———. *The Pictorial History of the Republican Party.* Secaucus, NJ: Castle Books, 1980.

Lorant, Stefan. *The Presidency.* New York: Duell, Sloan and Pearce, 1951.

Shade, William G., and Ballard C. Campbell. *American Presidential Campaigns and Elections.* Armonk, NY: M.E. Sharpe, 2003.

Emigration Societies

Emigration societies were formed to assist groups of people who chose to emigrate (to leave a birthplace, to go and live in another country or part of the country). These societies of colonization may have been organized by a church, but often were funded by towns or countries needing to increase their population, usually in the form of more laborers.

These societies helped organize emigrants by securing passage on a ship or with an overland guide. They arranged for supplies, equipment, stock, and other necessities for the journey. Some societies also chose who would emigrate and who would not.

The first widespread "western fever" struck Vermont and New Hampshire in the 1830s and 1940s. In the fall of 1835, the Reverend Sylvester Cochrane, a Congregational minister from Vermont, visited present-day Michigan for the purpose of permanently locating there. Struck by the sparseness of population, he returned to Vermont to sell the idea of establishing a colony of New England citizens within the township. He successfully convinced forty-two families to join him, and during 1836 the first groups arrived, forming Vermontville, Michigan.

Especially after the financial collapse of 1837, the lure of economic opportunity, including the promise of gold, pulled and tugged New Englanders westward. Emigrants moved to southern Michigan, northern Illinois, and southeastern Wisconsin in order to set up trading posts on the frontier and to create new farms and ranches.

By 1843 the "Great Migration" marked the starting of the Oregon Trail. Initially, about a 1,000 people traveled west; then hundreds of thousands, possibly upward of 500,000, followed on a multitude of overland trails. Emigration societies continued to form during this time. The Oregon and California emigration society shared information and set in motion emigration plans. From 1840 through 1846, emigrants headed from the United States to Oregon Territory traveling with family groups, extended families, or emigration societies composed of neighbors from the same town. Protestant missionaries joined the early emigrant mix heading to Oregon. In 1841 the first emigrant wagon train (the Bidwell-Bartleson party) arrived in what is now the state of California.

California belonged to Mexico at the time and was sparsely settled by cattle ranchers. Mexico expected emigrants to become Mexican citizens and join the Catholic Church. However, this idea did not appeal to most U.S. citizens. Emigrant societies continued to settle their clients there, but shunned the Mexican government until California became a possession of the United States following the 1846 Mexican-American War.

When gold was discovered in 1848 in California, the ensuing gold rush altered emigration patterns. Those migrants were mostly young males. Families still predominantly chose Oregon. More and more trail services (trading posts, forts, bridges, and ferries) sprang up to provide protection, respite, and necessities, making overland travel easier.

The Church of Jesus Christ of Latter-day Saints (Mormons) was the most extreme of all emigration organizations. Not technically an emigration society, nevertheless the church organized the migration of all its members in 1846–1847 from Nauvoo, Illinois, to a new city they founded in what they called Zion (now Utah). When the church began converting members in foreign countries, including England, Scotland, Wales, Italy, and Scandinavia, it also organized immigration programs to help those members gather to Zion. The migration to Great Salt Lake City of about 70,000 Mormons encouraged others to move west to establish forts, trading posts, ferries, and other business opportunities.

Kansas emigration societies were formed in the 1850s in Montpelier, Rutland, and Randolph, Vermont; Sutton and Londonderry, New Hampshire; and other eastern states. Rutland's Vermont Kansas Relief Company was formed "for mutual defense and protection" to aid emigrants to Kansas; its funds were devoted solely to "men of good character." Money was raised as well by the Vermont legislature, which passed an appropriation to help Kansas pioneers. The intent was to flood the territory of Kansas with anti-slavery citizens who would ensure the defeat of slavery under the principle of popular sovereignty. There were emigration societies in the South as well, but these failed to mobilize anywhere near the number of settlers sent by the New England emigration societies.

Like many emigrants, northerners moved as family groups in a pattern of chain migration, with earlier settlers encouraging others to join them. As historian Susan Gray suggested, Yankees in particular tended to form various organizations for the purpose of colonization. These emigration societies purchased land and established tight communities with the familiar institutions of school, church, and township government.

The Children's Aid Society, founded in 1853 in New York, sent orphans from New York by "orphan train" to the farming states of the Midwest: Kansas,

Ohio, Michigan, and Iowa. Many of these children became field hands, but some found loving families. This idea of sending out children to schools to be trained for farmwork was adopted in London in 1870 by Annie MacPherson, the Scottish evangelist.

Following the Civil War, freed slaves sometimes organized groups to migrate from the South to the lands beyond the Mississippi River. A Tennessee-born African-American named Benjamin Singleton was the sponsor of one such group, leading a large number of his fellow former slaves to settle in Kansas. Singleton advertised in Nashville on March 18, 1878, that on the following April 15, the "Real Estate and Homestead Association" would depart from the city "in pursuit of Homes in the Southwestern Lands of America, at Transportation Rates." Before the so-called Exodus of 1879 was over, nearly 40,000 African-Americans had resettled from the South to the Midwest, many of them in Kansas, where they organized all-black townships such as Nicodemus.

The almost universal feeling of the pioneer emigrants was that the trip was one of the hardest things they had done in their lives, but also was one of the most memorable, most rewarding, most cherished, and, for some, most enjoyable. Without the emigration societies, westward expansion would have been much more difficult.

Melody Groves

See also: Burnett, Peter Hardeman; California Trail; Mexican-American War; Mormon Church; Mormon Trail; Oregon Trail; Overland Trail.

Further Reading

Burnett, Peter H. *Recollections and Opinions of an Old Pioneer.* Santa Barbara, CA: Narrative Press, 2004.

Marcy, Randolph B. *The Prairie Traveler: A Handbook for Overland Expeditions.* New York: Harper & Brothers, 1859.

Nixon, Joan Lowry. *The Orphan Train Adventures.* New York: Delacourte Books, 1987.

Unruh, John D., Jr. *The Plains Across: The Overland Emigrants and the Trans-Mississippi West, 1840–60.* Urbana: University of Illinois Press, 1979.

Emory, William H. (1811–1887)

The U.S. Army Corps of Topographical Engineers was one of the most important elements in America's move westward. Surveying, mapping, and documenting much of the trans-Mississippi region, particularly in the years prior to the Civil War, the small but important unit counted among its members many men who later in their careers became icons in American political and military history. None, however, was more important to America's westward surge than William H. Emory.

Born in Queen Anne's County, Maryland, on September 11, 1811, Emory came from a distinguished and influential family that had expanded its plantation into one of the largest in the South. John C. Calhoun secured Emory an appointment to the U.S. Military Academy at West Point in 1827 and, following four years of intense study, Emory graduated in 1831 and was assigned to the 4th Artillery as a second lieutenant. Among Emory's friends at West Point were Joseph E. Johnston, Jefferson Davis, and Henry Clay Jr. Not entirely satisfied with his role in the artillery, Emory resigned his commission in 1836 upon his appointment as assistant United States engineer. This position prepared him for entry in 1838 into the recently organized Corps of Topographical Engineers. His reentry into the army that year was coupled with another significant event—his marriage to the great-granddaughter of Benjamin Franklin.

Emory's most important role in his long career with the topographical engineers occurred during the Mexican-American War when he was assigned to Colonel Stephen Watts Kearny's Army of the West, whose mission was to occupy New Mexico and California. Departing from Fort Leavenworth in late June 1846, the army made its way along the Santa Fe Trail and across the Great Plains to Bent's Fort, a large fur-trading post perched along the north bank of the Arkansas River in present-day southeastern Colorado. From there the troops traversed the dry, hot countryside of southern Colorado and conquered the high, treacherous pass at Raton, New Mexico. They entered Santa Fe on August 18, and achieved the conquest of New Mexico without a shot being fired.

A few days later, Kearny ordered Emory to build a fortification, named Fort Marcy in honor of U.S. secretary of war William L. Marcy, upon an eminence overlooking the city. In late September, Kearny and elements of the Army of the West departed Santa Fe for California and the second phase of the mission. In California, Emory fought in the Battle of San Pasqual and in several other skirmishes and was brevetted, first to captain and days later to major, for his outstanding service in the field.

Following the end of the war in 1848, Emory was assigned to serve as chief astronomer on the boundary survey between California and Mexico. After the United States acquired additional Mexican territory as a result of the Gadsden Purchase in 1853, Emory worked as commissioner of the newly organized U.S.-Mexican Boundary Survey to complete the earlier work in light of the new land cessions.

Emory's post–Corps of Topographical Engineers career included army service in Kansas, Utah, Indian Territory, and Texas. By 1861, when the Civil War broke out, he was a lieutenant colonel serving on the Texas frontier. Despite his Southern background, he served throughout the war in the Union army and distinguished himself in several battles, ending the conflict with the rank of major general. In 1876 he retired after four-and-a-half decades of service to the army and died on December 1, 1887, in Washington, DC.

Emory's enduring legacies to the nation's westward expansion are the two works he produced while serving with the Topographical Engineers. *Notes of a Military Reconnoissance {sic} from Fort Leavenworth, in Missouri, to San Diego, in California, Including Parts of the Arkansas, Del Norte, and Gila Rivers* was published by the federal government in 1848 and documents Emory's tenure with the Army of the West. The three-volume *Report on the United States and Mexican Boundary Survey*, published in 1857, describes the boundary work he performed as commissioner of the survey.

James A. Crutchfield

See also: Army of the West; California, Conquest of; Corps of Topographical Engineers; Kearny, Stephen Watts; Mexican-American War; Mexican Boundary Survey.

Further Reading

Norris, L. David, James C. Milligan, and Odie B. Faulk. *William H. Emory: Soldier-Scientist*. Tucson: University of Arizona Press, 1998.
Viola, Herman J. *Exploring the West*. Washington, DC: Smithsonian Books, 1987.

Empresario System

In 1820 Moses Austin took his proposal to settle American families in Spanish Texas to the authorities there. He could not have envisioned how his idea would be expanded upon in later years. After the Spanish were expelled from Mexico in 1821, the new Mexican government adopted Austin's vision as a means of populating their northern province and

providing a buffer against Comanche incursions. The system the Mexicans set up was modeled after the successful San Felipe colony operated by Stephen Austin, Moses's son, who had taken over implementing the plan after the untimely death of his father. By 1825 a set of rules and regulations was in place governing immigration.

Upon approval of an application to act as an agent for the Mexican government, a land speculator, or *empresario*, was allotted a large tract of land of his own choosing in Texas for the express purpose of importing settlers of good character to populate, cultivate, or otherwise improve it. Under the Mexican empresario system, each agent had six years to recruit settlers and populate this parcel of land. In return, the empresario received five leagues (22,142 acres [8,961 ha]) of rangeland and five labors (886 acres [359 ha]) of farmland for every 100 families settled. Settlers received one labor of land (177 acres [72 ha]) if married. An unmarried man received only about one-quarter of a labor (44 acres [18 ha]). The impresario was responsible for upholding the laws of Mexico within his area and vouching for the good character of new immigrants under his influence, receiving no land bounty until his contract was fulfilled.

Potential colonists met certain requirements of the Mexican government. They first had to become Mexican citizens and either be Roman Catholic or, if not, convert to that religion. Speaking the Spanish language was not absolutely necessary, but was encouraged by a provision in the impresario's contract. That document called for the establishment of schools within his domain wherein the language was to be taught. The impresario was expected to build a Catholic church to further the practice of the state religion. Each colonist had six years to pay a nominal fee for his land, usually around thirty dollars, and had to occupy and cultivate the property he was granted because foreign residents were not allowed to own land in Mexico. In return for meeting the requirements, the new colonist was exempt from Mexican taxes for a period of several years while he made his land productive.

Roughly twenty-five empresario grants were awarded by the Mexican government from 1825 on, with preference given to Mexican-born applicants. Only a few were successful. Some of these were located close to Stephen Austin's San Felipe colony, which had been in existence for the longest time and which he oversaw with strict adherence to Mexican law and the requirements of his position. Other empresarios of note were Green DeWitt and Martin de Leon, whose grants were located southwest of Austin's colony. Others succeeded in settling some families on their grants, but not in sufficient numbers to qualify the empresarios to receive their land bounties. They included Haden Edwards, David G. Burnet, Ben Milam, and Lorenzo de Zavala. Absolute failures were the grants of Sterling Robertson, Arthur Wavell, and James Powers.

The Mexican empresario system was a unique colonization concept that, by its very nature, brought two distinct cultures, Anglo-American and Hispanic, into conflict. Mismanagement and abuses of the system contributed to its general failure, with the notable exception of Austin's San Felipe colony. The large influx of Americans into Texas for the purpose of colonization, and the unwillingness of Mexican-born citizens to occupy that distant province, led to disproportionate population. By the outbreak of the Texas Revolution in 1835, the Anglo-American inhabitants of Texas outnumbered the Spanish-speaking, or Tejano, inhabitants by nearly five to one. That most of the immigrants were content to abide by the rules and restrictions placed upon them by the Mexican government mattered little in the long run. Conflict was inevitable and unavoidable, eventually leading to open warfare between the two groups.

Rod Timanus

See also: Austin, Moses; Austin, Stephen F.; Mexican Land Grants; Texas Revolution and Independence.

Further Reading

Fehrenbach, T R. *Lone Star: A History of Texas and the Texans.* New York: Macmillan, 1991.
Tijerina, Andres. *Tejanos and Texas Under the Mexican Flag.* College Station: Texas A&M University Press, 1994.

End-of-Track Towns

As the railroad crossed the continent, mountains, rivers, canyons, and a variety of topographical features forced the construction crews and engineers to stop long enough to build bridges, cut difficult grades, or stage equipment for building over difficult ground. End-of-track towns—sometimes called hell-on-wheels towns—came into existence at strategic points like the crossings of the Platte River, Green River, and Bear River. In one way, calling them end-of-track towns was a misnomer, since tracks sometimes had already passed through the town or had not yet reached it. What went on in these communities gave them their color.

Saloons, dance halls, gambling, and a town filled with more men than women created an electric environment. Leigh Freeman, the writer, editor, and outspoken voice of the hell-on-wheels towns in Wyoming Territory, wrote in the *Frontier Index* in 1868 that Green River had daily fights and random shootings. According to one military commander in town, the jail had room for only the worst criminals; the other criminals were set free. Added to the shootings, drinking sprees, and houses of prostitution was the fact that the towns sprang up almost overnight. The street alternated between mud and dirt. The buildings came down with ease. The jail in Laramie City had a roof that could be lifted off. The saloons looked more like shacks than places of business. Considering that most of these towns consisted primarily of tents, any wooden building was a welcome sight.

The end-of-track town did serve a function. Needed services like laundries, clothing stores, restaurants, hotels, post offices, and blacksmith shops were found in them. The communities attracted diverse entrepreneurs and workers. Irish merchants, Jewish shop owners, and Chinese laundrymen all opened businesses at various end-of-track towns. Blacks, Indians, veterans of the Civil War, Englishmen, Swedes, and Scotsmen all found their way into these towns. Women, while not as numerous as men, filled a variety of roles. Traditional roles such as "keeping house" occupied many women, who also found legitimate work as saloon and shopkeepers.

The end-of-track town served as the hub of activity for railroad workers along the transcontinental railroad from 1867 to 1869. At end-of-track towns like Laramie City, in present-day Wyoming, Mormon emigrants loaded their goods on old wooden-wheeled wagons headed to Salt Lake City, Utah. Freighters transferred goods from steel-wheeled trains to wagons and headed to the grading camps sprinkled all along the future railroad right-of-way. Mile-long wagon and mule trains left the end-of-track towns every week. Telegraph lines from the end-of-track towns extended in both directions. The wild, rip-roaring nature of the towns masked their logistical significance along future railroads.

All major railroads built across the plains, mountains, and basins of the West after 1869 had their own version of the end-of-track towns, but the Union Pacific and Central Pacific Railroad camps set the tone. The noises and images of Chinese cooks, Irish blacksmiths, and nightly parties became the stereotype of what these towns sounded and looked like. Mythically and factually they became a western reality. In myth they were rooting, tooting, gambling, drinking establishments with a circus environment; in reality they served a unique function as repair facilities, logistical centers, and providers of services like hotels, restaurants, and clothing shops.

Dudley Gardner

See also: Central Pacific Railroad; Transportation, Land.

Further Reading

Athern, Robert G. *Union Pacific Country*. Lincoln: University of Nebraska Press, 1976.

Griswold, Wesley. *A Work of Giants*. New York: McGraw-Hill, 1962.

Kraus, George. *High Road to Promontory*. Palo Alto, CA: American West Publishing, 1969.

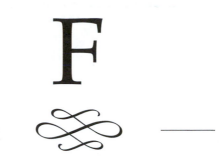

Factory System

Stirred to action by the Indian Wars in the Old Northwest that culminated in the Battle of Fallen Timbers, President George Washington persuaded Congress in 1795 to establish a network of government-sponsored trading posts known as "factories," designed to gain the confidence and loyalty of the tribes arrayed along the American frontier. Through an appropriation of $150,000 intended to establish a self-supporting capital fund, Congress authorized the president to establish the trading houses, which were to maintain the capital fund through profits from the sale of furs.

The Office of Indian Trade—or "factory system" as it was commonly known—was a unique institution in the development of U.S. Indian policy. Ostensibly created to increase harmony with the tribes, the factories were really intended to control the Indians economically and to attract the lucrative fur trade to the United States while counteracting British influence, which still remained strong with the tribes of the Old Northwest. A total of twenty-eight stores were eventually established, but no more than a dozen were ever in operation at one time.

In the beginning, the Purveyor of Public Supplies administered the factory system under the Secretary of War, but in 1806 Congress established the position of Superintendent of Indian Trade and moved the office from Philadelphia to Georgetown in Washington, DC. Two individuals served as superintendent of Indian Trade: James Mason, 1806 to 1816, and Thomas L. McKenney, 1816 to 1822.

As conceived, the factory system should have succeeded. The trading houses were to stock quality merchandise and offer it at little more than cost to the Indians in a fair exchange for their furs. Factors were to be literate, trustworthy, and interested in Indian welfare. It was anticipated that in time a vast network of houses would serve all the frontier tribes, making them completely dependent upon the government for trade goods. Thus, the factories, rather than expensive military garrisons, would control the tribes under the assumption that the threat of depriving them of trade goods would keep the Indians friendly and peaceful. However, Congress handicapped the system by failing to give it legislative permanence. The act establishing the system lapsed after three years and it continued thereafter only through the passage of additional enabling acts of one or two years' duration. Nonetheless, the factories were moderately successful until the War of 1812, which completely disrupted the trade network. Several houses were destroyed or abandoned, while the others had to stock inferior American-made products since British goods were no longer available.

After the war the system found itself saddled with a large inventory of worthless merchandise while having to compete with American traders, who could offer the Indians superior products as well as alcohol in exchange for their furs. Furthermore, there was a rising sentiment in the country that it was unfair for the federal government to compete with private industry in the marketplace. The system continued its precarious existence until May 1822 when Congress, led by Senator Thomas Hart Benton, abolished it after a massive lobbying effort directed by John Jacob Astor and the American Fur Company.

Herman J. Viola

See also: American Fur Company; Astor, John Jacob; Benton, Thomas Hart; Crooks, Ramsay; McKenney, Thomas L.; Stuart, Robert.

Further Reading
Peake, Ora Brooks. *A History of the United States Indian Factory System, 1795–1822.* Denver: Sage Books, 1954.

Viola, Herman J. *Thomas L. McKenney, Architect of America's Early Indian Policy: 1816–1830.* Chicago: Sage Books, The Swallow Press, 1974.

Fallen Timbers, Battle of

With the signing of the Treaty of Paris in 1786, the United States found itself with vast tracts of land ripe for settlement west of the Appalachians. The promise of land for veterans of the Revolutionary War set up potential conflicts with the various tribes of the Ohio territory. Working under the Articles of Confederation, the Congress passed the Land Ordinance of 1785, which encouraged the settlement of lands claimed by Indian tribes. As a result, a confederation of Indian nations, including the Miamis, Delawares, Shawnees, Kaskaskias, Wyandots, and several other tribes, formed to treat with their American neighbors. The Western Indian Confederacy (also referred to as the Western Confederacy) asserted that the boundary between Indian lands and the lands of the United States had been established at the Ohio River in 1768 by the Treaty of Fort Stanwix. The administration of President George Washington did not agree with this interpretation. Congress passed the Northwest Ordinance of 1787, which admitted that lands then settled by Indians were their possessions. However, it opened unsettled lands to settlement by Americans. The British encouraged resistance by the Western Indian Confederacy as a way of making difficulty for their former colonies.

When negotiations failed, war broke out between the Indian Confederacy and the United States. Known by a variety of names, including Little Turtle's War and the Ohio War, this conflict was a stern test for the fledgling United States. Starting in 1786, the United States and the tribes of the Confederacy began raiding along the borders, resulting in hundreds, if not thousands of deaths. In 1790 and 1791, the U.S. Army was handed two of its worst defeats at the hands of Indians (the Battles of Maumee and the Wabash) in the history of the nation. After these disasters, several of Washington's peace emissaries were murdered by tribesmen.

Washington tapped General "Mad Anthony" Wayne, hero of the Revolution, to set things straight in the Northwest. Wayne was a strict disciplinarian whose iron hand ensured that the army that the Western Confederacy faced was significantly stronger than the rustic militia that had failed so miserably in the earlier battles. He used the pause in hostilities during negotiations to build and train his legion.

General Anthony led his forces, known as the Legion of the United States, out to assert American hegemony in 1793. Warriors of the Confederacy waited as the army approached, building fortifications along the way. The Indians held fast near present-day Toledo, Ohio, at a position whose scores of uprooted trees gave it the name Fallen Timbers. When Wayne's army reached the battlefield, his force numbered roughly 3,000 fighters. The 1,500 tribesmen were outnumbered and gave way as cavalry was sent to roll up their flank. Each side suffered less than fifty killed, but the power of the Indian Confederacy had been severely disrupted. The Indians retreated to British Fort Miami, hoping for protection from that quarter, only to be rebuffed by their former ally. General Wayne swept away Indian settlements. The defeat at Fallen Timbers was instrumental in forcing the Indians to treat with the U.S. government and led to the signing of the Treaty of Greenville in 1795.

Terry A. Del Bene

See also: Greenville, Treaty of (1795); Harrison, William Henry; Little Turtle; St. Clair, Arthur; Tecumseh; Wayne, Anthony.

Further Reading

Dillon, Richard H. *North American Indian Wars*. New York: Facts on File, 1983.

Utley, Robert M., and Wilcomb E. Washburn. *The American Heritage History of the Indian Wars*. New York: American Heritage, 1977.

Withers, Alexander Scott. *Chronicles of Border Warfare or, a History of the Settlement By Whites, of Northwestern Virginia, and of the Indian Wars and Massacres in that section of the State with Reflections, Anecdotes, etc.* Cincinnati: Robert Clarke, 1895.

Fannin, James Walker (1804–1836)

James Walker Fannin, Jr., who for a brief period of time in 1836 served as commander-in-chief of the Republic of Texas Army, was born on January 1, 1804, near Marion, Georgia, the illegitimate son of a plantation owner. He was adopted and raised by his grandfather, James Walker, and as a teenager briefly attended the University of Georgia. In 1819 he enrolled in the U.S. Military Academy under the name James F. Walker, but left in 1821 before graduating. Returning to Georgia, he became a merchant and soon married. In 1828 he and his wife and two daughters moved to Columbus, Georgia.

Fannin moved his family to Texas, then still part of Mexico, in 1834, settling near Velasco, where he established a sugarcane plantation and began importing slaves from Cuba, although slavery was outlawed in Mexico. When rumblings of discontent with the Mexican government began to surface among American-born colonists in Texas, Fannin took the forefront of those advocating open rebellion in 1835. With the rank of captain, he fought against Mexican soldiers in the first battle of the revolution at Gonzales, later distinguishing himself during the siege of San Antonio in a skirmish with Mexican forces while co-commanding a rebel scouting party with James Bowie. Promoted to colonel, Fannin then assumed command of the forces occupying the old Spanish presidio (fort) of La Bahia at Goliad. There he proved to be a weak and indecisive commander, preferring to lead by committee vote among his junior officers rather than by his own initiative. By early 1836 at La Bahia, Fannin commanded around 500 men, most of them newly arrived from the United States. Unlike the Alamo, the mission located 90 miles (145 km) away in San Antonio, Fannin's post was actually constructed as a fortress and he believed his command to be safe behind its walls.

When the Mexican army launched its siege at the Alamo in February 1836, Texas officials sent messages throughout Texas pleading for assistance, especially hoping that the sizable garrison at Goliad would respond. Fannin initially refused to march his men to the aid of the Alamo, however, and only at the urging of his officers, who threatened mutiny, did he make a half-hearted effort to do so. The march was a fiasco and, when a supply wagon broke down, Fannin ordered his men back to Goliad after advancing only 8 miles (13 km).

Following the Alamo's fall on March 6, General Sam Houston ordered Fannin to abandon Goliad and march his troops to Victoria. Ever indecisive, Fannin delayed his departure for various reasons, and when the march did finally get under way, his command was surrounded on the open prairie by Mexican forces. After a fierce battle, Fannin surrendered and his men were returned as prisoners to Goliad, where more than 300, including Fannin, were executed on March 27, 1836.

Rod Timanus

See also: Alamo, The; Crockett, Davy; Goliad, Battle of; Texas Revolution and Independence.

Further Reading
Brown, Gary. *Hesitant Martyr in the Texas Revolution: James Walker Fannin.* Plano: Republic of Texas Press, 2000.
Hopewell, Clifford. *Remember Goliad: Their Silent Tents.* Waco, TX: Eakin Press, 1998.

Fetterman Massacre
See **Red Cloud's War**

Filibusters

During the 1840s and 1850s, filibusters (the name derived from a Dutch word meaning "freebooter,") engaged in privately sponsored military invasions of several Latin American nations. These expeditions (also known as filibusters), principally directed at Mexico and the Central American states, were an extreme expression of a public sentiment that favored the aggressive expansion of the United States. To many American citizens in the era of Manifest Destiny, filibusters were outlaw heroes who were actively bringing the freedom of the American republic to the inhabitants of less fortunate nations.

Many filibusters, influenced by nationalistic dreams of American expansion, were inspired to take military action by the sectional divisions that increasingly dominated the internal politics of the United States through the 1850s. Their appetite for expansion whetted by Mexican concessions in the Treaty of Guadalupe Hidalgo (1848), filibusters imagined that U.S. ownership of the northern Mexican states of Sonora and Chihuahua was inevitable. Although support for filibustering crossed regional and political lines, many filibusters were Southerners, or had Southern political sympathies. A significant motive for invading Mexico was to realize a prevalent Southern dream of expanding the institution of slavery into new territories to the south. The annexation of all or part of Mexico and Central America as slave states would increase the congressional power of the South and bring parity into the U.S. Senate. At least one organization, the Knights of the Golden Circle, was formed to advocate the creation of a southern empire for slavery and to formally support filibustering raids directed at Mexico.

Between 1850 and 1860 several filibustering expeditions penetrated into Mexico from Texas and California. In 1853 Tennessee native William Walker, known to the public as "the gray-eyed man of destiny," led his first filibuster into the Mexican states of Sonora and Baja California. With forty-five men, Walker managed to capture the town of La Paz in Baja, California, and declare himself president of the independent republic of Sonora. When the United States cut off Walker's supply line, however, he quickly retreated to California, where he was prosecuted for violating the Neutrality Act. A sympathetic jury cleared Walker on all counts.

Equally notorious was the filibuster led by another Tennessee native, former California state senator Henry A. Crabb, who invaded Sonora in 1854. He and his followers were quickly captured by local authorities; they were all executed in 1857, their bodies left unburied in the desert as a warning to others. Texas Ranger James Callahan led a filibuster into Mexico with the stated goal of recovering runaway slaves in 1855, while José María Jesús de Caravajal led three unsuccessful invasions of Tamaulipas in the 1850s. Although filibustering was an illegal act, in violation of both U.S. and international law, the repeated attempts of President James Buchanan's administration in 1859 and 1860 to purchase Sonora indicate that the goals, if not the methods, of the filibusters were very much in line with the expansionist dreams of the federal government.

Although most expansionist filibusters had designs on Mexico, the most infamous filibustering expedition was William Walker's invasion of Nicaragua. Despite the failure of his initial filibuster into Mexico, Walker was able in 1855 to raise a regiment of fifty-eight recruits in San Francisco to assist Nicaraguan revolutionaries in a civil war. The expedition was successful, and, in 1856, Walker, now the general of an insurgent group of Nicaraguan and American rebels, declared himself president of the new government. The United States initially recognized Walker's administration but, by 1857, he was at odds with American commercial interests in Nicaragua and was forced to surrender to the U.S. Navy. Walker led two more unsuccessful filibusters to Central America before he was captured by the British Navy, turned over to Honduran authorities, and executed by a firing squad in 1860.

Although most filibusters were native-born white American men, not all were American citizens or espoused expansionist principals. The notorious filibuster Narciso López, a native of Venezuela, used New Orleans as a base from which to conspire to launch four successive attacks on the Spanish empire in Cuba. The federal government stopped two of these expeditions before they left the United States. López's final expedition ended when he was captured by the Spanish and executed in Havana in 1851.

Incidences of filibustering declined in the late 1850s as the sectional divide in the United States grew, and filibustering lost its appeal in the 1860s as the Civil War engulfed the nation. The term was resurrected in the 1880s to refer to obstructionist and lengthy speeches in Congress.

Sarah Grossman

See also: Manifest Destiny.

Further Reading

Brown, Charles H. *Agents of Manifest Destiny: The Lives and Times of the Filibusters.* Chapel Hill: University of North Carolina Press, 1980.

Carr, Albert Z. *The World and William Walker.* New York: Harper & Row, 1963.

Greenberg, Amy S. *Manifest Manhood and the Antebellum American Empire.* New York: Cambridge University Press, 2005.

May, Robert E. *The Southern Dream of a Caribbean Empire: 1854–1861.* Baton Rouge: Louisiana State University Press, 1973.

Firearms

The firearms of westward expansion were many—muskets, rifles, pistols, and derringers—and varied in design—flintlock, percussion, and paper and metallic cartridge firing. During the eighteenth and nineteenth centuries alone, literally hundreds of types and models of firearms were used by Indians, explorers, long hunters, mountain men, cattle ranchers, the military, and the rest of the groups that set their sights on the frontier. Three of the most notable are covered here.

U.S. Model 1803 Rifle

History has failed to record Meriwether Lewis's logic in selecting the U.S. Army Model 1803 rifle as the weapon of choice for his expedition to the Pacific Ocean. Whatever the reason, he requisitioned fifteen of the rifles from the Harpers Ferry Arsenal along with a long list of other weaponry and equipment. The Model 1803 was the first regulation rifle ever adopted by the U.S. Army. It was a flintlock weapon that fired a .54-caliber lead ball weighing a half-ounce. Before Model 1803's introduction, army personnel were issued a variety of muskets—smoothbore guns—the latest version being Model 1795.

Army officials were aware of the legendary accuracy of the domestically produced Kentucky and Pennsylvania rifles that had been in use on the frontier for years. They were excited about the potential of Model 1803, since its rifled barrel—like that of the Kentucky and Pennsylvania varieties—assured much greater accuracy at longer distances than did the smoothbore barrel of the musket.

The Harpers Ferry Arsenal eventually produced about 20,000 units of the Model 1803 rifle between the years 1803 and 1819. Although the weapon was officially replaced by Model 1817, the 1803 model continued to be standard issue as late as 1836. The fact that some contemporary authorities believe Model 1803 served as the prototype for the immensely popular "Plains" rifle—commonly used by a generation of mountain men throughout the American West—testifies to the efficiency of this well-designed rifle.

Sharps Single-Shot Rifle

Although the Sharps single-shot, percussion carbine was extremely popular on both sides during the Civil War—even being crudely copied at the Confederate armory in Richmond—the rifle version of the versatile weapon came truly into its own in the hands of the buffalo "hide" hunters in the years following the great conflict. Indeed, probably no firearm in U.S. history had a more dramatic and enduring effect on the final conquest of the American West than the Sharps rifle.

The Sharps was the weapon of choice for multitudes of hide hunters who frequented the Great Plains in search of the mighty American bison during the 1870s and 1880s. In those days, the prairie teemed with bison, or buffalo, as the animals were more commonly called. Some reliable estimates placed their numbers in the millions. With the rapid demise of the animal at the hands—and Sharps rifles—of the commercial hide hunters came the final defeat and displacement of thousands of Plains Indians who could no longer survive without their primary food source. Like other weapons before and after it, the Sharps rifle was gradually replaced by more sophisticated, repeating firearms. By then, however, its place in history was assured.

Colt Single-Action Army Revolver

Since the Colt single-action army revolver, sometimes called the "Peacemaker," was first produced in 1873, it probably has had more stories written about it, more movies and TV shows highlighting it, and more testimonials given for it than just about any other American-made weapon. Although a variety of metallic cartridges and the firearms to use them existed before 1873, it was the advent of the Colt single-action revolver that year, along with the Winchester Model 1873 lever-action rifle, that guaranteed the new technology's triumph over the previously popular paper cartridge and the more primitive muzzle-loading systems. Plus, it was a two-way proposition; the metallic cartridge's rapid acceptance assured the success of the single-action revolver, as well as scores of other models made by Colt and its competitors.

The first Colt single-actions were manufactured primarily for the U.S. government. Officials of the army's ordnance department much preferred them to products manufactured by Colt's competitor, Smith & Wesson. Between 1873 and 1891, the Colt factory furnished more than 37,000 of the highly acclaimed single-actions to various governmental entities.

The pistol was particularly popular with the American military establishment (George Armstrong Custer's 7th U.S. Cavalry was armed with it on the ill-fated Little Bighorn battlefield), and its success soon spilled over to the civilian population. During the last quarter of the nineteenth century, the performance of the legendary pistol in the hands of the ever westward-marching American—cowboy, soldier, outlaw, and lawman alike—made it, probably above all others, the firearm that won the West.

James A. Crutchfield

See also: Bison, American; Hide Hunters; Lewis and Clark Expedition; Long Hunters.

Further Reading
Crutchfield, James A. *A Primer of the North American Fur Trade.* Union City, TN: Pioneer Press, 1986.

Peterson, Harold L., and Robert Elman. *The Great Guns.* New York: Grosset & Dunlap, 1971.

Russell, Carl P. *Firearms, Traps, & Tools of the Mountain Men.* New York: Alfred A. Knopf, 1967.

———. *Guns on the Early Frontiers.* New York: Bonanza Books, 1957.

Fitzpatrick, Thomas "Broken Hand" (1799–1854)

Thomas "Broken Hand" Fitzpatrick was one of the most prominent of all the mountain men. Born in Ireland in 1799, he immigrated to America when he was nineteen years old. According to the explorer John C. Frémont, Fitzpatrick received his moniker from the Indians after an exploding rifle shattered one of his hands. Well-educated but adventurous, the young man joined William Ashley's 1823 expedition up the Missouri River and was present at the battle with the Arikara.

Fitzpatrick roamed the Rocky Mountains for years and rubbed elbows with all of the great and near-great mountain men of the period. At the 1830 rendezvous, he, along with his friends Jim Bridger, Milton

Sublette, Henry Fraeb, and Jean B. Gervais, purchased the Smith, Jackson, and Sublette Company and called the new entity the Rocky Mountain Fur Company. After that outfit's failure a few years later, Fitzpatrick joined Bridger, Sublette, Andrew Drips, and Lucien Fontenelle in establishing Fontenelle, Fitzpatrick, and Company.

After retiring from the mountain trade, Fitzpatrick became a guide for emigrants traveling the Oregon and California trails. His first mission in that capacity was to escort the 1841 wagon train to the Pacific coast, a job that he performed with impeccable precision. One of the grateful travelers commented afterward that, had it not been for Fitzpatrick, the entourage would never have reached California. In addition to helping out weary homesteaders on the westward-reaching trails, Fitzpatrick also guided John C. Frémont on his second exploring expedition to the Rocky Mountains in 1843.

When war broke out with Mexico in 1846, Fitzpatrick was hired to escort General Stephen Watts Kearny and his Army of the West from Bent's Fort to Santa Fe and beyond. Halfway to California from New Mexico, the army met Kit Carson on the trail and Carson was persuaded to assume Fitzpatrick's job of guiding the army the rest of the way to the Pacific while Tom carried dispatches from Kearny back to Washington, DC.

While in the capital city, Fitzpatrick was appointed Indian agent for the Upper Platte and Arkansas rivers region, a position he filled with dignity, expertise, and understanding. He organized the great treaty-signing at Fort Laramie in 1851, which brought peace to the region until 1854, when the army violated some of the treaty's articles and attacked a peaceful Indian camp following a dispute over a cow. Lieutenant John L. Grattan and several army troops were killed in the incident. Later, the army built a series of illegal forts along the Bozeman Trail, further violating the treaty. Fitzpatrick unsuccessfully advocated an agency for Cheyennes in Colorado that included much of the traditional tribal lands, but federal Indian policy—which advocated confining the tribes into ever smaller reservations, thus eliminating their food sources and leading to their demise—rejected the proposal. Rather than take up land along the South Platte, the tribe was situated on the Arkansas River, where they were living at the time of the Sand Creek Massacre in 1864.

Three years after the treaty, Fitzpatrick again traveled to Washington, DC, to brief officials on the status of Indian affairs in his region. While there, he became ill with pneumonia and died on February 7, 1854. Perhaps "Broken Hand's" greatest compliment came a decade after his death when Chief Black Kettle of the Cheyennes exclaimed, "Major Fitzpatrick was a good man. He told us that when he was gone we would have trouble, and it has proved true."

James A. Crutchfield

See also: Arikara War; Army of the West; Carson, Kit; Horse Creek Treaty (1851); Mexican-American War; Rocky Mountain Fur Company.

Further Reading

Hafen, LeRoy R. *Broken Hand: The Life of Thomas Fitzpatrick, Mountain Man, Guide and Indian Agent.* Denver: Old West, 1973. Reprint, Lincoln: University of Nebraska Press, 1981.

Flathead

This Indian nation called themselves *Salish*, meaning "people." The Salish occupied the Columbia River area, but originally had come from east of the continental divide. Flatheads occupied a broad area including parts of modern Montana, Wyoming, Idaho, and British Columbia. They spoke a language from the Salish language family. Salish speakers spoke twenty-three related languages, which were characterized by dialects consisting overwhelmingly of verbs.

This group of Salish was called Flatheads because they did not practice binding the heads of infants so as to deform the vault of the skull. Head deformation was a common practice among neighboring tribes, so the unaltered heads of the Flatheads appeared flat in comparison.

The Flatheads scratched out a difficult existence in the mountains and valleys of their homeland. Berries and tubers were their staples, supplemented by hunting and fishing. The Flatheads did not have access to the huge herds of buffalo on the plains and hence were not able to support large populations like the tribes of the vast prairies.

Flatheads lived in small communities in houses made of bark and reeds. Sometimes they lived like the Plains Indians in skin tents. Their primary rival was the Blackfoot tribe. Were it not for the rugged terrain where the Flatheads lived, their powerful enemy might have been able to overwhelm them. Flatheads met with the Lewis and Clark Expedition in 1805, supplying the newcomers with horses. The explorers thought them very much like the Shoshones with a much different language. They speculated that the Flatheads might be related to the Welsh, a theory that, at the time, was postulated for several Indian groups due to numerous members of some tribes possessing pale skins and blond hair, as well as the similarities of some Indian words to counterparts in the Welsh language. In the light of modern science, this theory has since been disproved.

In 1855 the Flatheads entered into the Hell Gate Treaty, ceding a portion of their lands in consideration for annuities, a blacksmith shop, and a signing bonus. As a result of this treaty, the Flatheads were concentrated on a reservation. The tribe further agreed to stop trading with the Hudson's Bay Company. A second treaty involving the Flatheads was signed later in 1855 and established peace with the Blackfoots.

Today, the Flatheads live on reservations in Montana and Washington State. The Montana reservation consists of almost 1.3 million acres (525,000 ha). The nation is thought to consist of roughly 7,000 members, most of whom live within the reservation boundaries, with roughly 1,400 living in Washington State.

Terry A. Del Bene

See also: Blackfoot; Lewis and Clark Expedition.

Further Reading

Fahey, John. *The Flathead Indians.* Norman: University of Oklahoma Press, 1975.

Fontenelle, Lucien (c. 1800–1840)

Born to a wealthy New Orleans family in about 1800, Lucien Fontenelle was one of the most important fur traders on the early American frontier. During his teenage years Fontenelle reached St. Louis, Missouri, and quickly joined the fur-trading profession.

He started his lifelong career in trading by working for the Missouri Fur Company, which brought him into constant contact with various Indian tribes along the Missouri River, beginning with the Omahas in northeastern Nebraska. During his early years with the Omahas (about 1820) he met and married an Omaha woman named Mío'bathi', or Bright Moon. Bright Moon was the daughter of Big Elk

(Ó'po'to'ga), chief leader of the Omahas in the early to mid-1800s.

Throughout the 1820s, Fontenelle operated the Bellevue trading post on the Missouri River. The Bellevue trading post—established by the Missouri Fur Company—traded regularly with the Omaha, Otoe, and Pawnee tribes, while it also served as a service and supply station on the Upper Missouri. Fontenelle's location at the post left him—like many traders—on the fringe of his own society. However, his primary interest in the fur trade business was profit, and he became a fairly competitive trader.

During his time at the Bellevue trading post, Fontenelle embarked on many trapping expeditions to the Rocky Mountains. By 1825 he had headed west to the Rocky Mountains on an expedition with a group of other fur trappers. Although they had hopes to create their own trading company, the group disbanded by 1828. Fontenelle returned to the Missouri River.

Upon the termination of the Missouri Fur Company in 1828, Fontenelle purchased the Bellevue trading post. In 1832 he sold the property to the Office of Indian Affairs. It was then used as the headquarters of the Indian agency for the Omaha, Otoe-Missouria, and Pawnee tribes. Fontenelle moved south and built a new trading post. He spent the last decade of his life operating his post and going on trapping expeditions to the Rocky Mountains. He died in 1840.

The oldest son of Lucien Fontenelle and Bright Moon (they had four sons and one daughter) was Logan Fontenelle, who became an influential leader and chief interpreter for the Omahas. Logan (Sho'géska, meaning "White Horse") inherited his position as chief leader of the Omahas from his grandfather Big Elk. Logan Fontenelle accompanied other Omaha chiefs to sign the Treaty of 1854, which sold most of the tribe's lands and restricted the Omahas to their reservation in northeastern Nebraska. Logan accompanied an Omaha buffalo hunting party in 1855 and was killed in an attack launched by another tribe.

Elaine M. Nelson

See also: Lisa, Manuel; Missouri Fur Company; Omaha.

Further Reading

Fletcher, Alice C., and Francis LaFlesche. *The Omaha Tribe.* Lincoln: University of Nebraska Press, 1992.

Wishart, David J. *An Unspeakable Sadness: The Dispossession of the Nebraska Indians.* Lincoln: University of Nebraska Press, 1994.

Forks of the Ohio

This little remembered location figured conspicuously in the history of the first surge westward by Anglo-Americans. On a cold winter's day in late 1753, twenty-one-year-old Major George Washington of the Virginia militia viewed the Forks of the Ohio River and observed in his journal that the place would be ideal for a major fortification, helping to set into motion events that assured the place a role in westward expansion.

By this time, the French population in North America stood at around 50,000, while the aggregate of British subjects neared the 1 million mark. With these rapidly growing numbers, rumors of troubling times ran rampant among the Indian tribes that lived along the upper Ohio River and its tributary system. Great Britain and France were on a collision course over who actually possessed the area, consisting of much of present-day Pennsylvania, Ohio, West Virginia, and Kentucky, with neither power willing to admit that the real owners were the natives who had hunted and fished the vast region for hundreds, if not thousands, of years. As the two European powers positioned themselves for control, the various Indian tribes looked on with growing awareness that nothing good could come out of the coming conflict.

For years, control of the Ohio River valley had been irrelevant since few white settlers had encroached upon the wilderness with intentions of permanently occupying it. In 1747 and 1749, however, the formation of two land-speculation concerns, the Ohio Company and the Loyal Company, by a consortium of British Virginians caught French officials' attention when they learned that the companies' goal was the introduction of hundreds of settlers into the region. France reacted by building several forts—among them Fort Duquesne at the Forks of the Ohio—to guard the Ohio River frontier.

The Forks of the Ohio, modern-day Pittsburgh, Pennsylvania, consisted of the peninsula created by the confluence of the Monongahela and the Allegheny rivers to form the Ohio River. Its strategic position was recognized not only by George Washington, but also by the French and British military establishments. During the French and Indian War, and following Fort Duquesne's desertion by the French in late November 1758, the conquering British army began work on Fort Pitt, located on the same site. Following its completion in 1761, the installation, with a garrison of between 300 and 400 troops, became a critical part of the British defense of the upper Ohio frontier and, in time,

the town of Pittsburgh grew rapidly outside its walls. Pittsburgh became a trading center for the region, with fur traders and Indians meeting to exchange wares, merchants hawking the latest goods from the East, and a large assemblage of nonmilitary men, women, and children clustered together in shoddy housing that hugged the fort's exterior walls.

During the spring of 1763, the noted Ottawa chief, Pontiac, assembled members of most of the warring Indian nations living east of the Mississippi River to Detroit and revealed to them his plans for the total expulsion of the British from the Great Lakes region. In May Fort Detroit was besieged by Pontiac's warriors, followed in quick succession by attacks on Fort Sandusky and the large fur-trading post at Michilimackinac, located at the meeting of the waters of lakes Michigan and Huron. In June the ripple effect of Pontiac's Rebellion reached Fort Pitt and Pittsburgh. On June 22, Fort Pitt came under attack, holding out until August 1, when all of the Indians left the area to intercept an approaching British relief column. A few days later the two foes met at a place called Bushy Run, where the Indians were decisively defeated by the relief column that marched into nearby Fort Pitt amid cheers of jubilation.

Following abandonment as a military post in 1772, Fort Pitt survived a few years longer before falling into ruin and being engulfed by the growing town of Pittsburgh. By then the revolution was over, the United States of America was a reality, and many of the region's inhabitants were casting hungry eyes toward the fertile lands and abundant fur-bearing animals of the West. Pittsburgh became a major outfitting point for westward exploration and migration. Boat-building establishments flourished. The keelboat Lewis and Clark used in their journey west was built at Pittsburgh and, indeed, an argument can be made that Lewis's departure from the town en route to St. Louis in 1803 was the real beginning of the "voyage of discovery." As towns were established further down the Ohio River, and as already existing cities were reached by boat, a thriving commerce was established between Pittsburgh and communities such as Cincinnati, Louisville, Natchez, and New Orleans. During a single year, more than 1,000 boats, carrying 20,000 people and 12,000 head of livestock, left the Forks of the Ohio for destinations west. For many years, along with Cumberland Gap situated at the Virginia-Kentucky-Tennessee borders to the south, the Forks of the Ohio and, subsequently, Pittsburgh, was a major funneling point for tens of thousands of emigrants headed west.

James A. Crutchfield

See also: Cumberland Gap; Land Speculation Companies; Transportation, Water.

Further Reading
O'Meara, Walter. *Guns at the Forks*. Englewood Cliffs, NJ: Prentice-Hall, 1965.

Fort Benton

Fort Benton was pivotal to the settlement of Montana Territory. Located on the plains of north-central Montana along the northern bank of the Missouri River, Fort Benton was often called the "birthplace of Montana."

The region surrounding the fort was originally Blackfoot territory. The Blackfoot, a collection of Algonquian-speaking tribes known collectively as *Siksika*, were not friendly to Americans. They traded exclusively with the British-run Hudson's Bay Company (HBC) until 1830, when Kenneth McKenzie, a partner in the American Fur Company (AFC), convinced the tribe to trade with AFC, which built several trading posts in the area for the Blackfoot. It was a profitable, but rocky relationship. By 1839 AFC had changed hands to Pierre Chouteau Jr. & Company, but people still referred to it as the "Company."

In the fall of 1845, Alexander Culbertson, a Company employee, built Fort Lewis, named for Meriwether Lewis, 3 miles (6 km) upriver from the present site of Fort Benton. It was difficult for the Blackfoot to reach Fort Lewis due to ice jams and floods. In the spring of 1847, Culbertson dismantled Fort Lewis and moved everything downriver to the present location of Fort Benton.

Culbertson's men originally constructed the new post, Fort Clay, using cottonwood timber; in 1850 workers began rebuilding it with adobe bricks. On December 25 of that same year, Culberson renamed the post Fort Benton after Missouri's Senator Thomas Hart Benton, a proponent of western expansion and friend of Pierre Chouteau Jr.

Keelboats brought goods 2,500 miles (4,000 km) upriver from St. Louis to trade with the Blackfoot for buffalo robes and furs. The boats then hauled hides and furs back to St. Louis for eventual sale in the eastern markets. In 1831 the steamboat *Yellow Stone* arrived at Fort Pierre in present-day South Dakota. The next year it traveled as far as Fort Union, in today's North Dakota. In 1859 the steamboat *Chippewa* tried to reach Fort Benton, but fell short by 12 miles (23 km). The next year, on July 2, 1860, the *Chippewa*, followed by the steamboat *Key West*, reached Fort Benton. This was as far as steamboats could travel due to a rock shelf in the riverbed upriver from Fort Benton.

In 1862 prospectors discovered gold at Grasshopper Creek in southwestern Montana, sparking a gold rush. Many miners came to the goldfields by way of the Missouri River steamboats disembarking at Fort Benton. The only time of year the steamboats could navigate the Missouri as far as Fort Benton was in the spring and early summer, when the river was swollen with runoff from melting snow. The trip from St. Louis to Fort Benton could take from two to three months, depending on conditions and river hazards. Steamboats hauled not only passengers, but also large amounts of mining supplies and equipment. In the heyday of riverboat traffic, thirty to forty steamboats arrived at Fort Benton annually.

In 1860 Lieutenant John Mullan completed a military wagon road linking Fort Benton with Fort Walla Walla, Washington. In addition to the military, civilians also used the 624-mile (1,000-km) Mullan Road as they traveled to the Montana and Idaho goldfields. Fort Benton was also the trailhead for other routes, such as the Whoop-Up Trail that led into Canada. In 1866 the Company sold the old trading post buildings to the Northwest Fur Company, which in turn sold them to the U.S. Army a few years later. The army used the buildings for storage until the mid-1870s.

With the mining and the liquor trade, Fort Benton erupted into a boomtown. It was a rough place with all types of con men, prostitutes, and gamblers. Thomas Francis Meagher, Civil War hero as leader of the famed Irish Brigade and acting governor of the Montana Territory, was on board a steamboat at Fort Benton the night of July 1, 1867, when he fell overboard. Searchers never found his body; some suspected foul play.

The town became a commercial center for the cattle industry and later for farmers. In 1887, with the completion of the railroad to Fort Benton, the riverboat era ended. Today, Fort Benton remains a commercial center for the area. Modern explorers use Fort Benton as a staging point to canoe the 149 miles (240 km) of the Upper Missouri National Wild and Scenic River.

Bill Markley

See also: American Fur Company; Benton, Thomas Hart; Blackfoot; Chouteau Family; Fort Union (North Dakota); Forts and Fortification; Hudson's Bay Company; McKenzie, Kenneth; Mullan, John; Mullan Road; Whoop-Up Trail.

Further Reading

Athearn, Robert G. *Forts of the Upper Missouri.* Lincoln: University of Nebraska Press, 1972.

Monahan, Glenn. *Montana's Wild and Scenic Upper Missouri River.* Anaconda, MT: Northern Rocky Mountain Books, 1997.

Robertson, R.G. *Competitive Struggle: America's Western Fur Trading Posts, 1764–1865.* Boise, ID: Tamarack Books, 1999.

Fort Bridger

Famed mountaineer Jim Bridger recognized that as the fur trade declined there was great opportunity in supplying the increasing numbers of farmers on their way to Oregon Territory. In 1843 Bridger and his partner Louis Vasquez constructed Fort Bridger on the Black's Fork River bottoms in today's southwestern Wyoming. This became the famous Fort Bridger that served to refit and supply emigrants bound for the rich farmlands of Oregon and California. The most important services offered at the fort were blacksmithing, livestock replacement, and consumer items.

In 1844 Sublette's Cutoff—also known as Greenwood's Cutoff—opened a route that avoided Fort Bridger. Substantial numbers of emigrants were pulled away from Bridger's business in favor of a shorter, drier route. Fortune returned in 1846 as the then unproven Hastings Cutoff appeared to offer a shorter route to California, once again passing through Fort Bridger. Jim Bridger took an active role in supporting the fraudulent route (which actually is longer and in large part unsuitable for wagon traffic). The mountaineer unabashedly confirmed the advantages of the route to the Donner Party. Following the Hastings route and confident in Bridger's honesty, the Donner Party became delayed in their journey and suffered horrendous losses of life when caught in the Sierra Nevada Mountains' early snows. When the stories of their cannibalism reached the world they became the most famous wagon company in history.

In 1847 the Mormon Pioneer companies passed through Fort Bridger on their way to their new Zion in the valley of the Great Salt Lake. This increased traffic to the route through Fort Bridger and did much to assure that the Hastings Cutoff became well used. The coming of the Mormons was a mixed blessing for Bridger and Vasquez as tensions between the local mountaineers and their Mormon neighbors grew. The California gold rush, starting in 1849, made ferries, fords, and trading posts highly lucrative. The Mormon

An 1850s lithograph depicts Fort Bridger, located on Black's Fork of the Green River in present-day southwestern Wyoming. Founded as a fur-trading post, the fort became a busy supply depot for wagon trains on the Oregon Trail. *(The Granger Collection, New York)*

newcomers wanted to share in the bounty. In 1853 territorial governor and Mormon leader Brigham Young rescinded all licenses for trading with Indians. Hearing that Bridger and Vasquez still traded arms and ammunition to the Indians, Young sent a Mormon posse to Fort Bridger. Jim Bridger wisely fled. The Mormons took possession of the post and its contents. Later that year Mormon families colonized the area. Fort Bridger fell into disrepair as the Mormons built Fort Supply to replace it. In a transaction still clouded in history, Mormons "purchased" the fort in 1855 but Bridger spent much energy trying to recoup his losses.

In 1857 relations between the Mormon Church and the U.S. government brought the two parties to the brink of war. President James Buchanan sent a 2,500-man expedition to build a fort in Utah and to help with the installation of a new territorial governor. The Nauvoo Legion, a church-operated militia of roughly 4,000 men, burned the prairies and important places ahead of the approach of army troops. Fort Bridger was consigned to the flames along with several U.S. supply trains near the Green and Big Sandy rivers, which had been carelessly exposed to attack. The U.S. Army found itself unable to press through the deep fall snows that choked the mountain passes into Great Salt Lake City, and had to take up winter quarters in several positions, including the ruins at Fort Bridger. The troops spent a rough winter in tents and huts on the Black's Fork River, having been forced to reduce rations. A negotiated agreement put an end to the Utah War before there were any pitched battles between the Mormons and the U.S. military. An outcome of the war was the establishment of a military base at Fort Bridger. Jim Bridger agreed to lease the post he had already sold to the Mormons for $600 a year with an option to purchase after ten years.

Under military control, Fort Bridger became one of the premier posts in the Rocky Mountain West. Astride routes to California, Utah, and Oregon, it had great strategic significance. The Pony Express established a station at the post in 1860, replaced by the telegraph in 1861 and supplemented by Ben Holladay's Overland Stage. During the Civil War, the post was almost abandoned completely as most troops in the West were sent to the war back East. As Indian conflicts increased during this same period, volunteer groups from California, Nevada Territory, and other states came to occupy the fort. A treaty with the Shoshones was signed there in 1863. During the military period, wagon roads were established from the fort, which served to encourage settlement of the local area. In 1866 Wells, Fargo established a station at Fort Bridger.

Soldiers from Fort Bridger helped maintain a shaky peace and to civilize the area. Vigilantism and lawlessness associated with the 1867 gold rush in the South Pass area required additional efforts on the part of the military stationed at Fort Bridger. Soldiers helped protect the coming of the Union Pacific route of the transcontinental railroad in 1868–1869. Fort Bridger remained a vital post until 1890, when the military decided to phase the base out. Today, large portions of the fort are owned and operated by the state of Wyoming as an historical park.

Terry A. Del Bene

See also: Bridger, Jim; California Trail; Donner Party; Forts and Fortification; Johnston, Alfred Sidney; Oregon Trail; Vasquez, Louis; Young, Brigham.

Further Reading

Frazer, Robert W. *Forts of the West*. Norman: University of Oklahoma Press, 1965.

Gowen, Fred R., and Eugene E. Campbell. *Fort Bridger: Island in the Wilderness*. Provo, UT: Brigham Young University Press, 1975.

Fort Clatsop

On November 17, 1805, Captains Meriwether Lewis and William Clark, along with their small contingent of explorers, reached the Pacific Ocean at the mouth of the Columbia River. After the U.S. purchase from France of the Louisiana Territory in 1803, President Thomas Jefferson had dispatched the two army officers and the Corps of Discovery to the western expanses of the territory with one of its primary missions to find a passage to the Pacific Ocean.

When the expedition arrived on the shores of the Pacific, winter was rapidly approaching and the mountain passes on a return trip would be impossible to cross, so the exploring party contemplated spending the winter in the Oregon country and returning home the following spring. Trading ships occasionally visited Oregon and Lewis and Clark hoped that they might make contact with a ship and send a message back to President Jefferson advising him of their progress, but they never sighted a ship during their stay.

The captains gave the members of the expedition the right to vote on what to do about the oncoming inclement weather. They had three choices. The first was to stay where they were and to pitch winter camp on the north bank of the Columbia River in present-day Washington. There, they would be close to neighboring Indian tribes and able to trade for food. The second choice was to return east toward home, a difficult option since the weather would be colder the farther inland they traveled. The third choice was to cross the Columbia to the south bank, where, according to the Indians, there were plenty of elk and deer. Everyone voted, including York, Clark's black slave, and Sacagawea, the Shoshone woman who had guided the party during the last half of the outward journey. All agreed to move to the south side of the river in present-day Oregon, erect a fort, and spend the winter.

The travelers selected a site in the forest not too far from the Pacific coast. Not only were they close to the elk herds, but also they could distill ocean water to make salt, which everyone craved except Clark, who had no taste for it. Furthermore, they were in a position to signal a ship if one should happen by and thus be able to send back reports to Jefferson.

The men began the tough job of cutting down trees for a palisade wall and buildings. Despite the constant rain and frequent gales of wind, they completed most of the fort by December 23, 1805. It was named Fort Clatsop after one of the local Indian tribes. The structure was built square-shaped, 50 feet (15 m) to a side, with gates at opposite ends. Two buildings were placed inside the walls. Enlisted men lived in one building. In the other structure were four rooms: one for Lewis and Clark to share; one for Sacagawea, her husband Charbonneau, and their small child; one to serve as an orderly room; and one to be used for a smokehouse to preserve meat.

The Corps members survived the winter mostly by hunting elk and deer. Occasionally they traded with Indians for roots, fish, and other meat, but the prices were very high. Many members took ill during their stay at Fort Clatsop due to poor nutrition and the constantly damp weather.

Since the expedition was military in nature, Lewis and Clark observed military discipline at the fort. A sentry was always on duty, and the gates were closed after sundown. Lewis spent much of his time writing about and sketching the flora and fauna of the Pacific Northwest, while Clark drafted maps of the country they had explored.

On March 23, 1806, the Corps of Discovery left Fort Clatsop to begin the long trip home. The expedition to the Pacific Ocean provided additional justification for the U.S. claim to Oregon. Today people can visit a replica of Fort Clatsop on the site of the original fort near Astoria, Oregon.

Bill Markley

See also: Charbonneau, Jean Baptiste; Charbonneau, Toussaint; Clark, William; Forts and Fortification; Lewis, Meriwether; Lewis and Clark Expedition; Louisiana Purchase (1803); Louisiana Territory; Sacagawea.

Further Reading

Ambrose, Stephen E. *Undaunted Courage: Meriwether Lewis, Thomas Jefferson, and the Opening of the American West.* New York: Simon & Schuster, 1996.

DeVoto, Bernard, ed. *The Journals of Lewis and Clark.* New York: Houghton Mifflin, 1953.

Moulton, Gary E., ed. *The Definitive Journals of Lewis and Clark.* Lincoln: University of Nebraska Press, 1986.

Ronda, James P. *Lewis and Clark Among the Indians.* Lincoln: University of Nebraska Press, 1984.

Fort Dilts

Emigrants crossing the prairie near the Little Missouri Badlands in current North Dakota hastily built Fort Dilts to defend themselves from attacking Hunkpapa Sioux warriors during September 1864. The Sioux were harassing people traveling through their territory to the Montana goldfields. General Alfred Sully's army engaged the Sioux while building military forts in the aftermath of the Minnesota Massacres of 1862.

That summer of 1864, James Liberty Fisk—captain and assistant quartermaster commanding North Overland Expedition for Protecting Emigrants, commissioned by the government to lead emigrant wagon trains to the goldfields—arrived with a military escort at the newly built Fort Rice on the Missouri River with a train of more than 100 wagons and 200 men, women, and children. At Fort Rice, Fisk asked Commander Colonel Daniel J. Dill for an escort of fifty cavalry troopers, which was granted reluctantly, allowing the wagon train to continue west from Fort Rice.

On September 2, 160 miles (260 km) west of Fort Rice and on the eastern edge of the Badlands, a wagon overturned as it descended a steep gulch. The wagon train continued on while a second driver and wagon and a rear guard remained to aright and fix the wagon before rejoining the wagon train. More than 100 Hunkpapa Sioux attacked the wagons and rear guard, killing 8 men. Sitting Bull most likely participated and was wounded in the fight. Jefferson Dilts, a guide and former corporal in the army, was the first of a rescue party from the wagon train to reach the isolated men. He fought and killed six warriors before he died with three arrows in his back. The Hunkpapas ransacked the wagons taking guns, ammunition, whiskey, wine, cigars, silverware, stationery, canned goods, and other valuables. The rescue party recovered the bodies and buried them.

The wagon train continued further west and camped for the night, with the Hunkpapas constantly harassing the emigrants. The next morning the train proceeded west another 3 miles (5 km) before the emigrants stopped, brought their wagons together, hitched plows to oxen, broke up sod, and built a 6-foot (1.8-m) high wall with loopholes, naming their fortification Fort Dilts, after Jefferson Dilts. The train had a borrowed howitzer from Fort Rice that helped keep the Hunkpapas at a distance.

Fanny Kelly, a white woman who had earlier been taken captive by some Oglalas in a raid on wagons traveling along the Platte River, was with the Hunkpapas and the Indians told her to write a note to the emigrants demanding they leave Hunkpapa territory and leave behind goods in tribute. Unknown to her captors, Fanny included in the note details about her captivity and a plea to be rescued.

Fisk did not trust the note and replied that Fanny needed to show herself. She did so and when Fisk realized she was telling the truth he began to negotiate for her release, but the ransom was too extravagant for the emigrants to pay and they did not trust the Hunkpapas to actually release Fanny. (She was later sold to the Blackfoot and then released at Fort Sully in Dakota Territory.)

Lieutenant Smith, the commander of the escort, and fourteen of his men secretly left Fort Dilts at night during a storm to summon help. The small party rode hard and after three days arrived at Fort Rice. Colonel Dill led a 900-man relief expedition, reaching Fort Dilts on September 20, to find that the Hunkpapas had tired of sniping at the fortification and left to hunt buffalo.

Dill subsequently refused Fisk's request for an escort to the goldfields, telling the emigrants they could return with him to Fort Rice, but were on their own if they continued west. The emigrants decided to return with Dill, and Fisk reluctantly accompanied them back to Fort Rice.

In many respects the siege at Fort Dilts became the model for Hollywood's vision of Indian warfare on the Plains. The wagons were drawn into a protective circle to stave off the attack of mounted assailants. As time and resources grew shorter in the besieged train, brave men slipped out under cover of darkness and brought the army to the rescue before it was too late. The siege was maintained from a distance by long-range sniping by tribesmen with very limited ammunition. At times, the emigrants were able to take their livestock outside the walls and allow the animals to graze.

Bill Markley

See also: Forts and Fortification; Indian Captivity; Lakota; Sioux; Sitting Bull.

Further Reading

Clodfelter, Micheal. *The Dakota War: The United States Army Versus the Sioux, 1862–1865.* Jefferson, NC: McFarland, 1998.

Hart, Herbert. *Pioneer Forts of the West.* Seattle: Superior Publishing, 1967.

Kelly, Fanny. *Narrative of My Captivity Among the Sioux Indians.* Ann Arbor: University of Michigan Library, 2005.

Utley, Robert M. *Frontiersmen in Blue: the United States Army and the Indian, 1848–1865.* Lincoln: University of Nebraska Press, 1981.

———. *The Lance and the Shield: The Life and Times of Sitting Bull.* New York: Ballantine Books, 1994.

Fort Hall

One of the busiest way stations on the Oregon-California Trail resulted from a failed business deal. As part of a concerted effort to become a force in the fur trade, Boston ice merchant Nathaniel Wyeth contracted with the Rocky Mountain Fur Company to deliver goods to their trappers at the 1834 rendezvous on Black's Fork in modern-day Wyoming. However, competitor William Sublette arrived first and forced Wyeth's would-be customers to buy his goods to discharge the company's debts to his firm.

With few options, Wyeth pushed along the trail to where the Portneuf River flowed into the Snake River in what is now the state of Idaho but was then part of the Oregon Country. There he established a post, intending to liquidate his goods in trade with Indians and trappers. He named the place Fort Hall in honor of one of his New England investors and soon pushed on to the Columbia River, leaving others to operate the outpost. Accompanying his party was Jason Lee, a minister on the way to Oregon to establish missions among the Indians and who became instrumental in attracting other settlers to the area.

Eventually, some 270,000 travelers bound for Oregon and California in the flood of emigration in the decades to come passed though the Fort Hall area, many stopping to purchase supplies and trade for fresh draft animals. This business, too, was a lost opportunity for Nathaniel Wyeth, who had sold Fort Hall in 1837 to the foremost competitor in fur trade–related commerce, the British conglomerate, Hudson's Bay Company. The British flag flew over Fort Hall in the disputed Oregon Country until the 1846 Oregon Treaty placed the site firmly within the boundaries of the United States.

Facing a declining fur business and increasing competition from Mormon settlers in Utah for emigrant trade, Hudson's Bay Company closed Fort Hall in 1856. The abandoned fort crumbled and decayed, leaving little trace of its existence until 1863, when the site took on a second life.

Indians in the area, primarily Shoshones, Bannocks, and Paiutes, had long clashed with emigrants and settlers. Trails through their traditional homelands—encompassing what is today western Wyoming, northern Utah, southern Idaho, and northern Nevada—became the most dangerous places throughout the emigrant era, with numerous attacks on travelers by Indians, and frequent abuse of Indian people and property by emigrants. Violence in the area climaxed with the Bear River Massacre in 1863, leading to treaties with the Shoshones and their eventual confinement on the newly established Fort Hall Indian Reservation. Many Shoshone bands were forced onto the reservation, with the Bannocks joining them later. Fort Hall, a community on the reservation, has since become the cultural center for the Shoshone-Bannock tribes and headquarters for numerous business enterprises and tribal government.

Modern-day visitors to southeastern Idaho get a sense of Nathaniel Wyeth's Fort Hall when visiting a museum and replica of the fort in Pocatello, about one dozen miles from the original.

Rod Miller

See also: California Trail; Forts and Fortification; Hudson's Bay Company; Oregon Trail; Rocky Mountain Fur Company; Shoshone; Sublette Brothers; Wyeth, Nathaniel Jarvis.

Further Reading

DeVoto, Bernard. *Across the Wide Missouri*. Boston: Houghton Mifflin, 1947.

Idaho Historical Society. "Fort Hall, 1834–1856" Idaho Historical Series No. 17. Boise, ID, 1968.

Madsen, Brigham D. *The Northern Shoshoni*. Caldwell, ID: Caxton Press, 2000.

Fort Jackson, Treaty of (1814)

The Treaty of Fort Jackson (Alabama) was negotiated by the hero of the War of 1812, General Andrew Jackson. American military leaders negotiated the terms of peace in most U.S. treaties before official commissioners were assigned. At the close of the War of 1812 and the Muscogee (Creek) Civil War, commonly called the Red-Stick rebellion, Jackson negotiated the settlement.

Its horrific defeat at the Battle of Horseshoe Bend in Alabama on March 29, 1814, forced the Creek Nation to seek terms of peace with the United States. The resulting treaty demanded full reparations from the Creeks to cover every expense paid by the Americans to prosecute the war. The ultimate form of currency was traditional Creek lands, and over 20 million acres (8 million ha) were signed away on August 9, 1814.

Jackson further demanded that the Creeks abandon any connection with the British or Spanish. The tribe fell under the exclusive protection and authority of the United States. Furthermore, the treaty authorized the construction of military forts, roads, trading houses, and command of all waterways. This article committed the Creek Nation to permanent military occupation and a position as a buffer to foreign powers.

Revenge played an important role in the negotiation of the treaty. Jackson called for all Creek prophets and military leaders to be turned over for imprisonment. This measure exacerbated the divisions between upper and lower towns of the Creek Nation. The result of this attempt to divide and conquer a people from within was indeed to intensify the internal bitterness and hostilities among the Creeks. Many Creeks, embittered by the war and the treaty, fled to Florida and organized as the Seminole Nation.

At the end of the War of 1812—and to protest America's actions toward the Creeks—the British added a stipulation to the Treaty of Ghent guaranteeing the rights of the Indians. In the added proviso, the United States agreed to honor all property and rights of Native American peoples before 1811. This was a way for the British to protect its former allies and trading privileges with the Indians. The Treaty of Ghent, signed in December 1814 in the Netherlands, nullified the provisions that Andrew Jackson had forced upon the Creek Nation. However, without enforcement or pressure from the British, the United States failed to honor the intent of the treaty with Great Britain. The Treaty of Fort Jackson continued for the next sixteen years, until Indian removal in the 1830s.

Kent Blansett

See also: Creek; Creek Wars; Jackson, Andrew.

Further Reading

Debo, Angie. *The Road to Disappearance: A History of the Creek Indians.* Norman: University of Oklahoma Press, 1979.

Remini, Robert. *Andrew Jackson and His Indian Wars.* New York: Penguin Putnam, 2002.

Fort Kearny (Nebraska)

Fort Kearny, situated in the middle of present-day Nebraska on the Platte River, was one of the most important way stations on the Great Platte River Road—the Oregon Trail, California Trail, and Mormon Trail. Emigrants took this road heading to California, Oregon, Utah, and other western destinations.

There were two Fort Kearnys. The U.S. Army built the first Fort Kearny in May 1846 on the west bank of the Missouri River, where today's Nebraska City, Nebraska, stands. The army named the fort after Colonel Stephen Watts Kearny of the 1st Dragoons, who selected the site. The army built this fort to protect emigrants, but, soon deciding that the post was in the wrong location to provide protection, abandoned it in May 1848.

In 1847 First Lieutenant Daniel P. Woodbury with the Corps of Engineers pioneered a road from the first Fort Kearny up to Grand Island on the Platte River near the present-day city of Kearney, Nebraska. This road became another major emigrant route. People soon called it the Old Fort Kearny Road. In May 1848, Woodbury began building a fort at the head of Grand Island on property that the army purchased from the Pawnees. Woodbury first called the new structure the Post at Grand Island, renaming it Fort Childs after his father-in-law, Major Thomas Childs of the 1st U.S. Artillery. The army changed the name to Fort Kearny after the late General Stephen Watts Kearny.

Good lumber was scarce at the new site, so the soldiers built most of the buildings out of sod. As time went on, they replaced some of these sod buildings with wooden structures. As at many other western posts, the army never built a wall around Fort Kearny. Indians never attacked it. The Pawnees were usually friendly to the whites, and the Lakota and Cheyenne war parties

Artist William Henry Jackson painted Fort Kearny, an army outpost in central Nebraska Territory, in 1865. Later the site of Nebraska City, the fort was a strategic convergence point and way station for several major trails carrying settlers west. *(MPI/Stringer/Getty Images)*

that occasionally came through the region were usually looking for the Pawnees to raid.

One of the distinguishing features of Fort Kearny was its flagpole. It was very tall with a large American flag flying from the top. The flag was the first thing travelers saw as they approached the fort and it gave many of them a sense of security.

All major trails leaving Missouri for the West funneled together just before reaching Fort Kearny, ensuring that anyone heading west on these trails passed by the fort, making it not only a place of protection, but also one where messages could be left. From Fort Kearny to Fort Laramie, the roads followed the north and south sides of the Platte River.

Tens of thousands of emigrants passed Fort Kearny—gold miners bound for California, Mormons on their way to Utah, and families looking for new beginnings in Oregon. The fort was there to assist emigrants, who could buy supplies, mend their wagons and equipment, and mail their letters back east.

The army permanently stationed soldiers at Fort Kearny and used the fort as a staging area for expeditions to fight hostile Indian tribes. The Omaha Scouts and Frank North's Pawnee Scouts used Fort Kearny as a temporary base.

As settlers developed communities in the West, freight wagons passed by the fort as well as stagecoaches. Pony Express riders had a station nearby. William F. "Buffalo Bill" Cody had his first jobs riding for the Pony Express and driving freight wagons and stagecoaches passing through Fort Kearny. Transcontinental telegraph lines soon reached the fort as they continued westward and, in August 1866, the Union Pacific's transcontinental railroad reached the vicinity of Fort Kearny. The railroad was on the north side of the river, however, making it difficult for railroad passengers to visit the fort.

With the railroad's arrival, troops were able to move rapidly to their destinations, enabling the army to reduce the number of forts it needed to garrison. Fort Kearny, guardian of westward expansion for many years, was a victim of its own success, and the army abandoned it in 1871. Today, Fort Kearny is a Nebraska state park. Although no original buildings exist, replicas have been constructed, and archeologists have uncovered original foundations and artifacts.

Bill Markley

See also: California Trail; Cody, William Frederick (Buffalo Bill); Forts and Fortification; Forty-Niners; Kearny, Stephen Watts; Mormon Trail; North, Frank Joshua; North, Luther Hedden; Omaha; Oregon Trail; Pawnee; Pawnee Scouts; Pony Express.

Further Reading

Frazer, Robert W. *Forts of the West: Military Forts and Presidios and Posts Commonly Called Forts West of the Mississippi River to 1898.* Norman: University of Oklahoma Press, 1972.

Mattes, Merrill. *The Great Platte River Road: The Covered Wagon Mainline Via Fort Kearny to Fort Laramie.* Lincoln: University of Nebraska Press, 1987.

Wilson, D. Ray. *Fort Kearny on the Platte.* Dundee, IL: Crossroads Communications, 1980.

Fort Laramie

Fort Laramie, located in present-day southeastern Wyoming on the north bank of the Laramie River near its confluence with the North Platte, was one of the nation's most important fur trade posts and, later, military establishments. It was a key way station for travelers along the Oregon, Mormon, and California trails, and it played an important role in treaty sessions that moved Plains Indians onto reservations. During its fifty-six years of operation, from 1834 to 1890, it witnessed the magnificent parade of westward expansion during the movement's heyday and climax. Fort Laramie was visited by many of the most significant historical figures of the times, including Alfred Jacob Miller, Thomas Fitzpatrick, Red Cloud, Marcus and Narcissa Whitman, William Selby Harney, Francis Parkman, and Stephen Watts Kearny.

Veteran fur trapper and trader William Sublette built the fort, originally named Fort William in his honor, in the spring of 1834, as another step in his and partner Robert Campbell's ambitions to compete with the powerful American Fur Company (AFC), whose headquarters were at Fort Union, situated at the confluence of the Yellowstone and Missouri rivers. The two men had constructed a post a few miles from Fort Union during the previous year, and their company's success had extracting a pledge from AFC to keep its trappers out of the Rocky Mountains for one year in exchange for Sublette and Campbell pulling out of the upper Missouri trade.

Soon renamed Fort Laramie, after a French trapper, Jacques La Ramie, who had been killed along the stream's banks in 1822 by Arapaho Indians, the post soon became a leading player in the mountain fur trade, rivaling in size and importance the noted Bent's Fort in southeastern Colorado. Alfred Jacob Miller, the artist who accompanied Sir William Drummond Stewart on his journey to the 1837 fur trappers' rendezvous and along the way visited Fort Laramie, painted the only

Fort Laramie in eastern Wyoming was founded as a fur-trading post in 1834 and taken over by the U.S. Army in 1849 to protect westward-bound settlers on the Oregon Trail. It later provided a key staging point for U.S. troops and supplies in the Indian Wars. *(MPI/Stringer/Getty Images)*

known images of the original post as it was designed and built by Sublette. He described it as situated about 800 miles (1,290 km) from St. Louis and constructed in the form of a quadrangle measuring about 150 square feet (14 sq m), with two bastions at opposite corners and a tower covering the entrance. The fort was built with massive, squared cottonwood logs.

Within a decade of its construction, Fort Laramie, by now falling into serious disrepair, became the property of the AFC, whose employees in 1841 built a second fort out of adobe a short distance from the original log post. The new structure was named Fort John, but almost everyone continued to call it Fort Laramie. Its walls measured about 167 by 121 feet (51 × 37 m), and within were eighteen rooms. In the meantime, the beaver population had played out and buffalo robes replaced the beaver in fur trade primacy.

The next group to frequent Fort Laramie was various units of the U.S. Army. By 1851 a much larger, more permanent army post was being built in the vicinity of the two earlier posts. This was the site of the conclusion of the 1851 Treaty of Fort Laramie, which relegated thousands

of Sioux, Cheyennes, Arapahos, Crows, Gros Ventres, and Arikaras to dependence upon an annuity payment system administered by the federal government.

The fort was almost abandoned during the Civil War, but as Indian hostilities along the overland mail and telegraph routes exploded, the fort was manned by large numbers of volunteers from a variety of states. Even Confederate prisoners of war choosing to serve out their imprisonment wearing blue uniforms served at the fort.

In 1868 Fort Laramie was the location of the signing of a treaty with northern Plains Indians that called for the army's evacuation of Forts Reno, C.F. Smith, and Phil Kearny, situated along the Bozeman Trail, and the placement of thousands of regional Indians on reservations with permission to leave in order to hunt, all in exchange for the Indians' promise not to attack American posts, railroads, or wagon roads. Despite the treaty, numerous conflicts between the army and various Indian tribes of the region followed, including the army's illegal reconnaissance of the Sioux's sacred Black Hills, the illegal construction of several army posts in violation of the treaty, an Indian attack on Northern Pacific Railroad workers and their military escort, and the infamous Battle of the Little Big Horn, in which several companies of the 7th Cavalry, commanded by Lieutenant Colonel George A. Custer, were annihilated by Sioux and Cheyenne warriors.

After most of the Indian tribes were subdued on the northern plains and the frontier had passed the military installations, vastly lessening the army's importance to the region, Fort Laramie held on a while longer. In 1875 the scientific party led by Walter P. Jenney and Henry Newton, supported by the 23rd Infantry commanded by Colonel Richard Irving Dodge, organized at Fort Laramie for its expedition into the Black Hills that precipitated the gold rush to that region. Between 1876 and 1887, as a way station, the fort accommodated thousands of passengers aboard the stagecoaches of the Cheyenne-Deadwood Stage line on their way to the Black Hills goldfields. By this time, the fort consisted of sixty-two separate structures surrounded by 35,000 acres (14,000 ha) of military reserve land. In 1886 the army recommended closing Fort Laramie, but the inevitable was delayed for another four years. Then, the reserve lands were opened for homesteading and the buildings were auctioned off for $1,417. Today the site is operated as a National Historic Site by the National Park Service.

James A. Crutchfield

See also: American Fur Company; Black Hills Expeditions; Campbell, Robert; Cheyenne; Cheyenne-Deadwood Trail; Fort Laramie, Treaty of (1868); Forts and Fortification; Oregon Trail; Red Cloud; Sioux; Sublette Brothers.

Further Reading

Hafen, LeRoy R. *Fort Laramie and the Pageant of the West*. Lincoln: University of Nebraska Press, 1984.

Hedren, Paul L. *Fort Laramie and the Great Sioux War*. Norman: University of Oklahoma Press, 1998.

Lavender, David. *Fort Laramie and the Changing Frontier*. Washington, DC: U.S. Department of the Interior, 1983.

Nadeau, Remi. *Fort Laramie and the Sioux Indians*. Englewood Cliffs, NJ: Prentice-Hall, 1967.

Fort Laramie, Treaty of (1868)

Peace negotiations between the United States and the tribes of the northern plains took more than two years to complete, but eventually tribal signatories to the Fort Laramie Treaty of 1868 were forced onto reservations, allowing settlers to claim former tribal homelands and emigrants to travel across the native territories. The treaty also allowed for overland roads and eventual construction of railroads.

During the Civil War (1861–1865), relations with the Plains Indians rapidly deteriorated into the largest Indian war experienced by the United States. Massacres at Bear River (1862) and Sand Creek (Colorado, 1864) and the mass execution at Mankato (Minnesota) of Santee Sioux, following their 1862 uprising, made clear the United States' intentions to take the remaining Indian lands by force. The massacre at Sand Creek was surpassed by the "bloody summer of 1865," when Julesburg, Colorado, was sacked and burned twice by Indian warriors, despite the presence of a military post nearby. U.S. troops, released from the war in the East by the collapse of the southern Confederacy, rapidly were transferred to the new seat of action.

By early 1866 principal leaders of many Indian nations were suggesting that the time for peace was at hand. The federal government called for a treaty council to convene at Fort Laramie in present-day Wyoming in early June. The government hoped to get concessions for the building of roads and forts within the prime hunting grounds of the Brulé and Oglala bands of the Sioux tribe. By mid-June roughly 2,000 members of these bands assembled at the fort and negotiations began. The U.S. War Department, anticipating a successful conclusion of the treaty, already had troops on the march for posting in the Sioux territories. Much to the chagrin of the negotiators, the troops arrived at Fort Laramie during the treaty negotiations, prompting leaders such as Red Cloud and Man-Afraid-of-His-Horses to withdraw. A sham treaty was concluded with a few headmen who remained, but the treaty of 1866 was worthless. The army had to fight to hold the posts subsequently built along the Bozeman Trail, in what became known as Red Cloud's War. The Fetterman Massacre in December 1866, a major setback for the military, fostered a more peace-oriented policy in the government's Indian affairs.

In July 1867, a law was passed establishing another peace commission to deal with tribes then hostile to the government. The commission included Generals William Tecumseh Sherman, Albert H. Terry, and William S. Harney, as well as N.G. Taylor, the U.S. Commissioner of Indian Affairs. It was an unusual peace commission because in the event that it failed to make peace, the secretary of war was empowered to mobilize 4,000 soldiers to fight the recalcitrant Indians. The commission presented to the Indians an edict to make peace or be obliterated, and attempted

General William Tecumseh Sherman and his peace commission meet with Cheyenne and Arapaho Indians in May 1868 to sign the Treaty of Fort Laramie. The agreement ended Red Cloud's War and set aside lands for the exclusive use of native tribes. *(MPI/Stringer/Getty Images)*

to meet with the northern plains tribes in September 1867. This proved impossible due to the continued fighting on the Powder River. A second attempt was made in November 1867, which also failed.

In April 1868, the commission finally was able to meet with the Brulés and then some of the Oglalas in May. The tribesmen successfully demanded abandonment of the forts on the Bozeman Trail. Red Cloud, waiting to see that the forts were actually abandoned, held out on signing the treaty until November. Red Cloud had won his war.

Actually, there were several Fort Laramie treaties signed in 1868. These included treaties with the Sioux (Brulés, Oglalas, Miniconjou, Yanktonais, Hunkpapas, Cutheads, Two Kettles, Sans Arcs, and Santees), Blackfoot, and Arapahos (April 29); Crows (May 7); and Cheyennes and Northern Arapahos (May 10). All the treaties provided for the establishment of a reserve of land for the exclusive and undisturbed use of the Indian Nations. The government was to build an agency near each reservation. The Indian Nations were to establish permanent settlement in the prescribed reservation, but were allowed to hunt unoccupied federal lands. Incentives were provided for Indians who wished to become farmers. The treaty also provided for an annuity to be paid in specified goods each September for the next thirty years. The government was also tasked to provide a physician, teachers, a carpenter, a miller, an engineer, a farmer, and blacksmiths.

Terry A. Del Bene

See also: Bozeman Trail; Fort Laramie; Harney, William S.; Lakota; Red Cloud; Red Cloud's War; Sand Creek Massacre; Santee Sioux; Santee Sioux Uprising; Sherman, William Tecumseh; Sioux.

Further Reading

Kappler, Charles J. *Indian Treaties, 1778–1883*. Mattituck, NJ: Amereon House, 1972.

Prucha, Francis Paul. *American Indian Treaties: The History of a Political Anomaly*. Berkeley: University of California Press, 1994.

Fort Leavenworth

Fort Leavenworth, Kansas, is the oldest continuously operating U.S. military installation west of the Mississippi River. It was key to the military establishment in the West during the nineteenth century.

After Major Stephen Long's map of his 1820 expedition across the Great Plains labeled the area "The Great American Desert," the federal government determined it was not worth settling and established a permanent Indian frontier. The army built a series of forts in a line ranging roughly from north to south at the edge of the frontier. These forts were intended to protect settlers and to prevent Indian tribes from warring against each other. One of this chain of forts was Fort Leavenworth.

In 1827 Colonel Henry Leavenworth led units of the 3rd Infantry Regiment up the Missouri River, well into Indian country, selecting the location for a new fort to be located 25 miles (40 km) north of present-day Kansas City. On May 8, the soldiers began to build the fort on a 150-foot (46-m) high bluff on the west bank overlooking the river.

The army named the fort after Colonel Leavenworth—Cantonment Leavenworth since it was temporary in nature. At first the men slept in tents and built a stonewall for defense. They then built temporary log cabins. By 1832, when the army designated Leavenworth a fort, the men had built officers' quarters, barracks, and a hospital using brick and wood. The initial stonewall eventually fell into disrepair and was never rebuilt since the danger of Indian attack was negligible.

As the government began moving tribes west to the permanent Indian frontier, it was important to try to keep the peace between the original inhabitants and the new tribes moving in. Accordingly, Fort Leavenworth was the scene of many peace councils between the tribes. Major John Dougherty, the Indian agent at Leavenworth, held the first major intertribal council in 1830. The council was a success and was attended by members of the Oto, Omaha, Ioway, Sac, Delaware, Shawnee, and Kickapoo tribes. This was followed by a second council the same year involving the Delaware and Pawnee people. The government was moving the Delawares to new lands just west of Fort Leavenworth and wanted to ensure that there would be no conflict with the Pawnees, who used those lands as hunting grounds.

The troops stationed at Fort Leavenworth also regulated trade with the Indian tribes. Congress passed a law in 1832 prohibiting liquor in Indian country, and the military tried to enforce this law by inspecting overland wagons, pack animals, and trade vessels heading up the Missouri River.

The Philadelphia portrait painter George Catlin visited the fort while traveling aboard the American Fur Company's steamboat *Yellow Stone* in 1832 during his quest to paint Indians. In the spring of 1833, the *Yellow Stone* again stopped at Fort Leavenworth with renowned scientist Prince Maximilian of Wied and artist Karl Bodmer. Prince Maximilian and Bodmer recorded the Indian way of life up the Missouri River to Fort Union and beyond.

Another original purpose for Fort Leavenworth was to protect traffic on the Santa Fe Trail that originated near the fort. The military provided escorts for shipments of goods to Santa Fe during times of Indian hostilities. As emigrants began to travel to the West Coast using the California and Oregon trails, the army also used Fort Leavenworth as a base of operations to protect them. Emigrants passed by the fort, but the army did not allow them to use the fort as a staging area or for resupply. Those needs were met by Weston, a settlement on the east bank of the Missouri across from the fort which Joseph More, a former army dragoon, founded in 1837 to provide goods and services for the soldiers stationed at Fort Leavenworth.

The army pioneered the Fort Leavenworth Road up to the St. Joseph Road, which then led to the Oregon Trail. Some forty-niners and other emigrants began taking this road, hoping it might provide a shortcut.

The army used Fort Leavenworth as a base of operations for military expeditions to impress the Indian tribes. These included Colonel Stephen Watts Kearny's 1845 expedition along the Oregon Trail to South Pass, as well as punitive expeditions such as Colonel William S. Harney's troop movement against the Lakotas after the Grattan Massacre at Fort Laramie in 1854.

When the Mexican-American War broke out in 1846, Kearny organized his Army of the West at Fort Leavenworth and marched west along the Santa Fe Trail, invading New Mexico and California. Two other military expeditions originated at Fort Leavenworth. One, headed by Colonel Alexander Doniphan, invaded and occupied Chihuahua, Mexico, and the other, led by Colonel Sterling Price, served in New Mexico.

During the 1850s and 1860s, Fort Leavenworth served as the chief military depot sending supplies and equipment to forts westward and into the Rocky Mountain region.

In 1857 the so-called Mormon War came to a head. President James Buchanan was concerned that the Mormons in Utah Territory might be in a state of revolt and would not accept his appointed territorial governor, Alfred Cummings. A force, later commanded by Albert Sidney Johnston in place of General Harney, who chose to remain in Kansas, left Fort Leavenworth for Utah to ensure the smooth replacement of Brigham Young as territorial governor.

During the Civil War, the Union held Fort Leavenworth. A Confederate force commanded by Major General Sterling Price advanced on the installation, intending to capture it, but Union troops led by Major General Samuel R. Curtis, whose headquarters were Fort Leavenworth, stopped the Confederate advance at Westport, Missouri, on October 23, 1864.

After the war, Fort Leavenworth was the headquarters of the Department of the Missouri until 1890, except during 1869–1870. It was responsible for the administration and supply of the army in Illinois, Missouri, Kansas, Colorado, New Mexico, and the Indian Territory. Today, it is a National Historic Landmark District.

Bill Markley

See also: American Fur Company; Army of the West; Bodmer, Karl; Buffalo Soldiers; California Trail; Catlin, George; Fort Kearny (Nebraska); Fort Laramie; Forts and Fortification; Forty-Niners; Harney, William S.; Johnston, Albert Sidney; Kearny, Stephen Watts; Leavenworth, Henry; Maximilian, Prince Alexander Philip; Mexican-American War; Mormon Church; Mormon Trail; Oregon Trail; Santa Fe Trail; Utah War.

Further Reading

Frazer, Robert W. *Forts of the West: Military Forts and Presidios and Posts Commonly Called Forts West of the Mississippi River to 1898.* Norman: University of Oklahoma Press, 1972.

Hunt, Elvid. *History of Fort Leavenworth, 1827–1937.* Fort Leavenworth, KS: Fort Leavenworth Historical Society, 1984.

Mattes, Merrill. *The Great Platte River Road: The Covered Wagon Mainline Via Fort Kearny to Fort Laramie.* Lincoln: University of Nebraska Press, 1987.

Partin, John W., ed. *A Brief History of Fort Leavenworth, 1827–1983.* Fort Leavenworth, KS: Combat Studies Institute, U.S. Army Command and General Staff College, 1983.

Robinson, Willard B. *American Forts: Architectural Form and Function.* Urbana: University of Illinois Press, 1977.

Fort Mandan

Fort Mandan was built in 1804 on the shores of the Missouri River during the second winter of the Lewis and Clark Expedition. The Mandans, accustomed to trading with a diversity of tribes and Europeans, welcomed the Americans as potential commercial partners.

During the trading season, the Mandan's villages of Matootonha and Rooptahee were visited by Crees, Cheyennes, Assiniboins, and Crows. Enemy tribes such as the Teton Sioux were counted among the traders. Meat, horses, buffalo hides, musical instruments, and even seashells were traded for Mandan corn, beans, and tobacco. President Thomas Jefferson was keenly aware of the Mandans' reputation as traders and instructed Meriwether Lewis specifically to establish commercial relations with them.

Construction of the fort began in November 1804, across the river from Matootonha. It was built of cottonwood, elm, and ash, triangular in shape, with a double gate facing the Missouri River.

The work consists of two rows of huts or sheds, forming an angle where they joined each other; each row containing four rooms, of fourteen feet square and seven feet high, with plank ceiling, and the roof slanting so as to form a loft above the rooms, the highest part of which is eighteen feet from the ground: the backs of the huts formed a wall of that height, and opposite the angle the place of the wall was supplied by picketing: in the area were two rooms for stores and provisions.

While at Fort Mandan, Lewis and William Clark brokered a peace agreement between the Arikaras and the Mandans. The Arikaras were a predominantly agricultural tribe that lived down river from the Mandans. The plan for the Arikaras to winter nearby resulted in conflict and the fragile peace agreement was broken.

The Corps of Discovery spent a considerable amount of time hunting, trading, and participating in rituals. Because of the friendly nature of the Mandans and the length of the winter, Lewis and Clark came to know them better than any other nation they encountered. They obtained vital logistical information regarding the country through which they would travel in the months ahead to reach the fabled short portage and the Pacific Ocean.

It was at Fort Mandan that Lewis and Clark met and hired a French fur trapper, Toussaint Charbonneau, and his Shoshone wife, Sacagawea. The explorers had learned that the Shoshones lived at the headwaters of the Missouri and it was the belief of both captains that Charbonneau and Sacagawea would be invaluable when the expedition reached the mountains. Lewis assisted in the birth of Sacagawea's child, Jean Baptiste, on February 11, 1805, by giving her a potion made from the rings of a rattlesnake's rattle.

The Corps of Discovery departed Fort Mandan on April 7, 1805, but it was not their final farewell to their winter quarters. Upon their return in August 1806, Lewis and Clark discovered the fort had burned to the ground. The cause of the fire was unknown, but prairie fires were a common occurrence. Lewis and Clark said good-bye to Charbonneau, Sacagawea, and Jean Baptiste at the burned-out works and headed east to give their report to President Jefferson.

The ever-changing banks of the Missouri River have covered up or swept away what remained of the fort. A replica of Fort Mandan now stands on the banks of the river near the fort's original location.

Larry D. Sweazy

See also: Charbonneau, Jean Baptiste; Charbonneau, Toussaint; Clark, William; Forts and Fortification; Lewis, Meriwether; Lewis and Clark Expedition; Mandan; Sacagawea.

Further Reading

DeVoto, Bernard, ed. *The Journals of Lewis and Clark*. New York: Mariner Books, 1997.

Field, Ron, and Adam Hook. *Forts of the American Frontier, 1820–91: Central and Northern Plains*. London: Osprey, 2005.

Robertson, R.G. *Competitive Struggle: America's Western Fur Trading Posts, 1764–1865*. Caldwell, ID: Tamarack Books, 1999.

Fort Osage

When Fort Osage was completed in the fall of 1808, it was the westernmost military establishment in the United States. The outpost was built 330 miles (530 km) up the Missouri River from St. Louis. William Clark, co-commander of the Lewis and Clark Expedition and later the U.S. Indian agent and governor of Missouri Territory, commented on the site of the future fort in June 1804, during his outbound journey to the Pacific Ocean, stating that the spot would be perfect for a fort and trading house.

By 1808 the Osage Indians were exhibiting considerable hostility toward the other tribes and the few white inhabitants who lived in the region along the boundary line separating the present-day states of Missouri and Kansas. The Osages were a warlike, Siouan-speaking tribe that migrated to the central prairie from the lower Ohio River valley at some distant time in the past. The people lived in earth-covered mound-shaped dwellings typical of the agricultural tribes that inhabited the middle Missouri River valley. Since acquiring horses, however, the Osages had adopted the buffalo culture of other Great Plains tribes and become proficient at hunting the great bison herds that roamed the prairie between the Mississippi River and the Rocky Mountains.

In June of 1808, Meriwether Lewis, the governor of Louisiana Territory, conferred with Clark about the recent incursions by the Osages. Lewis pointed out to Clark that the government had failed in several attempts to pacify the Osages and to persuade them to return a number of stolen horses and other property to their rightful owners. Even White Hare, the principal chief of one of the subdivisions of the tribe, the Great Osages, had admitted that he could no longer restrain the warriors of his tribe from committing depredations among their neighbors.

In order to establish a military presence in the region, as well as to provide a trading house, or "factory," for the nearby Indian tribes, the federal government proposed the construction of a fort on the spot that William Clark had commented upon four years earlier. Shortly afterward, Captain Eli B. Clemson and George C. Sibley, the factor-to-be at the new post, departed for the site accompanied by a company of 1st U.S. Infantry troops and wagons laden with trading supplies for the Indians. Clark arrived at the new post, initially named Fort Clark, on September 4 and immediately dispatched Captain Nathan Boone, son of Daniel Boone, to communicate with the Osages and to invite them to the fort for talks and trade. Treaties with the Osage headmen soon provided for the relinquishment of practically the entire current state of Missouri plus the northern half of Arkansas in return for $1,200 cash and promises of $1,500 dollars worth of merchandise every year thereafter.

By the end of 1809, the government trading house at Fort Osage, ably managed by George Sibley, had outperformed every other factory within the system and boasted more than $22,000 in assets. The fort's early success was an indicator for the future and it consistently ranked among the most profitable trading houses in the nation. However, the War of 1812 and its accompanying export restrictions, coupled with the increasing difficulty and expense of procuring merchandise for the factories, caused financial difficulties within the system and Fort Osage was abandoned in June 1813, although trading functions were reopened in August at Arrow Rock, a few miles down the Missouri.

By spring 1814, the Osages were again displaying hostility toward Americans in the region, but peace was restored with the ending of the War of 1812. During the fall of 1815, George Sibley returned to Fort Osage and reopened it as a government factory. A small contingent of army troops reoccupied the fort in July 1816, but most of the garrison left once again in 1819 to work on the construction of Camp Missouri (later called Fort Atkinson) located near Council Bluffs several miles upriver.

In 1822 Missouri senator Thomas Hart Benton succeeded in dismantling the factory system and on November 5 of that year, trading operations at Fort Osage ceased. A few army troops had returned to the outpost in 1820, but with the closure of the trading facility the fort lost its military significance as well. It was permanently abandoned in 1827. By then, the frontier had passed this important outpost on the Missouri, and the line of settlement had moved a little farther to the west. There, the fur trade was centered in the Rocky Mountains, conducted by either "free" trappers, who owed their allegiance to no one, or by employees of large, privately owned companies formed expressly for the purpose of trapping and trading in furs. During its brief heyday, however, Fort Osage was one of the most important military and trading establishments west of the Mississippi River.

Today, the reconstructed outpost is located in present-day Sibley, Missouri, a few miles east of Kansas City.

James A. Crutchfield

See also: Benton, Thomas Hart; Clark, William; Factory System; Forts and Fortification; Osage.

Further Reading

Crutchfield, James A. "Indian Trade Program Established 200 Years Ago." *The Tombstone Epitaph* 114:10 (October 1994).

Frazer, Robert W. *Forts of the West.* Norman: University of Oklahoma Press, 1965.

Fort Phil Kearny (Wyoming)

Fort Phil Kearny is the best known of the three forts built on the Bozeman Trail in 1865 and 1866. Fort Phil Kearny was located between the junction of Piney Creek and Little Piney Creek, 14 miles (23 km) north of present-day Buffalo, Wyoming. In the spring of 1866, General John Pope ordered Fort Reno moved about 40 miles (64 km) west and rebuilt as a four-company outpost with two additional forts constructed at the Bighorn River and the upper Yellowstone Valley. In June Colonel Henry B. Carrington, commander of the Mountain District, decided not to abandon Fort Reno but to keep it active and to establish Fort Smith at the Bighorn River and Fort Phil Kearny.

Colonel Carrington, four companies of the 18th Infantry, and the regimental band left Fort Reno on July 10, 1866, and arrived at Piney Creek on July 13 to establish the outpost. Carrington selected the site on July 14, and the post grounds were surveyed and occupied on July 15. A week later the new fort on Piney Creek was officially named Fort Phil Kearny, for Major General Phil Kearny, who was killed September 1, 1862, at the Battle of Chantilly, Virginia. Captain Tenodor Ten Eyck, the first post commander, was replaced by Colonel Carrington in October.

The fort was constructed in the fall. The large stockade was built first, followed by barracks, commissary and quartermaster buildings, a hospital, band quarters, officers' quarters, headquarters office, and a sutler's store. With 700 soldiers and numerous civilians fulfilling military contracts and operating private businesses, the post quickly became a small town in the heart of Indian territory. Oglala war leaders Red Cloud and Man Afraid of His Horses formed an alliance of tribes to resist the military occupation, beginning a conflict known as Red Cloud's War. Several skirmishes in the fall culminated in the disastrous Fetterman Massacre on December 21, in which Captain William J. Fetterman and his entire command and two civilians were killed.

In January 1867, Carrington was removed from command and replaced with Lieutenant Colonel Henry W. Wessells. During the winter, food supplies were low, and deep snow cut off all communication with Fort Smith. Indian raids on the post herds resumed in May. Colonel John E. Smith took over command of the fort in July. On August 2, 1867, troops were successful at the Wagon Box Fight at the fort's wood camp when new breech-loading rifles gave them a decided military advantage. Another major engagement occurred in November 1867 when Lieutenant Edmond R.P. Shurly's command was attacked and besieged a few miles from the fort. In March 1868, as a result of the Treaty of Fort Laramie, orders were issued to prepare to abandon the Bozeman Trail forts. Withdrawal movements began in June, and on August 1 the last troops moved out of Fort Phil Kearny. Indian warriors burned the fort almost immediately.

Susan Badger Doyle

See also: Bozeman Trail; Carrington Family; Cheyenne; Forts and Fortification; Powder River Expedition (1876); Red Cloud; Red Cloud's War; Sioux.

Further Reading

Brown, Dee. *The Fetterman Massacre.* Lincoln: University of Nebraska Press, 1971.

Carrington, Frances C. *My Army Life and the Fort Phil Kearney Massacre.* Boulder, CO: Pruett, 1990.

Carrington, Margaret Irvin. *Absaraka, Home of the Crows.* Lincoln: University of Nebraska Press, 1983.

Monnett, John H. *Where a Hundred Soldiers Were Killed: The Struggle for the Powder River Country in 1866 and the Making of the Fetterman Myth.* Albuquerque: University of New Mexico Press, 2008.

Smith, Shannon D. *Give Me Eighty Men: Women and the Myth of the Fetterman Fight.* Lincoln: University of Nebraska Press, 2008.

Fort Robinson

Fort Robinson, located in northwestern Nebraska, was important to American westward expansion and military development, serving to support exploration of the Black Hills and controlling Indian tribes.

In 1868 United States authorities concluded peace with the Lakotas and other tribes at Fort Laramie, Wyoming. As part of the treaty, the government established the Red Cloud Agency for the Oglala band of the Lakotas on the White River just south of the Great Sioux Reservation. Trouble eventually erupted when members of the Miniconjou branch of the Lakotas began raiding the agency's livestock and firing their weapons at agency buildings. On February 9, 1874, a Miniconjou warrior murdered Frank Appleton, the acting agent, and on the same day, near Laramie Peak, 40 miles (65 km) west of Fort Laramie, Wyoming, Indians attacked and killed Lieutenant Levi H. Robinson and Corporal John C. Colman while they were out hunting.

These events created fears that the Lakotas would kill all white people at Red Cloud Agency. Dr. John J. Saville, the agent, asked the Fort Laramie commander, Colonel John E. Smith, for troops to protect the agency. Smith led cavalry and infantry troops 100 miles (160 km) to Red Cloud Agency, setting up camp on March 5, an action that caused the Minneconjous to flee the area. The camp was at first simply called Camp at Red Cloud, but Smith soon renamed it Camp Robinson after Lieutenant Levi Robinson. Believing that the troops were too close to the agency, Smith moved the campsite across the White River, eventually replacing military tents with buildings, including officers' quarters, barracks, storerooms, offices, a guardhouse, a hospital, workshops, stables, and a bakery. The men did not build a palisade around the fort although there were some rock fortifications present.

The army used Camp Robinson as a base from which to send troops north to patrol the Black Hills, which were part of the Great Sioux Reservation. After Lieutenant Colonel George Armstrong Custer's 1874 expedition to the Black Hills reported the discovery of gold, a large number of prospectors illegally entered the region. Troops at first evicted the miners, then decided to negotiate a treaty that would allow for federal control of the area. When Red Cloud and other Sioux leaders rejected treaty conditions, the government—represented by the Allison Commission—attempted to buy the region. When those efforts also failed, subsequent orders directed the Indians to report to the agencies by

January 31, 1876. This directive, along with reduced rations, restrictions on arms and ammunition sales to the Indians, and restrictions on Indian hunting south of the Platte River, drove many tribesmen to leave their agencies. It also set up the final major battles of the northern Plains Indian wars, including those in the Powder River Basin and at the Little Big Horn. By the winter of 1876–1877, the tribes, under constant harassment, began to return to the agencies. Crazy Horse, one of the great leaders of the Oglalas, surrendered at Camp Robinson on May 6, 1877; on September 5, he was killed in a scuffle as soldiers attempted to put him in a cell at Camp Robinson's guardhouse.

Deciding that Camp Robinson would remain a permanent military facility, in January 1878 the army renamed it Fort Robinson. That same year, the government moved Red Cloud Agency to White Clay Creek within the Great Sioux Reservation and renamed it Pine Ridge Agency.

By 1877 the government was concerned about the close alliance of the Northern Cheyennes and Lakotas and attempted to break it up by forcing the Northern Cheyennes to move to Indian Territory, present-day Oklahoma, to live with the Southern Cheyennes. Many of the Northern Cheyennes, lacking rations, became ill in the unfamiliar climate. During the autumn of 1878, many of them—led by Dull Knife and Little Wolf—fled the Territory and headed back to their northern homeland. Fort Robinson troops captured Chief Dull Knife, along with 150 men, women, and children, and took them to the fort, where they gave the Cheyenne refugees quarters in one of the barracks. The government decreed that the Cheyennes must return to Indian Territory; the Indians resisted. On the night of January 9, 1879, Dull Knife and his followers broke out of the barracks. Over the next two weeks, they kept up a running battle with the troops. In the end, the army killed sixty-four men, women, and children and recaptured the rest, again holding them at Fort Robinson before eventually allowing them to move to reservation lands.

One of four all-black army regiments, the U.S. 9th Cavalry, arrived at Fort Robinson in 1885. The post became the regimental headquarters for these Buffalo Soldiers from 1887 to 1898. They served on the Pine Ridge Reservation when the Oglalas began practicing the Ghost Dance religion and fighting broke out. The Fremont, Elkhorn, and Missouri Valley Railroad reached Fort Robinson on May 11, 1886, increasing the importance of Fort Robinson as a military transfer point.

In the twentieth century, the military used Fort Robinson as a training ground for cavalry horses.

During World War II, the army trained dogs (the K-9 Corps) at the fort; it became the site of a German prisoner-of-war camp in 1943. In 1948 the army transferred Fort Robinson to the U.S. Department of Agriculture, which used it for a research station. Today, Fort Robinson is a Nebraska State Park open to the public.

Bill Markley

See also: Allison Commission; Black Hills Expeditions; Buffalo Soldiers; Cheyenne; Cody, William Frederick (Buffalo Bill); Crazy Horse; Custer, George Armstrong; Custer Expedition; Dull Knife; Fort Laramie; Fort Laramie, Treaty of (1868); Forts and Fortification; Ghost Dance; Powder River Expedition (1876); Red Cloud; Red Cloud's War; Sioux.

Further Reading

Buecker, Thomas R. *Fort Robinson and the American West, 1874–1899.* Norman: University of Oklahoma Press, 2003.

Frazer, Robert W. *Forts of the West: Military Forts and Presidios and Posts Commonly Called Forts West of the Mississippi River to 1898.* Norman: University of Oklahoma Press, 1972.

Hedren, Paul L. *First Scalp for Custer: The Skirmish at Warbonnet Creek, Nebraska, July 17, 1876.* Lincoln: Nebraska State Historical Society, 2005.

Schubert, Frank N. *Buffalo Soldiers, Braves and the Brass: The Story of Fort Robinson, Nebraska.* Shippensburg, PA: White Mane, 1993.

Fort Snelling

Fort Snelling was established in 1820 at the confluence of the Mississippi and Minnesota rivers, where the twin cities of Minneapolis and St. Paul now stand. The fort, built on a site purchased from the Dakota Indians by Zebulon Pike in 1805, was used by the U.S. Army in many roles throughout its history and still serves as home base for reserve units from various branches of the military services.

When Zebulon Pike ventured north from St. Louis in 1805 to explore the upper Mississippi River, one of his assigned goals was to secure a strategic river site for a future fortification. When he arrived at the juncture of the Mississippi and St. Peter's (Minnesota) rivers, he met with the Santee leader Little Crow (not to be confused with the Dakota leader, Taoyateduta, or Little Crow, of the 1860s Great Sioux Uprising). Pike traded Little Crow goods worth about $200 in exchange for 1,000 acres (400 ha) of land along the rivers.

Nothing was done to fortify this position for almost fifteen years, but after the War of 1812, the army was eager to build a network of forts along important transportation routes on the Northwest Frontier. Thus, in 1819, soldiers from the 5th Infantry Regiment, under the command of Lieutenant Colonel Henry Leavenworth, arrived at the site and built an encampment called Camp Coldwater. The following summer saw the beginning of construction on the fort, under the leadership of the regiment's new commander, Colonel Josiah Snelling. The installation was initially called Fort St. Anthony, for the waterfall on the Mississippi 6 miles (10 km) upriver. By 1825 the post was completed and named after Snelling, its first commander and visionary designer. In addition, the army built a grist mill at St. Anthony Falls, established an Indian agency, carved out roads in the surrounding countryside, and planted and harvested crops nearby to sustain the troops quartered there.

Over the next three decades, Fort Snelling became the key outpost on the upper Mississippi River. It helped maintain peace between the Dakota and Ojibwa Indians, who were traditional enemies, and became a meeting place for traders, soldiers, settlers, travelers, and Indians. A number of transplanted Canadians from the failed Selkirk colony settled near the fort in the late 1820s. When the army began evicting these settlers from the area in 1839, they moved downriver a few miles and founded Pig's Eye Landing, soon to become the city of St. Paul.

By 1849 the importance of the fort had begun to decline. Minnesota had become a territory, St. Paul was the center of government, and much of the surrounding land had been sold to white settlers. Treaties with the Dakotas had moved them further north and west, where new installations (Forts Ripley, Ridgely, and Ambercrombie) had been established. The frontier had moved westward, and the future of Fort Snelling was in question.

It appeared that Fort Snelling's military mission was over in 1858, the year Minnesota was admitted to the Union. Franklin Steele, a former sutler at the fort, negotiated the purchase of the post and 8,000 surrounding acres (3,200 ha) for $90,000. Steele intended to sell lots and to create a city on the grounds of the former military reservation, but his plans were thwarted by repercussions from the financial panic of 1857, and the business venture languished. Steele used the fort as a sheep pen, and Minnesota held its first state fair on the old parade grounds in 1860. However, the civilian role played by Fort Snelling was to be short-lived.

In April 1861, after Confederate forces captured Fort Sumter, South Carolina, Minnesota governor Alexander Ramsey offered to raise a regiment of volunteers in response to President Lincoln's appeal for soldiers. Meanwhile, the state adjutant general arranged with Steele for the use of the former fort and it became the mustering and training center for ten state volunteer infantry regiments during the Civil War. Many of the troops trained at Fort Snelling went east and south to fight in the war, while some were kept in the state to guard the frontier. In August 1862, troops from Fort Snelling joined others under Henry Sibley to quell the Great Sioux Uprising.

After the Civil War, General William T. Sherman declared that Fort Snelling would become an army administrative center. It served as headquarters for the Department of Dakota for the next two decades and became home base for the U.S. 3rd Infantry Regiment in 1889. Fort Snelling expanded its facilities to keep up with its changing roles, serving as a training center for junior officers, as well as for cavalry and artillery units. During World War II, a Japanese language school was established there, and over 300,000 troops were trained or processed through the various facilities at the fort. The end of the war also brought an end to Fort Snelling's active military role. Since 1946 it has mainly served as a host for reserve and National Guard units. The original fort has been largely renovated and restored to its appearance in the early nineteenth century.

Jim Ersfeld

See also: Forts and Fortification; Leavenworth, Henry; Pike, Zebulon M.

Further Reading

Hall, Steve. *Fort Snelling: Colossus of the Wilderness.* St. Paul: Minnesota Historical Society Press, 1987.

Ruche, Francis Paul. *Broadax and Bayonet: The Role of the United States Army in the Development of the Northwest, 1815–1860.* Lincoln: University of Nebraska Press, 1967.

Fort Stanwix, Treaty of (1768)

The Proclamation Line of 1763 was established to prevent the uncontrolled movement of western settlement into Indian country and avert the increasing hostilities between British colonials and Native Americans. After the French and Indian War (1754–1763) and Pontiac's Rebellion (1763–1766), the British lacked the necessary resources to wage another western territorial war. The line was intended to thwart another costly, armed conflict. However, colonials within these borderlands pushed further into Kentucky and the West. The proclamation line was ignored, a defiant act against British rule.

The first Treaty of Fort Stanwix, parleyed in 1768 in New York, was designed to assuage the growing pressures by colonists to settle in the Ohio River valley. The British negotiated the treaty with the Haudenosaunee or Iroquois Confederacy (Mohawks, Cayugas, Senecas, Oneidas, Onondagas, and Tuscaroras). The Iroquois were a powerhouse of military, economic, and diplomatic strength in the Northeast. Peaceful relations were necessary, as the British colonials had been weakened by constant warfare. The Iroquois were instrumental in playing off both the French and British during the French and Indian War. Peaceful relations with the Iroquois Confederacy were absolutely necessary to ensure peace along the frontier.

In 1768 the six chiefs of the Iroquois Confederacy signed a document acknowledging receipt of £10,460 in exchange for land in the Ohio Valley ceded to the British under the Treaty of Fort Stanwix. *(The Granger Collection, New York)*

The British were unaware that the Iroquois lacked the proper authority to relinquish lands in the Ohio River country. The Lenapes (Delawares), Mingos, and Shawnees all held traditional land title to this region. The unauthorized sale of this land culminated in further hostilities between British settlers and Indians. While the 1763 Proclamation Line was renegotiated to encourage movement west, it also provoked Lord Dunmore's War in 1774.

The Shawnees and Mingos formed an intertribal alliance, under the leadership of Cornstalk, to push colonial settlers who had advanced on Mingo communities. The alliance launched attacks on Pennsylvania settlements in reprisal for past atrocities. Virginia, fearful that Pennsylvania might claim parts of the Ohio, organized a militia to destroy the alliance. After Lord Dunmore's War, the Shawnees accepted the boundary lines prescribed under the initial Fort Stanwix treaty. During the American Revolution, Americans used the new boundary line to secure tribal alliances against the British.

Kent Blansett

See also: Fort Stanwix, Treaty of (1784); Pontiac; Proclamation of 1763; Shawnee.

Further Reading

Prucha, Francis Paul. *American Indian Treaties: The History of a Political Anomaly.* Berkeley: University of California Press, 1994.

Richter, Daniel K. *The Ordeal of the Longhouse: The Peoples of the Iroquois League in the Era of European Colonization.* Chapel Hill: University of North Carolina Press, 1992.

Fort Stanwix, Treaty of (1784)

In New York, at the end of the American Revolution, the newly formed United States of America, under the Articles of Confederation, negotiated a second Treaty of Fort Stanwix with the Haudenosaunee or Iroquois Confederacy.

During the Revolutionary War the Iroquois had split their allegiances between the British and Americans, and by war's end the Iroquois Confederacy represented the greatest military threat to the young American nation. As a result, one of George Washington's first acts as president was to order the burning of Iroquois villages and crops by General John Sullivan. This slash-and-burn campaign earned Washington the name Town Destroyer by the Iroquois. Washington knew that the subjugation of the Iroquois was the key to controlling access to the Ohio River valley.

The Onieda and Tuscarora tribes were excluded from the treaty for their loyalty to the United States. The famed Mohawk warrior Thayendanegea (Joseph Brant) refused to participate in the treaty negotiation because it lacked representation from the thirteen states, while Mohawk leader Kanonraron (Aaron Hill) argued that the Haudenosaunee were an independent nation autonomous from British or American rule. Seneca Chief KaiũtwahÃkũ (Cornplanter) argued for the continuation of the boundary line established in the 1768 Fort Stanwix Treaty.

Commissioner Oliver Wolcott, General Richard Butler, and Arthur Lee represented the United States. Their goal was to promote the peace and seek the return of prisoners. General Butler refused to acknowledge Iroquois demands. The commission redrew existing boundary lines and claimed the new territories by right of conquest and reparation for the war. In addition, the commission arrested Iroquois leaders present at the negotiation to pressure the quick release of prisoners held by the nations.

Once again the Iroquois signed away land outside of their jurisdiction. Many of the western tribes lacked representation at the signing and the commissioners made the mistake of assuming that the Iroquois were empowered to negotiate for the western tribes. The state of New York protested the treaty and claimed that under the Articles of Confederation only the states had the right to negotiate treaties. The Treaty of Fort Stanwix was quickly pushed through Congress and abrogated the states' right to intervene.

While the second Treaty of Fort Stanwix set many precedents, it negotiated the further push for western settlement beyond the Appalachians. The treaty also forced a split with the Mohawks as many sought refuge with the British in Canada. Today, the Mohawks have reservations in both the United States and Canada.

Kent Blansett

See also: Fort Stanwix, Treaty of (1768).

Further Reading

Graymont, Barbara. *The Iroquois in the American Revolution.* Syracuse, NY: Syracuse University Press, 1975.

Taylor, Alan. *The Divided Ground: Indians, Settlers, and the Northern Borderland of the American Revolution.* New York: Vintage Books, 2007.

Fort Union (New Mexico)

Fort Union was considered one of the most important and influential forts of the Southwest. It guarded the Santa Fe Trail, served as a base providing protection against hostile Indian tribes, held the territory for the Union Army during the Civil War, and became the supply depot for all military forts and functions in the Southwest.

The Santa Fe Trail, the main trading route between the Missouri River settlements and Santa Fe, New Mexico, had been in use by American traders since 1821. The trail forked at the Cimarron Crossing of the Arkansas River. One branch, called the Cimarron Cutoff, angled southwest through the desert. The Mountain Branch was 100 miles (160 km) longer and went through the Raton Mountains. Each branch had its advantages and disadvantages. The two branches rejoined at the Mora and Sapello rivers about 100 miles east of Santa Fe.

With the outbreak of the Mexican-American War in 1846, General Stephen Watts Kearny led the Army of the West over the Santa Fe Trail, capturing the Southwest. At the end of the war, the United States acquired New Mexico and with it problems with the local tribes—Apaches, Navajos, and others.

The army stationed troops in towns, but this was ineffective in combating hostile Indians and protecting settlers and commerce. C.M. Conrad, the secretary of war, ordered Lieutenant Colonel Edwin V. Summer, 1st Dragoons, to move the troops closer to the Indian tribes. Summer moved the troops out of Santa Fe, which had been the department headquarters and supply depot.

The troops traveled east on the Santa Fe Trail until they were at the juncture of the trail's two branches, where the military began construction of Fort Union on July 26, 1851. The site had a good supply of water, grass for the animals, and wood for fuel, although it was also replete with rattlesnakes. The soldiers did a poor job of construction. There later were complaints about the poor workmanship and horrible quarters. The men preferred to sleep outside.

In 1854 the army used Fort Union as a base of operations against the Jicarilla Apaches, who had been raiding settlements and travelers on the Santa Fe Trail. After several inconclusive skirmishes, on Christmas Day, 1854, the Utes and Jicarillas attacked the town of Hardscrabble, today's Pueblo, Colorado, killing fifteen men and making off with two women as well as cattle. The warriors followed this with an attack on a settlement near current Alamosa, Colorado. Colonel Thomas

T. Fauntleroy led units including the 1st Dragoons out of Fort Union. The command pursued and attacked the Utes and Jicarillas at night, routing them. The Utes and Jicarillas soon sued for peace.

In 1860 when Comanches and Kiowas were attacking and robbing travelers on the Santa Fe Trail, troops from Fort Union patrolled the trail and escorted wagon trains and stagecoaches, as well as mail shipments as far as the Arkansas River. Other troops were dispatched to intercept the raiders. After skirmishes in 1860 and 1861, the warriors finally promised to leave the Santa Fe Trail travelers alone.

By August 1861, the Civil War had erupted and many of Fort Union's officers resigned their commissions to fight for the Confederacy. Fearing bombardment should Confederate artillery be placed on a nearby mesa top, Colonel Edward R.S. Canby ordered the Fort Union garrison to begin construction of a second Fort Union a mile away. The new Fort Union had an eight-pointed star-shaped earthwork surrounding it. The men considered the star fort also a poor facility. The earthen walls began to crumble, the barracks' roofs leaked, and the interiors were damp.

In January 1862, Confederate Brigadier General Henry H. Sibley began his invasion of New Mexico from Fort Bliss, Texas. Sibley's plans were to invade New Mexico, capture the forts, including Fort Union, and all their supplies, and from there capture Denver and the Colorado goldfields. Sibley's plans were working; Union forces were either defeated in battle or retreated before his advance. Almost all that stood between the Confederate army and Denver were the crumbling fortifications of Fort Union and the small post at Fort Garland, in Colorado, west of the Sangre de Cristo range.

Colorado volunteer regiments under the command of Colonel John P. Slough reinforced the regular army troops at Fort Union. The Confederates, under the command of Major Charles L. Pyron, were on the move eastward from Santa Fe to Glorieta Pass on the Santa Fe Trail. Slough sent Major John M. Chivington and 400 soldiers to the pass, where they ran into the Confederates on March 26, 1862. Chivington's men were able to hold the Confederates at the pass until Slough arrived with 900 troops and artillery. After a stalemated battle, Chivington's men were able to find and destroy the Confederate supply wagons. Pyron had no choice but to fall back. The Confederates eventually had to abandon all of New Mexico.

In 1863 Brigadier General James H. Carleton ordered construction of a new fort and arsenal close to the star fort. The army built the post, which was completed in 1866, of adobe and brick. Fort Union became the general supply depot for New Mexico Territory and served as a base for further operations against Apaches, Kiowas, and Comanches.

With the construction of the Atchison, Topeka, and Santa Fe Railroad into New Mexico, the army no longer needed the supply depot. The fort was abandoned in 1882 and closed in 1891. The government eventually returned the land and the buildings to the original landowner's family. Today, Fort Union is a national monument run by the U.S. Park Service.

Bill Markley

See also: Apache; Chivington, John M.; Comanche; Forts and Fortification; Kearny, Stephen Watts; Kiowa; Navajo; Santa Fe Trail; Ute.

Further Reading

Frazer, Robert W. *Forts of the West: Military Forts and Presidios and Posts Commonly Called Forts West of the Mississippi River to 1898.* Norman: University of Oklahoma Press, 1972.

Robinson, Willard B. *American Forts: Architectural Form and Function.* Urbana: University of Illinois Press, 1977.

Utley, Robert M. *Fort Union National Monument, New Mexico.* National Park Service Historical Handbook Series No. 35. Washington, DC: National Park Service, 1962.

———. *Frontiersmen in Blue: The United States Army and the Indian, 1848–1865.* Lincoln: University of Nebraska Press, 1981.

Fort Union (North Dakota)

Fort Union, located on the Missouri River in present-day North Dakota near the Montana border, was one of the most important and the longest operating American fur-trading posts on the frontier, doing business from 1828 to 1867. Its purpose was to establish and maintain trade with the Indian tribes of the Northern Plains; in so doing, Fort Union developed its own unique culture.

In 1827 John Jacob Astor, principal partner of the American Fur Company, purchased the Columbia Fur Company with the condition that some of Columbia Fur's partners become involved in American Fur. Pierre Chouteau Jr., member of an esteemed St. Louis fur-trading family and a noted leader in the business, had already teamed up with Astor, and with the acquisition of Columbia Fur Astor picked up another important partner, Kenneth McKenzie, who, together with Chouteau, greatly increased profits for the company.

With Astor's acquisition, the Columbia Fur Company became known as the Upper Missouri River Outfit as part of the American Fur Company's Western Division. McKenzie managed the outfit with Chouteau in charge of the Western Division. People eventually called the American Fur Company "the Company" and any competitor "the Opposition."

McKenzie based the old Columbia Fur Company at Fort Tecumseh, near modern Fort Pierre, South Dakota. McKenzie and Chouteau believed they could make more money by drawing trade with the Cree and Assiniboine tribes from the powerful Hudson's Bay Company (HBC), but to do so they needed to establish a strong presence further up the Missouri River. Accordingly, in 1828 McKenzie sent traders up the Missouri to its confluence with the Yellowstone River. The men proceeded a few miles further up the Missouri and built a cabin for trading with the Assiniboines. The ensuing business was profitable, prompting McKenzie to build a fort near the trading cabin. He named it Fort Union and transferred his headquarters from Fort Tecumseh to the new post, which became the largest fur installation on the Missouri River at the time, eventually measuring 237 feet (72 m) long on the east and west walls and 245 feet (75 m) long on the north and south walls.

The American Fur Company controlled most of the trade with the tribes of the upper Missouri, trading manufactured goods for beaver pelts, buffalo hides, and other furs. McKenzie wanted to establish trade with the Blackfoot tribe and his chance came in 1830. The Blackfoot had always traded exclusively with the Hudson's Bay Company and considered all Americans their enemies as far back as their run-in with Meriwether Lewis during the Corps of Discovery's return from the West Coast in 1806. McKenzie sent Jacob Berger to the Blackfoots, inviting them to Fort Union to discuss trade prospects. Berger, an old Hudson's Bay trapper and friend of the Blackfoots, contacted tribal leaders and brought a tribal delegation to Fort Union. After McKenzie provided presents and promised a good exchange for their furs, the Indians agreed to trade with the company. They also gave permission for the company to build a trading post in their territory. McKenzie sent James Kipp up the Missouri into Blackfoot territory, and by October 1831 he had built the first of several forts: Fort Piegan, 11 miles (18 km) downstream from present-day Fort Benton, Montana. Trade was brisk, and by the spring he had traded all his goods for Blackfoot furs. In November 1831, McKenzie developed and concluded a treaty of peace and friendship between the

Blackfoot and Assiniboine tribes, an accommodation that was good for trade.

In mid-1832, John Jacob Astor sold his share in the company to Pierre Chouteau Jr., and other partners. The same year, McKenzie authorized the building of Fort Cass on the Yellowstone River at the mouth of the Bighorn River in Crow country. McKenzie and the Upper Missouri Outfit now had trading relations with all the major tribes in the Upper Missouri River basin. McKenzie was called "the King of the Upper Missouri" and rightly so as he controlled most of the trade with the tribes. The opposition traders tried to make inroads, but the hard-driving McKenzie eventually drove them out of business.

On June 17, 1832, the company's steamboat *Yellow Stone* arrived at Fort Union to the firing of the fort's cannon and cheers from the crowd of onlookers. The *Yellow Stone* was the first steamboat to travel up the Missouri River. Onboard were Pierre Chouteau, Jr., and the artist George Catlin, who was painting and writing about the tribes of the West. Steamboats increased the Upper Missouri Outfit's efficiency to move furs, hides, and trade goods faster and easier.

McKenzie traveled to St. Louis and Washington, DC, and returned to Fort Union on June 23, 1833, aboard the company's steamboat *Assiniboine* accompanying German Prince Maximilian of Wied, and his personal artist, Karl Bodmer. Maximilian had served in a regiment of the Royal Prussian Army during the Napoleonic Wars and had previously explored Brazil. By 1833 he was studying the native peoples and natural history of North America. Maximilian and McKenzie had similar interests and became good friends.

By the 1840s, most of the trade with the tribes was in buffalo robes. The Lakotas began to move into the territory, battling the local tribes and displaying hostility toward the Fort Union traders. The U.S. Army sent troops and supplies to the fort in 1864. The fur and hide trade eventually became unprofitable and in June 1865 the company sold the fort to the Northwest Fur Company. Due to the continued decline in trade and attacks by the Lakotas, the Northwest Company sold the post to the U.S. Army, which soon dismantled it to use as building materials for Fort Buford.

The National Park Service acquired the Fort Union site in 1966. After the completion of several archeological digs, a replica of the fort was built, which today serves the region as a major tourist attraction.

Bill Markley

See also: American Fur Company; Astor, John Jacob; Blackfoot; Bodmer, Karl; Catlin, George; Chouteau Family; Forts and Fortification; Hudson's Bay Company; Maximilian, Prince Alexander Philip; McKenzie, Kenneth.

Further Reading

Barbour, Barton H. *Fort Union and the Upper Missouri Fur Trade.* Norman: University of Oklahoma Press, 2001.

Christian, Shirley. *Before Lewis and Clark: The Story of the Chouteaus, the French Dynasty That Ruled America's Frontier.* New York: Farrar, Straus and Giroux, 2004.

Jackson, Donald. *Voyages of the Steamboat Yellow Stone.* New York: Ticknor & Fields, 1985.

Robertson, R.G. *Competitive Struggle: America's Western Fur Trading Posts, 1764–1865.* Boise, ID: Tamarack Books, 1999.

Thompson, Erwin N. *Fort Union Trading Post: Fur Trade Empire on the Upper Missouri.* Medora, ND: Theodore Roosevelt Nature and History Association, 1986.

Fort Vancouver

Fort Vancouver, established in 1825 near the mouth of the Columbia River as headquarters for the Hudson's Bay Company (HBC), became an important fur-trading outpost and center of operations for the company as it sought to control the huge fur empire drained by the Columbia. When the first emigrants reached the end of the Oregon Trail in the 1840s, the fort became a critical supply point thanks to the largesse of the company factor, Dr. John McLoughlin.

The HBC, a London-based fur-trading company, had been granted a royal charter in 1670 giving exclusive Canadian trapping rights to the British over all the land that emptied into Hudson's Bay. HBC's North American headquarters was at York Factory, on the edge of the bay. HBC was forced into a coalition with the rival North West Company (NWC) in 1821, and the merger produced a monumental force that within a few years had spread the HBC to the Pacific Coast.

At this time, the Pacific coast area was occupied jointly by the United States and Great Britain. Rumors flew that the eventual boundary between the two countries would be the Columbia River. Wanting to protect their interests in the area, HBC officials sent Dr. John McLoughlin, a Canadian medical doctor, to set up headquarters and serve as factor at the company's trading hub. He was directed to denude the area of beaver, but first he established his operations on the south bank of the Columbia River at Fort George (current Astoria, Oregon). Knowing this was definitely on the American side of the river, he relocated to the

Fort Vancouver, located on the Columbia River near today's Portland, Oregon, was headquarters of the Hudson's Bay Company in the Pacific Northwest from 1825 to 1849 and then became the first U.S. Army post in the region. It is depicted here in 1860. *(MPI/Stringer/Getty Images)*

north bank, slightly upstream from the mouth of the Willamette River, and built Fort Vancouver. The site selected was flat and had easy access to the Columbia, yet it was just outside the flood plain. HBC wanted the fort to be self-sufficient, as food was costly to ship.

The palisade protecting the fort measured 750 feet (227 m) long, 450 feet (137 m) wide, and about 20 feet (6 m) high. Inside, forty buildings were used for housing, warehouses, a school, a library, a pharmacy, a chapel, a blacksmith shop, and a large manufacturing facility.

Although it was a fur trade post, it employed more people and more ethnic groups in agriculture than any other activity. The population of the fort and the surrounding area consisted primarily of French-Canadians and Métis, who were a mixture of French-Canadian and American Indian, but also it counted several English, Scots, Irish, Hawaiians, and a wide variety of Indians, including Iroquoians and Crees. Because of this mix, many languages were spoken at the fort, such as Canadian French and the Chinook jargon, interlaced with Chehalis, English, French, and Hawaiian. While the most common spoken language was French, company records and official journals were kept in English.

Every year, ships from London dropped off trade goods and supplies in exchange for furs. The fort's influence extended across 700,000 square miles (1.8 million sq km), from the Rocky Mountains to the Hawaiian Islands (at that time called the Sandwich Islands), and from Alaska into Mexican-controlled California. Fort Vancouver watched over 34 outposts, 24 ports, 6 ships, and 600 employees. It was the largest settlement of non-natives west of the Great Plains at the time.

During the 1840s, about 40 percent of Fort Vancouver's laborers were Hawaiian. When the British ships docked in the Hawaiian Islands to take on supplies and other goods, such as rum and coral, Hawaiian natives were offered short-term, renewable contracts with HBC. The Hawaiians gained a reputation as skillful hands aboard ship, because, unlike most sailors of that day, they could swim. Once they arrived, they joined the workforce at Fort Vancouver, which quickly became the center point of social, cultural, and economic activity. The residential village, comprised of employees, their families, and others, was known as Kanaka Village because of the number of Hawaiians living there.

Outside the fort proper there was additional housing, as well as fields, gardens, orchards, a shipyard, a distillery, a tannery, a sawmill, and a dairy. The agricultural industry expanded to cover almost 30 miles (48 km) along the Columbia River and 10 miles (16 km) north from the riverbank, and included grazing areas, large-scale cropping, ornamental gardens, and orchards. Many trades flourished, among them, blacksmithing, baking, carpentry, and cooperage, all helping to expand the physical size of the post. Eventually, there were a salmon store and a hospital built during the peak of malaria epidemics.

The Oregon Treaty in 1846 set the United States–British border at the 49th parallel, instead of the Columbia River, as had been widely predicted. By this time Fort Vancouver was firmly planted in U.S. territory and political pressure forced HBC to relocate its headquarters in 1849 to Fort Victoria, part of today's Victoria, British Columbia.

After HBC moved out, the Columbia Barracks (later renamed Vancouver Barracks) was set up river from Fort Vancouver and was used as housing and storage. The army renamed both areas Fort Columbia, later changing back to Fort Vancouver. With each year came diminished fur trade, but additional settlers and U.S. Army involvement.

Fort Vancouver and HBC factor Dr. McLoughlin provided important support for the early American emigrants who had followed the Oregon Trail west. Many weary travelers reached the end of the trail with few—and in some cases no—supplies to see them through their first winter in the Oregon Country. They relied heavily on the largesse of McLoughlin and the company, and that support enabled them to successfully establish new homes.

By 1861 the population at Fort Vancouver had dropped to fifty, and in 1866 a fire destroyed the entire compound. The fort was rebuilt, including two double-story barracks on opposite sides of the parade ground, each with kitchen and mess. Eleven buildings served as officers' quarters. It was from this post that General Oliver O. Howard reported to command federal troops in their effort to force the Nez Percé Indians onto the reservation in Idaho Territory in 1877, an incident that led Chief Joseph and other Nez Percé leaders to strike eastward in an effort to avoid reservation life.

Fort Vancouver remained active through World War II, when Vancouver Barracks was used as a staging area for the Seattle Port of Embarkation. It closed its doors in 1946.

Melody Groves

See also: Chief Joseph; Forts and Fortification; Howard, Oliver O.; Hudson's Bay Company; McLoughlin, John; Oregon Trail.

Further Reading

Division of Publications, National Park Service. *Fort Vancouver.* Handbook 113. Washington DC: U.S. Department of the Interior, 1981.

Sinclair, Donna. *Our Manifest Destiny Bids Fair for Fulfillment, An Historical Overview of Vancouver Barracks, 1846–1898.* Portland OR: Center for Columbia River History, 1999.

Walker, Dale L. *Pacific Destiny: The Three-Century Journey to the Oregon Country.* New York: Forge Books, 2000.

Fort Wise, Treaty of (1861)

In February 1861, Cheyenne leaders Moke-tav-a-to (Black Kettle) and Wokai-hwoiko-masl (White Antelope) along with Arapaho leader Hósa (Little Raven) signed a treaty with U.S. representatives at Fort Wise in Kansas Territory. The treaty was negotiated just ten years after the Fort Laramie Treaty and ceded additional lands protected under the previous treaty. Both the Cheyenne and Arapaho leaders relocated their people to a smaller reservation along the Arkansas River.

Unique to the Fort Wise Treaty, the new reservation lands were divided into individual allotments to make way for private ownership. This redistribution of land effectively sought to disenfranchise and erode traditional tribal government, as well as change the communal nature of tribal society. By encouraging the private ownership of land, the U.S. government pushed the Cheyennes and Arapahos into a system of assimilation and acculturation.

Annuities of $450,000 were promised to the tribes for a period of fifteen years by the discretion of the secretary of the interior and appointed Indian agents. Most of the funding was to promote "civilization" programs in schooling and agricultural development. These added to the political attempts to disrupt and forever alter the free-range lifeways of both nations.

Despite the unique stipulations of the treaty, the government failed to protect the Cheyennes and Arapahos from further U.S. expansion. Soon railroads, stage lines, and cattle drives led to further encroachment onto Indian lands. These trespasses further exacerbated tensions between Americans and the Cheyenne and Arapaho nations.

The result was the rise of mob violence in the form of the "Bloodless" 3rd Colorado Volunteer Cavalry led by Colonel John Chivington, a Methodist minister who used his title and voice to promote fears and hatred toward Native Americans. On the cold and bitter morning of November 29, 1864, Chivington signaled a charge on a sleeping village near Sand Creek in southeastern Colorado. By daybreak it had become one of the most horrific massacres of men, women, and children in U.S. history. Over 160 Cheyennes and Arapahos were killed and mutilated under Chivington's orders. Eventually, Black Kettle and his people relocated again to Oklahoma Territory and settled near the Washita River.

The Fort Wise Treaty and the massacre at Sand Creek foreshadowed the Great Plains wars to follow.

The next year was known as the Bloody Summer of 1865. The treaty placed the Cheyennes and Arapahos under the protection of the U.S. government, but failed to protect them and instead further eroded their territory.

Kent Blansett

See also: Arapaho; Black Kettle; Cheyenne; Chivington, John M.; Sand Creek Massacre; Washita Engagement.

Further Reading

Fowler, Loretta. *Tribal Sovereignty and the Historical Imagination: Cheyenne-Arapaho Politics.* Lincoln: University of Nebraska Press, 2002.

Hoig, Stan. *The Sand Creek Massacre.* Norman: University of Oklahoma Press, 1961.

Prucha, Francis Paul. *American Indian Treaties: The History of a Political Anomaly.* Berkeley: University of California Press, 1994.

Forts and Fortification

Forts and fortification have been a part of westward expansion in North America since the first European colonists landed on its shores. Many prehistoric American Indian groups, such as the Mississippian and Ancestral Puebloan cultures, had long traditions of building palisades and walled villages for protection against marauding neighbors.

Early Spanish adventurers built forts and garrisons called *castillos* and *presidios* in Florida, Texas, the Southwest, and California. The French built forts in the Mississippi River valley, in the Great Lakes region into Canada, and even in western Pennsylvania with Fort Duquesne at the site of present-day Pittsburgh. British colonists built forts in the thirteen colonies along the east coast. These forts were to protect European colonists from each other, Indian tribes, and sea-going pirates. As the colonies grew, they competed with each other for natural resources and were also brought into larger, more complex conflicts of imperial expansion in Europe. Fort building increased during the French and Indian War and the Revolution.

As the United States moved westward, Americans used six basic types of forts—military forts, civilian community forts, house forts, commercial trading posts, nonfort structures used as forts, and temporary forts serving an immediate need.

The purpose of early American military frontier forts was to protect settlers. These forts were typically stockades with blockhouses such as those built by General "Mad" Anthony Wayne—Forts Washington, Recovery, and Defiance in Ohio, and Wayne in Indiana.

Pioneers built civilian community forts on the frontier for mutual protection. Fending for themselves, these settlers built stockades with blockhouses. Two famous civilian community forts are Boonesborough, Kentucky, founded by Daniel Boone, and Fort Nashborough, Tennessee, named for Revolutionary War hero Francis Nash, which grew into modern Nashville.

House forts were prevalent on the early frontier. The fort could be a log cabin or a stone farmhouse, modified with loopholes for firing positions and stocked with supplies necessary for defense, where people knew they could gather in times of attack. One such house fort was the Hagenbuch Farmstead in Pennsylvania, which during the French and Indian War was used as a place of refuge for neighbors and to garrison troops.

Commercial trading posts were used to trade with Indian tribes for furs and hides. These forts, such as Fort Union, North Dakota, ranged far ahead of any military or other civilian forts. These usually had stockades and blockhouses to protect the traders and the trade goods. Many commercial trading forts were located along the Mississippi and Missouri rivers—the frontier's superhighways that were used as conduits for trade goods sent upriver and for hides and furs that floated back down.

During periods of conflict, people used any structure they could find to fortify when attack was imminent. Probably the most famous structure that was not a fort but that defenders used as a fortification was the Alamo mission building in San Antonio, Texas, during the Texas Revolution in 1836. The compound was a poor choice as a defensive position, as witnessed by its recurring capture by assaulting forces.

Finally, people built temporary forts to use for a short duration, such as Fort Mandan, North Dakota, and Fort Clatsop, Oregon, which Meriwether Lewis and William Clark's Corps of Discovery used for shelter and protection during the winter and then abandoned. Temporary forts could be anything thrown together to withstand attack, such as circled wagons or even plowed-up sod, as was the case of Fort Dilts in western North Dakota in 1864.

As the nation pushed past the eastern woodlands and into the trans-Mississippi region, the army built forts along what was called the permanent Indian frontier. These forts stretched along a line north to south—Fort Snelling, Minnesota; Fort Leavenworth, Kansas; and Fort Smith, Arkansas. As emigrants began traveling west along the California and Oregon trails, they needed protection and assistance. The government built Fort Kearny in what became Nebraska and acquired commercial forts such as Fort Laramie and Fort Bridger in today's Wyoming; Fort Hall, in present Idaho; and Fort Vancouver in what became Washington.

After the Mexican-American War and the settlement with Great Britain on the Oregon Territory boundary, the United States achieved its manifest destiny by acquiring a vast new territory extending to the Pacific Ocean. The permanent Indian boundary vanished. The nation had communities, rural populations, and travelers in Texas, the Southwest, California, and Oregon to protect from hostile Indian tribes. This meant retaining some of the original Mexican presidios and building new forts, such as Fort Union in present-day New Mexico near the end of the Santa Fe Trail. The army established additional forts to protect the country's borders and to prevent Apache and Navajo marauders from raiding into Mexico.

The army constructed forts out of local materials, adapting to the climate and terrain. Early American forts were constructed of wood and stone, but as the frontier advanced across the plains, wood became scare. In some areas, especially the Southwest, the army constructed forts out of mud or adobe bricks. The selection of relatively weak building materials signaled a recognition that the army was concerned with defense against lightly armed Indians or marauders, not well-equipped European-style armies. The cannon-ball-deflecting Vaubanesque geometric posts and reinforced brick and stone casemates familiar in the East are not found in the American West. The army selected fort locations based on what it needed to protect, the best defensive position, and a good supply of fresh water, hay for animals, and wood for fuel.

As the army built forts, local economies developed near them. Ranchers and farmers provided crops, cattle, and horses to the army. Entrepreneurs sold luxury items and provided entertainment.

Although guerrilla warfare had raged for years in Bleeding Kansas, in April 1861 Confederate forces attacked Fort Sumter, South Carolina, beginning the Civil War. Union and Confederate armies struggled for control of the West from Missouri to the Southwest. Forts throughout the western states and territories were built and changed hands depending on the fortunes of war.

After the Civil War, most new forts were built to hem in the Indian tribes, keeping them from new settlements, farms, and ranchlands. The army was now building forts without blockhouses and outer walls except for isolated posts in hostile Indian Territory, such as Fort Phil Kearny along the Bozeman Trail in Wyoming. The reason for forgoing walls was that the military believed that the posts were so strong that the Indians could not afford to make massed assaults on them. So to save on funds, the army built wall-less forts. The hollowness of this concept was exposed when in 1864 a few warriors rode through the parade ground of Fort Laramie and stole the mounts of a returning patrol while the officer in charge of that parade was reporting the absence of Indians for 10 miles (16 km) around the fort.

The typical fort of the post–Civil War era was laid out around a parade ground, at the center of which was a flagpole with the American flag at the top. Officers' quarters, enlisted men's barracks, hospital, and offices lined the edges of the parade ground. Small communities tended to grow around the fort, providing additional warning of approaching danger.

Officers and, in some cases, enlisted men brought along their wives and children. There were schools for children, and the women engaged in social get-togethers. The soldiers and their wives broke the monotony and daily drill of the post with parties, theatricals, dances, games, and parades. Other forts could be dull affairs where no action was taking place. The men became depressed during their isolation, especially during the heat of summer and the cold of winter.

Forts such as Fort Robinson, Nebraska, and Fort Yates, North Dakota, were built to monitor the Indians on their reservations, keep them from moving off, and prevent the entry of white squatters and desperados onto the reservations. Thousands of places in the West were temporarily fortified by the military. Telegraph and stage stations often were surrounded by well-placed rifle pits. Short-term camps to accommodate surveys, patrols, wagon trains, observation, resource gathering, and heliograph stations often had temporary fortifications around them. Important river fords and ferries had their defensibility improved at a time of crisis.

As railroads advanced into the West, they made it faster, easier, and less expensive to move troops and matériel to areas where they were most needed when hostilities arose. The railroads reduced the number of forts needed, and many were closed.

Today, the military still uses some of the old forts such as Forts Leavenworth and Riley in Kansas and Fort Meade in South Dakota, where the fort's band first played the "Star Spangled Banner" each evening at retreat before it became the national anthem. Other forts—such as Fort Robinson in Nebraska, Fort Larned in Kansas, and Fort Laramie in Wyoming—have become historical sites open to the public, while others, such as Fort Sully, South Dakota, have vanished.

Bill Markley

See also: Alamo, The; Bent's Fort; Boonesborough, Kentucky; Bozeman Trail; Fort Bridger; Fort Clatsop; Fort Dilts; Fort Hall; Fort Kearny (Nebraska); Fort Laramie; Fort Leavenworth; Fort Mandan; Fort Phil Kearny (Wyoming); Fort Robinson; Fort Snelling; Fort Union (New Mexico); Fort Union (North Dakota); Fort Vancouver; Nashville.

Further Reading

Downey, Fairfax. *Indian-Fighting Army.* New York: Bantam Books, 1963.

Frazer, Robert W. *Forts of the West: Military Forts and Presidios and Posts Commonly Called Forts West of the Mississippi River to 1898.* Norman: University of Oklahoma Press, 1972.

Robertson, R.G. *Competitive Struggle: America's Western Fur Trading Posts, 1764–1865.* Boise: Tamarack Books, 1999.

Robinson, Willard B. *American Forts: Architectural Form and Function.* Urbana: University of Illinois Press, 1977.

Schuler, Harold H. *Fort Sully: Guns at Sunset.* Vermillion: University of South Dakota Press, 1992.

Utley, Robert M. *Frontiersmen in Blue: The United States Army and the Indian, 1848–1865.* Lincoln: University of Nebraska Press, 1981.

Waddell, Louis M., and Bruce D. Bomberger. *The French and Indian War in Pennsylvania, 1753–1763: Fortification and Struggle During the War for Empire.* Harrisburg: Pennsylvania Historical and Museum Commission, 1996.

Forty-Niners

The discovery of gold on the South Fork of the American River in California on January 24, 1848, ignited what historians have called the largest voluntary migration in human history, the California gold rush. The *California Star* published the news on April 1, and when copies of the newspaper reached New York in August, the first outbreaks of gold fever began to spread. After the U.S. War Department put a tea caddy containing more than 14 pounds (6 kg) of California gold on display in Washington, DC, the infection became an international mania. One contemporary, John Berry Hill, recalled that gold fever was as terrible as the itch and that if one caught it, neither fire nor grease would cure it.

The rush quickly became a worldwide phenomenon, luring miners from South America, Hawaii, China, Australia, and Europe. By January 1, 1849, every ship passage from New York to the West Coast was sold out for months. About 16,000 so-called Argonauts rounded Cape Horn in 1849, while 4,624 hardy souls sailed to Panama, crossed the isthmus to the Pacific, and then competed to buy a ship's ticket to San Francisco. The demand for quick passages led to the development of extreme clipper ships such as the *Flying Cloud*, which sailed from New York to San Francisco in eighty-nine days, setting a record that stood for 140 years. In April some 50,000 gold seekers began departing Iowa, Missouri, Arkansas, and Texas for their personal El Dorado in wagons and on mule-back. Most headed up the Platte River, and by July 4 gold seekers were scattered along the trail from Chimney Rock to Thousand Springs, near present-day Wells, Nevada.

The rush across the plains began as a race against time and ended as a struggle for survival. Seven men reached the Dry Diggings (now Placerville, California) on July 21, and G.W. Paul brought the first wagons to Sutter's Fort a few days later. As many as 35,000 Americans crossed South Pass in 1849. This enormous surge in migration stripped the trails of forage and littered the wagon road with thousands of dead oxen and mules. Indians did little to bother the vast throng, but cholera swept through the unsanitary camps on the Platte River, killing hundreds, if not thousands. The crowd ignited a burst of trail exploration that led to the opening of a wagon road from Salt Lake to Los Angeles (and Death Valley), the creation of the Hudspeth Cutoff between Soda Springs and the Raft River, and a brief revival in the use of the Hastings Cutoff (made infamous by the Donner Party tragedy of 1846). Many desperate forty-niners among the rearguard of the golden horde left the established road down the Humboldt River on an alleged shortcut, Lassen's Cutoff, which turned out to be 200 arduous miles (320 km) longer than the traveled road. Fearing disaster, military governor Persifer Smith spent $100,000 to rescue the last families on the trail. By November most emigrants had reached the mines.

By 1854 the population of California had swelled to more than 300,000. The California gold rush created the pattern repeated after later mineral strikes in Australia, Nevada, Colorado, Idaho, and Montana.

Will Bagley

See also: California Trail; Donner Party; South Pass; Sutter's Fort.

Further Reading

Holliday, J.S. *Rush for Riches: Gold Fever and the Making of California*. Oakland and Berkeley: Oakland Museum of California and University of California Press, 1999.

Rohrbough, Malcolm J. *Days of Gold: The California Gold Rush and the American Nation*. Berkeley: University of California Press, 1997.

Fraser, Simon (1776–1862)

Fur trader and explorer Simon Fraser made an intrepid exploration of the great 870-mile (1,400-km) long river that bears his name and charted much of what became the Canadian province of British Columbia while employed by the North West Company (NWC), the fur-trading enterprise headquartered in Montreal.

Born in 1776, in Mapletown, New York, Fraser came from Scottish Highlander stock. His father was a British army captain who was taken prisoner by the American forces at Saratoga and died in an Albany jail. Fraser's mother moved to Montreal with her children in 1784 and after rudimentary schooling, Simon, whose uncles were in the fur trade, was apprenticed to the NWC when he was sixteen. For some years he worked for the company in its Athabaska department, along the huge lake that straddles northern Alberta and Saskatchewan provinces. He was raised to a full partnership in the NWC in 1805 and given responsibility for all the company's operations west of the Rocky Mountains.

Between 1789 and 1793, Alexander Mackenzie (1764–1820) of the NWC traversed Canada from Montreal and, with a party of voyageurs, succeeded in crossing the Canadian Rockies to the Pacific Ocean in the first recorded transcontinental crossing of North America north of Mexico by a European. In the autumn of 1805, Simon Fraser picked up where Mackenzie left off, exploring and setting up fur trade posts on the Peace, Parsnip, and Pack rivers, and in 1808 on the river later named after him in today's south-central British Columbia. The descent of the Fraser River became one of the most harrowing explorations in North American history, with Fraser and his party of twenty-four men encountering hostile natives, switchbacks and canoe-wrecking rapids, long and laborious portages, and the near-mutiny of the crew. This expedition, along with Fraser's other explorations, led to the eventual setting of Canada's boundary with the United States at the 49th parallel, and to the first European settlement in what became British Columbia.

Fraser was reassigned to the Athabaska area of the NWC in 1809 and for five years was in charge of the Mackenzie River district, then was dispatched to the Red River area of Manitoba. There he was briefly caught up in the conflict between the Nor'westers of the NWC and the Hudson's Bay Company's Red River Colony. Fraser, as an NWC partner, was arrested and transported to Montreal, where he was quickly released.

He retired from the company in 1818 and settled on 240 acres (100 ha) of farmland he had purchased earlier near Cornwall, Ontario, on the banks of the St. Lawrence River. He married in 1820, fathered five sons and three daughters, and in 1837 served as a militia officer in the 1837 Canadian rebellions against Catholic exclusion and mass immigrations into Canada from the United States, among other grievances.

Fraser died on August 18, 1862, on his farm, the last surviving partner of the NWC. Catherine Macdonell Fraser, his wife of forty-two years, died the next day and is buried with him in the Catholic Cemetery near his home. In 1965 Fraser's life was commemorated in the opening of Simon Fraser University in Vancouver, British Columbia.

Dale L. Walker

See also: North West Company.

Further Reading

Hume, Stephen. *Simon Fraser: In Search of Modern British Columbia*. Madeira Park, BC: Harbour, 2008.

Lamb, W. Kaye. *The Letters and Journals of Simon Fraser, 1806–1808*. Toronto: Macmillan Company of Canada, 1960.

Fredonian Rebellion

The Fredonian Rebellion of 1826–1827 was a significant conflict in a series of difficulties between Anglo-American settlers of Texas and Mexican officials. The rebellion's principal player, Haden Edwards, was born in 1771 in Virginia, the son of a wealthy land speculator who became a U.S. senator. Inspired by Moses and Stephen F. Austin, Edwards traveled to Mexico City in 1823 to obtain a colonization contract in Texas.

Two years later, Edwards was appointed *empresario* of a 100-square-mile (250-sq km) region surrounding Nacogdoches in Texas—*empresario* being a title issued by the Mexican government to individuals who brought in new settlers in exchange for land grants. His contract called for him to settle 800 families, but he was required to honor the land grants of early settlers. Nacogdoches was the oldest community in Texas, and numerous established settlers were angered when Edwards decreed that all residents must produce titles to their grants and pay substantial land fees. Ignoring growing unrest, in December 1835 Edwards certified the election of his son-in-law as *alcalde*, or mayor, of Nacogdoches. The young man represented new emigrants who did not yet own land titles, and old settlers were convinced that his election was fraudulent.

The older residents protested to Mexican officials in San Antonio, and in March of 1826 the election results were reversed. When word of the conflict reached Mexico City, the Edwards *empresario* contract was nullified. Edwards, who already had invested heavily in his Texas enterprise, resorted to extreme measures. In November 1826, he sent three-dozen armed men to arrest the commander of the small Mexican garrison in Nacogdoches, along with other officials. A semblance of a trial convicted these prisoners of corruption and oppression, and decreed their removal from office. When word of the illegal proceedings reached San Antonio, a force of 130 government *soldados* (soldiers) was ordered to Nacogdoches. The most prominent *empresario*, Stephen F. Austin, expressed his opposition to Edwards and urged his own colonists not to support the rebels.

On December 21, 1826, Edwards, his brother Benjamin, and others signed a declaration of independence from Mexico. The declaration proclaimed the Republic of Fredonia, stretching from the Sabine River to the Rio Grande. On January 4, 1827, the Fredonian rebels successfully defended the Old Stone Fort in Nacogdoches from an attack by local opponents. Hoping to acquire allies, Edwards arranged a treaty with neighboring Cherokee Indians, promising to give them the northern portion of the Fredonian Republic. In the end, however, little support was forthcoming for the rebellion and by late January the column from San Antonio, reinforced by Austin and a company of his settlers, advanced on Nacogdoches. On January 28, Edwards and his small band of rebels fled to Louisiana, and the Fredonian Rebellion sputtered to an inglorious end.

Although Austin and other Anglos had opposed the Fredonian Rebellion, the specter of revolution alarmed Mexican officials. Their alarm was increased by a subsequent inspection of Texas, resulting in an 1830 law designed to halt further Anglo immigration. By then, however, the tide of immigration was inexorable, and attempted restrictions against Anglos only led to a series of conflicts and, in 1835, to revolution.

Bill O'Neal

See also: Austin, Stephen F.; Empresario System; Texas Revolution and Independence.

Further Reading
McDonald, Archie P. "Fredonian Rebellion." *New Handbook of Texas*. Vol. 2. Austin: Texas State Historical Association, 1996.
———. *Nacogdoches, Texas, A Pictorial History*. Virginia Beach, VA: Donning, 1996.

Frémont, John C. (1813–1890)

Among the most audacious personalities in western American history, John Charles Frémont has fascinated both biographers and fiction writers for over a century. His explorations of the Rocky Mountains and Great Plains, his role in the Bear Flag revolt and subsequent conquest of California, his controversial Civil War career, and his clandestine marriage to the teenage daughter of a powerful U.S. senator form a genuine historical romance of nineteenth-century America.

The son of a French adventurer's liaison with the daughter of an eminent Virginia family, Frémont was born in 1813, in Savannah, Georgia, and then moved with his unmarried parents to Nashville, Tennessee, and after his father's death in 1818, to Charleston, South Carolina. At age fifteen he enrolled in Charleston College, but was expelled just a few months prior to graduation. (Some years later he appealed for and was awarded a bachelor's degree from the college.)

In 1833 Frémont met the eminent Charleston native Joel Poinsett—physician, botanist, former minister to Mexico, and future secretary of war. Poinsett used his influence to find a position for Frémont as a mathematics instructor on the U.S. warship *Natchez*, bound for South America. During 1836 Frémont served as surveyor on a railroad route through Ohio, Kentucky, and Tennessee; two years later Poinsett again assisted him in obtaining an appointment as second lieutenant in the army's topographical engineers. The commission enabled Frémont to accompany French explorer Joseph N. Nicollet on a mapping journey to the Dakota and Minnesota territories and another to the Rocky Mountains in 1842, in which Frémont succeeded to command when Nicollet fell ill.

Between these assignments Frémont met Senator Thomas Hart Benton of Missouri, a tireless exponent of western exploration and expansion. Young Frémont fell

John C. Frémont gained prominence as a western explorer in the 1840s, helped conquer California in the Mexican-American War, ran for president as a Republican in 1856, and briefly commanded the Union's Department of the West in the Civil War. *(Kean Collection/Getty Images)*

in love with Benton's daughter Jessie, barely seventeen years old, and despite the eleven-year age difference the couple eloped and married on October 19, 1841. Eventually, with his beloved daughter's persuasion, the senator's ire subsided and his son-in-law was welcomed into the family.

The 1842 exploration of the North Platte River and the South Pass of the Rocky Mountains included among its twenty-one members the veteran mountain man Christopher "Kit" Carson, who became the explorer's trusted guide and lieutenant who would contribute markedly to Frémont's reputation as the "Pathfinder."

The second expedition, in 1843, revisited the South Pass and then turned southeast toward the Great Salt Lake, proceeded on to Fort Hall on the Snake River, and crossed into the Oregon country in mid-October. From Fort Boise Frémont headed his party south to Alta California despite strained relations between Mexico and the United States. After leading his party

into the Sacramento Valley and Sutter's Fort in March 1844, Frémont returned overland to Washington, DC, arriving there in August to spend seven months dictating his account of the expedition to Jessie.

In November 1845, Frémont once again arrived at Sutter's Fort, now with sixty-two men, ostensibly to map the Sierra Nevada foothills and the Oregon Trail. In May 1846, after Mexican authorities ordered him to leave the province, he received messages believed to be from the U.S. secretary of state and Senator Benton informing him that war with Mexico was imminent. From his participation in the brief "Bear Flag" uprising by Sacramento Valley settlers in June until the Mexican surrender of Alta California on January 13, 1847, Frémont was at the forefront of the far western theater of the Mexican-American War. His imperious nature was an irritant to his superiors such as Brigadier General Stephen Watts Kearny, commander of all American military forces in California. As a result of confrontations with this old-school general, Frémont was court-martialed at Fort Leavenworth on charges of mutiny, disobedience of orders, and conduct prejudicial to order. After the trial he was allowed to resign his commission.

In 1848 the Frémonts settled near San Francisco Bay. The Pathfinder made a fortune in the California gold rush, built a lavish estate in Monterey, and, following California statehood in 1850, served briefly in Washington as a senator. His exploration career ended tragically during the winter of 1848–1849 when he led a party to locate a railroad route through the central Rockies, this time lacking Kit Carson who was by then farming near Taos, New Mexico Territory. In the San Juan Mountains of southern Colorado, 10 of his 33 men and all of his 120 pack mules died from starvation and exposure.

Frémont was nominated as the first Republican candidate for the presidency of the United States in 1856, but did not actively participate in the campaign and lost the election to James Buchanan by about a half-million popular votes out of the over 3 million cast. During the Civil War, his importance to the Republican Party resulted in his appointment as a political general. He served as a major general in command of the new Department of the West, but was removed by President Abraham Lincoln after suffering military losses, including the Battle of Wilson's Creek in August of 1861. General Frémont's unauthorized proclamation at the end of August ordering all Missouri slaves to be freed also angered the president. The order preceded Lincoln's Emancipation Proclamation by more than a year.

Despite these setbacks, in March 1862 the Pathfinder was named head of the army's new Mountain

Department, serving in western Virginia. This last chance at military glory failed, and after suffering a string of battle losses against Thomas "Stonewall" Jackson during the Shenandoah Valley Campaign, Frémont resigned from the army.

In postwar years Frémont returned to California and involved himself and his fortune in mining, railroad promotion, and other enterprises that proved financially disastrous. In 1878 political cronies orchestrated his appointment as territorial governor of Arizona, primarily to relieve his poverty, but he resigned in 1883 and for some years thereafter the Frémonts were dependent upon Jessie's publication earnings. He died of peritonitis in a Manhattan rooming house on July 13, 1890, and is buried in the Rockland County Cemetery in Sparkill, New York.

Jessie Benton was a student in a girl's seminary when she met and fell in love with Lieutenant John C. Frémont, eleven years her senior. Self-confidant, intellectual, politically shrewd, and a brilliant writer, she collaborated with her husband in writing the best-selling books and articles on the explorations that made him famous, and she wrote much of his *Memoirs of My Life*, published in 1886. She survived her husband by twelve years, dying on December 27, 1902, in Los Angeles.

Dale L. Walker

See also: Bear Flag Revolt; Benton, Thomas Hart; California, Conquest of; Carson, Kit; Elections, Presidential; Manifest Destiny; Mexican-American War.

Further Reading:

Chaffin, Tom. *Pathfinder: John Charles Frémont and the Course of American Empire*. New York: Hill & Wang, 2004.

Denton, Sally. *Passion and Principle: John and Jessie Frémont, the Couple Whose Power, Politics, and Love Shaped Nineteenth-Century America*. New York: Bloomsbury USA, 2007.

Frémont, John C., and Jessie Benton Frémont. *Memoirs of My Life*. Chicago: Belford, Clarke & Co., 1886; various reprint editions.

Roberts, David. *A Newer World: Kit Carson, John C. Frémont, and the Claiming of the American West*. New York: Simon & Schuster, 2001.

Frontier Theory

In 1890 the director of the U.S. Census Bureau declared that unsettled regions of the country were so interspersed with pockets of habitation that a clear frontier line no longer existed. The realization of that event has been hailed by historians ever since to signify and define the closing of the American frontier and the end of the nation's westward expansion. The movement lasted nearly 300 years and spanned the North American continent from the Atlantic Ocean to the shores of the Pacific.

Three years after the above pronouncement, Frederick Jackson Turner (1861–1932), a professor of history at the University of Wisconsin, read a paper titled "The Significance of the Frontier in American History" before members of the American Historical Association at Chicago. His recitation signaled the genesis of an important hypothesis known as the "frontier theory" in American history. More than a century after Turner's presentation, the theory, although argued by some authorities, is still accepted today, with varying degrees of modification, by a large segment of American historians.

The theory postulates that the rise and success of the United States were direct results of the frontier experience of hundreds of thousands of migrating people and the hardships they endured over decades of ever-westward expansion. It posits that American democracy, society, and politics have all been tempered by the pushing westward of the frontier. "Social evolution," as Turner called it, was the result of the fortitude of miners, homesteaders, trappers and traders, and a host of other migrants—all of them facing extreme hardships caused by nature, geography, and conflict with newly confronted natives. "To the frontier the American intellect owes its striking characteristics," Turner wrote, adding that it was due to that "coarseness and strength combined with acuteness and inquisitiveness; that practical, inventive turn of mind, quick to find expedients; that masterful grasp of material things, lacking in the artistic but powerful to effect great ends; that restless, nervous energy" that the "composite nationality" of Americans was formed.

Although the evolution of the American character was Turner's raison d'être for developing the frontier theory, it is interesting to note that other historians have applied the theory to the national characteristics of other large, one-time wilderness regions of the world: Brazil, Australia, and Russia.

James A. Crutchfield

Further Reading

Billington, Ray Allen. *America's Frontier Heritage*. Albuquerque: University of New Mexico Press, 1993.

Turner, Frederick Jackson. "The Significance of the Frontier in American History." In *Annual Report*, American Historical Association. Washington, DC: Government Printing Office, 1894.

G

Gadsden Purchase (1853)

At the end of the Mexican-American War in 1848, the Treaty of Guadalupe Hidalgo stipulated that Mexico cede two-fifths of its territory to the United States. The 200,000 square miles (518,000 sq km) of land the United States thus acquired included most of present-day California, Utah, Nevada, Arizona, and New Mexico. A strip of the vast land lying south of the Gila River in what is now Arizona and New Mexico soon became prime real estate, although it remained under Mexican ownership and the control of marauding bands of Indians.

With a desire to build a southern railroad connection between California and Texas, Secretary of War Jefferson Davis, future president of the Confederate States of America, in 1852 sent James Gadsden to Mexico City to negotiate the purchase of that strip of land. Gadsden, himself in partnership with a group of investors and railroad builders, was happy to comply in his official capacity as U.S. minister to Mexico. When the deal was struck in 1853 with Mexican dictator Antonio López de Santa Anna, the United States agreed to pay Mexico $10 million for 45,535 square miles (117,900 sq km) of land. The 30-million-acre (12.1-million-ha) territory, roughly the size of the state of Pennsylvania, would cost the United States only 53 cents an acre. The area agreed upon lay west of the Rio Grande, south of the Gila River, and east of the Colorado River. Congress ratified the Gadsden Purchase, known in Mexico as the Treaty of La Mesilla, in 1854 but reduced the purchase price to $7 million, or 33 cents an acre. The purchase was unpopular on both sides of the border.

Opposition to the sale was so strong in Mexico that Santa Anna was overthrown and forced into exile in 1855 for his part in the transaction and for squandering the money received. Gadsden was removed from his position as minister in 1856, more for meddling in Mexican politics and affairs of state than for the deal he had brokered. Many in the United States thought that the price paid was excessive for such a desolate parcel, but reconciled the expense against all of the territory that had been acquired in the Treaty of Guadalupe Hidalgo four years earlier.

The Gadsden Purchase was one of the last major land acquisitions the United States undertook on the North American continent. The deal helped establish a new and permanent boundary between the southwestern United States and northern Mexico, which remained an inhospitable territory for many years. By 1877 the Southern Pacific Railroad tracks stretched to Arizona from California. Not until 1883, however, was the line coming from Texas linked with the Southern Pacific. Once completed, the railroad extended from New Orleans to Los Angeles and provided a southern route of commerce and transportation across the desert Southwest.

Rod Timanus

See also: Central Pacific Railroad; Davis, Jefferson; Santa Anna, Antonio López de.

Further Reading

Ambrose, Stephen E. *Nothing Like It in the World*. New York: Simon & Schuster, 2001.
Devine, David. *Slavery, Scandal, and Steel Rails*. Bloomington, IN: iUniverse, 2004.
Wheeler, Keith *The Railroaders*. Alexandria, VA: Time-Life Books, 1985.

Gall (c. 1840–1894)

Hunkpapa war chief, adopted son of Sitting Bull, and pivotal figure in the Battle of the Little Bighorn, Gall was born about 1840 in a Lakota village on the Moreau

River in present-day South Dakota. Lakota tradition states that his mother named him Pizi (gall) after witnessing him eating the gall bladder of a freshly killed buffalo. Others maintain the name derived from his bitter nature.

At an early age he became a skilled horseback fighter against such Lakota enemies as Crows, Assiniboines, and the Salish people of the Bitterroot Valley of southwestern Montana; as an adult he fought the U.S. Army and civilian whites. He rode with Sitting Bull and 1,600 Sioux in the Battle of Killdeer Mountain, Dakota Territory, on July 28–29, 1864, against a force of 3,000 Union soldiers under Brigadier General Alfred Sully. Among his significant fights before the Custer battle, he joined Sitting Bull in 1872 and 1873 in derailing plans by the Northern Pacific Railroad to build its transcontinental railroad through Yellowstone Valley. The two Hunkpapa chiefs attacked the soldier-escorts of Northern Pacific's surveyors and succeeded in delaying the railroad's plans for six years.

Gall and Sitting Bull were among the Lakotas who refused to attend the Fort Laramie Treaty signing in the spring of 1868, which set aside the Black Hills as the exclusive domain of the Great Sioux Reservation. Gall did lead a small delegation to Fort Rice in Dakota Territory where he eloquently denounced the treaty, then changed his mind and endorsed it. In an 1869 gathering of Sioux chiefs on the Rosebud River he again, and finally, rejected the treaty, thereafter becoming a war chief among "nontreaty" Indians under Sitting Bull and Crazy Horse of the Oglalas.

The treaty provisions began unraveling in 1872 with white encroachments into the treaty-protected territory, and in 1874 when Lieutenant Colonel George A. Custer brought an expedition into the Black Hills and effectively opened the area to gold miners. Army troops were dispatched to protect the miners from attacks by "hostiles"—the Sioux who regarded the lands as sacred hunting grounds, precisely as the Fort Laramie Treaty stated—and this trespassing raised the curtain on the Little Bighorn fight of June 25, 1876, in which Gall played a prominent role.

Sitting Bull and Gall's Hunkpapa village was among the first to be struck by Major Marcus Reno's 7th Cavalry troops, during which two of Gall's wives and four of his children were killed, reputedly by Reno's Arikara scouts. Upon finding the bodies of his family, Gall vowed to kill his newfound enemies with the hatchet. He led his Hunkpapa horsemen in driving Reno's battalion from the Lakota camp and sweeping north to join Crazy Horse's force in the attack on Custer's remnant.

After the battle Gall accompanied Sitting Bull into exile in Saskatchewan, but in January 1881, he surrendered to the United States army and settled on the Standing Rock reservation in Dakota Territory where he became a farmer, a judge on the reservation's Court of Indian Offenses, preached assimilation with the whites, and was baptized as Abraham Gall into the Episcopal Church. He died peacefully on December 5, 1894.

Dale L. Walker

See also: Black Hills Expeditions; Custer, George Armstrong; Lakota; Sitting Bull.

Further Reading

Greene, Jerome A., ed. *Lakota and Cheyenne: Indian Views of the Great Sioux War, 1876–1877.* Norman: University of Oklahoma Press, 2000.

Larson, Robert W. *Gall: Lakota War Chief.* Norman: University of Oklahoma Press, 2007.

Utley, Robert M. *The Lance and the Shield: The Life and Times of Sitting Bull.* New York: Henry Holt, 1993.

Garrard, Hector Lewis (1829–1887)

Hector Lewis Garrard's name is indelibly linked with the American West through the publication of his colorful book documenting a journey to the southwestern part of the country during 1846–1847.

Born in Cincinnati, Ohio, on June 15, 1829, Garrard's first brush with the West was revelatory. Upon reading Colonel John C. Frémont's report of his 1842–1843 foray into the Rocky Mountains, Garrard, with his parents' blessing, left home for Taos, New Mexico, by means of the Santa Fe Trail. It was July 1846, and the United States was at war with Mexico, the fight spilling over into what would become Garrard's western base, Bent's Fort (alternately referred to as Fort William), located along the Arkansas River in present-day southeastern Colorado.

Established in 1832, this adobe fortress was the Gibraltar of the American Southwest, a bustling hub employing 100 men. Trade in beaver furs and buffalo robes was brisk and Indians were omnipresent. William Bent—the fort's manager and cofounder along with his brother, Charles—was married to a Cheyenne Indian woman and many of her kinsmen, along with their Arapaho allies, pitched their tepees nearby. Here Garrard met a host of notables, including Cerán St. Vrain, Christopher "Kit" Carson, and Jim Beckwourth, recording their tales and his reflections. Twice he encountered another romantic wayfarer, George Frederick Ruxton, whose books would be compared to his own; both men were observant, young, enthusiastic, and possessed a keen ear for dialect.

Adopting mountain ways, Garrard feasted on stewed dog and buffalo hump-meat, tongue, and intestines, and wore fringed buckskins, leggings, and a loincloth. At Fort Mann he battled Comanches, thinking that a genuine Indian raid made his western sabbatical more complete. He deeply respected the close brotherhood of the mountain men, although many of them were willing to kill and scalp with impunity. He relished their company and camaraderie, preserving images of their half-Indian dress and odd speech. On February 4, 1847, he witnessed frontier justice—the mass hanging of six Pueblo and Mexican conspirators of the Taos Revolt, a bloody affair in which twenty Americans (including Charles Bent) were slain, their bodies mutilated. Garrard's telling of the trial and the grim aftermath of the swaying, wildly convulsing bodies, suspended and tethered neck-first to lariats, is the only first-hand account of the episode.

After ten months of mountain life, Garrard returned to Ohio and in 1850 published his colorful memoirs, *Wah-to-yah and the Taos Trail* (Wah-to-yah, "The Breasts of the World," were the Spanish Peaks, twin pinnacles located in the Rocky Mountains' southern range near Bent's Fort). Garrard became involved in banking and land speculation, journeyed to Minnesota where he met his wife and sired four children, wrote two other books that did not sell well, became a physician, and finally returned to Ohio. He died in Lakewood, New York, on July 7, 1887, at the age of fifty-eight.

Wah-to-yah and the Taos Trail, for some unknown reason written under the name Lewis Hector Garrard, rather than Hector Lewis Garrard, remains Garrard's legacy of westward expansion, one far too often overshadowed by Francis Parkman's more literary *Oregon Trail*.

Ted Franklin Belue

See also: Bent Brothers; Bent's Fort; Ruxton, George A.F.; Santa Fe Trail; Taos Revolt.

Further Reading

Blevins, Winfred. *Give Your Heart to the Hawks: A Tribute to the Mountain Men.* New York: Avon Books, 1973.
Crutchfield, James A. *Tragedy at Taos: The Revolt of 1847.* Plano: Republic of Texas Press, 1995.
De Voto, Bernard. *Across the Wide Missouri.* New York: Houghton Mifflin, 1947.
Garrard, Lewis H. *Wah-to-yah and the Taos Trail.* Norman: University of Oklahoma Press, 1955.

Gass, Patrick (1771–1870)

One of the Lewis and Clark Expedition's most important participants, and one of the few who left a written record of the journey, Patrick Gass was born in Falling Springs, Pennsylvania, on June 12, 1771. His family moved several times after his birth, finally settling in Catfish Camp, now known as Washington, Pennsylvania. As a young man Gass developed a love of travel and exploration that served him well throughout his life. In 1793 he joined a trading expedition to New Orleans and returned to Philadelphia via ship by way of the island of Cuba. He then became a carpenter's apprentice, a trade he pursued until 1799, when he joined the army.

For the next few years, Gass was stationed at various outposts along the American frontier in both infantry and artillery units. By 1802 he was serving in Illinois Territory at Kaskaskia, and in early 1803 volunteered to join the newly formed Lewis and Clark Expedition to explore Louisiana Territory. Over the protests of his commanding officer, and only after the intervention of Captain Meriwether Lewis himself, Gass became a member of the Corps of Discovery. One of his first tasks was to use his carpentry skills to help build living quarters at Camp DuBois on the Mississippi River opposite St. Louis, Missouri, where the expedition finished its preparations for the westward journey. Being literate, he also began to keep a daily journal.

In 1804, on the trip up the Missouri River in boats, squad leader Sergeant Charles Floyd became ill and died suddenly, the only man lost in the entire two-year journey. Gass was elected by the men to become squad leader and was promoted to the rank of sergeant. He proved to be an able and well-liked leader whose skills as a carpenter proved invaluable to the success of the expedition. He was called upon to keep the expedition boats in working order, repairing masts and plugging leaks, and also plied his craft in the construction of the two forts in which expedition members wintered. Fort Mandan, in present-day North Dakota, and Fort Clatsop, on the Pacific coast of Oregon, were both sturdy, functional collections of log structures that served as home for the expedition in the winters of 1804 and 1805.

In 1806, upon the return to St. Louis of the successful expedition, Gass mustered out of the service and returned east to Wellsburg, Virginia. Unlike many of his comrades who returned to the West as hunters and trappers, Gass seemed content to rejoin civilization. When he died on April 3, 1870, at nearly ninety-nine years of age, he had seen his expedition journal published, served in the War of 1812, and at age fifty-nine married a woman forty years his junior with whom he fathered seven children. He had witnessed the election of eighteen presidents, one of whom, James Buchanan, had been a boy when Gass had worked on his father's house as a carpenter in 1794. Gass saw the United States grow to thirty-eight states, and he outlived every other member of the Lewis and Clark Corps of Discovery.

Rod Timanus

See also: Fort Clatsop; Fort Mandan; Lewis and Clark Expedition.

Further Reading

Clarke, Charles G. *The Men of the Lewis and Clark Expedition.* Spokane, WA: Arthur H. Clark, 2001.

DeVoto, Bernard, ed. *The Journals of Lewis and Clark.* New York: Houghton Mifflin, 1981.

MacGregor, Carol Lynn, ed. *The Journals of Patrick Gass.* Missoula, MT: Mountain Press, 1997.

Geronimo (c. 1823–1909)

Controversy about Geronimo, also called Goyahkla ("One Who Yawns"), begins at birth; historians cannot agree as to the time or the place. Time ranges from the period of a great meteor shower in 1823 to June 1829. His birthplace is often listed as near present-day Silver City, New Mexico; Clifton, Arizona (No-doyohn Canyon); the headwaters of the Gila River; or Turkey Flats, both also in Arizona. Some have suggested he was born in Mexico among the Nednhis (a band of the Chiricahua Apaches). Even though he was undoubtedly a Bedonkohe (a band of the Chiricahuas), some historians believe that his father, Taklishim, son of Bedonkohe chief Mahko, might have been in Mexico for a visit to friends or relatives with his wife, Juana, who may have been a captive of the Mexicans.

In his youth, Geronimo lived in a time of relative peace, a condition not common among the Apaches. As a boy, he learned of Ussen the-Giver-of-Life, White Painted Woman, the Water Spirit, and other Apache beliefs. Taklishim, his father, taught him to hunt and told him stories of his grandfather, Mahko, and his greatness. When Geronimo was old enough, he worked his family's plot of ground, probably about 2 acres (.8 ha), cultivating corn, beans, and pumpkins.

While he was still a young boy, a party of Nednhis visited his tribe. Among them was another young boy named Juh (pronounced "Ho"). Geronimo and Juh

The Apache leader Geronimo (*seated, center left*) meets with U.S. General George Crook (*third from right*) at Canyon de los Embudos in the Sierra Madre in May 1886. Geronimo surrendered, then fled, and turned himself in again in September. (*Camillus S. Fly/Stringer/ Getty Images*)

remained friends throughout life, with the latter marrying Geronimo's favorite cousin, Ishton. Shortly after Juh's visit, Taklishim died and although he was not yet a man, Geronimo's childhood came to an end.

In 1846 Geronimo married Alope; the couple had three children. In March 1851, members of Geronimo's band were camped near Janos in Mexico. While the men were in town trading, Colonel José Maria Carrasco attacked the camp, killing or capturing most of the inhabitants. Among the dead were Geronimo's wife, children, and mother. Hatred of the Mexicans was hereafter burned in his heart.

With the help of leader Mangas Coloradas, Geronimo sought help from Cochise's Chokonen band of the Chiricahuas. When they set out to avenge the death of Geronimo's family, Cochise agreed to join, as did Juh. All were undoubtedly under the overall command of Mangas Coloradas. At Arispe in Sonora, Mexico, during the following summer, the allies stood toe-to-toe with the Mexican infantry and cavalry and, in about two hours, took possession of the battlefield. Many Apaches consider this fight their most glorious victory over the Mexicans. Geronimo may have been allowed to direct tactical movements during the battle as he had suffered most at the hands of the Mexicans. It is likely that during this battle Geronimo received the name that he made famous.

Although Geronimo was never a chief, history often considers him one. This might partially result from his long years of rebellion and because he often acted as spokesman for Juh, chief of the Nednhi, who stuttered, especially when excited. Geronimo was a medicine man and was believed to have great powers of perception and vision. His words often were sought in council.

In September 1851, Geronimo saw his first white men. West of Apache Pass, he and several of his warriors met with a survey party and communicated as well as they could without interpreters. They camped near each other and traded goods—buckskins, blankets, and ponies in exchange for shirts and provisions. The Apaches also brought the surveyors some game, which the Americans paid for with money.

When Mangas Coloradas took up arms against the Americans in 1860, Geronimo participated along with Cochise. Geronimo's fame came after the death of Cochise in 1874. The Chokonen band was removed from its reservation and relocated to the San Carlos Reservation, as were Geronimo's people. The new homeland proved unacceptable to most of the Chiricahua bands for several reasons: it was hot, dry, mosquito-laden in August, barren, relatively flat, disease-ridden, lacked game and water for productive agriculture, and was inhabited by other tribes hostile to the Chiricahuas. Plus, a shortage of rations and supplies made dissent unavoidable.

Several times in the late 1870s, Geronimo left the reservation only to be captured and returned. He divided his time between raids into Mexico and farming on the San Carlos Reservation until May 1885, when he left the reservation with thirty-five warriors and 109 other men, women, and children. On March 1, 1886, they were surrounded by federal troops. Exhausted and hopelessly outnumbered, he surrendered. On the way back to Fort Bowie, Geronimo, fearing reprisal hanging, managed to escape with Nai'che, son of Cochise, eleven warriors, and a few women and boys.

During the final campaign against Geronimo, more than 5,000 troops and 500 Indian scouts and auxiliaries were put into the field, about 20 percent of the entire U.S. Army. At a conference in Skeleton Canyon, Arizona (near the present town of Douglas), General Nelson Miles induced Geronimo to surrender once again, promising him that he would be returned to Arizona after an indefinite period of incarceration elsewhere. The promise was not kept. Geronimo was instead imprisoned in Florida and later moved to Fort Sill, Oklahoma, where he died on February 17, 1909.

Stoney Livingston

See also: Apache; Cochise (Cheis); Mangas Coloradas; Miles, Nelson A.

Further Reading

Debo, Angie. *Geronimo: The Man, His Time, His Place*. Norman: University of Oklahoma Press, 1988.

Lockwood, Frank C. *The Apache Indians*. Lincoln: University of Nebraska Press, 1987.

Roberts, David. *Once They Moved Like the Wind*. New York: Touchstone, 1993.

Ghost Dance

Although the Ghost Dance is routinely believed to have originated with Jack Wilson's teachings, the round dance, or prophet dance, can be traced back to the days before European contact with North America. Noted anthropologist James Mooney was one of the first to thoroughly study the round dance and its associative meanings. Enculturation and diffusion are two diverse explanations for common rituals among distant Indian tribes. Enculturation establishes boundaries within a society, and diffusion describes the spread of language, religions, and ideas from one culture to another, which would explain the seemingly universal practice of the round dance in various and often unrelated tribes.

The Ghost Dance, as it came to be known in the late nineteenth century, was performed first in present-day Nevada, among the Paiutes, according to the teachings of Jack Wilson. Wilson's Paiute name was Wovoka. Wilson's father died when he was fourteen, and he was taken in by David Wilson, a white rancher, who introduced the boy to the English language and Christianity.

In about 1870, a Paiute named Tävibo prophesied that the earth would swallow all the white men and that all the dead Indians would return to life and be free of the white man's rules and control. Wilson adopted Tävibo's vision, which incorporated the circle dance and stressed clean living, honesty, and living in peace with other cultures. Violence of any kind prevented salvation. There was a distinct Christian influence to the prophecy with references to a messiah, a supreme being (one God), and the promise of immortality, all of which seem counter to the events that eventually played out at the death of Sitting Bull, the tragedy at Wounded Knee, and the demise of the Ghost Dance.

At its inception, the Ghost Dance spread rapidly across the West, reaching the farthest corners of California and Oklahoma. The Ghost Dance transformed from tribe to tribe, with ingrained belief systems affecting the ritual itself. However, at the core were the belief and the hope that the white man would be wiped from the face of the earth and the old ways restored to Indian life.

One of the outgrowths of the Ghost Dance tradition was the belief that the wearing of Ghost Shirts could repel bullets. Ghost Shirts were actually vests sanctified by a prophet. The origin of the belief is uncertain, but James Mooney argued that the concept came from the Mormon endowment garment, which was believed to protect the true believer from any kind of physical harm. Chief Kicking Bear introduced the Ghost Shirt to his people, the Lakota Sioux, in 1890. The view of the Sioux was more militant than the pacifist preaching of Jack Wilson. The Lakotas introduced a new element to the Ghost Dance, the concept of a renewed earth. According to this view, all evil will be washed away from the earth, including the removal of the white man from traditional Indian lands.

It was the confluence of beliefs, fear, and anger that brought the Ghost Dance to Wounded Knee in 1890.

The U.S. government broke a treaty with the Lakota Sioux in February 1890. The Great Sioux Reservation of South Dakota was broken into five smaller reservations to make way for homesteaders from the East. The Lakotas were separated and forced to live as much like the whites as possible. The Indians were encouraged to farm and raise livestock, and they were forbidden to teach their children traditional languages or cultural beliefs. Christianity was the only acceptable religion.

The Bureau of Indian Affairs (BIA) was charged with aiding the Lakota Sioux by supplementing food and hiring whites to act as teachers for the tribe. The taskmasters, who decided to teach the Indians to farm, did not consider the difficulty of cultivating crops in the inhospitable and almost arid South Dakota region. A drought soon settled in and the crops perished in the heat. The BIA responded callously, blaming the failure of crops on "Indian laziness." With starvation serving as standard living conditions in much of the Indian nation, it was no surprise that anger turned to desperation, creating a perfect environment for Jack Wilson's message to thrive.

Kicking Bear, who had traveled previously to Nevada and sat with Wilson, brought the message of the Ghost Dance to Sitting Bull when he visited Standing Rock Reservation in October 1890. It was not long before the news of the Ghost Dance and the Ghost Shirts spread throughout the reservation. White homesteaders and the government soon became aware of the Ghost Dance religion. Most troubling was the prophecy that they would be banished from the western frontier. As panic and fear of sustained violence set in, the government felt it had no choice but to respond with a show of force.

On December 12, 1890, an arrest order for Sitting Bull was issued. Three days later, forty-three Indian police officers went to Sitting Bull's cabin to arrest him. A squadron of cavalry was not far away, set to back up the Indian police. Sitting Bull was asleep, unaware of what was about to take place. When the police entered the cabin, Sitting Bull awoke and agreed to go with them peacefully.

Outside the cabin, a large group of followers of the Ghost Dance assembled. The police were massively outnumbered. A member of the crowd fired a shot, wounding Lieutenant Bull Head, the man leading Sitting Bull out of the cabin. Bull Head returned fire and accidentally shot Sitting Bull—then another member of the Indian police shot Sitting Bull in the head. A full-scale shoot-out rang out, and several men on both sides died before the cavalry arrived to intervene.

The massacre at Wounded Knee followed almost two weeks later. One hundred fifty-three Lakota Sioux died and the Ghost Dance all but vanished. In an 1892 interview with James Mooney, Jack Wilson said he had stood before God in a vision that precipitated the introduction of the Ghost Dance religion. He believed in the vision until his death in 1932.

Larry D. Sweazy

See also: Lakota; Sioux; Sitting Bull; Wounded Knee.

Further Reading

Brown, Dee. *Bury My Heart at Wounded Knee: An Indian History of the American West.* New York: Holt, Rinehart & Winston, 1970.

Hittman, Michael. *Wovoka and the Ghost Dance.* Lincoln: University of Nebraska Press, 1998.

Mooney, James. *The Ghost Dance Religion and the Sioux Outbreak of 1890.* Lincoln: University of Nebraska Press, 1991.

Glass, Hugh (c. 1780–1833)

Neither Hugh Glass's exact birth date nor place of birth (perhaps Pennsylvania) is known. By the time he began his illustrious trapping career with the Ashley-Henry party in 1823, his associates were already calling him "Old" Glass. If anyone had reason to look "old," it surely was Glass. Before his entry into the fur trade, he had already lived through more adventures than most men do in a lifetime. He had been a captive of the notorious pirate Jean Lafitte, and operated as a brigand himself until he outwitted his captors and fled into the Texas wilderness, where he resided with the Pawnees for several years.

Glass eventually reached St. Louis, where he read William Ashley's advertisement for "one hundred men to ascend the Missouri to the Rocky Mountains." He joined the expedition, along with such soon-to-be notables as Jim Bridger and Jedediah Smith. As later events proved, Glass's "mountain man" years were even more adventuresome and dangerous than his early days as Lafitte's captive and his sojourn among the Pawnees. Surviving a skirmish with the Arikara tribe in 1823, in which he was wounded in the knee, he volunteered to go with Major Andrew Henry to the Yellowstone River to trap beaver in virgin territory. It was while he was on this foray that Glass attained immortality among his associates and future generations of fur trade historians.

While on a hunting detail for Henry, Glass was severely mauled by a grizzly bear. His condition was so serious that he was thought to have only a few hours to live. Accordingly, Henry detailed two men, John Fitzgerald and Jim Bridger, to stay with the old man until he died and to give him a proper burial. But Old Glass would not die and instead held on to life with a tenacity that caused apprehension for the two men entrusted with his care. After several days of watching the comatose Glass, Bridger and Fitzgerald, in fear of being discovered by hostile Indians, took all of their companion's possessions and left him to die alone in the wilderness.

Glass's luck came through once again, however. Through sheer willpower, he survived the ordeal and made his way—first at a crawl, then at a slow walk—across 300 miles (480 km) of wilderness to Fort Kiowa. Filled with thoughts of vengeance, Glass finally caught up with Bridger, but decided to spare the youth due to his inexperience. Meanwhile, Fitzgerald joined the U.S. Army and claimed federal protection from the angry mountain man.

Glass trapped throughout the Rocky Mountains for several more years. His ordeal with the grizzly bear had made him a living legend. In later years, he pursued his trade in the north, around Fort Union on the Missouri River, until 1833, when his old foes, the Arikara, killed him along the Yellowstone River.

James A. Crutchfield

See also: Arikara War; Bridger, Jim; Henry, Andrew.

Further Reading

Myers, John. *The Saga of Hugh Glass: Pirate, Pawnee, and Mountain Man.* Lincoln: University of Nebraska Press, 1963.

Glenn-Fowler Expedition

Hugh Glenn, who with his partner Jacob Fowler explored much of the region around the headwaters of the Arkansas River in present-day Colorado, was born on January 7, 1788, in Berkeley County, Virginia (now West Virginia). In his early twenties, Glenn moved to Cincinnati where he soon became involved in providing supplies for American troops during the War of 1812. It was during this period of his life that he met Fowler. A surveyor by profession, Jacob Fowler was well suited to being an explorer and mountain man. Born in Maryland on

March 1, 1764, he participated in several Indian skirmishes in the Old Northwest Territory, including General Arthur St. Clair's disastrous defeat in November 1791, at the hands of the Miami chief Little Turtle and his confederation of 2,000 Miami, Shawnee, Chippewa, Delaware, and Ottawa warriors. Fowler was one of the few survivors in the greatest defeat ever suffered by the U.S. military at the hands of Indians. He later served as a quartermaster with General William Henry Harrison's army during the War of 1812.

By 1821 Glenn and Fowler had joined forces and planned a trip far up the Arkansas River to trap and trade with the Indians. Their party left Fort Smith, Arkansas, in September, and for the next ten months scoured the present-day southern Great Plains and Front Range of the southern Rocky Mountains for furs. On Sunday, January 6, 1822, Fowler wrote in his journal:

> Went up to the Warm Spring Branch and soot [set] two traps but the Weather is So Cold I beleve the bever Will not Come out—duglass [George Douglas, one of Fowler's trappers] in the Evening on driving up the Horses Reports Some Buffelow In Sight the Hunters Will look for them In the morning.

Glenn and Fowler are generally credited with being the first white Americans to frequent the region around today's Pueblo, Colorado, which later became a favorite gathering place for mountain men. While exploring the upper reaches of the Arkansas, the traders learned of Mexico's recent declaration of independence from Spain and, after Glenn traveled to Taos in early 1822 to meet with Mexican officials, he sent back word that he had obtained permission to trap and hunt in the vast territory. Regrouping in New Mexico, the two men and their companions then trapped along the Rio Grande and in the far reaches of the Sangre de Cristo Mountains before departing for Missouri on June 1, 1822.

Following the expedition, Glenn participated in later ventures to the West, but his rapidly failing finances sent him back to Cincinnati, where he died on May 28, 1833. Jacob Fowler died at Covington, Kentucky, on October 15, 1849.

James A. Crutchfield

Further Reading

Fowler, Jacob. *The Journal of Jacob Fowler.* Minneapolis: Ross & Haines, 1965.

Glidden, Joseph (1813–1906)

Three men—a hardware merchant, a lumberman, and a farmer—all living in DeKalb, Illinois, came away from the 1873 county fair with visions of creating a better type of fencing material than the one they had seen demonstrated there. The farmer, Joseph Farwell Glidden, soon conceived, patented, and manufactured his version of barbed wire. It was destined to change the West and continues to be widely used into the twenty-first century.

Rails, stone walls, and hedges had been used commonly to control livestock and proclaim property lines in the East, but these materials often were scarce commodities on the Great Plains, where homesteaders converged by the thousands following the Civil War and had significant areas to enclose with fencing. These settlers were in need of a practical means of protecting croplands from damage caused by roaming herds of wild buffalo and semi-domesticated longhorns. Also searching for a better method, a few large-scale ranchers who were determined to quell livestock theft and trespassing had put up miles of expensive board fences. Family-oriented nesters, advocates of free rangelands, and profit-driven stockmen became locked in deadly conflict. The arrival of barbed wire eventually resolved many complicated issues of land and livestock management, but not without a struggle.

Born on January 18, 1813, in Charleston, New Hampshire, Glidden called his design of wire "The Winner," and patented it on October 20, 1874. Although not the first barbed wire invented, Glidden's brand became the most readily available fencing material on the market. By converting his wife's coffee mill and a hand-operated sharpening stone, he fashioned prototypical examples, and soon greater lengths were being mass-produced by twisting two No. 9 smooth wires and adding diagonally cut barbs at intervals every few inches.

Glidden eventually took the lead in barbed wire production by winning patent rights battles, forming partnerships, and promoting research and development to increase demand for his product. He sold his one-half interest in the resulting company in 1876 and the operation was moved to Worcester, Massachusetts, where it became known as Washburn and Moen Manufacturing Company. The enterprise eventually was absorbed by U.S. Steel Corporation and by 1880 its annual output was topping 80 million pounds of fencing wire.

Promotion in Texas, potentially the greatest market, was accomplished by example. Glidden and his partner, Henry Bradley Sanborn, established the Panhandle Ranch, stocked it with cattle, and built a barbed wire fence to effectively control the operation. Representing Glidden's product in his own unique way was John Warne Gates, who made bold claims about the quality of the barbed wire and who implemented an unconventional bit of salesmanship by enclosing a herd of longhorn cattle with barbed wire in downtown San Antonio. When the pen successfully held the restless cattle, local hardware merchants hurriedly purchased—and quickly sold out of—the new product that had been proved on sight to the doubting stockmen, who were now eager to try out the wire on their own ranches.

Joseph Glidden died in DeKalb, Illinois, on October 9, 1906. At the time of his death he was one of the richest men in the United States, having based his million-dollar fortune on patent royalties and profits collected from the design and sale of barbed wire.

Dan R. Manning

See also: Barbed Wire; Cattle Frontier; Open Range.

Further Reading

Clifton, Robert T. *Barbs, Prongs, Points, Prickers, and Stickers.* Norman: University of Oklahoma Press, 1970.

Lea, Tom. *The King Ranch.* 2 vols. Boston: Little, Brown, 1957.

McCallum, Henry D., and Frances T. McCallum. *The Wire That Fenced the West.* Norman: University of Oklahoma Press, 1965.

Goliad, Battle of

Following the fall of the Alamo in March 1836, General Sam Houston withdrew the Texan army he had gathered, some 500 strong, at Gonzales ahead of the advancing Mexican forces. He sent orders to Colonel James Fannin at Goliad to retreat with his 400 men to Victoria. Fannin received his orders on March 14, but delayed his departure for several days while he waited for expeditionary parties he had sent out to return or send word of their whereabouts. When he finally decided to begin his retreat, five days had elapsed, and Mexican cavalry scouts could be seen from the walls of the fort.

A heavy morning fog concealed the evacuation on March 19, but as the column of wagons and carts departed Fannin ordered that everything left behind be burned. The resulting smoke and flames alerted the nearby Mexican force, 550 men under the command of General Jose Urrea, that something was afoot. While the Mexicans mounted a pursuit, Fannin and his men moved slowly north across the open prairie toward Victoria. As the fog burned off, Fannin called a halt, after marching only 6 miles (10 km), to rest and reorganize.

When the march resumed, Fannin's small detachment of cavalry scouted ahead, reaching the tree-lined Coleto Creek without encountering any enemy activity. But the Mexican cavalry was closing in from the south and came within sight of the column after it had moved only a few more miles. Coleto Creek was only one mile (1.6 km) away and, although his officers urged him to seek the safety of the trees and the water supply there, Fannin ordered the wagons to be formed into a large square with cannons set up at each corner to repel the Mexican attack. The Mexican cavalry encircled Fannin's position, dismounted, and attacked on foot. Though they suffered heavy losses, the attackers succeeded in pinning down their quarry until the slower-moving Mexican infantry arrived and began to take up positions. Fannin's cavalry, safely under cover of the trees by Coleto Creek, made no attempt to rejoin the command and simply rode away.

As the afternoon wore on, Fannin's troops repulsed several bayonet charges by the Mexican infantry and cavalry charges by the Mexican lancers. But the Texans, especially the wounded, suffered terribly under the broiling sun without water to quench their thirst. Fannin was wounded in the leg, but continued to command vigorously. Nightfall brought an end to the day's hostilities, but the Mexican artillery arrived after dark and was soon in place. A few artillery barrages the next morning convinced Fannin that his position was too exposed and hopeless, so when Urrea offered to accept his surrender he complied. His troops were disarmed and marched back to Goliad.

On March 27, 1836, Fannin and more than 300 of his men were executed by the Mexican army in and around Goliad. The bloody slaughter provided a rallying cry for angry Texans everywhere, and the call to arms "Remember Goliad!" joined "Remember the Alamo!" whenever patriots gathered.

Rod Timanus

See also: Alamo, The; Fannin, James Walker; Texas Revolution and Independence.

Further Reading
Hardin, Stephen L. *Texian Iliad.* Austin: University of Texas Press, 1994.
Hopewell, Clifford. *Remember Goliad: Their Silent Tents.* Waco, TX: Eakin Press, 1998.

"Gone to Texas"

Beginning in the mid-1830s, the phrase "Gone to Texas," usually abbreviated as GTT, was used by Americans immigrating to Texas to begin a new life.

Mexico had declared its independence from Spain in 1821. The new country included today's Texas, New Mexico, Arizona, Nevada, California, and large parts of Colorado, Utah, and Wyoming. Texas particularly presented a major concern to Mexican authorities since most of it was unexplored wilderness inhabited by Indians who were not overly friendly to white interlopers. To assist with the development of the unstable area, the Mexican government opened many parts of Texas to neighboring Americans, encouraging them to relocate and become citizens.

As thousands of Americans accepted Mexico's invitation, government officials in Mexico City realized, too late, that their state of Texas was quickly becoming overrun by the new arrivals. The decision of Mexico to then close the borders of Texas to American entry was a factor in the soon-to-erupt War of Texas Independence.

The Texas Declaration of Independence was adopted at Washington-on-the-Brazos in March 1836. After the fall of the Alamo on March 6 and Sam Houston's victory at San Jacinto in April, officials of the newly formed Republic of Texas set about trying to establish a working government. Huge land grants were handed out to all newcomers for free. A single male received 640 acres (260 ha), or 1 square mile (2.5 sq km) of land, while a family was given twice that amount.

Because of this generous land policy, the population boomed. In 1836 the population was counted at 35,000; by 1847 (when Texas joined the United States), about 140,000 people called Texas home. Ninety percent of those newcomers were from the United States, the overwhelming portion from southern states. They came on foot or horseback or by stagecoach, although roads were crude. Many of the emigrants were farmers; others were tradespeople and wealthy plantation owners who came with their slaves. However, quite a few were debtors running from their creditors. The message "GTT," or "Gone to Texas,"

was often painted on gates and doors of the homes in the East, telling family and friends, and possibly the law, that the former inhabitants were gone for good. It was considered a great joke to chalk "GTT" on people's suitcases at a stagecoach station, suggesting that the suitcase owners had either plunged into bankruptcy and needed to start a new life or that a sheriff with a warrant was on their trail.

Reaching Texas, however, was no laughing matter. Rivers overran banks and many newcomers sickened. But the speculators, adventurers, fugitives from debt and the law, ruffians, homesteaders, and honorable working people all saw an opportunity for advancement when they settled the area.

Melody Groves

See also: Alamo, The; Austin, Stephen F.; Houston, Sam; San Jacinto, Battle of; Texas Revolution and Independence.

Further Reading
Campbell, Randolph. *Gone To Texas: A History of the Lone Star State.* New York: Oxford University Press, 2004.

Goodnight, Charles (1836–1929)

Among the West's most recognized and successful cattlemen, Charles Goodnight was born on March 5, 1836, and moved to Texas at age nine, riding with his family from their southern Illinois farm to their new home near Nashville-on-the-Brazos in Milam County. He is known for forging cattle trails that allowed movement of herds from Texas to more northerly areas, effectively helping settle the region.

With only six months of formal education, Goodnight worked a variety of jobs including farm hand, race jockey, and freighter, but found his true calling in the 1850s when he began raising cattle. In 1857 Goodnight and his partner, stepbrother John Wesley Sheek, started a ranch in the Keechi Valley.

Goodnight served with the Texas Rangers as a scout and guide from about 1860 to 1864. After the Civil War, he formed a partnership with Oliver Loving to drive a herd of cattle west and north to New Mexico and Colorado territories, envisioning not only a market but also the opening of new ranges. The route they blazed, eventually stretching all the way to Cheyenne, Wyoming, became known as the Goodnight-Loving Trail and was used by many drovers.

In 1869 Goodnight established the Rock Cañon

Ranch on the Arkansas River near Pueblo, Colorado, and a year later married Molly Dyer. He continued to thrive in the cattle business, working with noted cattle barons such as John Wesley Iliff, John Chisum, and the Thatcher brothers, but was financially crippled by the Panic of 1873.

After losing his Colorado landholdings, Goodnight founded a new ranch in the vast Palo Duro Canyon, south of current Amarillo in the Texas Panhandle. There, in 1877, he partnered with Denver capitalist John G. Adair to create the JA Ranch and, as ranch manager, expanded the ranch's range and herds over the next eleven years. In 1878 he blazed another cattle trail, the Palo Duro–Dodge City Trail, when he took a herd to the Kansas railhead. By 1885, when Adair died, the JA Ranch encompassed a sprawling 1.325 million acres (535,200 ha) and had more than 100,000 cattle.

Later enterprises included the Inter-State Land Company and the Goodnight-Thayer Cattle Company, and Goodnight often is credited with helping bring law and order to the Panhandle. He also introduced Hereford bulls to improve the quality of his herds, bred bison with polled Angus cattle to create the "cattalo" cross, and grew wheat. Goodnight helped save the American bison, or buffalo, from possible extinction, raising a herd on his ranch and shipping bison to zoos as well as to Yellowstone National Park. He even staged buffalo hunts for his friend, Comanche leader Quanah Parker, and often fought for Indian rights. Other ventures included a failed mining enterprise in Mexico, and an equally unsuccessful stab as a movie producer.

Molly died in 1926, and Goodnight remarried the following year, wedding twenty-six-year-old Corinne Goodnight. They struck up a friendship because they had the same surnames, and she later nursed him back to health after a serious illness. In his later years, he spent his winters in Phoenix, Arizona, where he died on December 12, 1929, at age 93. He was buried next to Molly in the cemetery in Goodnight, Texas.

Johnny D. Boggs

See also: Cattle Frontier; Goodnight-Loving Trail; Loving, Oliver.

Further Reading

Hagan, William T. *Charles Goodnight: Father of the Texas Panhandle.* Norman: University of Oklahoma Press, 2007.

Haley, J. Evetts. *Charles Goodnight, Cowman and Plainsman.* Norman: University of Oklahoma Press, 1949.

Goodnight-Loving Trail

In the spring of 1866, at a time when most Texas cattlemen were trailing beef to Kansas or Missouri, Charles Goodnight and partner Oliver Loving decided to take a chance and drive a herd to New Mexico Territory, where officials needed beef at Fort Sumner to feed Mescalero Apache and Navajo Indians being held at the Bosque Redondo Reservation.

On June 6, Goodnight, Loving, eighteen cowboys, and 2,000 head of Longhorns began the journey, leaving Young County and following the old Overland Mail Company stage route southwest, crossing the parched West Texas countryside until reaching Horsehead Crossing on the Pecos River. The summer heat and lack of water proved costly; 300 Longhorns died before reaching the river and another 100 head were drowned or trampled when the cattle rushed to the waters of the Pecos.

Still, Goodnight and Loving went on. At Horsehead Crossing, the trail crew left the Overland mail route and followed the Pecos into New Mexico Territory, where they sold part of the herd at Fort Sumner for $12,000 in gold. Goodnight returned to Texas to start another herd while Loving took the remaining stock north—following the Pecos toward Las Vegas, New Mexico, then traveling along the Santa Fe Trail over Raton Pass into Colorado, through Trinidad and Pueblo and on toward Denver—where cattleman John Wesley Iliff purchased the herd. Loving rejoined Goodnight in New Mexico, establishing a ranch south of Fort Sumner at Bosque Grande, supplying cattle during the winter of 1866–1867 to the fort and as far away as Santa Fe. That spring, the partners returned to Texas and began another drive, but Loving was wounded in a fight with Comanche Indians near the Pecos River. With the help of Mexican traders, Loving reached Fort Sumner, where he died of infection on September 25. Goodnight continued the drive, but changed the route, shortening it while taking advantage of the waters in the northeastern part of the territory. The trail crossed the Gallinas Valley, moved north to Capulin Mountain, and then turned northwest to Raton Pass. Once in Colorado, Goodnight established a ranch 40 miles (64 km) northeast of Trinidad at Apishapa Canyon.

The trail added another leg in the spring of 1868 when Goodnight contracted with Iliff to bring a herd to Cheyenne, Wyoming. This time, Goodnight turned east of Denver, crossing the South Platte River near present-day Greeley and following Cow Creek to Cheyenne and the Union Pacific Railroad. Later changes by Goodnight had the trail leave the Pecos River at Fort Sumner and follow Alamogordo and Cuervo creeks and the Canadian River to Cimarron Seco before turning north through Trinchera Pass—thereby avoiding the toll Dick Wootton charged at Raton—and on to Colorado.

Goodnight would drive cattle to Cheyenne over the trail only once more, but other cattlemen would take advantage of the route Goodnight and Loving had blazed, herding cattle along the Goodnight-Loving Trail—sometimes called the Goodnight Trail—until the arrival of the railroads in the early 1880s ended the need for the trail.

Johnny D. Boggs

See also: Cattle Frontier; Goodnight, Charles; Long Walk; Loving, Oliver.

Further Reading

Forbis, William H. *The Cowboys.* Alexandria, VA: Time-Life Books, 1973.

Haley, J. Evetts. *Charles Goodnight, Cowman and Plainsman.* Norman: University of Oklahoma Press, 1949.

Graduation Act (1854)

The Graduation Act of 1854 was the culmination of a decades long American sectional struggle over public land policy that pitted western states against eastern states. Sandwiched between two other major public land acts—the Preemption Act of 1841 and the Homestead Act of 1862—the Graduation Act enabled the federal government to sell some of its subprime lands to settlers at prices believed to be consistent with market values. This resulted in increased revenues to the U.S. government from land sales, a higher tax base for the states possessing the sold acres, and a greater number of settlers occupying the western states.

In the first half of the nineteenth century, most public land in the United States was valued and sold at $1.25 to $2.00 per acre (.4 ha), the result of various acts and ordinances on the books since 1796. Prime land in the western states being settled during this period easily sold at those prices. Poorer land, however, tended to be bypassed as pioneers sought and found new rich lands in their continual push westward. As a result, vast tracts of land were left vacant and unsettled in states east of the ever-moving frontier.

These states sought more settlers and the resulting increase in tax revenues, services, and social benefits if land were offered and sold at lower prices. The eastern states, however, opposed cheaper prices for federal land, believing that the nation overall would suffer from decreased land sales revenue in the long run. Graduated (cheaper) prices for lower-quality land were discussed and argued for decades prior to 1854, but no action was taken, despite the support for lower prices by the House of Representative's Committee on Public Lands, three presidents (Andrew Jackson, Martin van Buren, and James K. Polk), and many congressmen, including the influential Thomas Hart Benton of Missouri.

The Preemption Act, which allowed squatters to purchase the land they had settled upon for a minimum of $1.25 an acre, was passed in 1841. Although seen as a concession to western states, it did little to encourage settlement on acreage deemed undesirable and overpriced. Although momentum was gathering for a homestead law that would provide land free to settlers, opposition to such a drastic measure was stiff. Advocates of graduation sought to position it as a compromise between the sectional factions that could not agree on the policy of free homesteads. Williamson R.W. Cobb of Alabama introduced legislation in the House of Representatives that based the price of unsold public land on the length of time it had been available for sale. Land unsold for ten years would sell for $1.00 per acre (.4 ha), with the price reduced by 25 cents per acre (.4 ha) for each additional five-year period it remained unsold. A minimum price of 12.5 cents per acre was set for lands on the market for thirty years or more. The House and Senate passed this bill into law in 1854. Over the next eight years, 77 million acres (32 million ha) of public land became available under provisions set by this act, with nearly 26 million acres (11 million ha) sold at an average price of 32 cents per acre. While only modest revenues accrued to the U.S. Treasury, undesirable land speculation occurred, and some states sold very little of their available public land. The Graduation Act brought many settlers to the nation's then-western states, setting the stage for the passage of the Homestead Act in 1862.

Jim Ersfeld

See also: Homestead Act (1862); Preemption Act (1841).

Further Reading

Hibbard, Benjamin Horace. *A History of the Public Land Policies.* Madison: University of Wisconsin Press, 1965.

Grant, Ulysses S. (1822–1885)

Ulysses S. Grant served as general-in-chief commanding the Union Army as the Civil War ended in April 1865. He later served as president of the United States from 1869 to 1877, and his two administrations significantly influenced the nation's westward expansion.

He was born and named Hiram Ulysses Grant on April 27, 1822, at Point Pleasant, Ohio, and as a boy learned farming and leather tanning from his father. When his congressman incorrectly transcribed Grant's name on his appointment papers to West Point, the boy decided not to correct it and he became known by his fellow cadets as Ulysses S. Grant, the name he carried throughout his life. He graduated from West Point in 1843, ranking in the middle of his class, and served in the military up through the outbreak of the Mexican-American War, fighting with distinction in Mexico.

After the war, Grant married Julia Dent from Missouri, a sister of a West Point classmate. He served at West Coast military posts without Julia, as his pay could not support her to be with him. In 1854 he resigned from the army to be with his family and tried a variety of jobs, including farming, to make ends meet.

At the outbreak of the Civil War in 1861, Grant, now living with his wife and children in Galena, Illinois, volunteered his services to his adopted state, and the governor appointed him colonel of the 21st Illinois Volunteer Infantry. By August 1861, following his success in converting rowdy and inexperienced farm boys into soldiers, he was appointed brigadier general of volunteers. Despite a less than stellar beginning in combat command at Belmont, Missouri, in early November 1861, Grant redeemed himself in Tennessee during February 1862 when he captured two strategic Confederate forts—Henry and Donelson—that commanded the Tennessee and Cumberland rivers and protected Nashville.

Serving with distinction throughout the war, he earned the nickname "Unconditional Surrender" Grant and won major victories with the capture of Vicksburg and the lifting of the siege of Chattanooga. In March 1864, President Lincoln appointed Grant general-in-chief of the Union Army. Grant superintended General George Meade's Army of the Potomac in Virginia from the Battle of the Wilderness through the Battle of Petersburg, directing the whole of the war effort while in the field. His activities eventually led to the surrender of Confederate General Robert E. Lee's army at Appomattox Court House on April 7, 1865.

In 1868 Grant, still lionized for his Civil War service, became the Republican nominee for president, and easily won in the November elections. He was an honest man, but many of his appointees were not, causing his administration to be wracked with scandal. Even so, Grant handily won reelection in 1872.

Several important events occurred during Grant's tenure as the nation's chief executive. He was a great supporter of the transcontinental railroad (completed in 1869), believing that it would unify the country and help settle the frontier. In 1872 he oversaw congressional approval to create Yellowstone, in the northwest corner of Wyoming, as the nation's first national park. The same year, he approved a mining act that still remains in effect.

Believing that the government needed to reform its dealings with Indians, Grant established his Indian peace policy in 1869. He appointed his good friend Ely Parker, a Seneca Indian and Civil War brigadier

Ulysses S. Grant, former commander of all Union armies during the Civil War, was elevated to the new rank of full general in 1866, the year of this photo. As president, Grant was a great supporter of the transcontinental railroad and westward expansion. *(Hulton Archive/Stringer/Getty Images)*

general, as commissioner of Indian affairs. Cases of politically appointed Indian agents stealing from the natives and mismanaging government programs ran rampant. In fact, Grant's own brother was involved in a kickback scheme that further embarrassed the president's efforts. Grant fired all but a few good Indian agents and appointed replacements from among the Quakers, a Christian denomination, and military officers. Congress retaliated in 1870 by making it illegal for military officers to hold civilian positions. Grant responded by filling the Indian agent vacancies with Protestant and Catholic clergy.

Grant appointed the independent Board of Indian Commissioners to advise the federal government on Indian policy. This board remained in existence until 1934. Grant believed Indians could be educated and trained to be farmers and mechanics, and his administration increased funding for Indian education. But he ordered army commanders such as Philip Sheridan and William Sherman to force uncooperative tribes to live on reservations.

Grant privately supported the recommendations of Sheridan and Sherman to control the Indians by destroying their source of food—the bison. The program was so successful that in 1874 Representative Greenberg L. Fort of Illinois introduced a bill to save the bison from extinction by prohibiting the killing of bison cows. The bill passed Congress, which sent it to President Grant for signature; however, the measure died as a pocket veto.

Later in life, Grant developed throat cancer. He wrote his memoirs with the support of Mark Twain, finishing them shortly before his death at Mount McGregor, New York, on July 23, 1885.

Bill Markley

See also: Bison, American; Indian Policy; Mexican-American War; Sheridan, Philip H.; Sherman, William Tecumseh.

Further Reading

Freidel, Frank. *Our Country's Presidents*. Washington, DC: National Geographic Society, 1983.

Grant, U.S. *Personal Memoirs of U.S. Grant*. 2 vols. New York: Charles L. Webster, 1894.

Hutton, Paul Andrew. *Phil Sheridan and His Army*. Norman: University of Oklahoma Press, 1999.

Perret, Geoffrey. *Ulysses S. Grant, Soldier and President*. New York: Random House, 1997.

Smith, Page. *The Rise of Industrial America, A People's History of the Post-Reconstruction Era*. Vol. 6. New York: McGraw-Hill, 1984.

Grattan Massacre

A perfect storm of events—and an imperfect cast of characters—combined at Fort Laramie in 1854 to initiate four decades of sporadic, often intense conflict between the United States and the Lakota people. On the surface the actions leading to the Grattan Massacre—otherwise known as the Grattan Fight or the Mormon Cow Incident—seemed almost trivial, if not ludicrous, in their recounting.

The signers of the 1851 Fort Laramie Treaty— the U.S. government and a vast delegation of Plains Indian tribes—had intended to ease conflicts between emigrants heading to California, Oregon, and Utah and the Native American groups who lived, hunted, and traded along the overland trail. For nearly three travel seasons the agreement to provide safe passage for American travelers had generally held. That peace came abruptly to an end on August 18, 1854, when a wagon train of Danish converts to Mormonism approached Fort Laramie on the North Platte River in present-day eastern Wyoming. Although late in the season for the heavier traffic to California and Oregon, late summer still saw several civilian parties on the trail with the Utah settlements as their ultimate destination. At the same time hundreds of Lakota and Cheyenne families chose to assemble near the fort to receive their government annuities as provided by the aforementioned treaty.

On that summer's day an emigrant lost his footsore ox to a Lakota arrow loosed by a hungry Miniconjou Lakota man. The ox's owner took his complaint to Second Lieutenant Hugh B. Fleming, 6th U.S. Infantry, the young and inexperienced commander of Fort Laramie, who on August 19 dispatched recent West Point graduate Brevet Second Lieutenant John L. Grattan, even younger and less experienced, to arrest the perpetrator. Over the objections of experienced Lakota headmen who sought to settle the dispute with diplomacy and not guns, Grattan left the fort with twenty-nine infantrymen (which was much of the garrison), two field pieces, and a drunken interpreter, headed for a Brulé Lakota village 8 miles (13 km) east of the fort. Here, nestled amid a camp of 1,000 warriors, sat the Miniconjou man's tepee.

Under these inauspicious conditions Grattan and his interpreter unwisely attempted to use bluff and bluster to make the arrest. A long discussion ensued between him and Lakota leaders Big Partisan, Conquering Bear, Man Afraid of His Horses, and Little Thunder, but the Lakotas' arguments fell on deaf ears.

A frustrated Grattan then attempted to intimidate the Indians with a volley from his guns. This resulted in a few damaged tepees, a mortally wounded Conquering Bear, and the fury of the enraged tribesmen unleashed upon the hopelessly outnumbered soldiers. Grattan fell early, next to a cannon, his body later found pierced with at least sixteen arrows. In the one-sided, running skirmish that followed, all but one member of the military party were soon killed. A single enlisted man managed to escape and hide, but died days later from his wounds, never able to tell his personal tale of the last stand.

The Indians soon turned their anger toward the nearby trading posts and ransacked them, principally to take their unissued government goods. They left alone the virtually unprotected military post. As a relative calm descended and they realized the significance of their actions, the Lakotas packed up and left the area. When Fort Laramie's remaining inhabitants sent word to the East of the debacle, military officials placed the blame for the "massacre" squarely on the Indians and planned a punitive expedition. The Indians long argued that it was a fair fight and one that they had not started.

In 1855 Colonel William S. Harney led a large force to punish the perpetrators. Ironically his target was the village of Little Thunder, one of the Lakota leaders who had tried to settle the initial dispute. During that season Harney's column of avengers passed the site of the fight, where the only evidence was a rude monument of sorts to the common grave of the lost command. Grattan reposed not with his men but at Fort Leavenworth, where his body lay unclaimed by his family. His gravestone is now a minor feature in the fort's national cemetery, serving as mute testimony to a brief career and the many wars to follow. The Grattan Massacre was the initial engagement in the first Sioux war, a conflict between two expanding powers, the United States and the western Sioux.

R. Eli Paul

See also: Blue Water Creek, Battle of; Fort Laramie; Harney, William S.; Lakota; Sioux.

Further Reading

Adams, George Rollie. *General William S. Harney: Prince of Dragoons.* Lincoln: University of Nebraska Press, 2001.

Hafen, LeRoy R., and Francis Marion Young. *Fort Laramie and the Pageant of the West, 1834–1890.* Glendale, CA: Arthur H. Clark, 1938.

Paul, R. Eli. *Blue Water Creek and the First Sioux War, 1854–1856.* Norman: University of Oklahoma Press, 2004.

Gray, Robert (1755–1806)

Robert Gray's achievements as a merchant seaman and explorer include his command of the first American ship to circumnavigate the earth and his discovery of the Columbia River estuary.

Born in Tiverton, Rhode Island, on May 10, 1755, Gray's history before 1787 is virtually unknown. He is believed to have served in the Continental Navy during the American Revolutionary War, or perhaps as a privateer, and sailed in trade vessels out of South Carolina.

In 1787 a company of Boston merchants pooled $50,000 to dispatch two trade vessels from Nantucket Roads to the northern Pacific on a fur-trading enterprise, the first such American venture. In command of the expedition, John Kendrick of Harwich, Massachusetts, sailed on the *Columbia Rediviva* ("Columbia Reborn"), a 212-ton (192-mt), 83-foot (25-m) merchantman with ten cannons and a thirty-man crew. Kendrick's second-in-command was the thirty-two-year-old Robert Gray, commanding the *Lady Washington*, a 90-ton (82-mt) merchant sloop.

The ships carried a cargo of scrap iron, salt beef, gunpowder, rum, tea, chocolate, and gimcracks and utensils for trade with coastal natives. After the ships lost sight of each other in a Cape Horn gale, Gray sailed on and brought his sloop into Nootka Sound, on the west coast of Vancouver Island, in September of 1788. Within a few days Captain Kendrick rejoined him and the traders spent a successful winter bartering with the natives for sea otter and other skins. In the spring, Kendrick ordered the furs loaded on the *Columbia* and turned the sloop over to Gray to sail to Canton. There, Gray sold the furs for more than $20,000, took on a cargo of tea, and sailed home to Boston. On August 10, 1790, after a three-year absence, the *Columbia* anchored off Nantucket, the first American ship to sail around the globe.

Gray was rehired by the company of Boston merchants two months after his triumphant return to the port, and now, as part owner of the *Columbia*, fitted out his ship for a new Pacific venture. In June 1791, he reached anchorage on an island above Juan de Fuca Strait, later part of the U.S.-Canadian boundary, and, while trading for sea otter pelts, was attacked by natives, but beat back the assault and burned a large native village in retribution.

In April 1792, Gray sailed the *Columbia* down the Pacific coastline and upon returning north on the 29th encountered the English exploring ship HMS *Discovery*, commanded by British navy captain George

Vancouver. Gray told Vancouver that he had recently visited the mouth of a river with an out-flowing current so strong that he was prevented from entering it, but on May 11, 1792, Gray brought the *Columbia* back to the estuary, braved the lashing seas, and after eleven days crossed the bar and anchored 10 miles (16 km) above the entrance. A party of thirty men sailed a cutter 30 miles (48 km) upstream, found a Chinook village, and soon after the ship was visited by numerous Indian canoes bringing furs to trade. Bad weather prevented the *Columbia* from escaping the estuary until May 20, by which time Gray named the river after his ship and claimed the territory around it in the name of the United States.

Gray participated in the Franco-American "Quasi-War" of 1798–1800, a maritime series of privateer adventures in South American waters. He died at sea, probably of yellow fever, in July 1806, near Charleston, South Carolina.

Dale L. Walker

See also: Astoria.

Further Reading

Nokes, J. Richard. *Columbia's River: The Voyages of Robert Gray, 1787–1793.* Tacoma: Washington State Historical Society, 1991.

Scofield, John. *Hail, Columbia: Robert Gray, John Kendrick and the Pacific Fur Trade.* Portland: Oregon Historical Society Press, 1993.

Walker, Dale L. *Pacific Destiny: The Three-Century Journey to the Oregon Country.* New York: Forge Books, 2000.

Great American Desert

"Great American Desert" was a term used in the early nineteenth century to describe a large part of the area lying west of the Mississippi River and east of the Rocky Mountains and encompassing much of the region today known as the Great Plains.

The Great American Desert was first described by army explorer Zebulon M. Pike following his journey to Spanish New Mexico in 1806–1807 and fourteen years later by Major Stephen H. Long who, in two different reports, wrote that the vast plains of the Western Hemisphere resembled the sandy deserts of Africa. Long's map of 1823 officially labeled the Great Plains as the Great American Desert.

This semiarid region, enveloping about 3.2 million square miles (1.2 million sq km), stretches from the Rocky Mountains eastward across Oklahoma, Kansas, Nebraska, and the Dakotas and from Texas northward to Alberta, Saskatchewan, and Manitoba in Canada. Carey and Lee's atlas of 1827 located the Great American Desert as an indefinite territory in present-day Colorado, Nebraska, Kansas, New Mexico, and Texas. Then, in 1838, the Bradford atlas expanded the desert to include the area from the Arkansas River through Colorado and Wyoming, including South Dakota and parts of Nebraska and Kansas. With each new atlas, the boundaries changed.

In many respects, Long's description of the Great American Desert slowed westward migration considerably. Since a desert was presumed unfit for cultivation, emigrants and travelers rushed across the region without much thought of inhabiting it. After the discovery of gold in California in 1848, upward of 42,000 emigrants crossed the Great Plains, but even then few people stopped to consider homesteading.

During the emigration period to Oregon, Utah, and California beginning in the 1840s, hundreds of thousands of people moved west, pouring across the plains. Many of them finally realized that the moniker "Great American Desert" was inaccurate. If millions of bison and tens of thousands of Indians could live on these plains, why could not Americans?

People eager to boost settlement, attract business, and ultimately seek railroad connections wanted the rest of the nation to realize that the Great American Desert was not a desert at all. So in the 1860s and 1870s they constructed a counter-myth and began calling the vast region the Great Plains, "the Garden," or "the Garden of the West," an agricultural paradise that offered enough space for thousands of people to fulfill their dreams.

To encourage settlement, Congress established a monthly mail route between the Missouri River and Salt Lake City, Utah, and another one between the Pacific coast and Salt Lake City. Another mail route was established across the "desert" from Independence, Missouri, to Albuquerque, New Mexico, in the early 1850s. However the real rush started in the summer of 1858 when gold was discovered along a stream tributary to the South Platte River, on the eastern slope of the Rocky Mountains in Colorado. Numerous stage lines sprang up, and in 1860 the Pony Express crossed the Great American Desert.

By 1869 the railroad steamed from coast to coast, traversing the region. Once irrigation was introduced, the "fruitless desert" became ripe with vegetation and people.

Melody Groves

See also: Long, Stephen H.; Long Expedition; Pike, Zebulon M.; Pike Expedition.

Further Reading

Annerino, John. *Desert Survivor: An Adventurer's Guide to Exploring the Great American Desert*. New York: Four Walls Eight Windows, 2001.

MacGregor, Greg. *Overland: The California Emigrant Trail of 1841–1870*. Albuquerque: University of New Mexico Press, 1996.

Parkman, Francis. *The Oregon Trail*. New York: Penguin Books, 1985.

Greeley, Horace (1811–1872)

A brilliant and bold newspaperman, social reformer, and presidential candidate, Horace Greeley was born in Amherst, New Hampshire, in February 1811, the son of an impoverished farming family. Abandoning formal schooling at age fourteen to help support his family, he learned the printer's trade and, after a newspaper apprenticeship in Vermont, moved to New York City. There, in 1834, with money assiduously saved, he published a political and literary journal, the *New Yorker*, which earned little revenue above its production costs and was therefore short-lived. However, his writings in support of the Whig party, in opposition to the policies of Jacksonian Democrats, brought him the attention of influential New Yorkers and, in 1840, the editorship of the *Log Cabin*. This weekly Whig-oriented paper became an important factor in the election of William Henry Harrison to the presidency in 1841 and led directly to Greeley's launching of the *New York Tribune*.

Eventually to be counted among the nation's greatest newspapers, the *Tribune* served as a mirror of Greeley's humanistic, egalitarian ideals. In his eloquent editorials he opposed monopolistic business practices, capital punishment, the Mexican-American War, land grants to railroads, the sale and consumption of liquor, and an array of other disparate issues. He favored the impeachment of President Andrew Johnson, agrarian reforms, women's rights, and Utopian and socialistic experiments. He was particularly interested in land reform and vigorously advocated that the federal government bestow land grants on eastern families with the provision that they move west to claim them. In this manner, he rationalized, not only would vast regions of the West become populated with ambitious, hardworking Americans, but the large eastern cities would be relieved of their overpopulation and all the problems that went with it. Through Greeley's efforts the *Tribune* became the unofficial newspaper of the fledgling Republican Party, founded in 1854, and reached a daily circulation of 300,000 by 1861.

Greeley's admonition to "Go West, young man, go West and grow up with the country" seems to have been a variation of his frequent urging that young, ambitious Americans should "Fly, scatter through the country—go to the Great West." Yet another variation was the sentence in the August 25, 1838, issue of his short-lived political and literary journal, *New Yorker*: "If any young man is about to commence the world, we say to him, publicly and privately, Go to the West." (The "Go West" quotation is sometimes attributed to John Soule, a reporter with the Terre Haute, Indiana, *Express*, but no evidence for the claim has surfaced.)

Greeley's anti-slavery stance began more than a decade before the Civil War, and he became among the most outspoken of the radical anti-slavery adherents, even criticizing President Abraham Lincoln for being dilatory in proclaiming emancipation. He wrote passionately to hasten postwar healing and in 1867 signed the bond to release Confederate President Jefferson Davis from prison.

Although he supported the election of Republican Ulysses S. Grant to the presidency in 1868, Greeley crusaded against the corruption of Grant's administration and agreed to stand as the 1872 presidential candidate of the new Liberal Republican Party. He was an energetic speaker, but he campaigned poorly and was mercilessly lambasted in the pro-Grant press and in Thomas Nast's caricatures in *Harper's Weekly*. While he gained the support of disaffected Democrats and nearly 3 million popular votes, he was soundly defeated by Grant.

During the campaign Greeley, in failing health, lost financial and editorial control of the *Tribune* and suffered yet another devastating loss a week before Election Day with the death of his wife of thirty-six years, Mary Cheney Greeley. The 1872 presidential balloting took place on November 5, the popular vote was tallied on November 29, and on that day, in a private hospital in Pleasantville, New York, Greeley died, a broken man.

Dale L. Walker

See also: Homestead Act (1862); Kansas-Nebraska Act (1854).

Further Reading

Cross, Coy F., II. *Go West Young Man! Horace Greeley's Vision for America*. Albuquerque: University of Mexico Press, 1995.

Greeley, Horace. *Recollections of a Busy Life*. New York: J.B. Ford, 1868.

Lunde, Erik S. *Horace Greeley*. New York: Twayne, 1981.

Seitz, Don C. *Horace Greeley: Founder of the New York Tribune*. Indianapolis: Bobbs-Merrill, 1926.

Williams, Robert C. *Horace Greeley: Champion of American Freedom*. New York: New York University Press, 2006.

Green River

This historically and geographically significant river is the main upper channel of the Colorado River. It flows 730 miles (1,174 km) from its source at the base of Gannett Peak in the Wind River Mountains of Wyoming to its confluence with the Colorado River, formerly known as the Grand River, in Canyonlands National Park. Fathers Francisco Dominguez and Silvestre Escalante, Spanish Franciscan missionaries exploring the western territory in 1776, called it the San Buenaventura; later explorers knew it as the Spanish River or the Rio Verde. By 1825, when General William Ashley visited the region, it generally was known as the Green River.

In 1811–1812, Wilson Price Hunt and his party of fur trappers called Astorians, who worked for the Pacific Fur Company became the first Americans known to have reached the Green River in Wyoming. Crossing a high pass in the Wind River Mountains, later named Union Pass by Captain William Raynolds in 1860, the Astorians followed the Green River south to the Hoback Rim and followed the Hoback River into Jackson Hole. In 1823 General William Ashley and Major Andrew Henry of Missouri partnered in a fur trade enterprise, the predecessor of the Rocky Mountain Fur Company. Ashley and Henry recruited 100 "enterprising young men . . . to ascend the river Missouri to its source." Among those employed in the company were Jedediah Smith, Jim Beckwourth, Thomas Fitzpatrick, and David E. Jackson. Other mountain men who joined them were Jim Bridger, Joseph Meek, and Kit Carson. "Meet Me on the Green" became a common parting call of these mountain men, referring to the practice of gathering somewhere along the Green River for the annual rendezvous. During the fur trade era, the Green River was the location for eight of the gatherings, in 1825, 1833–1837, and 1839–1840. The Green River Basin was the heart of fur-trapping country, and the Green River and its tributaries were recognized as one of the most important beaver habitats in the Rockies.

John Wesley Powell launches his second expedition down the Green and Colorado rivers in 1871. This journey yielded what his first mission, two years earlier, did not: a map, photographs, scientific descriptions, and biological and geological specimens. *(Stringer/Getty Images)*

Ashley was among the first to explore the river itself. Constructing a bullboat (a bowl-shaped vessel made from several buffalo skins) along the banks of the river, he and some of his men traveled down the river as far south as possible in their crude craft. It was not until 1869 that John Wesley Powell and his men would travel farther along the river's course.

Many geographers, geologists, and historians consider the Green River to be the main tributary of the Colorado River. Until the 1920s the Colorado River was known as the Grand River from its source near the continental divide in Colorado to its confluence with the Green River in Utah. According to Roy Webb, it was during the 1920s that Colorado legislators and the Chamber of Commerce of the State of Colorado realized that the river flowing through the northwestern part of their state appeared nowhere on published maps as the Colorado River. They pressured the newly created United States Board of Geographic Names to eliminate the name "Grand" and call it the Colorado River along its entire length. The Utah legislature supported this move. An act of Congress in 1922 made the change official. Some who disagree with this decision support the idea that it could just as easily be called the Green River along its entire length.

Tamsen Emerson Hert

See also: Ashley, William Henry; Henry, Andrew; Hunt, Wilson Price; Powell, John Wesley; Rendezvous.

Further Reading

Blackstock, Alan. *A Green River Reader.* Salt Lake City: University of Utah Press, 2005.

Linford, Dee. *Wyoming Stream Names: A Bicentennial Publication.* 2nd ed. Cheyenne: Wyoming Game and Fish Commission, 1975.

Webb, Roy. *If We Had a Boat: Green River Explorers, Adventurers, and Runners.* Salt Lake City: Bonneville Books/University of Utah Press, 1986.

Greenville, Treaty of (1795)

The Treaty of Greenville, signed in 1795, gave the United States sole authority over trade with the Indian tribes of the Ohio River valley, preventing any foreign power from holding trade privileges among the Wyandot, Lenape (Delaware), Shawnee, Ottawa, Anishnabe, Pottawatomie, Miami, Eel River, Wea, Kickapoo, Piankeshaw, and Kaskaskia tribes. The treaty signaled the end of warfare between Miami leader Mishakinaquah (Little Turtle) and his confederacy against the United States.

In 1790 the confederacy had defeated General Josiah Harmer and 1,400 soldiers at the Battle of Maumee. Little Turtle scored an even bigger success in 1791, defeating General Arthur St. Clair and 2,000 soldiers at the Battle of the Wabash. After Little Turtle orchestrated several successful attacks on American supply lines and a failed attack on Fort Recovery, General Anthony Wayne launched a full assault on the Indian confederacy. The British, sparked by Little Turtle's success against the Americans, offered military aide to the confederacy. However, at the Battle of Fallen Timbers, Wayne's force surprised the Indian leader and, when the Indian warriors fled to a British fort, the doors remained closed. Several years later this defeat would inspire another warrior, the Shawnee Tecumseh, to establish a larger intertribal movement intended to forever alter whites' encroachment onto native lands.

Wayne negotiated the Treaty of Greenville as the lead military commander against the Indian confederacy. Most of the tribes within the confederacy had been excluded from the 1784 Fort Stanwix Treaty and were fighting to protect their lands from settlers expanding further west. Negotiations started in June 1795 at Fort Greenville in present-day Ohio, and the final document was signed by August. Over three months of talks produced a treaty that renegotiated the settlement lines and ceded most of Ohio to the United States.

The United States quickly established factories or trading houses among the defeated Indian nations. These factories prevented any foreign trade and required all traders living among the tribes to be licensed by the U.S. government. Not only did this give American traders exclusive rights, but also it regulated the economic exchange between settlers and the tribes. The treaty placed the tribes under the exclusive protection of the United States.

The Treaty of Greenville serves as an early example of treaty making on the frontier of the Northwest Territory. However, the new Treaty of Greenville lines were not immediately drawn and lacked the proper enforcement. Tribal-controlled lands were quickly eroded by the constant influx of settlers into the Ohio Territory. Many tribes refused to sign and continued to see the push of settlers as an assault on their sovereignty. Responsibility to carry out the treaty ultimately fell upon William Henry Harrison, governor of Indiana

Territory. Harrison's command grew in direct confrontation with Tecumseh and his brother Tenskwetawa's renewed confederacy. Between the eventual War of 1812 and the leadership of Tecumseh, the Treaty of Greenville proved ineffectual in stopping the violence on the northwest frontier.

Kent Blansett

See also: Fallen Timbers, Battle of; Fort Stanwix, Treaty of (1784); Harrison, William Henry; Little Turtle; St. Clair, Arthur; Tecumseh; Wayne, Anthony.

Further Reading

Edmunds, R. David. *Tecumseh and the Quest for Indian Leadership.* New York: Pearson Longman, 2007.

Prucha, Francis Paul. *American Indian Treaties: The History of a Political Anomaly.* Berkeley: University of California Press, 1994.

Gregg, Josiah (1806–1850)

In his book *Commerce of the Prairies*, published in New York in 1844, Josiah Gregg left future generations a classic account of his life as a trader in Santa Fe. The book is a gold mine of information about the Santa Fe Trail and the geography, geology, and ethnology of the region through which it passes. Indeed, the subtitle of Gregg's masterpiece, "The Journal of a Santa Fe Trader During Eight Expeditions Across the Great Western Prairies, and a Residence of Nearly Nine Years in Northern Mexico," describes the contents very well.

Gregg was born on July 19, 1806, in Overton County, Tennessee. His father was a wheelwright, and the family moved frequently from place to place. By the time Josiah was eight years old, he was living at the edge of the western frontier in Missouri. He was a sickly lad, but grew up to become an intelligent, well-educated man, disciplined in mathematics, surveying, and literature.

About the year 1830, Gregg again became ill. He had always been a consumptive-type person, but exactly what his latest illness was has never been determined. He was studying law at the time, and perhaps the pressures of his work, coupled with his age-old disposition to illness, overwhelmed him. In any event, his physician advised him to take the next wagon train to Santa Fe. Thus began his romance with the American Southwest and the Santa Fe Trail.

Gregg's journey must have temporarily cured

him, because between 1831 and 1840, he made eight trips across the southern Great Plains on the Santa Fe Trail. During some of his journeys, he spent several months at a time in Santa Fe, which he came to know and to love as much as any town he had ever visited. Drawing upon training in medicine that he had received as a young man living in Kentucky, Gregg practiced his art among the poor inhabitants of New Mexico. His real love, however, was the recording of every event, every strange sight, and every peculiar sound that he witnessed. With a keen eye for observation, Gregg, in his *Commerce of the Prairies*, gave readers a complete study of the Santa Fe Trail and its surroundings. He was one of the first writers to recognize the importance of the bison to the economy of the American Indian tribes. He was also among the first to understand that the continued killing of the bison for sport and hides would eventually lead to extinction of the species.

Gregg traveled the Santa Fe Trail so many times that he was well qualified to describe the best camping places along the route and to give distances between them. He reported in his book that the total mileage from Independence, Missouri, to Santa Fe was 775 miles (1,250 km); from Council Grove, where the individual wagons were usually organized into trains, the distance to Santa Fe was 625 miles (1,005 km). Both these routes were measured along the shorter Cimarron Cutoff.

Gregg's book is also important because it gives figures about the yearly traffic along the trail. In one particularly interesting part, he describes the number of wagons and men who traveled the trail in the years between 1822 and 1843, as well as the value of the merchandise for those years. Chapters on mining, the New Mexican government, Indians, agriculture, wildlife, and history, among other subjects, make Gregg's *Commerce of the Prairies* one of the most important books ever written about the Santa Fe Trail.

Gregg eventually left the Santa Fe trade to pursue other interests. During the Mexican-American War, he served as a newspaper correspondent, and later he immigrated to the California gold fields. On February 25, 1850, when he was only forty-four years old, Gregg fell from his horse and died instantly. Today, his body lies at the spot of his death, near Clear Lake, California.

Josiah Gregg, through the magic of the written word, brought the romance and mystery of the Santa Fe Trail to anyone who would take the time to read his wonderful book.

James A. Crutchfield

See also: Becknell, William; Santa Fe Trail.

Further Reading

Fulton, Maurice Garland, ed. *Diary & Letters of Josiah Gregg.* 2 vols. Norman: University of Oklahoma Press, 1941 and 1944.

Gregg, Josiah. *Commerce of the Prairies.* Edited by Max L. Moorhead. Norman: University of Oklahoma Press, 1954.

Horgan, Paul. *Josiah Gregg and His Vision of the Early West.* New York: Farrar, Straus and Giroux, 1979.

Grinnell, George Bird (1849–1938)

American conservationist and ethnologist George Bird Grinnell was born in Brooklyn, New York, in 1849; his father was an eminent banker and his grandfather a ten-term U.S. congressman. In his boyhood, Grinnell's family moved to Ossining, New York, and by chance gave special meaning to his middle name when they settled on land once owned by John James Audubon, the celebrated ornithologist and artist. Young Grinnell became friends with Audubon's widow and sons and spent his youth hunting and fishing with his friends and beginning the nature studies that became his life's work.

At Yale University Grinnell studied under Professor Othniel Charles Marsh (1831–1899), the preeminent paleontologist of his era. Graduating in 1870 (he received a Yale doctorate ten years later), Grinnell had the good fortune to take part that year in Marsh's fossil-hunting expedition into Nebraska, Kansas, Wyoming, Colorado, and Utah. During the six-month-long investigation, Marsh and his students unearthed the remains of several species of early horses, rhinoceroses, turtles, birds, and rodents, plus fossilized mosasaurs (marine reptiles) and a wing-bone fragment of a pterodactyl.

As a graduate student, Grinnell accompanied Lieutenant Colonel George Armstrong Custer's 1874 Black Hills exploration as a naturalist. During this expedition he studied the Pawnee, Gros Ventre, and especially the Cheyenne tribes of the region, and for the rest of his life he served as a tireless advocate for the rights and fair treatment of Native Americans. Grinnell's best-known literary works are *The Fighting Cheyennes* (1915) and the two volumes of *The Cheyenne Indians* (1923).

In 1875, after an exploration of Yellowstone National Park, Grinnell became dedicated to protecting the park from commercialization and neglect. In this effort he was later joined by future president Theodore Roosevelt, with whom he forged a bond of friendship.

Together with such other environmentalists as John Burroughs and John Muir, Grinnell had great influence on Roosevelt's unprecedented conservation record as president.

Grinnell edited the sportsman's magazine *Forest and Stream* (later *Field and Stream*) for thirty years and used it as a forum for the preservation of Yellowstone's wonders, especially its buffalo. In 1873 he warned that this survivor of the Ice Age, numbering at one time 30 million in North America, would be extinct by the end of the century unless stringent efforts were made to protect the species.

The 1880s became Grinnell's most active conservationist decade. In 1885 he explored the glacier in northwestern Montana that now bears his name (he was influential in establishing Glacier National Park in 1910); in 1886 he helped organize the first Audubon Society; in 1887 he joined Theodore Roosevelt in forming the Boone and Crockett Club of gentleman hunters and wilderness protection advocates.

In 1925, when Grinnell received the Theodore Roosevelt Distinguished Service Medal, President Calvin Coolidge told him few people had done as much "to preserve vast areas of picturesque wilderness for the eyes of posterity."

Grinnell died on April 11, 1938, at age eighty-nine. The *New York Times* obituary called him "the father of American conservation."

Dale L. Walker

See also: Audubon, John James; Cheyenne; Custer Expedition.

Further Reading

Grinnell, George Bird. *The Fighting Cheyennes.* Norman: University of Oklahoma Press, 1955.

Hagan, William Thomas. *Theodore Roosevelt and Six Friends of the Indian.* Norman: University of Oklahoma Press, 1997.

Punke, Michael. *Last Stand: George Bird Grinnell, the Battle to Save the Buffalo, and the Birth of the New West.* New York: HarperCollins, 2007.

Reiger, John F., ed. *The Passing of the Great West: Selected Papers of George Bird Grinnell.* New York: Scribner's, 1972.

Guadalupe Hidalgo, Treaty of (1848)

The Treaty of Guadalupe Hidalgo was signed by representatives of Mexico and the United States in the village of the same name on February 2, 1848. The treaty ended the Mexican-American War and ceded to the United States nearly 1.2 million square miles (3 million sq km) of the present-day Southwest, encompassing all previously held Mexican territory north of the Rio Grande and Gila River. The United States paid Mexico $15 million for the cession, plus $3.25 million for American claims against the Mexican government. The U.S. Senate ratified the treaty on March 10, with a vote of thirty-eight to fourteen, with twenty-six Democrats and twelve Whigs voting for ratification and seven Democrats and seven Whigs voting against. Mexico ratified the treaty fifteen days later.

Most hostilities between the two nations had already formally ceased earlier, and on June 12, American troops permanently evacuated Mexico City. On July 4, President James K. Polk declared the Treaty of Guadalupe Hidalgo "official." The price tag for the American involvement in the war amounted to nearly $98 million. More than 11,000 soldiers died from disease, while only 1,721 were killed in combat; 4,102 more were wounded.

An adjustment to the treaty was made in 1853 with the completion of the Gadsden Purchase, wherein the United States acquired from Mexico the stretch of land lying between the original northern treaty line and the present-day boundary of the two nations.

James A. Crutchfield

See also: Gadsden Purchase (1853); Mexican Boundary Survey; Mexican-American War; Polk, James K.

Further Reading

Goetzmann, William H. *Exploration and Empire: The Explorer and the Scientist in the Winning of the West.* Austin: Texas State Historical Association, 1993.

Gwin, William McKendree (1805–1885)

Born in Sumner County, Tennessee, on October 9, 1805, William McKendree Gwin earned a medical degree in Kentucky, and launched his political career as U.S. congressman from Mississippi in 1841, continuing in 1850 as one of the first U.S. senators from the new state of California.

He moved to California in 1849, the first year of the great gold rush in the Sacramento Valley north of San Francisco, and purchased land in the town of Paloma in Calaveras County. There he founded a placer gold mine that made him rich and allowed him to concentrate his time on politics.

Gwin's political experience served him well when he was elected as one of the forty-eight delegates to California's constitutional convention at Monterey in the fall and winter of 1849 and became a signer of the original California Constitution. Then, upon the admission of California as the thirty-first U.S. state in September of 1850, he was elected as a Democrat to the U.S. Senate. He first served from September 1850 to March 1855, the term highlighted by his duel with California congressman Joseph Walker McCorkle on June 1, 1853. Their conflict, a patronage dispute, was settled with rifle shots, although neither man was injured.

Gwin returned to the Senate in 1857 and served through the opening year of the Civil War. He became known as a Southern sympathizer and pro-slavery advocate during the conflict, and clashed frequently with another California senator, David C. Broderick, a Unionist and Free Soil Party member who opposed expansion of slavery in the western states and territories.

Gwin was responsible for congressional bills beneficial to California. These include creation of a mint, a navy yard, and military installations, and encouragement of American designs to purchase Alaska from czarist Russia. He also gave his influential backing to the Pony Express enterprise of 1860–1861 to carry mail between St. Joseph, Missouri, and Sacramento, California.

After touring Southern states on the eve of the Civil War, Gwin returned to California where his Democratic Party suffered severely in the 1861 elections. He returned to Mississippi, but after losing his plantation to Union forces he moved with his family to France.

Gwin had once envisioned an enclave—a state within a state—of Southern secessionists in California, and in Paris in 1864 he proposed an even more fantastic idea to Emperor Napoleon III. At the time, Maximilian I, brother of Emperor Francis Joseph of Austria, ruled Mexico. Maximilian had been persuaded by Napoleon III to take the Mexican crown and Gwin proposed that the French emperor use his influence to permit the emigration of Southern slaveholders to the Mexican state of Sonora. The militaristic Napoleon III seemed interested in the project, but Maximilian wisely rejected the idea.

At the end of the Civil War, Gwin returned to the

United States and to California, where he lived quietly as a gentleman farmer and respected pioneer. He died in New York City on September 3, 1885.

Dale L. Walker

See also: California, Conquest of; Pony Express.

Further Reading

O'Meara, James. *Broderick and Gwin: The Most Extraordinary Contest for a Seat in the Senate of the United States Ever Known; A Brief History of Early Politics in California*. San Francisco: Bacon, 1881. Reprint, Whitefish, MT: Kessenger Publishing, 2007.

Quinn, Arthur. *The Rivals: William Gwin, David Broderick, and the Birth of California*. New York: Crown, 1994.

Thomas, Lately. *Between Two Empires: The Life Story of California's First Senator*. Boston: Houghton Mifflin, 1969.

Harney, William S. (1800–1889)

Born in Haysborough, Tennessee, a few miles from Nashville, on August 22, 1800, William Selby Harney served the United States in a lifelong military career that began in 1818. He played a pivotal leadership role in the era of western expansion throughout the nineteenth century.

In 1825 Harney joined the expeditions of Colonel Henry Atkinson and Benjamin O'Fallon, which allowed him to be present at one of the first treaty signings with Indian tribes of the upper Missouri River. He then served as General Zachary Taylor's assistant inspector in the 1832 Sauk and Fox wars and participated in the Second Seminole War in Florida in 1837. Harney's role in these events earned him the reputation of a brute soldier and an Indian fighter.

Between 1846 and 1848, Harney was appointed colonel during the Mexican-American War. In 1854 he received a special request to organize and lead an expedition against the Sioux Nation. This campaign, which began in the summer of 1855, was sparked by the military's desire for retaliation for the previous year's Grattan incident (also called Grattan Massacre) near Fort Laramie. The incident, which involved the theft of a Mormon emigrant's cow by a young Lakota, resulted in the death of twenty-nine white soldiers, including Lieutenant John Grattan.

Harney led the 1,000-member expedition against the Sioux the next year, eventually locating and destroying a Lakota village on Blue Water Creek in current western Nebraska. The attack, known as the Ash Hollow Massacre or the Blue Water Creek incident, ended with more than 100 dead Lakota men, women, and children. Harney quickly earned the name "Mad Bear" from the Lakotas, along with several other nicknames including "Hornet," "Squaw Killer," and "White Beard."

Following this attack, Harney doggedly pursued the Lakotas from Fort Laramie across Dakota Territory to Fort Pierre. Traveling with his expedition was Second Lieutenant Gouverneur Kemble Warren of the Army Corps of Topographical Engineers. Warren was requested to discuss the resources found on the route through Western Dakota Territory. He reported that much of the land was not suited for settlement. However, two years later, on an expedition devoted solely to the Black Hills, Warren provided the first comprehensive report on the region (including a discussion of gold) and stated that an inevitable war with the Lakotas should be pursued near the Black Hills area. Harney's campaign in 1855 ultimately drew the Euro-American presence closer to the Black Hills, a region that remains a controversial subject among the Sioux in modern America.

Harney's 1855 campaign was also responsible for pushing the Lakotas away from the overland trails, forts, and newly settled and traveled areas on the American frontier. This campaign, known commonly as the first Sioux expedition on the northern plains, has been interpreted as the origin of the era of violence in this region that ensued a decade later. As the leader, Harney set the example for military strategy in future conflicts with Indians in the region.

Following his retirement in 1863, Harney played a role in peace commissions and treaty negotiations with tribal leaders between 1865 and 1867. In 1868 he established three agencies for the Sioux Nation along the Missouri River. He died on May 9, 1889, in Orlando, Florida.

Elaine M. Nelson

See also: Atkinson, Henry; Blue Water Creek, Battle of; Grattan Massacre; Lakota; Sioux; Taylor, Zachary; Warren, Gouverneur Kemble.

Further Reading

Adams, George Rollie. *General William S. Harney: Prince of Dragoons.* Lincoln: University of Nebraska Press, 2001.

Clow, Richmond L. "General William Harney on the Northern Plains." *South Dakota History* 16 (1986): 229–248.

Paul, R. Eli. *Blue Water Creek and the First Sioux War, 1854–1856.* Norman: University of Oklahoma Press, 2004.

Harrison, William Henry (1773–1841)

As first territorial governor of Indiana and general in the U.S. army, William Henry Harrison played a pivotal role in the subjugation of the Indian tribes of the Old Northwest Territory. His victories over the Shawnees at Prophet's Town (Battle of Tippecanoe) in November 1811 and at the Battle of the Thames on October 5, 1813, during the War of 1812, opened up thousands of square miles lying between the Ohio River and the Great Lakes to ever westward-expanding white occupation.

Harrison was born on February 9, 1773, at Berkeley Plantation along the James River in Virginia, the son of former Virginia governor, signer of the Declaration of Independence, and Revolutionary War veteran Benjamin Harrison. Leaving medical school before graduation, young Harrison joined the army, migrated westward across the Appalachian Mountains to Fort Washington (now Cincinnati, Ohio) in the Northwest Territory, and began his long career as an Indian fighter. Arriving on the frontier shortly after the disastrous defeats by Indians of Generals Josiah Harmer and Arthur St. Clair, he later served under General Anthony Wayne and participated in the army's victory at the Battle of Fallen Timbers in 1794.

When Indiana Territory, consisting of present-day Indiana, Illinois, Wisconsin, and parts of Michigan and Minnesota, was carved out of the western sections of the Northwest Territory in 1800, Harrison was appointed territorial governor, a role he fulfilled for the next twelve years. As the second war with Great Britain approached, he again immersed himself in military affairs and was commissioned a brigadier general in August 1812 and promoted to major general the following year. After his victory at the Battle of the Thames, he retired from the army in May 1814, receiving a gold medal from Congress in 1818 for his service.

Harrison settled on a tract of land near Cincinnati, and for the next few years, the hero of Tippecanoe tried his hand at farming. In 1816 he was elected to the

Later the ninth president of the United States, William Henry Harrison rose to fame in the early 1800s as an Indian fighter in the Old Northwest Territory. Victories over the Shawnee and neighboring tribes opened the region between the Ohio River and Great Lakes to white settlement. *(The Granger Collection, New York)*

U.S. House of Representatives, where his criticism of Andrew Jackson made the two men enemies, and then served in the Ohio state senate and the U.S. Senate. In 1836 he ran for president on the Whig ticket but was handily defeated by Martin Van Buren, Jackson's handpicked successor. Four years later, with fellow Virginian John Tyler as his running-mate, Harrison was elected chief executive over the incumbent Van Buren, utilizing the Whig Party's slogan "Tippecanoe and Tyler, too."

Harrison's tenure as president lasted only one month. On the day of the inauguration, he adamantly refused to cover his head or wear a heavy coat despite the extremely cold and inclement weather. He took ill soon afterward and died of pneumonia on April 4, 1841, the first president to die in office. His service to the nation as president was so short-lived that his wife of nearly half a century, the former Anna Tuthill Symmes, failed to reach the White House from their Ohio home before his death.

James A. Crutchfield

See also: Fallen Timbers, Battle of; Tecumseh; Thames, Battle of the; Wayne, Anthony.

Further Reading

Dillon, Richard H. *North American Indian Wars*. New York: Facts on File, 1983.

Hurt, R. Douglas. *The Ohio Frontier: Crucible of the Old Northwest, 1720–1830*. Bloomington: Indiana University Press, 1998.

Owens, Robert M. *Mr. Jefferson's Hammer: William Henry Harrison and the Origins of American Indian Policy*. Norman: University of Oklahoma Press, 2007.

Hayden, Ferdinand
(1828–1887)

Considered one of America's most popular and celebrated public scientists of the 1870s, Ferdinand Vandeveer Hayden popularized the American West through his numerous explorations of the states and territories between the Missouri River and the Rocky Mountains.

Hayden was born in Westfield, Massachusetts, on September 7, 1828, and upon his parent's divorce and his mother's remarriage, he was sent to live with relatives in Rochester, Ohio, early in 1841. At sixteen he left for Oberlin, 15 miles (24 km) away, and enrolled in the Preparatory Department of Oberlin College. Graduating in August 1850, he taught for a year and a half in Ohio district schools. Encouraged to obtain a medical degree, Hayden attended Albany Medical College, graduating in 1854.

Immensely interested in natural history and geology, Hayden sought every opportunity to work in the field—especially in the American West. He had an uncanny ability to identify representative fossils in an area and after several excursions up the Missouri River was recognized as an excellent collector of specimens. From 1853 to 1862, he accompanied several expeditions in the western territories from the White River badlands to the confluence of the Yellowstone and Bighorn rivers. On his first trip he found thirty-four new species of invertebrate shells and, on a later trip, found the first fossils of American dinosaurs. In 1856 Hayden met Jim Bridger, the famed mountain man, who recounted tales of the wonders of the region where Hell bubbled up. In 1859 Hayden circumnavigated the Yellowstone region with Captain W.F. Raynolds, a trip that contributed to his interest in further exploring that region.

These experiences whetted his appetite for conducting his own expeditions. However, western exploration was put on hold with the outbreak of the Civil War.

Dr. Hayden enlisted in the Union Army in 1862 as a surgeon. By the end of the war, he was serving as the chief medical officer for the Army of the Shenandoah. He was honorably discharged in June 1865.

From 1865 to 1872, Hayden was an auxiliary professor of geology and mineralogy at the University of Pennsylvania. The terms of this appointment allowed him to continue explorations in the western territories. The opportunity to conduct his own expedition came in 1867 when he was appointed the director of the Geological Survey of Nebraska. For the next twelve years he led one of the most successful geological and geographical surveys in the American West. From Nebraska the survey expanded to include Wyoming, Colorado, and portions of Utah, Idaho, and Montana. It was his 1871 exploration of the Yellowstone region that was his greatest achievement.

The Hayden Survey was the first official scientific expedition to visit Yellowstone. Upon the explorers' return to Washington, the photographs of William Henry Jackson and the illustrations and paintings of Thomas Moran demonstrated to the American public that the wonders of the Yellowstone did indeed exist. More than providing evidence of the geysers and hot springs, Hayden identified the headwaters of the Yellowstone, Snake, Madison, Gallatin, and Green rivers. But the Hayden Survey "discovered" more than Yellowstone. On one of the Colorado expeditions, members identified the Mount of the Holy Cross as well as some of the earliest Anasazi cliff dwellings in the Southwest.

In 1879 the "great surveys" were combined into one agency—the U.S. Geological Survey—that still exists today. Despite Hayden's role as leader of the most successful of the western surveys, did not receive the directorship. He died following a lengthy illness on December 22, 1887, at the age of fifty-nine. Historians and biographers largely ignored him and his contributions to the expansion of the American West until the late twentieth century. Two places are named in honor of this pioneer of geology and promoter of westward expansion—Hayden, Colorado, and the Hayden Valley in Yellowstone National Park.

Tamsen Emerson Hert

See also: Bridger, Jim; Hayden Survey; Jackson, William Henry; Moran, Thomas; United States Geological Survey.

Further Reading

Cassidy, James G. *Ferdinand V. Hayden, Entrepreneur of Science*. Lincoln: University of Nebraska Press, 2000.

Foster, Mike. *Strange Genius: The Life of Ferdinand Vandeveer Hayden*. Niwot, CO: Roberts Rinehart, 1994.

Hayden Survey

The Hayden Survey was one of the four "great surveys" initiated after the Civil War. Established in 1867 as the Geological Survey of Nebraska with Ferdinand Vandeveer Hayden as "geologist-in-charge," it was later officially designated as the Geological Survey of the Territories (1869–1873) and the United States Geological and Geographical Survey of the Territories (1873–1879). All four surveys demonstrated the federal government's support for the economic development of the western states and territories.

Upon Nebraska's entry into the Union in 1867, Dr. Ferdinand Hayden—who had extensive experience exploring the West—organized the expedition to examine geologic formations, collect fossils and minerals, make barometrical observations, and develop a geological map. Hayden was instructed to produce numerous illustrations of specimens, landscapes, and other features of the terrain. He produced all these results with the assistance of skillful individuals who possessed geological, paleontological, artistic, and photographic experience. When the survey was terminated in 1879, more than $700,000 had been spent on the explorations, which extended from New Mexico to Montana. The effort employed more than 200 men as cooks, packers, journalists, photographers, artists, and scientists. This team mapped 417,000 square miles (1 million sq km) and produced 21,142 pages of documentation, most of it later published as reports, monographs, and maps.

During its twelve years of operation, the Hayden Survey conducted fieldwork in some of the most remote areas of the American West. Following operations in western Nebraska and along the front range of the Rocky Mountains in 1868, the survey expanded its work to Colorado and New Mexico in 1869. The 1870 season found the men back in southeastern Wyoming, exploring the Laramie range, the upper valleys of the North Platte and Sweetwater rivers, and the Laramie Plains all the way to the northern edge of the Uinta Mountains in the southwestern part of Wyoming Territory.

It was the 1871 expedition into the region of the Yellowstone that brought fame to the Hayden Survey as well as to select members of its staff. As early as 1856 Hayden had been intrigued with the Yellowstone region and determined to return to authenticate the geological wonders of the area as well as to identify the headwaters of the major rivers that flow out of northwestern Wyoming. His plans for this expedition were in place long before the preliminary report of Gustavus Doane was available or Nathaniel Langford gave public lectures about the region. Accompanying the Hayden Survey to the Yellowstone region was photographer William Henry Jackson and artist Thomas Moran. Jackson's photographs are considered the most important contributions of this trip, although Moran's

Members of the Hayden geological survey make camp at Red Buttes, Wyoming Territory, in 1870. Hayden's four federally sponsored expeditions produced an extensive scientific record of some of the most remote areas of the American West. *(Time & Life Pictures/Getty Images)*

watercolors and his oil painting of the Grand Canyon of the Yellowstone also are significant. These works, coupled with Hayden's public support of the national park idea, helped create Yellowstone National Park. Hayden drew the map indicating the boundaries of the proposed park. The survey continued its work in Yellowstone in 1872.

From 1873 to 1876 Colorado and the central Rockies were the focus. During this time the Mount of the Holy Cross and the cliff dwellings near Mancos were discovered, bringing more national attention to the survey. In 1877 Hayden published *The Atlas of Colorado*. The final years of the survey, 1877–1878, were spent mapping areas of Wyoming, Idaho, and Montana.

According to Richard Bartlett:

> The Hayden Survey fulfilled its basic function of mapping the West and laying the foundations for much of the knowledge we possess of its natural beauty, but its accomplishments did not stop there. It also served another valuable purpose. Through the journalists and photographers who accompanied its expeditions, it popularized the wonders of the West and gave to the rest of the world a new and more accurate image of western scenic wonders.

Additionally, the Hayden Survey served as the model for the new U.S. Geological Survey, which consolidated the work of the four "great surveys" in 1879.

Tamsen Emerson Hert

See also: Hayden, Ferdinand; Holmes, William Henry; Jackson, William Henry; Moran, Thomas; United States Geological Survey.

Further Reading

Bartlett, Richard A. *Great Surveys of the American West*. Norman: University of Oklahoma Press, 1962.
Goetzman, William H. *Exploration and Empire: The Explorer and the Scientist in the Winning of the American West*. New York: History Book Club, 1993.
Lundberg, Ann E. *The Geologist and the Great West: An Historical Review of the Geological Survey of the Territories Under F.V. Hayden*. Laramie: Department of Geology and Geophysics, University of Wyoming, 1989.

Hayfield Fight
See Red Cloud's War

Heap, Gwinn Harris (1817–1887)

In 1853 Edward F. Beale, commissioner of Indian affairs in California, former U.S. Navy officer, and close friend of John C. Frémont, undertook an expedition to explore and chart a route through the central portion of the American West for a potential transcontinental railroad. Thomas Hart Benton, a powerful senator from Missouri, an advocate for a central rail route through the West, and Frémont's father-in-law, sponsored this project. Beale chose his cousin, Gwinn Harris Heap, to accompany him on the journey to chronicle its events and course. Heap's account of this expedition, *Central Route to the Pacific*, became a landmark journal of western American exploration and an important tool in the sectional struggle for the location of the impending transcontinental railroad.

Gwinn Heap was born in Chester, Pennsylvania, in 1817. His father was named U.S. consul to Tunis in 1825; thereafter, Heap spent much of his youth overseas. He became acting consul to Tunis in 1839 and remained in the Middle East until 1846, when he returned to the United States. Heap was a government clerk in Washington, DC, when Beale asked him to join the expedition. Beale's successful journey was skillfully recorded by Heap. His account of the trip, in the form of letters and journal entries, was sent back to Senator Benton, who had it published in the nation's prominent newspapers. After returning to the East Coast in 1854, Heap had the journal, along with a detailed map of the expedition's route and an impressive collection of his drawings, published as a book. Benton, who assisted Heap in getting the work published, used the volume's words and images to promote his dream of a central rail route both to the public and to his political colleagues.

Heap then traveled to Egypt and Turkey, where he and his brother-in-law, David Dixon Porter, acquired camels for shipment to the United States; the U.S. Army wanted to test their usefulness in the desert expanses of the American West. In 1857 the secretary of war assigned Edward Beale to survey a military wagon road between New Mexico and California and to assess the effectiveness of the imported camels in this environment. Heap joined the expedition as Beale's second-in-command, but early in the journey, following a dispute with Beale, resigned and returned to the East Coast. Heap later served in the Civil War by helping his brother-in-law, now Admiral Porter, procure and arrange transportation for the Union navy's supplies. After the war, he again went overseas. Heap was appointed consul to Belfast, Ireland, in 1866, consul to Tunis in 1867, and finally consul general at Constantinople, where he served until his death in 1887.

Jim Ersfeld

See also: Beale Wagon Road; Benton, Thomas Hart; Frémont, John C.; Railroad Surveys, Transcontinental.

Further Reading

Heap, Gwinn Harris. *Central Route to the Pacific, with Related Material on Railroad Explorations and Indian Affairs by Edward F. Beale, Thomas H. Benton, Kit Carson, and Col. E. A. Hitchcock, and in Other Documents, 1853–54.* Edited by LeRoy R. Hafen and Ann W. Hafen. Glendale, CA: Arthur H. Clark, 1957.

Henry, Andrew
(c. 1770s–1832)

Andrew Henry is one of the unsung heroes of America's westward expansion and the western fur trade. While his partner, General William Ashley, is a household name among western historians and aficionados, Henry operated so much in the background that his fame today is far less than his associate's. Henry's exact date of birth is uncertain, but it is believed to be sometime between 1773 and 1778. From his birthplace in Pennsylvania, he moved to Nashville, Tennessee, then to Louisiana Territory, where he operated a lead mine near present-day Potosi, Missouri. When Manuel Lisa organized the St. Louis Missouri Fur Company in 1809, Henry was one of the incorporators.

Henry was with Lisa on the 1809 trip upriver when their party met mountain man John Colter and persuaded him to join them and return to the wilderness. The following year, Henry oversaw the construction of a fur post at the Three Forks of the Missouri River and, for the next few months, he and his small party combed the upper river basin for furs. Hostile Blackfoot Indians, however, cut short his sojourn at the Three Forks, and while one half of his group returned to St. Louis, Henry guided the other half farther up the Madison River. Later in the year, he established the first American fur post west of the Continental Divide (one of several stockades named Fort Henry) on the Snake River in present-day Idaho.

Fatigued from his hazardous ordeals in the fur trade, Henry retired to his lead mines in Missouri. When the War of 1812 broke out, Henry and Ashley teamed up to supply the U.S. Army with much-needed lead and saltpeter required for ammunition. He attained the rank of major in the Missouri volunteer infantry and forever afterward was called Major Henry. Between the end of the war and 1822, he again associated himself with Ashley and became the recruiting agent when the general advertised for "enterprising young men" to accompany his expedition up the Missouri River.

Henry and a complement of trader-trappers went upriver in the spring of 1822 and built a small post, another Fort Henry, at the mouth of the Yellowstone River. Although Henry encountered trouble with the Blackfoot when he tried to trap on their lands, he was still in the area the following year when the Arikaras confronted Ashley further down the Missouri. By the time Henry and a relief column of trappers arrived at the scene, the conflict was over, and he returned to the fort on the Yellowstone.

Henry stayed in the fur business until his retirement in 1824, when he moved back to his farm in Washington County, Missouri. When he died at his home on January 10, 1832, a St. Louis newspaper eulogized him as one of the earliest and most enterprising trapper-traders to explore the wilderness of the Rocky Mountains and called him a man who was noted for his honesty, intelligence, and business acumen.

James A. Crutchfield

See also: Arikara War; Ashley, William Henry; Rocky Mountain Fur Company; Smith, Jedediah.

Further Reading

Clokey, Richard M. *William H. Ashley: Enterprise and Politics in the Trans-Mississippi West.* Norman: University of Oklahoma Press, 1980.

Morgan, Dale L. *Jedediah Smith and the Opening of the West.* Indianapolis: Bobbs-Merrill, 1953.

Hidatsa

The Hidatsas, a Siouan people, were called Minitaris by the Mandan Indians and Gros Ventre by French trappers and traders. Lewis and Clark referred to their village as that of the Little Minnetarees. Three villages, or groups, made up the whole of the Hidatsa: Hidatsa Proper; the Awatixa, a smaller group; and the Awaxawi. The largest of the three villages was Hidatsa Proper (Hidatsa), whose inhabitants' own name for themselves meant "willows."

Karl Bodmer, the great Swiss artist of the American West, painted this Hidatsa warrior performing the ceremonial Dog Dance in 1833. The Hidatsa were a Siouan-speaking tribe of the upper Missouri River region. They were decimated by smallpox and war. *(Library of Congress)*

The language of the Hidatsas is akin to that of the Crow. In fact, the Hidatsas claim to have descended from the Crows, separating from them at some early time because of a quarrel over a buffalo hunt. Each of the three Hidatsas villages spoke in dialects that were distinct from the others.

Migrating from Miniwakan, or Devils Lake, in present-day North Dakota, the tribe met the Mandans at the mouth of the Heart River. The Mandans and the Hidatsas attempted to join as one tribe, but ongoing conflicts caused them to remain physically apart. The Mandans, known as adept traders in the region, aided the Hidatsas after the separation by helping them build new villages not far from their own.

In 1804 Lewis and Clark encountered the Hidatsas in three villages at the mouth of the Knife River. Expedition members spent the winter of 1804 with the Mandans in two villages a few miles further down the Missouri, and frequently interacted with the Hidatsas.

The artist George Catlin visited the Hidatsas in 1832. Catlin remained with the tribe and the Mandans

for several months, sketching and painting, in an effort to faithfully document their life. The paintings later accompanied Catlin as he toured Europe. A year later, German explorer, ethnologist, and naturalist Prince Alexander Philip Maximilian zu Wied-Neuwied visited the Hidatsas with the artist Karl Bodmer. Bodmer, just twenty-four years old when he embarked on the 5,000-mile (8,000-km) expedition, is best known as a watercolor artist. Like Lewis and Clark, Prince Maximilian and Bodmer spent the winter with the hospitable Hidatsas and Mandans. Bodmer returned to Europe after the trip and was a founding member of the Barbizon group of artists.

A severe smallpox epidemic that swept the Great Plains did not leave the Mandan or Hidatsa Indians untouched. The dread disease nearly exterminated the Mandans in 1837–1838, leaving only 150 survivors. The same outbreak reduced the Hidatsas to about 500 members. Survivors of the two tribes united and in 1845 moved up the Missouri. There they built a village at Like-a-Fishhook bend, in close proximity to the Fort Berthold trading post.

The Hidatsa and Mandan tribes were joined by the Arikaras in 1862. Neighboring lands were set apart as a reservation for them, and the three tribes are still today based out of the Fort Berthold Reservation in North Dakota. The tribes are now collectively referred to as the Three Affiliated Tribes.

Larry D. Sweazy

See also: Arikara; Bodmer, Karl; Catlin, George; Disease; Lewis and Clark Expedition; Mandan; Maximilian, Prince Alexander Philip.

Further Reading
Ahler, Stanley A., Thomas D. Thiessen, and Michael K. Trimble. *People of the Willows: The Prehistory and Early History of the Hidatsa Indians.* Grand Forks: University of North Dakota Press, 1991.

Matthews, Washington. *Ethnography and Philology of the Hidatsa Indians.* Washington, DC: Government Printing Office, 1877.

Hide Hunters

During the mid-to-late 1860s, thousands of men displaced by the American Civil War moved from eastern war-torn states west across the Mississippi River to the rich hunting grounds of the central plains. There they started an industry that became an integral part of the country's policy of manifest destiny—hunting buffalo.

The American Plains Indians used every part of the buffalo to sustain life, and in order to supply themselves with great numbers of this extremely important animal, the tribesmen followed the herds on their annual north-south migrations stretching from Sioux lands on the Canadian border southward to Nebraska and, among the southern tribes (Arapahos, Cheyennes, Pawnees, and Comanches), from present-day Oklahoma south into Texas. Upon arrival on the Great Plains, white settlers from the East, looking for a new start and "free" land, killed the buffalo for only its meat to feed themselves and their families.

Professional hunters—more entrepreneurial than the settlers and farmers with families—soon followed and found a commercial outlet for the buffalo's meat. They took only the choice cuts and the animals' tongues, smoked them in large pits dug on the hunting ranges, salted and dried the meat, and hauled it in wagons to butchers in nearby towns. These men also sold buffalo meat to the railroads for their workers, now building rail lines across the Great Plains. The rest of the animal was left on the Plains to be scavenged by crows, vultures, wolves, and coyotes.

To the Plains Indians, the wastefulness displayed by Anglo-Americans and their encroachment on what was perceived as Indian hunting territories caused contention and much bloodshed during the mid-nineteenth century. The ruthless harvesting of bison meat continued until, in 1870, almost by accident, a new use for the buffalo was discovered. Josiah Wright Mooar, a nineteen-year-old Vermonter who had moved to the West in search of adventure, was eking out a small living cutting and hauling wood for the U.S. military at Fort Hays, Kansas, when local entrepreneur and hunter Charles Rath asked Mooar to help supply buffalo hides for well-known fur dealer W.C. Lobenstein, located in Leavenworth, Kansas. Mooar oversupplied Rath's needs and sent fifty-seven leftover hides to his brother, John Wesley Mooar, in New York City. A Pennsylvania fur dealer there, intrigued by the mound of thick, furry hides, purchased them and eventually discovered that the warm, thick winter hides could be tanned and made into lap robes for the horse and buggy trade of the urban East. From that meager beginning, J. Wright Mooar and thousands of others proved that, although it was a filthy, cold, and time-consuming occupation, hide hunting was also a very lucrative one.

The American bison provided a short-lived but lively business in hides, meat, and later, even bones. Meat hunting continued as well, but hide taking eventually became the primary industry. Hunters killed buffalo and skinned and cured the hides for sale in centrally located markets throughout the plains of North America. To facilitate the efficiency of the hunter, Lobenstein sent agents onto the hunting ranges, purchased hides "on the ground," and sent his own wagons out for the collection of the hides. He then distributed the harvest to merchants in towns like Dodge City and Caldwell, Kansas; Fort Worth, Denison, and Fort Griffin, Texas; and Kit Carson and Granada in eastern Colorado. From those towns, now that the railroads had reached them, hundreds of thousands of buffalo hides were shipped east and, in some instances, on to England where buffalo hide leather was used for military equipment.

As the big animals became scarce in Kansas, the hunters spread out into surrounding areas—Nebraska, eastern Colorado, Indian Territory (Oklahoma), and south into the Panhandle of Texas. The latter territory was opened to hunters by none other than the adventurous J. Wright Mooar and some of his friends who had braved the Comanche Indians to follow the buffalo. When the Texas herds were winnowed during the winter hunting season of 1878–1879, hunters then looked far north to the smaller herds of the Dakota and Montana territories and, in a few instances, into Canada.

By the mid-1880s, the millions of the American bison that had once populated North America had essentially disappeared and the American Indians, who had depended upon the buffalo for their very lives, were displaced to reservations and forced to become dependent upon the U.S. government for their subsistence. In fact, the over-zealousness of the hide hunter worked hand in hand with federal policy to remove the Indians from their original homelands in order to make more room for white settlers. General Philip H. Sheridan, when addressing the Texas Legislature in 1875, pleaded with lawmakers to kill a proposal to protect the last of the state's buffalo herd. In his opinion, the men who destroyed the bison were heroes and should be given a medal with a rendition of a dead buffalo on one side and a discouraged Indian on the other. Telling the legislators that the hide hunters had done more in the last two years to alleviate the "Indian question" than the entire army had done in the previous two decades, Sheridan heaped praise on the hunters for destroying the Indians' commissary.

The decimation of the American bison was a tragedy, on the one hand, resulting in the almost complete disappearance of the largest existing American land mammal. On the other hand, however, it provided reason for towns to spring up in convenient places across the Great Plains that later were useful during the construction of railroads, which in turn became important in another phase of the westward expansion of the United States—the cattle ranching industry.

The buffalo hide hunting industry had lasted a mere fifteen years, but had an overarching impact on the lives of people in the West. Today, after almost a century of conservation efforts, the buffalo population is making a steady comeback with current herds numbering in the tens of thousands.

Sharon Cunningham

See also: Cattle Frontier.

Further Reading

Dary, David. *The Buffalo Book: The Saga of an American Symbol.* New York: Avon Books, 1975.

Gilbert, Miles, Leo Remiger, and Sharon Cunningham. *Encyclopedia of Buffalo Hunters & Skinners.* 2 vols. Union City, TN: Pioneer Press, 2003 and 2006.

McHugh, Tom. *The Time of the Buffalo.* New York: Alfred A. Knopf, 1972.

Robinson, Charles M., III, and Robert K. DeArment. *The Buffalo Hunters.* Abilene, TX: State House Press, 1995.

Holladay, Ben (1819–1887)

Ben Holladay, born in Kentucky, on October 14, 1819, and raised in Weston, Missouri, learned the wagon trade business from his father while helping him lead wagon trains west through the Cumberland Gap. He began his adult career in the mercantile business and soon gained contracts furnishing supplies to General Stephen Watts Kearny in the Mexican-American War. By 1849 Holladay, now an accomplished businessman, moved west where he established a group of mercantile houses and transportation services spread from Salt Lake City to San Francisco. It is during this period that he is given credit for introducing the Concord stagecoach into the West by purchasing Abbott and Downing's signature vehicle of the era. Establishing a stronghold on the business, Holladay furthered his enterprise when he acquired the Butterfield Overland Dispatch, renaming it the Holladay Overland Mail and Express Company. He eventually became known as the "Stagecoach King."

In the spring of 1861, Holladay allowed his Pike's Peak stage line to service the Central Overland California and Pike's Peak Express Company during the infant stages of the Pony Express. He supported the effort by extending credit to the backers of the Pony Express for horses, feed, and other supplies. As the primary creditor, Holladay eventually controlled the financial aspects of the short-lived company.

Due to the Indian uprisings along the Oregon Trail and the increasing need to deliver the mail to points west, such as Denver, Holladay established service on the new Overland Trail through Colorado Territory. With government approval, his coaches were rolling over the new route by mid-summer 1862, and mail was soon being delivered to Denver. By 1864 Holladay's stage line business had expanded along the Overland Trail across present southern Wyoming. He controlled a near monopoly on the mail, freight, and passenger services between Missouri and Salt Lake City; a distance of over 2,500 miles (4,025 km) of stage lines across the West.

In 1866 Holladay sold his routes to Wells Fargo Express for a reported $1.5 million. Relocating in Oregon, he formed the Northern Pacific Transportation Company, operating from Alaska to Mexico, as well as the Oregon and California Railroad Company. He also had controlling interests in several gold and silver mines, real estate properties, and retail establishments along the west coast. By the age of fifty, Ben Holladay, "Stagecoach King" turned transportation mogul, was a multimillionaire.

In Oregon, Holladay established Portland's first horse-car line, which was pulled over iron rails from a downtown turntable. He also established two hotels in the city, and, after a few years, he had a monopoly on the Portland shipping enterprise.

Everything changed for Holladay, as it did for thousands of Americans, when, on September 18, 1873, the stock market crashed. He lost control of the Oregon and California Railroad and spent the remaining years of his life battling lawsuits due to the complexity and failure of his many financial enterprises, eventually losing his homes and various real estate properties. The man who brought the stagecoach to the West and furthered westward transportation on several levels, died in Portland, Oregon on July 8, 1887.

Linda Wommack

See also: Overland Trail; Pony Express; Russell, Majors, and Waddell; Transportation, Land; Wells, Fargo & Company.

Further Reading

Hafen, LeRoy R. *The Overland Mail, 1819–1869.* Norman: University of Oklahoma Press, 2004.

Newell, Gordon, and Joe Williamson. *Pacific Coastal Liners.* New York: Bonanza Books, 1959.

Holmes, William Henry (1846–1933)

William Henry Holmes, whose long life spanned the period between the Mexican-American War and the Great Depression, was best known for the detailed illustrations he provided during Ferdinand V. Hayden's scientific explorations of the Yellowstone region (1871–1872) and Colorado (1873–1876) as well as Clarence E. Dutton's survey of the Grand Canyon (1879). His topographical drawings, later issued as part of Hayden's monumental *Geological and Geographical Atlas of Colorado* (1877) and Dutton's *Tertiary History of the Grand Canyon District* (1882), are unexcelled in their beauty and accuracy.

Born near Cadiz, Ohio, in 1846, Holmes received art training as a young man and in 1871 was hired by the Smithsonian Institution to provide illustrations for paleontological reports. The quality of his art came to the attention of Ferdinand Hayden of the U.S. Geographical and Geological Survey, who appointed him geologist-artist for the upcoming scientific exploration of the Yellowstone region. The sketches, drawings, and topographical renditions that Holmes produced for Hayden brought him almost instant recognition, and Hayden invited the artist to accompany him on his next assignment, the mapping of Colorado Territory. It was on this journey that Holmes drew the first-ever artistic rendition of the Mount of the Holy Cross—a simple, yet wonderfully executed pencil sketch—and also explored and mapped the vast ruins of Mesa Verde, an area now a national park in southwestern Colorado.

Following his later tenure with Dutton's survey of the Grand Canyon, Holmes's interest gradually shifted from geology to ethnology, no doubt prompted to some degree by his wanderings throughout Mesa Verde during the mid-1870s. He taught for a while at the University of Chicago and served as head curator of anthropology at the Field Museum of Natural History in that city. When his friend Major John Wesley Powell, longtime director of the Bureau of American Ethnology (BAE), died in 1902, Holmes became his successor, with the title of "chief" rather than "director." Although Holmes was not a BAE staff member at the time, his friendship with Powell went back many years and Powell had often called upon Holmes to provide artwork for BAE bulletins and periodicals. The two men were founders of the notable Cosmos Club and the Anthropological Society of Washington, DC.

After serving for seven years as chief of the BAE, Holmes left his post and became head curator of anthropology at the U.S. National Museum within the structure of the Smithsonian Institution. Later, he became the first director of the newly organized National Gallery of Art, also a Smithsonian museum. He died in 1933.

James A. Crutchfield

See also: Hayden, Ferdinand; Hayden Survey; Powell, John Wesley; United States Geological Survey.

Further Reading

Bartlett, Richard A. *Great Surveys of the American West*. Norman: University of Oklahoma Press, 1962.
Viola, Herman J. *Exploring the West*. Washington, DC: Smithsonian Books, 1987.

Homestead Act (1862)

When President Abraham Lincoln signed the Homestead Act into law in 1862, he fulfilled a campaign promise to advocate agricultural production and support a government-backed homestead measure. Both were accomplished and backed in supporting legislation with federal aid for westward railroad construction and the establishment of the Federal Department of Agriculture.

Advocated by Westerners for many years, the Homestead Act went into effect on January 1, 1863. It became one of the most important congressional acts implemented during the nineteenth century in the effort to permanently settle the lands west of the Mississippi River, giving the right to men, and in some situations to women, of all socioeconomic strata to establish their own farms or small ranches.

The new law provided the opportunity for essentially anyone to file for a quarter section of federal public land (160 acres [65 ha]). Claimants were required to be the head of a family, or an individual over the age of twenty-one, or meet a military service requirement. One significant aspect of the law was the requirement that the applicant must not have raised arms against the United States or given aid and comfort to its enemies (a significant requirement at the time of enactment, given the ongoing Civil War).

To gain title, the applicant paid an $18 filing fee. Land title was issued free and clear after the applicant had resided on the land for five years and made improvements, such as home building and/or

The Homestead Act of 1862, which granted 160 acres (65 ha) of free land to any settler, triggered a massive westward migration. Nearly 1 million Americans filed claims between 1863 and 1890, the greatest period of farm establishment in the nation's history. *(American Stock Archive/ Getty Images)*

agriculture. Other means of claiming western land were allowed under various other laws such as by preemption, or under claims related to planting trees (timber claims) or reclaiming desert lands (desert claims), though fewer acres were ever ultimately transferred to individual ownership under such provisions. Homesteading was a difficult objective not easily achieved, as those who made homestead claims found that environmental conditions were quite different in the arid West from the more humid East. Water was often scarce, the land itself was drier, and the winds could be quite severe.

Homesteaders built sod homes and lived in constant fear of hailstorms, drought, prairie fires, windstorms, and blizzards. Other threats from nature were the swarms of locusts and grasshoppers that wiped out entire crops. Although initially most homesteaders were male, eventually women took advantage of the law and claimed land in their own names. Sometimes they undertook improvements in cooperation with a sister, or near acreage owned by fathers and brothers; other women struck out solely on their own and made successful claims.

The Homestead Act of 1862 has often been referred to as one of the most significant government acts for American citizens in history. During the westward migration following the Civil War, some 270 million acres (109 million ha) of western land were developed in the form of homesteads, ranches, and farms, and they gave rise to communities across the region. Yet the Homestead Act was not without its faults. While 160 acres (65 ha) was a generous amount of free land, in the West it was often a liability. With the lack of water, it was difficult to farm the acreage adequately. For ranchers in the high altitudes, or on the dry grasslands, a quarter section of land could not support a cattle ranch. A U.S. Geological Survey conducted in 1879, reported that each steer required ten acres of grazing.

For the ranchers, other problems soon surfaced. Encroachment of land, particularly near rivers and streams, became problematic for large ranch owners, while conversely, homesteaders were often threatened or so harassed by stockmen that they would sell out or simply leave; in extreme cases they were killed. Predatory stock rustling led to range wars and set up the end of the open range when barbed wire fencing became a necessity.

Additional provisions to the original Homestead Act were subsequently enacted. Even so, the federal homestead laws are important primarily because they provided an incentive in the form of easily obtainable land for settlement of the American West.

Linda Wommack

See also: Barbed Wire; Graduation Act (1854); Preemption Act (1841); Timber Culture Act (1873).

Further Reading

Davis, William C. *The American Frontier.* Norman: University of Oklahoma Press, 1992.

Gruver, Brooks. *Rebecca: An American History.* New York: New York City University Press, 1972.

Lindgren, H. Elaine. *Land in Her Own Name.* Norman: University of Oklahoma Press. 1996.

Hopewell, Treaty of (1785)

At the conclusion of the Revolutionary War the United States sought opportunities to negotiate treaties with those Indian nations formerly allied with the British. One of the greatest threats in the South was a southeastern confederacy of tribes. The young nation established a commission to negotiate the terms of the Treaty of Hopewell with the Muscogee (Creek), Cherokee, Choctaw, and Chickasaw nations.

Five commissioners were appointed: Benjamin Hawkins, Andrew Pickens, Joseph Martin, Lachlan McIntosh, and William Perry. Four of them, minus Perry, first met with the Creeks, who adamantly refused any treaty negotiations with the Americans. After these failed negotiations, the commissioners gathered in South Carolina in late November 1785, to urge the Cherokees to accept their terms. This negotiation, which became known as the Treaty of Hopewell, was the first official covenant negotiated between representatives of the U.S. government and the Cherokee Nation.

Like the 1784 Treaty of Fort Stanwix, the Hopewell treaty established new boundary lines, established the United States as the protector of the Cherokees, restored prisoners of war, and granted the Americans the exclusive right of trade. In addition, the treaty provided for a Cherokee deputy to be sent to Congress. As part of the treaty, the Cherokees ceded a large portion of today's middle Tennessee lying between the Duck River on the south and the Cumberland River on the north, as well as a sizable parcel of land in North Carolina lying east of Asheville and stretching between the state's borders with Tennessee and South Carolina. Nine hundred and eighteen Cherokees attended the gathering, but only thirty-seven chiefs and principal men of the tribe actually participated in the signing. The Cherokees who attended the signing were awarded trade goods valued at about $1,300. They were told that the payment was so small because only the chiefs and headmen had been expected at the signing.

The next two treaties were negotiated with the Choctaws and the Chickasaws in early January 1786. While the treaties followed a similar format as the Cherokee treaty, neither tribe was afforded a deputy position in Congress.

Like the previous Fort Stanwix treaty, the boundary lines defined in the Hopewell Treaty lacked proper backing and left the enforcement to the Cherokees, Choctaws, and Chickasaws. The southern states under the Articles of Confederation viewed congressional authority over their western lands as an assault on their sovereignty, and hostilities escalated as southern states ignored the provisions of the treaty. By the 1830s these clashes led to the Indian Removal Act. The deliberations with the Cherokees pointed to the future and John Marshall's landmark Supreme Court decision to claim the Cherokees as a "domestic dependent nation."

The Treaty of Hopewell signed in 1785 was the first of a long list of negotiations between the U.S. government and various Indian nations that extinguished native title to thousands upon thousands of square miles of the present-day country. The settlers were pushing for more and more real estate, and the regions further west were the next logical spaces to be occupied. In later years, the same scenario occurred again and again as other Indians ceded other lands to the newly arrived settlers until eventually the entire continent, from coast to coast, became the possession of the newcomers.

Kent Blansett

See also: Cherokee; Chickasaw; Choctaw; Fort Stanwix, Treaty of (1784); Nashville.

Further Reading

Kappler, Charles J., ed. and comp. *Indian Affairs: Laws and Treaties.* Vol. 2. Washington, DC: Government Printing Office, 1904.

Prucha, Francis Paul. *American Indian Treaties: The History of a Political Anomaly.* Berkeley: University of California Press, 1994.

Royce, Charles C. *Indian Land Cessions in the United States.* Eighteenth Annual Report of the Bureau of American Ethnology. Washington, DC: Government Printing Office, 1899.

Strickland, Rennard. *Fire and Spirits: Cherokee Law from Clan to Court.* Norman: University of Oklahoma Press, 1982.

Hopi

Descendants of the cliff-dwelling Anasazi (more recently called Ancestral Puebloan) culture, the Hopis are believed to have settled and farmed in northern

Arizona as early as 500 C.E. and to have occupied three mesas on the southern flanks of Black Mesa in northeast Arizona since the period of 900–1000 C.E. The Hopi village of Oraibi dates to the mid-twelfth century and is the oldest continually inhabited settlement in the United States. The Hopis call themselves *Hopitu*, "Peaceable People."

Masters of "dry farming" (depending upon the natural precipitation of summer rains and winter snow melt for irrigation), the Hopis planted farms and gardens in terraced washes and valleys between their mesas. Crops included many varieties of corn plus beans, squash, melons, pumpkins, and fruit. Raising livestock also became important in Hopi life. The people were at the mercy of periodic droughts, but otherwise, due to the remoteness of their villages, remained for 1,000 years isolated and peaceful in their high desert villages of stone and adobe.

Hopi religion is centered on spirits representing the cycle of life, death, and rebirth. Both the spirits and the colorful, doll-like figures that depict them are known as kachinas (or katsinas). Hopi ceremonies include a snake dance and a rain ritual. Hopi culture is regarded as one of the best-preserved Native American cultures in North America.

The Hopi people first encountered Europeans in 1541 when an advance guard of Spanish conquistadors under Francisco Vásquez de Coronado passed through the Black Mesa region in their search for the legendary (and mythical) Seven Cities of Gold. Fifty years passed before the Spaniards returned, escorting Franciscan priests and establishing a mission among the Hopi tribe. While unsuccessful in suppressing the native religion in favor of Catholicism, the Europeans bartered for horses, burros, cattle, sheep, and the vegetables and fruits from the Hopis' gardens and orchards. Unfortunately, the result of these trade relations was the introduction of diseases theretofore unknown to the natives—smallpox in particular—epidemics of which decimated the Hopis and other Puebloan populations.

In 1680 the Hopis joined other Pueblo people in a revolt against Spanish colonization. The temporarily successful rising, centered in New Mexico, forced the Spaniards to retreat toward El Paso del Norte (present-day El Paso), but the conflict ended in 1792 with the reconquest of Santa Fe by the Europeans. The Hopis in their near-impenetrable mesa-top communities or those who sought refuge among the nomadic Navajos were largely unaffected by the revolt itself; however, they endured intermittent conflicts with the Spanish interlopers, including the invasion of grazing lands and water sources and raids on Hopi villages, until 1821, when Spain recognized Mexico's independence.

The Hopis have had ongoing land disputes with their neighbors, the Navajos, dating from the 1820s, when Navajos took over certain Hopi lands. In 1882, in the administration of President Chester A. Arthur, 2.5 million acres (1 million ha) of land were set aside for a Hopi reservation encompassing the three mesas in northern Arizona Territory.

The twelve Hopi villages atop the three mesas today have a population of about 10,000, most of whom work outside the reservation.

Dale L. Walker

See also: Apache; Navajo.

Further Reading

Courlander, Harold, and Enrico Arno. *The Fourth World of the Hopis: The Epic Story of the Hopi Indians as Preserved in Their Legends and Traditions.* Albuquerque: University of New Mexico Press, 1971.

Hack, J.T. *The Changing Physical Environment of the Hopi Indians of Arizona.* Cambridge, MA: Harvard University Press, 1942.

Waters, Frank. *Book of the Hopi.* New York: Viking Press, 1971.

Horse Creek Treaty (1851)

In early 1851 Congress appropriated $100,000 to hold a treaty council with Indian tribes at Fort Laramie to bring peace and stability to the region. Indian agent Thomas Fitzpatrick recognized the devastation that the tides of emigration were causing to resources along the trails. So far the Indian nations had been tolerant of the emigration, but their forbearance was unlikely to last forever. Commissioner D.D. Mitchell, superintendent of Indian affairs, and Fitzpatrick arrived at Fort Laramie in July and sent messages to various Indian tribes to come to the fort at the start of September. In the latter days of August, the great nations of the Northern Plains began to gather at the fort. The garrison was placed on alert; roughly 200 dragoons were on hand to maintain order between tribal groups that were traditional enemies.

Members of the Sioux, Assiniboine, Arapaho, Cheyenne, Gros Ventre, Mandan, Crow, and Arikara tribes showed up for the council. When Chief Washakie and the Eastern Shoshone bands arrived, their grand procession into the fort was marred by an attempted attack by a Sioux warrior, who had to be intercepted by an interpreter. The incident could have turned the council into the largest Indian battle recorded on the Great Plains. Following the foiled attack upon Chief Washakie, the Eastern Shoshones did not take further part in the council and instead returned to their homelands. It was not until the 1863 Fort Bridger Treaty that the Eastern Shoshones entered into a treaty with the United States.

The vast numbers of Indians present, estimated at 10,000, took the planners by surprise, and they decided to move the entire council to a place with better grass to support the enormous herds of horses. A site with rich bottomlands between Horse Creek and Spring Creek, east of Fort Laramie near the present Wyoming-Nebraska border, was selected. The treaty takes its name from Horse Creek. The council site consisted of a great hoop of tepees with the eastern end of the circle left open. Only the most respected personages were allowed places within the great hoop.

The negotiations took roughly two weeks. The council took on many of the airs of a pageant, with demonstrations of horsemanship, battle tactics, and clothing finery. On September 17, 1851, the tribes present signed the Horse Creek Treaty (also known as the Fort Laramie Treaty). The treaty bound the participants to peaceful relations and friendship. The United States received the right to build roads and military posts within the lands of the Indian nations. The United States agreed to provide protection to the tribes against the depredations of American people and to provide an annuity of $50,000, in specie or goods, for a minimum of ten years. The Indian nations agreed to make restitution for any wrongs committed after the ratification of the treaty. The treaty established tracts of land as official tribal territories.

After the signing of the treaty, a large wagon train bearing the first year's annuity of $50,000 worth of goods arrived. It took the headmen two days to distribute the annuity to their people, after which the participants returned to their territories.

Terry A. Del Bene

See also: Fitzpatrick, Thomas "Broken Hand"; Fort Laramie; Fort Laramie, Treaty of (1868); Washakie.

Further Reading

Hafen, Leroy R., and Francis Marion Young. *Fort Laramie and the Pageant of the West.* Lincoln: University of Nebraska Press, 1938.

Kappler, Charles J. *Indian Treaties, 1778–1883.* Mattituck, NY: Amereon House, 1972.

Houston, Sam (1793–1863)

Sam Houston, who along with Stephen Austin arguably can be considered the "father" of Texas, was born in Rockbridge County, Virginia, on March 2, 1793. His father died while Houston was a youngster, and his mother and the rest of the family moved to the neighborhood of Maryville, Tennessee, in 1807. At the time, Cherokee Indians still roamed the wilderness of the southern Appalachian Mountains, and young Sam left home to live with the tribe for a period of three years, cultivating his skills as a woodsman and warrior and forever instilling in him a deep respect for America's native people.

In 1813, when he was twenty years old, Houston joined the U.S. Army and quickly rose in rank from private to first lieutenant before retiring after five years service. During his tour of duty, he saw action against the Creeks at Horseshoe Bend in Alabama in March 1814, sustaining three severe wounds. The army's commander, General Andrew Jackson, learned of his valor and the two men became lifelong friends.

Houston's post-army career included studying law and succeeding to a series of important positions in the Nashville area, including district attorney, adjutant-general for the state of Tennessee, major general of the Tennessee militia, U.S. representative, and, finally, governor of Tennessee in 1827. During the early days of his governorship, his brief marriage ended tragically and he abruptly resigned the post and moved to Arkansas to, once again, take up a several-year residency with his friends the Cherokees, a contingent of whom had already left their homelands in the East and migrated beyond the Mississippi River. There, he married a Cherokee woman and was adopted into the tribe.

While in Arkansas, Houston made frequent trips to neighboring Texas, which at the time was still under control of Mexico but was rapidly becoming a destination for Anglo-American settlers intent on its separation from the mother country. Eventually leaving his Indian wife, Houston moved to Texas, where his personality and no-nonsense opinions on political affairs soon made him a favorite among his neighbors and associates. In late 1835 he was named major general of the Texas army. Two days after he signed the Texas Declaration of Independence on March 2, 1836, he was made commander-in-chief of the army.

Within days of the signing of the declaration, the Mexican army commanded by General Antonio López de Santa Anna overran the Alamo in present-day San Antonio, killing all of the mission's defenders. Three weeks later, several hundred more Americans, under the leadership of James W. Fannin, were massacred by the Mexican army near Goliad. Houston's response was rapid and deadly. On April 21, he launched a surprise attack upon the resting Mexican troops on the banks on the San Jacinto River, near today's Houston. Within fifteen minutes, the small Texas army had killed or captured 1,400 Mexicans while suffering only 35 casualties, one of whom was Houston himself, who was wounded in the ankle. The capture of Santa Anna the following day assured the independence of Texas.

Houston served as the first elected president of the Republic of Texas from 1836–1838, but his efforts to gain annexation of the new country to the United States failed, primarily because American officials feared the new entity would espouse slavery. Houston was succeeded by Mirabeau B. Lamar and, in the meantime, married a third time, eventually siring eight children. He then replaced Lamar for a term as third president. In late December 1845, President James K. Polk approved legislation making Texas a state within the Union. Upon statehood, Houston faithfully served his constituency for fourteen years in the U.S. Senate, after which he was elected governor in 1859, despite his strong pro-Union position, unpopular with pro-South Texans. Despite his Virginia and Tennessee roots, Houston refused to take the oath to the Confederacy and was forced to resign the governorship in 1861. After retiring from government service to his farm near Huntsville, Houston died on July 26, 1863.

James A. Crutchfield

See also: Alamo, The; Austin, Stephen F.; Empresario System; Goliad, Battle of; "Gone to Texas"; Polk, James K.; San Jacinto, Battle of; Santa Anna, Antonio López de; Texas Annexation; Texas Revolution and Independence; Tyler, John.

Further Reading

Haley, James L. *Sam Houston*. Norman: University of Oklahoma Press, 2004.

James, Marquis. *The Raven: A Biography of Sam Houston*. Indianapolis: Bobbs-Merrill, 1929; various reprint editions.

Howard, Oliver O. (1830–1909)

Union Army general during the Civil War, founder of a university, civil rights activist, author, and Indian

fighter, Oliver Otis Howard was involved in several historic moments in the history of American westward expansion. He is probably best remembered as the soldier who, in 1877, pursued Chief Joseph and the Nez Percé Indians for 1,500 miles (2,400 km) across the northern Rocky Mountains and Great Plains, intent on forcing them to leave their homelands for a reservation in Idaho.

A native of Leeds, Maine, Howard was born on November 8, 1830, and graduated from both Bowdoin College and West Point. During the Civil War he fought for the Union Army at the first Battle of Bull Run, Fair Oaks in the Peninsula Campaign (where he lost an arm; he was later awarded the Congressional Medal of Honor for his valor), Chancellorsville (where his 11th Corps was routed by General Stonewall Jackson's famous flank attack), and Gettysburg (where on the first day he assumed command of John Reynolds' corps and suffered heavy losses before regrouping on Cemetery Hill). Howard later served with General William T. Sherman and commanded the Army of the Tennessee, participating in the Battle of Atlanta, the famous March to the Sea, and the Carolina campaigns that ultimately brought the South to its knees.

Following the war, President Andrew Johnson appointed Howard head of the Freedman's Bureau, designed to protect and assist newly freed slaves. He proved to be a man of compassion while earning contempt from white southerners and many northerners for his support of black rights. He worked diligently to integrate his church in Washington, DC, and helped establish the all-black university named in his honor in the nation's capital.

President Ulysses S. Grant sent Howard to the American Southwest in 1872 to meet with the Chiracahua Apache leader Cochise and bring an end to the lengthy guerrilla warfare against American settlers in the region. He met the challenge with great courage and tenacity, ultimately securing peace and negotiating an agreement giving Cochise and the Apaches a reservation of their choosing. His work and compassion once again earned him the enmity of those who wanted the Indians treated more harshly.

Another monumental challenge was presented to Howard in 1877 when he was dispatched to Oregon in an effort to persuade the Nez Percés, led by Chief Joseph, to leave their homeland in the Wallowa Valley of northeastern Oregon for a reservation in Lapwai, Idaho. The Nez Percés refused, and Joseph, with fellow Nez Percé leaders and hundreds of their people, led Howard and the U.S. Army on an epic "retreat" across Idaho, Wyoming, Yellowstone National Park, and Montana. General Howard and Lieutenant Colonel Nelson Miles ultimately subdued the Nez Percés at Bear Paw Valley, just a scant 40 miles (64 km) from sanctuary in Canada. Howard never lost sight of the underlying moral issue involved in this controversial confrontation and argued without success to allow Joseph and the Nez Percés to return to their Oregon home.

Howard later was appointed superintendent of the U.S. Military Academy at West Point and commander of the Department of the Platte and Division of the East. After retiring from the army, he moved to Vermont and authored several books, including an autobiography and a biography of Chief Joseph. He also continued his work on behalf of educational and religious causes. He died on October 26, 1909, at Burlington, Vermont.

Gene Bryan

See also: Apache; Chief Joseph; Cochise (Cheis); Nez Percé.

Further Reading

Green, Jerome. *Nez Percé Summer of 1877*. Helena: Montana Historical Society Press, 2000.

Howard, O.O. *Autobiography of Oliver Otis Howard*. New York: Baker and Taylor, 1907.

Moulton, Candy. *Chief Joseph: Guardian of the People*. New York: Forge Books, 2005.

Wert, Jeffry D. *The Sword of Lincoln*. New York: Simon & Schuster, 2005.

Woodworth, Steven E. *Nothing but Victory: The Army of the Tennessee, 1861–1865*. New York: Alfred A. Knopf, 2005.

Hudson's Bay Company

The English-chartered Hudson's Bay Company (HBC) was the first and, for many years foremost, fur-trading organization in North America, preceding its competition by scores of years. The result of a gift from King Charles II to his cousin, Prince Rupert, Duke of Bavaria, in 1670, the huge grant gave Rupert and his associates the sole right to trade with the numerous Indian tribes living in the widespread territory that drained into Hudson Bay.

In 1779 HBC introduced the "point" blanket to the American fur trade. Short, indigo-colored lines or "points" dyed into the blankets indicated the number of beaver pelts for which each blanket, based upon its quality, should be exchanged. The scheme was highly successful, and from that time on, blankets became a universal medium of exchange between traders and Indian tribes.

Growth of the company was rapid as it extended its chain of trading posts, or "houses," throughout its domain. It monopolized the Indian trade for many years, and not until 1783 did serious competition develop with the establishment of the North West Company (NWC). Formed by several smaller, independent operators called "pedlars," the NWC went head to head with HBC for dominance of the lucrative Canadian fur trade until 1821, when the two giants merged operations under the HBC's name.

North West traders had established an early influence within the current United States when they acquired John Jacob Astor's outpost, Astoria, during the War of 1812. The HBC, however, had few dealings with the Indians in that region until 1824, when it moved the headquarters for its Columbia District to Fort Vancouver on the Columbia River in present-day Washington from Fort George (the former Astoria, which had been transferred to the newly reorganized HBC with the merger in 1821). From Fort Vancouver, chief factor Dr. John McLoughlin oversaw a vast empire consisting of large areas of present-day Washington, Oregon, Idaho, Montana, Wyoming, and British Columbia.

When the question of ownership of the Oregon Country was finally decided in 1846, HBC influence south of the new international border waned. By then beaver populations had become severely diminished in the Rocky Mountains and the era of the fur trade was on the decline. By 1870 HBC had sold all of its Canadian land originally contained in Rupert's Land to the British Crown for £300,000, in exchange for the right to retain its 120 fur outposts. A new vision captured HBC management as the twentieth century opened: the development of a chain of department and general goods stores. By 1981 the company had become the tenth largest corporation in Canada, employing 42,000 people, and had extended its interests to oil and gas production, real estate development, and tobacco distribution, all the while maintaining its long-held position as the world's number one fur-trading operation. Today, the nearly 350-year-old company, having since 1987 divested itself of all of its fur auction houses and 178 stores, concentrates on its remaining department stores and real estate holdings. It maintains its position as one of Canada's premier commercial institutions.

James A. Crutchfield

Carts of fur belonging to the Hudson's Bay Company arrive for shipment at Calgary, Alberta, Canada, in the 1870s. The English joint-stock enterprise was chartered in 1670 to trade in fur and colonize North America. It controlled much of Canada for centuries. *(The Granger Collection, New York)*

See also: American Fur Company; Astoria; McLoughlin, John; North West Company.

Further Reading

Crutchfield, James A. *A Primer of the North American Fur Trade.* Union City, TN: Pioneer Press, 1986.

Lavender, David. *Fort Vancouver.* Washington, DC: U.S. Department of the Interior, 1981.

Newman, Peter C. *Empire by the Bay: An Illustrated History of the Hudson's Bay Company.* New York: Viking Penguin, 1989.

Hunt, Wilson Price (1783–1842)

Rather than epitomizing the rough-and-tumble "mountain man" character with whom he so often rubbed elbows, Wilson Price Hunt was an educated businessman who gravitated toward the fur trade after catching the eye of John Jacob Astor, the founder of both the American and the Pacific Fur companies. Born in Asbury, New Jersey, in 1783, Hunt migrated to St. Louis in 1804 and went into the mercantile business. His success caught Astor's attention in 1810

and the fur magnate chose the twenty-seven-year old merchant to head his Pacific coast operations and to lead an overland party to the mouth of the Columbia River, where he would construct a fort and become the chief operating officer. After traveling to and from Montreal and Fort Michilimackinac, Michigan, to recruit personnel and obtain supplies, Hunt and his party of sixty trappers and voyageurs left St. Louis on October 21, 1810, for the long trip up the Missouri River. About the same time, Astor discharged a second group to travel by sea to the same destination.

Hunt and his companions spent the winter at the mouth of the Nodaway River, near the present-day Missouri, Nebraska, Kansas border. Leaving camp in April 1811, the group proceeded upriver, finally reaching the Pacific coast on February 15 of the following year. There, they found that the sea-borne party on the *Tonquin* had already arrived the previous spring and built a fur post appropriately named Astoria.

Hunt later spent time in Alaska and the Hawaiian Islands (then called the Sandwich Islands) watching over Astor's fur interests before news of the War of 1812 sent him back to Astoria. When he arrived at the post, he found that most of the other Astor employees had deserted the place, but had left all of the furs and supplies behind. While he was searching for another ship to rescue the valuables, North West Company employees occupied Astoria and took over its operations.

Indignant that he had not been advised that Astor interests had actually sold Astoria to the North West Company, Hunt returned to New York, via China, arriving there in October 1816. Completing his business there, Hunt returned to St. Louis the following year. His final years in St. Louis were good ones; he was a successful merchant and large landowner. He became postmaster of St. Louis in 1822 and held the largely political post for eighteen years. He died in his adopted city on April 13, 1842.

James A. Crutchfield

See also: American Fur Company; Astor, John Jacob; Astoria; North West Company.

Further Reading

Irving, Washington. *Astoria: Or, Anecdotes of an Enterprise Beyond the Rocky Mountains*. Lincoln: University of Nebraska Press, 1982.

Lavender, David. *The Fist in the Wilderness*. Garden City, NY: Doubleday, 1964.

I

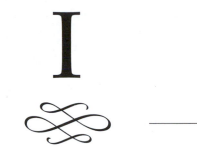

Independence, Missouri

Some 250 miles (400 km) upstream from its confluence with the Mississippi, the Missouri River meanders into a decided right-angle turn until its waters flow from the north. Not far from this turn, on high ground just southeast of the outside bend of the elbow, lies Independence, Missouri, an important outfitting and gathering point for westbound travelers on the Oregon, California, and Santa Fe trails. Plentiful water from "Big Springs," as the area was called originally, made the location even more desirable.

Part of the traditional homelands of the Missouri and Osage Indians, the area's first white settlement, the fur-trading post of Fort Osage, was established by William Clark in 1808. As more mountain men and traders journeyed west, additional opportunists and settlers set up shop in the area. Thousands of oxen- and mule-drawn wagon trains came and went from Independence, hauling trade goods to Santa Fe and returning with gold, silver, furs, and other goods, as well as mules and the jackasses that became the foundation stock for the famous Missouri mules. Spanish law decreed this trade illegal but it proceeded nonetheless, becoming officially sanctioned with Mexican independence in 1821.

In 1827 population growth led to the establishment of Jackson County, with Independence named the county seat. The slave-built log building used as the courthouse during business hours is said to have served as a pigpen overnight, with the public's morning entry preceded by a band of sheep to absorb the fleas.

An unprecedented influx of settlers arrived in Independence beginning in 1831 when Joseph Smith, Jr., founder and prophet of the newly organized Mormon Church—The Church of Jesus Christ of Latter-day Saints—designated the place "Zion" and the location of the "New Jerusalem" God had commanded the Saints to establish. Clashes with existing residents over politics, religion, and a variety of other incompatible practices led to unrest and violence. By 1833 continued Mormon presence in Independence became untenable and the Saints were pushed into sparsely settled regions farther north; they were expelled from the state altogether by 1839, moving to Nauvoo, Illinois.

The onset of extensive migration to Oregon in the early 1840s and the glut of gold-seekers rushing to California in 1849 increased the importance of Independence as a supply and gathering point. Thousands of wagon trains formed here, rolling out of the town square to points west. The village claimed a near monopoly in outfitting travelers for several years. However, other communities sprouted along the Missouri River to compete for the business of supplying emigrants with equipment and provisions, including Westport a few miles to the west and St. Joseph. Attempts to fend off competition included the establishment of the first railroad west of the Mississippi, the Missouri and Independence Railroad. Incorporated in 1849, the 4-mile (6.5-km) long mule-drawn affair was built to carry freight from the river landing to the center of town. Shifting sandbars in the river blocked the wharf, rendering the railroad useless, and operations ceased in 1852.

The city grew with the westward migration, its location favorable to numerous enterprises in service to the increasing population centers in the West. Stagecoach service to Santa Fe, through Fort Bent, along a post road officially designated by the U.S. government, began in 1850. That same year, a mail route was established to Utah Territory, with connections to California, and several other express and travel routes launched from Independence in later years.

Unrest over slavery and sectionalism in the 1850s found Independence embroiled in border wars as pro-slavery "bushwhackers" traded violent raids with the rival anti-slavery "jayhawkers" across the border in

Kansas Territory. Growing violence and the eventual onset of the Civil War divided loyalties in Independence and throughout the border region, with support for both the Confederacy and the United States among the citizens. Independence never regained its prominence or importance after the war. A faction of the Mormon Church, split from the main body after Joseph Smith's murder in 1844, returned to Independence and later established the Reorganized Church of Jesus Christ of Latter-day Saints (now the Community of Christ), which grew to become an important landowner and visible presence in the community, along with a number of other, smaller offshoots of Mormonism.

Visitors to Independence today can get a sense of the city's importance in westward expansion with stops at several museums and historic sites. Prominent among them is the National Frontier Trails Center, with extensive information and exhibits interpreting travel along the Santa Fe, Oregon, and California trails.

Rod Miller

See also: California Trail; Fort Osage; Mormon Church; Oregon Trail; Santa Fe Trail; Westport and Westport Landing, Missouri.

Further Reading

Hickman, J.V. *History of Jackson County Missouri.* Greenville, SC: Southern Historical Press, 1990.

The History of Jackson County Missouri. Cirardeau, MO: Remfre Press, 1966.

Wilcox, Pearl. *Jackson County Pioneers.* Independence, MO: Jackson County Historical Society, 1990.

Indian Captivity

The Indian captivity narrative has been part of American literature and history for about 300 years. From the beginning, European men, women, and children were captured by Indians, and the threat of capture was a real danger for generations of Americans on the frontier. Many people wrote books about their captivity and some of them became best sellers, with the topics expanded to include political aims, religious expression, spiritual allegory, and sensational adventure.

Although a western overland trip could be hazardous, the stay-at-home frontier settlers faced a greater threat of captivity. No comprehensive statistics are available for the entire western movement; however,

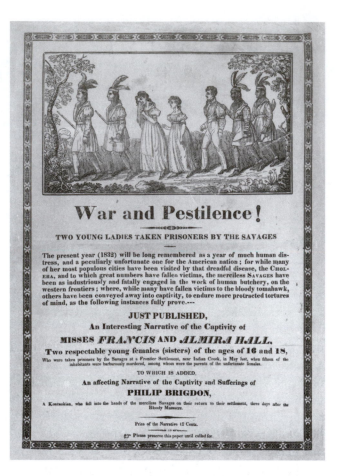

An 1832 broadside advertises the "affecting narrative" of the capture of two white women by "savages" in Texas. Indian captivity narratives, a popular genre for decades, evoked the danger of the frontier and stoked anti-native sentiment. Some were fictitious. *(MPI/Stringer/Getty Images)*

from 1540 to 1820, estimates range from 5,000 to 10,000 people captured by Indians along the Texas-Sonora border alone. One estimate is that about 400 people were captured within 100 miles (160 km) of Parker County, Texas. By 1855 Comanches from the Southwest held 2,000 prisoners. About 1,000 Americans were taken captive between 1860 and 1875. About 300 white captives were taken in the 1862 Santee Sioux uprising in Minnesota.

These tens of thousands of captives were taken for a number of reasons: for revenge, for ransom, as replacements of tribal members, and as slaves. Indian slaveholding was a pre-Columbian practice that was given fresh impetus when Indians realized that they could raid other tribes and sell captives to Europeans. In the West, the early Spanish and French traders gave the tribes an outlet for their captives, and the number of captives incorporated into the tribes lessened as Europeans stimulated the profit motive. Spanish, Mexicans, and Indians seemed to accept the established process of capture, ransom, intermarriage, or slavery, but it was a situation that Americans would not tolerate. Because Indians needed guns and ammunition, horses, cattle, and captives were necessary commodities; one of the reasons Americans tried to get Indians onto reservations was to break the captive exchange economy and begin free labor capitalism. When the cycle of capture and ransom ended, the Indians became dependent on wage labor.

Studies of eastern captivities between 1675 and 1763 show that about 62 percent of the captives were male and 52 percent were adults and that girls acculturated into Indian life better than boys. In the West, 35 percent of the captives were male and 25 percent were adults. In the East there was a slight preference for capturing older males, while in the West there was a significant preference for young females, but they did not acculturate well at all.

It is estimated that in New England, 54 percent of captured girls between ages seven and fifteen refused to return to their white families. Other views hold that roughly one-third of female captives stayed with the Indians. In the West, only one girl out of forty in that age group stayed or returned to the Indians, or tried to, when given the choice. The one girl who wanted to remain was Cynthia Ann Parker, who was captured when ten years old and spent twenty-four years with the Indians. Yet Parker is universally cited as proof that white girls preferred to remain with the Indians. As for boys in the West, only 4 percent returned to live with the Indians.

One reason that women did not prefer to stay with their captors in the West was that western tribes sexually abused female captives more than did eastern tribes. One study of western captivities shows that of the eighty-three women who were thirteen or older, 58 percent were raped, while only 7 percent stated that they were not compromised.

Several books summarize the white captive experience, speculating as to why some prisoners preferred death to capture, while others were more easily assimilated into the tribe. It appears that family background, religious training, race, national origin, and length of time held were not significant in determining how easily a captive would assimilate, although length of captivity did increase the likelihood of assimilation. Age was the critical factor. With few exceptions, children captured under the age of twelve were more easily "Indianized," with twelve being the limit for girls and fourteen the limit for boys.

There were thousands of white captives. Almost all of them had bad experiences, especially in the West, where most of the captured women were raped. There, most of them never assimilated, nor did they return to the Indians if given such an opportunity. Although there were notable exceptions, a captive was almost assured of a horrible ordeal, even more so in the West than in the East.

Greg Michno

See also: Oatman Girls' Captivity; Parker, Cynthia Ann; Parker, Quanah.

Further Reading
Brooks, James F. *Captives and Cousins: Slavery, Kinship, and Community in the Southwest Borderlands.* Chapel Hill: University of North Carolina Press, 2002.

Derounian-Stodola, Kathryn Zabelle, and James Arthur Levernier. *The Indian Captivity Narrative, 1550–1900.* New York: Twayne, 1993.

Heard, J. Norman. *White Into Red: A Study of the Assimilation of White Persons Captured by Indians.* Metuchen, NJ: Scarecrow, 1973.

Michno, Gregory, and Susan Michno. *A Fate Worse Than Death: Indian Captivities in the West, 1838–1885.* Caldwell, ID: Caxton Press, 2007.

Indian Policy

Governmental policies toward the first inhabitants of the Americas were complex and constantly evolving during the centuries. Policies developed in relation to local factors, international politics, and often-overlooked Native American attitudes toward dealing with the newcomers. Establishment of viable European colonies required at least tacit assistance from Native American inhabitants, and often the groundwork was prepared as devastating European and Asian diseases decimated indigenous populations. But it is far too simple to envision Indian policies as a choice between extermination and acculturation. Policies included isolation, economic interdependence, economic dependence, extermination, civilization, acculturation, removal, concentration, and absorption.

The early days of colonial expansion on the continent were seen as a period of adjustment for both cultures. Native American and European cultures and technologies competed for dominance. Europeans dominated in metallurgy and chemistry, while Indians dominated in agriculture and medicine. Both Europeans and Native Americans took captives and proselytized each other, seeking spiritual and political advantages. Native American cultures contained democratic institutions and personal freedoms uncommon in imperial Europe, some of which guided the development on the continent of an experiment in democracy that became the United States of America. On the other side of the coin, both European and Native American cultures practiced slavery and were adept at pressing victims captured from each other into this dark economic system.

In the sixteenth century, Europeans had little concern with the rights of individual Indians. Collectively, Indians became economic surrogates for trading with the interior, allies, enemies, and often invisible parts of the landscape. Adherence to the Doctrine of Discovery allowed Europeans to carve up the continent, paying almost no attention to the millions of inhabitants who were already there.

In the eighteenth century, the pattern of expansion to suit European-style agriculture continued. The American colonies became a small part of the geopolitical balance of power in Europe, and the European empires sought allies among their Native American neighbors. There was an explosion of treaty making as colonial governors sought to defang potential dangers created by neighboring Native American confederations siding with Continental enemies. The colonies reached deep into the interior of the continent through a complex trade network. Economic and military dependence upon Native Americans made the politics somewhat less local and put the issue of Indian policy in a geopolitical context. The wars in Europe deeply involved the North American colonies.

With the defeat of France in 1763 Great Britain took over as the dominant European power in North America. Almost immediately the Native Americans felt a shift in Indian policy. No longer needed for their military strength, the Indian allies and foes of the British alike felt a dramatic cooling in relationships. Trading became far less favorable and colonies seemed intent on further expansion, cutting up tribal lands almost with impunity. The resulting conflict, called Pontiac's Rebellion, steeled the British government to take an even harder line with its Native American neighbors. The British instituted germ warfare and were ruthless in quelling hostilities. The government attempted to impose strict borders and control commerce through construction of a series of forts along the frontier. The Plan of 1764 quickly unraveled as commercial interests ignored imperial edicts. Land jobbers acquired new property through murder and intimidation, setting off local conflicts.

The coming of the American Revolution upset the entire house of cards. The combatants sought allies. Many tribes viewed joining the British as a chance to strike back at the colonists. The League of the Iroquois split. With the loss of the American colonies in 1783, the British abandoned their former Indian allies to their fate. The Native Americans now had to face a new power that regarded them as enemies. The new American government became determined to civilize the frontiers. Firm boundaries established by treaties were considered temporary measures until the need arose for further cessations of land by the Native Americans. The expansion of the "higher" American society was considered by the U.S. government as a benefit to the Native Americans. The Indians believed otherwise. As the century came to a close, tribal armies inflicted a series of serious defeats upon the newcomers. The new government realized it had to become more accommodating. Congress passed a series of trade and intercourse acts that once again established boundaries, forbade settlement beyond the frontiers, and started an official policy of civilizing the tribes. Trading posts were established. The U.S. government hoped that friendly commerce and self-interest would encourage the Indians to adopt lifeways more like those of the whites. This policy envisioned separate but similar Indian communities of farmers and tradesmen, not the complete acculturation of the tribes as was seen among groups like the Cherokees and the Creeks.

In the nineteenth century, the Jefferson administration continued the policy that would push Indians toward "civilization." Ultimately, President Thomas Jefferson hoped for absorption of the Native Americans into American culture through the teaching of agriculture, technology, art, and literature, supplemented by intermarriage. Treaties were sought with tribes to acquire lands for settlement and these settlements were envisioned as the seeds of absorption.

The policy of absorption failed because of the War of 1812. Once again, the British were successful in finding numerous Native American allies. Even though many tribes sided with the United States or remained neutral, at the end of the conflict the U.S. government tended to paint all Indians with the same broad brush: they were enemies. The United States was determined to exert its dominion over tribes within its lands. A chain of new forts was intended to prevent the British in Canada from ever again raising the tribes against the U.S. government. The government-sponsored trading post system was reestablished.

In 1823 the cornerstone of American Indian policy was laid by the U.S. Supreme Court under Chief Justice John Marshall. Henceforth, Native American nations were dependent, domestic nations, under the steerage of the government. Such nations had diminished sovereignty and were incapable of managing their own international policies. Ultimately, the U.S. government owned the Native American lands. The government's policy was for the continued advance of settlement, with Native Americans either being assimilated or moving out of the way. Congress established schools on Native American reservations to be the instruments of assimilation. Under President Andrew Jackson, many tribes were uprooted from their lands in the East and sent to an uncertain future in the West. Removal was not limited to this short period of time, but remained a policy and tool of expansion for decades to come. There were thoughts of combining the removed tribes into a Native American state, but these plans did not materialize.

The end of the war with Mexico in 1848 put hundreds of thousands of Native Americans under U.S. control. It also placed recently removed tribes once again squarely in the path of unbridled expansion. Posts were established in the West to establish order. Indian affairs were moved from the War Department to the Department of the Interior in 1849. The government continued a program of acculturation and building tribal prosperity, hoping this would be an avenue to peaceful expansion. Treaties released Indian lands for settlement and allowed the government to further concentrate the Native Americans. The concentration policy, an outgrowth of the removal policy, seemed necessary if the new settlers were to be kept apart from the tribes.

Once again, events ran ahead of the policies. The 1848 discovery of gold in California resulted in an international torrent of newcomers into the West. Tribes in the vicinity of the mining communities were obliterated from the face of the earth almost overnight. Tribes along the main routes of travel to the goldfields found themselves facing increasing levels of conflict with the emigrants. New cities, such as Great Salt Lake City and Denver, sprang up setting off a series of conflicts as Indians were pushed into the lands of other tribal groups. Like stones dropped into a pool of water, the disturbances sent waves of conflict across the West. The Wild West was born.

With the coming of the Civil War, the issue of Indian allies gained importance once again. The overall goal of both the Union and Confederate governments was acculturation, but the war forced many tribes to choose sides in a conflict not of their making. The Union government was somewhat paranoid about the Confederacy creating an uprising of tribes in the West. However, it was the Lincoln administration's actions of denuding the West of soldiers, increasing traffic along the overland trails (as a result of conscription and homesteading acts), and being late with annual payments that set off the largest conflict with Native American tribes. Fighting raged from Minnesota to California. Federal troops fighting the Navajos allowed prisoners to be sold into slavery in Mexico at a time when the president was freeing slaves in the Confederacy. Massacres of Indians at places like Bear River and Sand Creek inflamed the greater Rocky Mountain West and the Plains into a scale of warfare heretofore unknown in those regions. In the Southwest, the Apaches fought both Confederate and Union soldiers with equal enthusiasm. Troops were diverted from the Civil War to restore order. As the Civil War came to a close, thousands of soldiers hoping to return to their farms were sent west to quell the conflict there. Tribes that sided with the Confederacy or otherwise fought the federal government felt a harsh hand. Concentration camps were established for hostile tribes such as the Apaches and Navajos, and the removal and concentration policies of the past took on a new and terrible aspect.

After the Civil War, the Grant administration considered returning Indian affairs to the War Department. William T. Sherman led a "peace commission" that was intended to remind the tribes that they had the options of accepting the terms of the U.S. government or suffering the consequences. This commission resulted in a diplomatic debacle that set off a new conflict, called Red Cloud's War. The U.S. was defeated in this war, as public opinion turned against further bloodletting. This ushered in Grant's peace policy. Under the peace policy, the days of roaming tribes were to come to an end. Native Americans were to be assigned to specific reservations where they would be isolated from the general American populace. There they would be acculturated though Indian schools and churches and made to remain peaceful. The assumption was that encroachment of settlements into former tribal lands must continue. A board of Indian commissioners was established to oversee Indian affairs. In 1871 Congress revoked the power of the tribes to enter into treaties and began an era of handling Indian affairs through legislation. Congressional intent was to give away as much federal land, including tribal lands, as possible.

There was substantial resistance to the peace policy in the latter part of the century, resulting in a series of conflicts. George A. Custer became an icon for failed Indian policies at the Battle of the Little Bighorn in 1876, and the nation was shocked by images of frozen corpses at a place called Wounded Knee in 1890. The shooting wars came to an end and the policies of civilization, removal, and concentration were allowed to proceed unimpeded. In 1887 the General Allotment Act continued a pattern of removing Indians from the land by removing "surplus" lands from tribal control and allowing leasing of allotments

In the twentieth century, the policies of the past were continued. Legislation such as the Dawes Severalty Act, approved in 1884, allowed substantial acreages of Indian lands to pass into non-Indian ownership.

Terry A. Del Bene

See also: Indian Removal Act (1830); Jackson's Indian Policy.

Further Reading

Brown, Dee. *Bury My Heart at Wounded Knee: An Indian History of the American West.* New York: Henry Holt, 1970.

Debo, Angie E. *A History of the Indians of the United States.* Norman: University of Oklahoma Press, 1970.

Fitzhugh, William W. *Cultures in Contact.* Washington, DC: Smithsonian Institution Press, 1985.

Josephy, Alvin M., Jr. *500 Nations.* New York: Alfred A. Knopf, 1994.

Rippy, J. Fred, and Angie E. Debo. *The Historical Background of the American Policy of Isolation.* Northhampton, MA: Smith College Studies in History, 1924.

Washburn, Wilcomb E. *Handbook of North American Indians.* Vol. 4, *History of Indian-White Relations.* Washington, DC: Smithsonian Institution Press, 1988.

Indian Removal Act (1830)

President Andrew Jackson signed the Indian Removal Act into law on May 26, 1830, as part of a larger U.S. government Indian removal policy that had been in place since the Jefferson administration. Indian lands lying between the Appalachian Mountains and the Mississippi River had long been sought after as the white population grew. Prior to 1830, Indians had been offered treaties, encouraged to sell their land, and offered resettlement in the West, beyond the current borders of the United States.

The Cherokees in the state of Georgia were the first people to experience the issue of forcible removal. In 1802 the state signed a compact with the federal government essentially rescinding all land titles held by the Cherokees within its boundaries. The agreement forfeited any claim to western lands that Georgia might obtain in the future.

Between 1814 and 1824, the federal government negotiated eleven treaties with the Creek, Cherokee, and Choctaw tribes. Migration was voluntary during this time, and only a small population of the three tribes actually moved to lands west of the Mississippi River.

By the mid-1820s, Georgia state legislators were losing faith in the federal government's ability to enforce the compact and remove the Cherokees. A new state constitution was adopted that gave the Cherokee Nation complete jurisdiction over its lands. The state courts, fully anti-Cherokee, were given the sole power to decide on the removal issue, since the federal government had been taken out of the picture. John Ross, chief of the Cherokee Nation, traveled to Washington in January 1829 to attempt to resolve the disputes between Georgia and the Cherokees. The secretary of war, John H. Eaton, informed Ross that President Jackson supported the right of Georgia to apply state law to the Cherokee Nation.

Indian removal had been a strong component of Andrew Jackson's presidential campaign in 1828. The passage of the act in 1830 was a realization of Jackson's election promise. National security was another reason given for Jackson's support of the Removal Act, given the disputes erupting in Georgia and bordering states. Even with President Jackson's support, passage of the Indian Removal Act was bitterly contested.

Strong support for the passage of the act was evident throughout the South, particularly in Georgia. The Southern states openly coveted the land held by the Cherokees and the other members of the Five Civilized Tribes—the Chickasaws, Choctaws, Creeks, and Seminoles. Opposition to the Removal Act came from pockets in the North, and it was especially contested by Christian missionaries, most prominently Jeremiah Evarts. Evarts was the editor of *The Panoplist*, a monthly magazine, from 1805 until 1820. Writing twenty-four essays under the name of William Penn, Evarts was a loud voice and lobbyist against Indian removal, especially of the Cherokees in Georgia. Prior to his personal battle to topple the passage of the Indian Removal Act, Evarts had convinced Congress and President John Quincy Adams to retain funding for the efforts to "civilize" all Native Americans east of the Mississippi. Other opponents of the act were Senator Theodore Frelinghuysen of New Jersey and Congressman David "Davy" Crockett of Tennessee.

Frelinghuysen gave a six-hour speech delivered over the course of three days to Congress against the Removal Act. He warned Congress, and the country, of the dire consequences if the legislation passed: "Let us beware how, by oppressive encroachments upon the sacred privileges of our Indian neighbors, we minister to the agonies of future remorse." The speech fell on deaf ears and Frelinghuysen faced heated criticism for mixing politics and religion.

Davy Crockett, a staunch supporter of squatter's rights in the West, took up the cause of the Indians based on the same principle of landownership. His opposition to the Removal Act was the primary cause of his reelection defeat in 1830, an action that eventually sent him to Texas to fight for its independence from Mexico.

After passage of the Removal Act, which stated that removal was to be voluntary, several leaders of the Five Civilized Tribes reconsidered their resistance to the policy. The first treaty signed after the act's passage was the Treaty of Dancing Rabbit Creek, signed with the Choctaws in Mississippi on September 27, 1830, and ceding their land east of the Mississippi for monetary compensation and land in the West.

Removal began in October of 1831 with 4,000 Choctaws moving west. Due to poor planning, they walked much farther than anticipated and many died, or arrived exhausted or ill the following spring. The next wave of Choctaws was much smaller, numbering 550, and the journey was worse than the first as the band suffered a cholera outbreak. The third wave of removal went more smoothly, though nearly 6,000 Choctaws chose to remain in Mississippi. Another removal effort began in 1842 with 3,000 of the remaining Choctaws moving to present-day Oklahoma under forced conditions.

The Cherokee Nation signed the Treaty of New Echota in 1835, moving the tribe to Oklahoma. Although it was never accepted by the elected Cherokee tribal leaders, this treaty, and the enactment of the Indian Removal Act, resulted in the Trail of Tears migration, which caused the deaths of 4,000 Cherokees.

Larry D. Sweazy

See also: Adams, John Quincy; Cherokee; Chickasaw; Choctaw; Creek; Crockett, Davy; Jackson, Andrew; Jackson's Indian Policy; New Echota, Treaty of (1835); Trail of Tears.

Further Reading

Foreman, Grant. *Indian Removal: The Emigration of the Five Civilized Tribes of Indians.* Norman: University of Oklahoma Press, 1989.

Satz, Ronald N. *American Indian Policy in the Jacksonian Era.* Norman: University of Oklahoma Press, 2002.

Wallace, Anthony F.C. *The Long, Bitter Trail: Andrew Jackson and the Indians.* New York: Hill & Wang, 1993.

Jackson, Andrew (1767–1845)

Andrew Jackson, seventh president of the United States, was born in North Carolina on March 15, 1767, the son of poor Scots-Irish farmers. As a young man, he studied law and moved to present-day eastern Tennessee, then to Nashville, where he practiced law and fell in love with Rachel Donelson Robards, the married daughter of John Donelson, co-founder in 1780 of the town. Rachel was in the process of divorcing Lewis Robards, who lived in Kentucky, and when she and Jackson were informed that the divorce had become final, the couple married. Sometime later, they learned that the divorce, in fact, was not actually finalized, and when, once again, word came that this time the transaction was valid, the Jacksons once more exchanged vows in order to make the marriage legal. The misunderstanding over Rachel's divorce and the couple's premature marriage caused much consternation and heartache for both in years to come.

When Tennessee became a state in 1796, Jackson was elected its first congressman and then served as U.S. senator. He sat on the Tennessee Supreme Court, was appointed a major general of the Tennessee militia, and, during the War of 1812, assumed the rank of major general of the U.S. Army. During March 1814 he decisively defeated the Creek Indians at the Battle of Horseshoe Bend in Alabama, then routed the British army at New Orleans in January 1815, a feat that made him a national hero.

Jackson also helped the United States to acquire Florida. He patrolled the Florida border during the First Seminole War (1817–1818) to keep slaves from escaping to the territory and to defend settlers against Seminoles and Creeks who raided across the border into Georgia. President James Monroe proposed purchas-ing Florida from Spain to eliminate the problem, but Jackson preferred to take it by force. Disregarding Monroe's orders, he invaded the territory, forcing Spain to protect Florida or cede it to the United States. Spain chose the latter, and Jackson became the first territorial governor of Florida in 1821.

In 1824 Jackson was defeated for the presidency of the United States by John Quincy Adams, but was elected to the office four years later. His campaign for the high office was a nasty one, with his political enemies bringing up the matter of his illegal marriage to Rachel so many years earlier. Whether or not as a result of the name-calling and innuendo, the bereaved Rachel died in Nashville in December 1828, never to see the White House and her husband as president.

During Jackson's presidency (1829–1837), certain white citizens protested the residency of Cherokee, Choctaw, Creek, Chickasaw, and Seminole Indians on eastern lands rumored to be rich in mineral wealth, and the Anglo-Americans' growing desire for land increased pressure on Jackson to expel the natives. Although the U.S. Supreme Court ruled in *Worcester v. Georgia* that the state of Georgia had no power to force the Cherokees out, Jackson instituted a policy of removal and Congress passed the Indian Removal Act of 1830, which resulted in the infamous Trail of Tears and other difficult relocations of eastern tribes of Indians to the trans-Mississippi West.

"Old Hickory" (Jackson earned the nickname during the War of 1812 because of his toughness) significantly affected American Indians and set a precedent for the federal government's relationship with them. His policy of removal opened up new territory to white settlers. His military actions resulted in the expansion of American territory. Contemporaries regarded him as the first frontier president, a representative of the common man. He was a strong proponent of a limited central government and held wide appeal as a self-made man. As president, he increased the powers of the chief executive's office and established a new political plank espousing the virtues and rights of the common man, resulting in his general political philosophy becoming known as Jacksonian Democracy.

Jackson died at Nashville at his home, The Hermitage, on June 8, 1845. As the first western president, he raised the profile of that region and left a great legacy for his younger protégé and neighbor, James K. Polk, to carry to the White House.

Meg Frisbee

See also: Adams, John Quincy; Creek; Creek Wars; Indian Removal Act (1830); Jackson's Indian Policy; Trail of Tears; War of 1812.

Further Reading
Remini, Robert V. *Andrew Jackson and His Indian Wars.* New York: Penguin, 2002.
———. *The Life of Andrew Jackson.* Newtown, CT: American Political Biography Press, 2003.

Jackson, David E. (1788–1837)

One of the Rocky Mountain fur trade's most brilliant, yet illusive, players was David E. Jackson. He was born in present-day West Virginia on October 30, 1788, the second son of rugged trans-Appalachian pioneers, and grew up in the vast wilderness expanses of the upper Ohio River valley. He married in 1809 and served in the War of 1812 as an ensign in the 19th Infantry, but saw no action. Resigning from the army in 1814, he moved to Missouri the following year.

Jackson was one of the group of adventurers who read with interest General William Ashley's 1822 advertisement for "enterprising young men" to ascend the Missouri River on a fur-gathering expedition. Although most of the ad's respondents were men in their late teens and early twenties—wild, single, and looking for excitement—Jackson was already in his mid-thirties and married with four children.

By mid 1822, Jackson accompanied Ashley's partner, Andrew Henry, up the Missouri River and helped establish Fort Henry at the mouth of the Yellowstone River. Following Ashley's arrival at the post in the fall with supplies, Jackson left with him and returned to St. Louis. The next year, Jackson was again with Ashley in a hard-fought battle with the Arikaras along the Missouri River. The Indians put up such a fight that

the 6th U.S. Infantry Regiment from Fort Atkinson, under the command of Colonel Henry Leavenworth, had to be called up for assistance. Jackson was remembered by some of his fellow adventurers as displaying exceptional bravery in that confrontation.

Jackson was present at both the first and second annual rendezvous and became a partner, along with Jedediah Smith and Andrew Sublette, in Ashley's old company when the general sold out in 1826. It appears that Jackson administered the day-to-day activities of the outfit, while Smith and Sublette explored and hauled furs to St. Louis and trade goods back to the mountains.

When he finally gave up trapping, Jackson participated briefly in the Santa Fe trade and was in the caravan with Jedediah Smith when Comanche Indians killed Smith in 1831. Jackson conducted mule trading in California before retiring to Missouri. He died in December 1837 of typhoid fever in Paris, Tennessee, where he had journeyed to collect on some investments. Jackson Hole, Jackson Lake, and the town of Jackson, all in present-day Wyoming, are named in his honor. Until 1993, when John C. Jackson published the biography of his kinsman, *Shadow on the Tetons: David E. Jackson and the Claiming of the American West*, precious little was known of the man who was a well-respected member of the mountain man brotherhood of the 1820s when the beaver trade was at its peak.

James A. Crutchfield

See also: Arikara War; Ashley, William Henry; Henry, Andrew; Leavenworth, Henry; Smith, Jackson & Sublette.

Further Reading
Jackson, John C. *Shadow on the Tetons: David E. Jackson and the Claiming of the American West.* Missoula, MT: Mountain Press, 1993.

Jackson, William Henry (1843–1942)

William Henry Jackson's life of ninety-nine years encompassed several professions—explorer, author, artist, historian, and pioneer photographer among them. In the latter career, he became celebrated as the man who brought to public attention images of the wonders of the Yellowstone River country, images that aided in the creation of Yellowstone National Park in 1872.

Photographer and artist William Henry Jackson, whose images of pioneers, Indians, and the American landscape chronicled the era of western expansion, prepares to photograph Laguna Pueblo, New Mexico Territory, in about 1880. *(The Granger Collection)*

Born in 1843 in Keeseville, New York, and spending his youth in Troy, New York, and Rutland, Vermont, Jackson was inspired by his mother, an eminent watercolorist. By his teens he had developed a passion for painting and seemed certain his life's work lay in art. After employment as a colorist and retoucher in a Troy photography studio—where he also learned camera and darkroom work—Jackson, then nineteen, enlisted in the 12th Vermont Infantry, served nine months in the Union Army, and was present at the battle of Gettysburg in July 1863.

In 1866, after successful work in a photographic studio in Rutland and an unhappy love affair, Jackson decided to see some of the world outside New England and made his way to Nebraska Territory, gateway to the far West, where he found employment with a freighting company. After learning the skills of a bullwhacker (driver of an ox-drawn freight wagon) and working his way across the West, he saw the unique potential in documenting in photographs—an art that by then had captivated him—the vast and then-unknown territories he had seen.

After setting up a studio in Omaha, Jackson began making photographs of Indians on the Omaha reservation and construction workers on the Union Pacific Railroad. In 1871 he joined an expedition into Wyoming Territory led by Dr. Ferdinand Hayden, a former army surgeon. Hayden had conducted an important government exploration and survey of the Yellowstone and Missouri Rivers in 1859–1860 and was returning to the area for further scientific work.

Jackson, with pack mules and a half-dozen men to move his heavy, unwieldy equipment (huge stereographic cameras, glass plates, developing chemicals, and tents), performed miraculously in impossible wilderness conditions, producing a treasure-trove of images of landmarks. His Indian portraits and pictures of the Colorado Rockies, the Grand Tetons, and the geyser and waterfall wonders and wildlife of the Yellowstone River country became a sensation when exhibited after his return east. The Yellowstone images became an important factor in the March 1, 1872, designation by the U.S. Congress of Yellowstone National Park, America's first national park.

From his studio in Denver, Colorado Territory, Jackson continued his photography of Western landmarks and people long after his government work ended, producing portraits and documenting railroad construction and mining boomtowns. In the early 1920s, after he passed his eightieth birthday, he returned to his first love—painting—and turned out over 100 oils, most with Western historic themes, all meticulously researched. He took up residence in Washington, DC, in 1924, and painted a series of Old West murals for the U.S. Department of the Interior building.

Jackson died on June 30, 1942, at the age of ninety-nine and was buried in Arlington National Cemetery.

The world's largest collection of William Henry Jackson's works—photographic images, sketches, and paintings—is located at the Scotts Bluff National Monument, near the town of Gering in western Nebraska.

Dale L. Walker

See also: Hayden, Ferdinand; Hayden Survey; Moran, Thomas.

Further Reading

Forsee, Aylesa. *William Henry Jackson: Pioneer Photographer of the West.* New York: Viking Press, 1964.

Hales, Peter B. *William Henry Jackson and the Transformation of the American Landscape.* Philadelphia: Temple University Press, 1996.

Jackson, William Henry. *Time Exposure: The Autobiography of William Henry Jackson.* New York: Putnam's, 1940.

Jackson's Indian Policy

"Andrew Jackson . . . was a patriot and a traitor. He was one of the greatest of generals, and wholly ignorant of the art of war. . . . He was the most candid of men, and was capable of the profoundest dissimulation. . . . A democratic autocrat. An urbane savage. An atrocious saint." So wrote James Parton, one of Jackson's earliest biographers, attempting to encapsulate the backwoodsman, soldier, duelist, lawyer, gambler, judge, and politician who became the seventh president of the United States.

He was probably the most contentious public figure of his age. Jackson's presidency (1829–1837) followed this polarizing pattern in a time of a national economic depression, bitter tariff debates, corruption under a "spoils system" (which Jackson's patronage helped create), struggles against the National Bank, and rampant industrialization. But of all national issues that identify the Jackson era, his policy concerning America's Indians has been characterized as creating one of the bleakest chapters in American history.

Jackson's study of the U.S. Constitution convinced him that Article IV, Section 3 ("New states may be admitted by the Congress into this union; but no new states shall be formed or erected within the jurisdiction of any other state . . .") denied the organization of sovereign Indian entities within the Union and prohibited designating state lands for such entities or "nations." A fact not lost on the pragmatic observer was that the growth of cities, of commerce and agriculture, were land-demanding advances and that the Indians, with their great tracts of tribal land, were obstacles to this land-hungry march of progress.

Jackson had advocated Indian "removal" to territorial lands west of the Mississippi in both of his presidential campaigns (in 1824, when he was defeated by John Quincy Adams, and in 1828). It was no surprise that in 1830 he signed the Indian Removal Act into law. The act authorized the president to negotiate purchase of certain tribal lands in the eastern and southern states, and make arrangements for the transportation and settlement of the Indian residents of these states to lands outside the existing U.S. border.

In 1830—although some Indian peoples from the East had already moved to reservation land in the as yet unorganized "Indian Territory" west of the Mississippi River—the Cherokees, Chickasaws, Choctaws, Creeks, and Seminoles continued to occupy their homelands in Georgia, Alabama, Mississippi, Tennessee, and the Carolinas. These tribes had adapted in varying degrees to white American life, including embracing the Christian religion, and thus were known as the Five Civilized Tribes.

Upon passage of the Removal Act, Jackson conducted the first negotiations in person. In Tennessee he stated unequivocally that there were to be no Indian states-within-states. The Cherokees, in presenting the most serious resistance to Jackson's policy, took the matter to the courts, and in 1832 the U.S. Supreme Court upheld the tribes' independence from state authority in *Georgia v. Cherokee Nation*. The state of Georgia ignored the high court's decision, and in 1835 a faction within the tribal governance signed the removal papers. Three years later, in the first year of the Van Buren administration, the Cherokees who refused to leave their ancestral lands were forced by an army of 7,000 federal troops to march westward. The Cherokees suffered 4,000 dead and countless others debilitated from exposure and starvation. The forced exodus is notorious in U.S. history as the "Trail of Tears."

Ultimately, the Indian removal policy became an indelible blot on the Jackson presidency. Stipulations in the treaty, such as those promising remuneration for the Indians' land and goods, safe transportation to the West, and allocation of food and shelter upon arrival, turned out to be hollow promises. Corruption among contractors and traders was often ignored by the Jackson administration.

In the wake of the Removal Act were such instances of Indian resistance as the Black Hawk War on the upper Mississippi in 1832, the Second Creek War of 1836, and the long and costly Second Seminole War of 1835–1842.

About 45,000 American Indians were relocated to the West during Jackson's presidency and about 100,000 were eventually relocated as a result of the 1830 Removal Act, most settling in what was known as Indian Territory, the present-day state of Oklahoma.

Dale L. Walker

See also: Cherokee; Chickasaw; Choctaw; Creek; Indian Removal Act (1830); Jackson, Andrew; New Echota, Treaty of (1835); Trail of Tears; Van Buren, Martin.

Further Reading
Brands, H.W. *Andrew Jackson: His Life and Times.* New York: Doubleday, 2005.
Meacham, Jon. *American Lion: Andrew Jackson in the White House.* New York: Random House, 2008.
Parton, James. *Life of Andrew Jackson.* New York: Mason Brothers, 1860.

Remini, Robert V. *Andrew Jackson and His Indian Wars*. New York: Penguin Books, 2002.

———. *The Legacy of Andrew Jackson: Essays on Democracy, Indian Removal, and Slavery*. Baton Rouge: Louisiana State University Press, 1988.

Schlesinger, Arthur M., Jr. *The Age of Jackson*. Boston: Little, Brown, 1950.

Jefferson, Thomas (1743–1826)

Through his acquisition of the Louisiana Territory from Napoleonic France in 1803 and dispatching the Lewis and Clark Expedition into the trans-Mississippi West in 1804, Thomas Jefferson, third president of the United States, became the father of westward expansion.

Born in Albemarle County, Virginia, on April 13, 1743, the son of a prosperous planter and landowner, Jefferson graduated from the College of William and Mary in 1762, studied law, and entered the Virginia House of Burgesses in 1769. His service in this legislature marked the beginning of a stellar political and diplomatic career. He served twice in the Continental Congress (1774–1775), as governor of Virginia (1779–1781), U.S. minister to France (1785–1789), secretary of state (1789–1793) under President George Washington, vice president (1797–1801) in the John Adams cabinet, and president of the United States (1801–1809). In 1772 he married Martha Wayles Skelton. Five children were born of the union.

An erudite, polished writer, Jefferson's congressional accomplishments included his writings on coinage and establishing a basic U.S. monetary unit, and his proposals—ahead of their time—that new western territories in the expanding United States should have the right of self-governance and at appropriate times in their development be admitted to the Union. He was a slave-owner who believed slavery to be immoral and proposed that the institution be prohibited in new territories after 1800.

In June of 1776, during the Second Continental Congress, Jefferson was appointed to lead a committee to draft the Declaration of Independence and at age thirty-three became its principal author.

In the first term of his presidency (1801–1805), Jefferson reduced the national debt by one-third, dispatched warships to fight Barbary pirates who were attacking American commercial vessels in the Mediterranean Sea, and, by a treaty signed in Paris on April 30, 1803, purchased the Louisiana Territory from France for $15 million. For that sum the United States gained 828,000 square miles (2.15 million sq km) of land between the Mississippi River and the Rocky Mountains, an area encompassing all of six future states and portions of nine others.

Just over a year after the Louisiana Purchase, Jefferson sent the Lewis and Clark Expedition of nearly fifty men up the Missouri River on May 14, 1804, to explore the newly acquired territory and beyond, in search of a water route to the Pacific. The expedition returned to St. Louis on September 23, 1806, a monumental success in its mapping of new territory, gathering of data and specimens, and acquiring ethnological knowledge. Although an American foothold in the Oregon Country was established, the expedition failed in its mission to find a navigable route to the Pacific Ocean. Among other exploring parties that Jefferson dispatched to gather information about the newly acquired territory was the one led by Zebulon M. Pike in 1806–1807, as well as the Dunbar-Hunter (1804–1805) and the Freeman-Custis (1806) expeditions.

Jefferson's second term in the presidency had him concentrating on keeping the United States free of involvement in Europe's Napoleonic wars. After his term of office ended, he retired to Monticello, his mountaintop home near Charlottesville, Virginia, and worked assiduously on the planning of the University of Virginia, chartered in January of 1819; its first classes were held in 1825.

Jefferson died at Monticello on July 4, 1826, the fiftieth anniversary of the Declaration of Independence. (On the same day in 1826, John Adams—the only other president to sign the Declaration—also died.)

Dale L. Walker

See also: Dunbar-Hunter and Freeman-Custis Expeditions; Lewis and Clark Expedition; Louisiana Purchase (1803); Louisiana Territory; Pike Expedition.

Further Reading

Brodie, Fawn. *Thomas Jefferson: An Intimate History*. New York: W.W. Norton, 1974.

Ellis, Joseph J. *American Sphinx: The Character of Thomas Jefferson*. New York: Alfred A. Knopf, 1996.

Malone, Dumas. *Jefferson and His Time*. 6 vols. Boston: Little, Brown, 1948–1982.

Peterson, Merrill. *Thomas Jefferson and the New Nation*. New York: Oxford University Press, 1970.

Jefferson Barracks

Jefferson Barracks was an important military base that supported nearly every facet of America's westward expansion into the trans-Mississippi and beyond. Established in 1826, the post holds the distinction of being the first permanent military base west of the Mississippi River. By the 1840s, it was the largest military post in the United States. Many of the nineteenth century's most famous military figures—Robert E. Lee, Ulysses S. Grant, William T. Sherman, Jefferson Davis, Zachary Taylor, Henry Leavenworth, and Stephen Watts Kearny—either served at Jefferson Barracks or passed through the installation.

In 1825 the U.S. Army obtained a land parcel of over 1,700 acres (690 ha) located 10 miles (16 km) south of St. Louis for the purpose of building a permanent military installation. Several companies of the 1st Infantry Regiment under Stephen Watts Kearny set up camp at the site in 1826 and began constructing the post. It was named Jefferson Barracks after former president Thomas Jefferson, who had died on July 4 of that year. It soon became the first basic training center for the infantry and was named the headquarters for the 6th U.S. Infantry Regiment in 1827.

The years 1832 and 1833 proved important ones for Jefferson Barracks. The first group of troops to deploy for conflict left the post for the Black Hawk War in April 1832. After the Sauk and Fox tribes had been defeated, the captured chief Black Hawk was taken to the barracks as a prisoner. During the following year, the 1st U.S. Dragoons, later to become the 1st U.S. Cavalry Regiment, was formed at Jefferson Barracks, and the post became a cavalry-training center. In later years, the 2nd and most of the 3rd U.S. Cavalry Regiments were formed, trained, and headquartered at Jefferson Barracks.

Jefferson Barracks also played a prominent role in the Mexican-American War and Civil War. In 1846 artillery units under Braxton Bragg assembled at the post before departing to join Zachary Taylor for his campaign against Monterrey. Stephen Watts Kearny embarked down the Santa Fe Trail from Jefferson Barracks, en route to seizing what is now most of New Mexico, Arizona, and Southern California. When the Civil War broke out in 1861, Missourians became embroiled in conflict and turmoil. In May 1861, troops from Jefferson Barracks under Nathaniel Lyon captured nearby Camp Jackson, which was manned by the state militia sympathetic to the Confederate cause. Lyon then marched on the state capitol, defeating state guards and militia at Booneville on the way. In late summer, he was killed at Wilson's Creek near Springfield. Later in the war, Sterling Price, victor at Wilson's Creek, invaded Missouri with a large Confederate force. Jefferson Barracks played a key role in assembling Union forces to defend St. Louis and central Missouri.

After the Civil War, Jefferson Barracks continued as a major military staging post. It assembled and trained troops used during the Spanish-American War, the insurrection in the Philippines, Pershing's punitive expedition against Mexico, and World War I. During World War II, the installation was used as an induction, training, and separation center and took on new functions in support of the Army Air Corps. Although declared surplus by the War Department shortly after World War II, Jefferson Barracks continues to headquarter reserve and National Guard units into the twenty-first century.

Jim Ersfeld

See also: Black Hawk; Black Hawk War (1832); Davis, Jefferson; Grant, Ulysses S.; Kearny, Stephen Watts; Leavenworth, Henry; Sherman, William Tecumseh; Taylor, Zachary.

Further Reading
Mueller, Richard E. "Jefferson Barracks: The Early Years." *Missouri Historical Review* 67 (1972): 7–30.
Prucha, Francis Paul. *The Sword of the Republic: The United States Army on the Frontier, 1783–1846.* New York: Macmillan, 1969.

Johnson County War

Late in the nineteenth century, Wyoming's northern rangeland was torn by the Johnson County War (also referred to as the Johnson County Invasion), a violent western collision pitting cattle barons and powerful politicians against homesteaders and rustlers. During the 1880s large cattlemen provided the backbone of Wyoming's economy, while the Wyoming Stock Growers Association (WSGA) was the territory's most powerful political force. But the vast cattle herds were plagued by rustlers—cowboys hoping to build a little herd of their own, or homesteaders and small ranchers trying to benefit from a couple of extra head of livestock, both of whom stole cattle. The WSGA employed stock detectives and legal teams, carefully building evidence against rustlers. However, often juries were comprised of small operators, and it proved virtually impossible to obtain convictions no matter how tight the case.

Cattlemen became willing to resort to extralegal violence at a time when lynching remained common in the West and South, and when capitalists from the East utilized violent strikebreakers. In 1889 six Wyoming ranchers lynched homesteaders Jim Averell and Ella Watson, the latter dubbed "Cattle Kate" in an attempt to brand her as a receiver of stolen cattle.

In 1890 a stock thief was lynched and two small operators were dry-gulched (killed without warning in a deserted place) in separate incidents near Buffalo, Wyoming, the seat of Johnson County. Frank Canton, former county sheriff and now a WSGA stock detective, became suspected as a dry-gulcher. Cowboy Nate Champion, a leader of the homesteader-cowboy-small rancher faction, had fought off an attack by Canton and several other stock detectives.

By 1891 a number of large ranchers had decided to launch an invasion of Johnson County, a hotbed of suspected rustlers. They collected a war chest of $100,000 and recruited more than twenty Texas gunmen. The Texans were mostly deputy U.S. marshals and posse-men from the federal court of Paris, Texas, and they were employed with the understanding that they would serve legal warrants against stock thieves. In April of 1891, the Texans arrived in Cheyenne, where they found horses, supplies, and weapons provided by the stockmen. Numerous ranchers and foremen—and a physician—were part of the expedition, and instead of warrants they carried a death list.

More than fifty men left the train at Casper, Wyoming, and began riding toward Johnson County in a blizzard. At the KC Ranch (in the current town of Kaycee, Wyoming) the invaders encountered Nate Champion and Nick Ray. In the attack that quickly unfolded the invaders fatally wounded Ray, but Champion stood off the invaders all day, until his cabin was set on fire and he was killed trying to escape. The daylong battle alerted residents in the countryside, and when the invaders approached Buffalo they found resistance had been organized. The invaders quickly became besieged by hundreds of angry citizens at the TA Ranch, 13 miles (21 km) south of Buffalo. For three days the outnumbered invaders engaged in a long-range rifle duel, until three companies of U.S. cavalrymen arrived from Fort McKinney, near Buffalo, to halt the fighting and take custody of the invaders.

Wyoming's acting governor, Dr. Amos W. Barber, responded to pleas from the WSGA, telegraphing Wyoming's senators, who awoke President Benjamin Harrison to obtain federal intervention on behalf of the invaders. The army transferred the prisoners to Fort D.A. Russell, outside Cheyenne and far from vengeful Johnson County.

Months of legal machinations followed. Future Supreme Court justice Willis Van Devanter devised a legal strategy that eventually bankrupted Johnson County and ended all proceedings early in 1893. These dramatic events on America's last frontier captivated novelists and filmmakers, inspiring such classics as *The Virginian* and *Shane.*

Although the Johnson County War ended with no convictions of any of the men involved in the killing of Champion or Ray, the WSGA subsequently reduced overt attacks on small homesteaders who had moved onto range earlier utilized by the big operators.

Bill O'Neal

See also: Cattle Frontier; Open Range; Vigilantism; Watson, Ella "Cattle Kate."

Further Reading
O'Neal, Bill. *The Johnson County War.* Austin, TX: Eakin Press, 2004.

Smith, Helena Huntington. *The War on Powder River.* Lincoln: University of Nebraska Press, 1966.

Johnston, Albert Sidney (1803–1862)

A career officer serving from the Black Hawk War to the Civil War, Albert Sidney Johnston was born in Washington, Kentucky, on February 2, 1803. He attended Transylvania University at Lexington and was later appointed to West Point, finishing eighth in the graduating class of 1826. While there he became acquainted with Jefferson Davis, and the two men remained close friends until Johnston's untimely death in 1862.

Johnston participated as a lieutenant in Black Hawk's war of 1832, becoming aide-de-camp to General Henry Atkinson. In 1834, when his wife became ill and nearly died, he resigned his commission and became a farmer. Two years later, he volunteered as a private to join the fight for Texas independence from Mexico. His military experience caught the attention of his superiors. Soon, the president of Texas, Sam Houston, made Johnston senior brigadier general in command of the Texas army, passing over Felix

Huston, who was in command at the time of Johnston's appointment. Offended, Huston challenged Johnston to a duel. Johnston accepted and chose pistols, even though his challenger had a reputation as an expert shot. The duel ended with Johnston severely wounded in the leg. Huston expressed regret and the two later became cordial.

The Texas command proved trying for Johnston as he lacked supplies and arms for his army and advocated invading Mexico to settle the issue of Texas independence once and for all. Discovering a plot by the Cherokee nation in Texas to join forces with Mexico in exchange for titled land, Mirabeau B. Lamar, Sam Houston's successor as president of Texas, ordered Johnston to drive the Cherokees from Texas soil. Johnston succeeded in this effort and the surviving Cherokees retreated to Arkansas. Soon many other tribes left Texas and returned to the United States, leaving their lands open to settlement by non-natives. Johnston was appointed secretary of war for the Republic of Texas and conducted several campaigns against the Comanches, soon becoming known as the scourge of the Indians.

War with Mexico erupted in 1846, but by then Texas was no longer a republic. It was part of the United States and Johnston was chosen to command the First Texas Rifles. After a training period, his unit set out for Mexico, but before it saw any fighting, most of the enlistments in his unit expired and the soldiers returned home, leaving Johnston without a command. General Zachary Taylor then appointed Johnston inspector general on the staff of General William O. Butler. At the Battle of Monterey (July 7, 1846), Johnston rallied retreating Ohio troops and directed a devastating barrage of fire at attacking Mexican lancers, turning them back and saving the American unit from near-certain annihilation.

In 1856 Colonel Johnston, as commander of the Department of Texas, carried on a successful campaign against the Comanches. The following year he was assigned the military command of an expedition into Utah to quell a Mormon "rebellion," replacing the original commander of the expedition, General William S. Harney. The Utah expedition, known as "Buchanan's Blunder," (named after incumbent president James Buchanan who had dispatched the troops to Utah) was hastily put into action too late in the year to escape the ravages of winter, and thus Johnston's command endured much hardship. The Mormon army burned grazing land, scattered army cattle, made off with supply wagons, and fortified Echo and Weber canyons, the only easy approaches

to Salt Lake City. Johnston joined his troops when they were nearing the Green River, in Wyoming. He pressed the straggling army forward, but was not fleet enough to avoid being shut out of the Valley of the Great Salt Lake by a blizzard. Johnston's army, now on short supplies and in need of additional livestock, wintered at Camp Scott and other encampments near the burned-out remains of Fort Bridger, Wyoming. The winter was severe, and survival of his command as a fighting unit can be attributed to his skills and ability as a leader.

By early spring of 1858, as Johnston was about to move his army against the Mormons, the Buchanan administration had a change of heart regarding the use of military force and Johnston was ordered to use restraint. After a series of negotiations between Mormon leader Brigham Young, Alfred Cummings, the newly appointed governor of Utah, and Thomas Kane, emissary from Washington, the Mormons agreed to put down their arms and accept the new governor. Despite his personal dislike of the Mormons and their way of life, Johnston demanded his troops show the utmost respect for them and their property.

In March 1860, Johnston left the Salt Lake valley and was reassigned as commander of the Pacific (California-Oregon), with headquarters in San Francisco. South Carolina seceded from the Union late in 1860, followed shortly by several other southern states. Before resigning his commission in the U.S. Army, Johnston relocated the weapons in the federal arsenal to Alcatraz Island to protect them from southern sympathizers. When his replacement arrived, Johnston left California overland to join Texas and the Confederacy.

Longtime acquaintance Jefferson Davis, president of the Confederate States, appointed Johnston as commander of the Department of Kentucky and Tennessee. At the time many considered Johnston the most talented officer in the Confederate Army. North of Corinth, Mississippi, near Shiloh Church in southwestern Tennessee, in early April 1862, Johnston's Confederates surprised a Union force commanded by General U.S. Grant. With victory near and Grant's army all but surrounded, Johnston suffered a mortal wound while directing his troops. He bled to death for want of a tourniquet, having dispatched his personal doctor to aid wounded federal troops. Johnston died April 6, 1862.

Stoney Livingston

See also: Black Hawk War (1832); Davis, Jefferson; Harney, William S.; Mexican-American War; Mormon Church; Texas Revolution and Independence; Utah War.

Further Reading

Johnston, William Preston. *The Life of General Albert Sidney Johnston: Embracing His Services in the Armies of the United States, the Republic of Texas, and the Confederate States.* New York: Da Capo Press, 1997.

Jones, Thomas ap Catesby (1790–1858)

Born in 1790, Westmoreland County, Virginia, of Welsh ancestry, Thomas ap Catesby Jones ("ap" is a Welsh indicator for "son of") entered the U.S. Navy in 1805 and spent the first several years of his service in the Gulf of Mexico suppressing piracy and the slave trade. A lieutenant during the War of 1812, he commanded a flotilla of five gunboats on Lake Borgne, Louisiana. On December 14, 1814, he engaged a convoy of British launches, carrying nearly 1,000 men. A musket ball in the shoulder wounded Jones and his gunboats were eventually overcome, but the action delayed the British landing at New Orleans and enabled General Andrew Jackson to gather his forces there for the subsequent successful battle.

In 1826, after a dozen years of routine sea and shore duties, Jones, on a government mission, performed a notable service in the Sandwich Islands (later Hawaii) when he assisted in negotiating a treaty with King Kamehameha III that granted favored trade status to the United States. In 1837 he was selected to lead the U.S. Exploring Expedition to the South Seas, a long-planned, multiyear enterprise. However, his disputes with the secretary of the navy and recurring health problems caused him to withdraw as commander of the expedition.

In 1841, promoted to the rank of commodore, Jones took over command of the U.S. Pacific Squadron and the following year a bizarre slip-up eclipsed the considerable accomplishments of his naval career. On October 18, 1842, Jones arrived off Monterey in his flagship *United States*, accompanied by the sloop-of-war *Cyane*. With a party of officers and sailors he came ashore and to the wonderment of port/presidio officials and townspeople, announced that he was taking possession of Alta California in the name of the government of the United States.

As it happened, when Jones's squadron lay at anchor off Callao, Peru, he received newspaper articles and dispatches that led him to believe the United States and Mexico were at war. Since there were no telegraphic sta-tions in the West and all military instructions came to Pacific outposts by way of Cape Horn, the commodore concluded that, in the absence of orders to the contrary, he needed to sail for California instantly and seize it. Otherwise Mexico might do something drastic, such as ceding the province to England.

The preemptive capture of Monterey ended the next day after Thomas O. Larkin, an American merchant in Monterey, found newspapers and commercial mail, all more recent than the material Jones had read at Callao, which proved no state of war existed between the two countries. After apologies to presidio officials, Jones had the Stars and Stripes lowered and sailed south to Los Angeles to tender similar regrets to the governor of Alta California.

Jones was temporarily relieved of his command but resumed it in 1848, commanding the naval forces in San Francisco Bay at the end of the Mexican-American War and during the California gold rush. In 1850 a court-martial found him guilty on charges of fraud and neglect of duty and suspended him from service for five years. In 1853 President Millard Fillmore reinstated Jones.

Commodore Jones died on May 30, 1858, in Fairfax County, Virginia.

Dale L. Walker

See also: Larkin, Thomas Oliver; Sloat, John D.; United States Exploring Expedition.

Further Reading

Gapp, Frank W. *The Commodore and the Whale: The Lost Victories of Thomas Ap Catesby Jones.* New York: Vantage Press, 1996.

Smith, Gene A. *Thomas ap Catesby Jones, Commodore of Manifest Destiny.* Annapolis, MD: Naval Institute Press, 2000.

Judah, Theodore D. (1826–1863)

Theodore Dehone Judah was a railroad visionary and one of the most ardent supporters of the transcontinental railway in America, paving the way for the creation of the vehicle that enabled manifest destiny. A brilliant civil engineer and tireless lobbyist, Judah devoted many productive years toward the realization of a railroad that stretched from the nation's central plains to the Pacific Coast.

Judah was born in Bridgeport, Connecticut, in 1826, the son of an Episcopalian minister. After his father's death, Theodore, at age thirteen, struck out on his own. He attended Troy Institute, now Rensselaer Polytechnic Institute, where he completed the Classic Course in engineering. Judah was then hired by the Schenectady and Troy Railroad as a surveyor. After gaining experience with several companies, Judah became the assistant to the chief engineer for the Connecticut Valley Railroad at the age of twenty. By the time he was twenty-seven he had completed a difficult project building a rail line down the Niagara Gorge between Lakes Erie and Ontario and become the chief engineer for the Buffalo, New York & Erie Railroad. His destiny, however, was in the West.

In 1854 Judah was hired by California's Sacramento Valley Railroad, the first railroad west of the Mississippi, as chief engineer. He performed a survey of the proposed route from Sacramento to Folsom in the California goldfields and supervised the construction of the line, completed in 1856. Over the next three years, Judah worked on several speculative projects that envisioned expanding rail lines into additional areas of California, but an economic downturn and other factors kept those concepts from reaching physical fruition. During this time, he began thinking of a rail line eastward through the rugged Sierra Nevada—a route that would link the West Coast with the midsection of America. The idea would consume Judah's imagination and energies for the rest of his life.

Judah threw himself into the effort of convincing businessmen and the federal government that a transcontinental railroad must be built. He participated in the Pacific Railroad Commission in San Francisco in 1859, and then went to Washington as a commission delegate to promote a unifying rail line. Intense sectional rivalry kept a national rail bill from being passed in Congress at that time, but the concept was gaining favor.

Judah returned to California to explore a possible route through the Sierra Nevada. Convinced that passage through this range was feasible, he set about creating the Central Pacific Railroad (CPRR) and its requisite financing. Finding no capital investment prospects in San Francisco, he finally was able to attract the interest of four Sacramento financiers: Mark Hopkins, Leland Stanford, Charles Crocker, and Collis Huntington. These men were to become the famous "Big Four" who pushed the CPRR eastward to Promontory, Utah.

After securing financing, Judah performed a detailed survey of the proposed route through California into Nevada. He then returned to Washington to continue lobbying for the passage of a transcontinental railroad bill. President Lincoln finally signed the Pacific Railroad Act into law on July 1, 1862. As work commenced on the CPRR line, however, Judah found himself increasingly at odds with the CPRR's Big Four. He pushed for quality of construction, while the Big Four stressed speed and profit.

When an impasse was reached in 1863, Judah ventured to the East Coast to secure capital for buying out the Big Four. While traversing the Isthmus of Panama, he contracted yellow fever and died in late 1863 at the age of thirty-seven. The man who had worked so tirelessly and successfully to unite the country by rail did not see the culmination of his dream.

Jim Ersfeld

See also: Central Pacific Railroad; Judah Survey; Pacific Railway Act (1862); Railroad Surveys, Transcontinental.

Further Reading
Hinckley, Helen. *Rails From the West.* San Marino, CA: Golden West Books, 1969.

Judah Survey

Perhaps the most daunting obstacle to the construction of the transcontinental railroad in the United States during the mid-nineteenth century was the presence of the lofty, rugged mountains in the West. Nowhere was the challenge of laying rails through, around, or over mountains more testing than in the Sierra Nevada of northern California. The route eventually used to navigate this terrain was the result of a survey completed in 1861 by railroad engineer Theodore Judah.

The Judah Survey was born in frustration, but also was the beneficiary of good fortune. Judah had been unable to convince either the federal government or local Californians to finance a railroad that would tie the Pacific Coast to the rest of the country. Returning in 1860 to Sacramento from an unsuccessful campaign for railroad legislation in Washington, DC, Judah decided that the only way to win support was to show exactly how the Sierra Nevada would be traversed, so financial backers and government officials could see the feasibility of his dream. To that end, he resolved to find the most practical route through the Sierras. His project started with a fortuitous stroke of good luck.

Judah's wife, Anna, told him that a man named Doc Strong, from Dutch Flats, California, wanted to show him an old wagon trail that led into the Sierra

Nevada mountains. It was in fact the route formerly used by overland migrants to get from Donner Lake to Dutch Flats, abandoned after the Donner Party disaster of 1846–1847. After seeing the wagon road, Judah knew that he had found the best way to pierce the Sierra Nevada. This route did not require a rail line to climb two steep ridgelines, a condition of all other known routes through the Sierras. Contemporary locomotives had sufficient power to scale the more moderate grades. The key element for a route through the Sierra Nevada had been found.

Confident that this breakthrough would attract investors for building the railroad, Judah drafted plans for such a company, publishing a pamphlet titled *Central Pacific Railroad Company of California* in November 1860. At first rebuffed by capitalists in San Francisco, Judah convened several meetings with potential subscribers for his enterprise in Sacramento. He succeeded in attracting a handful of them—most notably the "Big Four": Charles Crocker, Mark Hopkins, Collis Huntington, and Leland Stanford—to become shareholders, and the Central Pacific Railroad (CPRR) of California was born. Judah began his detailed survey of the planned route between Sacramento and the California-Nevada state line in the spring of 1861. By September he had completed the survey and presented it to the officers and directors of the CPRR. It featured moderate grades, avoided crossing over major canyons and rivers, and minimized the number of tunnels required. It was a feasible route and, in retrospect, the optimal one.

Judah returned to Washington as the agent for the new railroad, seeking federal government aid and subsidies for his company. He published and distributed reports of his survey to government officials and congressmen and lobbied hard and successfully for a transcontinental railroad bill. On July 1, 1862, President Abraham Lincoln signed the Pacific Railroad Act, enabling the building of a rail line that united the country's east and west coasts. Theodore Judah, and the survey he conducted, had made this bold step possible.

James Ersfeld

See also: Central Pacific Railroad; Donner Party; Judah, Theodore D.; Pacific Railway Act (1862); Railroad Surveys, Transcontinental.

Further Reading

Evans, Harold, with Gail Buckland and David Lefer. "Theodore Dehone Judah." In *They Made America*. New York: Little, Brown, 2004.

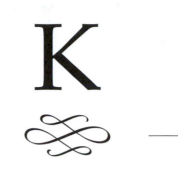

Kansas-Nebraska Act (1854)

In the mid-nineteenth century the United States teetered on the brink of civil war. The weighty issue of slavery drove a wedge between the states and threatened the very existence of the young republic. Much of the drama played out in Congress as pro-slavery states struggled to maintain their parity with anti-slavery states. The disposition of new territories fanned the flames of discord. Most of the huge tracts of lands acquired in the Louisiana Purchase and the war with Mexico were unsuitable for growing cotton, the main type of agriculture in the slave states. It was inevitable that as new states were created from these lands the control of Congress must pass to the anti-slavery forces. States that allowed slavery continually threatened war and secession, resulting in a search for creative solutions to bring in new states without upsetting the delicate balance of power.

In January 1854, Senator Stephen Douglas of Illinois introduced the legislation: "An Act to Organize the Territories of Nebraska and Kansas." Under the Missouri Compromise of 1820, both Kansas and Nebraska should have been admitted to the union as free-soil territories. Douglas promoted the principle of popular sovereignty as his selling point to pass the legislation. Under this principle the residents of the territories were to vote upon whether slavery was to be allowed there. If either Kansas or Nebraska voted for fostering the institution of slavery, the precarious balance of power in Congress could be maintained a while longer. In the more likely outcome that both territories would vote against slavery, Douglas hoped that the power of the plebiscite might cool the passions of the slave-holding states and preserve the union intact.

On the surface it seemed to be the most democratic of compromises. However, the passage of the act started a civil war in Kansas that predated the Civil War by roughly six years. No one foresaw the Herculean efforts of both sides to affect the outcome of the referendum. Societies sprang up throughout New England to raise capital and send emigrants to flood the plains of Kansas with free-soil voters. Similar efforts were made in the slave-holding states, but the burgeoning population and wealth of the northern states were better able to equip waves of anti-slavery emigrants in numbers the slave-holders could not match.

The neighboring state of Missouri provided a great advantage to the pro-slavery forces. Missourians passed a variety of anti-free soiler resolutions, including declarations that Kansas already was a slave-holding territory. Missourians were encouraged to move their human property across the border into Kansas with all haste. They did so and quickly held elections wherein they controlled all save one polling place.

The political conflict resulting from the tyrannical control of the territory by the minority pro-slavery faction, in a land that was overwhelmingly inhabited by free-soilers, dragged on for years. The pro-slavery government used every means at its disposal to cow those arrayed against it. Free-soiler emigrants were turned away by the territorial authorities. In response to violence and election fraud, the free-soilers attempted to impose their own government, located in Topeka, even going so far as to elect Charles Robinson as governor. The governors appointed by President Franklin Pierce and later President James Buchanan did not recognize the Topeka government.

Governor Andrew H. Reeder endorsed the fraudulent election of the territorial legislature and issued certificates of election for the representatives. He directed that the new territorial legislature be called into session. The pro-slavery legislature convened in the new border town of Pawnee on July 2, 1855. Reeder later soured on the pro-slavery government

283

and coined the phrase "border ruffians" to describe the emigrants from Missouri. Reeder was beaten by one of those ruffians, Dr. J.H. Stringfellow, editor of the *Squatter Sovereign*. Pierce removed Reeder, setting into motion a veritable revolving door of territorial governors, including Wilson Shannon, John W. Geary, Frederick P. Stanton, and Robert J. Walker. The territorial governors were chosen so as to be acceptable to the pro-slavery politicians. Most had a similar history of eventually coming into conflict with the pro-slavery leadership. Governor Geary, having survived one assassination attempt, eventually resigned, fearing that the next attempt by the pro-slavery men to take his life would be successful.

Kansas became a battleground as murder begat murder. The free-soiler community of Lawrence was sacked and burned. John Brown sought to avenge the burning of Lawrence at Pottawatomie Creek via the savage murders of five pro-slavery men. It was in this period of internecine warfare that the legend of "Bleeding Kansas" was born. Estimates are that fifty-six murders and untold property damage were the result of the several years of conflict.

The U.S. Army sought to restore order, although, like the territorial government, the soldiers tended to side with the pro-slavery factions. The flood of free-soilers increased, causing many discouraged pro-slavery people to return to Missouri. The Pierce administration chastised territorial governor Geary for failing to clean out the nest of free-soil rebels in Topeka, even though under Geary's leadership the violence diminished. The drama in Kansas had a great effect on the election of 1856, which pitted the new Republican Party's candidate John C. Frémont against Democrat James Buchanan. The violence in Kansas worked in Frémont's favor.

The influx of settlers from both sides into the territory created great difficulties for the territorial government. The surveys necessary to complete the land patents had not been completed. Additionally, many of the new settlers chose to settle in lands where the rights were held by Indian nations. The settlement issues raised the level of friction between the already-hostile factions.

In 1857 the pro-slavery legislature pushed its agenda forward and, overriding the veto of the governor, called for a constitutional convention to be held at Lecompton. The free-soil Kansans were unconvinced that the plebiscite was to be a fair one. They boycotted the election. Buchanan accepted the pro-slavery Lecompton constitution despite an investigative committee's report detailing problems with the plebiscite.

Congress forced a second plebiscite that was boycotted by the pro-slavery faction. The resulting overwhelming defeat of the document opened the way for the drafting of the free-soil Wyandotte constitution in 1859. Kansas was admitted as a free state in January of 1861. Nebraska was admitted as a state in 1867.

Terry A. Del Bene

See also: Douglas, Stephen A.; Elections, Presidential; Missouri Compromise (1820).

Further Reading

Brown, George W. *Governor Walker With the Rescue of Kansas from Slavery.* Rockford, KS: G.W. Brown, 1881.

Levine, Bruce. *Half Slave and Half Free: The Roots of the Civil War.* New York: Hill & Wang, 1992.

Monaghan, Jay. *Civil War on the Western Border, 1854–1865.* Lincoln: University of Nebraska Press, 1955.

Stampp, Kenneth M. *America in 1857: A Nation on the Brink.* New York: Oxford University Press, 1990.

Kearny, Stephen Watts (1794–1848)

The youngest of thirteen children of a prominent lawyer and landowner in Newark, New Jersey, Stephen Watts Kearny was born on August 30, 1794, and as a young man, attended Columbia University in New York City for two years before joining the New York Militia and choosing the army for his life's work. As a lieutenant in the U.S. 13th Infantry, he fought in the Battle of Queenston Heights on the Niagara frontier on October 13, 1812, where he was wounded and taken prisoner by the British.

Following the War of 1812, in 1819, he was promoted to captain, joined a regiment in Iowa, and began a long term of service in the Western territories at Council Bluffs, Iowa; Fort Smith, Arkansas; Fort Atkinson, Nebraska; and St. Louis, with brief sojourns in Detroit; Baton Rouge, Louisiana; and with expeditions across the Missouri River to the Yellowstone. He led minor campaigns against the Winnebagos in Wisconsin, Poncas and Mandans on the Missouri, and Choctaws on the Texas border, but his opportunity for significant military work was stalled until 1826, when he was promoted to the colonelcy and command at Jefferson Barracks in St. Louis.

In St. Louis in 1830 Kearny married eighteen-year old Mary Radford Clark, the stepdaughter of soldier-explorer William Clark, co-commander of the Lewis and Clark Expedition of 1804–1806. In the long years of his Jefferson Barracks tenure, Kearny organized a unit of dragoons, a form of heavy cavalry he may have seen during action in the War of 1812, and eventually expanded the unit to be designated the 1st U.S. Dragoon Regiment. (In 1861 the U.S. War Department reorganized the dragoons as the 1st Regiment of Cavalry.)

In 1842, Kearny, now a colonel, took command of the Third Military Department of the Army, responsible for guarding 1,000 miles (1,600 km) of Louisiana Purchase frontier lands. Headquartered in St. Louis, he came to know Missouri's foremost citizen, Senator Thomas Hart Benton, Benton's teenaged daughter Jessie, and Jessie's husband, John Charles Frémont of the Army's Corps of Topographical Engineers.

In 1845 Kearny led an expedition along the Oregon Trail to the South Pass of Wyoming, holding a council with the Lakota tribes near Fort Laramie and returning to Fort Leavenworth, Kansas, by way of Fort Bent and the Arkansas River. The expedition gave his five companies of dragoons experience in the daily travails of a wilderness march and familiarity with the Santa Fe Trail.

On May 13, 1846, the day war was declared against Mexico, the U.S. secretary of war ordered Kearny to ready his 1st Dragoons for a long overland march and to recruit 1,000 volunteers for the "Army of the West," as his mobile command was designated. His further orders were to lead his army to the province of New Mexico, capture its capital of Santa Fe, and annex the territory to the United States. Once order and government were established in New Mexico, he would proceed south and west and seize the province of Alta California.

New Mexico proved to be a bloodless campaign and was duly occupied on August 18, 1846, with Kearny, headquartered in Santa Fe, named military governor. He departed the territory on September 25 with 300 mule-mounted dragoons. On October 6, after learning from dispatch rider Christopher "Kit" Carson that California had already fallen to U.S. forces under Commodore Robert Stockton, Kearny sent 200 of his dragoons back to Santa Fe and continued on westward with his 100-man escort.

On December 6, 1846, after an arduous 850-mile (1,370-km) trek across the southwestern deserts, Kearny was wounded and his weakened force suffered heavy casualties in a battle with *californio* lancers at the Indian village of San Pasqual (near present-day Escondido). His occupation of San Diego became possible only with reinforcements from Stockton. Under a fragile joint command the two officers fought two further skirmishes near Los Angeles in January 1847 and were proceeding toward Monterey when news reached them that the last Mexican forces had surrendered to Frémont on January 13, 1847. After a controversy between Kearny and Stockton over authority to organize a provisional government in California, Kearny's position was upheld.

In February 1848, Kearny was ordered to join General Winfield Scott's army of occupation in Mexico City and served briefly as military commander of the capital and of Vera Cruz. His service in Mexico ended in July 1848, when he contracted yellow fever and was sent home. That month he was promoted to major general. He died in St. Louis on October 31, 1848, from the effects of the fever he had contracted in Mexico.

Dale L. Walker

See also: Army of the West; Bear Flag Revolt; California, Conquest of; Frémont, John C.; Stockton, Robert Field.

Further Reading

Clarke, Dwight L. *Stephen Watts Kearny, Soldier of the West*. Norman: University of Oklahoma Press, 1961.

Turner, Henry Smith. *Original Journals of Henry Smith Turner: With Stephen Watts Kearny to New Mexico and California*. Norman: University of Oklahoma Press, 1966.

Walker, Dale L. *Bear Flag Rising: The Conquest of California, 1846*. New York: Forge Books, 1999.

Keil, William (1812–1877)

Wilhelm Keil (known in America as William Keil) was born March 6, 1812, in Prussia. He immigrated to the United States with his wife, Louise Ritter, in 1836. They lived a short time in New York and then moved to Pittsburgh, where William opened a pharmacy and called himself "doctor," a title he used for the rest of his life. Keil became a Methodist preacher, but within a few years severed his ties with the Methodists and established a communal congregation in Deer Creek, Pennsylvania, organized around a cooperative structure based on community ownership and equality of work and profit. In 1844 he gathered a group of 200 followers and founded the Bethel Colony in Missouri. Although the Bethel Colony was successful Keil was dissatisfied with Missouri, and in 1853 he sent scouts to find a new location in the West. A year later two of the scouts returned and reported they had found a likely location on Willapa Bay in Washington Territory.

In May 1855, several of the members of the Bethel Colony prepared to migrate to Washington Territory. Four days before their departure date, Keil's nineteen-year-old son Willie died of malaria. Keil had promised Willie he could drive the lead wagon. Wanting neither to delay the wagon train's departure nor to leave Willie behind, Keil arranged to have the body put in a wooden, lead-lined coffin and covered with Golden Rule whiskey (from the Bethel Colony distillery) to preserve it. Willie's coffin rode in the lead wagon to Willapa Bay, where he was buried near present Menlo, Washington.

After wintering at Willapa Bay, Keil decided that the location was too remote and unsuitable for developing a self-sufficient agricultural community and began scouting the Willamette Valley. He found a promising spot south of Oregon City, and in 1856 purchased land and a working mill. Keil named the colony Aurora Mills for his daughter and served as the first postmaster. People continued to come from Bethel, and the colony grew and prospered. The Aurora colonists believed in hard work and simple living. They built homes, businesses, schools, and mills. Colony orchards made Aurora a prominent fruit-growing region. Their manufactured goods were among the first in the Northwest. With the construction of a hotel, Aurora became a stage stop along the territorial highway. When the railroad was built through Aurora, four trains a day stopped at the colony hotel for meals.

At its peak in 1868, the Aurora Colony boasted about 600 people and 15,000 acres (6,100 ha). William Keil continued as the acknowledged leader of the colonists' personal lives and finances until he died on December 30, 1877. Without a strong leader, the Aurora Colony dissolved, and the land was distributed to individual families. Dissolution became final in 1883, and Aurora's businesses and industries became privately owned—many of them operated by former colony members and their descendants.

Susan Badger Doyle

See also: Donation Land Claim Act (1850).

Further Reading

Duke, David Nelson. "A Profile of Religion in the Bethel-Aurora Colonies." *Oregon Historical Quarterly* 92:4 (Winter 1991).

Harris, Patrick J. "William Keil and the Aurora Colony: A Communal Society Crosses the Oregon Trail." In *Religion and Society in the American West*, ed. Carl Guarneri and David Alvarez. Lanham, MD: University Press of America, 1987.

Nash, Tom, and Twilo Scofield. *The Well-Traveled Casket: Oregon Folklore.* Eugene, OR: Meadowlark Press, 1999.

Kern Brothers

The Kern brothers were artists and scientists whose works portrayed sites all over the American West in the mid-nineteenth century. Edward M. (Ned) (b. October 26, 1823), Richard H. (b. 1821), and Benjamin J. (b. August 3, 1818) were all from Philadelphia and became members of the Philadelphia Academy of Natural Sciences. The two younger brothers accompanied several of the scientific expeditions undertaken by the U.S. Army Corps of Topographical Engineers during what is known as the Great Reconnaissance. Their work is intertwined with John C. Frémont's expeditions to find a route for a Pacific-bound railroad. Although their employers expected them to produce scientific renderings of the geographical features, flora, and fauna, they created several portraits that reflected the spirit of Romanticism. Some of the most famous works in the collective Kern portfolio are watercolor scenes of the Southwest, including local Indians and natural settings. They also kept official journals of their travels, which added to the body of knowledge about the West. The Kerns' written and artistic contributions to the many volumes describing the West helped introduce the western landscapes to the American public.

Edward was a trained artist and the first Kern brother to venture west. He worked as a topographer on the third Frémont expedition from 1845 to 1847, replacing Charles Preuss in the party. He sketched the south shore of the Great Salt Lake in Utah and ventured through the Sierra Nevadas in California with famed mountain man Joseph Walker, traversing the dangerous river that would later bear his name after he nearly drowned in it. In California, in addition to the Kern River, Edward's namesakes include Kern County, Kernville, and the Kern Valley. Edward also mapped the route from Walker Lake in northern California to the San Joaquin Valley.

Besides his work as an artist, Edward inadvertently became a military man. Frémont first entrusted him with prisoners housed at Fort Sutter taken during the Bear Flag Revolt. Frémont then commissioned him first lieutenant in the California Battalion at the outbreak of the Mexican-American War in 1846. Kern commanded Fort Sutter and also organized rescue efforts for the Donner Party. He continued to sketch the area and its inhabitants during his sojourn in the region. Shortly after the California Battalion disbanded in 1847, he returned to Philadelphia.

Edward's brothers Benjamin, a physician, and Richard, also a topographer and artist, soon joined him on his adventures. The three men accompanied Frémont's fourth expedition in 1848, whose mission was to survey the 38th parallel as a possible railroad route. The explorers, along with famed mountain man Bill Williams as guide, ran into serious trouble when they were stranded in the San Juan Mountains in southern Colorado. Several of the group died while others trekked out and eventually found safety in Taos, New Mexico. Ute Indians killed Benjamin on March 14, 1849, when he returned to the mountains two months later to collect baggage left behind after the party's escape. Edward blamed Frémont for the tragedy, but Frémont forged ahead to California, leaving the rest of the party waiting for rescue. Edward and Richard continued to work while they were marooned in New Mexico, and Richard produced one of his most famous pieces resulting from the ill-fated expedition, his watercolor *Valley of Taos, Looking South, N.M., 1849.*

The two remaining brothers joined the company of Colonel John N. Washington on the expedition against the Navajos in 1849. On that mission, they passed Canyon de Chelly, which Richard painted. They also investigated and captured in color Chaco Canyon and the Zuñi complex. Richard painted Acoma and was one of very few white men at that time to see the inside of a kiva, a Pueblo meeting chamber. Edward returned to Philadelphia in 1851, but Richard stayed on in the Southwest. He traveled with Captain Lorenzo Sitgreaves across the desert to San Diego and recorded the likenesses of several tribes, including the Yampais, for the first time.

Richard was also a member of other parties tasked with finding a route for the planned transcontinental railroad. He worked with the expedition of Captain John Gunnison, who was studying a proposed route along the 38th parallel. Gunnison's group set out in late summer 1853 and many of the party did not survive the mission, victims of a horrific episode known as the Gunnison Massacre. Richard was a veteran of several scrapes with Indians throughout his many journeys, but the encounter with them under the command of Gunnison would be his last. On October 26, 1853, the Utes killed him, Gunnison, and five others in the massacre along the Sevier River in Utah.

Richard and Edward had both begun new surveys in 1853, but the surviving brother crossed the Pacific Ocean rather than the Rocky Mountains on his trek. He was the official artist with the Ringgold Expedition to the North Pacific from 1853 to 1856. He later aided the U.S. Navy as it charted a route from California to China. He sketched and painted scenes such as *View of the Coast of Japan* during this time, and scholars have referred to his work from this period as his best.

Edward served under Frémont briefly during the Civil War as part of scouting missions. The two had apparently reconciled. He was discharged in 1861 when Frémont lost his command of the western department. He died of an epileptic seizure in Philadelphia on November 23, 1863.

The contributions of the Kern brothers as artists, explorers, and collectors of scientific data were significant to America's understanding of the West. They mapped and sketched major areas in the Southwest, Utah, and California. Edward and Richard helped plot potential routes for the transcontinental railroad. Richard's artwork offered some of the first examples of indigenous life in the Southwest, and they would inspire future artists, especially in New Mexico. Edward's efforts helped open the door to Japan and the Far East as well as the American West. The Kerns were not quite mythic rough-and-rugged explorers, but rather curious Romantics with wanderlust for the West who became frontiersmen.

Meg Frisbee

See also: Frémont, John C.; Williams, William "Old Bill."

Further Reading

Hine, Robert V. *In the Shadow of Fremont: Edward Kern and the Art of American Exploration, 1845–1860.* Norman: University of Oklahoma Press, 1982.

Viola, Herman J. *Exploring the West.* Washington, DC: Smithsonian Books, 1987.

Weber, David J. *Richard H. Kern: Expeditionary Artist in the Far Southwest, 1848–1853.* Albuquerque: University of New Mexico Press, 1985.

King, Clarence (1842–1901)

Clarence King, the geologist-in-charge of the U.S. Geological Exploration of the 40th parallel, was responsible for leading one of the four most important post–Civil War scientific surveys in the trans–Mississippi West. Covering a band of territory nearly

Clarence King headed the Geological Exploration of the 40th parallel, a federal survey of the Great Basin from western Nevada to eastern Wyoming, from 1867 to 1872. The eight-volume survey report won acclaim from the scientific community. *(George Eastman House/Getty Images)*

100 miles (160 km) wide and situated primarily north of the 40th parallel, it traversed the region from just east of Cheyenne, Wyoming, to the Nevada-California border, west of Pyramid Lake, Nevada.

King was an unlikely candidate to be the leader of the years-long survey that covered the wild, barren, and desiccated expanses of the Great Basin. Before his death, he would become associated with some of America's leading statesmen, scientists, authors, and businessmen, among them Henry Adams, Louis Agassiz, William Dean Howells, J.P. Morgan, Baron Rothschild, Bret Harte, John Hay, and Albert Bierstadt. Born into a well-to-do family of China merchants in Newport, Rhode Island, on January 6, 1842, King graduated from Yale University's Sheffield Scientific School in 1862. Primarily due to the poor health of his

childhood friend and schoolmate James Terry Gardner, King and his friend headed for California soon after graduation. When the pair arrived on the West Coast in 1863, they soon learned that the noted geologist Josiah Whitney was involved in a scientific survey in California and King was hired on. Out of his California sojourn came not only four years of valuable experience working under the direction of one of the nation's most respected geologists, but also a volume of his recollections entitled *Mountaineering in the Sierra Nevada*, the first of several books and papers he authored over the next thirty years.

Upon his return to the East with Gardner, King launched a campaign to obtain approval for a government-sponsored geological survey along the 40th parallel, an idea the two men had conceived on their return home from California. In early 1867—armed with recommendations from his former employer, Josiah Whitney; from Spencer Baird, who one day would become the second secretary of the Smithsonian Institution; and from the eminent Swiss-born naturalist Louis Agassiz—King persuaded U.S. Army authorities to organize the United States Geological Exploration of the 40th parallel, with himself in charge. The results of the massive survey, which kept King and his large party busy in the field from 1867 until 1872, were published in seven volumes and an atlas between 1870 and 1880.

In 1879 King was appointed the first director of the newly organized United States Geological Survey. He served in the position for one year before retiring to private endeavors. Over the next score of years, he dabbled in mining, traveled extensively throughout Europe, and socialized with wealthy and influential friends back in the United States before succumbing to tuberculosis in Phoenix, Arizona, on December 24, 1901.

James A. Crutchfield

See also: United States Geological Survey.

Further Reading

Bartlett, Richard A. *Great Surveys of the American West.* Norman: University of Oklahoma Press, 1962.

Viola, Herman J. *Exploring the West.* Washington, DC: Smithsonian Books, 1987.

Wilkins, Thurman. *Clarence King: A Biography.* Revised and enlarged edition. Albuquerque: University of New Mexico, 1988.

Kiowa

Prior to their encounter with Spanish explorers in the mid-eighteenth century, the Kiowas inhabited villages near the Three Forks of the Missouri River headwaters in southwestern Montana. They gradually migrated southward, and under the influence and teachings of the Crow people, with whom they were friendly, the Kiowas evolved into expert horsemen and nomadic buffalo hunters.

In 1805 Lewis and Clark learned that the Kiowas were living along the North Platte River in southern Wyoming, but horseback mobility, migrating buffalo herds, and conflicts with Cheyennes, Arapahos, and other Plains Indians drew the tribe southward to the Arkansas River country of Colorado and Kansas.

Kiowa tradition has it that their progress was halted by Comanche claims to all the territory south of the Arkansas, but the two tribes eventually formed a lasting peace and thereafter traded and made war together. The Kiowas and their Comanche allies became known for their incessant raids on frontier settlements in Oklahoma, Texas, and as deep into Mexico as Durango. Historians of the Southwestern Indian wars count the Kiowas and Comanches as the most bloodthirsty toward whites of all tribes north of Apache territory.

Notable among the conflicts between Kiowas and whites on the Texas frontier were the two battles at Adobe Walls, the ruins of an abandoned fort on the Canadian River in the Texas Panhandle. In the first of these, on November 26, 1864, a force of 300 volunteer cavalrymen out of Fort Bascom in northeastern New Mexico attacked a Kiowa village of some 150 lodges near Adobe Walls. Before the day ended, Colonel Christopher "Kit" Carson's troopers, with the aid of two mountain howitzers, met and defeated a force of some 1,500 Kiowas, Comanches, and Cheyennes as they defended their camps. A year later the Kiowa chief Dohasan and his people were consigned to a reservation in southwestern Oklahoma.

The Second Battle of Adobe Walls was fought a decade later, on June 27, 1874, between about 700 Comanche, Kiowa, Southern Cheyenne, and Arapaho tribesmen and a party of 28 buffalo hunters camped one mile from the adobe ruins. After a five-day siege, with only minor casualties on either side, the Indians withdrew. This seemingly insignificant conflict led to the Red River War of 1874–1875, in which the Kiowas and neighboring tribes fought the U.S. Army in more than twenty skirmishes in the Texas Panhandle. In the summer of 1875, the Red River War ended with the surrender at Fort Sill, Oklahoma, of Comanche war leader Quanah Parker and his band. The last remnant of the Kiowas came into Fort Sill later in the year. The surrender marked the end of Indian warfare on the southern plains and the final removal of the tribes to reservations in Indian Territory, opening the region further to white settlement.

By the time of their surrender in 1875, the Kiowas numbered fewer than 2,000. The tribe was dogged for nearly thirty years by white man's diseases: cholera in 1849, the year of the greatest California gold rush migration across the West; smallpox in 1861–1862; and measles in 1877. The 1989 U.S. census reported a national populace of 4,800 Kiowas.

The Kiowas experimented briefly with the Ghost Dance religious movement of 1890, but abandoned it after the massacre at Wounded Knee, later adopting the peyote "religion" of the Comanches. Gradually, the Kiowa people were assimilated into white culture.

The tribal complex is located just west of Carnegie, Oklahoma.

Dale L. Walker

See also: Adobe Walls, Battles of; Apache; Cheyenne; Comanche; Ghost Dance; Parker, Quanah; Wounded Knee.

Further Reading

Corwin, Hugh D. *The Kiowa Indians: Their History and Life Stories*. Lawton, OK: Privately printed, 1958.

Mayhall, Mildred P. *The Kiowas*. Norman: University of Oklahoma Press, 1962.

Nye, Wilbur S. *Bad Medicine and Good: Tales of the Kiowas*. Norman: University of Oklahoma Press, 1962.

Laclède Liguest, Pierre de (1729–1778)

Pierre de Laclède Liguest was the founder of St. Louis, which originated as a trading post named after his patron saint, King Louis IX of France.

Laclède was born into a middle-class family on November 22, 1729, in Berdous, France. He graduated from the Académie d'Armes de Toulouse, where he not only received a military education but also learned agriculture, milling, engineering, and foreign languages. He was generous and honest, always looking out for the less fortunate.

In 1755 Laclède brought a group of settlers to New Orleans and began working on agricultural and other business ventures. When fighting between France and Great Britain broke out in the French and Indian War, he joined the French army and was placed on the staff of Colonel Gilbert Antoine de Maxent, who liked the younger Laclède and took him under his wing.

Laclède met Marie Thérèse Chouteau who, with her small son Auguste, had been deserted by her husband, René Chouteau, who was living in France. Laclède and Marie Thérèse wanted to marry, but the Catholic Church and the French government did not recognize divorce. Defying church and state, the couple lived together as husband and wife. A son, Pierre, was born in 1758, followed by three sisters. Since Marie Thérèse and Laclède were not legally married, they had to give the children the last name of Chouteau.

The governor of Louisiana gave Maxent trading rights on the west bank of the Mississippi River and all of the Missouri River. Maxent and Laclède formed a partnership, with Maxent providing the capital and Laclède traveling upriver to trade with various Indian tribes. In 1763 Laclède journeyed up the Mississippi River with Auguste and a band of workers in order to establish a trading post. In December, he located a good site for his trading post on high ground on the west bank of the Mississippi just below the mouth of the Missouri River. This well-situated site provided easy access for upstream Missouri, Mississippi, and Illinois River tribes. Laclède spent the winter at Fort Chartres on the east bank of the Mississippi River, and on February 14, 1764, he sent fourteen-year-old Auguste and a work crew back to the trading post site to begin clearing the land and constructing the buildings.

Laclède arrived in early April, bringing with him people from the Fort Chartres area to settle near his new post, which he named St. Louis. The newcomers learned in December that France had transferred Louisiana to Spain in a secret treaty, but they saw little change in the way the region was governed.

After Laclède finished building his home and trading post, he sent for Marie Thérèse and the other children. The trading post was an instant success with the Osage and other tribes, who learned to respect Laclède for his honest dealings. In 1778 Laclède traveled to New Orleans to compile a shipment of trade goods. He was not feeling well and wrote a will, possibly having a premonition that death was near. On May 27, he was returning upriver when he died of natural causes. Because of his leniency in the extension of credit, he left extensive debts, but he had trained Auguste and Pierre in the art of business and had instilled in them honor and compassion. The Chouteau brothers were poised to become one of the great trading families of the Old West.

Bill Markley

See also: Chouteau Family; Osage; St. Louis, Missouri.

Further Reading

Christian, Shirley. *Before Lewis and Clark: The Story of the Chouteaus, the French Dynasty That Ruled America's Frontier.* New York: Farrar, Straus and Giroux, 2004.

Foley, William E., and David C. Rice. *The First Chouteaus: River Barons of Early St. Louis.* Urbana: University of Illinois Press, 2000.

Lakota

The Plains Indians known as the Lakotas developed a distinctive culture centered on horsemanship and buffalo hunting. When white pioneers and the military advanced into their territory, the Lakotas fought back. They are one of three linguistically related tribes who refer to themselves as Lakotas, Dakotas, and Nakotas. These are the same word, meaning "alliance of friends," but spoken in three distinct dialects. French and later English explorers and traders called these people Sioux, a misnomer derived from a Chippewa word, Naduwessi, meaning "snakes" or "enemies."

The Lakota people divide themselves into seven councils or family groups: Sicangu or Brulé, Oglala, Hunkpapa, Minniconjou, Sihasapa or Blackfeet, Oohenumpa or Two Kettle, and Itazip or Sans Arc.

The Lakotas lived to the west of the Dakotas and Nakotas in present-day Minnesota. After acquiring horses and firearms, the Lakotas expanded into present-day South Dakota and North Dakota, eventually as far west as the Bighorn Mountains in Wyoming. The Lakotas worshiped Wakan Tanka, the Great Mystery.

They went on vision quests to learn what their purpose in life was to be. They strove to live up to the Lakota virtues—bravery, fortitude, generosity, and wisdom—given to them long ago by White Buffalo Calf Woman.

The men hunted, protected the villages, and went on raids. The women tended the homes, raised the children, and advised the men. Tribal government was a loose confederation of older, experienced men who sat in council and made decisions that were considered best for the tribe. There was no one overall leader of the Lakotas, but people were attracted to and followed great leaders such as Red Cloud, Spotted Tail, Crazy Horse, Gall, American Horse, and Sitting Bull.

The United States' first major encounter with the Lakotas occurred in 1804 when the Corps of Discovery, led by Meriwether Lewis and William Clark, met the Brulés at the confluence of the Bad and Missouri Rivers at present-day Fort Pierre, South Dakota. The cool-headed action on the part of Black Buffalo diffused a situation that could have turned hostile when the Indians wanted more presents than the Corps of Discovery was willing to share.

During the first half of the nineteenth century, an uneasy truce existed between the white traders pushing their way up the Missouri River and the Lakotas. At times the Lakotas traded furs and

A delegation of Lakota led by Chief Red Cloud (*seated, second from left*) visited Washington, DC, in the aftermath of the Great Sioux War in 1877. A treaty forced the Lakotas to sell the Black Hills—ceded to them in 1868—back to the U.S. government. (*Library of Congress*)

buffalo robes for manufactured items such as guns, powder, ammunition, knives, and household goods. As settlers and the military encroached on Lakota territory, they fought back to hold on to their lands and traditions. In August 1854, a Lakota butchered a crippled, stray cow near Fort Laramie. Soldiers were sent to apprehend the man who had butchered the cow, a fight broke out, the soldiers were killed, and a Lakota leader fatally wounded in what has become known as the Grattan incident. The following year soldiers retaliated against the Lakotas with an attack at Blue Water Creek in Nebraska. There would be other confrontations over the military encroachment into Lakota Territory with the development of the Bozeman Trail (1866–1868) and later during the Great Sioux War (1876–1877), which included the Battle of the Little Bighorn. Crazy Horse, Sitting Bull, Gall, and other leaders took part in those battles. Eventually they all surrendered and agreed to live on the Great Sioux Reservation.

In 1888 Congress passed the Sioux Act, breaking up the Great Sioux Reservation into six smaller reservations and selling off the rest of the land. The last major incident with the Lakotas ended during the Ghost Dance movement in 1890 at Wounded Knee on the Pine Ridge Reservation.

Today, Lakota reservations are located in South Dakota and North Dakota—Standing Rock, Cheyenne River, Lower Brulé, Pine Ridge, and Rosebud. Many Lakotas live away from the reservations, but still take pride in continuing their traditions as they participate in all aspects of mainstream American life.

Bill Markley

See also: American Horse; Blue Water Creek, Battle of; Crazy Horse; Custer, George Armstrong; Custer Expedition; Dawes Severalty Act (1887); Fort Laramie, Treaty of (1868); Gall; Ghost Dance; Grattan Massacre; Red Cloud; Red Cloud's War; Sioux; Sitting Bull; Spotted Tail; Wounded Knee.

Further Reading

Bray, Kingsley. *Crazy Horse*. Norman: University of Oklahoma Press, 2006.

Clodfelter, Micheal. *The Dakota War: The United States Army Versus the Sioux, 1862–1865*. Jefferson, NC: McFarland, 1998.

Larson, Robert. *Gall*. Norman: University of Oklahoma Press, 2007.

Smith, Rex Alan. *Moon of Popping Trees*. Lincoln: University of Nebraska Press, 1981.

Utley, Robert M. *The Lance and the Shield: The Life and Times of Sitting Bull*. New York: Ballantine Books, 1994.

Lamar, Mirabeau B. (1798–1859)

Mirabeau Buonaparte Lamar—second president of the Republic of Texas (1838–1841) and vice-president in Sam Houston's first administration (1836–1838)—inherited the presidency as the country began to feel the economic pains of rapid growth and the need to bring Texas into the modern age through road and school improvement. Although his administration was less than stellar, he did succeed in establishing a firm foundation upon which Texas's later educational program was grounded, a feat that earned him the sobriquet "father of Texas public education."

Born on August 16, 1798, near Louisville, Georgia, Lamar grew up the son of wealthy plantation owners. Educated at the best private academies, as a youngster he showed a keen interest in fine horses, fencing, oil painting, and poetry. He published newspapers in both Georgia and Alabama and served as a Georgia state senator for one term. When defeated in the 1832 and 1834 races for a seat in the U.S. Congress, he decided to move to Texas with his friend and neighbor, James W. Fannin, whose name would become legend in the months to come.

Lamar had scarcely arrived in Texas before he became involved in the independence movement. During his return to Georgia to settle his personal affairs, the incidents at the Alamo and Goliad (where his friend, Fannin, was executed by Mexican troops) occurred, and he returned to Texas at once, enlisting in the army as a private. At the Battle of San Jacinto in late April 1836, he distinguished himself and was given a battlefield promotion to colonel of cavalry, followed ten days later by his appointment as secretary of war in provisional president David G. Burnet's cabinet. Four weeks later Burnet appointed him to the role of commander in chief of the Texas army, a position he did not fill due to the army's dislike for him.

In October 1836, Lamar was elected vice-president of Texas and served a little more than two years with President Sam Houston, a political opposite. Two years later, the anti-Houston faction ran Lamar for president and he won the election unopposed. Taking office on December 10, 1838, Lamar stepped into a political mire. Only the United States so far had recognized the independence of Texas, and Lamar made it a priority to seek additional recognition from the major European powers, a task in which he succeeded when Great Britain, France, and Holland opened diplomatic relations with the republic. He had to contend with a burgeoning national debt; the republic's total annual income was $500,000, while the outstanding debt had already risen to $7 million. Relations with various Indian tribes had to be refined, and, unfortunately for several of them—the Cherokees, themselves relatively new arrivals in Texas, and the warlike Comanches—official treatment was harsh.

Lamar devised a scheme to fill the republic's coffers by opening commercial trade with the merchants of Santa Fe and other markets in New Mexico (which Lamar, like all Texans, believed was actually part of Texas). The mission was a total failure and resulted primarily in the capture and imprisonment by Mexicans of many of the participants.

Following his three-year administration, Lamar retired from politics, but later, in Washington, DC, lobbied for the annexation of Texas by the United States. He served as a lieutenant colonel with General Zachary Taylor during the Mexican-American War, was appointed U.S. minister to both Nicaragua and Costa Rica, began work on a massive history of Texas that was never completed, and wrote poetry before he succumbed to a heart attack on December 19, 1859, at his plantation in Richmond, Texas.

James A. Crutchfield

See also: Alamo, The; Fannin, James Walker; Goliad, Battle of; Houston, Sam; Mexican-American War; San Jacinto, Battle of; Texan Santa Fe Expedition; Texas Revolution and Independence.

Further Reading
Ramsay, Jack C., Jr. *Thunder Beyond the Brazos*. Austin, TX: Eakin Press, 1985.

Land Speculation Companies

In the trans-Mississippi West, America's private citizen response to the call of manifest destiny received its impetus from the earlier explorations of mountain men and army engineers, government-sponsored railroad surveys, gold and silver rushes, free government land, and the surge of the great migrations across numerous overland trails. In the East, however, half a century earlier, the success of westward expansion was in many cases due to private enterprise in the form of land speculation companies.

From the very beginning of European settlement in North America, adventurers and entrepreneurs were driven to search out new lands for settlement by privately chartered companies that owned, primarily from royal gifts to the companies' principals, millions of acres of uncharted land in the wilderness. Thus in 1606, King James I of England granted a charter to a group of investors and businessmen for the establishment of the Virginia Company, which was divided into the Virginia Company of Plymouth, with authority to colonize and administer present-day New England, and the Virginia Company of London, whose oversight focused on the southern portions of the Atlantic seaboard and whose efforts resulted in the founding of Jamestown in 1607. From this beginning until the middle of the eighteenth century, America's original thirteen colonies grew and prospered.

During the years immediately prior to the French and Indian Wars, several land speculation entities were formed, two of the most important being the Ohio Company, established in 1747, and the Loyal Company, formed two years later. Among the Ohio Company's founders were Augustine and Lawrence Washington, the first president's half-brothers, and the corporation's goal was to settle 200,000 acres (81,000 ha) (augmented two years later by an additional 700,000 acres [283,000 ha]) of prime land located in the upper Ohio River valley. The Loyal Company's holdings consisted of a parcel of land stretching to the Appalachian Mountains along the Virginia-North Carolina border.

Following the Revolutionary War and assurance of American independence from Great Britain, land speculators again made an impact on westward expansion. Anxious to populate remote regions of the frontier with eastern-dwelling settlers, officials of these companies made tracts of land available to practically any comers at attractive prices. Some of the establishments were fraudulent, like the Yazoo Company, which during 1789 and 1795 purchased 25 million acres (10 million ha) of present-day Mississippi from an equally corrupt Georgia legislature, fully aware that the expanse was still Indian territory. Others, like the Transylvania Company, were directly responsible for the colonization of large numbers of families in remote territory, such as the settlement of Nashville, which the company's principal shareholder, Richard Henderson, directed.

It is interesting to speculate whether or not America's first great surge westward would have succeeded as well as it did if, during those early days of expansion across and beyond the Appalachian Mountains, no privately held land companies had existed.

James A. Crutchfield

See also: Boonesborough, Kentucky; Nashville.

Further Reading

Alvord, Clarence. *The Mississippi Valley in British Politics*. Whitefish, MT: Kessinger, 2008.

Horsman, Reginald. *The Frontier in the Formative Years, 1783–1815*. New York: Holt, Rinehart and Winston, 1970.

Lander, Frederick W. (1821–1862)

Frederick Lander was born into a Massachusetts seafaring family on December 17, 1821. There was little in his childhood to suggest his potential for being a railroad worker, explorer, engineer, poet, writer, and soldier. He was trained at the Franklin & Phillips, and Dummer academies, where he learned civil engineering. While working in his brother's ice business in the 1840s, Lander met Grenville Dodge, and the two youths took an instant liking to one another and became lifelong friends. Dodge followed Lander into Norwich University, America's first private military school. Later, both would have successful careers building railroads.

At the conclusion of the Mexican-American War, railroad expansion to the Pacific coast became feasible. Seeking the best route, the U.S. government commissioned a study under the leadership of Jefferson Davis, who chose Isaac Stevens to direct the topographical survey. Stevens, the top member of West Point's graduating class of 1839 and a former student of Franklin & Phillips Academy, offered Lander the chance to work on the history-making railroad survey.

Lander killed the first buffalo on the survey, explored into Canada searching for the source of the Souris River, and scouted foothills and passes in the Rocky Mountains. As time progressed, Lander had a falling-out with Stevens that almost turned to gunplay. Stevens's party linked with that of George Brinton McClellan, coming from the east, and Lander was entrusted with several tasks left undone by McClellan, including examining the passes of the Cascade Mountains. Lander also explored a route to Puget Sound along the Columbia and Cowitz rivers.

Lander spent the winter of 1853–1854 with his brother Ned, a judge in Olympia, Washington Territory, using his time there to garner support for an independent expedition to examine the route of the Platte River for the railroad. The subsequent 1854 expedition involved exploration of the South Pass of the Rockies and the Great Divide Basin. Lander was traveling east when he happened to encounter Grenville Dodge, now a farmer. Lander and Dodge struck up their old friendship, but Lander pressed on to Washington to promote the central railroad route through South Pass, later returning to Boston to document his findings, which he self-published. His pamphlet shot down Stevens's northern route in favor of the central route for a transcontinental railroad.

For the next two years Lander labored as a civil engineer, worked on a railroad from Indiana to Canada, followed the lecture circuit, and consulted on western expansion projects, such as the national wagon roads planned for South Pass, Honey Lake, and Fort Kearny. In 1858 he was hired to command construction of that road west of South Pass to the City of Rocks in present-day Idaho.

In 1859 Dodge had a chance encounter with Abraham Lincoln. The two spoke for two hours about the transcontinental railroad, especially the benefits of Lander's central route. This conversation helped to mold history. That year Lander returned to South Pass to continue improvements on his road. This was Lander's most unusual expedition as it included artists such as Albert Bierstadt, Henry Hitchings, and Francis Seth Frost. Lander also published 1,000 copies of a guide to attract people to the national wagon road, which led roughly 13,000 emigrants to follow the Lander Road that season.

At the start of the Civil War, Lander, an ardent Unionist, served in the campaigns in western Virginia, which raised his former associate George Brinton McClellan to lead the Army of the Potomac. Lander's artillery fired the first shots of the first land battle of the conflict at Phillipi. Lander quickly rose to the rank of brigadier general. On March 2, 1862, Lander's remarkable life ended suddenly when he succumbed to congestive chills (probably pneumonia).

Lander is remembered for his work on the national wagon road, which now bears his name. However, his brilliant explorations of a central route for the transcontinental railroad bore fruit years after his death.

Terry A. Del Bene

See also: Lander Cutoff; Railroad Surveys, Transcontinental; South Pass.

Further Reading

Ecelbarger, Gary L. *Frederick W. Lander: The Great Natural American Soldier*. Baton Rouge: Louisiana State University Press, 2000.

Lander Cutoff

Facing growing political influence in the West, Congress passed the Pacific Wagon Road Act early in 1857 to provide the first federal funds to develop an overland wagon road. It appropriated $300,000 to survey and construct the "Fort Kearney [*sic*], South Pass, and Honey Lake Wagon Road." W.M.F. Magraw became superintendent, but the project's chief engineer was Frederick William Lander, a brilliant railroad expert whose western exploits had already made him famous. "Magraw is an ignorant blackguard, totally unfit for the head of such an expedition," Captain John Phelps concluded at Fort Laramie, "while the chief engineer of the party is." After the drunken Magraw volunteered to serve in the Utah Expedition, Lander became superintendent in 1858. He reported "the completion of the Overland Wagon Road" in September 1860.

The project made minor improvements at the start and end of the California Trail, but the work centered on South Pass, where Lander sought a route that avoided several difficult river and desert crossings. The Lander Cutoff began at the ninth crossing of the Sweetwater River and ended on the Snake River. The road Lander located in 1857 and opened during the next two years rejoined the "old Emigrant road" at Fort Hall, 229 miles (369 km) from its start. Better supplied with water, grass, and wood, it was about 60 miles (97 km) shorter and infinitely more scenic than traditional routes. But, as Randall Hewitt wrote in 1862, the road traversed "a mixture of level plains and hills—some of them very steep and rough—hollows and sloughs."

Even though many travelers, such as Royal D. Ross in 1863, thought the cutoff was "built to enable the emigrants to avoid the Mormon settlements in Utah," most of the workers Lander hired were Mormons, and he praised their character and efficiency. Lander brought a "full corps of artists" with him in 1859, including the brilliant Albert Bierstadt, whose paintings are some of the earliest of the overland road, while the landscapes the expedition inspired are legendary.

Some 13,000 emigrants used Lander's Road during the summer of 1859. Gold rushes to Idaho and Montana generated more traffic. It became a preferred route during the Civil War; the army estimated that 8,000 travelers used it in 1862. Wagons followed the trail until at least 1912, and the total number of people who crossed the cutoff probably topped 100,000.

No modern highway traces Lander's route. Its creator died a Union general in 1862, but his most enduring monument is his trail which still "spans the plateau south of the Wind River Range, winds its way to the heights of a three-way continental divide, fords swift mountain streams, passes through mountain meadows and tight canyons, and finally rolls out onto the Snake River Plain," as historian Peter T. Harstad wrote. "In the well-worn ruts of this nineteenth-century wagon road can be seen a mingling of practicality and romanticism—qualities deeply imbedded in the westward movement as well as in the character of F.W. Lander."

Will Bagley

See also: California Trail; Lander, Frederick W.

Further Reading

Ecelbarger, Gary. *Frederick W. Lander: The Great Natural American Soldier.* Baton Rouge: Louisiana State University Press, 2000.

Harstad, Peter T. "The Lander Trail." *Idaho Yesterdays* 12:3 (Fall 1968).

Houston, Alan Fraser, and Jourdan Moore Houston. "The 1859 Lander Expedition Revisited: 'Worthy Relics' Tell New Tales of a Wind River Wagon Road." *Montana: The Magazine of Western History* 49:2 (Summer 1999).

Larkin, Thomas Oliver (1802–1858)

The first (and only) U.S. consul to the Mexican province of Alta (Upper) California, Thomas O. Larkin served an important role in the subsequent annexation of California in the Mexican-American War.

Born in Charlestown, Massachusetts, in 1802, Larkin worked as a bookbinder and storekeeper as a young man until taking advantage of an offer of employment from his half-brother, John B.R. Cooper, a sea captain who was opening a business on the California coast. In September 1831, Larkin sailed on a merchant ship around Cape Horn to Yerba Buena (later San Francisco), arriving there in April 1832.

In 1833 he married Rachel Hobson Holmes, a widow from Massachusetts, while working as clerk and factotum for John Cooper in Monterey, capital of Alta California. After a year Larkin was able to open his own store, and within a few years he built a flourmill in Monterey, a sawmill in Santa Cruz, and established himself as an entrepreneur, trader, and exporter. He conducted business in lumber, livestock, flour, and furs with the Sandwich Islands (now Hawaii), the Pacific ports of Mexico, and even became involved in the China trade.

The home he built in Monterey for Rachel and his growing family, the first two-story structure in the town, became a gathering place, with fine dinners, music, and dances, for American and other foreign dignitaries and visitors to the town.

Larkin's business successes in Alta California are attributable to his natural diplomatic skills and to the laissez-faire attitude of provincial officials so far from the seat of government in Mexico City toward its small foreign population. He never took Mexican citizenship, yet was able to conduct his business ventures, and acquired wealth and eminence, through the many changes in California's governance.

Larkin was keenly attuned to the growing instability in California in the 1840s among American settlers in the north of the province, and to the burgeoning expansionist views, which he shared, of those who wished to see the United States stretch its boundaries westward to the Pacific. In 1842 he helped smooth over the premature "capture" of Monterey by American warships, and in 1845 he became a confidential agent for the U.S. State Department. His instructions as agent were to take advantage of any signs of unrest among the *californios*—Spanish-speaking natives of the province—and to cultivate their support of annexation by the United States. For these services Larkin came to the attention of President James K. Polk, who in 1846 appointed him U.S. consul to Alta California.

Larkin was an active observer of the rebellion of American settlers in northern California in the summer of 1846 and became a participant in its aftermath, the annexation of Alta California in the Mexican-American War, during which he served as adviser to all the main military figures of the campaign.

Larkin and his family took up residence in San Francisco after the war and he prospered in the economic boom of the 1848–1850 gold rush, served as a member of the state Constitutional Convention that met in Monterey in 1849, and grew immensely wealthy from investments in land, mines, and railroads.

He contracted typhoid fever in the town of Colusa, north of Sacramento, and died on October 27, 1858.

Dale L. Walker

See also: Bear Flag Revolt; California, Conquest of; Jones, Thomas ap Catesby; Mexican-American War.

Further Reading

Hague, Harlan. "The Jumping Off Place of the World: California and the Transformation of Thomas O. Larkin." *California History* (Winter 1991/1992).
———. *Thomas O. Larkin: A Life of Patriotism and Profit in Old California.* Norman: University of Oklahoma Press, 1990.
Soule, Frank, John H. Gihon, and James Nisbet. *The Annals of San Francisco.* Berkeley, CA: Berkeley Hills Books, 1999. Reprint of 1854 edition.

Leavenworth, Henry (1783–1834)

A career army man, Henry Leavenworth figured prominently in America's westward expansion since he led the military contingent, forever afterward known as the "Missouri Legion," up the Missouri River in 1823 in an attempt to rescue General William Ashley's fur trappers from hostile Arikara Indians. According to some of his contemporaries, Leavenworth's failure to totally subdue the Indian tribe when he had the opportunity—and his decision to allow them to go largely unpunished for their unwarranted attack on Ashley—only served to strengthen future native resistance to the rapidly expanding Missouri River fur trade.

Leavenworth was born on December 10, 1783, in New Haven, Connecticut, the son of a colonel in the American Revolution. As a young man he studied law and was admitted to the New York state bar in 1804. When the War of 1812 broke out, he raised a company of volunteers from his home county and was appointed its commander. Later in the year, he was commissioned a captain of the 25th U.S. Infantry Regiment and subsequently was promoted to major and transferred to the 9th Infantry. On July 5, 1814, he was brevetted to lieutenant colonel for conspicuous conduct at the Battle of Chippewa in Canada, and ten days later was brevetted to colonel for distinguished service at Niagara Falls. Following the war, Leavenworth was instrumental in establishing several army posts throughout the upper Mississippi and middle Missouri River basins in response to the government's desire to fortify its northwestern frontier.

Leavenworth was serving in the 6th Infantry Regiment as the commander of Fort Atkinson in present-day Nebraska when the Arikara incident—the nation's first conflict between the army and a trans-Mississippi Indian tribe—occurred in 1823. Leaders of the Arikaras, a war-like tribe that alternatively expressed friendship and hatred for white traders and trappers traveling the Missouri River, refused to allow General William H. Ashley and his fur brigade to pass their villages, located along the river in today's South Dakota. A vicious conflict ensued, Ashley's men retreated down the river, and Leavenworth—bolstered by 6 infantry companies, several volunteer trappers from Manuel Lisa's Missouri Fur Company, and about 750 Sioux warriors—marched toward the villages. Upon his arrival in August, Leavenworth launched a half-hearted attack upon the tribe, and then parleyed for a cease-fire, to which the Arikaras agreed. While the two sides argued about the return of General Ashley's stolen merchandise, most of the Arikaras fled in the night, leaving Leavenworth and the trappers (the Sioux had since deserted) alone to celebrate their questionable victory.

After the Arikara campaign, Leavenworth went on to other army assignments, among them the establishment of Fort Leavenworth in 1827. He died on July 21, 1834, while on assignment near the Washita River.

James A. Crutchfield

See also: Arikara War; Ashley, William Henry; Fort Leavenworth.

Further Reading

Berry, Don. *A Majority of Scoundrels.* New York: Harper & Brothers, 1961.

Clokey, Richard M. *William H. Ashley: Enterprise and Politics in the Trans-Mississippi West.* Norman: University of Oklahoma Press, 1990.

Nester, William R. *The Arikara War: The First Plains Indian War, 1823.* Missoula, MT: Mountain Press, 2001.

Sunder, John E. *Joshua Pilcher: Fur Trader and Indian Agent.* Norman: University of Oklahoma Press, 1968.

Leavenworth and Pike's Peak Express

With the discovery of gold in the Rocky Mountains in 1858, a new group of travelers rushed westward toward Denver City. In an effort to meet the demand, William H. Russell, of the freighting firm Russell, Majors, and Waddell, formed a partnership with his old friend John S. Jones, a veteran freighter with over ten years on the trails of the Great Plains who had previously worked as a subcontractor for Russell's firm. With Jones's experience and Russell's knowledge, the two were able to secure a ninety-day money grant,

which they used to purchase supplies, equipment, and 1,000 Kentucky mules to be used in establishment of the Leavenworth and Pike's Peak Express. The grant also paid for the survey for a new and shorter route directly west across Kansas and Colorado. William Green Russell, who had discovered gold in the Rocky Mountains the previous year, led the survey.

Bypassing the old Oregon Trail, which lay farther north, the Leavenworth and Pike's Peak Express chose a shorter, more southern route that left Leavenworth, Kansas, and continued west to Denver City, following the Solomon and Republican rivers. In April 1859, twenty-seven stations, roughly 25 miles (40 km) apart, had been selected and supplied. Initial trips proved the route viable, and service was inaugurated. The new route was received with enthusiasm by travelers, including Horace Greeley, editor of the *New York Tribune*, who provided early important reports about the new gold strikes and routes to the region.

Miners and businessmen of the Rockies were particularly pleased with the quicker freight deliveries. On May 11, 1859, after only three weeks of business along the new route, Russell and Jones purchased the transportation firm of John M. Hockaday, who held a government mail contract providing service to Salt Lake City. The new owners soon rerouted the service to Colorado, with the first shiny Concord stagecoaches Denver City had ever seen rolling into town on July 9, 1859.

However, just two months later, Russell was forced to redirect his freight line and thereby his deliveries, to satisfy the government contract he had purchased from Hockaday. He abandoned the new direct route across Kansas and began following the overland route from Fort Kearny. This led to involvement of Russell's other partners, Majors and Waddell, and effectively ended the Leavenworth and Pike's Peak Express, although under their expanded business Russell, Majors, and Waddell continued freight services to the West, providing quick, efficient mail deliveries and eventually leading to establishment of the Pony Express.

Linda Wommack

See also: Greeley, Horace; Pony Express; Russell, Majors, and Waddell.

Further Reading

Lee, Wayne C., and Howard C. Raynesford. *Trails of the Smoky Hill.* Caldwell, ID: Caxton Press, 1980.

West, Elliott. *The Contested Plains: Indians, Goldseekers, and the Rush to Colorado.* Lawrence: University Press of Kansas, 1998.

Leonard, Zenas (1809–1857)

Zenas Leonard spent the first twenty-one years of his life in Pennsylvania. Born on a farm in Clearfield County on March 19, 1809, the young man eventually moved to St. Louis around 1830, where he took a position as clerk with a fur company, Gantt and Blackwell. Later becoming a free trapper, Leonard participated in the 1832 rendezvous and fought the Blackfoot in the Battle at Pierre's Hole, writing at length about the event in his highly important and useful book, *Narrative of the Adventures of Zenas Leonard, A Native of Clearfield County, Pa. Who Spent Five Years In Trapping Furs, Trading With The Indians, &c., &c., of The Rocky Mountains*, published in Clearfield, Pennsylvania, in 1839.

In 1833 Leonard hired on with the Benjamin Bonneville outfit and accompanied Joseph Walker to California, crossing the modern-day states of Utah and Nevada en route, thus becoming one of the first white men to see the wonders of Yosemite. He later trapped among the Crow Indians in the Yellowstone region and in the Wind River Range of today's Wyoming. After visiting his home in Pennsylvania in 1835, Leonard returned to the West and established a trading post near the site of the old Fort Osage factory (present-day Sibley, Missouri), also operating a boat along the Missouri River. It was apparently while there that he compiled the narrative of his life in the Rocky Mountain fur trade.

Leonard was married and fathered two girls and a boy. He died at his Missouri home on July 14, 1857, and is buried nearby in the Sibley Cemetery.

James A. Crutchfield

See also: Bonneville, Benjamin Louis; Pierre's Hole, Battle of; Walker, Joseph R.

Further Reading

Gilbert, Bil. *Westering Man: The Life of Joseph Walker, Master of the Frontier.* New York: Atheneum, 1983.

Leonard, Zenas. *Adventures of Zenas Leonard, Fur Trader.* Edited by John C. Ewers. Norman: University of Oklahoma Press, 1959.

Lewis, Meriwether (1774–1809)

Soldier, explorer, and proconsul Meriwether Lewis was born near Charlottesville, Albemarle County, Virginia, on August 18, 1774. His father, John Lewis, a former army officer in the Revolutionary War, died in 1789. Meriwether quit school at age eighteen and in 1794 volunteered as a militiaman in the suppression of the Whiskey Rebellion in the Monongahela Valley of Pennsylvania. That taste of military adventure was followed in the summer of the same year with service as a junior officer of the regular army in the Battle of Fallen Timbers in Ohio where he was befriended by fellow Virginian William Clark, a captain in General Anthony Wayne's forces.

After valuable service on the western frontier, Lewis rose to a captaincy in the 1st Infantry Regiment in 1800 and a year later received the momentous appointment of private secretary to President-elect Thomas Jefferson, a friend of the Lewis family. Jefferson had planned a transcontinental exploration for several years and Lewis, who undertook scientific studies as part of his secretarial duties, was named to command the expedition after its approval by Congress in January 1803.

In May of 1804, Lewis and his chosen co-captain of the "Corps of Discovery," William Clark, led their company of soldiers, hunters, and boatmen in ascending the Missouri River, and in September 1806 returned to St. Louis from their epic 8,000-mile (13,000-km) journey across uncharted wilderness to the Pacific and back. In October Lewis traveled on to Charlottesville, where a letter from the president awaited. Jefferson wrote of his "unspeakable joy" over successes of the expedition, and in February 1807 appointed Lewis governor of Louisiana Territory.

Before traveling on to St. Louis, seat of his governorship, the explorer settled expedition accounts, arranged for publication of a book on the enterprise based on his and Clark's journals, and served briefly as Jefferson's representative at Aaron Burr's treason trial in Richmond in August 1807. He also contracted a fever, believed to be malaria, for which he dosed himself with various medications, including laudanum, a dangerous, addictive opiate.

In March of 1808, over a year after his appointment, Lewis reached St. Louis where he was reunited with Clark, now superintendent of Indian Affairs for Louisiana Territory. During his seventeen months as governor Lewis dealt expertly with various political, military, and Indian problems, and even arranged to finance publication of the *Missouri Gazette*, the first territorial newspaper. His personal life and health faltered, however: he made poor land investments and verged on bankruptcy, drank heavily, and continued to nurse his ailments with opiates.

In early September 1809, he departed St. Louis by flatboat to Chickasaw Bluffs (now Memphis) to begin a horseback journey to Washington, DC. During the afternoon of October 10, Lewis and his small entourage reached the Natchez Trace, the old trade path running north out of Natchez through the valley of Tennessee to Nashville. At twilight Lewis and his party arrived at a remote inn called Grinder's Stand, about 70 miles (113 km) southwest of Nashville, and there, in the night or early morning hours of October 10–11, Meriwether Lewis, age thirty-five, died of gunshot wounds to his chest and head. While there were rumors of murder from the outset, both Jefferson and Clark were satisfied that he had killed himself out of despair over his health and perceived failures in his personal and professional life.

Dale L. Walker

See also: Clark, William; Jefferson, Thomas; Lewis and Clark Expedition; Louisiana Purchase (1803); Louisiana Territory; Natchez Trace.

Further Reading

Ambrose, Stephen. *Undaunted Courage: Meriwether Lewis, Thomas Jefferson, and the Opening of the American West.* New York: Simon & Schuster, 1996.

Bakeless, John. *Lewis and Clark: Partners in Discovery.* New York: William Morrow, 1948.

Dillon, Richard. *Meriwether Lewis: A Biography.* New York: Coward-McCann, 1965.

Lewis and Clark Expedition

Years before he took office in March 1801 as third president of the United States, Thomas Jefferson had envisioned an exploration into the lands west of the Mississippi, a vast *terra incognita* that he viewed as being of paramount importance to the future of the country. In a confidential message to Congress he set forth preliminary plans to explore these lands "even to the Western Ocean" and Congress responded in February 1803, approving a preliminary sum of $2,500 to finance an expedition to ascend the Missouri River to its source and continue westward to the Pacific.

Adding immediacy and legality to the daring enterprise was the president's diplomatic coup that culminated in Paris on April 30, 1803. On that date a treaty was signed in which the United States paid $15 million to Napoleonic France to acquire Louisiana Territory—827,000 square miles (2.2 million sq km) of some of the richest wilderness land in North America. This vast region, doubling the size of the nation, lay between the Mississippi River and beyond the Rocky Mountains, the territory to be traversed under Jefferson's exploration plan.

To command the Corps of Discovery, as he designated the expedition, the president selected his private secretary, Meriwether Lewis, age twenty-eight, and Lewis in turn called upon his friend, army colleague, and fellow Virginian William Clark to serve as co-captain. They were to lead a group of army volunteers, hunters, and boatmen, and map the party's progress up the 2,300-mile (3,700-km) long Missouri River and westward. As they proceeded, they were to complete scientific observations, collect specimens of flora and fauna, and contact and befriend any Indian tribes they encountered, with the objective of opening a fur trade with the natives.

Back east, Lewis gathered supplies, arms, ammunition, tools, medical implements and medicines, food, clothing, scientific instruments, books, maps, and a collection of ironware, knives, beads, cloth, ribbons, vermillion paint, and other goods as trade items and gifts for the native people they would visit en route to the Pacific. He also supervised construction of a 55-foot (17-m) long, 8-foot (2.5-m) wide shallow draft keelboat with a square sail and oars, as well as two pirogues (flat-bottomed canoe-like boats). On the trip from Pittsburgh down the Ohio River, Lewis rendezvoused with William Clark, and on the Wood River in Illinois near the confluence of the Missouri and Mississippi they set up their winter camp.

The expedition of nearly fifty men pushed off on May 14, 1804, "under a jentle brease," as Clark noted, and, averaging 12 to 14 miles (19–22.5 km) a day, reached present-day Omaha, Nebraska, on August 3. On August 20, near modern Sioux City, Iowa, the Corps suffered its sole fatality when Sergeant Charles Floyd, a Kentuckian in his early twenties, died of what is believed to have been a ruptured appendix.

Toward the end of October, in modern North Dakota the explorers reached the villages of the Mandan and Minnetaree tribes at the mouth of the Knife River and built Fort Mandan, their winter quarters. Along

Frontispiece   A Canoe striking on a Tree.   Page 320.

JOURNAL
OF THE
VOYAGES AND TRAVELS
OF
A CORPS OF DISCOVERY,

Under the command of Capt. Lewis and Capt. Clarke
of the army of the United States,

FROM THE MOUTH OF THE RIVER MISSOURI THROUGH
THE INTERIOR PARTS OF NORTH AMERICA
TO THE PACIFIC OCEAN,

During the Years 1804, 1805, and 1806.

CONTAINING

An authentic relation of the most interesting transactions
during the expedition; a description of the country;
and an account of its inhabitants, soil, climate, curiosities, and vegetable
and animal productions.

BY PATRICK GASS,
One of the persons employed in the expedition.

WITH GEOGRAPHICAL AND EXPLANATORY NOTES.

THIRD EDITION—WITH SIX ENGRAVINGS.

[Copy-right secured according to Law.]

PRINTED FOR MATHEW CAREY,
NO. 122 MARKET STREET,
PHILADELPHIA.

1811.

In 1807–1811, Patrick Gass, a sergeant in the Corps of Discovery, became the first member to publish a journal of the Lewis and Clark Expedition, including woodcut engravings. Lewis and Clark's own History of the Expedition appeared in 1814. (*MPI/Stringer/Getty Images*)

the route, as they had made contact with native people, Lewis explained to them, with the help of interpreter George Drouillard (son of a French-Canadian father and Shawnee mother) the purpose of their peaceful mission.

That winter the French fur trader Toussaint Charbonneau and his Shoshone wife Sacagawea joined the expedition as interpreters. Sacagawea's people lived near the headwaters of the Missouri, the Corps' destination as it departed Fort Mandan on April 7, 1805, after sending the keelboat, loaded with scientific specimens and Indian artifacts, back downriver with a dozen men.

Now numbering thirty-two men, one woman, and Sacagawea's baby son Jean-Baptiste (whom Clark nicknamed "Pomp"), the expedition traveled in two pirogues and several dugout canoes into present-day Montana, discovering a profusion of animal life—buffalo, wolves, bighorn sheep, and grizzly bears among them—en route. In late July the Corps reached the Three Forks of the Missouri—the river's headwaters—and on August 12 portaged across the Continental Divide. Five days later, Lewis, scouting ahead with three men, stumbled upon a Shoshone village whose chief turned out to be Sacagawea's brother. From him the captains purchased twenty-one horses and a mule and on the last day of August proceeded north into the valley of the Bitterroot River.

After an eleven-day ordeal in crossing the Bit-

terroot Range, fighting blizzards, plummeting temperatures, and starvation, the expedition reached the homelands of the Nez Percé people in present-day northern Idaho, where they recovered their strength. In early October, after fashioning dugout canoes and entrusting their horses to their Nez Percé friends, the explorers descended the Clearwater, Snake, and Columbia rivers and reached the Pacific Ocean on October 16, a year and a half and 4,100 miles (6,600 km) after departing their Wood River camp at the mouth of the Missouri.

For their winter quarters, Corps of Discovery workers built a stockade and outbuildings on the south side of the Columbia estuary (near today's Astoria, Oregon), named it Fort Clatsop for a nearby Indian tribe, and spent a miserable winter of incessant rain and cold. After five months at Fort Clatsop, and with weather clearing, the expedition departed on March 23, 1806, on the return journey. The Corps of Discovery recovered its horses from the Nez Percé caretakers and in June, after abandoning their dugouts, portaged across the Bitterroots in fair weather.

After crossing the Continental Divide, on July 3 the captains divided the party temporarily to enable Lewis to explore the Marias River, a Missouri tributary to the north of the homeward trail. In their camp on July 26 Lewis's party found some Blackfoot raiders attempting to steal their horses and guns and opened fire on the thieves, killing two. Fearing retaliation, Lewis and the men rode all day before resting. They rejoined Clark's party at the confluence of the Yellowstone and Missouri rivers on August 11 and reached St. Louis on September 23, 1806.

"In obedience to your orders," Lewis wrote to the president, "we have penetrated the Continent of North America to the Pacific Ocean and sufficiently explored the interior of the country to affirm that we have discovered the most practicable communication which does exist across the continent."

Among the expedition's accomplishments were the extensive mapping and geographical, geological, and ethnological data compiled by the co-captains; the massive flora and fauna information and specimens gathered; the precedent set for further exploration of the trans-Mississippi West by military and civilian parties; the first steps toward an extensive fur trade among the native tribes; and the foundation for American claims to the Oregon country. The total cost of the expedition to the federal government was $38,727.

Dale L. Walker

See also: Charbonneau, Jean Baptiste; Charbonneau, Toussaint; Clark, William; Drouillard, George; Fort Clatsop; Fort Mandan; Gass, Patrick; Jefferson, Thomas; Lewis, Meriwether; Louisiana Purchase (1803); Louisiana Territory; Ordway, John; Sacagawea.

Further Reading

Ambrose, Stephen. *Undaunted Courage: Meriwether Lewis, Thomas Jefferson, and the Opening of the American West.* New York: Simon & Schuster, 1996.

Jones, Landon Y. *The Essential Lewis and Clark.* New York: Ecco Press, 1999.

Lavender, David. *The Way to the Western Sea: Lewis and Clark Across the Continent.* New York: Harper & Row, 1988.

Moulton, Gary, ed. *The Lewis and Clark Journals: An American Epic of Discovery.* Lincoln: University of Nebraska Press, 2003.

Lisa, Manuel (1772–1820)

Lewis and Clark had been back from the Pacific Coast only a year, Jim Bridger was still a three-year-old tot playing in Richmond, Virginia, and William Ashley's dreams of a Rocky Mountain fur empire were fifteen years in the future when Manuel Lisa first took a flatboat expedition up the Missouri River in 1807 in search of plentiful beaver. Born of Spanish parentage on September 8, 1772, in New Orleans, Lisa had

already dabbled in the Indian trade in the old Northwest Territory, among the Osage tribe, and in the distant markets of Santa Fe, so he was well prepared to launch this first American trading venture among the Missouri River tribes.

Lisa's effort resulted in the construction of Fort Raymond at the confluence of the Bighorn and Yellowstone rivers. The expedition was successful enough that the Spaniard began planning a second upriver journey as soon as he arrived back in St. Louis in the fall of 1807. Two years later, he masterminded the organization of the St. Louis Missouri Fur Company, usually simply called the Missouri Fur Company. His partners included some of the elite of St. Louis, including William Clark, Andrew Henry, Pierre Chouteau, and Reuben Lewis, among others.

For the next several years, Lisa and his struggling company met with mixed success. Cash flow was always a problem, and frequent forays with hostile Indian tribes in the upper Missouri River basin added to his difficulties. In 1814 the Missouri Fur Company went out of business and Lisa occupied his time with the formation of other partnerships, performing his duties as sub-Indian agent for the tribes located above the Kansas River, and entering into two marriages. In 1819 he established a new Missouri Fur Company.

After organizing the new company, Lisa made one more upriver trip, but was stricken with an unknown illness while on that journey and died on August 12, 1820. He was buried in present-day Bellefontaine Cemetery in St. Louis. The company helm passed to Lisa's lieutenant, Joshua Pilcher, who ran the outfit for a few more years before it, too, passed into history. Despite Lisa's trials and tribulations and the mixed successes of his various enterprises, he was one of the most important men to work in the western fur trade. His friendship, understanding, and genuine interest in furthering the welfare of the various Indian tribes with whom he dealt were legendary. He laid the groundwork for the American fur trade with a total of thirteen trapping expeditions up the Missouri River and its tributaries, and deserves far more credit than he is usually given.

James A. Crutchfield

See also: Ashley, William Henry; Bridger, Jim; Missouri Fur Company; Pilcher, Joshua.

Further Reading

Oglesby, Richard Edward. *Manuel Lisa and the Opening of the Missouri Fur Trade.* Norman: University of Oklahoma Press, 1963.

Little Bighorn, Battle of the
See Custer, George Armstrong

Little Turtle (c. 1752–1812)

Michikinqua, known to Americans as Little Turtle, became chief of the Miami nation of the Ohio Territory as a young man. He was the son of a chief, born about 1752 on the Eel River, just north of the future Fort Wayne in Indiana Territory, the town named for Little Turtle's great nemesis, General "Mad Anthony" Wayne.

Michikinqua's life before the end of the Revolutionary War is unknown. His name arose after the Treaty of Paris of 1783 when the Ohio country was recognized as a sovereign territory of the United States and opened to settlement. The steady stream of emigrants crossing the Appalachians and creating white settlements in these Ohio lands inevitably caused conflicts. It was in this violent arena that Little Turtle and his Miami people, with their capital at Kekionga in the northwest of the current state of Ohio, wrote their page in history.

Until 1790 the Miami and other tribes were able to defend their ancestral lands by small raids and sorties against the white settlers, but when the eastern colonies created a national government, the picture changed radically: President George Washington of the new United States used his authority to send a military force into the Ohio country in retaliation for Indian depredations. Command of the expedition was given to Brigadier General Josiah Harmar (1753–1813) of Pennsylvania, who had served with Washington in the late war. Near the Miami stronghold of Kekionga, Harmar's force of 350 regulars and 1,000 militiamen met Little Turtle and his Miami fighters plus a number of Shawnees (including the future Shawnee chief Tecumseh), Delawares, and Wyandots—about 1,000 warriors total. After a four-day battle, October 19–22, 1790, Harmar, suffering high casualties and desertions among the militia volunteers, quit the field in defeat.

Succeeding Harmar in command of troops dispatched to the conflict that came to be known as Little Turtle's War was another Pennsylvanian and Continental Army veteran, General Arthur St. Clair.

On November 4, 1791, St. Clair led two regular army regiments and a force of militiamen into battle against Little Turtle's Miamis and their Shawnee allies near the headwaters of the Wabash River. The result was the worst defeat of an American army by Indians in history, with over 600 American soldiers killed in action as opposed to a small fraction of Indian dead.

Even with such a resounding victory, Little Turtle had no faith that the tribes would prevail over the Americans and urged peace negotiations but failed to convince his followers. Meantime, in 1793, an army of nearly 5,000 men, commanded by General Anthony Wayne, reached the Ohio Territory. Finally, after a long training period, on August 10, 1794, Wayne led 3,000 of his troops into battle at a wilderness area known as Fallen Timbers near present-day Toledo, Ohio. Wayne's seasoned soldiers soundly defeated Little Turtle's Miamis and the confederation of Shawnees, Delawares, and other tribes. The American victory led to the signing of the Treaty of Greeneville (Ohio Territory) in 1795, which ended the war. Ten tribes of the territory signed the treaty that ceded much of present-day Ohio to the United States.

In 1797 Little Turtle visited several eastern cities and was able to meet President Washington in Philadelphia. He died in Fort Wayne, Indiana, on July 14, 1812.

Dale L. Walker

See also: Fallen Timbers, Battle of; Greenville, Treaty of (1795); St. Clair, Arthur; Wayne, Anthony.

Further Reading

Anson, Bert. *The Miami Indians*. Norman: University of Oklahoma Press, 1970.

Hurt, R. Douglas. *The Ohio Frontier: Crucible of the Old Northwest*. Bloomington: Indiana University Press, 1996.

Young, Calvin. *Little Turtle, Me-she-kin-no-quah, the Great Chief of the Miami Indian Nation, Being a Sketch of His Life, Together with That of Wm. Wells and Some Noted Descendants*. Fort Wayne, IN: Fort Wayne Public Library, 1956.

Long, Stephen H. (1784–1864)

Stephen Harriman Long was one of a handful of U.S. Army officers who played a vital role in examining the West at a time when almost nothing was known of the region between the Mississippi River and the Rocky Mountains.

Soldier, engineer, and inventor, Long was born in Hopkinton, New Hampshire, on December 30, 1784. He was the second child of Moses and Lucy Long, the former having served in the 9th Massachusetts Line of the Continental Army during the Revolutionary War. After the war, Moses farmed and engaged in the cooper's trade making casks and barrels, and Stephen learned both skills. In 1805 or 1806 he entered Dartmouth College, where he obtained what was then known as a classical education. Following graduation in 1809, he taught school in New Hampshire and after a year was named principal of a school in Germantown, Pennsylvania.

A handsome youth with a penchant for organization and detail, Long also possessed a natural mechanical aptitude, which might have remained merely a hobby had it not been for Brigadier General Joseph Gardener Swift. The general took note of a hydrostatic engine that Long had co-designed and persuaded the young man, restless and dissatisfied with his career as a public educator, to become a civilian engineer. Soon Long was working on the defenses of New York harbor. Later, Swift induced Long to join the Army Corps of Engineers. From 1815 to 1816, he served on the West Point faculty as assistant professor of mathematics. On April 29, 1816, he requested a transfer to the newly created Corps of Topographical Engineers with the brevet rank of major, thus beginning a long career as engineer and army explorer.

During his first years as a topographical engineer, Long led five small expeditions through the upper Mississippi River valley, reporting on the various Indian tribes and suitable sites for military posts. In 1819 he married Martha Hodgkiss (sometimes spelled Hodkiss or Hotchkiss). During the next twelve years they had five children; one son would become an engineer and another would graduate from West Point. Although Long appears to have been a devoted father and family man, his assignments often compelled him to be absent for extended periods.

The event for which Long is best remembered is his scientific trek to the Rocky Mountains in the spring of 1820 in search of the sources of the South Platte, Arkansas, and Red rivers. Although historians have generally been critical of Long's expedition because it failed to achieve all that it set out to accomplish, the mission stood as the first truly scientific effort to penetrate and make observations of the Great Plains. Long's Peak, one of Colorado's most majestic, honors Stephen Long, as does the city of Longmont. It was Long who coined the phrase "Great American Desert," a description that supported Zebulon Pike's earlier "Great Sandy Desert."

Although his expedition was regarded as something much less than successful, the army continued to regard Long as a valued asset. In 1823 General Alexander Macomb, chief of engineers, asked Long to undertake yet another exploring party up the Minnesota (then St. Peters) and St. Croix rivers to report on the country and determine the Canadian-United States boundary line. Unlike his 1820 mission, this one proved successful. Upon his return, Long chronicled the journey in a book that was published in 1824 and included contributions from other members of the expedition.

In 1826 Long was promoted to lieutenant colonel and thereafter engaged in various railroad surveys. Later, he was promoted to the rank of full colonel and appointed head of the Corps of Topographical Engineers. In 1863 the Topographical Engineers merged with the Corps of Engineers and Long was demoted from bureau head to the ranking colonel in the corps. In 1863 he was placed on the army's retired list and died the following year.

Jerry Keenan

See also: Corps of Topographical Engineers; Great American Desert; Long Expedition; Pike, Zebulon M.; Pike Expedition.

Further Reading

Benson, Maxine, ed. *From Pittsburgh to the Rocky Mountains: Major Stephen Long's Expedition, 1819–1820*. Golden, CO: Fulcrum, 1988.

Goetzmann, William H. *Army Exploration in the American West, 1803–1863*. Austin: Texas State Historical Association, 1991.

Kane, Lucille M., June D. Holmquist, and Carolyn Gilman. *The Northern Expeditions of Stephen H. Long*. St. Paul: Minnesota Historical Society Press, 1978.

Wood, Richard G. *Stephen Harriman Long, 1784–1864: Army Engineer, Explorer, Inventor*. Glendale, CA: Arthur H. Clark, 1966.

Long Expedition

On June 6, 1820, Major Stephen Harriman Long of the U.S. Army Corps of Topographical Engineers headed west from the Missouri River with a party of twenty-two men, including scientists, guides, and a small military escort. Long's orders were to locate the sources of the Platte, Arkansas, and Red rivers.

Long's party had originally been part of a larger undertaking whose objective was twofold: to establish a strong American presence in the region as a deter-

Major Stephen H. Long and his party meet with Pawnee Indians during his expedition to the Rocky Mountains in 1819–1820. It was the first scientific exploration of what Long called the "Great American Desert," between the Missouri River and Rockies. (*The Granger Collection, New York*)

rent against British expansion and to gain control over the Indian tribes in the area. The plan called for a strong military force to move up the Missouri River on steamboats as far as the Yellowstone River; thus, it was officially known as the Yellowstone Expedition.

The expedition had actually gotten under way during the spring of 1819, but progress was slow and by September it had been forced to go into winter quarters at Engineer Cantonment near Council Bluffs. Long, meanwhile, returned to the East, where he received new orders. Unhappy with both progress and cost, a penurious Congress canceled the use of steamboats and authorized Long to procure horses as a mode of transportation for his new assignment.

From Engineer Cantonment, Long proceeded west along the north side of the Platte, crossing over to follow the South Platte where the river divided. Near the end of June, the party reached the Front Range of the Rockies, where they sighted the eminence that would be named Long's Peak. Here the party turned south, following the Front Range to the mountain that Zebulon Pike had first seen in 1805. The botanist Edwin James, Lieutenant William Swift, and an old mountain man, Joe Bissonette, climbed to the summit. It was Long's intention to name the mountain James

Peak, after Edwin James, but Pike's name was already firmly entrenched.

After taking longitude and latitude measurements, the party continued south to the Arkansas River, where Long divided his party. One group under Captain John Bell traveled down the Arkansas, while Long—in company with Edwin James and several others—continued south until they found what they believed to be the Red River. Instead of seeking its source, however, Long continued downstream, only to find that the river emptied into the Arkansas and was not the Red at all but the Canadian River.

Some historians have been critical of Long for his failure to locate the headwaters of the rivers he had been directed to explore. However, his expedition stands as the first serious scientific examination of the region lying between the Missouri River and the Rockies. His discovery of the Canadian River, although accidental, was important because it shed new light on the river systems of the Southwest.

Earlier, Zebulon Pike had called the region a "Great Sandy Desert," a description supported by Long, who called it the "Great American Desert." In either case, it was an assessment of the region that discouraged agriculture and settlement for many years.

Jerry Keenan

See also: Corps of Topographical Engineers; Great American Desert; Long, Stephen H.; Pike, Zebulon M.; Pike Expedition.

Further Reading

Goetzmann, William H. *Army Exploration in the American West, 1803–1863*. Austin: Texas State Historical Association, 1991.

Wood, Richard G. *Stephen Harriman Long, 1784–1864: Army Engineer, Explorer, Inventor*. Glendale, CA: Arthur H. Clark, 1966.

Long Hunters

The long hunter can arguably be called the eastern equivalent of the far better known, but much later, mountain man of the American West. For a period of about twenty years during the 1760s to the 1780s, scores of these intrepid adventurers—so called because of the long periods of time they absented themselves from home and family—explored thousands of square miles of virgin territory in the present-day states of Tennessee, Kentucky, and Virginia.

The long hunters preceded the more domesticated farmers and merchants who moved from the settlements of North Carolina and Virginia to take up lands in Kentucky and Tennessee. Their primary profession was hunting, but a by-product of inestimable value was their exploration of vast expanses of largely untrodden territory situated across the Appalachian Mountains that only a few years later would be invaded by thousands of settlers.

Although the collective exploits and contributions of the long hunters are well known, only the names of a few have passed down in history, the most notable being Daniel Boone, who blazed the forerunner of the Wilderness Road from the treaty grounds at Sycamore Shoals (today Kingsport, Tennessee) to the bluegrass region of Kentucky where he founded Boonesborough. Others—James Smith, Uriah Stone, Kasper Mansker, Henry Scraggins, Isaac Lindsay, Thomas Sharpe Spencer, and the Bledsoe brothers, Isaac and Anthony—were among those who scouted out the Cumberland River country years before Nashville and the surrounding region were permanently settled.

Like several mountain men of a later age whose reputations reached heroic proportions even in their own lifetimes, long hunters were revered by their fellows as bigger than life. One of them, Thomas Sharp Spencer, spent the winter of 1776–1777 in the hollow of a giant sycamore tree near Nashville. He carried a flintlock rifle that he called "Little Lucy," and reliable reports document that he weighed nearly 400 pounds (181 kg) and sported feet so large that he earned the nickname "Big Foot."

Like the era of the mountain men, the time of the long hunters was brief. They defined the leading edge for the colonial assault upon the trans-Appalachian frontier, providing the stories and eyewitness accounts that lured so many farmers and shopkeepers to abandon their "civilized" life back east and head across the mountains to see what was on the other side. They were, indeed, one of the earliest and most important elements of America's westward expansion.

James A. Crutchfield

See also: Boone, Daniel; Boonesborough, Kentucky; Nashville.

Further Reading

Crutchfield, James A. *Early Times in the Cumberland Valley*. Nashville, TN: First American National Bank, 1976. Reprint, Nashville: Williams Press, 1977. Reprinted as *A River Through Time: Man's Emergence and Early Settlement Along the Cumberland River*. Franklin, TN: Cool Springs Press, 1995.

Parks, Edd Winfield. *Long Hunter: The Story of Big-Foot Spencer*. New York: Farrar & Rinehart, 1942.

Long Walk

Throughout 1860 the canyons and mesas of Navajo land echoed with the movements of armed parties. The Navajo homeland, situated among four sacred mountains in the Four Corners of present-day Arizona, New Mexico, Colorado, and Utah had long resisted incursions from outside cultural groups. Determined to break the Navajos' power, the U.S. Army, augmented by Ute and Pueblo Indians and New Mexicans, attempted an ambitious pincer movement against the scattered bands of Navajos. Interrupted by the coming of the American Civil War in 1861, the military turned its attention to dealing with Confederate General H.H. Sibley's invasion of New Mexico.

In 1862, following a sharp campaign against the Mescalero Apaches, Colonel James H. Carleton considered a suitable place of detention for the Mescaleros who were unfortunate enough to have been captured. Despite difficulties with supply and a penchant to flooding, Carleton selected a site in the Pecos River valley at Bosque Redondo in New Mexico. There he established Fort Sumner and moved Mescalero prisoners to the Bosque. Fort Sumner was intended to serve as a concentration and reeducation facility, "civilizing" tribesmen while keeping them separated from the general populace. Carleton did not intend for the Mescaleros to be alone in their confinement. Since Navajo land was rumored to possess great mineral and agricultural wealth, the military planned its return to the majestic canyons, opening opportunities for settlement and civilization.

The start of the invasion was heralded by the establishment of Fort Wingate on the eastern slopes of the Zuni Mountains in New Mexico. Seeing the construction, the Navajos were concerned about the fort's implications. A delegation of eighteen headmen led by Barboncito and Delgadito traveled to Santa Fe to sue Colonel Carleton for peace. The Navajo peace overtures were rebuffed.

On April 11, 1863, Carleton ordered an expedition under Christopher "Kit" Carson to assemble. On June 15, preparations were ready and Carson was ordered to enter the Navajo strongholds, establish a depot, and then prosecute a vigorous war. Carson made excellent use of his Ute guides and men experienced in fighting the Navajos. On June 23 a message was sent ahead to the Navajos announcing that all wishing to avoid war must turn themselves in at Forts Canby or Wingate by July 20.

Unlike the 1860 engagements, this campaign featured raiding parties as opposed to the converging movements of large military forces. Small groups were better suited to finding and defeating the nimble Navajo bands. As the military swept through the canyons and mesas of the Navajo homeland, the soldiers and their supporters burned vital Navajo fields and confiscated and slaughtered livestock. This assured that starvation would soon become a foe more daunting than the soldiers' bullets. A Navajo peace delegation appeared at Fort Wingate on October 21. The terms presented by the military were simple: those who surrendered were going to be sent to the Bosque Redondo; those who did not surrender were going to die. Only 180 Navajo surrendered.

With the arrival of 1864, the snows were piled deep on the mesa tops and the Navajos were on the verge of starving. In January the army switched back to its former large-unit tactics. One detachment was under the command of A.W. Pheiffer, while Kit Carson led the larger unit. Both commands aimed for the Navajo stronghold at Canyon de Chelly in northeastern

Arizona. Pheiffer's men encountered Navajo warriors in Canyon del Muerto and were forced to encamp. On January 13 Carson split his force, sending one party along the northern rim of Canyon de Chelly while the second traversed the southern rim. Following an initial surrender by some sixty Navajos over the next few days, hundreds of starving Navajos surrendered. The soldiers returned to their forts to await the coming of spring. Throughout the winter more starving Navajos surrendered.

On March 4 more than 2,000 Navajos began their 400-mile (640-km) trek from Fort Canby to Fort Sumner, enduring horrendous conditions. Those who were unable to continue the march were shot. Roughly 126 died the first week alone; the total number who died on the march was never recorded. Navajos continued to surrender during this period, and numerous parties were forced to make their own "Long Walk." A group of 2,400 made the march in mid-April, through heavy spring snows. Once again, the loss of life was substantial.

Before the war, the army had estimated that as many as 5,000 Navajo Indians lived in the region— it was a gross underestimate. Soon there were 6,000 Navajo prisoners, as well as the 400 Mescalero Apaches originally incarcerated at Bosque Redondo. The supply situation was impossible. In order to stretch supplies, the military was put on half rations throughout the department, and the Indians' rations were even slimmer. Efforts were made to clear 3,000 acres (1,200 ha) for growing corn. The prisoners were starving, almost naked, and many did not survive to harvest time. Then cutworms wiped out the ripening corn crop. Hail and early frosts damaged supplemental crops from farms outside Fort Sumner. The only things in abundance at Fort Sumner were the hungry prisoners, whose numbers swelled to 8,000 from continued military pressure on the Navajos.

Tensions between the Navajo and Apache prisoners mounted. Many Apaches managed to slip away. Navajo farmers tripled their efforts of the previous season and planted almost 9,000 acres (3,640 ha) of corn. The result was the same as in 1864: the cutworms destroyed the crops in the field. Modest wheat and pumpkin crops helped sustain the hungry population. Raids by Plains Indians and others ran off much of the livestock, adding to the suffering.

By the end of 1865 it was clear even to the military that the experiment at Fort Sumner was failing. Navajos were escaping in ever-increasing numbers. After investigating conditions on the reservation, Congress decided to see if another planting season could bring relief. With the failure of the crops of 1866, Carleton was removed from command and the tribesmen put under civil authority. Their suffering continued as the government vacillated about how best to deal with horrendous conditions at Fort Sumner. In June 1868, the Navajos were returned to their homeland among the four sacred mountains. The Long Walk of the Navajos remains one of the defining events in Navajo history.

Terry A. Del Bene

See also: Apache; Carson, Kit; Navajo.

Further Reading

Bailey, Lynn R. *Bosque Redondo: The Navajo Internment at Fort Sumner, New Mexico, 1863–1868.* Tucson, AZ: Westernlore Press, 1998.

———. *The Long Walk.* Tucson, AZ: Westernlore Press, 1988.

Sides, Hampton. *Blood and Thunder: An Epic of the American West.* New York: Doubleday, 2006.

Louisiana Purchase (1803)

On April 30, 1803, U.S. officials, under the direction of President Thomas Jefferson, purchased Louisiana from France for $15 million, doubling the size of the country. Overnight, more than 827,000 square miles (2.1 million sq km) were opened to American exploration, trade, and expansion. The Louisiana Purchase, which included a large part of the Mississippi River basin and most of the Missouri River basin, stretched from the port city of New Orleans on the Gulf of Mexico north to the present border with Canada and westward from the Mississippi River to the frontiers of New Spain in the southwest and the Oregon country in the northwest.

When France lost the French and Indian War to Great Britain and its American colonial allies in 1762, French influence in North America was crushed. Britain claimed all American territory from the Atlantic Ocean to the Mississippi River, as well as Canada. France, not wanting Britain to claim Louisiana as well, ceded its vast western empire to its ally Spain who held possession of the region until 1800, when it ceded it back to France with the signing of the Treaty of San Ildefonso. Although France once again owned Louisiana, the Spanish continued to administer the region. In early 1803, officials closed New Orleans to American shipping.

With congressional approval, President Thomas Jefferson instructed Robert Livingston, the U.S. ambassador to France, and James Monroe, a special envoy, to try to buy a small segment of Louisiana—that part surrounding New Orleans—for $2 million so western farmers could resume shipments of goods through the city. French officials refused the sale until they realized they had lost control of French interests in Haiti, which meant that they had no strategic need for Louisiana. In a surprise move, on April 10, 1803, François de Barbé-Marbois, France's finance minister, told Monroe and Livingston that they could buy not only New Orleans but all of Louisiana if they so desired. The plenipotentiaries agreed to the French proposal, believing that Jefferson and Congress would approve.

Although the U.S. Constitution did not authorize the purchase of land, it did authorize treaties, and this deal fell under that realm. Jefferson was unsure about the acquisition and some members of the opposition party, the Federalists, opposed it, but Congress ratified the treaty on October 25, 1803. The United States took possession of lower Louisiana at New Orleans, December 20, 1803, and upper Louisiana at St. Louis on March 9, 1804. Soon after, Jefferson instructed Meriwether Lewis and William Clark to lead the Corps of Discovery up the Missouri River to explore the nation's new acquisition.

Bill Markley

See also: Jefferson, Thomas; Lewis and Clark Expedition; Louisiana Territory; Monroe, James.

Further Reading

Christian, Shirley. *Before Lewis and Clark: The Story of the Chouteaus, the French Dynasty That Ruled America's Frontier.* New York: Farrar, Straus and Giroux, 2004.

Jones, Landon Y. *William Clark and the Shaping of the West.* New York: Hill & Wang, 2004.

Kukla, Jon. *A Wilderness so Immense: The Louisiana Purchase and the Destiny of America.* New York: Alfred A. Knopf, 2003.

Louisiana Territory

Louisiana Territory was an 800,000-square-mile (2.15-million-sq-km) tract of North American land originally claimed by France that roughly encompassed the territory lying east to west between the Mississippi River and the Rocky Mountains and north to south between the frontiers of Canada and New Spain. France's claim to the region was established in 1673 when Louis Joliet and Jacques Marquette explored the Mississippi River as far south as the Arkansas River. In 1682 René-Robert Cavelier, Sieur de La Salle, sailed the entire length of the Mississippi to the Gulf of Mexico, thereby reasserting France's ownership.

In 1762, at the end of the French and Indian War, France ceded the vast region to Spain as compensation for Spain's allegiance during the conflict and in order to keep the territory out of British control following its victory. After the American Revolution, the young nation of the United States began to cast a covetous eye on the lands to the west when its expansion inland from the Atlantic coastline was halted at the Mississippi. In 1792 an American trading ship sailing along the Pacific coast explored the Columbia River, in present-day Washington and Oregon, and a territorial claim to that river, and its tributaries, was made in the name of the United States even though England considered it part of Canada.

Alarmed at what it perceived as American encroachment from the east and northwest, Spain threatened to cut off the port of New Orleans, and in effect the entire Mississippi River, to American commerce. However France, after its own revolution and now a dominant world power under the leadership of Napoleon Bonaparte, enticed Spain to return Louisiana Territory to French control in 1800. President Thomas Jefferson then sent emissaries to France in 1801 with an offer to purchase the city and port of New Orleans in an effort to keep American trade moving up and down the Mississippi River unhindered. Napoleon delayed the negotiations until 1803, when, seeking badly needed income to fund a losing confrontation against rebellious Haitian slaves, he countered with an offer to sell the entire Louisiana Territory to the United States. Without hesitation, Jefferson jumped at the opportunity.

At the conclusion of the sale, the United States took possession of the territory in an official ceremony held in the city of St. Louis at the confluence of the Mississippi and Missouri rivers. Acting as representative of the United States was Captain Meriwether Lewis, who immediately set off up the Missouri River at the head of the Corps of Discovery to explore and chart the newly acquired lands while seeking a water route to the Pacific Ocean. Upon the return of the Lewis and Clark Expedition in 1806, Lewis was appointed the first governor of the Louisiana Territory. His expedition co-commander, William Clark, later succeeded him.

Much of Louisiana Territory was administratively divided into six large subdivisions, the St. Louis, St. Charles, Arkansas, Cape Girardeau, Ste. Genevieve, and New Madrid districts. The remainder was designated as Upper Louisiana Territory. Each district would eventually be subdivided into smaller territories. In 1812 the name Louisiana Territory was changed when the state of Louisiana was admitted into the Union. The original territory was renamed Missouri Territory to avoid any confusion with the new state, but kept all of its counties, districts, and governing agencies intact. The population continued to grow, and stood at 25,000 by 1814.

With the acquisition of Louisiana Territory and the later settlement of the Oregon dispute, the United States became a truly continental nation, stretching from the Atlantic Ocean to the Pacific. It was the beginning of a new era, one that ushered in an unprecedented period of exploration and expansion.

Rod Timanus

See also: Lewis and Clark Expedition; Louisiana Purchase (1803); San Ildefonso, Treaty of (1800).

Further Reading
Gilbert, Bil. *The Trailblazers*. Alexandria, VA: Time-Life Books, 1973.

Wall, Bennett. *Louisiana: A History*. Wheeling, IL: Harlan Davidson, 1997.

Loving, Oliver (1812–1867)

Oliver Loving was born on December 4, 1812, in Hopkins County, Kentucky. He married Susan Doggett Morgan in 1833, and spent the next ten years farming and raising a family in Muhlenberg County before moving to Texas with his brother and brother-in-law's families. Arriving in Peters Colony in 1843, the Lovings continued to farm, moving from county to county while Loving also dabbled in the freighting business. The year 1855 found the Lovings running a store and ranching around Keechi Creek, and it was here, in Palo Pinto County, that Loving became a noted cattleman and drover.

Loving first sent a herd up the Shawnee Trail to Illinois in 1857; he drove 1,500 head to Colorado three years later to feed the miners in Denver, and during the Civil War sent cattle to feed Confederate forces along the Mississippi River. The end of the war left Texas ranchers struggling with plenty of cattle but no nearby market. In 1866 Loving heard of cattleman Charles Goodnight's plan to drive a herd west to New Mexico and Colorado territories: "If you will let me go," Loving told Goodnight, "I will go with you."

The two men formed a partnership, and began the long drive in June, using a trail that basically followed the old Overland Mail Company stagecoach route southwest to the Pecos River, and then up along the Pecos to Fort Sumner, New Mexico. Part of the herd was sold there to feed Mescalero Apache and Navajo captives, but Loving continued north with the rest of the stock, selling the remaining cattle in Colorado. This route, eventually reaching Cheyenne, Wyoming, became known as the Goodnight-Loving Trail.

Loving and Goodnight continued their partnership and began another drive in the spring of 1867 from Texas to New Mexico. Loving rode ahead of the herd with "One-Armed" Bill Wilson, and near the Pecos River they ran into a party of Comanche Indians who attacked and seriously wounded Loving in the arm and the side, although both he and Wilson managed to escape. Desperately weak, Loving sent Wilson back to the herd and continued across the land, without food, for seven days before being rescued by Mexican traders. They took him to Fort Sumner, where Goodnight, surprised to learn Loving was still alive, rejoined his friend.

After much delay, a doctor amputated Loving's arm to prevent the spread of blood poisoning, but Loving grew weaker. With his friend dying, Goodnight promised to bury Loving in Texas. On September 25, 1867, Loving died and was buried at Fort Sumner, but after Goodnight completed the drive to Colorado, he returned, had the remains exhumed, and took Loving home. On March 4, 1868, Loving was reinterred, with Masonic honors, at Greenwood Cemetery in Weatherford, Texas.

Oliver Loving has been honored with a Texas county and New Mexico town named after him. Larry McMurtry's novel *Lonesome Dove*, loosely based on the story of Goodnight and Loving, was awarded the Pulitzer Prize, and later adapted into a critically acclaimed television miniseries.

Johnny D. Boggs

See also: Cattle Frontier; Goodnight, Charles; Goodnight-Loving Trail.

Further Reading

Haley, J. Evetts. *Charles Goodnight, Cowman and Plainsman.* Norman: University of Oklahoma Press, 1949.

Hunter, J. Marvin, ed. *The Trail Drivers of Texas.* Austin: University of Texas Press, 1985.

Lozen (late 1840s–1886)

In the late 1840s, about 60 miles (100 km) northeast of present-day Silver City, New Mexico, a baby named Little Sister was born into the Warm Springs band of Apaches. The Warm Springs Apaches called themselves Chihenne or "Red Paint People," after the color of the clay the men used to paint their faces. Ethnologists later included them in the larger group called Chiricahua Apaches.

The territory sacred to Little Sister's people lay on the eastern side of the mountains known as the Black Range. Located on a small tributary of the Rio Grande, it had at its center a spring called Ojo Caliente. It was a country of piñon and juniper trees, waterfalls, hot springs, deep canyons, high grassy meadows, and impressive formations of red rock.

Little Sister had three sisters and a brother, Victorio, who was about twenty years older. Apache customs required siblings, and even cousins, of the opposite sex to avoid each other. A cousin was considered the same as a brother or sister, and the customary rules of strict decorum and avoidance pertained to both.

Since Apache girls and women were expected to hunt small game and guard their camp, they trained with the boys. Little Sister continued her training until she could ride and shoot as well as the boys and beat them in footraces.

When an Apache girl reached puberty, her people organized a ceremony called *da-i-dá*. During four days of feasting, dancing, and rituals, the young woman possessed the power to bestow blessings and receive supernatural abilities. At about that time, Little Sister acquired the spirit gifts of healing, horse magic, and the ability to sense enemies before they came into view. Her nephew, Kaywaykla, described how she summoned this last gift of far-sight. She stood on high ground and stretched out her arms, palms up. She looked at the sky and circled slowly while singing to Ussen the Creator. When she felt a tingling in her hands, she stopped and extended them in the direction of the enemy. According to Kaywaykla, when hostile forces were close, her palms turned almost purple.

Tall, broad-shouldered, and athletic, Little Sister earned the name Dexterous Horse Thief, or Lozen. Because of her physical skills, military wisdom, and her gift of far-sight, warriors welcomed her presence on raids. Apache wives sometimes traveled with war parties, but Lozen was the only single woman known to be accepted as an equal in battle. The men also invited her to sit in council with them. To many of the Apaches, she was a holy woman.

In 1877 U.S. soldiers rounded up the Chihennes and marched them west to the San Carlos reservation in southern Arizona. There they had to live with hundreds of others Indians, some of whom were their enemies. Inadequately housed, clothed, and fed, many of Lozen's people contracted smallpox and other diseases. When her band decided to flee, Lozen helped steal the horses that made escape possible.

From 1878 until 1886, approximately 400 Chihennes lived on the run, traveling thousands of miles across New Mexico Territory and the Mexican states of Sonora and Chihuahua. To survive they raided supply trains, ranches, and forts. Their children went to bed with food pouches tied to their belts, in case soldiers attacked. Sudden violence was so pervasive that a child might live a decade or more before learning that people could die from something other than a violent act. Even though siblings and cousins of opposite sexes were supposed to avoid each other's company, Lozen rode with her brother in their many battles with the U.S. Army. Victorio called her his "right hand." He said she was a shield to her people and was strong, brave, and a cunning strategist. To protect Lozen's reputation from those who would not understand her unique status as warrior, shaman, and healer, Apaches did not mention her until many years later. What is known about her comes from her people's eyewitness accounts.

Her nephew Kaywaykla said that while being pursued by American soldiers, about forty Chihenne families came to the Rio Grande. Their mounts refused to cross the flooded river until Lozen arrived on a beautiful black horse. Holding her rifle over her head, she rode into the swiftly running water and led the others across the river to Mexico.

In 1880, after months of hiding south of the border with Mexico, the council decided to return to their home at Ojo Caliente. Lozen volunteered to stay behind with a pregnant Mescalero Apache until the baby was born. She and the mother traveled on foot with the child until Lozen could steal a horse and, weeks later, deliver the woman to her people.

While Lozen was traveling with the mother and child, her brother and his followers rode into an ambush set by Mexican soldiers. Victorio and seventy-seven others were killed. Apaches believed that if Lozen had been with them, she could have warned them of the trap.

In 1881, during a battle at Cibicu, U.S. soldiers noted an Apache woman who rode into the crossfire. Lozen drove off a train of army mules loaded with enough ammunition to enable her people to fight on. In another firefight, she crawled out from behind cover to retrieve a heavy bag of ammunition.

By 1886 Geronimo and a few other Apache leaders were still evading the 5,000 soldiers who hunted them, but warfare had taken a toll. Their people were exhausted and hungry. Many of their relatives had been captured and exiled to Florida. Geronimo sent Lozen and another woman to arrange a meeting with Lieutenant Britton Davis.

In September 1886, Geronimo, along with Lozen, a handful of warriors, and their women and children boarded a train in southeast Arizona. After a 1,500-mile (2,400-km) journey, Lozen died of tuberculosis at the Mount Vernon barracks in Alabama. Her people buried her in an unmarked grave so it could not be found and desecrated.

Lucia Robson

See also: Apache; Geronimo.

Further Reading

Ball, Eve. *In the Days of Victorio: Recollections of a Warm Springs Apache.* Tucson: University of Arizona Press, 1994.

———. *Indeh: An Apache Odyssey.* Norman: University of Oklahoma Press, 1980.

Roberts, David. *Once They Moved Like the Wind: Cochise, Geronimo, and the Apache Wars.* New York: Simon & Schuster, 1993.